Images of Strategy

To the Wilsons and the Mitchells

IMAGES OF STRATEGY

Edited by

*Stephen Cummings
and David Wilson*

with

*Duncan Angwin
Chris Bilton
John Brocklesby
Peter Doyle
Bob Galliers
Karen Legge
John McGee
Sue Newell
Andrew Pettigrew
Chris Smith
Robin Wensley*

Blackwell
Publishing

© 2003 by Blackwell Publishing Ltd
except for editorial material and organization © 2003 by Stephen Cummings and David Wilson

BLACKWELL PUBLISHING
350 Main Street, Malden, MA 02148-5020, USA
9600 Garsington Road, Oxford OX4 2DQ, UK
550 Swanston Street, Carlton, Victoria 3053, Australia

The right of Stephen Cummings and David Wilson to be identified as the Authors of the
Editorial Material in this Work has been asserted in accordance with the UK Copyright, Designs,
and Patents Act 1988.

First published 2003 by Blackwell Publishing Ltd

3   2005

Library of Congress Cataloging-in-Publication Data has been applied for

ISBN-13: 978-0-631-22609-3 (hardback)
ISBN-10: 0-631-22609-5 (hardback)
ISBN-13: 978-0-631-22610-9 (paperback)
ISBN-10: 0-631-22610-9 (paperback)

A catalogue record for this title is available from the British Library.

Set in 10 on 12 pt Bembo
by SNP Best-set Typesetter Ltd, Hong Kong
Printed and bound in the United Kingdom
by TJ International, Padstow, Cornwall

The publisher's policy is to use permanent paper from mills that operate a sustainable forestry
policy, and which has been manufactured from pulp processed using acid-free and elementary
chlorine-free practices. Furthermore, the publisher ensures that the text paper and cover board
used have met acceptable environmental accreditation standards.

For further information on
Blackwell Publishing, visit our website:
www.blackwellpublishing.com

Contents

Contributors

Duncan Angwin is lecturer in strategic management at Warwick Business School, University of Warwick. His primary area of research is strategic perspectives on mergers and acquisitions. Recent publications include *Implementing Successful Post-acquisition Management* (2000). He has also published in *Long Range Planning*, *European Management Journal*, *Strategic Change Journal*, and in practitioner publications such as *Eclectic*, *Journal for the Institute of Bankers*, and *Management Today*.

John Brocklesby is professor of management studies at Victoria Management School, Victoria University of Wellington, New Zealand. He completed his doctorate at Warwick Business School. His research interests include strategic management, knowledge in organizations, systems-theory and autopoiesis and he has published on these topics in a range of management and OR/systems journal.

Chris Bilton is director of the MA in Creative and Media Enterprises at the Centre for Cultural Policy Studies at the University of Warwick. His research interests include the relationship between creativity and organization and the place of micro-businesses in the creative industries. He is currently working on a book on cultural missionaries and on a special edition of the *International Journal of Cultural Policy* devoted to the creative industries.

Stephen Cummings is professor of strategy at Victoria Management School, Victoria University of Wellington, New Zealand. He was a lecturer in strategic management at Warwick Business School from 1997 to 2002. His research interests include the history of strategy and management and the development of corporate ethos. He is the author of *ReCreating Strategy* (2002).

Peter Doyle is professor of marketing and strategic management at Warwick Business School. Previously he has taught at the London Business School, Stanford University and INSEAD. He is the author of *Value-Based Marketing* (2000), and *Marketing Management and Strategy* (2002). His research currently focuses on how marketing impacts on shareholder value.

Bob Galliers is provost of Bentley College, USA, and research professor, Department of Information Systems, London School of Economics. Previous to these posts he was Dean of Warwick Business School and head of the School of Information Systems at Curtin University, Perth, Western Australia. His research interests include business information systems strategy and the attendant management of change issues; the management of knowledge; and intra- and inter-organizational systems. Key publications include *Strategic Information Management* (2002, with D.E. Leidner); *Rethinking Management Information Systems* (1999, with W. Currie). He is also editor-in-chief of the *Journal of Strategic Information Systems*.

Karen Legge is professor of organizational behaviour at Warwick Business School, University of Warwick. Her research interests revolve round the critical analysis of

HRM, the management of change and organizational ethics from a postmodern perspective informed by discourse analysis. She is also editor (with Robin Wensley) of the *Journal of Management Studies*.

Sue Newell is trustee professor at Bentley College, USA, while on a two-year leave of absence from the Department of Management, Royal Holloway, University of London. She has worked previously at Warwick Business School, Aston University and Birmingham University. She was one of the founding members of the *ikon* (Innovation, Knowledge and Organizational Networking) research unit at Warwick and her research interests remain within this broad area of innovation and knowledge management. She is a co-author of *Knowledge Work and Knowledge Workers* (2002) and the author of *Creating the Healthy Organization* (2002), as well as numerous articles in academic journals.

Andrew Pettigrew is professor of strategy and organization at Warwick Business School and has previously held appointments at Yale and Harvard universities and London Business School. His research interests include new forms of organizing and company performance in Europe, Japan and the USA, and the making of strategy and the building of strategizing capabilities. He has authored and co-authored many books and articles on these themes.

Chris Smith is lecturer in strategic management at Warwick Business School. He has eclectic interests in strategy and strategic management as it is understood and manifest across different contexts, cultures and eras. His current research is centred on the strategic orientation of senior managers in recently incorporated public bodies, in the UK.

Robin Wensley is professor of strategic management and marketing and Deputy Dean at Warwick Business School. He recently co-edited *The Sage Handbook of Marketing* with Bart Weitz and retains an interest both in the longer-term issues of competitive market evolution and also the questions of relevance as it applies to social science research generally and management research specifically. He is co-editor of the *Journal of Management Studies* (with Karen Legge), a council member of the ESRC and Chair of the Council of the Tavistock Institute of Human Relations.

David Wilson is professor of strategy at Warwick Business School. His research interests include strategic decision making, organizational change, innovation and implementation. He has authored and co-authored many books and articles on these themes. He is the editor-in-chief of the journal *Organization Studies*.

Preface

'A fable to begin, often referred to, seldom known:

The Blind Men and the Elephant
By John Godfrey Saxe (1816–87)
It was six men of Indostan
To learning much inclined,
Who went to see the Elephant
(Though all of them were blind)
That each by observation
Might satisfy his mind.

The First approached the Elephant,
And happening to fall
Against his broad and sturdy side,
At once began to bawl:
"God bless me but the Elephant
Is very like a wall."

The Second, feeling of the tusk,
Cried, "Ho! What have we here
So very round and smooth and sharp?
To me 'tis mighty clear
This wonder of an Elephant
Is very like a spear! . . . [and so on].

We are the blind people and strategy formation is our elephant. Since no one has had the vision to see the entire beast, everyone had grabbed hold of some part or other and "railed on in utter ignorance" about the rest.' Henry Mintzberg et al. (the introduction to Strategy Safari, 1999)

This is fine start, but are we really objective observers looking in at the same static object? Furthermore, is this elephant (a.k.a. strategy) going to stand idle while six men touch him? What if the elephant had a temper? Or, even better, a sense of humour? Moreover, what if strategy was not a 'solid' object? What if there were more than one elephant; or more than one type of animal? What if we took a subjective view that assumed that different people saw different things when they thought of strategy? To accommodate these questions we would recognize the need for these different images to compete with one another, and for their coexistence to stimulate debate, hybrids and new images and ways of seeing. We would then not so much be in the position of the blind men, but the elephant: looking from the inside-out rather than the outside in. A clever elephant would acknowledge many different images of strategy. It would be the combination of these images that would inform the path taken as the elephant went on its particular way.

Stephen Cummings, Robin Wensley, David Wilson

In this introductory chapter the rationale for and philosophy behind Images of Strategy *are outlined. We argue that the conventional twentieth-century history of management and strategy leads us to unquestioningly assume that organizations are, for all people at all times, triangular hierarchies; that strategy is enacted by 'the men at the top', and that it is about long-term planning, directing, organizing and controlling. At a philosophical level, we deconstruct this history before reconstructing an alternative vision – one based on a broader 'pre-modern' heritage. Here, organization could take many forms and strategy could, correspondingly, be many things and be seen through many images. At a practical level, we use the analogy of how people are oriented and animated by maps to argue that this broader heritage simply reinstates a more pragmatic view of how everyday people use many different frameworks in developing strategy in complex environments over time.*

1   Images of Strategy

STEPHEN CUMMINGS AND DAVID WILSON

The young lieutenant of a Hungarian detachment in the Alps sent a reconnaissance unit into the icy wilderness. It began to snow immediately, and unexpectedly continued to snow for two days. The unit did not return. The lieutenant feared that he had dispatched his own people to death. However, on the third day the unit came back. Where had they been? How had they made their way? 'Yes,' they said: 'We considered ourselves lost and waited for the end. We did not have any maps, compasses or other equipment with which to ascertain our position or a probable route out. But then one of us found an old tattered map in a seldom used pocket. That calmed us down. The map did not seem to quite fit the terrain but eventually we discovered our bearings. We followed the map down the mountain and after a few wrong turns eventually found our way.' The lieutenant borrowed the map and had a good look at it. 'This isn't a map of the Alps,' he said. 'It's a map of the Pyrenees.'

Karl Weick, Substitutes for Strategy *(1987)*

The vignette above is extremely popular in courses that deal with strategy. The analogy is immediately recognizable. The notion that the value of a map, just like the value of a strategic framework, model or image, comes not just from its ability to represent the environment objectively in all its detail, but from its ability to focus minds and help people take a particular course, strikes a chord. This analogy, indicating the relationship between map and the individual process of *mapping* a particular journey, is the key to understanding the unique philosophy of images of strategy.

An organization's strategy can be described as its 'course', its onward movement in space and time, where it goes and where it does not go. Strategic frameworks, images and theories should be to an organization what the map was to the Hungarian soldiers. They can help people to orient themselves or *think strategically*, by offering a language by which complex options can be simply understood, communicated, bounced around and debated, enabling a group to focus in order to learn about themselves and what they want to achieve, and locate themselves in relation to their environment.

They can also foster *acting strategically* by getting people beyond indecision so as to begin the process of mapping and taking a course.

In other words, strategy frameworks, images or maps help people to do their own mapping, thereby kick-starting an oscillating thinking–acting, or 'strategizing', process which instils a momentum that brings other choices and possibilities to the fore. It may not get people 'down the mountain' in a straight line, but it gets things moving, and when things move other things come into view. In short, the interaction between the general map and the mapping of a particular course *orients* and *animates*, and no course is likely to be effectively taken without a measure of each of these things. Indeed, the question we are most often asked is probably 'How do you tell a good strategy from a bad one (beyond the obvious *post-hoc* financial measures)?' The best answer we have is that a good strategy, whether explicit or implicit, is one that both orients a company and animates it (see Figure 1.1).

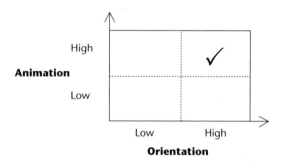

Figure 1.1 Strategy = orientation plus animation

Academic writing on strategy almost disappeared up an alley of its own making in the 1990s. 'Turf wars' were fought over which 'school', image or set of maps most accurately represented strategy, or by which set of criteria strategic decisions should be made. Some said strategy was instigated at the top of the organizational triangle and required logical forethought and rationally *designed explicit plans*. Others argued that strategy might be formalized by those at the top, but in reality this was where the 'rubber met the sky' – strategy actually happened at the 'base' of the company. Here salespeople met customers, research scientists met test tubes, and ideas were formulated. Good ideas developed on the ground would then *emerge* into policy from the *bottom-up* (see Figure 1.2).

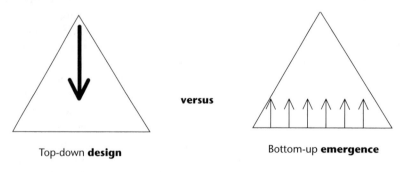

Figure 1.2 Top-down design versus bottom-up emergence

Some claimed industrial economics as the discipline to which we must look for foundations. Others countered that psychology, history and political science were more useful means of grasping the strategy nettle. The disagreements became so fractious that scholars despaired that we could not even come up with a logically coherent definition of the field, and wrote editorials asking: 'Were the many decades of vigorous development wasted? Does anybody at least *know* what strategy is?'

Thinking through how people use maps enables us not to get caught up in this ultimately fruitless line of debate. Let us say that you have arranged to meet a friend at a small pub in the country. It is about a three-hour drive from the city where you live. How many maps or images would you use to get there? Probably quite a few:

- A motorway map to plan the direction of the route, key interchanges, how long it should take you and so on before you set out.
- A street map of your city to determine the best exit and how you might get there.
- A map indicating the location of service stations if you found you needed to stop for gas or other supplies.
- A more detailed road map would be useful if you encountered roadworks on the motorway and wanted to find a quicker alternative route.
- A map drawn on the back of an envelope by your friend the last time you met, indicating the key turns and landmarks as you leave the motorway exit and approach the pub, would come in handy.
- And, a 'psychological map' of the friend who drew that map, indicating why he might draw or pick out things in the way he does would also help.

In addition you will consult road signs along the way and your onboard navigational system if you have one. If you have passengers with you no doubt you will debate some of the options in terms of the maps and signs.

The point is that for even a simple journey no one map exists that captures all perspectives, information and knowledge – attempting to create one would result in an almighty mess – and no single map can be objectively defined as 'the best'. You get where you are going by *combining* or *going between* your knowledge of where you want to get to and a number of different maps – maps compiled by a number of different people from different disciplinary pictures that provide *differing images*. What helps you in mapping and taking a course is a montage of fragments from these images networked together in your mind for the purposes of that particular journey. In the perilous situation that the Hungarian army platoon found themselves, one map, no matter how dubious, was better than none. In the more 'everyday' example described in the paragraph above, many maps or images are better than one.

Images of Strategy argues that it is useful to think of strategy in these terms. We believe that it is not important to ascertain 'what strategy is' without logical contradiction; or 'whether strategy is top-down planning or bottom-up emergence'. It is more useful to see what we can understand about our particular organizations by looking at how strategy develops through each of these images. It is also limiting to think of organizations through the image of the triangle, a traditional notion that the top-down versus bottom-up debate seems to reinforce and an assumption that has pervaded modern strategic thinking, as explored later in this chapter. It is not helpful to argue whether economics or psychology or ethics provides the correct background needed to understand strategy and make strategic choices (that is like arguing that the *London A-Z* is better than a London Tube map). It is more useful to ask how the various frameworks each provides may help us configure or understand particular strategic courses. It is not useful to argue, for example, that Michael Porter's strategy frameworks are too simplistic to represent accurately the real world. This misses the point that the strength of a simple, not overly detailed map (the back of the envelope, the Tube map), is its simplicity. Indeed, even a map of a related but different terrain (e.g. the Pyrenees may be a mountain but it is a different mountain) can stimulate debate and help orient and animate.

Different images of strategy, like different maps attempting to picture a complex world, project different relationships between objects and structures. Recognizing this immediately calls into question the notion that there should be one best image, school or map of strategy that most objectively represents the way things really are for organizations. Moreover, it questions the approach of many traditional strategy academics who sought to develop ever more exacting representations of the strategy process and present them as better, or more evolved, than others. The detail incorporated into these maps (an example is provided later in this chapter) prevents people from being able to see quickly and debate their own particular situation. In other words getting too caught up in developing all-encompassing world-views or convoluted planning procedures hinders the individual mapping process. Things tend to become bogged down in exacting orientation: all plotting and planning and no animation or action. However, this recognition also questions the response of many academics who took great delight in deconstructing and dismissing all images of strategy as too simple to capture the complexity of business. This is perhaps even less useful to scholars and managers. It is hard to engage in mapping particular courses if you do not have any maps to begin with. Things tend to become all animation and no orientation, a lot of charging about to no end.

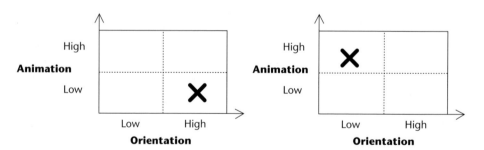

Figure 1.3   Low animation, high orientation; and high animation, low orientation

In this book it is argued that the art of strategy lies both in the combination of frameworks, images or maps and the choice of their focus (e.g., the big picture versus certain detail), toward mapping an organization's particular course. It is like the art of orienteering, like being an explorer moving into territories that are not certainly charted. Interestingly this is the view of strategy that influenced the civilization that gave us the term, the Ancient Greeks. The Greeks likened a military or political strategist (*strategos*) to a helmsmen on inshore vessels who had to *weave* their maps of the territory and their understanding of the prevailing currents with their ship's purpose and their own skill with a rudder. The Greeks likened strategic wisdom to *oscillating* between different positions and perspectives toward a particular purpose. *Images of*

Strategy seeks a return to a similar vision which encourages the reader to connect with *many* perspectives, models or images of strategy in terms of their ability to help you orient and animate organizations, or understand how they are currently animated and oriented. What is meant by this may be further explained by developing the map analogy in the light of the ancients' different approach.

In the sections that follow, there is related the history of what maps have depicted and how people have sought to use them to the history of the meaning of the word strategy. This discussion is divided into three parts:

- the first focuses on an ancient or 'pre-modern' approach;
- the second investigates how this perspective was challenged and changed by 'modern' scientific thinking in the last half of the second millennium and how this informs conventional views of strategy and its recent fractious either/or debates;
- the third outlines an approach more in keeping with a 'postmodern' landscape.

Pre-modern Maps and Mapping: The Subjective Web

Plate 1.1 shows a map that immediately offends modern sensibilities. It appears naïve. It is drawn as if its maker was standing on the ground in the middle of the tangled web that is his or her town. Some things are drawn in (e.g., houses), but others are left out (e.g., elevations). The church is not to scale. However, despite these things (and

Plate 1.1   The subjectivity of pre-modern mapping: 'Plan des dimes de Champeaux'; a fifteenth-century map
Source: 'Plan des dimes de Champeaux'; Archives Nationales de France.

because of them), this map is, to borrow the words of one young executive who was recently shown the map as part of a perception exercise, 'more real than maps we're used to'.

It is 'more real' because it shows the things experienced in everyday life and it is drawn from a personal perspective. Here the houses and the oversized church indicate their relative importance to the mapmaker and his community. It is 'more real' in the same sense that a map drawn on an envelope by a friend indicating how to find a pub means more than a road atlas. It relates to particular aspects and it is imbued with a personality. This is why it is animating, useful and memorable (indeed even if you leave such a map at home by mistake its mental 'imprint' will likely still guide you). Pre-modern mapping emphasized the personal or sensuous rather than the rational and objective qualities of spatial order. Subsequently, pre-modern maps were involving and organic in the sense that they could be added to, re-interpreted and/or modified in the light of a particular traveller's experiences. A sense of relief could easily be added so that the map depicts hills, valleys or other important milestones and particular indicators of progress (e.g., watch out for the shop near the tree).

But how could the ancients countenance such subjective relativism? It may have been because they lacked a knowledge of perspective or because it was only later that emerging capitalist states would require objective grids to determine land ownership, but it was also due to their different way of conceiving people's relationship with the world. Rather than the prevalent modern view of gaining certain objective knowledge from a detached perspective, over and above particular events, the ancients saw the world subjectively. Because they saw the individual human being as a 'microcosm' of the universal 'macrocosm' (see Plate 1.2) the Ancient Greeks, for example, sought knowledge by finding certain characteristics in themselves before then going on to form relationships with other things by seeing analogical connections. Thus they viewed animals, vegetables and land as intelligent organisms with particular 'personalities' and purposes. Prior to modernity, opium made one drowsy because poppies had a dormant 'gait', not because the drug had a corpuscular structure that acted on physiological structures in such a way as to cause a relaxed state. Similarly, the reason why a paste made from walnut skins cured external head injuries was that the nut of the fruit looked like a human brain. The modern world has since determined other, more scientific reasons, for this phenomenon.

In the pre-modern world, *webs* of knowledge developed by interpreting the signs that linked beings and things. This interpretation required maintaining a 'sympathetic' connection with the experience of, or 'stepping into the shoes of', other beings rather than detaching oneself and breaking down their mechanistic components. Over time, a particular individual would be seen as connected to a particular constellation of stars, which was associated with the stories told of a particular god, and these were linked to the nature of particular plants, and so on (see Plate 1.3).

Given the subjective, interpretative and unfolding nature of knowing, wisdom was also perceived differently by the ancients. From their foundation myths to their belief in *many* personable gods and goddesses (who had particular penchants and were not all-seeing and all-knowing unlike the unitary Judeo-Christian deity), they assumed an unresolvable tension between, and mutuality of, chaos and cosmos (or order). Consequently, the Greeks did not see wisdom as being able to represent the order of things with objective certainty so that things could be predicted and controlled, but as 'metos'. Metos meant the ability to *oscillate* or steer a course between:

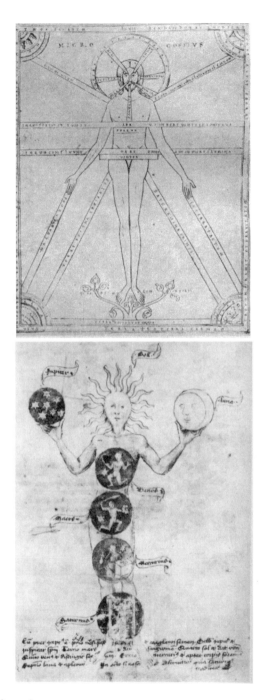

Plate 1.2 Pre-modern microcosms
Sources: Top – Munich (Bayr. Staats-Bibl., ms. Lat. 13003, f.7v);
bottom – Copenhagen (Kongel-Bibl., Gl. KGL.S.78, f.8r).

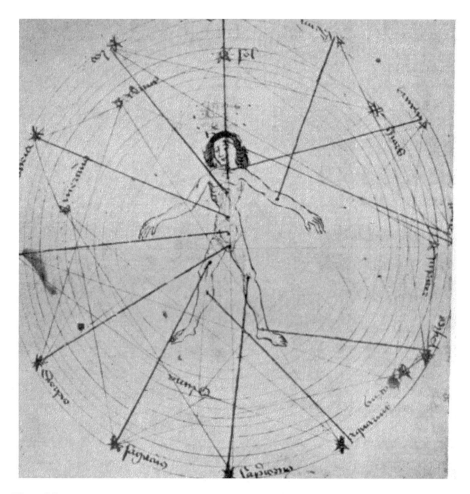

Plate 1.3   Pre-modern microcosmic webs of knowledge
Source: Vienna (Nat-Bibl., ms.2359, f.52v) (web at top right superimposed).

(1)   the world of order or *cosmos*, of forms, laws or maps; and
(2)   the world of *chaos*, of the multiple, the unstable and the unlimited nature of affairs;

in order to engage in mapping a prudent course.

Metos was characterized by an ability to bring to bear a number of different frameworks with which to confront particular situations at any given moment and move quickly between these two realms. To be 'polyvalent' or more multiple; to be sufficiently wily to bend one's course of action and be able to go in many different directions as needs be. It is for this reason that Odysseus, so admired by the Greeks, was given the epithet 'resourceful', and lauded as 'expert in all manners of contending'. His greatness lay in the ability to bring the right interpretation or experiences or image to bear so as to determine the best move for him given the way a situation was unfolding.

These pre-modern approaches to mapping and knowing relate to the original meaning of the word 'strategy'. The progenitor of strategy is the title of 'strategos', developed in 508 BC in conjunction with the democratizing organizational reforms of Kleisthenes who instituted ten tribal divisions as military and political sub-units of Athens. The new units cut across traditional regional boundaries to create a matrix structure with each 'slice' effectively the whole in microcosm. Each tribe was to be commanded by an elected strategos – a title developed by compounding: 'stratos' (an army spreading out over the ground), and 'agein' (to lead).

Kleisthenes' restructure paralleled increasing military and political complexity. Warfare had developed to a point where sides increasingly relied upon a network of many different types of units fighting on several different fronts, depending on particular circumstances, and direct democracy required responding to many different points of view.

The organizational image influencing this conception of strategy was therefore somewhat different from the modern triangular view. It was contextual and amorphous, more like the web illustrated in Plate 1.3. In keeping with this and with the conception of metos, strategy here was thus about oscillating between order and uncertainty. It was about detached long-term forethought, planning and ordering in advance of corporate action. However, as the frontlines were the best place to read the 'becoming' mood of events, to implement plans or to adapt and change plans as events emerged or unfolded, strategoi were at once expected to be at or connected to the nodes where action took place (either physically or relationally). Thus, strategy also happened here, either in the person of the strategos or developed by others better placed to reinterpret things.

Furthermore, given that the organizational form operated on many different fronts at once, depending on particular circumstances, strategy had to 'spread out' according to the form that the organization took at a particular point in time. Hence, strategy occurred at all levels and parts of what we would see as the organizational hierarchy, as a blend of what we might call strategy, tactics and operations. The Athenians, given this conception, would have had trouble comprehending the 'wars' between the top-down design and bottom-up emergence schools of thought. Strategy was about the interplay of design and emergence, in the same way that metos required oscillating between cosmos and chaos, model and circumstance, map and mapping. Ordered maps or design in advance of action provided necessary impetus, but once underway the art of strategy lay in 'working with the flow' as unforeseen opportunities rendered plans less than optimal, just like an expert helmsman.

Modern Maps and Mapping: The Triangle and the Objective Grid

The microcosm was the commonplace means of depicting knowledge relationships in Europe until it vanished suddenly at the end of the sixteenth century. This disappearance coincided with changes in mapping and linked in to changes in deity (from many

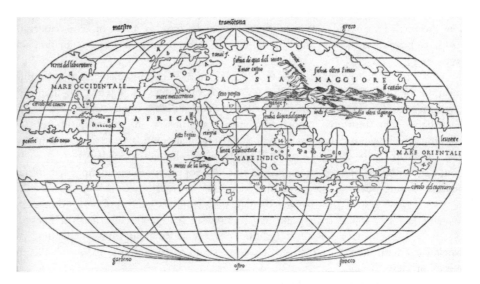

Plate 1.4   The objective grids of modern mapping – a sixteenth-century map
Source: Woodcut world map on an oval projection, from Bordone's *Isolario* (Venice, 1528).

personable gods and goddesses to one all-seeing, all-knowing, all-planning, all-organizing, all-directing, all-controlling God). Moderns imagined how the world would look to God, from outside and above, and were able to apply general mathematical principles to what was increasingly seen by capitalist nation-states, as 'the problem of objective representation' (Plate 1.4). Modern maps hence became universal unchanging grids for the general representation and control of phenomena in space; they were no longer open to subjective interpretation and development.

The ensuing 'mind shift' is often illustrated by the new 'geometry' of Elizabethan portraiture (Plate 1.5), which shows the human mind (and particularly the Crown) over the world of operations, indicating the power over affairs granted by an objective view above the 'big picture'. While monarchs are not so bold as to use this imagery now, it is still utilized by the heads of global corporations and management consultancies (see Plate 1.6).

This triangular conception, with Man's mind best placed at 'the top' to look down upon life's workings objectively, is borne out by the shape of the scientific method that emerged, through a series of development in the seventeenth and eighteenth centuries:

(1)   Galileo's refutation of the Aristotelian view that all things are animated by a unique purpose in keeping with their particular 'personality' and should thus be studied differently;
(2)   Descartes' detachment of matter (best understood in terms of underlying mechanistic functions) from the human mind (the only thing unable to be understood in these terms and subsequently 'over and above' matter); and
(3)   Newton's combination of empirical observation, inductive and deductive logic and hypothesizing toward certain general laws.

These discoveries led to the development of the modern scientific method (Figure 1.4).

Plate 1.5 The modern gaze – Elizabethan portraiture (showing the world as 'subject' to the monarch 'over and above')

Source: Top – the 'Armada' Portrait (1588), reproduced by kind permission of the Marquess of Tavistock and the Trustees of the Bedford Estate; bottom – the 'Ditchley' Portrait (1592), showing the monarch standing over a map of England and Wales; reproduced by kind permission of the National Portrait Gallery.

Plate 1.6 The new modern monarchs? Top – chairmen of KPMG and Ernst & Young; bottom – advertisement for a recruitment fair for management consultants
Source: Top – © Adrian Sherratt/Times Newspapers Ltd, London (21 February 1998). This photograph accompanied an article entitled 'KPMG Chief Proposes Far-reaching Changes'; bottom – image from front cover of brochure entitled 'Rekrutierung von Top-Consulting Nachwuchs in Deutschland' (July 2000).

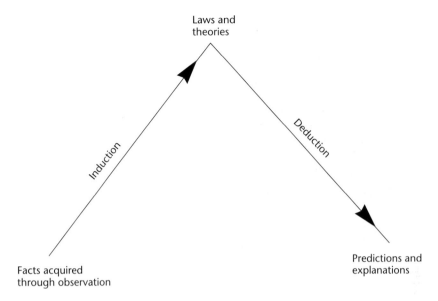

Figure 1.4   The geometry of the modern scientific gaze
Source: Chalmers, 'What Is This Thing Called Science?' (1999).

In a Europe troubled by religious and civic uncertainty the likes of Descartes' quest for certainty over particular sensual differences was well received. The subsequent discovery of universal material laws by way of the scientific method, like Newton's theory of gravitation, inspired others to apply it in an increasing number of spheres. The existence of many disparate schools of thought in Europe to this point, a manifestation of pre-modernity's acceptance of subjectivity and different interpretations, would gradually be overcome. The late seventeenth century witnessed the development of state-run knowledge institutes (e.g., The British Royal Society, The Académie française), with the expressed aim of 'bringing together all manner of different thinkers from different traditions'. All serious inquiries would be carried out and centralized by way of the scientific gaze.

The organization of the new objective knowledge being gathered would also follow the triangular hierarchical form. Once a unitary scientific method was established, thinkers could forgo time spent developing and justifying methods and get on with specializing and probing particular branches, knowing that others would be taken care of in a similar fashion. The Prospectus of the 1780 *Encyclopédie*, one of a number of new works bringing together the observations of experts in different fields, illustrates the form well. Here 'general manager' of the project Denis Diderot announced that forming the 'tree of all knowledge' was the 'first crucial step' in the volume's planning. While knowledge now had many branches, sub-branches and leaves, they could all be connected back to a unitary stem, a universal strategic plan of attack: scientific 'raison' or reason (Plate 1.7).

The nineteenth and twentieth centuries witnessed the replication of arboreal-triangular form toward greater certainty and order of explanation with regard to Man's

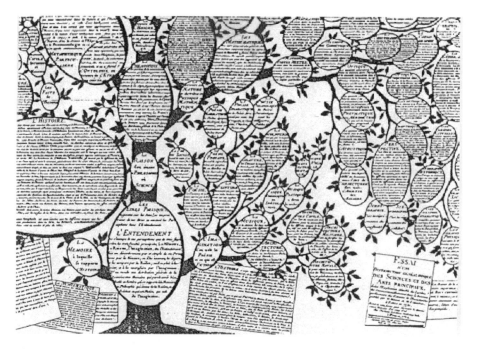

Plate 1.7   The modern 'Tree of knowledge' – the schema underlying Diderot's *Encyclopédie*, with 'Raison' as the central unifying trunk
Source: Frontispiece of volume 1 of the index of *Encyclopédie* (Paris: Hermann, 1751–80); only a portion is shown here.

place in the world: from Darwin's trees of evolution, showing the commonality of our origins, to the biological hierarchies found in textbooks (Plate 1.8). Knowledge or wisdom, given this perspective, was no longer subject to particular circumstances or individual re-interpretation; it was no longer time- or context-dependent; it was no longer about metos. It was about discovering and representing the essential stability that underlies particularities toward *ever more complex and certain images*, furthering the stock of cosmos and reducing chaos, about improving the representational quality of maps and reducing the individual guess work in mapping.

Because corporate strategy, as we tend to understand it today, was born in the middle of the twentieth century, the height of scientific or modernist optimism, it is exclusively fashioned upon these images. Alfred Chandler's classic 1962 definition of strategy 'The determination of the basic long-term goals and objectives of an enterprise', is premised upon the diagram reproduced in Figure 1.5 (a mirror image of Diderot's Tree); an enterprise that Chandler saw as having 'two specific characteristics: *many distinct operating units* managed by a *hierarchy of salaried executives*'. To this day strategy is subsequently seen by textbooks as management at the highest, overriding and most detached level 'the planning, directing, organizing and controlling of a company's strategy related (i.e., higher level and longer-term) decisions'. The geometrical image upon which this view was based was fleshed out by Igor Ansoff. Ansoff began his work by identifying a gap between:

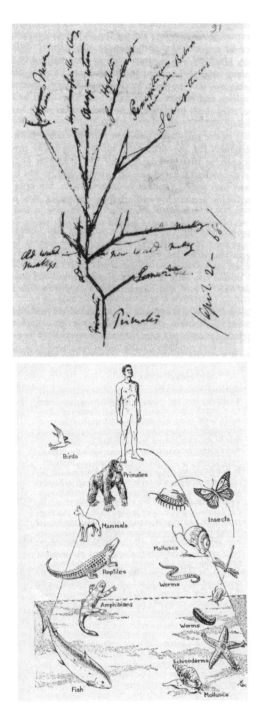

Plate 1.8 Darwin's Tree, showing the relation of Man to other primates and the modern biological triangle

Source: Drawing by Charles Darwin (21 April 1868), courtesy of Cambridge University Library; J.T. Bonner, *The Ideas of Biology* (Fakenham: Cox & Wyman, 1962).

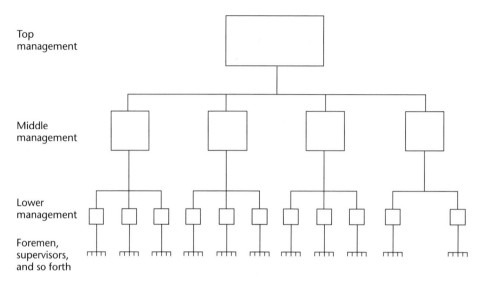

Figure 1.5 Chandler's view of organization
Source: Chandler, *The Visible Hand* (1977).

- increasingly complex business environments and multi-business firms, which created a desire for foresightful ways of positioning companies in order to exploit environmental change; and
- a current theory set based on the prevailing microeconomic theoretical conception of the firm. This view saw organizations as simply turning resources into outputs through a production function and assumed that managers just manipulated the factors under their control to maximize profits and offered managers little decision-making guidance as to how they could take different positions.

Ansoff defined strategy as 'a rule for making decisions pertaining to a firm's match to its environment' and set out to 'enrich the theoretical conception of the firm'. This 'enrichment' involved adding a layer on top of the microeconomic theory of the firm called 'management process', and outlining three distinctive action or decision areas: administrative or tactical, operational and strategic (see Figure 1.6):

- *Administration* related to establishing the central stem of management and logistic processes.
- *Operations* related to the maximization of operational efficiency within the process parameters set by the administration.
- *Strategy* related to establishing an organization's overall relationship to its environment It is, therefore, carried out by the 'men at the top' – those best placed to gain an objective 'global' view, forecast and represent changes in the environment and position and control corporate development accordingly.

The classical, or 'design', school thus perceives strategy as separate from, overseeing and proceeding, organizational action in a linear-hierarchical manner. It is about developing the most accurate and objective grid-map of the environment possible, then ori-

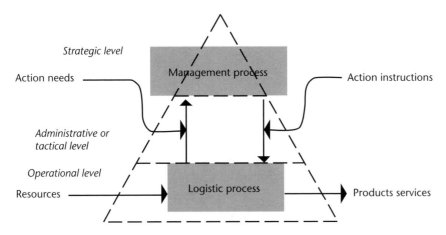

Figure 1.6 Ansoff's development of strategy
Source: H.I. Ansoff, *Business Strategy* (1969) (levels superimposed).

enting or positioning the company, and formulating rational plans as to where the company will move in the future.

Ansoff and Chandler's triangular-hierarchical image matched that of the foundational reports into the organization of business schools – 1959's Carnegie and Ford studies. These reports concluded that in order to counter the disparate 'organic' growth of programmes with differing contributing 'specialisms', it had to be realized that 'economics has traditionally provided the only theoretical framework for the study of business'. Economics then became the central stem to which other courses in a management degree would be connected. Having outlined this central gaze and then using it as a basis on which to determine a properly ordered range of contributing subjects, the studies advocated the standardization of the curricula's super-level or 'sharp end'. They recommended the development of 'capstone courses' that would allow students to 'pull together what they have learned in the separate business fields'. These tips of the educational triangle would become courses in 'corporate strategy'. As Kenneth Andrews noted, the ensuing 'establishment of Business Schools provided the basis for the education of strategic managers and the divisionalized structure of organizations provided the form for them to work within'.

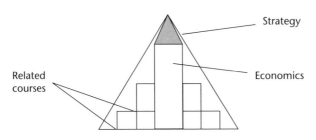

Figure 1.7 Strategy as a capstone

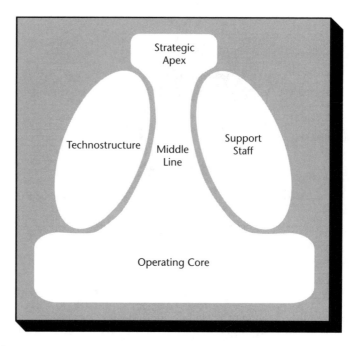

Figure 1.8   Mintzberg's 'organic' organization – the generic underlying functions
Source: H. Mintzberg, *Structures in Fives: Designing Effective Organizations* (© H. Mintzberg, 1983, second edition); reproduced by permission of Pearson Education Inc., Upper Saddle River, NJ.

It was this triangular-hierarchical view and its promotion of strategy as a top-down environmental map-drawing affair that Henry Mintzberg sought to bring down in the first half of the 1990s. However, in opposing this, 'emergence' theorists reasserted the triangle as the image with which we think strategy.

In the early 1970s, Mintzberg's research found that practising managers were far less rational and foresightful map-makers than the literature on management supposed. In the late 1970s and early 1980s, he led the way in prescribing a more 'organic' view of organizations. Mintzberg sought to get beyond the standard mechanistic 'boxes and lines' hierarchy by seeing organizations as shaped by generic elements (a strategic apex, a middle co-ordinating stem and a broad operating base where the action takes place – see Figure 1.8). The end result, while less rigid, is still essentially triangular.

Mintzberg's challenge to the 'classical' design view of strategy shows the influence of these two earlier projects. Mintzberg argued that the views of Ansoff and others were dependent on 'the fallacy of detachment', the belief that thinking and doing are separate. Managers were not rational, logical, directors – their courses were influenced by politics and historical or patterns of behaviour over time. Consequently, Mintzberg found that the interaction crucial to strategy does not happen between top executives and the environment – it occurs where employees at the operational base of the organization interact with one another and react to or anticipate customer needs and wants.

Over time, the mapping that goes on here may create patterns of behaviour that filter up the apex to be formalized in plans (or maps), but strategy did not come from the top. Mintzberg and other emergence theorists subsequently argued that 'real strategy' emerges 'bottom-up'.

The debate between what became known as the 'emergence' school and the planning or 'design' school, began fairly inclusively (Mintzberg called for an opening up of the definition of strategy to include patterns, perspectives and ploys, *in addition* to planning and positioning). However, things became increasingly polarized in the first half of the 1990s. In so doing, they reflected one of the modernity's key tenets: 'objective representationalism'; the idea that the purpose of knowledge is to represent, without logical contradiction, the 'ways things really are' or the linear, functional causes of actions. Given this, finding opposing schools of thought is problematic for any field seeking to develop as a modern science. Hence, there appeared to be much at stake. Mintzberg's views became more strident in a series of published debates with Ansoff, and he was backed up by new strategy gurus such as Gary Hamel, C.K. Prahalad and Ralph Stacey, who 'uncompromisingly rejected conventional strategic management frameworks, with their trite future-mission statements and flimsy strategic plans'.

Ansoff, however, was clear that the evidence he was continuing to gather backed up the planning view of how strategy really develops, an assertion reaffirmed by heavyweights such as Michael Porter. Porter, whose models build upon microeconomic and design school premises (the arrangement of Porter's value chain and the horizontal line of his five forces of industry – see Figure 1.9 – replicate the microeconomic input–process–output model that Ansoff 'enriched'), and are still the most popular modern strategy grids, entered the fray in a *Harvard Business Review* article titled 'What is Strategy?' Here he argued that the 'new dogma', based on the mistaken belief that strategy happens 'further down' organizations, was leading to several problems and a subsequent lack of focus on 'real strategy'. The best remedy, Porter said, was a 'reconnection' with the classical design view.

By the late 1990s the debate between the emergence and design camps was being described by eminent commentators as 'tectonic', indicating how seemingly fundamental it had become. However, tracing strategy back to its ancient fundaments, as we did in the previous section, might have led to a different conclusion. In a world where strategy was about both design and emergence, about what we call strategy and tactics and operations, or where many competing schools of thought were normal, such a chilly polarization could not have set in.

However, the protagonists in the 1990s' debate did not recognize the pre-modern perspective as a point of reference. Indeed, one of the reasons that Mintzberg's ideas were 'reactionary', and consequently a mirror image of his top-down opponents, was that he identified Ansoff as where corporate strategy began and as what he was opposing. Mintzberg did mention the Ancient Greek origins of the concept in an earlier article, but disparaged them as a simpler version of the top-down planning approach. Stacey was similarly dismissive of strategy's ancient military heritage, seeing it as a reason why we have a mistaken top-down view of strategy. The ancient world-view was misconstrued as a less refined and less educated version of our own.

What we want to put forward in *Images of Strategy* is another way of looking at strategic development – a way that circumvents the 'tectonic debates'; a way that seeks to *acknowledge and combine*:

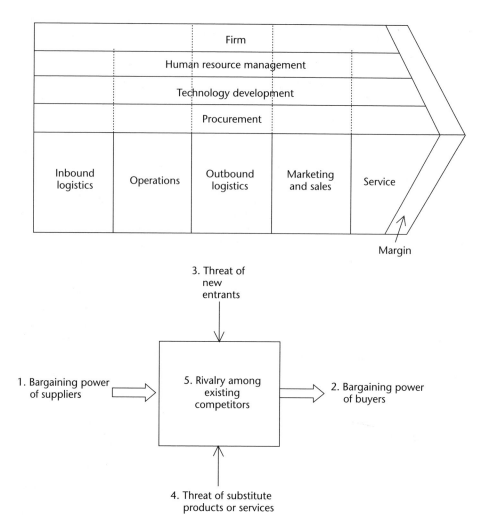

Figure 1.9 Porter's generic value chain and five forces of industry models
Source: Reprinted with the permission of Free Press, a division of Simon & Schuster Inc., from *Competitive Advantage: Creating and Sustaining Superior Performance*, by Michael E. Porter (© 1985, 1998, Michael E. Porter); and *Competitive Strategy: Techniques for Analyzing Industries and Competitors*, by Michael E. Porter (© 1980, 1998, Free Press).

(1) pre-modern notions such as the subjective web and the interaction between design and emergence (so as to incorporate the notions of emergent or unfolding process of *mapping* that are perhaps lost sight of by the design approach), and

(2) many of the *maps* or images born of the over and above design approach to strategy (maps that aid individualized mapping, a factor that was lost sight of by many of the emergence theorists who sought to bring down the top-down view).

This is an approach to strategy based on oscillating between these two realms to create individualized 'montages' toward taking particular courses.

Postmodern Maps and Mapping:
The Networked Montage

I am a great lover of these processes of division and generalization; they help me to speak and think.

Socrates, in Plato's Phaedrus (c.406 BC)

At the beginning of this new millennium we are beginning to see a further change in the way people conceive of strategy. And, once again, Mintzberg is at the forefront. Under his leadership, a forum discussed the state of strategy in 1996's *California Management Review*. Paying particular reference to the way that Honda Motorcyles' entry into the US had been seen by some to be the result of top-down design and by others as the emergence of patterns following chance events on the 'ground', they concluded that both images were right. In the light of this, Richard Pascale's final reflections argued that there is a useful and necessary tension between design and emergence and, subsequently, that most important strategic capability is 'agility', the ability to move from and to plans faster than one's competition – a conception uncannily like metos.

Moving further beyond the either/or debates, Mintzberg's 1998 *Strategy Safari* outlines many different strategy 'schools' and concludes that no one is better than the others. 'We are like blind men', says Mintzberg:

> Each of us, in trying to cope with the mysteries of the beast, grabs hold of some part or the other [but all are looking at the same] elephant . . . To academics this represents confusion and disorder, whereas to others [like Mintzberg] it expresses a certain welcome eclecticism.

Mintzberg has also got beyond the image of organization as a triangle, claiming that the generic triangular hierarchy of boxes and lines that we call organization charts are now 'irrelevant'. 'Organigraphs' (subjective 'mind-maps' containing any number of different shapes that symbolize and 'convey meaning') are where it's at and managers must now 'create a customized picture of their company' (see Chapter 9, 'Strategy as Systems Thinking' for more on Mintzberg's 'organigraphs'). This new thinking is in keeping with an emerging discourse about organizations as networks and a moving away from the conception of value chains to relational value webs (a theme developed in more detail in Chapter 5, 'Strategy as Orchestrating Knowledge').

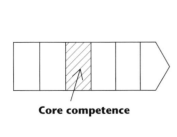

Core competence

Value chain

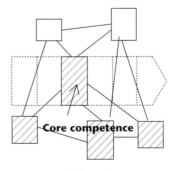

Core competence

Value web

Figure 1.10   Value chain to value web

However, like much that is 'new' in management, these ideas lag a long way behind developments in social theory, philosophy and the arts from which we might learn much. By the 1970s, cultural commentators were already beginning to write of the exhaustion of the 'modernist' world-view and a re-appreciation of pre-modern subjectivity. Modernism's reductionist approach to searching for the underlying functional laws of all things, combined with the relentless quest for 'the new', had led from non-representational impressionist art to cubism (the distillation of objects into their essential boxes and lines) to abstractionism, and on to the 'white canvas' as the encapsulation of all things – an encapsulation to which no individual could relate. In architecture it had led to the international style – the same building everywhere based on the universal maxims of essentialism, functionality and efficiency, no matter the local context; and in modern music, from atonality to noise to absolute silence.

Jean-François Lyotard expressed the attempt to get beyond the corner that a dogmatic modernism had painted itself into as 'postmodernity' in 1979. 'The ground-zero of contemporary culture', Lyotard claimed, 'must be eclecticism.' Five years before, Theodore Levitt was proclaiming that globalization, best practice and advances in communications technology were bringing us ever closer to homogenized universal products and services; Lyotard was arguing otherwise. The same information technology was actually leading, he claimed, to a greater global appreciation of local difference. This enabled individuals to move beyond the quest for keeping up with singular international styles and develop their own particular identities through the establishment of webs of relationships between different things. In postmodernity, Lyotard wrote: 'One is free to listen to reggae, watch a Western, eat McDonald's for lunch and local cuisine for dinner, wear Paris perfume in Tokyo and retro clothes in Hong Kong.'

In keeping, people became increasingly incredulous toward 'meta-narratives': universal maxims or criteria over and above particular instances (e.g., science, communism, capitalism, global policies) that claimed to capture the essence of things through averages and general laws and tell individuals what norms they must follow. Postmodernity sees the re-appreciation or embracing of particular paths and many different views, and playful combinations of styles taken from different traditions and time zones according to individual or local preferences. Illustrative examples include:

- London's Tate Bankside gallery – a power station rebuilt using leading edge modern technology in order to reinvigorate its distinctive 1930s' facade.
- Cindy Sherman's photography, showing how one person at once has a core and many contradictory aspects depending on the context.
- Design commentators reviewing chair design through the twentieth century and determining an iconic style for each decade, before reaching the 1990s and claiming that what matters now mixing and matching classical elements from other decades according to the vision of a particular designer.
- *Billboard* and other music magazines' increasing struggle to classify new music into traditional categories such as 'R&B', 'country', 'jazz', 'rock', and 'indie'.
- Customized trainers with individualized patterns scrawled over old generic canvases (see Plate 1.9).

While the 'shapes' of the modern industrial era were the triangle, the tree and the causal line of production, we appear now to be witnessing a return to the individualized nodal constellations of pre-modern times. At the time Lyotard was writing about the 'postmodern condition', Gilles Deleuze and Félix Guattari were anticipating these

Plate 1.9 A postmodern form: 'Customized trainer (from Burro)'
Source: Photograph © Ian Nolan, first appeared in *Guardian Weekend*, 15 December 2001; reproduced by kind permission of Ian Nolan.

developments in their arguments against the 'trees, roots, and radicles' upon which modern 'arborescent culture' was based. While they did not seek to dismiss the standard 'trees that people had growing in their heads' for classifying things, they advocated more chaotic 'underground stems, aerial roots, adventitious growths and rhizomes' as alternative images. They subsequently favoured 'nomadology' as an approach to knowledge: individual wandering and eclectic combinations or networks of elements, rather than one common path toward greater objectivity. This alternative 'shape' is apparent in the cities in which many of us now live. According to geographer David Harvey, the postmodern city is:

> A labyrinth, honeycombed with such diverse networks of social interaction oriented to such diverse goals that the encyclopaedia becomes a maniacal scrapbook filled with colourful entries which have no determining rational or economic scheme.

Hugh Pearman, cultural commentator with *The Sunday Times*, has recently related this postmodern turn to the changing shape of cars. The use of the same global-standard ergonomic principles, best practice benchmarking, and focus groups representative of a global society as the key 'yay' or 'nay-sayers' in prototype development, meant that most new cars came to look much the same. Rather than develop a model to which some were passionate about connecting, the aim for increasingly risk-averse manufacturers was for the greatest number of people to be unoffended by the look of the product. Consequently, Pearman claimed that 'Weird French cars ceased to be weird, Japanese cars stopped being ugly, the Americans toned down their once incredible styling in the name of international sales.'

However, this homogenization made it impossible to express an individual identity through a new car (vindicating famously anti-focus group inventors such as James Dyson, who likes to contrast the Hillman Avenger – focus-group approved; and the Mini – the vision of one designer). This, combined with the realization that margins can only decrease if all companies are competing on the same dimensions, is now driving manufacturers to take new risks in order to create market niches.

Pearman claims that manufacturers now want their products 'to look distinctive and are discovering the joys of "localism" and pluralism'. Hence:

- Chrysler's PT Cruiser (a people-mover/1950s' hot-rod cross) is part of what it describes as its 'yestertech' range, combining retro-styling and modern technology. Only 41 per cent of the company's focus group members liked the PT and 26 per cent hated it – usually more than enough to kill off a prototype.
- BMW's reinvigoration of the very British Mini.
- Toyota's recent claim that 'Our global strategy used to center on "world cars", which we would modify slightly to accommodate demand in different markets. To-day our focus is shifting to models that we develop and manufacture for selected regional markets.'
- Rover's advertising uses images of non-politically correct pursuits such as hunting, nudism and boxing to convey the idea that not everyone will like the car but those that do will love it.

The change of emphasis caught some manufacturers on the hop. Citroën and Renault, once leaders in quirky styling, are now responding to consumers being unsure of their 'identity' and seeing its new cars as resembling last year's Fords. Meanwhile Jaguar, more concerned to project its past into the present, has kept loyal customers and is attracting new customers impressed by the doughty British character of their cars. (The most important test for Jaguar 'focus groups' is whether they recognize a prototype, without badging, as a Jaguar – if more than 90 per cent do not, then it does not go to production no matter how good a car it may be.)

Correspondingly, Doug Daft, the new CEO of the global icon Coca-Cola, describes the company's new vision as 'Think local, act local'. Levi, whose standard jeans have become global currency, now see 'mass-customization' (enabling individual customers to work with Levi's technicians to mix and match features into a combination that has a particular 'identity') as its most exciting new development. Instead of companies deciding to become more centralized or more decentralized, the talk is now of 'centralized-decentralization'. Paradoxical phrases such as 'glocalization' and 'lo-glo strategies' are bandied about. Pop-management books are entitled *Thriving on Chaos*, *The Age of Unreason* and *The Individualized Corporation*. And, in the year 2000, *The McKinsey Quarterly* concluded that while modelling performance on best-in-class competitors is an aspiration often offered by consultants and bought by companies as a badge of soundness, 'best practice does not equal best strategy'. Industries where best-practice copying has been widespread seem to witness declining average margins as competitors are forced to compete on price for customers who can no longer differen-tiate their products on any other grounds.

However, it would be foolish to suggest that 'Levittian' globalization is not hap-pening at the same time. For example:

- VW's development of the 'new' Beetle has been enabled by a global chassis that is the same for a Seat or a Golf, and Ford's quirky Ka is just a Fiesta with curves.
- Jaguar can maintain its identity because of operating under the auspices of the giant Ford conglomerate.

- Local marketing strategies may differ, but a Coke is still a Coke.
- 'Best practice' benchmarking continues to play a role in cutting operational costs.

Postmodernism, therefore, should not be thought of as the death of the global or the modern and the imposition of a 'new world order', but as the paradoxical networking of global and local, general and individual modern and premodern, for specific purposes. Bernard Cova's excellent *The Postmodern Explained to Managers* subsequently describes postmodernism as a series of paradoxes and a breaking down of either/or distinctions:

FRAGMENTATION *WITH* GLOBALIZATION,

HETEROGENEITY *WITH* UNIFORMITY,

PASSIVE CONSUMPTION *WITH* ACTIVE CUSTOMIZATION,

INDIVIDUALISM *WITH* TRIBALISM,

OLD *WITH* NEW.

So in this increasingly paradoxical and uncertain world what use are traditional images of strategy? Academics such as Stacey claim that this new world of complexity means that conventional strategy frameworks are 'trite' and 'flimsy' and that the image of strategy as rational planning is 'redundant'. A recent paper by David Knights described Porter's 'generic strategy matrix' (see Figure 1.11), a typical top-down positioning grid, as a classic example of the 'myth of progress that underlies the demand for stable and positive management knowledge'.

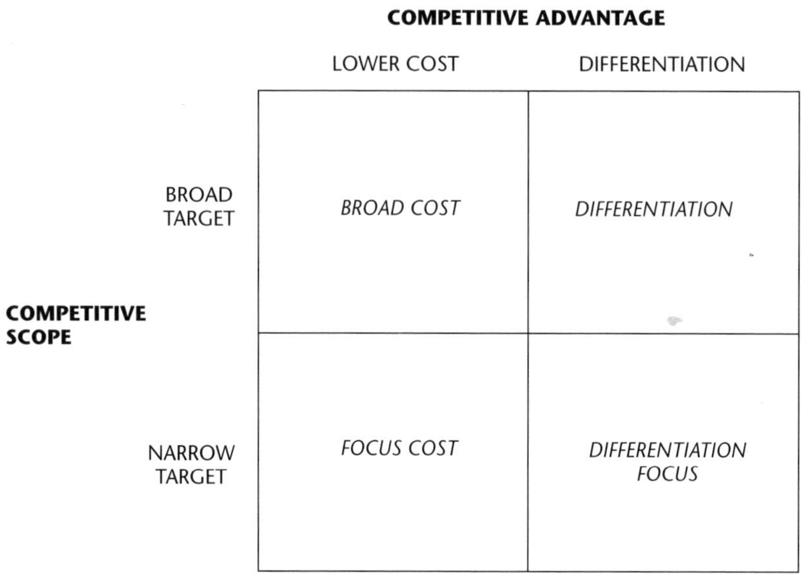

COMPETITIVE ADVANTAGE

	LOWER COST	DIFFERENTIATION
BROAD TARGET	*BROAD COST*	*DIFFERENTIATION*
NARROW TARGET	*FOCUS COST*	*DIFFERENTIATION FOCUS*

COMPETITIVE SCOPE

Figure 1.11 Porter's generic strategy matrix
Source: Reprinted with the permission of Free Press, a division of Simon & Schuster Inc., from *Competitive Strategy: Techniques for Analyzing Industries and Competitors*, by Michael E. Porter (© 1980, 1998, Free Press).

Knights claims that despite the fact that Porter's model is too simple to reflect the reality for managers, they continue to cling to it. Furthermore, says Knights, it detracts from giving attention to 'subjectivity' by 'disciplining modern management regimes into emulating it'. However, thinking of a postmodern map and how it is used might lead us to other conclusions. One such image is Harry Beck's London Underground map (Plate 1.10). Here geographic representation is eschewed for one man's diagram. It may not be rational in an objective representational sense, but it does not claim to be. Everybody knows that the distances between lines and stations are not 'factual'. However, Beck's map is memorable and open to nomadology, individual customization or montage. Indeed, as Beck said, the map 'must be thought of as a living and changing thing, with schematic "manipulation" and spare part osteopathy going on all the time'. Subsequently, anyone who has lived in or visited London will find their own lives being understood, networked and communicated in relation to particular parts of it. It is not reality (see above it for that), but its symbols have become language and people interact with it to schematize their lives in ways that are useful to them in making decisions and taking particular courses.

Paradoxically, simple, open, non-representative images such as the tube map help us outline our individuality in these labyrinthine postmodern times. Borrowing from Plato's premodern perspective, such 'processes of division and generalization help us to speak and think'. Seeing images of strategy thus, rather than as objectively representations of how the world really is, we could argue that they can *be used in individualized ways to actually enhance subjective mapping*. Contrary to the views of Knights and Stacey described above, *Images of Strategy* suggests that a further postmodern paradox is that simple strategic images have never been more useful than they are in these increasingly complex times.

To illustrate, let us explore some 'trite' and 'flimsy' images of strategy in this postmodern manner. If the story of the Hungarian army unit (on p. 1) is the anecdote most remembered by our students of strategy, the model that managers we have taught remember most is likely this simple expression:

cost + margin = selling price (of a unit of product or service)
　　　margin × units = profit

The beauty of these equations is that any strategy for any for-profit company can be analysed, and should be justifiable, in these terms. A viable strategy must, over time, enable profit to improve by way of:

- reducing costs and/or
- increasing selling price and/or
- increasing units sold.

If a strategy cannot be justified in these terms for the long term, it is hard to see why a for-profit company would take it. People like this expression because it is easy to remember, and it enables them to quickly assess proposals, ask difficult (but pertinent) questions, and make decisions.

Of course, the logic of these equations is very similar to that behind Michael Porter's 'generic strategy matrix' (GSM pictured in Figure 1.11), which has, as its base, the idea that all companies must gain some 'competitive advantage' from either focusing on *reducing costs* or differentiating their offerings so as to command a higher *selling price*. Porter creates a two-by-two matrix out of this by crossing competitive advantage with 'competitive scope' (i.e., number of *units* sold, number of distribution channels used,

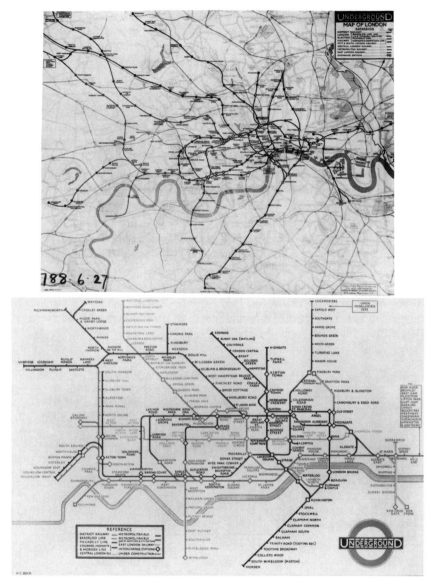

Plate 1.10 Harry Beck's 'postmodern' map (bottom) and the more geographically representative map that it replaced
Source: Top – Underground Map of London, *c.* 1927; bottom – Harry Beck's 1933 Underground Map of London. Both maps reproduced with the kind permission of the London Transport Museum.

etc.). Here the choice is *broad* or *narrow*. Thus a grid comprising four generic positions is developed. Porter condemns those 'stuck in the middle', those who have failed to choose between cost or differentiation, and broad or narrow, and subsequently cannot identify which of the four strategic positions is theirs.

We can demonstrate a model such as the GSM's limitations and worth from an individualized postmodern perspective by revisiting our earlier car industry discussion. The car industry is now characterized by value-webs or relational connections created through alliances and mergers. Some of these webs appear to work better than others. One such concern is the Ford Group. After initially attempting to impose 'The Ford Way' upon Jaguar (according to Jaguar people at least), the Ford management has now taken a step back. It recognizes that it benefits from being associated with a Jaguar that maintains its own identity within the focused differentiation segment, and so leave it 'to do its own thing'. Thus it does not undermine the distinctive *differentiated* Jaguar style, but seeks to network it into the core Ford identity wherever possible to help on *cost reduction*. This 'soft-merger' relationship is similar to that with Volvo (and Land Rover and Mazda). Ford seeks to increase its average selling prices through association with Volvo's differentiated competitive advantage (safety technology), while using its operational expertise and global muscle to reduce Volvo costs. Thus one can better understand the Ford Group's strategy by superimposing a particular pre-modern type web of relationships over Porter's general modern grid (see Figure 1.12).

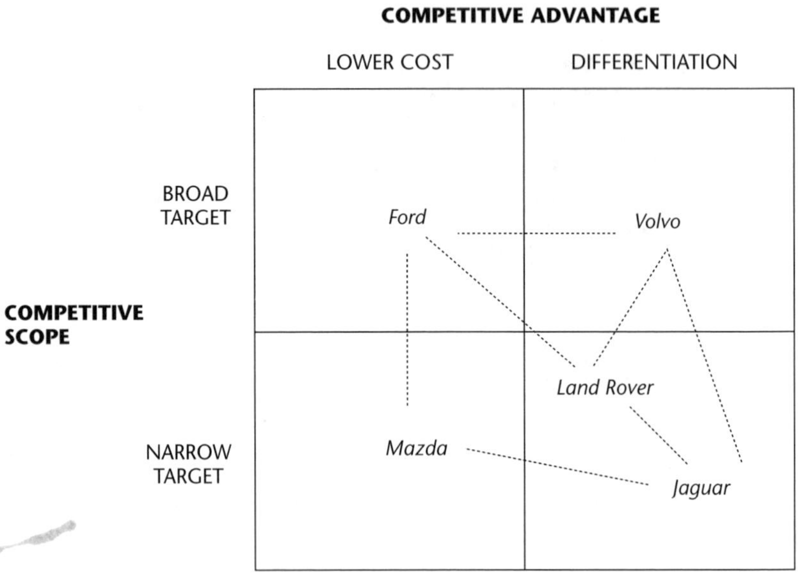

Figure 1.12 The modern GSM crossed with a premodern relationship web

Other companies and groups in the industry may also be quickly and simply mapped out and analysed in this manner:

- The VW group works well by networking particular identities in all four segments. However, draw them out and you will begin to recognize that a key challenge for VW is not to let the sharing of costs across the group lead to all of its marques being perceived as too 'samey' with all gravitating to the middle. This would result in Seat cannibalizing VW sales and VW cannibalizing Audi sales and so on.

- BMW succeeded in positioning Rover to produce the 75, a car directly competing with its own marques in the broad-differentiated segment, and then did not know what to do with it.
- Citroën, whose sameness problems were cited earlier, is attempting to refocus on differentiating itself (in the end it cannot compete just on cost reduction) and Renault appointed Patrick le Quemert as their new head of design with a mandate to bring more 'Frenchness' to the brand.

Porter's notion that companies must be clear in understanding their positioning or identity still rings true. However, the idea that one must choose to *either* reduce costs or focus on differentiation and not be 'stuck in the middle' may be a little outdated in these individualized and network-oriented times. (Indeed, Honda is a great example of a company profiting from being in the middle because it knows it is there for a good reason, which marks it out from its competitors.) Despite this, however, Porter's images, with input or modification in terms of particular concerns, provide great grids upon which ideas can be divided, generalized, spoken and thought as a starting point for debate as to a company's future direction.

Indeed, one of the main reasons that Porter's images are so popular is that their simplicity enables people to interpret them in different ways, work their own thinking into them and express their ideas in ways to which people can quickly relate. Moreover, their simplicity and openness enable people to customize models by combining them into their own particular 'hot-rods'. For example, we have seen managers create montages that help them understand particular situations by 'bolting' a PEST analysis onto the five forces to facilitate a fuller discussion on the factors influencing their industry (see Figure 1.13). (Indeed, one of the questions we often like to press MBAs with in order to get them thinking 'outside the box', is 'why are there five forces of industry?'.)

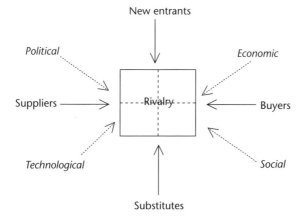

Figure 1.13 Porter's five forces + PEST = nine forces of industry

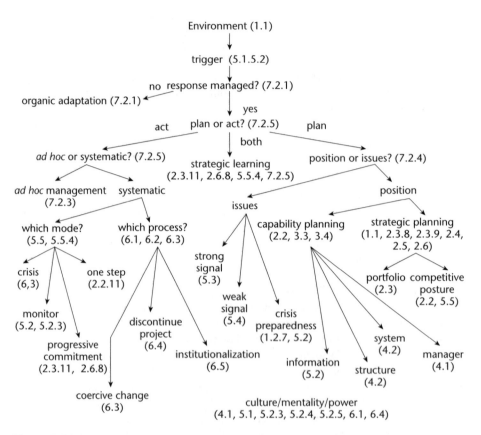

Figure 1.14 A more representative or all-encompassing strategy framework
Source: Figure entitled 'Tree of Strategic Management', from H.I. Ansoff, *Implanting Strategic Management* (1984) (© H.I. Ansoff); reproduced by permission of Pearson Education Inc., Upper Saddle River, NJ.

There are many more complex models than these now available that seek to represent strategy in more objectively representative ways that encapsulate 'the global picture' all at once (see Figure 1.14, for example). However, we have found that in a world where one meta-narrative's ability to represent reality objectively is doubted, these are less effective than more basic forms, such as the GSM or C + M = SP, that allow interpretation, connection and 'play'. The more complex, 'technical' or representative a model is, the more it alienates people, closes off debate, and prevents them incorporating their own ideas or networks of relationship. In fact we argue that while useful images must be regarded as having some 'sympathy with' or connection to the situation faced, their lack of accuracy actually inspires a greater compulsion to 'take ownership' of strategic situations by using these maps as a starting point and then doing one's own mapping.

While academics such as Stacey may be right in saying that conventional strategy frameworks are 'trite' and 'flimsy' and that strategy is much more than this, the call to make such images 'redundant' may be a case of throwing out the baby with the bath water. While things *are* more complex than a two-by-two matrix, good strategies often come from the interaction between local individuals and such images. As with the Hungarian army example or with the tube map, these images need not objectively represent the world all in one. Their divisions and generalizations animate and orient people, they provide a shared language, they act as sounding boards and points of convergence – even if people choose to disagree with them and debate why. So long as we recognize them as such there is no need for belittling – strategic thinking is the richer for them.

David Harvey's *The Condition of Postmodernity* begins with this quotation from Jonathan Raban's *Soft City*, a novel about a London life:

> For better or for worse the city invites you to remake it, to consolidate it into a shape you can live in. Decide who you are, and the city will again assume a fixed form around you. Decide what it is, and your own identity will be revealed, like a map fixed by triangulation.

There could be no better expression of the worth of exploring many different strategic images in the postmodern manner described here, to see which may be particularly useful to connect with, which help you triangulate or begin mapping your own particular concerns. The onus is, first and foremost, on individuals to know themselves and their particular companies. Know this and you can resourcefully use many different frameworks to good purpose. Do that and you will develop a further understanding of your own and other companies and be able to use more frameworks to greater effect. And on it goes, with the strategic manager adding more images and becoming ever more insightful and resourceful. Case box 1.1 gives further food for thought in this regard.

Case Box 1.1   Porter's Power

Power, a pub/restaurant group, has grown fast through successful acquisitions. It now owns many big name brands, including 'Mr Beef, 'MJ's' and 'Pizza Court'. To aid the company's co-ordination as it grows, managers need to think through how these various identities relate to one another. The diagram and dialogue below came about as the result of encouraging a group of these managers to use Porter's frameworks to express their own ideas about where the company was going, with a particular emphasis on Mr Beef.

> Manager 1: Basically, I saw Mr Beef as being a family pub/restaurant, but a bit better than the competition – differentiated. However, over time this has been kind of forgotten. It's been easier to focus on cost reduction and it's drifted back into the broad-cost segment. The interesting development is Happy House [Happy House is a children's restaurant/playground that had been established within a number of Mr Beef pubs]. These have proved really popular and are differentiated and focussed on kids, obviously. So, what do we do? Perhaps we need to revamp Mr Beef and move it into the differentiated end again?

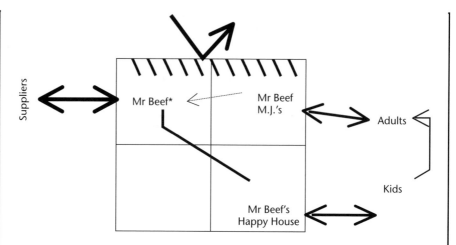

Manager 2: 'Maybe, but there it's almost directly competing against MJ's.'

Manager 1: 'And surely Mr Beef is such a big chain now that we should be in the broad-cost segment? If you add in that part of Porter's five forces of industry that's where we can really exercise power over suppliers by using our size as a buying strength.'

Manager 2: 'But what about the disparity between Mr Beef and Happy House? If we continue with your bringing in the five forces and look at the other side of things, buyer power, we all know that for family pub/restaurants it's kids who often make the buying decision. We can't afford to damage that link by letting Happy House slide the way of Mr Beef.'

Manager 3: 'Sure, but if we realize the difference and the relationship between the two, then surely we can benefit at both ends of the value chain: a strong link into key suppliers and a key hook into a special type of buyers.'

Manager 4: 'Yeah, in a way, if we could do this, and get the best of both sides, then this could be a source of competitive advantage hard to replicate. It would create a real barrier to new entrants up at the top of the box there.'

1. *How did using basic strategy grids aid these managers? How might this conversation have gone differently without using the grids?*
2. *While the above discussion may not represent a pure application of the logic of Porter's models, how have these managers benefited by customizing these models?*

Note: (The identities of this organization and its business units have been disguised). A version of this case first appeared in *Recreating Strategy* (Sage 2002) by S. Cummings.

Images of Strategy – a User's Guide

Creativity comes from the co-agitation or shaking together of already existing but previously separate areas of knowledge, frames of perception or universes of discourse.

Arthur Koestler, The Act of Creation

Knowledge so conceived is not a series of self-consistent theories that converge towards an ideal view . . . It is rather an ever increasing ocean of mutually incompatible alternatives, each single theory, each fairy-tale, each myth that is part of the collection forcing others into greater articulation and all of them contributing, via this process of competition, to the development of our consciousness.

Paul Feyerabend, Against Method

It might be thought that the approach advocated in *Images of Strategy* is similar to Mintzberg's earlier described *Strategy Safari*. However, it is different in key respects. Briefly exploring its similarities and differences, not only in contrast to *Strategy Safari* but also in contrast to other strategy texts, is a good place to begin this outline of how *Images of Strategy* can be used to best effect. And this exploration might best be guided by adapting our earlier developed (on p. 2) animation/orientation matrix (see Figure 1.15).

The first books written on strategic management in the 1950s and 1960s were written from a singularly *industrial economics* basis. While they provided a means of orienting organizations in terms of this logic, they were generally fairly dry and often failed to inspire or animate managers.

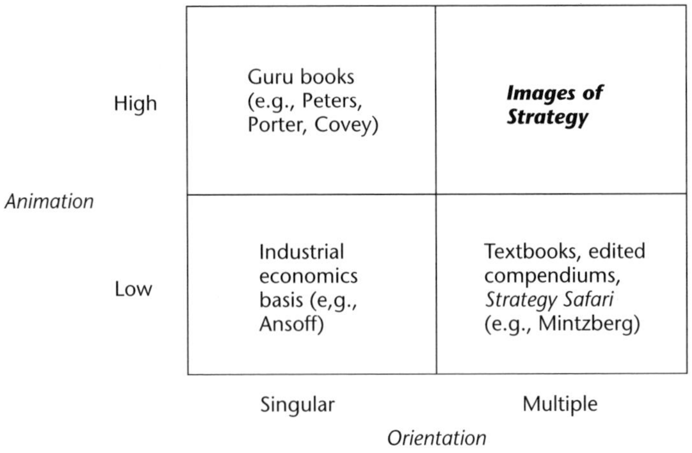

	Singular	Multiple
High	Guru books (e.g., Peters, Porter, Covey)	***Images of Strategy***
Low	Industrial economics basis (e,g., Ansoff)	Textbooks, edited compendiums, *Strategy Safari* (e.g., Mintzberg)

Animation (vertical axis)

Orientation (horizontal axis): Singular — Multiple

Figure 1.15 *Images of Strategy* related to other books

Writers such as Porter built on this thinking, taking strategy into the realm of pop-management *gurus* such as Tom Peters and Stephen Covey by weaving in practical examples and simple checklists and frameworks that were more easily related to and hence more animating. However, these guru books were also singular in their orientation; their logic was based on the view and subsequent images of the individual author. Moreover, these books increasingly became like a fast-food meal – initially tasty, easy to digest and causing a great deal of action in one's stomach, but lacking in lasting effect. While executives may have disembarked transatlantic flights excited by having just read such books, their generic and prescriptive nature often failed to provide the means by which managers could orient or understand or debate their particular company in relation to others or the environment.

The strategy *textbooks and edited compendiums* of strategic thinking, which have become increasingly prevalent in the past decade, moved beyond this tendency to have to choose between either this guru recipe or another, by listing many strategic images by which managers could think their companies. However, their length and dry objective manner, their focus on facts and technical approaches rather than unfolding examples where best answers are by no means clear, and their general lack of a particular philosophy generally meant that the reader's initial animation often collapsed under the weight of all their means of orientation.

Perhaps the most advanced of the multiple means of orientation genre is Henry Mintzberg et al.'s *Strategy Safari*. This outlines the different extant strategy 'schools' and encourages managers to be eclectic. *Images of Strategy* shares this interest in eclecticism, but it also picks up on some of *Safari's* weaknesses. *Safari's* objective overview of existing schools by its singular authors is a useful survey, but we find that it often fails to animate managers. Too often it leaves them asking 'so what should I do now that I've read it?'. Like most safaris, one is guided around as an interested observer rather than an active participant and creator of one's own particular path.

Furthermore, in order to stimulate these particular paths, *Images* advocates a broader and more eclectic range of images of strategy than that contained in Mintzberg's more structured survey. *Safari* is constrained by its reporting on defined schools that have established themselves in the past 40 years and what Mintzberg describes as the strategy tree with its branches 'the basic [modern] disciplines – economics, sociology, anthropology, political science, biology'. *Images of Strategy*, by contrast, is not 'one elephant' looked in at from established perspectives, but personal images from the subjective perspectives of several enthusiasts who want you to take part in their ideas. *Images of Strategy* takes a subjective perspective, assuming strategy depends on who is doing the looking and how that looking is done. To borrow a quotation by William Blake from Duncan Angwin's chapter on 'Strategy as Exploration and Interconnection', 'The eye altering alters all'. Thus in the chapters to follow:

- Stephen Cummings investigates *ancient philosophy* as a means of developing images beyond those provided by conventional approaches to business *ethics* in 'Strategy as Ethos'.
- Karen Legge connects us to an understanding of how *human resource management* and the *linguistic* turns that surround it shape organizational development in 'Strategy as Organizing'.
- Robin Wensley draws on *physics, logic* and *game theory* and beyond to think of strategy as about people's predetermined assumptions in 'Strategy as Intention and Anticipation'.
- John McGee draws on the *economics* and *knowledge* literatures to challenge us to rethink the conventional shape of organizations and the traditional roles of managers in 'Strategy as Orchestrating Knowledge'.
- Bob Galliers and Sue Newell investigate the *human and technology interface* and its influence on strategy in 'Strategy as Data Plus Sense-Making'.
- Chris Bilton trawls his *theatrical* and arts experiences to help us think about how we might develop strategy more *creatively* in 'Strategy as Creativity'.
- Duncan Angwin takes from his background in *historical geography* and knowledge of *explorers* to develop interesting images for exploring aspects of mergers and acquisition in 'Strategy as Exploration and Interconnection'.

- John Brocklesby and Stephen Cummings visit *systems and cognitive biological theories* to see if they may contain images useful for aiding strategy in 'Strategy as Systems Thinking'.
- Andrew Pettigrew reflects on the roles played by *history* and *politics* in shaping the *process* and *context* of strategy in 'Strategy as Process, Power and Change'.
- Peter Doyle seeks to reconnect strategic thinking with the discipline of *marketing* through the image of *shareholder value* in 'Strategy as Marketing'.
- Chris Smith utilizes his background in psychology to look at how strategy is often shaped by our love and need for tangible *financial* figures in 'Strategy as Numbers'.
- And, David Wilson draws on his 25 years of research on the cusp of *organizational analysis* and strategy in 'Strategy as Decision Making'.

Each chapter contains case boxes which provide examples and questions designed to test your knowledge and stimulate debate.

The final chapter draws the different chapters' images together into an integrative framework for thinking through how you might use different images of strategy to orient and animate organizations. This chapter also presents an integrative case.

While the chapters listed above may seem disparate, as they have emerged from first draft to last, we, as editors, have been pleased to recognize the 'base notes' that underpin them. They appear to us as indicative of the particular ethos of Warwick Business School, to which each of the authors is, in some way, connected. These base notes include:

- A *breadth of influences*, which fits with a business school that draws on being part of a fully fledged university, rather than a stand-alone entity communicating only with business concerns.
- A *combination of some fairly 'heavy' theory with practical case examples*, reflecting the ground that we have traditionally sought to occupy by bringing together theory and practice.
- This 'bringing together' relates to our desire to *deconstruct conventional thinking*, but so as to enable *re-constructions that people can use*, not a scorched earth from which we walk away with shrugging shoulders.
- The importance placed throughout on *context and temporality* is reflective of how we have tended to draw on fields like anthropology, sociology and history as much as economics and finance when thinking about management and strategy.
- The recognition that any discussion of strategy requires *forethought* with *regard to the nature of organization* indicates how we have tended to operate on the boundary between what has conventionally been seen as strategic management and organization theory.
- And finally, *Images of Strategy* is characterized by the idea that the world of business is *too complex to allow us to prescribe easy, one-best way prescriptions*.

We hope that you find the images that are built out from these hubs challenging and engaging. However, we do not claim them to be the be all and end all of strategic thought. To think that would be to misunderstand the role of a good creative reader. In Karen Legge's words 'students must be producers of knowledge, not just consumers'. We trust that readers will respond to the spirit in which this book is developed by offering up their own images to add to what we present here. We even offer a web site (www.blackwell.co.uk/resources/images) that invites contributions to what we hope is an organic and ongoing body of work.

Relatedly, it is useful to take a pre-modern attitude to the reading of this book. Plutarch, biographer of ancient strategists, contended that we should read the stories and ideas of such people as a means of stimulating our own unique style: 'A colour', he wrote:

> is well suited to the eye if its bright and agreeable tones stimulate and refresh the vision, and in the same way we ought to apply our intellectual vision to those models which can inspire it to attain its own virtue. [Such a model is] no sooner seen than it rouses the spectator to action, and yet it does not form his character by mere imitation, but by promoting . . . a dominating purpose [to come from within].

We hope that the images we outline, processes of division and generalization that aid speaking and thinking about strategy, or maps that enable mapping, will stimulate and refresh your own strategic vision. However, none of these images will prescribe what you must do, each individual must bring his or her particular purpose and understanding into the mix in order to 'triangulate' or analyse his or her situations. Nigella Lawson provides a useful parallel in bemoaning the 'tyranny of the recipe' in her recently published *How to Eat*. Having several good recipes is a starting point, she explains, but a good chef must be more than this – he or she must have their 'own individual sense of what food is about'. Hence she encourages readers to develop and critique her recipes and think of her book as 'a conversation we might be having'.

Like the Ancient Greeks, and like Nigella, this book thinks of strategy as the *oscillation between* recipes, maps or images, and particular practical chaotic realities. We hope that after years of debating which image best represents the way strategy really is, we might now see the value in being Able to connect to many. One is more likely to reach a *particular destination* by using a Tube map *in combination* with a *London A-Z in combination* with a map drawn by a friend on the back of an envelope. These, *in combination* with other environmental signs picked up along the way, will provide a basis for constructive debate with those travelling with you and, subsequently, a platform for developing impetus. We think that the images of strategy presented here should be used in a similar vein. The measure of this book's success will be the extent to which the reader finds it increasing his or her resourcefulness in connecting them to an increasing number of ways to think about strategy that they can bring to bear in their own chaotic worlds: making them more multiple, more mobile or more polyvalent; making their strategic intelligence more wily and supple so as to help them to think (and un-think) in many directions before deciding the path on which it is best for them to set out. And if there is a picture that expresses this individual building of multidirectional connections then it is the microcosm shown in Plate 1.3.

Consequently, *Images of Strategy* needs not be read in a linear fashion from the first chapter to the last or from strategic to tactical to operational levels like a standard strategy text. Instead, wander over it. Read it as a nomad. Pick up bits that you think are interesting or that connect with your own experiences within organizations past and present, or bits that you think you might usefully apply to give you impetus into the future. We believe that this is where creative problem solving comes from, from different traditions being connected together and, to use Arthur Koestler's phrase, 'shaking hands' in the light of particular purposes and circumstances (see Plate 1.11).

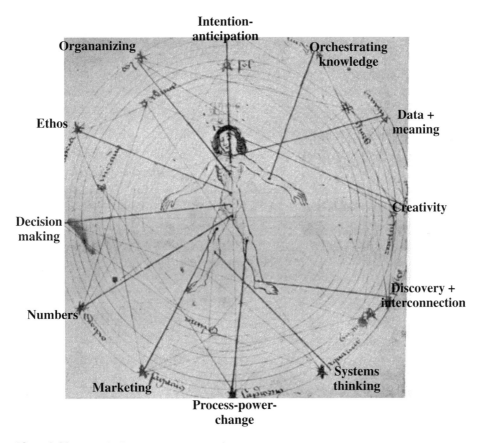

Plate 1.11   Individually connecting images of strategy

In any event, the complexity of a postmodern world, and the subsequent realization that organizations *must accentuate their differences* in order to maintain a sustainable competitive advantage, mean that 'intellectuals' cannot prescribe what individual managers must do. That is a matter for those who determine particular goals in specific contexts. A matter for you. In the words of postmodern philosopher Michel Foucault, 'The intellectual can no longer play the role of the advisor. The project, tactics, and goals to be adopted are a matter for those who do the fighting. [The best] the intellectual can do is provide instruments of analysis.'

Strategy for too long has been driven by academics and consultants looking from the 'outside-in' and offering generic best-practice prescriptions. It is time for the strategic identity of corporations to come from the 'inside-out'. We hope that the images that we have found useful over the years refresh your strategic vision toward mapping a course across your own uncharted territories.

Source Material and Recommended Further Reading

The Hungarian soldier's story at the head of this chapter is taken from a chapter by Karl Weick titled 'Substitutes for Strategy', in J. Teece (ed.), *The Competitive Challenge* (Cambridge, MA: Ballinger, 1987).

A good overview of the 'turf wars' between strategy's bottom-up emergence and top-down planning schools can be gained by reading the exchange between Henry Mintzberg and Igor Ansoff in *Strategic Management Journal* 11 (1990) and 12 (1991). An edited version is reproduced in B. De Wit and R. Meyer (eds), *Strategy: Process, Content, Context* (London: ITP, 1998). Mintzberg's *The Rise and Fall of Strategic Planning* (New York: Free Press, 1994), develops the 'anti-establishment' argument further. Ralph Stacey's *Dynamic Strategic Management for the 1990s* (London: Kogan Page, 1990) is perhaps even more vitriolic. Michael Porter's *Harvard Business Review* article 'What is Strategy?' (Nov.–Dec. 1996) shows the 'empire striking back'. The despairing editorial quotation on page 2 is from Milan Zeleny's 'The Fall of Strategic Planning', *Human Systems Management*, 16, 1997.

For more on how pre-modern ways of seeing and knowing are different from modern views see R.G. Collingwood's *The Idea of History* (London: Oxford University Press, 1960); M. Foucault's *The Order of Things: An Archaeology of the Human Science* (London: Tavistock, 1970); A. Gabbey's 'The Mechanical Philosophy and its Problems', in J.C. Pitt (ed.), *Change and Progress in Modern Science* (Dordrecht: Reidel, 1985); and C. Taylor's 'Overcoming Epistemology', in K. Baynes et al. (eds), *After Philosophy: End or Transformation?* (Cambridge, MA: MIT Press, 1987). J. Seznec's *The Survival of the Pagan Gods* (Princeton, NJ: Princeton University Press, 1953) reproduces several ancient microcosms. Nietzche's *The Birth of Tragedy* (various publishers) is a useful synopsis of the appreciation of Dionysian and Apollonian forces in the Ancient Greek world. For more on *metos*, see M. Detienne and J-P. Vernant, *Cunning Intelligence in Greek Culture and Society* (Sussex: Harvester, 1978). D. Harvey's *The Condition of Postmodernity* (Oxford: Blackwell, 1990) nicely describes the change of perspective from pre-modern to modern with particular reference to mapping.

E. Kearn's 'Change and Continuity in Religious Structures After Cleisthenes', in P.A. Cartledge and F.D. Harvey (eds), *Crux* (London: Imprint, 1985) and S. Cummings and J. Brocklesby 'Toward *Demokratia*: Myth and the Management of Change in Ancient Athens', *Journal of Organizational Change Management*, 10, 1997, provide background on Kleisthenes' reconfiguration of Athens. For a discussion of how this organizational structuring and pre-modern thinking influence the Greek's approach to strategy see S. Cummings, 'Pericles of Athens – Drawing from the Essence of Strategy', *Business Horizons*, Jan.–Feb. 1995.

Roy Strong's commentaries on Elizabethan portraiture, for example, *Gloriana: The Portraits of Queen Elizabeth the 1st* (London: Thames & Hudson, 1987) provide a good starting point for an understanding of the geometry of the modern gaze. The cause of the 'mind-shift' is generally put down to advances in technology in most histories of science. However, A. Giddens' *The Consequences of Modernity* (Stanford, CA: Stanford University Press, 1990) gives a good account of the importance of the rise of Europe's nation-states and organized capitalism and colonialism in shaping the modern representational objectivist way of seeing. S. Toulmin's *Cosmopolis: The Hidden Agenda of Modernity* (New York: Free Press, 1990) puts the case for the change toward privileging certain objective knowledge being related to a Europe fed up with religious and social divisiveness in the seventeenth century. R.S. Westfall's *The Construction of Modern Science* (New York: Wiley, 1971) and R. Dawkins *The Blind Watchmaker* (Harmondsworth: Penguin, 1991) provide good accounts of the development of the modern scientific method. *The Scientific Revolution in National Context*, edited by R. Porter and M. Teich (Cambridge: Cambridge University Press, 1992), builds upon these and describes the emergence of centralized knowledge institutions. The best concise combined review of all of these aspects is S. Shapin's *The Scientific Revolution* (Chicago: University of Chicago Press, 1996).

To see how the shape and perspective of modern scientific reasoning and bureaucracy influence what are considered to be the origins of corporate strategy, read the introductions to A. Chandler's influential *Strategy and Structure* (Cambridge, MA: MIT Press, 1962) and *The Visible Hand* (Cambridge, MA: Harvard University Press, 1977). Also, look at I. Ansoff's *Corporate Strategy* (New York: McGraw-Hill, 1965), and his introductory chapter of *Business Strategy*. 'Toward a Strategic Theory of the Firm' (Harmondsworth: Penguin, 1969). The Ford and Carnegie reports (F.C. Pierson, *The Education of American Businessmen*, New York: McGraw-Hill, 1959; R.A. Gordon and J. Howell, *Higher Education for Business*, New York: Columbia University Press) outline the shape of business schools. L.W. Porter and L.E. McKibbon's *Management Education and Development – Drift or Thrust in the 21st Century* (New York: McGraw-Hill, 1988) shows how the model laid down in 1959 has really only been tinkered with. K. Andrews' *Harvard Business Review* article 'Toward Professionalism in Business Management' (March–April 1969) comments on how Chandlerian bureaucracy and the organization of business schools inform one another.

The best comprehensive survey of postmodernism in all its forms is D. Harvey's *The Condition of Postmodernity*. Important postmodern documents include J.-F. Lyotard's *The Postmodern Condition: A Report on Knowledge* (Manchester: Manchester University Press, 1984), G. Deleuze and F. Guattari's *Anti-Oedipus* (New York: Viking, 1977), and *Mille-Plateaux: Capitalism and Schizophrenia* (London: Athlone, 1988). Umberto Eco's *Reflections on 'The Name of the Rose'* (London: Minerva, 1994) is a readable series of insights into the exhaustion of modernism and the subsequent rise of the postmodern view using his famous novel as an exemplar. For something more focused upon the impact of postmodernism on management, B. Cova's 'The Postmodern Explained to Managers: Implications for Marketing', *Business Horizons* (Nov.–Dec. 1996) brings the issues down to earth in a simple but not simplistic manner.

The state of strategy is discussed by H. Mintzberg, R. Pascale, M. Goold and R. Rumelt in 'The "Honda Effect" Revisited', *California Management Review*, 38, 1996. Mintzberg's latest thinking can be found in *The Strategy Safari: A Guided Tour Through the Jungles of Strategic Management* (Englewood Cliffs, NJ: Prentice-Hall, 1998); and 'Organigraphs: Drawing How Companies Really Work', *Harvard Business Review*, Sept.–Oct. 1999. The pop-management books mentioned in this chapter are T. Peters' uneven *Thriving on Chaos* (London: Macmillan, 1988); C. Handy's interesting but fairly lightweight *The Age of Unreason* (London: Business Books, 1991); and C. Bartlett and S. Ghoshal's very good *The Individualized Corporation* (New York: HarperBusiness, 1997). On the breakdown of the either/or choice between centralization and decentralization see S. Cummings' 'Centralization and Decentralization: The Never-ending Story of Separation and Betrayal', *Scandinavian Journal of Management*, 11, 1995. The revelation that 'Best practice does not equal best strategy' comes from an article of the same name by P. Nattermann, *McKinsey Quarterly*, 2, 2000, 20–5.

Michael Porter's 'generic strategy matrix' and 'five forces of industry' are built up in *Competitive Advantage* and *Competitive Strategy* (New York: Free Press, 1985 and 1980 respectively). For a briefer description of these and many other useful strategy frameworks like PEST, S. Harding and T. Long's *MBA Management Models* (London: Gower, 1998) is an excellent resource. David Knight's article critiquing Porter's models in particular and simple theories of management in general is 'Changing Spaces: The Disruptive Impact of a New Epistemological Location for the Study of Management', *Academy of Management Review*, 17, 1992.

Mr. Beck's Underground Map (K. Garland, London: Capital Transport Publishing, 1994) is a fascinating account of one man's vision and the uniquely memorable London Tube map. The novel *Soft City* by Jonathan Raban was published in 1974 (London: Collins).

Plutarch's ideas regarding the importance of being inspired by strategos models form the introduction to his 'Life of Pericles' (*The Rise and Fall of Athens*, Harmondsworth: Penguin, 1960). Nigella Lawson's words come from *How to Eat: The Pleasures and Principles of Good Food* (London: Random House, 1999). Arthur Koestler's notion of creative decision making stemming from different traditions, 'shaking hands' to solve particular problems can be explored in greater detail in *The Act of Creation* (London: Hutchinson, 1964).

The overuse of 'best practice' has led to a reinvestigation of how a sustainable competitive advantage must spring from things that cannot be easy copied or engineered. Other chapters will examine how the tacit 'knowledge' that is embedded in an organization's particular relationships has thus come to be seen as key. This chapter starts at the core of an organization. It looks at how a corporate **ethos**, similarly difficult to replicate because of its organic, emergent nature and dependence on history, can provide another new form of competitive advantage. Unfortunately, recent attempts to introduce aspects into strategy that might have informed us about ethos have proved disappointing, generally resulting in bland mission statements applicable to any organization and generic corporate value statements that always list the same adjectives. However, research now suggests that people have never thought of companies as if they were lists of values, but as different people or 'characters' and, as such, are happy to attribute different value systems to them so long as their behaviour is consistent. Using this thinking and the notion of 'ethos', the idea that every being has a 'distinctive genius' can be a fruitful way of guiding strategy by accentuating differences rather than conforming to generic standards. This chapter looks at ways of determining and developing your company's ethos and how this can help focus strategic decision making.

2 Strategy as Ethos

STEPHEN CUMMINGS

Things have changed since the likes of Peter Drucker and Milton Friedman's assessments that business ethics was a 'non-subject'. As managers have come to wield more power in society, the claim that 'ethics is other people's concern, we just do the managing', has ceased to wash. In addition, the 'freeing up' of access to global information networks has enabled an increasingly cynical public to find out more about what companies are doing in various locations and effectively network and organize themselves against companies' actions if they see fit. Management has had to respond, and this response has seen the rise of the field called business ethics. This last decade in particular has witnessed an increasing awareness in the importance of 'doing business ethically'. It is a sign of the times that companies such as Royal Dutch Shell and British Petroleum now sponsor reports titled 'Profits and Principles – Does There Have to be a Choice?' These reports conclude that 'Tomorrow's successful company can no longer afford to be a faceless institution that does nothing more than sell the right product at the right price.'

The idea, addressed by statements such as this and in business ethics in general, is that companies must now all be 'good'. However, this has led to a somewhat limited approach to ethics being applied in the corporate world. Because of its historical conception of itself as being built upon beliefs particular to the modern age, and because ethical approaches are now often sold by external consultancies, business ethics has come to emphasize general objective 'goods' and common codes or values, things that can be bought off the shelf and applied to many organizations at once from the 'outside-in'. Strategy has taken the application of 'ethics', 'philosophy' and 'values' to be about organizations developing the same externally imposed ideal or average identity, about imposing the *same face* on all.

Such an approach might work well in a world with one clearly defined universal set of values and if organizations were all made up the same – a world shaped by the generalizing gaze of the triangle and the objective grid described in Chapter 1, where all organizations followed the same bureaucratic hierarchical form and operated according to the same logic. But, paradoxically, the forces for globalization that are leading to a heightened awareness of business ethics are at once driving a juxtaposition of local traditions that is leading many to question the belief in universal goods. Hence, in a world where people are increasingly aware that not to acknowledge that different local traditions sponsor different beliefs as to what is right is both short-sighted and imperialistic, and where the cost advantages of applying universal business processes are not the only motivator for customers, such an approach seems lacking.

The main reason why commentators now confess that the codes of conduct and well-meaning missions that spring from 'an ethical approach' have little impact on the formation of strategy, and why most involved with strategy fail to see business ethics as a particularly informative construct, is no longer that they believe that ethics has no place in business. It is rather that in a time where people are recognizing that 'best practice' copying cannot be effectively applied to strategic thinking, where it is recognized that strategy is about determining and expressing how you are different from your competitors, business ethics appears focused upon bounding organizations to act 'in accordance' or all be the same.

Let us explore the decline of 'best practice' a bit further by critiquing its application to strategy from two angles: first, from a simple economics perspective and, second, from a social or psychological perspective.

If firms seek to copy others (and are advised by an increasingly small number of consulting firms in the process) then their products and services and values become increasingly similar. And when that happens, the main means of customer differentiation between competitors is price. Competition is therefore reduced to a price war, and, because everyone's costs are similar (because they have sought to replicate best practice production methods), everyone's margins decline (one study has shown that this sort of 'strategic herding' led to a 50 per cent decline in margins in the five years to 1999 among German wireless telecommunications providers). In other words, cream is only a treat worth stretching for when the rest of the bottle is milk, and everything being creamed is a recipe for stagnation. As managers become more focused on developing the 'technologies' necessary for copying, the less concerned and able they are to promote substantive innovation, or to get anything different 'out of the bottle'.

From a social or psychological point of view, we can analyse the decline of best practice in the twenty-first century by taking the classic motivation theories of Maslow and Herzberg and combining and playing around with them in a postmodern manner to create the 'reed' diagram in Figure 2.1.

While Maslow suggested that all humans move from satisfying food and shelter needs at base; up to safety needs; then on to belongingness or family or love needs; then once this is satisfied status; and finally self-actualization at the tip of the triangle, nowadays we do not believe that people are so uniformly linear. While our lower order or physiological needs may be common, as people satisfy their basic needs, such as food, shelter, safety and efficiency, they generally look for ways to differentiate themselves. People want different things and once their basic needs are satisfied they increas-

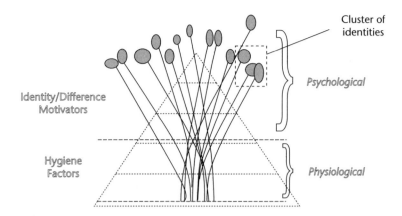

Figure 2.1 A reed model of motivational differentiation

ingly seek to differentiate from others by associating with products that express or augment their identity. For some people, family or a sense of community is most important to their sense of identity; for some it's a particular type of status; for others an individual form of self-actualization.

If we add in Herzberg's idea that there are some things that really motivate us to go that little bit extra, and others that are simply 'hygiene factors' – things that we expect and so therefore take for granted (e.g., cleanliness in a restaurant, air bags in cars), so that their presence does not act as a motivator but their lack is a positive demotivator – we can say that increasingly, in the West at least, the physiological functions of a product or service are hygiene factors. If this is the case, then the motivators are increasingly the stuff of 'identity' (advertisers seem aware of this dynamic – when was the last time that you saw an advertisement that focused solely on the mechanistic functions of a product or service?). This is why the big global food brands emerged at the turn of the twentieth century (Coca-Cola, 1886; Heinz Ketchup, 1876; Colgate Toothpaste, 1896; Kellogg's Corn Flakes, 1906), when production technology was available to produce them and there was a population whose correspondingly 'basic needs' were as yet unfulfilled. Beyond another burst after the Second World War, very few new 'universal' brands such as these have emerged. It is also why most of the big commodity brand producers have, in recent times, had to look for growth in 'less developed' countries as the West is increasingly characterized by what we might call 'lower need saturation'.

Thus, the basic attributes of products or services – function, efficiency, safety, cost, etc. – increasingly become 'hygiene factors'; things that dissatisfy customers if they are not present but do not motivate them to purchase if they are. Motivators to purchase are thus increasingly the things about a product or service that go beyond these hygiene factors to indicate a particular identity or lifestyle choice. And, because people are different, it is increasingly difficult for one company to be all things to all people – to hit all of the reed-heads at the top of the diagram in Figure 2.1. Hence, there may no longer be a general 'one best way'. It depends upon which particular identity or cluster of identities you are trying to target or relate to.

It is an interesting exercise to think of an industry with which you are familiar and ask what are the things about this product or service that are hygiene factors and what are the real motivators, and to ask how this has changed over the past 20 years. But as a general example think of cars. Two decades ago you might not purchase certain cars because you worried that they would be unreliable, unsafe or function poorly. Now through mergers, strategic alliances, reverse engineering and other forms of best practice copying, all cars have got the basic needs covered. For example, not so long ago jokes were made about the function and safety of Skoda and Hyundai cars in this regard. Now it is almost impossible to differentiate them from the more established manufacturers in the categories in which they compete, therefore making these technological aspects more hygiene factors than motivators to purchase. (In classical strategy terms, while these hygiene factors may be increasingly 'critical success factors' they are decreasingly sources of 'competitive advantage'.) This leaves more established manufacturers with three options:

(1) compete on price (very difficult given their historical sunk costs);
(2) rely on systems of tacit knowledge built up over time between people in the organization (explored further in Chapter 5, 'Strategy as Orchestrating Knowledge' and Chapter 9, 'Strategy as Systems Thinking'); and/or
(3) turn to the one thing that they have that cannot be readily reproduced.

Hence, most of the established marks are trying to differentiate themselves by connecting to particular identities or a particular ethos. Look at car advertising, it says increasingly less about physical function and more and more about image.

Identity or ethos, wound up as it is with history, is almost impossible to replicate, whether it be a person's, a nation's, or a company's. Bill Clinton got to the White House in the early 1990s with the catchphrase 'It's the economy, stupid'. However, ten years further on it might be more effective to recognize that it is 'also about identity, stupid'. And identity is something that must grow organically, over time, from the 'inside-out'.

A recent evaluation of a medium-sized financial organization provides a good illustration of how ethics have entered into the strategy arena in a similarly limited best-practice way. This organization had, like many of its competitors, employed consultants to help them to construct 'corporate values'. Seven were agreed upon:

CREATIVITY	PROFESSIONALISM
INTEGRITY	TEAMWORK
RESPECT	HUMOUR
COMMITMENT	

However, upon reviewing the value statements of its competitors, it was found that most, apart from humour, were common across all companies. As the general manager said to me upon seeing this, 'If everybody is doing this then these are just hygiene factors. We need some added-value values' (later sections of this chapter will look at how we attempted to do this, by expanding upon the humour dimension). Case Box 2.1 below provides a further example of how such a generalized, objective and external approach to ethics and values can diminish rather than add value to a particular identity, ethos or ethic of an organization at a time when such things have never been more strategically important.

Thus, there appears a discrepancy between current views of business ethics and the multi-cultural, eclectic, or postmodern, environments in which organizations must now

Case Box 2.1   How External Consultants and 'Best Practice' Can Diminish an Organization's Ethos

The New Zealand Police have a reputation as being one of the least corrupt law-enforcement bodies in the world. Up until the early 1990s, this simple ethos or mission guided them:

'To work with the community to maintain the peace.'

However, as was often the way with public service organizations in the 1990s, the New Zealand Police were increasingly encouraged to utilize external consultants in order to help them move closer toward 'best practice' and be seen to be more 'accountable'. One of the first services that such consultants generally offered was the creation of a new mission statement. Hence, after much development work, 1992 saw the launch of New Zealand Police's new mission:

'To contribute to the provision of a safe and secure environment where people may go about their lawful business unhindered and which is conducive to the enhancement of the quality of life and economic performance.'

Curiously, while the later statement is five times longer it says no more of substance than the first (indeed, by making no mention of how, or by what strategy, its stated aims should be achieved – contrast 'To work with the community . . .' with 'To contribute . . .' – it says less). Subsequently, the second statement is far less memorable and more confusing in terms of how it might be operationalized.

1. *What would have led the consultants involved to come up with the 1992 statement?*
2. *Why might the 1992 statement mean less than the one it replaced?*

Postscript: In recent times the NZ Police have been promoting a new 'strapline' which appears to seek to recapture the spirit of the ethos outlined above: 'safer communities together'.

in multicultural, postmodern environment

act. In response, this chapter attempts to reconceptualize and broaden our understanding of business ethics by incorporating a pre-modern outlook. A vision where ethics was closer to what we now might call character, individual *ethos* or personal consistency than objective universal ethical goods. It is an approach that business ethics has largely written out of its constitution. How it has done so and the implications of this are explored in more detail in the paragraphs that follow. The nature of what an ethos-based approach to strategy would mean is then explored.

The Modern Conception of Business Ethics

With a broad enough perspective one may discern two basic approaches to ethics:

(1) codes of behaviour, and
(2) forms of subjectification.

Codes of behaviour refer to collective rules of conduct that exist above or *outside* of particular actors. These may be used to prove actions right or wrong and thus provide the means to channel individual behaviour in a common, normal or ideal direction. Forms of subjectification refer to individuals constituting or 'rejuvenating' themselves as subjects of moral conduct from the *inside-out*, through the development of relationships for self-examination and according to self-delineated, rather than externally imposed, criteria.

A similar distinction is often drawn between *deontic* and *aretaic* ethics. The former, from the Ancient Greek *deos* meaning 'duty' (in Modern Greek *deos* now means 'fear'), views ethical questions with appeal to some external code of rights and responsibilities toward others. The latter, from the Greek *arete* meaning virtues or personal excellence, is about working on an individual's particular purpose in life, character or *telos*. Most ethical systems in most societies incorporate elements of both of these modes. Business ethics has focused almost entirely on the general *deontic* code.

One need only examine the mainstream literature of business ethics to observe this particular constitution. For example, *Blackwell's Encyclopedic Dictionary of Business Ethics* summarizes ethics in terms of the *deontic* and *aretaic* branches described above and notes that the *deontic* strands harbour business ethics' 'most popular and highly developed approaches'. Its entry on a virtue approach explains that:

> It is not clear . . . that any kind of business could fit the virtue model. [It] distinguishes between the internal and external good of practices. The virtues help us to achieve the internal good of a practice (e.g., effective teaching in academia); external goods such as wealth inhibit the development of those virtues. Business necessarily involves a focus on the external good of wealth, and so precludes the virtues.

Consequently, the *Dictionary of Business Ethics* explains that what managers need from business ethics is 'an orderly way to think through the moral implications of a policy decision – a perspective and a language for appraising the alternatives available from an ethical [i.e., a *deontic*-objective] point of view'. A top-selling strategy compendium similarly informs us that business ethics is about 'the codes of behaviour over and above everyday behaviour that professional and business people agree among themselves constitute the proper way to deal with the general public and each other'. A leading strategy text explains what business ethics should do in the 'model of ethical decision making' reproduced in Figure 2.2. An ethical standpoint consequently means taking an objective position, identifying how action may impinge upon 'stakeholders', evaluating stakeholder rights relative to general or external moral principles, and then using the outcomes of this analysis to provide restrictive boundaries.

Business ethics, as it is currently constituted, is thus largely devoted to codifying general ethical principles, about the study and development of collective charters that provide rules enforceable by objective bodies for individual people, organizations, industries and professions to act in accordance with. On this view, ethics is nothing to do with *arete* or individual subjectification. Indeed, we are told by leading texts that subjects cannot 'create their own morality'; that 'the manager's role if it were derived from ethical theory would focus on society and other individuals rather than on self-interest'. Why this particular constitution should be the case may be better understood by considering the history that business ethics acknowledges. The *Dictionary of Business Ethics* tells us that while the field is 'at least as old as commerce itself, in the modern

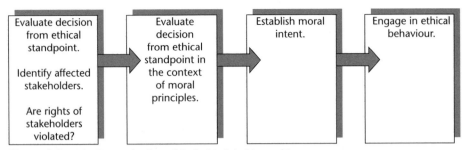

Figure 2.2   A leading textbook model of ethical decision making
Source: C.W. Hill and G.R. Jones, *Strategic Management: An Integrated Approach* (New York: Houghton-Mifflin, 1998).

period [and it is from here its discussion begins] we can date it from the industrial revolution'. Given this point of origin, it may be no surprise that the establishment of business ethics 'piggybacks' upon the particular views of this period – the post-Enlightenment moral tradition.

The 'Enlightenment' of the seventeenth and eighteenth centuries is in many respects the finest flowering of the style of thinking called 'modernism'. Thinkers here sought to move beyond reliance on tradition and custom and the acceptance of individual difference with regard to the constitution and purpose of all things, including humans. Newton's scientific method was increasingly applied to the 'human race' so as to abstract the general characteristics of the 'species' and difficult-to-measure particularities were put to one side or seen as 'secondary'. These general characteristics were then used to establish universal 'tables' comprising categories and measures that could be used as universal backdrops against which particular cases could be assessed. Rather than constellations of unique relationships within particular communities, people became discrete objects subject to general laws and norms. Medical science developed these tables by averaging the data gathered in modern bureaucratic hospitals and clinics – institutions that in turn administered life on the basis of the norms thus defined. Psychiatry and psychology did the same by studying cases and gathering statistics in asylums run according to bureaucratic principles, while criminology drew on centrally organized penal systems. Indeed, the belief that society as a whole could be seen in this way (with bureaucracy as *the* form of organizing and where an individual's behaviour could be detached from his circumstances and traditions and isolated as a 'case' to be judged against general laws, where the common ideals and procedures for operations in society could be specified in advance), supported the belief in a science of ethics that worked toward the provision of general norms of moral action. Consequently, in the period that business ethics takes to be its origin, the word 'moral' only pertains to what is *generally good* and bad, or right and wrong, and ethics is correspondingly defined as the science of 'how we ought to live', with an emphasis on the general 'we'.

Modern developments also added further to the advance of codes of conduct. Given modernity's dismissal of the influence of 'surface' traditions and the belief in liberty and equality, general codes of behaviour became a necessary social component. Without recourse to the guidance of tradition, belief in some overriding restrictions or rules of practice, rules not thought subjective or infringing upon 'basic human rights or norms', became necessary. Hence, in addition to general laws of normality, *common codes* of practice outlining patients' or criminals' rights, doctors' responsibilities and so forth, became increasingly commonplace.

By the nineteenth century, the development of common norms and common codes led thinkers such as Sidgwick to declare that a new 'ethical science' was arising from the application of 'the same disinterested curiosity to which we chiefly owe the great discoveries of physics'. Indeed, modernism appeared, by this time, to have gone a long way toward filling the gap left by the dismissal of traditional beliefs. The eighteenth and nineteenth centuries' ethical doctrines matched developments in other sciences in rejecting the Aristotelian view of people as having a specific *telos* comprising their many individual roles that implied case-specific ways of acting toward particular ends. At the same time, the modern bureaucratic/triangular way of seeing, with general norms below and detached objective observation points above particular instances, encouraged seeing ethics as the perfection of general codes as opposed to the development of a particular *arete* toward a specific *telos*. Moreover, the modern perspective, mixed with the egalitarian and self-sacrificing Christian vision of the period, saw modernity dismiss an *aretaic* ethics as *selfish*. In fact, an *aretaic* approach came to be regarded as not really ethics at all and was subsequently forgotten.

When 'corporate culture' became popular in organizational analysis in the 1980s and the 1990s, many of the frameworks developed to measure the general effectiveness of an organization's culture contained dimensions called 'ethics' or 'moral integrity', indicating how ethics had come to be something that was a discrete element that could be objectively measured and copied from one organization to the next as 'best practice'. With ethics separated out from an individual's particular being, the concept of ethical codes, missions and moral values as things that could be objectively measured, generalized, abstracted and transferred best-practice style became possible, then prevalent, and eventually the only way of thinking ethics with regard to organizations.

The Historical Limits of Modern Business Ethics

When ethics emerged as something that management should be concerned with (according to the *Dictionary of Business Ethics* 'with Baumhart's revealing 1961 study', the first to show 'that ethical issues and problems were important because they were found in every industry, in most companies, and on all levels of the managerial pyramid'), it reflected the heritage described above. Its influences are limited to the modernist top-down triangular perspective and the subsequent quest for general codes outlining common norms while *arete* is not part of its consciousness. While business ethics arose as a field in its own right in the 1960s, it looked back to the halcyon days of the eighteenth and nineteenth centuries for a heritage. Correspondingly, its development mirrors the fate of ethics in general since this period and ethics' subsequent difficulties with regard to having practical effect. Business ethics' attempts to outline *essential* goods and to satisfy all people led, first, to approaches that were difficult to apply to a company's direction or, second, approaches that were so bland as to be next to meaningless. Third, in an attempt to take a firmer stance, business ethics reverted back to the economic logic of efficiency that added nothing more to the economic models that companies were already using.

Limited application

Stakeholder theory, which is claimed to be based on utilitarian principles and maximizing the happiness of all concerned, is currently business ethics' most highly developed approach with respect to actively influencing an organization's decisions. In a stakeholder approach, an organization's duties to those potentially affected by their future development are written down (usually in mission statements or corporate credos). Its limitations may be explored with reference to perhaps the most widely regarded statement of a corporation's duties with regard to stakeholders' interests and rights (see Johnson & Johnson's Credo, Figure 2.3).

I once made the mistake of suggesting that the Credo was so long that no employee could remember much of it let alone take it seriously in an MBA class where two of the participants happened to be J&J employees. They quickly pointed out that the company did take the Credo extremely seriously and that employees were expected to know it (a point they proved by reciting most of it back to the class). The Credo is indeed something that J&J sees as very important, and something that it claims guides its decision making. Its prominence has contributed greatly to J&J's strong reputation as one of the world's most ethical companies.

At the end of 1982, J&J fell victim to industrial terrorists who claimed to have injected cyanide into an unspecified number of Tylenol capsules. Seven people in the Chicago area died. Leading strategy textbooks often outline what happened next; J&J immediately withdrew all Tylenol capsules from the US market, at an estimated cost to the company of $100 million. At the same time the company embarked on a comprehensive communication effort targeted at the pharmaceutical and medical communities. By such means, J&J successfully presented itself to the public as a company that was willing to do what was *right*, regardless of the cost. As a consequence, the Tylenol crisis enhanced rather than diminished J&J's image. Indeed, because of its actions, the company was able to regain its status as a market leader within months. The Credo, it was argued, had shown them the way.

However, in February 1986 another person died in New York after taking a tainted Tylenol capsule and many commentators revisited the case. In 1983, shortly after the first crisis struck, J&J had developed 'caplets', smooth-coated capsule-shaped tablets that could not be penetrated with a foreign substance. Some now argued that if J&J's first responsibility really was to doctors, nurses, patients and mothers and fathers, then the capsules should have been replaced with caplets. James Burke, then chairman of J&J, countered that if 'we get out of the capsule business, others will get into it' and that to do so would be, in any case, a 'victory for terrorism'. Others were more cynical, pointing to J&J's huge investments in capsule-making facilities, a survey that 59 per cent of capsule users would not be willing to switch to caplets, and projections that such a move would result in $150 million pre-tax charge against first-quarter earnings and cost the company between 60 and 80 cents a share. These things, they argued, made doing 'what was right' seem like the wrong thing to do. It was claimed that, in reality, J&J's 'final responsibility', to shareholders, had triumphed over their 'first'.

But then, is it really a drug company's role to act as 'big brother'? Surely all J&J could do was to offer people advice and alternatives, and then it was up to the individual? If J&J had done all that these critics seem to have expected it would soon be bankrupt, which would compromise all of its other responsibilities. The FDA concluded

---

Our Credo

We believe our first responsibility is to the doctors, nurses and patients, to mothers
and fathers and all others who use our products and services.
In meeting their needs everything we do must be of high quality.
We must constantly strive to reduce our costs in order to maintain reasonable prices.
Customers' orders must be serviced promptly and accurately.
Our suppliers and distributors must have an opportunity
to make a fair profit.

We are responsible to our employees, the men
and women who work with us throughout the world.
Everyone must be considered as an individual.
We must respect their dignity and recognize their merit.
They must have a sense of security in their jobs.
Compensation must be fair and adequate and
working conditions clean, orderly and safe.
We must be mindful of ways to help our employees fulfill
their family responsibilities.
Employees must feel free to make suggestions and complaints.
There must be equal opportunity for employment, development
and advancement for those qualified.

We must provide competent management, and their actions
must be just and ethical.
We are responsible to the communities in which we live and work
and to the world community as well.
We must be good citizens – support good works and charities
and bear our fair share of taxes.
We must encourage civic improvements and better health and education.
We must maintain in good order
the property we are privileged to use,
protecting the environment and natural resources.

Our final responsibility is to our stockholders.
Business must make a sound profit.
We must experiment with new ideas.
Research must be carried on, innovative programs developed
and mistakes paid for.
New equipment must be purchased, new facilities provided
and new products launched.
Reserves must be created to provide for adverse times.
When we operate according to these principles,
the stockholders should realize a fair return.

Johnson & Johnson

Figure 2.3   Johnson & Johnson's Credo (reproduced by courtesy of Johnson & Johnson)

that it should not direct or pressure J&J into such an action, and that the decision was
'a matter of J&J's own business judgement'. In any event, it is hard to see how the
Credo on its own could have provided J&J with the best judgement as to what
the company *ought* to do.

In addition, multinational companies are also increasingly concerned about what statements such as 'we are responsible to our employees' in their codes can be taken to mean.
As organizations increasingly act across national boundaries, notions of 'responsibility' are

problematized. Does this mean that companies are 'responsible' to employees in all of the countries in which they operate in the same ways? Should their healthcare benefits, insurances and even salaries be the same? These increasingly asked questions, in combination with increasingly bold lawyers and litigious interest groups, are now making companies balk before committing their duties to paper in this level of detail.

These examples do not suggest that J&J is an unethical company. Rather, they illustrate the limitations of any general code. The proliferation of information technology, mobile populations, multinational corporations and so on, have brought about an environment where different cultures and traditions wash across one another, resulting in the disintegration of the homogeneous socio-cultural canvas and the objective view with which such codes work best. The increasing acceptance of diverging interests and the recognition that measuring and comparing 'stakeholder utility' is impossible, make balancing stakeholder benefits an unworkable objective.

Limited meaning

From a modernist perspective there seem two responses possible to the above: either make codes more detailed so they represent every eventuality, or reduce them to essentials so that codes do not specify particular responsibilities that could be criticized or prosecuted. The first response has resulted in some mission statements being so convoluted that they could not possibly be remembered or applied, while still falling short of anticipating every eventuality in a complex world. The second response has been more commonplace. However, the drive to create shorter, more essential, mission statements and corporate values, tied up as it has been with most companies using the same set of consultant advisers and the effects of internal groupthink, has made 'mission' the past decade's most popular target for corporate satirists. Most prominent among them is Scott Adams, creator of the Dilbert cartoon strip. Adams' combination of a keen knowledge of corporate foibles and biting wit makes his commentaries strike a chord with most managers. About mission statements he writes:

> If your employees are producing low-quality products that no sane person would buy, you can often fix that problem by holding meetings to discuss your Mission Statement. A Mission Statement is defined as 'a long awkward statement that demonstrates management's inability to think clearly'. All good companies have one. Companies that don't have Mission Statements will often be under the mistaken impression that the objective of the company is to bicker among departments, produce low-quality products, and slowly go out of business. That misperception can easily be cured by writing a mission statement such as this: 'We will produce the highest quality products, using empowered team dynamics in a new Total Quality paradigm until we become the industry leader'.

Other Dilbert examples of inanely meaningless, but plausible, missions include: 'We enhance stockholder value through strategic business initiatives by empowered employees working in new team paradigms'. As with most of Adams' humour, it is funny because it is scarily close to the truth. (Indeed, Adams has posed as a management consultant and impressed management boards with mission statements like 'to scout profitable growth opportunities in relationships, both internally and externally, in emerging, mission inclusive markets, and explore new paradigms and then filter, communicate and evangelize the findings'.)

Case Box 2.1 provides one example of an organization attempting to say something that meets external criteria while not disenfranchising anyone or anything that ends up 'fudging' and saying less, but there are many others that could be pointed to. The root of most problems experienced by one company with which I worked recently could be traced to its mission statement: 'to satisfy the needs of our customers, shareholders and employees with exceptional business efficiency and superior service'. It turned out that this statement confused most employees (let alone customers) as they sought to make real decisions. For example, customer service and repair teams claimed that it gave them mixed messages. If they were called out to a repair job at 5 p.m. should they respond and bill the extra overtime to the company (= superior service) or leave the job until the next morning (= greater efficiency)? In similar vein, other commentators have criticized mission statements such as these for setting in stone vacuity and indecisiveness. One recent article in *The Guardian* bemoaned missions such as a gas company's 'Piping gas for you'; a university's 'Setting new challenges, creating new opportunities'; and a government department's 'Investing as people' as pointless on grounds of the 'inversion test'. If you invert sentences such as these you get a ridiculous statement for the organization (i.e., 'Not setting new challenges . . .'), indicating that a company has not really made a substantive decision as to how its character will be different within an industry.

Not unlike the criticisms levelled at modern abstract art as it disappeared toward essential nothingness (e.g., the blank white canvas), the codes, values and mission statements promoted by a business ethics influenced by modernism are now criticized for attempting to satisfy all without offending any. Criticized for being so devoid of meaning for the particular organizations they seek to serve that they are of little use as positive guides to action. Subsequently, many researchers and practitioners now see this kind of mission production and stakeholder ethics as 'wishy-washy', 'blandening', 'empirically problematic' or worse 'fundamentally misguided and incapable of providing better governance'.

Limited development (or back to where we started)

Business ethics' search for a universal overriding good that appears more tangible, justifiable and practically applicable in response to the 'catches' observed above, has seen it fall back upon the economic logic that many may have considered to be its purpose to overcome. In an attempt to provide more concrete or less 'wishy-washy' guidelines for business ethics, the language of economics is blended with utilitarianism. 'Moral common sense is [at the end of the day] disciplined by a single dominant objective: maximizing net expectable utility', explains the *Dictionary of Business Ethics*, and this generally 'manifests itself as a commitment to the social value of market forces'.

Primeaux and Stieber's recent output in business ethics' leading journals is exemplary in this regard. It advocates identifying the 'principles of business itself' as firm foundations upon which 'the ethics of business should be drawn'. These principles turn out to be 'defined in terms of neoclassical economics' because 'the firm's ethics should be economically determined'. Unsurprisingly, the principles or foundations of business ethics turn out to be 'economic efficiency', 'profit maximization' and 'opportunity cost'. Consequently, to find a 'common ethical language', Primeaux and Stieber argue that we must understand profit 'as a means of representing human achievement and social good' and define the 'inherent ethical absolutes of business in terms of economic effi-ciency'. Thus, we may situate 'ethical decision making for business within opportunity-cost decision making', and 'reserve judgment, in the final analysis, to the market'. Or, in other words, 'accept profit maximization and the efficiencies of profit maximization as the primary standard of judgment'

Business ethics' interpretation of history frames it as the provision of general codes to be applied from above and spoken in the modern humanist terms of the general 'utility of all concerned'. In the final analysis, because agreement as to what this tan-gibly might mean and practically effect has proved elusive, the general good arrived at amounts to 'efficiency'. It is now easy to see why strategists should now find business ethics, thus conceived, not to be a particularly useful concept. It is a logic, based on the microeconomic theory of the firm and offering only common assumptions about the way that capitalist economies work, that provides no guidance for differentiated or 'value-added' decision making. It seems to bring us back to where this chapter began, that ethics only makes sense to business if it is subsumed into economics. That, as Mathur and Kenyon's recently published *Creating Value: Shaping Tomorrow's Business* claims: 'financial performance must be the ultimate yardstick of business' and that 'busi-ness merely has an ethically neutral, financial reason for existing'.

Companies are people too?

No wonder, given the limitations described above, that managers should feel disap-pointed after having gone though a 'value development' exercise to the point of claim-ing that they need some 'added-value values' to *really* guide their strategy. Recognizing the limitations of a solely *deontic* approach is one reason why people have begun to think again as to whether it might be worth reconnecting to the *aretaic* channel. Another reason for this rethink is that there is growing evidence to suggest that people do not conceive of companies as lists of objective stakeholder responsibilities, mission statements or lists of values. It appears that they tend to make sense of them as if they were like other people. Hence, while they are increasingly concerned with a corpo-ration's efforts to be ethical in a *deontic* sense, people are at once happy to accept that different companies will, and should, have a 'face' that is unique. They do not expect a corporation, any more than an individual, to be able to be all things to all people, and do not seem to trust them when they attempt to.

For example, market research carried out into terrestrial television channels in the United Kingdom has revealed that people attributed particular characters and, corre-spondingly, different standards to each channel (see Case Box 2.2). Perhaps, this high-lights a postmodern paradox, that in a poly-dimensional world it is better to have a particularly clear sense of one's different 'personality' so that people can make well-informed choices as to who they want to connect or relate to, rather than attempting to represent all things or try to dutifully be all things to all people?

Perhaps this is why Jaguar never really suffered the problems that other cars did as modernist essentializing practices led to its designs looking increasingly bland and 'samey'. The aim of its 'focus groups' was not to determine the average of what a cross-section of people all thought was good (or not bad), but to ensure that at least 80 to 90 per cent of the group could identify a new prototype, without badging, as a Jaguar – as a continuation of the particular Jaguar 'personality'. Whether that appealed to the majority of the people that made up the focus group was not so important.

By the same token, when British Airways (BA) unveiled its new 'global identity' in June 1997 the multi-ethnic liveries that were daubed on tail fins and promotional materials over the traditional Union Jack flags were meant to consolidate BA's sense of itself as 'the world's favourite airline' in the new 'global village'. It seemed to make good sense. But by the year 2000 the fins were being repainted in red, white and blue and advertisements were featuring P.J. O'Rourke's odes to 'Britishness'. Apparently, it was not the protests from within the UK (from Margaret Thatcher down) that hurt BA as much as the protest from groups of Asian customers. They felt that the Union flag had personified a particular type of service that they wished to associate with and that BA's inconsistency was messing with this. Seemingly learning from this failed attempt to be all things to all people, Lufthansa was recently reported to be putting pressure on British Midland (in which it had a 20 per cent stake) not to drop the word 'British' from its name as it sought to expand its presence in the marketplace. Lufthansa's management apparently believed that the British association connected the company to a unique and particular ethos of safety and quality of service. (British Midland subsequently became BMI – British Midland International.)

Case Box 2.2   Channel 5

Channel 5, Britain's newest terrestrial (non-cable) television channel has a problem. Unlike its competitors, it does not have a personality. Consequently, viewers do not know what to expect from it and, subsequently, seem less likely to build a relationship with it.

British researchers have recently demonstrated that viewers tend to have clear images in their minds about the personalities of the television channels they watch. BBC 1 was seen as staid and 'establishment', but reliable – the Queen Victoria of channels. BBC2 was seen as an enthusiastic educator – something between an old professor and a trendy teacher, with a touch of social worker keen to save the world. ITV was seen as jolly, lively and 'more normal', but also a bit 'dodgy', with something of a used-car business about it. Channel 4 was identified as a 'Richard Branson' – entrepreneurial, dashing and risk-taking, but often pushing the boat out a bit too far.

The researchers also found that people do not apply the same ethical standards to each channel. For example, it appeared that one reason for making a customer complaint was if a programme delivered something at odds with the customer's anticipations of the channel's personality, thereby causing dissonance that led to the relationship between viewer and channel to be questioned. A racy programme shown on Channel 4 would receive less complaints than the same programme shown on BBC 1 – partly because of the profile of the people tuning in to each (those watching Channel 4 were likely people who had already decided that their ethos was okay with them), but also due to 'viewer expectations'. Using the same logic, when Channel 4 recently took over from the BBC the rights to show cricket matches, it knew that it would have to show them in a more dynamic, less traditional way – otherwise viewers would wonder 'what on earth is happening to Channel 4?' The message seems to be that customers can tolerate difference more than they can inconsistency.

Channel 5's problem is that their programming seems particularly inconsistent: a unruly mix of half-baked game shows, 'soft-porn', and 1960s wildlife programmes. It is hard to see any positive pattern to it and thus it is hard for any significant segment of the population to 'connect' with. This is partly due to circumstances beyond its control. It is young and it could be said that it is still finding its way (no infant arrives with a personality completely intact). Plus, just after a highly successful launch where the Spice Girls were used as the channel's spokespeople (indicating a bright, optimistic, youthful image), the five Spices became four, and those four seemed to go their own separate ways, making it difficult for Channel 5 to build upon the initial success of the launch. However, confusion still seemed to reign regarding what 5's character should be 18 months after the 'personality research' described above came out. Channel 5 executives recently announced that the channel was going to reposition itself dramatically – moving away from its salacious programming to become a 'family broadcaster emphasizing popular entertainment'. However, this did seem to have been compromised somewhat when one Channel 5 senior executive was reported to be demanding that his channel be allowed to show more explicit sex.

Channel 5 is not the only channel that is working on its personality. ITV has recently launched separate cable-only channels, with significantly different personalities, that will allow it to show a more diverse range of programming without compromising its 'flagship', and the BBC is reportedly not entirely happy about the staid Queen Victoria image. The BBC's public service remit is to 'serve all people', and, in response to what its own research defines as an increasingly fragmented and multi-cultural market, different delivery methods and more consumer choice, it is currently asking itself how, BBC 1 in particular, should change its 'personality' to better match the new environment.

1. Is Channel 5 doing the right thing in its latest attempt to 'rebrand' itself?
2. If you were advising the BBC, what would you suggest they do about BBC1's character?
3. What can we learn about organizations and strategy making from this research into the way that people relate to television channels?

This case is based on reporting in *The Times* ('Who's Your Favourite Television Channel', 2 September 1998), *The Guardian* ('Channel Filth' Plays the Family Card', 12 August 2000), and *The Independent* ('Channel 5 Boss Demands Explicit Sex on Television', 21 August 2000).

Ethos: The Aretaic Alternative?

Ethic. A. adj. *(now usually* ETHICAL.*) 1. relating to morals (i.e., 1. Concerned with the distinction between good and bad or right or wrong, 2. Adhering to conventionally adhered to standards of conduct). 2. Treating of moral questions and of ethics as a science. B.* sb. *1.a. The science of morals. b. A scheme of moral science. 2. The department of study concerned with the principles of human duty.*

Ethos. character, a person's nature or disposition 1. The characteristic spirit, prevalent tone of sentiment of a people or community; the 'genius' (i.e., distinctive spirit) of an institution or system.

The Comprehensive Oxford English Dictionary

Ethics and ethos have come to have very different meanings, despite having a common root in the Greek language. Modernism's quest for greater representative accuracy combined with a desire to identify universals has seen the definition of ethics, provided above, become the basis of our limited understanding of what business ethics is. While the recent emphasis on business ethics in corporations has been useful and helpful for many, the limitations associated with the *deontic* approach that it promotes and the recognition that people seem to connect to organizations as if they were particular people, is now encouraging some to look to *aretaic* alternatives. These alternatives are about developing upon a *characteristic spirit* or *distinctive 'genius'* rather than conforming to the same standards and common duties.

The development of these alternatives to business ethics draws on the rethinking of ethics in general that has taken place over the past few decades, where modernity's emphasis on foundational rule-based codes has been increasingly questioned. Prominent among the questioners is Michel Foucault. Foucault questioned the 'search for a form of morality acceptable to everybody, in the sense that everybody should submit to it'. He found that with the postmodern idea that an essential human 'self' may not be a natural given, the view of morality as obedience to a code of rules was now diminishing. Foucault believed that we must take advantage of this breach by establishing an alternative approach to ethics – one where we 'give style to our characters by surveying all the strengths and weaknesses of our particular nature and fitting this into an artistic plan'. However, Foucault found that such an approach had been lost in our times. He consequently decided to seek such an alternative by looking prior to modernity's dismissal of *arete* and forms of subjectification and was drawn to the Ancient Greeks – particularly the ethics of Aristotle.

'Good', Aristotle stated, could not be 'a common characteristic responding to one Idea', as life contained too many different 'categories'. Subsequently, Aristotle sought to reaffirm the more common Greek understanding of ethics that Plato (with his view that 'goodness' could be a single, self-subsistent entity) had attempted to overcome. During the early phases of modernity, Aristotle's thinking was targeted as symbolic of all that was wrong with prevailing thinking. Moderns, firm in their newfound belief that the goal of science and philosophy was the discovery of general truths and universal propositions, were far more inspired by Plato's arguments for ideal forms that could be abstracted in order to direct general progress. Thus, 'Aristotelianism', the dominant mode of thought in the West until the seventeenth century, was dumped, and the Greeks' approach to ethics, tarred with the Aristotelian brush, was thus forgotten. That it consequently remains largely untouched by modern thought made Foucault think that it might be capable of 'stretching' our thinking today. Perhaps the Greeks' alternative thinking can also be revisited in order to provide an alternative theoretical basis with which to reconceptualize business ethics?

Aristotle began with the notion that the end of an action was *eudaimonia*, which translates as 'happiness', but in a quite particular sense. *Eudaimonia* is not 'pleasure' for it cannot be short-lived. And the happiness that Aristotle expected the virtuous actor to pursue was not, as the utilitarians would have it, the whole world's 'general happiness'. It was rather the *individual* happiness of a particular actor. The *eudaimon* is thus the person who fulfils himself by achieving his 'heart's desire', and he who does so is, according to Aristotle, 'virtuous'. However, because Aristotle recognized that there are many ways people could fulfil themselves and many different ends they could pursue toward *eudaimonia*, to act in accordance with virtue depended on one's particular character or combination of characteristics. 'Virtue', he claimed, 'is a purposive disposition relative to the individual.'

Aristotle's *Ethics* consequently involved three elements: the un-reflective individual, the individual as they could be if they fulfilled their particular character and purpose in life (*telos*), and the moral bearing that would allow one to 'fare well' from one to the other. Morality, therefore, hinges upon knowing one's *telos*, an awareness that could only come from self-reflective contemplation or 'subjectification' – making oneself a subject of personal inquiry and reviewing what one knows about oneself and the traditions to which one relates or 'knowing thyself'. If one knows oneself, he is aware of what his particular character and subsequently his *telos is* and 'is' can indicate 'ought' with regard to what one must do to act virtuously. Knowing one's *telos* would also enable one to know the difference between one's current abilities and what one could be, so that they could begin to contemplate the bearing that could help them 'carry' them toward their *telos*.

This individualized approach to ethics, combined with the fact that ethics was, for the Greeks, a practical subject, meant that no general behavioural code could be appealed to. Because practice is contingent on the particularities of the situation faced, ethics could not be treated with the same clarity as mathematics or chemistry. In keeping with ancient notions of education, an individual's moral tutelage could be further furnished by stories, left to posterity, of virtuous people making particular decisions, but these could not be imitated as 'best practice' – they could only inspire one toward self-reflection and developing a sense of one's own virtuosity. Moral tutelage came from connecting these examples to one's own experiences and traditions and learning not by imitation but by comparison with one's own particular strengths and inspiration. Hence, ethical precepts or principles could only be related to specific situations by means of the sort of perception born of *prudence* gained from a reflective understanding of one's *telos* and a familiarity with analogous situations.

'Prudence' required one to develop a teleological understanding by which one could keep 'faring well' on one's 'life journey'. This wayfaring, claimed Aristotle, could be informed by the 'Doctrine of the Mean'. This suggested that each virtuous act exists between two vices (e.g., between a 'rash' and a 'cowardly' action exists a courageous action; or between 'bankruptcy' and 'self-serving' exists what company X must do to be ethical). However, this could not provide general prescriptions either. Virtuosity was not about adhering to a universal behavioural mid-way point, but acting in accordance with one's particular disposition and abilities, or one's own individual 'mid-way point'. The contemplative, virtuous person would know his character and his own particular limits when faced with a situation. He would also know which 'side of vice' he would more likely veer toward so that he could guard against this.

Consequently, we can say that helmsperson X will be prudent, therefore virtuous, therefore morally correct, if upon confronting a particular helming situation he can:

(1) know his purpose or *telos* as a helmsperson;
(2) connect to the traditions and stories of good helming might suggest in such a circumstance, and;
(3) know what the two vices (e.g., too ponderous or too rash) either side of a good action might be;
(4) know how his disposition might lead him to one or other of these courses of ruin;

(5)   know how his *particular* skill-set within this ought subsequently be put to good use.

This means that helmsperson X might act in ways that are different from those chosen by helmspersons Y or Z if they were faced with the same circumstances, but they all added to the helming community. Because people would be aware of the subsequent strengths and weakness of each, informed choices could be made as to which might best be chosen for particular purposes or missions.

Knowing one's *telos* would enable one to know where best to direct their energies *and* the price one must pay for this direction, because connecting to a specific *telos* means making choices (the great blues trumpeter, for example, will find that this ability will often distract him from attending to life's other pleasures or even other styles of trumpet). Consequently, the virtuous person, according to Aristotle, had an *eudaimonia* that was subject to imperfection. That is to say, one could not be master of all trades or generally good. Aristotle illustrated this by noting that everybody knows that 'Those who have a great many friends and greet everybody familiarly are felt to be friends of nobody.' Aristotle claimed that if one's network (of interests or friends) became too large then they would veer into the vice of obsequiousness where they would be faced with the joy of one friend or interest conflicting with the sorrow of another, thus being unable to be a virtuous actor toward both. The difficulty that the Greeks would have with the application of stakeholder theory is readily apparent.

The claim, quite logical from a modern (or Judeo-Christian) perspective, that this approach to ethics is purely self-serving and anarchic, may be countered by noting that ethos, with a subtle difference of intonation, also meant 'custom'. Ethos may be egotistical, but for the Greeks ego was wrapped up in building with manners and traditional links with one's past and one's communities. An individual character always implied a particular series of relationships – with friends, family, workmates, and the community at large – and the traditions embodied in these. Instead of modernity's scientific approach which separated out the individual as a discrete object subject to essential general principles, people here were conceived as dynamic constellations that could be worked upon. The Ancients took for granted a view of the self not as something pre-given to keep pure and unsullied (as in the Christian conception of soul or a modern material object), but as constituted by one's particular developing community of relationships and 'crafting' of oneself in the light of these (hence Foucault's analogy of the 'artistic plan'). Consequently, *eudaimonia* could not come from self-aggrandizement. It required securing the recognition of the communities within which one acted. Thus, the ultimate consideration for the prudent individual, having reflected on his character, is how his differences could complement those of his peers (e.g., how helmsperson X's differences complemented helmsperson Y's).

Knowing one's strengths and limits, the virtuous person would seek to be recognized as different from others and at once be 'completely integrated', 'on good terms with himself' or 'self-loving' and thus consistent in his character. This would enable them to win the recognition and trust of others within the wider community. Consequently, for the Greeks, virtuosity was characterized by an effort to give one's own life a unique story in which one could recognize oneself, be recognized by others and in which 'posterity could find an example'. But this was not *the* 'best practice' example.

The influence of this thinking on the likes of Heidegger, Nietzsche and Foucault is clear, and, particularly, Heidegger's half-existentialist idea of 'throwness' – that we have choices but at the same time these are limited by our being cast in particular directions by our past individual connections and traditions – and Nietzsche's belief that universal codes could only ever be artificial and limiting constructions. Nietzsche also believed that the Greek attitude toward personal ethics offered interesting ways of thinking beyond modernism. Inspired by the cynic Diogenes, Nietzsche liked to remark that rather than general codes 'what is truly irrefutable', in any philosophy, is what is 'personal', and that 'image of any individual could be conveyed with three anecdotes' or stories, more than with any number of principles.

Following Nietzsche, Foucault argued that 'arts of existence' had been lost as Christianity's and then humanism's focus on commonality downplayed individual difference. Here a self-ethics could only be equated with self-absorption, self-centredness and irrationality. Thus, the pre-Christian Greek idea of the relation with oneself and the nurturing or crafting of this relationship also particularly inspired him. In contrast to an approach to ethics that provoked the self to define itself in terms of a system of rules posited as universal, this was an attitude that enjoined a commitment to the elaboration of an 'œuvre that carries certain aesthetic values and meets certain stylistic criteria'. A process of shaping and developing the self according to personal standards in relation to particular communities.

Not seeing a dichotomy between being self-focused and community-minded, the 'self-aesthetics' that Foucault subsequently promoted did not see the individual as separate from social relations. Foucault noted that 'the pleasures of the other' must be seen in conjunction with the pursuit of a self-aesthetics, concluding that self-aesthetic practices are not something that the individual invents by himself, but patterns that an individual finds in his culture that he must work with. For Foucault, as for the Greeks, ethics or ethos is thus about 'deportment', about finding a way of 'carrying oneself' in a community in a manner that is distinctive enough to enable others to recognize you as a member of the community *and* think you exemplary in your difference; about leaving an impression so as to stand out *and* complementing a community so as to be remembered favourably.

Moral philosopher Alasdair MacIntyre gives reasons why the likes of Foucault's recovery of ethos may be pertinent now. He argues that those who sought to apply the modern methods to morality created an unresolvable tension. In a humanistic manner typical of the times, they believed that everyone had the same potentiality, disconnecting the way an individual 'is' from implying how they 'ought' to act. Thus, they took the first and the last elements of Aristotle's ethical scheme: the untutored individual and the moral precepts that allow him to pass from this to something better, but wished to remain silent about the second, silent about particular ends. Hence, they required a general, secular end that appeared neutral and disinterested and this turned out to be 'efficiency'. Consequently, MacIntyre argues that we now possess only a simulacrum of morality. We continue to talk and act as though we have recourse to frameworks for thinking about and resolving moral issues, but, in reality, moral debates can find no terminus. Moral questions thus end up going unresolved or being answered in terms of an impersonal economic efficiency. MacIntyre asserts that we must return to an Aristotelian ethics, recognizing that removing particular traditions and individual ends from morality results only in anarchic individualism hemmed by 'blandening general codes' that defer substantial debates, while the march of general progress continues to homogenize society. 'Blandening general codes' seem in many ways where the emphasis on ethics and values in management has thus far led us. Perhaps such a return to an Aristotelian ethics or ethos might also provide a means of offering organizations something that they can use to positively, rather than restrictively, inform them as to particular strategic directions?

Ethos-Driven Strategy – Strategy From the Inside Out

> *Twofold arguments concerning the good and bad are put forward by those who philosophize. Some say that good is one thing and bad another, but others say they are the same, and that a thing might be good for some persons but bad for others, or at one time good and another time bad for the same person. I myself side with those who hold the later opinion.*
>
> Dissoi Logoi, author unknown, fifth century BC

How might the idea of recovering an aretaic approach to ethics and the analogy that an organization is like an individual character, distinctive spirit or particular genius, positively influence an organization's development? The following paragraphs provide some ideas.

First, strategy as ethos would encourage organizations to base action not on ethical questions such as: 'what is expected of us?', 'how can we conform?' and 'how do we act in accordance?' Instead it would focus them upon questions such as:

- 'Who are we?'
- 'If our organization were a person, who or what would it be like?'
- 'How and why is this different from the "personality" of our competitors?'
- And, when faced with particular circumstances: 'how must we act in order to be true to or consistent with our character, personality or "distinctive spirit"?'

Ethos-driven strategy would consequently begin with a desire for those within an organization to know itself, develop its own 'artistic plan', 'œuvre' or 'style'. Actions would be scrutinized less from the perspective of how they directly affect external stakeholders and more on the degree to which they flow from and reinforce an internal character. Hence, organizations would not seek to please everyone. For example, customers would not always be right (some customers' particular wants cannot be met while staying true to company X's virtues and so should be referred on to others within the community, such as company Y or company Z, whose character is more in tune with such demands). An *aretaic* approach would, in this way, encourage organizations to develop and promote 'their legitimate strangeness' (to appropriate René Char, Foucault's favourite poet).

How could an organization's 'legitimate strangeness', character or ethos be further developed? The following paragraphs explore three ways. The first, which picks up on this chapter's earlier example of the financial services company that decided it needed 'added-value values' (which we shall call 'Virtue Finance' for the purposes of this discussion), comes by way of Diogenes, Nietzsche and Aristotle. The second draws upon Deleuze's summary of Foucault's attempts to 'think differently' about ethics. The third revisits and reinterprets some useful ideas with regard to developing an organization's mission.

Ethos as individualized or 'added value' values

Returning to the example of Virtue Finance (the company that found that their 'values' were shared by their competitors and thus were 'hygiene factors'), how might a company such as this begin to develop its differentiated ethos or 'added-value values'? Nietzsche's and Diogenes' notion of a character being able to be captured in 'three anecdotes' is one way. Exploring its one unique corporate value, 'humour', and probing what Virtue Finance people actually took that to mean beyond the abstract adjective, teased out stories such as this:

> There is a particular broker who is a Spurs [Tottenham Hotspurs Football Club] supporter who always calls us as opposed to our bigger rivals, even though he's advised otherwise, because he enjoys the mid-week banter with the people here who support other London teams. The banter usually takes longer than the business!

This may not seem much, but it indicates several differentiating virtues. For example, virtue finance:

- is about developing personal relationships with its buyers and suppliers;
- is about keeping staff for lengthy periods so it can develop these relationships;
- is not large and grey and all business;
- that it may not be the biggest is a weakness but its smallness can be made a virtue or a strength if they work at it, and so on.

Thus, a suitable way to begin to reflect on and understand an organization's ethos would be through highlighting a few such anecdotes towards developing a profile or 'œuvre' rather than a restrictive code. Such exemplars may be sought in reflection upon:

- traditions and history;
- funny stories of how employees have done, or do, things;
- key defining crises faced in the past and how it responded to these;
- how the organization consequently does things in the present;
- its historical relations with others and how these shape its make-up;
- its view of what it expects of itself; and,
- how people recognize the organization in contrast to others.

Such an œuvre is likely, due to the personal idiosyncrasy of its elements, to be more memorable and more difficult for competitors to replicate than a code or list of principles.

Applying Aristotle's Doctrine of the Mean can further develop an organization's ethos. If anecdotes, like the one from Virtue Finance above, characterize virtues, what actions either side of them indicate vices?

On the one side, the abovementioned broker could call virtue finance and be met with a *surly matter-of-factness*. The effect of this action would be more damaging to VF's standing than the same action would be to another company's (e.g., a bigger, cost-focused organization) because coming from VF such behaviour is unexpected and confusingly inconsistent.

On the other side, if VF's small talk became *too familiar* it could seem unprofessional.

This *familiarity* is the 'side of vice' that VF's disposition is more likely to veer toward. Thus, it needs its people to be particularly on guard against it.

The profile that emerges from such a process would work strategically as does a novelist's sketch of a character. This usually incorporates character profile and his or her purpose and key historical relationships with others, so as to enable an author to begin with an idea of the range of reactions a character ought to have to situations that emerge as the narrative unfolds. Hence, virtue finance knows, for example, that its ethos ought to promote a strategy that:

- involves the brokers that it has close relationships with in some capacity in evaluating its future development;
- is wary when considering growth opportunities and efficiency measures (such as timing telephone calls) if they impinge on its virtues (e.g., the personal touch; long-standing relationships).

And virtue finance knows, in this manner, how its particular character should be maintained and developed as it has some idea of what type of character it is and can easily imagine how this type of ethos would develop over time.

Four folds of ethos

This ethos-driven approach might be given more structure through the application of Deleuze's summary of Foucault's investigations into thinking ethics differently. Deleuze saw Foucault's work in terms of four 'folds of subjectification'. These folds distinguish an individual and are shaped differently by each subject, be it a society, field of knowledge, organization or individual. But in each case it takes four folds to constitute a distinctive ethical whole:

1. The first fold concerns the *material part of the being*, around which everything else folds. At a personal level, the Greeks saw this as the body and its pleasures, the *aphrodisia*. For Christians it was the flesh and its desires and was treated very differently. An organization might question itself here along the lines of:

- 'What is the core business or resource/s around which everything hinges?';
- 'How are these to be spent and restrained?';
- 'What needs to be done to ensure that they are sustained and replenished?'

2. Next is the fold of *power relations or the rules that one follows* as it is always according to particular rules that one monitors one's material being. Thus, it makes a difference whether one chooses to evaluate oneself in terms of natural, divine, scientifically rational or aesthetic values for example. Here an organization may ask:

- 'What "rules of living" are we bound by?';
- 'What codes do we look up to and wish to evaluate ourselves against?';
- 'What rules are applied for making decisions about our direction?'

That codes are incorporated here indicates that an ethos-driven approach to strategy would not seek to dismiss general codes, credos or principles — its aim is rather to add to the ethical 'folds' that may be related to and to encourage seeing codes, in themselves, not as the be all and end all. (Case Box 2.3 highlights how just discussing the nature of a corporate code can be a useful exercise.)

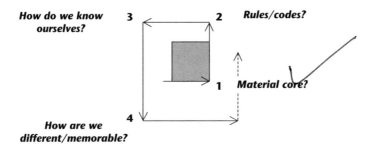

Figure 2.4   Ethos as four folds of subjectification (after Gilles Deleuze)

3.   The third fold is that of *knowledge*. How does an individual seek to know their self? For the Greeks this was primarily through contemplation about one's self and one's relations with friends, gods and traditions; for Christians it is more dependent upon one's relationship with God; for modernists the truth of human workings will be revealed by science. Of this fold, an organization may ask:

- 'What relationships are particularly important to us in defining our self?' (again, this will require making choices and seeing certain relationships are more important, or bigger, than others – in the same way that the pre-modern map in Chapter 1 showed the church and the homes as larger than they materially might be);
- 'Whose reactions allow us to see ourselves reflected?';
- 'What research allows us to know ourselves and how we are seen by others?'

4.   The final fold is the *line of the outside*. This constitutes an 'interiority of expectation', in which the individual recognizes him or herself as different from others. For the Greeks, the aim here was to define a unique but complementary and thus aesthetically pleasing life story. Organizations may correspondingly ask of themselves:

- 'What particular things do we (and don't we) do?';
- 'How will this difference in the way that we carry ourselves enable us to be recognized?';
- 'What do we see as our *telos* or particular *raison d'être*?; how do we want to be remembered?';
- 'What is this organization's style and how is that different from others?'

This leads us back to, and should replenish thinking about, the first fold or the material core of the organization.

Underlying all this is the simple idea that organizations are like characters, and like particular people. When we as individuals relate to others we easily capture all of this complexity. We understand that our friends have a particular ethos that indicates all sorts of things about them, but it may not be the same as our own. Because we know this, we have an idea of how they might act in particular situations. They do not always refer to codes of conduct, but we still consider them ethical, in their own way. If we wanted to describe them to another in anything more than a superficial sense, we would likely characterize them by relaying a few anecdotes. Organizations are like people too.

Case Box 2.3   Discussions Towards a Code

In March 2001, a spokesperson for the campaign for an oath to set global ethical standards for scientists announced that they were 'dropping the future pursuit of it'. It wasn't so much a lack of interest or failing to see it as an important issue that had stalled it, as the inability for the many bodies concerned to agree the wording of a common code. However, as one executive director of a leading scientific research society said, 'I'm sceptical about the practicality of an oath that can be widely applied, but the spirit of the discussions that led toward the oath may be more important than the oath itself.'

1. *Why might discussions toward an ethical code be more important than actually determining that code?*

This case draws on 'Science body snubs "impractical" ethics oath',
The Times Higher Education Supplement, 2 March 2001

Mission revisited

This ethos-based way of looking also encourages us to revisit 'mission', a concept that was largely thrown out with the bath water on account of examples of it becoming subject to the sort of satire described earlier and management's desire to quickly move on to 'the next big thing'. Mission statements were rightly derided as they were increasingly doled out by external consultants and academics rather than developed from within, and subsequently became increasingly bland, 'samey' and timid.

Our word 'mission' is a derivative of the Indo-European (*s*)*meit*, meaning to throw or send. One of the first senses of *meit* appears to have been to throw dung at a wall to dry for fuel, hence the word 'smite' from the meaning 'spot on the wall, where the dung strikes'. Stemming from this is the Latin *mittere* or *missus*, meaning to let go, to cause to go, to send, throw or cast. Hence the emergence of mission (the task on which one is sent or feels compelled to act out) and related words such as missile (a weapon thrown forward), dismiss (a sending away), demise (death, a sending away), emit (send forth), permit (send through) and premise (a foundation or proposition sent forth). Extrapolating this into an organizational context, one can see mission as the particular intent, spirit or 'genius' that constitutes an organization's trajectory that casts and carries it into the future in a particular direction toward its particular goals and targets. This is, of course, quite close to the concept of ethos being developed here. Perhaps the best framework for thinking about an organization's mission is that developed in the early 1990s at the Ashridge Management Centre in the UK. The Ashridge model outlines four elements that, if they reinforce one another to the point where the whole is greater than the sum of the parts, create such a 'sense of mission' that is far more helpful than any grand mission statement. The organization whose behaviour standards or 'actions' match its 'purpose' and whose particular 'values' reinforce its 'strategy' is generating this sense of mission whether or not it writes anything down.

We may return to it to inspire a further means for conceptualizing an alternative, ethos-based approach to an organization's ethics and, subsequently, their strategy. Here we may say that a strong ethos emerges if an organization's *telos* is reinforced by particular 'values', which inspire particular 'actions' by employees which then both

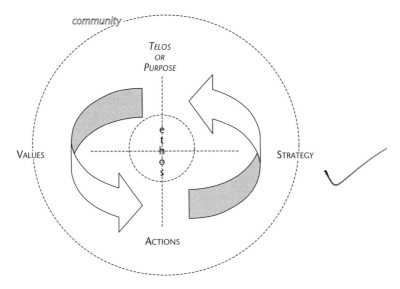

Figure 2.5 The circle of corporate ethos
Source: After A. Campbell, D. Young and M. Devine's Ashridge Mission Model in A. Campbell, D. Young and M. Devine, *A Sense of Mission*

drive and reflect the organization's 'strategy' for working toward its *telos* (see Figure 2.5).

We can use this diagram to reflect on the success of the New Zealand Police's traditional ethos: 'To work with the community to maintain the peace' (see Case Box 2.1). These words reflect the *telos* of the NZ Police, convey a particular set of values, and a sense of how staff should act toward achieving a particular strategy. Over time these things have reinforced one another and gathered strength and meaning so that the 'mass', the ethos, that they embody is far more than the combined weight of the individual words mentioned above. And this ethos has been able to be replenished even as the community around them has developed. (*The Economist*'s 'To take part in a severe contest between intelligence, which presses forward, and an unworthy, timid ignorance obstructing our progress', which has served it since 1873, Marks & Spencer's 'To continually raise the standards of the working man and woman', or *The Independent*'s 'Great minds don't think alike', are other good examples of missions that express an individualized ethos in this way.)

You may further examine how the four elements depicted in Figure 2.5 can create a vicious circle and generate a sense of ethos or, if they are out of alignment, create a vicious circle and subsequent downward spiral by relating the framework back to the television channel examples in Case Box 2.2, or by reflecting on organizations with which you are familiar (in Chapter 14 at the conclusion of this book it may be related to the rise and fall of Marks & Spencer).

The limits of ethos: 'authenticity'

'Authenticity' can be taken two ways. First, philosophers such as Heidegger claim that to simply absorb the ways and traditions handed down by our friends, family and culture is to be inauthentic. To be 'authentic' means critically questioning how things like this influence your character and then, to some extent at least, consciously shaping your own identity in the light of this self-reflection. Taken this way, it might appear that the frameworks that may be used to develop a more individualized or ethos-driven approach to ethics, as developed in the paragraphs above, would give corporations licence to do as they feel *and* then claim to be both ethical and authentic. However, while it is important for organizations to consciously reflect on their ethos if they are to be authentic, a second sense of the word 'authentic' and an increasingly networked society guards against organizations simply picking this or that ethos 'off the shelf'.

To be 'authentic' also means that your identity must be based on something genuine. It cannot therefore be invented out of thin air. It must be based on some characteristic. Indeed, in the words of David Lewis and Darren Bridger's recently published *The Soul of the New Consumer*, while it clearly helps in this day and age if a company's identity is connected with something creative and original, these creative or original aspects must connect to genuine aspects of the past, a particular:

- *time*; and/or
- *place*; and/or
- event or series of *events*

in order for that identity to be 'authentic' and that company to be considered *credible*.

As Aristotle insisted, virtuous persons must reflect some consistency of action over time if they are to be trusted. Thus, a company can reflect on the past and change but it cannot completely betray its history or traits any more than a friend can convince you that he is a new person because he is wearing a new outfit. For example, while British Petroleum may have had good internal reasons for changing its identity to 'Beyond Petroleum' in 2000, the move was criticized in newspaper editorials from London to New Zealand as inauthentic 'beyond belief given that less than 1 per cent of BP's revenues came from renewable sources of energy'. These editorials claimed that BP actually stood 'unmatched in the annals of British business for its contribution to keeping industry supplied with the energy it needs'. BP should be proud of this background and build upon it, they argued. It should 'proclaim itself for what it is, instead of masquerading, quite absurdly, as some kind of rival to Greenpeace'. These arguments seemed to strike a chord, and it was not long before BP was downplaying the change. Subsequently, organizations cannot chose an ethos willy-nilly or buy one off the shelf. Hewlett-Packard's emphasizing the notion of it being different because it is, at core (or on the 'first-fold'), like inventors in tin-sheds, washes because this rings true with its history, as does Jaguar's emphasizing how it is always being about 'little bits of history repeating'. Even new organizations have to work with and build upon the character of those who have formed it. While you cannot make something out of nothing, ethos-driven strategy is a matter of going back to the future – of picking out those elements or 'waves' that you want to build upon and then *surfing*; or promoting these for all they are worth.

Moreover, a company's ethos has to operate within a community (see Figure 2.6). So, while a company, like a character, cannot be all things to all people, it must be something to enough people. It must have some network of others that choose to relate to it. No character can afford to be disenfranchised. To illustrate this, we often show a video called *Roger & Me*. It is about filmmaker Michael Moore's attempts to get the then CEO of General Motors, Roger Smith, to visit the city of Flint,

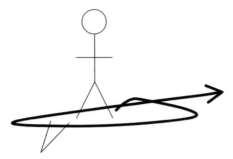

Figure 2.6 Managing ethos as surfing already forming waves

Michigan, the birthplace of GM, to see for himself the disintegration of the social fabric of the town since GM closed down its factories there. Often such films are shown in relation to case studies showing how other companies have been good and highlight how GM's decision was evil. However, most who watch the film say they would not necessarily change the decision to relocate to climes where production costs were lower. The thing that galls, and which subsequently caused GM the most damage when the film came out, was that GM appeared to be unwilling to confront the issue. It appeared unwilling to be up-front and straight about the choices it was making, and seemed to believe that the community that was once important to it was now nothing to do with it. Conditions may have meant that it had to change its relationship with Flint, but it should not have washed its hands of the implications of its decision.

Thus, from an ethos-driven perspective, a company such as Bodyshop *ought* to honour its hometown and keep its interests there because it is upon such values that the company is explicitly founded and profits from. Not to do so would be inconsistent. But, the same need not apply to a company such as GM, which competes on different bases. However, companies such as GM, like all companies from this alternative ethical perspective, must be forthright about their differences and the choices that they have made. Then individuals have the free access to the information they need to choose whether they wish to connect to them or another organization given their particular needs.

It is interesting to note that recent cases indicate that developments in information technology may be enabling a more *aretaic* approach now by exercising an influence similar to that of the public communities in which Aristotle thought. Influenced by a greater transparency promoted by, and 'community discussions' on, the Internet, many companies are currently 're-crafting' their characters. Nike and McDonald's are prominent examples of organizations that have had to re-evaluate and re-shape their virtues in light of these developments while recognizing that they cannot completely change their strategic direction or satisfy all stakeholders at once.

Conclusion

Know thyself

Ancient Greek proverb

In an episode of *The Simpsons*, Grandpa breaks the family television set. On their way to buy a replacement, Bart asks his mother if they can get one shaped like a New York Diner from 'The Sharper Image'. Lisa pleads that they buy one constructed according to age-old traditions by Hopi Indians. Their mother reminds them that they 'can't afford to buy anything from any company that has a philosophy'. Traditionally, approaches to business ethics have alienated many assuming that there is a general sense of angelic goodness that should be aimed for. While this may be possible for trendy-niche players, it means that for others ethics becomes 'something for other people' or something to be paid not much more than lip service. While all organizations must operate within communities and thus respond to certain stand-ards of acceptability if they are not to be ostracized, just because an organization seeks to focus on lowering costs or serving an older demographic does not mean that it does not have an ethos. (Think, for example, about why SouthWest Airlines so regularly tops customer satisfaction ratings in the US.) *A* more *aretaic* approach may enable many companies to more substantively think about and debate their ethical standpoints and bring ethics on to the agenda in places where it has not previously been.

This does not mean that we should overthrow conventional approaches to business ethics. Rather, in a postmodern way, a more pre-modern *aretaic* appreciation should be *added* to the modern focus on *deontic* codes in order to give people within organiza-tions, more to think on, bounce around and create with. But we should recognize that in environments not dominated by bureaucratic commonality, where people have less faith in general goods, or products and services that please all people (or plans that authentically satisfy all stakeholders), environments where organizations cannot be 'best friends with everybody', the concept of ethos may proactively inform a company's direction in ways that business ethics thus far has not.

However, in developing this approach we must be wary of falling into the same traps. Because organizations are 'thrown' by the wash of the past into the future in unique and historically influenced directions, everyone has a unique history to be built upon, a *unique ethos*. Thus we should avoid seeking to transplant 'best practice' values from one organization to another and using external consultants considered expert because of their detached objectivity and having performed similar tasks across many organizations. If ethos is about exploring what comes from the inside-out rather than what might be imposed from the outside-in, about knowing thyself, then the onus for developing ethos must fall back onto the people within particular organizations. It is they who embody that company's way of proceeding and perhaps best know the company's idiosyncrasies or 'genius'. In this way, by helping organizations to develop the 'face-to-face' nature of relations between themselves and those they seek to deal with, and by encouraging them to accentuate the differences that make individual personalities and organizations endearing, ethos may fruitfully connect the realms of ethics and strategy.

Case Box 2.4 and Case Box 2.5 enable you to develop your ability in this regard. The first provides an example for debate that illustrates how a particular ethos can evolve to fruitfully inform a strategy over time. Case Box 2.5 examines how in this fragmenting world a core ethos may be extended into a 'family' of differ-ent but related characters in order to serve different 'identity clusters' (see Figure 2.1). How you respond to it may cause you to reflect back upon question 2 in Case Box 2.2.

Case Box 2.4 From Jack Dee to 2-D

In the early 1990s, Jerry Goldberg, brand manager at Scottish Courage Breweries, oversaw the appointment of up-and-coming deadpan comedian Jack Dee as the spokesperson for John Smith's Bitter. 'When John Webster at DDB (the advertising agency responsible for the campaign) suggested Dee we weren't worried about whether he'd be big', reflected Goldberg. 'The fact was that his personality suited the brand's "no-nonsense" positioning.' Five years on, the Jack Dee campaign, with 50 awards to its name, was widely regarded as having helped propel John Smith's from number 16 to number 4 in the UK beer market, toppling Tetley's from its market-leader perch in the 'bitter' segment for the first time. In December 1995, John Smith's sales were almost two percentage points behind Tetley's. Three years later, they were 4.5 per cent ahead. In 1998 Scottish Courage decided to replace Jack Dee.

The Jack Dee campaign had re-energized a beer with a long, solid history; a beer that had personified the honest, straight up, 'no-frills just good taste' ethos of a bitter first brewed in Tadcaster, Yorkshire, 240 years ago. Now a new creative team came up with 'no-nonsense man', a cardboard cutout synthesis of an 'average bloke' pictured with a pint of John Smith's. A new agency, GGT, said that it would continue with the 'no-nonsense' image.

Jerry Goldberg's successor as brand manager explained that the new 'no-nonsense man' campaign would take 'the "no-nonsense" proposition one step further – our new frontman is the ultimate no-nonsense celebrity'. Scottish Courage's marketing manager claimed that 'no-nonsense man aims to show the beer's down-to-earth positioning in an involving way. It conveys all the product-values. It has the potential to become a cult star.'

Even though Jack Dee was by no means everybody's' favourite comedian, the momentum generated by the Jack Dee image had helped put John Smith's in a position where it looked well placed to leapfrog Guinness as the UK's third top selling beer (after Carlsberg and Fosters). However, after the launch a survey by *Campaign* magazine showed that 67 per cent of people thought that 'no-nonsense man' image was less effective than Jack Dee. A year on and the general consensus among industry and media commentators was that 'no-nonsense man' lacked the impact of the previous campaign and that, despite Scottish Courage not giving up on him, he was 'not catching on'. No-nonsense man had not become a 'cult star'. John Smith's had not overtaken Guinness.

By 1999 Goldberg had moved on to become brands director for lagers at Scottish Courage and was overseeing another highly successful campaign – Fosters' 'He who thinks Australian, drinks Australian'. Jack Dee hosted the British Advertising and Design Awards that year. One magazine's review of the night describes how 'the audience loved it when he riffed about "the days when John Smith's advertising used to win awards" and baited "Anyone here from GGT?" with a "You haven't won anything".' Whether he was genuinely bitter or just being funny was hard to tell. But then it always is with Jack Dee.

1. *What did Jack Dee provide for John Smith's that 'no-nonsense man' couldn't?*
2. *How could the Jack Dee campaign help focus a positioning strategy, and help Scottish Courage at once revive and change John Smith's brand and corporate values?*

3. As the case mentions, Jack Dee was never the most popular of comedians. Would a more generally appealing comedian have been even better for John Smith's?

4. Does the 'He who thinks Australian . . .' ethos 'work'? If so, why?

The case contains elements from *Marketing*, 'Lager Than Life' (23 April 1998); *Marketing* 'John Smith's in £10 m Sales Push' (9 September 1998); *Marketing*, 'Media Case Study: John Smith's' (23 September 1998); *The Scotsman*, 'Cardboard Cut-out With Cult Status' (24 September 1998); *Campaign*, 'Live Update' (25 September 1998); and *Campaign*, 'Design and Advertising Brave an Uneasy Alliance' (14 May 1999)

Postscript: in 2002 'no nonsense man' was replaced in John Smith's advertising by another up and coming comedian: Peter Kay.

Case Box 2.5   Ethos 'Families'

After working through the Channel 5 case (Case Box 2.2) as a preparatory exercise, a group of managers from a bank, based in the UK but increasingly, through mergers and acquisitions, present in other countries, settled down to discuss the ethos of their corporation and its current strategy. They began to think of the corporation in terms of its personality.

This was not an easy exercise for them, indicating that the corporation's personality or *ethos* was not particularly clear. One thing they were clear of, though, was that one of their leading competitors had recently got it all wrong. Barclays Bank had just launched a media campaign extolling the virtues of its 'bigness'. Celebrities such as Anthony Hopkins and Robbie Coltrane told the camera that 'people want things "big" – and they want a big bank'. According to the research done by these managers, people may have wanted some of the benefits that a big bank offered, but they also liked the idea of dealing with a bank that 'felt' small, who valued particular personal relationships.

Eventually, they came up with three possible personality types: James Bond, the current CEO of the bank and Michael Palin. After some discussion, Palin was thought best. The idea of Bond appealed to many, particularly the male members of the team. However, it was quickly decided that while his British, suave demeanor and his unruffled 'shaken not stirred' character could fit nicely, his risk-taking and attitude to women (an interesting character to have a 'fling' with, but not a very safe long-term bet) probably did not fit the image the bank wanted to present. Many thought that having a well-liked CEO step forward and lead the company from the front, in the spirit of Victor Kiam or Richard Branson, would have been particularly powerful. However, others countered that his personality could be problematic given that it was not well known to those outside the company and that the 'heart' would be pulled out of the corporation when he, inevitably, left. So in the end it was Palin – the ex-*Monty Python* turned world-travelling documentary maker – who won out. He is British, but had made a second career of combining this very British nature with embracing foreign cultures and appearing completely sympathetic to their differences. His television shows were the epitome of the 'when in Rome' ethos. He is also, said one manager 'a nerd, but with a broad good nature and a sense of humour underneath it – unlike James Bond you can associate this with a bank'.

While they could not have avoided thinking of strategy while thinking of characters, the managers then turned to focusing specifically on how the articulation of this personality or ethos could be related to a strategic position.

Using Porter's Generic Strategy Matrix (Chapter 1), they placed Palin firmly in the middle of the competitive advantage distinction between costs and differentiation. 'It's a very Palin-like position', said one manager. 'He just understands different perspectives.' They also felt that his wide-ranging appeal ('you can watch his show with the kids and even teenagers kind of like him because of the *Monty Python* connection') put him firmly at the broad end of the broad/narrow scope distinction.

'I guess this fits with our strategy,' another manager continued. 'Like all banks we're increasingly having to cut processing costs. Globalization is increasingly giving us opportunities to do that. At the moment we're switching a lot of our data processing and clearing stuff to India and places like that.'

Another interjected: 'But we maybe have to be careful about this, what with concerns with business ethics and so on.'

'Sure, sure, we can't abuse different people – maybe the Palin image can help us formulate our approach to that. But we have to cut costs to compete. But at the same time one of the strongest things our market research is telling us is that most of our customers like having a branch. They like the idea of a branch manager or someone they can talk to in a branch about them. So, one of the ways that we are going to try and differentiate ourselves increasingly is by having a strong local branch presence while others are closing theirs down. So I guess what I'm saying is that we have to look both ways – toward new suppliers for cost saving and to existing and new customers to differentiate, even though keeping the branches open and staffed costs us a lot.'

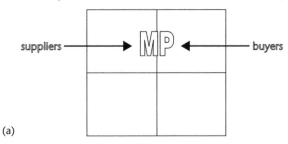

(a)

There was general agreement about this logic and the first figure presented here was developed. Another manager expanded on it: 'And we do, through our traditional presence in the High Street, have a broad appeal – in fact, we have to cover a lot of fixed costs so we really have to be broad to shift the "units" needed to perform.'

Moving on to expansion issues, the bank had recently announced two new initiatives: an Internet banking option and a tailored investment-banking arm. These two companies had been launched under different names, to avoid diminishing the brand image of the parent. However, all the managers present believed that it was important to realize how the various parts of the expanding company fitted together so that the most could be made of the synergies and cost reductions available to the group.

It was suggested that the Internet banking operation enabled the company to put forward a low-cost bundle of products and services to a particular market, while the personalized investment banking advice offered by the other arm sat in the differentiated and more exclusive segment. 'Together', said one manager, 'perhaps they could be seen as "the Palin children" – the same sort of values having been bred into them but they are more dynamic, more focused on what they want to do and a little bit less risk averse' (as the second figure seeks to represent).

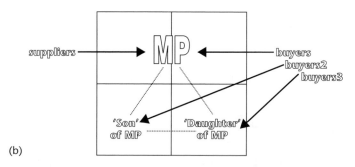

(b)

Nobody present knew whether Mr Palin would have been receptive to an approach with a proposal that could have led to these ideas being used in the public arena. Nor did anyone know whether Mr Palin had any children. But perhaps neither of these things mattered, for the time being at least. A group of managers had a clearer idea of what their organization was and what it was not and could, from there, begin to think about how they would move into the future.

1. Why shouldn't the bank have gone with the CEO or Bond? Surely these 'characters' would have been more personal or more exciting?
2. How are ethos and strategy related?
3. Outline the ethos of your company or an organization that you are familiar with. How should it be driving that company's strategy?

Note: (The identity of this organization has been disguised.)

Source Material and Recommended Further Reading

Abraham Maslow focused specifically upon the links between individual needs and work rewards, offering a perspective based upon the relative value individuals place on various rewards. Individuals are predisposed to satisfying these needs in a specific order – a hierarchy – ranging from physiological to self-actualization (physical comfort to challenge and achievement). Frederick Herzberg provided the Motivation-Hygiene Theory, whereby there are two types of motivators – those which provide job satisfaction (motivators) and those which merely prevent dissatisfaction (hygiene factors). Abraham Maslow, *Motivation and Personality* (Harper & Row: New York, 1970). Frederick Herzberg, B. Mausner and B. Snyderman, *The Motivation to Work* (Wiley: New York, 1959).

The report 'Profits and Principles – Does There Have to Be a Choice?', from which the quotation in the first paragraph in the chapter is taken, was published by Royal Dutch Shell in

1997. A good critique of best practice applied to strategy is 'Best practice does not equal best strategy', P.M. Nattermann, *McKinsey Quarterly*, 2, 2000, 20–5.

A more academic critique of the limits of business ethics is provided in S. Cummings, 'The Resurfacing of Self-Aesthetics as an Alternative to Business Ethics', in S. Linstead and H. Hopfl (eds), *The Aesthetic Organization* (Newbury Park, CA: Sage, 2000), pp. 212–27. B. Kjonstad and H. Willmott's 'Business ethics: restrictive or empowering?', *Journal of Business Ethics*, 14, 1995, 445–64) is another good critique of how business ethics is used only to provide general boundaries rather something that might be developed individually. G. Starling's 'Business Ethics and Nietzsche', *Business Horizons*, May–June 1997, 2–12, provides another, very entertaining, alternative perspective to business ethics.

The Blackwell Encyclopedic Dictionary of Business Ethics is edited by P.H. Werhane and R.E. Freeman (Cambridge, MA: Blackwell, 1997). Other good examples of how business ethics tends to be conceived of only from a *deontic* or external perspective can be found in T. Donaldson, *Corporations and Morality* (Englewood Cliffs, NJ: Prentice-Hall, 1982); T.L. Beauchamp and N.E. Bowie, *Ethical Theory and Business* (Englewood Cliffs, NJ: Prentice-Hall, 1993); and *The Economist's Pocket Strategy* (Harmondsworth: Penguin, 1994). P. Primeaux and J. Stieber have published a wealth of material on how economic efficiency provides the measures of business ethics, including *Profit Maximization: The Ethical Mandate of Business* (San Francisco: Austin & Winfield, 1995); and 'Managing business ethics and opportunity costs', (*Journal of Business Ethics*, 16, 1997, 835–42).

E. Steinberg's 'The Defects of Stakeholder Theory', in *Corporate Governance Quarterly Research and Theory Papers*, 5(1) (Oxford: Blackwell, 1997), is a good overview of the views against adopting stakeholder-based approaches given their limitations. The debates raised here are developed further in the 1999 edition of *The Academy of Management Review* (vol. 24, no. 2). Scott Adams' views on mission statements are taken from *The Dilbert Principle* (London: Boxtree Press, 1997).

Foucault's interest in ethics is described in M. Gardiner 'Foucault, Ethics and Dialogue', (*History of the Human Sciences*, 9, 1996, 27–46). Aristotle's *Ethics*, often published as *The Nichomachean Ethics* is available in a number of formats, including *Aristotle: Ethics* (Harmondsworth: Penguin Classics, 1976). J. Urmson's *Aristotle's Ethics* (Oxford: Blackwell, 1988), is a good academic summary of some of Aristotle's key themes and differences relative to modern thinking. The connection between the thought of Foucault, Aristotle, Nietzsche and Diogenes is covered in J. Miller, *The Passion of Michel Foucault* (New York: Simon & Schuster, 1993). Deleuze's understanding of Foucault's work in terms of the four folds of subjectivity is developed in *Foucault* (Minneapolis, MN: University of Minnesota Press, 1988).

For more on MacIntyre's thesis regarding ethics and modernity see his *After Virtue – A Study in Moral Theory* (London: Duckworth, 1981).

The emergence of our understanding of mission is outlined in S. Cummings and J. Davies 'Mission, Vision, Fusion', (*Long Range Planning*, 27, 1994, 147–50). Figure 2.5, 'The circle of corporate ethos' is based on 'The Ashridge Mission Model', developed in A. Campbell, D. Yeung and M. Devine's *A Sense of Mission* (London: FT/Pitman, 1993).

The Soul of the New Consumer, by David Lewis and Darren Bridger, is published by Nicholas Brearley (London, 2001).

The notion of ethos can be connected to emergent ideas relating to corporate identity, M. Schultz et al.'s *The Expressive Organization: Linking Identity, Reputation and the Corporate Brand* (Oxford: Oxford University Press, 2000) is an excellent collection of new thinking on this theme.

Several of the themes addressed here are backgrounded and developed further in S. Cummings *Recreating Strategy* (London: Sage, 2002).

*Defining organizing as 'how people make sense out of chaos to develop patterned regularities of behaviour over time', this chapter argues that in order to understand strategy we must reflect on this **organizing** process. It builds upon the ideas put forward in the 'Strategy as Ethos' chapter and contends that language plays a vital part in organizing, in accentuating aspects of the past and projecting values onto the future in order to make sense of the present. It then sets out to investigate how companies refer to their employees (as 'commodities', 'assets', 'team members', etc.)*

indicates a particular ethos embodied in a particular organizational form; a particular approach to learning; and thus a particular strategic approach. This chapter argues that by recognizing the subconscious link between 'naming humans' and strategy we can become more effective strategists, and develops the image of the strategist as a circus ringmaster who must balance the organization's particular need for control with the freedom and chaos necessary for innovation and dynamism to emerge.

3 Strategy as Organizing

KAREN LEGGE

Conventionally, strategy is seen as a purposeful, future-oriented activity represented by abstract things such as 'plans' and 'objectives'. As Henry Mintzberg and his colleagues put it, 'Ask someone to define strategy and you will likely be told that strategy is a plan, or something equivalent – direction, a guide or course of action into the future, a path to get from here to there.' But while we can anticipate the future, in a sense, we never experience it, as our direct experience, even our reflections on the past and anticipations of the future, is inescapably in the present. The past and the future, in other words, are always seen through the eyes of the present. Hence the view that strategy can equally be seen as an emergent sense-making activity, a present-day interpretation of the past that, with the benefit of hindsight, identifies consistency of behaviour as that behaviour unfolds over time.

This, of course, is exactly what organizing is all about – developing purposeful patterned regularities of behaviour out of our unfolding lives, or more precisely, creating narratives (i.e., names and stories) that interpret and represent behaviour as such. Whereas 'organization', as an abstract concept, sits happily with other strategy abstractions such as 'plans', 'organizing', as a verb, is focused on people and their behaviour developing over time. The problem for us as we organize in this way is that people's behaviour can be inconsistent as well as consistent, unpredictable as well as predictable, uncertain as well as certain. Indeed, it must be partly inconsistent – otherwise our lives would be completely determined, uncreative and undynamic (and, I would add, not worth living). Thus organizing, and, by analogy, strategizing, is about reconciling our paradoxical need for both pattern or consistency and the freedom to be unpredictable or creative as we move from the past into the present toward the future.

We can explore this further by adopting a 'Derridean perspective'. The French philosopher Jacques Derrida argues that societies resolve the underlying uncertainty and ambiguity of life as it unfolds by naming things according to simple binary oppositions (e.g., good and evil; civilized and barbarous; global and local; progress and regress). The meaning of words is thus constituted through binary oppositions, in which one term is privileged over a marginalized term. So, 'organizing' is defined by and contains its opposite through the implication that without organization there would be 'disorganization'. Hence, the process of organizing is the activity of creating order, patterned regularities of behaviour or sensible narratives of that behaviour, out of a potential disorder. However, because both must exist for the other to make sense, the terms are co-dependent. Thus while we might hope that good might overthrow evil, or organization overthrow disorganization, both must continue, eternally. Furthermore, Derrida demonstrates that because binary distinctions are socially or culturally constructed rather than fundamental, they can be deconstructed and we can show how things could be different. For example, we might ask why globalization has come to be seen as progressive and thus necessary, or even inevitable. Could we argue that localization might be just as viable or useful?

The lists of binary oppositions shown below (with the privileged or positive term first and the marginalized or negative term second) highlights the organizing or strategizing problem:

ORGANIZATION	DISORGANIZATION
CERTAINTY	UNCERTAINTY
AUTONOMY	CONTROL
INNOVATION	STAGNATION

The conventional view (in Western society at least) is that organization is better than disorganization; and that certainty is better than uncertainty (uncertainty is bad for the markets!). However, the bind is that the wholesale achievement of these things runs contrary to our simultaneous desire for autonomy (over control) and innovation (over stagnation). In this chapter I take the view that organizing is about creating environments that mediate (or allow people to mediate) this tension, and that different organizations (being mini-societies) can follow different strategies to do so. Some will err on the side of creating certainty and control and stagnation and others on the side of innovation and autonomy and disorganization. However, every strategy will of necessity contain elements of 'both sides' – even if one side is more 'sub-text' than explicit. Knowing how a particular organization organizes in this way will thus give us valuable insight into its implicit emergent strategy (which is not always the same thing as its plans!), and the potential strengths and weaknesses of this strategy.

But how might we see or know the approach an organization is taking? Derrida argues that one can see what a society privileges and marginalizes in its use of language. The most commonly cited example in recent times has been the binary opposition of white and black. In the Western world white, often unwittingly, is privileged. We can see this by looking at the 'spin' that our language puts on it *vis-à-vis* black. Think of terms such as 'whiter than white'; 'a white knight'; 'the future looked black', 'blackguard', 'blackball' and 'black magic'; and think about the stories they connect to and what images or messages they consequently convey. Subsequently, I propose the following methodology: that we look at how organizations organize and strategize by looking at how they use language: names and stories, to describe their members.

Thus, in this chapter I explore strategy as the sense-making processes and associated narratives of organizing people at work. What continuities/discontinuities can we construct in examining over time (but from today's perspective) activities aimed at creating patterned regularities of behaviour in organizational members? This will involve a consideration of how employees, work and organization are regularly 'reinvented' in the light of dominant interpretations and changing management fashions. Yesterday's machine bureaucracy becomes today's multidivisional firm and tomorrow's networked organization. One theme is constant though: that strategy as 'organizing' is not about overthrowing chaos or uncertainty, it is about managing the contradiction inherent in our need for both chaos and order, certainty and uncertainty. For example, it is between the extraction of surplus value and its realization in the marketplace, between the exercise of control and the generation of commitment, between stability and change.

Strategy as organizing, from this perspective, picks up on a further image – that of the circus, replete with tightrope walkers, jugglers, lion-tamers, bareback riders and clowns, in the nominal control of an orchestrating ringmaster. The good ringmaster must mediate between the ever-present threat of chaos (without which the circus would fail to entertain) and the necessity of order (without which everything would collapse). Each ringmaster's (or strategist's) style or 'grip' will be a combination of the firm and the tenuous, the disciplined and the dexterous.

This chapter is structured into four main sections. First, a discussion on the images of organizational members conveyed by the names that we give them. Second, how images of organizational members are reflective of strategy. Third, images of organizational members as reflective of organizational structure (note the reassuring Chandlerian ordering here, that structure follows strategy – a debatable point to say the least!). And, finally, a discussion on the tensions and contradictions between these images and the role of the ringmaster in balancing them in a world where people are savvier about spin.

Images of Organizational Members

How are people at work represented in discourses about organizing? Management literature is replete with famous discourses on the nature of people at work. Some notable examples include Frederick Taylor's classic description of the ideal handler of pig-iron as 'a man . . . so stupid and phlegmatic that he more nearly resembles in his mental make-up the ox than any other type', and Douglas McGregor's 'theory X and theory Y'.

Taylor's view of the employee was of a child who lacked the maturity to recognize what was best for him. McGregor argued that the common assumption of the working man, captured in Taylor's description, was a *cog in a machine* needing to be controlled by a manager/father-figure (theory X). This behaviour, McGregor claimed, was 'not a consequence of man's nature . . . but of industrial organizations'. Subsequently, it needed to be replaced by an opposite and more truthful understanding of how people are motivated. McGregor termed this theory Y: that humans are intrinsically commit-

Theory X Workers are stupid and lazy 'cogs' and thus have to be bribed and coerced to do their jobs. Management is thus about control.	**Theory Y** People are intelligent beings who are intrinsically motivated to work and to achieve. Management is thus about harnessing, unleashing and co-ordinating commitment.

Figure 3.1   'Theory X' versus 'theory Y'

ted to work and to achieve, thus organizations should grant them more autonomy to achieve their goals and seek to align these goals with those of the organization. That McGregor's work is currently being revitalized indicates how people love simple dichotomies. It also indicates how little management theory has advanced in the past four decades.

But one need not delve into the recesses of management theory to see images of organizational members. They are everywhere in everyday language. Note the heading that began this section, in itself is an act of representation. Organizational 'member' has connotations of value and inclusivity entirely absent in the labels of 'worker' and 'employee', which through signalling what they are not – 'manager' and 'employer' – carry connotations of hierarchy and, through such vertical differentiation, of exclusion. The language of employment reflects prevailing beliefs about the nature of work and the social and economic order.

Thus, for example, the rise of the factory system and large-scale organization, the dominance of the machine in imagery as well as actuality and the symbiotic assertion of an instrumental, technical rationality, gave rise to a view of people at work as a depersonalized labour input. People were represented as 'hands' in the act of heavy manual working. (Henry Ford apparently used to complain that 'every time he asked for another pair of hands it came with a brain attached'.) The verb 'to labour', consequently became the noun 'labour', to describe people at work.

To take a Derridean view again, and to be sensitive to the historical 'traces' of the word 'labour' as it relates to childbirth, this also evokes a negative understanding of work as hard, exhausting and painful, possibly even dangerous, but at the same time a worthy activity with potentially good outcomes. Thus embedded in this label are also connotations of the Protestant work ethic, the importance of deferred gratification and the avoidance of being labelled 'workshy'; at the very least to be part of the 'deserving' rather than the 'undeserving' poor. We should note that the most famous US models of motivation not only take a pyramidal form (as in Maslow's 'hierarchy of pre-potency', which mirrors the modern triangular hierarchies that inform strategy – see Chapter 1), or contain binary oppositions (as in theory X/theory Y, or Herzberg's 'motivators' and 'hygiene' factors), but also rest on an assumption of the intrinsic value of 'work' as a potential source of recognition and 'self-actualization', as a route to both becoming 'one of the elect' and of being recognized as such.

Marketplace images	Commodity Resource Asset Customer
Community images	Family member Team member

Figure 3.2 Images of organizational members

Clearly, in a Western world of outsourced commodity manufacturing and the celebration of professional services 'staffed' by knowledge workers, such language has fallen from favour (no wonder McGregor is popular again!). But in a capitalist system the commodification of labour is never far away. Today, 'strategy as organizing' speaks of reducing the 'headcount' (note: 'head' rather than 'hands') in order to improve shareholder value. However, this is not the only prevalent image of organizational members. As I have argued elsewhere, employees may be represented in terms of images of the marketplace (for example, 'commodity', 'resource', 'asset' and 'customer') and of the community (for example, 'family member', and 'team member'). The market (which seeks innovation *and* stable 'fundamentals'), and the community (with its desire to allow freedom or happiness or fulfilment *and* order), serve as excellent, but significantly different, analogies for what organizing is seeking to achieve. Subsequently, these images serve to tell us much about differing philosophies/strategies of organizing and I explore them in greater detail in the paragraphs that follow.

Images of the marketplace 1: the employee as commodity

Prior to the guild system and rise of the Protestant work ethic, the image of work in Western society had been grim – most famously seen as fit only for slaves in ancient societies. As suggested above, the Industrial Revolution, the factory system and the rise of employment/unemployment as the 'normal' status of most 'ordinary' people, gave rise to a grim image of work being equated with that of the employee as a labour input, a commodity, something to be bought and sold. Today, this is most evident in the models of 'new' organizational forms, such as Atkinson's model of the 'flexible firm' (developed at the right-wing Institute of Manpower Studies).

These models are replete with a new range of representations. In particular, rather than being 'labour', employees are now 'core' or 'periphery' and, if the latter, part of the 'contingent' workforce. Moreover, the 'contingent' workforce may constitute 'outsourced' and 'insourced' employees where their commodified status is evident. Thus, leaving aside the issue of freelance knowledge workers who, while subcontracted, are more correctly represented as independent entrepreneurs, the bulk of labour in subcontracted organizations is a *commodity* in the sense of being an input brought in to minimize the costs and optimize the profits of the contractor. The visibility of these employees is not as 'people at work' but as 'costed labour inputs' which can then be reflected in competitive pricing.

Insourcing

☞ Enhances flexibility (turn on and off like a tap)

☞ No legal or psychological contract with the individual

☞ Outsource management problems associated with non-core staff

☞ Greater cost efficiency (on average 15 to 20 per cent)

Figure 3.3 An employment agency's summary of the key benefits of insourcing

As John and Kate Purcell point out, a similar case exists with insourced labour. Agency contracts, providing generic and easily replaceable skills (e.g., data-inputting, telesales), are more usually concerned with cost than with quality and there is real pressure for cost reduction. A worst-case scenario is where what is now termed the client organization's 'labour procurement' function itself becomes outsourced and needs to prove its worth by securing a reduction of agency charges in order to secure its own contract renewal. Labour as a commodity is therefore seen in terms of a market exchange transaction, as a variable cost and, indeed, hardly as human at all. John Purcell cites an overhead slide from an employment agency's presentation that encapsulates this position. Figure 3.3 shows the key benefits (naturally from the contracting client's perspective – a commodity has no views of its own), that it sought to attribute to insourcing. In other words, the image of the employee is that of a commodity ('turn on and off like a tap'). And, if a commodity, the organization can wash its hands of responsibilities (no legal or psychological contract, outsource management problems), all in the interests of an economic rationality ('greater cost efficiency').

Images of the marketplace 2: the employee as resource/asset

The second, very different, market image is that of a *resource* or *asset*. This is the image beloved of company reports:

'Our most valued asset is the people who work for us'
'We pride ourselves on "Investing in People"'.

Here the employee is presented as the source of the organization's value added and competitive advantage; an asset to be cherished and developed (as long as it continues to be defined as an asset) rather than a cost to be minimized.

Organizations favouring this image, often professional service firms, engage in related imagery. They refer to 'the war for talent', and the need for 'golden hellos' and 'golden handshakes'. (Note the reinforcing, if contrasting, imagery here: the preparedness to 'fight' for a valued resource, which is then greeted as a 'friend'. Deconstructing this meaning, the 'friend' has the potential to become a competitor or enemy, if she remains unrecruited or leaves, hence the need also for 'golden handcuffs'.)

As an asset, there is a stress on developing reciprocal commitment. Employees are offered 'high-commitment' human resource management (HRM) practices and, in return, in theory at least, they offer attitudinal commitment (rather than the resigned behavioural compliance asked of the employee as commodity). This, it is argued, will result in 'higher performance', particularly for the long term. Rather than a back-grounding or denial of a psychological contract between the employee and the organization, it is seen as integral to the relationship and may be expressed in terms of a commitment to no compulsory redundancy.

Images of the marketplace 3: the employee as customer

The third, and perhaps now most popular image of employees, is that of the employee as *customer*. From Adam Smith onwards, apologists for market society have privileged the choices of consumers over the skills of producers. Admittedly, this is not always apparent. Indeed, in the recent celebration of the 'enterprise culture' in the Thatcherite UK society of the 1980s, a case could be made for the reverse – a eulogizing of the producer. The dual meaning of enterprise, as a noun ('the commercial enterprise') and as a verb (to be 'enterprising, by showing initiative, energy, independence, a willingness to take risks and accept responsibility for one's actions') come together in the presentation of the entrepreneur (for example, Richard Branson and Bill Gates) as hero. Indeed, Mintzberg and his colleagues represent the entrepreneurial school of strategy formation very much in terms of proactive 'visionary leadership'. But this is to background the essence of entrepreneurial success – a recognition of the sovereignty of the consumer and the need to respond to (or manipulate) her demands.

The consumer is presented as the epitome of the autonomous individual, creating and recreating successive identities through patterns of eclectic, self-fulfilling and liberating consumption, where freedom of choice is exercised to the full. If post-industrial, postmodern society privileges consumption over production, the provider of goods and services that fuel consumption is best portrayed in the language of consumption. Hence the fashion for representing the employee as the 'internal customer'.

The employee as 'internal customer' has a complex and symbiotic relationship with the employee as 'external customer'. The representation of employees as internal customers is intimately bound up with issues of quality and responsiveness to the external customer. This can be seen most clearly in Japanese-style 'lean' production systems, awash with total quality management (TQM) and just-in-time (JIT) initiatives. The employee, embedded in process-oriented organizing systems, has the 'right' to demand that inputs received conform to agreed specifications and, as supplier to the next process, the obligation to satisfy the needs of the next 'customer'. If the essence of a customer is to exercise choices, logically the employee, as internal customer, has to be afforded an element of job discretion and, as is appropriate in a world of customer sovereignty, this is represented as 'empowerment'.

In fact, given the fragility of lean production systems and lean organization generally, if responsiveness to the customer is to be achieved, this is not only desirable but also necessary. The fragility of lean production systems makes them highly vulnerable to workflow contingencies and employee lack of co-operation; hence generating employee flexibility, commitment and trust is vital. This calls for organizing a high-trust working environment, at least in theory, where employees can be relied upon to exercise their discretion, but in the employer's interest. The employer, also as customer, buys co-operation in order to achieve external customer satisfaction, the foundation of organizational viability.

And, just as people at work are represented as customers, as Paul du Gay and Graeme Salaman point out, external customers are now represented as people at work, indeed, as managers, as 'customers are made to function in the role of management . . . as customer satisfaction is now defined as critical to success'. In fact, external customers often *are* people at work as, co-opted in the 'McDonaldization' of society, they perform activities once the preserve of employees, through a whole range of self-service activities. For example, filling cars with petrol (pump attendant), stocking the supermarket trolley (sales assistant), collecting food and clearing tables at fast food outlets (waiter), using cash machines and telephoning/interest banking (bank cashier) and so on.

In summary, given the images and stories that surround 'customer' in our society, the representation of employees as customers has a positive up-beat ring to it:

- Customers have choices (empowerment).
- Customers have to be listened to (participation).
- Customers have sanctions (they can boycott goods and services – read withdrawal of co-operation if the effort–reward bargain deteriorates); and, of course,
- 'The customer is always right.'

All this takes place, so the spin would have it, in healthy 'lean' organizations, (so different from those 'fat' bureaucracies), where employees were supposedly disabled by suffocating red tape and where the external customer always came last.

Now let us turn from these 'detached' marketplace images to contrasting images of community: the employee as belonging to an organizational 'family' or 'team'.

Images of the community 1: the employee as family member

The values that underpin the marketplace images of the employee (individualism, free choice and economic rationality) are backgrounded in favour of collectivism, consensus and a social rationality (i.e., stressing the importance of social bonds and loyalties) in communitarianism. From this standpoint the employee is presented as a member of a social organization where the bonds are not those of contractual exchange, but of socially embedded reciprocities.

The communities to which the employee is portrayed as belonging generally comprise two representations: the family and the team. The images of family and team are both essentially unitaristic, assuming at the very least common goals, reciprocal loyalties and mutual support. A third possible community analogy, communities of labour solidarity, trades unions and professional associations rarely appears in managerial discourses. This is perhaps not surprising, given that they are represented as institutions that offer competing and potentially conflicting ideologies and loyalties. It was notable in the 1980s that the managerialist Thatcherite administration waged war on both unions and professional associations and referred to union members as a 'conscript army'. This very phrase suggests the invalidity of such representations of solidarity: employees, it is suggested, do not choose to join unions and are held against their will. Hence, we are left with two conventional community images: the family and the team.

The organization as family and the employee as *family member* are, of course, models of paternalistic employee relations. The image relies on a very traditional (idealized?) and hierarchical model of the family, with the father (read management) having control over the children (read non-managerial employees). The image of the wife and mother has resonances with the personnel function, not only because of the latter's female/welfarist image, but, presented as the 'oily rag'/'man-in-the-middle', personnel also has the motherly image of intervening with the father on the children's behalf. However, as in traditional families, although the father may exercise control, it is meant to be benevolent and for the ultimate good of all family members – hence the notion of benevolent paternalism. Further, this benevolence is not exercised solely in a Kantian mode of dutiful rationality, but is softened by affective bonds that underwrite a concern to treat family members as ends in themselves, each person being valuable in its own right.

The family may have its squabbles internally, but will fiercely protect each member against criticism from outsiders and aim to present a united face to the outside world. Hence representing the employee as a family member simultaneously asserts the following values:

(1)   hierarchy – but each employee having her own value and place;
(2)   control – but a caring paternalistic kind of control;
(3)   unity against competition; and
(4)   the pursuit of managerially/paternally defined goals – with internal conflict de-emphasized, indeed, trivialized.

Above all, just as individual family members' interests, in theory at least, are subordinated to what is in the family's interests as a whole, so employees, as members of the organizational family, in their own eyes (if they have swallowed the rhetoric) or in management's eyes alone (if they have not), should subordinate their interests to the organization. As with families, this may be justified by arguing that the family's/organization's well-being is the best guarantor of each family member's/employee's well-being.

This image survives for the same reasons that paternalism survives – the belief that caring and efficiency are mutually supportive rather than in conflict. As Edward Cadbury put it in 1912, writing of his welfare paternalism at Bournville, '. . . the supreme principle has been the belief that business efficiency and the welfare of employees are but different sides of the same problem'.

But this image is under threat. First, the traditional picture of the family on which paternalism rests is on shaky foundations. Today the word 'family' is as often associated with the words 'breakdown' and 'dysfunctional' as with 'happy' – symbolically questioning not only the unitaristic consensus of organizations but the existence of a long-term relationship between the employee and the organization. Gone are the jobs-for-life assumptions on which paternalism was predicated.

Second, just as in a family one is accepted largely for what one is rather than for what one does, so in traditionally paternalistic organizations there was tolerance of individual differences in (some might say 'lack of') performance, as long as it was accompanied by the appropriate attitudes of loyalty and deference. Today, as is evidenced even by the so-called 'sophisticated paternalism' embodied in bundles of 'high-commitment' HRM practices (of which more in a moment), although 'appropriate attitudes' are still to the fore (now defined as 'flexibility', 'a willingness to learn', 'team-player', and so on), tolerance of poor performance is now extremely limited. Selection is based on competence in aptitude tests as well as on attitudinal correctness, and rewards are contingent on performance. Further, the concept of 'empowerment' flies in the face of paternalism's view of employees as potentially wayward children (which seems fairly close to Taylor's archaic view).

Images of the community 2: the employee as team member

The 'team' image, in its principal manifestation, is in some ways an updating of the 'family'. If we take the team as a sporting metaphor, we can isolate a few key images:

(1) Members work together in pursuit of a common goal (e.g., victory!).
(2) Each member has a specialist role to play, but recognizes that the interests of the team override those of individual members – the charge of 'prima donna' signifying disapprobation when these priorities are reversed.
(3) There is the implication of reciprocal obligations supported by affective bonds of comradeship, shared interests and even mutual enjoyment; and,
(4) Just as the father is the head of a traditional family, so teams have 'captains' or 'leaders'.

In several respects, however, the images differ. Following the sporting analogy, membership of a team is usually voluntary, for a limited period and dependent on performance. Membership of a family of origin, notwithstanding earlier comments about family breakdown, from the children's perspective at least, is not chosen and conventionally it is for life and only tenuously linked to performance. Hence, as already suggested, while the family image appears to relate to earlier periods of organizing, this team image satisfies the present-day demand for attitudinal correctness combined with a concern for high performance but with a recognition of the insecurities of employment. If the performance of the team falters, erstwhile 'stars' run the risk of being dropped or transferred, along with the sacking of the manager.

However, the image of the team has other connotations. As the introduction to this chapter indicated and point (2) above makes clear, autonomy and control are not a simple either/or choice: these two opposites imply one another and hence coexist. As Parker and Slaughter make clear, the positive connotations attached to our everyday conception of teams rest on the assumption of the co-operation of specialists towards a common goal, rather than that of interchangeable members:

> In fact, the main place in our language where 'team' implies interchangeable members is where it refers to a team of horses – beasts of burden of equal capabilities yoked together to pull for a common end (determined by the person holding the whip).

In such a team (virtually a 'chain gang') membership is not voluntary and the nature and pace of work are prescribed by whoever has the 'whip-hand'. This projects an image of work being hard, not to say oppressive, and lacking any potential for enjoyment. It also suggests that work will be the same, day in, day out, and relieved only by the odd rest day.

This is very much the picture of teamworking at the Nissan car plant in Sunderland (in the north-east of England) as painted in Philip Garrahan and Paul Stewart's famous study and typified in terms of peer surveillance and 'management-by-compliance'. Team membership is not voluntary in the sense that the alternative is unemployment and life on diminishing state benefits. As such, this 'teamworking' has much in common with the fragmented, standardized, externally paced, Tayloristic work of 'cogs' in the machine. Here the 'team' is comprised of the cyborg of a fused man/machine, epitomized by the Ford assembly lines. Hence we may see a negative sub-text beneath the positive text with regard to 'team member'.

Images of Organizational Members as Reflective of Strategy

What might these images of employees tell us about emergent strategies of organizing people at work? First, a little history.

The lowly world of personnel management

Certainly if we take a conventional view of strategy, what Mintzberg and his colleagues have termed the design, planning and positioning schools, organizing people at work is either invisible or, at best, what John Purcell has termed, a 'third-order', functional strategy. (Note that the term 'functional' refers us back to images of inputs, machines and *cogs*.) Thus it is subservient to corporate, 'first-order' strategy: dealing with the long-term direction of the firm; and 'second-order' business strategy: dealing with internal operating procedures and relationships between different parts of the organization (see Figure 3.4).

The supposed specialists in managing people at work – personnel and industrial relations managers – were, for the greater part of the twentieth century, marked by their low status and exclusion from formal (i.e. important) top-down strategy making. Indeed, two examples will suffice to demonstrate their unenviable position. Drucker, in 1961, famously commented that:

> Personnel administration ... is largely a collection of incidental techniques without internal cohesion. As personnel administration conceives the job of managing worker and work, it is partly a file clerk's job, partly a housekeeping job, partly a social worker's job and partly fire-fighting to head off union trouble or to settle it ... the things the personnel administrator is typically responsible for – safety and pension plans, the suggestion system, the employment office and the union's grievances – are necessary chores. I doubt

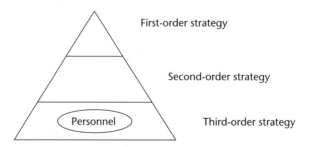

Figure 3.4   Three orders of strategy and the position of 'personnel management'

though that they should be put together in one department for they are a hodge-podge . . . They are neither one function by kinship of skills required to carry out the activities, nor are they one function by being linked together in the work process, by forming a distinct stage in the work of the managers or in the process of the business.

A scene from the film *Dirty Harry* makes a similar point more forcibly. Harry Callahan, the 'hero' of the movie, having overstepped the mark in the use of forceful persuasion in his policing activities, is summoned by his superiors and informed that he is to be transferred to personnel. With a curling lip and contemptuous look he snarls, 'Personnel is for assholes.'

Either way the message is clear. Personnel management was crap and, as such, had no place in the higher echelons of management where real strategizing supposedly took place.

The low status of personnel management was partly caused by and reflected in a swinging between two different styles of managing people at work: that of 'caring' (personnel) and of 'controlling' (management). If the former was reflected in welfare and sophisticated paternalism, where employees were seen as *family members*, and in consultative approaches, the latter was apparent in what Purcell and Sisson have termed 'constitutionalist' and 'standard modern' styles of collectivist employee relations management, where employees were largely seen as *commodities*.

The reason for this pendulum, as I have discussed in detail elsewhere, was partly a chasing of the latest management fashion in a desperate search for higher status and credibility. But it can also be attributed to personnel specialists' role in mediating a major contradiction embedded in capitalist systems: the need to achieve both the control and consent of employees. In Marxist terms, organizing people at work involves a major problematic: how to achieve both the extraction of surplus value at the point of production and its realization in the marketplace, through both the enacting and obscuring the commodity status of nominally free labour. In Weberian terms, the problematic is to mediate the tensions between formal (or 'instrumental') and material (or 'substantive') rationalities.

The rise of human resource management

Enter human resource management (HRM) in the 1980s. There has been much debate by commentators such as David Guest, John Purcell, John Storey and Tom Keenoy as to what HRM 'really' is and, subsequently, whether it is different from old-style personnel management. For many years, especially in the United States, human resource management was just another term for personnel management. As Barbara Townley put it, both terms referred to the management of the problematics in the employment relationship and of the indeterminacies in the employment contract. In the early 1980s, however, several factors came together:

- increased globalization of markets and perceived intensification of competition;
- the rise of the 'enterprise culture' and an emphasis on 'shareholder value';
- the Japanese 'Janus' (both threat and icon – at least in the 1980s) and its resulting 'models of excellence'; and
- the decline in trades union pressure and the changing nature of work and the workforce.

These factors forced people to reconsider prevailing images of employees. When this was combined with the disillusionment with traditional personnel management, senior managers woke up to the importance of human resources in the achievement of competitive advantage, and to a recognition that HRM/personnel management was too important to be left to lowly personnel specialists.

Indeed, whether HRM was considered to be different from personnel management largely depended on one's point of comparison. Sharp distinctions emerged if the normative aspirations of HRM were compared with the descriptive practices of personnel management, but otherwise faded into several different emphases, all of which, though, according to Peter Boxall, pointed to HRM, in theory at least, being an essentially higher level strategy task than personnel management. As Alan Fowler put it, the real difference between HRM and personnel management is not 'what it is, but who is saying it'. In a nutshell then, HRM represents the discovery of personnel management by chief executives and their elevation to being designers of 'the machine' rather than merely the oil that greased the cogs in it. Hence the idea of strategic human resource management starts off by resting on assumptions of mechanistic top-down strategy making.

The evolution of different styles of HRM

The movement of HRM issues, from being subject to organizational and managerial assumptions to being in a position to influence assumptions, has been a key factor in the development of different HRM schools of thought. Different commentators now espouse different models and approaches to strategic HRM. However, given that HRM still builds on many implicit organizational assumptions, these still echo the 'caring' and 'control' images to which personnel management was subject. Consequently, one major distinction may be found between the Michigan School's 'hard' model of HRM, reflecting what has been termed a controlling 'utilitarian instrumentalism' and the 'soft', 'mutuality' model of the Harvard School, more reminiscent of a caring 'developmental humanism'.

The hard model stresses HRM's focus on the critical importance of the close integration of human resources policies, systems and activities with business strategy, requiring that they are not only logically consistent with and supportive of business objectives, but achieve this effect by their own coherence. Note that in terms of Mintzberg and his colleagues' schools of strategy, this approach is sympathetic with their prescriptive design, planning and positioning schools. From this perspective, employees are regarded as a headcount *commodity* or *resource* (of more or less value, depending on business strategy) to be managed in exactly the same rational, impersonal way as any other resource, that is, to be exploited for maximal short-term economic return. Thus its focus is on 'human *resource management*'.

In contrast, the soft, 'developmental humanism' model, while still emphasizing the importance of integrating human resource (HR) policies with business objectives, sees this as involving treating employees as valued *assets*, a source of competitive advantage through their commitment, adaptability and high quality (of skills, performance, and so on). Employees are seen as proactive and resourceful rather than as passive inputs into the productive process. Rather than exploitation and cost minimization, the watchwords in this model are investment and value-added, of '*human resource* management'. From Mintzberg and his colleagues' perspective, this has resonance with their 'cultural' school of strategy. This is also consistent with narratives of organizing that see people at work as both *assets* and as *family* or *team members*.

Termed variously the 'high-commitment' (HCM), 'high-performance' or 'mutuality' model of HRM, at an operational level, soft HRM was seen to comprise policies such as:

- careful recruitment and selection emphasizing 'traits' and 'competencies';
- extensive use of systems of communication;
- teamworking with flexible job design;
- emphasis on training and learning;
- involvement in decision making with responsibility (empowerment);
- performance appraisal linked to contingent reward systems.

The soft model of HRM, throughout the 1990s, has become increasingly recognized as the exemplar of what HRM, as a distinct philosophy of managing the employment relationship, was all about. In the binary opposition of hard versus soft, soft is privileged. Relatedly, given that in the binary opposition between strategic and operational, strategic is increasingly privileged, throughout the 1990s, particularly among US commentators, this model has come to be equated with 'strategic HRM', reflecting the popularity of resource-based views of strategy in its belief in acquiring and developing employees as *assets* and valued *family or team members*.

In many ways, this reflects the interests of HR specialists and academics alike. As already mentioned, fitting HR policy and practice to 'business' strategy always leaves HR as the 'third-order' strategic decision, designed to reinforce prior 'first-order' decisions about portfolio planning and 'second-order' decisions about organizational design and operating procedures, as a still reactive if no longer as powerless as 'hodge-podge', traditional personnel management. The resource-based view of strategy accords a more proactive role to HRM as it can be valued not just for reinforcing predetermined business strategies, but for developing strategic capability, improving the long-term resilience of the firm.

Different HRM styles as reflective of strategizing

These two strands of sense-making about organizing people at work – hard and soft, and their related images of employees – raise a major question about precisely what has traditionally been meant in the HRM literature by 'integrating HRM with business strategy'. Integration appears to have two meanings according to Baird and Meshoulam:

(1) the contingent integration of particular HRM strategies with corporate strategy; and
(2) the universal integration, or complementarity and consistency, of soft 'mutuality' HRM policies aimed at generating employee commitment, flexibility, quality and the like.

These two meanings, in actual fact, are incompatible with one another. The problem is that while 'fit' with business strategy would argue such a *contingent* design of HRM policy and practices, integration and consistency with the 'soft' human resource values, associated with 'mutuality', would argue a *universalistic* approach. This distinction is critical, as the contingent and universalistic approaches rest on very different and contradictory theoretical perspectives about organizational competitiveness.

The universalistic approach is consistent with institutional theory and arguments about mimetic organizational isomorphism. In other words, the assumption here is that organizations that survive and prosper do so because they identify and implement the most effective, 'best' policies and practices. As a result, successful organizations, through a process of survival of the fittest, get to look more and more like each other through practices such as benchmarking and so on. In HR terms this equates with the belief that people are the source of sustainable competitive advantage and that treating them as assets − better still as 'resourceful' assets − by way of the HCM model will always pay off, irrespective of circumstances.

The contingent approach question this logic. If all organizations adopt the same 'best practices', paradoxically, as competitive convergence develops, competitive advantage for individual organizations is lost. Rather, consistent with resource-based value theories, contingency approaches argue that sustained competitive advantage, in Barney's terms, rests on developing unique, non-imitable competencies. Further, it is not concerned solely with people management but, as Porter would have it, 'grows out of the entire system of activities'. Hence, the contingency approach recognizes the importance of idiosyncratic contingencies that result from causal ambiguity and path dependency. And that sustainable competitive advantage results not from dutifully following universal 'best practices', but from knowledge about how to combine, implement and refine the whole potential range of HR policies and practices to suit the organization's idiosyncratic contingencies.

Integration taken to mean 'fit with business strategy', however, links well with traditional strategy approaches that have argued against their being 'one-best way'. Indeed, it is tempting to suggest links with the distinction between focusing on gaining competitive advantage through cost reduction or through differentiation, made in Michael Porter's 'generic strategy matrix', and the employee images I have discussed. Here we might associate a hard approach of seeing and naming employees as *cogs* or *commodities* as consistent with a strategy of focusing on being lowest cost providers. An approach of caring for employees as *family* or *team* members might be consistent with competing on differentiation. An approach of seeing employees as *resources* or *assets* might be as somewhere in between, a position which has been called being a 'best-cost' provider − an organization that has lower prices relative to others selling at a similar quality level in its segments.

To take the point further, in certain situations choosing HCM policies *may* be appropriate to driving the business strategy. HCM appears the logical choice where employee discretion is crucial to the delivery of added value and reciprocal high trust relations are essential to organizational performance. Such a situation is often equated with organizations pursuing a strategy of producing high value-added goods and services, in a knowledge-based industry, pursuing organic growth rather than asset management. But if the organization's chosen business strategy is to compete in a labour-intensive, high-volume, low-cost industry, generating profits through increasing market share by cost leadership, such a policy of treating employees as assets may be deemed an expensive luxury. For such an organization, the HR policies that may be most appropriate to driving strategic objectives are likely to involve treating employees as a variable input and cost to be minimized.

**Type of competitive advantage
being pursued**

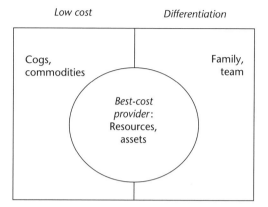

Low cost   *Differentiation*

Cogs,
commodities

Family,
team

*Best-cost
provider*:
Resources,
assets

Figure 3.5   Employee images loosely applied to Michael Porter's generic strategy matrix

While the distinctions described above provide an excellent 'thinking tool' for stimu-lating debate in your organization, we should be wary of oversimplification. It would be a mistake to reduce things to simple discrete either/or choices. Indeed, it would be a mistake to see these two contrasting models of HRM as necessarily unconnected. HRM, in line with the 'soft' HCM model, for example, may only be viable if the organization is seen to be economically successful or 'hard'. This brings home the already described idea that at the heart of the distinction between 'hard' and 'soft' models of HRM lies the fundamental contradiction that organizing people at work is called upon to mediate – the need to achieve both the control and consent of em-ployees. It also brings home the view that there is not one universally 'best' or 'good' approach to HRM and 'naming' employees. Although referring to people as 'team members' may sound great and make managers feel good about themselves, if it does not fit with what an organization is trying to achieve it will likely just create dissonant expectations and confuse people. Moreover, in an increasingly spin-savvy world it may just incite cynicism rather than commitment.

Thus, just as organizational strategy may require the interconnection of different generic approaches (see Chapter 1 for examples), integrating HRM with business strat-egy may require 'joined-up' fragmentation. For example, the design and implementa-tion of an employment contract that veers towards control (with assumptions of labour as a commodity, embedded structural conflict, low trust and transactional contracts) for some groups of employees, but consent (with assumptions about the employee as a valued team member, a unitary frame of reference, high trust and relational contracts) for others. With this in mind it is not surprising that Tom Keenoy likens HRM to both 'a wolf in sheep's clothing' and to a hologram, 'a phenomenon [that] may possess and can project a variety of mutually implicated identities'.

Images of Employees as Reflective of Organizational Structure

So far this discussion has focused on a major tension in representing and organizing people at work: between images that value employees and management practices that focus on 'caring' for such an asset and those that devalue employees and focus on the 'control' of a potentially recalcitrant commodity. While there are the contradictions within these simple dichotomies, their usefulness can be extended to a consideration of organizational forms. If, as Chandler classically maintained, structure follows strategy, we might expect them to mirror strategies of organizing people at work. And, at least in the discourses about appropriate organizational designs, this is so.

Cogs, commodities and customers: lean machines

The employee as *commodity*, by definition, is treated as an object, a discrete 'thing', not as a person. The images associated with the person as non-human object, for example, as something that can be processed (passive mode) or as a 'cog in the wheel' or a cyborg (active mode) evoke the image of a machine. 'Machine' imagery of organization structure has two well-known depictions: that of Mintzberg's 'machine bureaucracy' and the 'lean' (and 'mean') machines of business process re-engineering.

A machine bureaucracy is characterized by large operating unit size, standardization of work processes, behaviour formalization, vertical and horizontal job specialization, usually functional grouping, vertical centralization and limited horizontal decentralization. It was epitomized in Fordism, in producer-driven systems of mass production of standardized goods for mass markets. It is deemed appropriate only to simple and stable environments and so is supposedly unfashionable today, although many of its elements have translated well to service sector industries that provide standardized services for mass markets, for example, fast food and financial services call-centres. As George Ritzer demonstrates, 'McDonaldization' now reproduces many of the features of machine bureaucracy through its adherence to the principles of instrumental rationality, expressed through a commitment to efficiency, calculability, predictability and control, embodied not only in fast food chains, but in banks, educational systems and healthcare. In philosopher Michel Foucault's terms, this is a crucial element in a society obsessed with secular control through measurement, normalization, surveillance and auditing.

'Lean organization' is a more fashionable machine and at first sight might *appear* more in tune with employees as assets than as commodities: a halfway house between machine bureaucracy and the 'learning organization'. In theory it has three main pillars:

- It is about organizing in such a way that value is added by minimizing 'waste', whether of materials, time, space or people, and by developing responsiveness to major stakeholders, most of whom (whether employees, suppliers or purchasers of goods and services) are defined as customers.
- It is about marrying together the 'hardware' of TQM quality procedures and associated 'Japanese' production processes (e.g., just-in-time, statistical process control, supply chain management, material resources planning, benchmarking) with the 'software' of HCM, 'soft' HRM policies.

- It involves the use of ICT-facilitated BPR to move from function-centred to process-centred organization, from differentiated specialists to multidisciplinary teamworking, from 'unresponsive' machine bureaucracy to flatter hierarchies.

In this structure, *in theory*, the principles of 'control' and 'caring' appear to come together.

However, apart from some exemplar motor manufacturing plants, it is debatable how far this model can be applied to the service sector and the bulk of manufacturing in the UK. Stephen Ackroyd and Stephen Proctor suggest that in much of the UK manufacturing industry, at least, a different form of lean organization exists. They argue that the typical British manufacturing firm is not a chemical, pharmaceutical or defence contracting firm (with high capitalization and relatively low employment), but firms that have grown through merger and acquisition, comprising a large number of decentralized production facilities producing a wide range of 'cash cow' goods for retail in mature markets. These firms favour tight control of financial performance from the centre, with a good deal of operational freedom allowed to plant management. In terms of production systems and working practices there is little evidence of high levels of investment in advanced technology or of multi-skilling or of 'soft' HCM.

They argue that the characteristics of the typical UK manufacturing firm, in its search for profitability, are that:

- Production is organized as cellular manufacture as it facilitates the calculation of marginal costs and the identification of unprofitable activities, while limiting the need for employees to develop a broad spectrum of skills.
- Advanced manufacturing technology is little used, except as additions to existing configurations of equipment.
- Employed labour contributes to flexibility as teams of semi-skilled workers performing a range of specific tasks and given some on-the-job training.
- Employees do not enjoy privileged status or high employment security, but compete with subcontracted labour and alternative suppliers (i.e., they are, in reality, more suppliers than customers).
- Production operations are considered as dispensable, separate segments, about which calculations of cost are regularly made.
- Management takes the form of intensified indirect control based on the allocation of costs.
- The high surveillance management regimes, associated with 'Japanese' lean production methods involving TQM, JIT and so forth, are not typical of British manufacturing as they exaggerate the quality of information available, thus taxing the willingness and ability of managers to appraise such information given the much reduced ranks of middle management and supervision.

This model of lean organization clearly lacks the coherency and logic of the 'Japanese' model of leanness that seeks to integrate organizational design, operations management and human resource management into one reinforcing whole. This is a form of 'leanness', motivated exclusively by concerns of cost-cutting, and is often accused of 'cutting muscle' rather than fat, of giving rise to the stressed-out anorexic organization. As such it resonates with the images of labour as a *commodity* rather than as a valued customer.

Assets, team players and family members: learning organizations

It was stated earlier that we now talk of employees in terms of 'head-count' rather than of 'hands'. Its not surprising, then, when employees are conceptualized as *assets* (and the assets in question are their skills and competencies), that organizations may be seen as brains or, to use the fashionable buzzword, as 'learning organizations'. Organizations that are stuffed full of *families* or *teams* of valuable 'knowledge workers'. This, it is commonly assumed, is 'the way forward', away from the archaic mechanistic structures described above.

There are many definitions of what constitutes a learning organization, but Marquardt and Reynolds' list of characteristics captures most of the salient points. For them a learning organization:

- capitalizes on uncertainty as a source of growth;
- creates new knowledge as a central part of competitive strategy;
- embraces change;
- encourages accountability at the lowest level;
- encourages managers to act as mentors, coaches and learning facilitators;
- has a culture of feedback and disclosure;
- has a holistic systemic view of the organization and its systems, processes, and relationships;
- has a shared organization–wide vision, purpose and values;
- has leaders who encourage risk taking and experimentation;
- has systems for sharing knowledge/learning and using it in the business;
- is customer driven;
- is involved in the community;
- links employees' self-development to the development of the organization as a whole;
- networks within the business community; provides frequent opportunities to learn from experience;
- avoids bureaucracy and turf wars;
- has a high trust culture;
- strives for continuous improvement;
- structures, fosters and rewards all types of teams;
- uses cross-functional work teams; and
- views the unexpected as opportunities to learn.

Graeme Salaman, however, puts it rather differently. He sees the learning organization as a sanitized version of the discourse of enterprise ('organization and employee as actively and autonomously committed to the achievement of flexible, responsive relationships with clients and employers'), that subsequently 'replace[s] an overtly commercial, market focus with the gentler psychological developmental language of learning'.

Although organizations as diverse as Ford and (the now imploded) Arthur Andersen publicly aspired to becoming a learning organization, the path is fraught with difficulties that render its wholesale achievement highly questionable (see Case Box 3.1 at the end of this chapter). Both Keep and Rainbird and Salaman give a good analysis of the problems. To begin with, as Karl Weick and Frances Westley perceptively remark 'Organizing and learning are essentially antithetical processes which means the

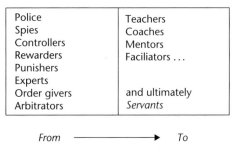

Figure 3.6 Changing roles of managers?

phrase "organizational learning" qualifies as an oxymoron. To learn is to disorganize and increase variety. To organize is to forget and reduce variety.'

Thus while organizations can live with single-loop learning, the double-loop learning (see Chapter 9, 'Strategy as Systems Thinking') of the learning organization is inimical to it. Further, the collectivist, democratic and unitarist assumptions of the learning organization run counter to the individualist, hierarchical and pluralist nature of conventional organizations in a capitalist economy. Issues to do with power and culture inhibit the development of a true 'learning organization' and the utopian future that it is often associated with.

To consider power first. The very fact of organizations' persistence and stability over time gives rise to a structuring that defines boundaries and levels – the horizontal boundaries that establish areas of expertise and the vertical levels that differentiate power and rewards. Such structures generate sectional interests, which, in a context of scarce resources, give rise to power struggles and, as Salaman puts it, 'the possibility of deference and careerism [and] strong motivation to distort, divert, censor data'. Knowledge and expertise have long been recognized as a potential source of individual power, assuming the knowledge is both scarce and considered valuable. Both of these aspects reinforce conventional hierarchies, as those looking for promotion have no incentive to share their 'scarce' knowledge with potential competitors, while, to echo Berger and Luckmann, 'he who wields the bigger stick has a better chance of imposing his definitions' (see Chapter 10 'Strategy as Process, Power and Change').

Then again, as Ewart Keep and Helen Rainbird point out, to develop a learning organization requires that managers' roles change from that of police, spies, controllers, dispensers of rewards and punishments, sources of expertise, order givers and arbitrators between competing claims (typical of a machine bureaucracy or the type of lean organization portrayed above) to teachers, coaches, mentors, facilitators, even 'servants' of 'empowered' teams (more reminiscent of an ideal-type 'Japanese' lean organization). But if this really were to happen, how could managers justify their differential status and reward? Further, the assumption that employees will willingly share their tacit knowledge with management (what Marxists refer to as 'mining the gold in the workers' heads') is unrealistic unless this sharing is fully rewarded. Adding to these limits are the issues of organizational and national cultures.

At the organizational level, shared values about conformity, deference, not treading on people's toes, group loyalty and risk avoidance are inimical to the learning organization's advocacy of freedom of speech, challenging taken-for-granted assumptions, welcoming criticism. Moreover, shared cognitive structures or 'recipes', while advantageously reducing data processing time when conditions are stable, may become counterproductive under changed circumstances, as both IBM and Marks & Spencer found to their cost. 'Recipes' restrict an organization's ability to learn by restricting environmental analysis or by influencing how data are analysed. Rather than flexibly responding to new signals from the environment, managers create their environments through shared sense-making and then respond to these enactments in ways that make them real. This is inconsistent with the learning organization's advocacy of managers reflexively questioning their own basic assumptions.

Finally, there is the issue of whether a national culture is likely to facilitate or inhibit the development of a learning organization. While Japan is often seen as facilitative, the UK, in contrast, is inhibitive. Keep and Rainbird, for example, point to the UK's chronic 'short term-ism', its preference for a growth strategy of merger and acquisition (facilitated by deregulated financial markets) rather than organic growth by way of R&D investment, its long working hours culture (leaving people with little time or energy for training), and its obsession with shareholder value and the bottom line as inimical to the development of a learning organization. Indeed, despite all the talk of 'learning organizations', they point to the prevalence of the 'McDonaldized', and lean and mean organizational forms in the UK, identified by Ackroyd and Proctor:

> The notion that a set of universalistic trends and competitive pressures is impelling organizations towards competition based on organizational learning is seriously flawed. Alternative avenues to competitive advantage remain viable, at least in the UK, and price-based competition continues to thrive above all in the service sector . . . many organizations, far from opting for the high skills route to competitive success remain wedded to standardized, low-specification goods and services where the main factor of competitive advantage is consistent delivery of relatively simple goods and services at a low price. This Fordist or Neo-Fordist strategy is in turn reflected in Tayloristic forms of work organization that minimize the opportunities for creativity and discretion.

Such organizations, in a deregulated labour market, are likely to be at the forefront of cost-reducing delayering and downsizing exercises, with their attendant effects on employee trust. Low trust is hardly conducive to collaborative learning.

Nevertheless, this organizational form matches well the rhetoric that promotes employees as the source of competitive advantage (*assets, resources, team players*, etc.), even if for most organizations advocating this organizational form, it remains a utopian aspiration rather than a realistic achievement.

Through a Glass Darkly: Tensions and Contradictions

The emergent 'hard' and 'soft' strategies of organizing people at work are continually in tension, reflecting as they do employers' simultaneous desire for both the control and consent of their employees. Here we have what Watson has termed 'the paradox of consequences'. Employers cannot always prescribe tasks in detail, particularly when the work is highly complex and the achievement of quality standards (so necessary to achieve competitive advantage/realization of surplus value in the market place) requires the exercise of employee discretion. In the interests of a flexible response to variances in day-to-day operational processes the employer would not wish to remove all worker discretion – indeed, 'flexibility', whether on the part of the employee or in terms of organizational forms, is a present-day mantra. Furthermore, although employers may wish to extract surplus value by minimizing labour costs, too aggressive a pursuit of this strategy may be self-defeating, not only through the potential loss of such labour to higher paying employers, but through the disabling of employees as potential direct or indirect purchasers of the goods and services produced. Unless employees also act as customers, surplus value cannot be realized in the economy at large, as evidenced by major economic recessions and the urgings of public figures, post-September 11th, to go out and spend.

Employers, then, may buy the right to control their employees' work but, in the interests of the achievement and realization of surplus value, they must give some leeway to their employees on a daily basis to exercise some control over the means of production, albeit ultimately in the employers' interests as much as the employees. In both cases, employers must enlist their employees'/customers' co-operation to ensure that their discretion as both workers and consumers is exercised for, rather than against, capitalism's interests.

In a sense, therefore, organizing people at work and advertising are two sides of the same coin, of 'manufacturing consent' or exercising 'hegemonic', ideological control, to quote Burawoy. But this carries its own contradictions. The creation of commitment to the job (whether by way of collusive game-playing or 'soft' HCM policies or the creation of a 'strong' corporate culture) may result in employee inflexibility, group-think and conservatism. At worst it may lead to an inward-looking solidarity and complacency that fail to recognize signals from either competitors or customers in a changing marketplace. Danny Miller has used an image from Greek mythology to characterize such blind arrogance – that of Icarus, who thinking he could fly to the sun, failed to recognize that his wax wings would melt as he approach the heat of the sun's rays (read strategies, structures and systems inappropriate for a changing, more challenging environment). Marks & Spencer and Equitable Life are good recent examples of the 'Icarus Paradox' (see Chapter 12; on 'Strategy as Numbers' for more on this).

These tensions and contradictions may be uncovered toward more informed discussions of strategic HRM choices, if we return to deconstruct the imagery of employees that we have already identified. In their different ways employees as 'customer' (choice), 'assets/resources' (value), 'sporting team member' (chosen, specialist team role) and 'family member' (valued, even loved) all have positive connotations. Employees as 'commodities' (undifferentiated, low value) or as chain-gang cogs (imprisoned, mechanized, slave labour) have a distinctly negative ring. There is a tendency too, as already mentioned, to attribute these images to different groups of employees: positive images with 'core' employees and negative images with the 'peripheral' or 'contingent' workforce. However, mindful of the control/consent tension in organizing people at work, it is possible to see negative meanings in the positive images and vice versa.

Deconstructing positive employee images

Let us begin with the employee as *customer*. The defining characteristic of a customer, so those that celebrate the market would have us believe, is the freedom to exercise choice. The internal customer in a TQM system can refuse to accept substandard inputs from an earlier production process and is empowered to stop the line to deal with process problems or product defects, before faulty work reaches another team or customer downstream.

But to what extent is this free choice? Just as external customers through advertising, brand development, cross-selling and promotions are manipulated into 'freely choosing' the products and services that the selling organization wishes them to buy, so internal customers' choices are constrained by processes of organizational socialization and other covert forms of what Barker has termed 'concertive' control. Thus according to Philip Garrahan and Paul Stewart, although at Nissan 'internal customers' (employees) have the 'choice' to stop the line, operators often choose not to, as they feel that if they regularly stop the line they will be identified as incompetent. As a result, they will rectify minor faults created by others upstream ('empowerment'?) because, if the line is stopped for a minor defect, the resultant check of all the work might reveal defects of their own making.

The tight control on all resources in lean production systems, and resultant labour intensification, can be presented as *freely chosen* by the employee as both internal and external customer. To the employee as external customer, lean production is presented as cost minimization, necessary to keep prices down (we all want that, right?). To the employee as internal customer, 'surplus' resources are presented as waste, a product that the consumer, by definition, has rejected or does not want and, therefore logically, necessarily and so with consent has to be eliminated. Thus, to borrow from Michel Foucault's terminology again, rather than free choice being exercised here, the employee as customer, through processes of examination and confession, internalizes and enacts management controls.

So it is with the other positive images. The employee as *resource/asset* is valuable, but the other side of a valuable resource is the imperative to 'exploit' it to the full. This alerts us to a negative meaning for valued 'core' employees – the long hours and workaholic lifestyle that may be the corollary to high salaries and benefits. In today's organizations, even if one has a highly challenging and potentially developmental job, and is part of an organization's core competency staff, the common complaint is of heightened pressure through increasingly demanding and shifting targets, in the context of diminishing resources, in the effort to achieve 'lean' organization. To survive many 'resources' develop a workaholic lifestyle so as to demonstrate how the most is being got out of them, before collapsing into 'burn out'. It is often said that few people on their deathbeds express a wish that they had spent more time in the office, but many regret that they did not spend more time with their families.

Team membership may have been seen to be one leg of a 'tripod of success' (along with flexibility and quality) by Peter Wickens, a personnel director at Nissan, Sunderland. But the same teams were seen to be a leg of a 'tripod of subjugation' through peer surveillance and 'management through compliance' by Philip Garrahan and Paul Stewart. 'Management through compliance', they argue, arises out of team-based working whereby, having made teams responsible for their own performance, it encourages them to harness peer pressure on delinquent members to secure compliance to managerially set targets, with the additional pressure of compliance to the sovereign customer being linked to job security.

Further, the nature of teamworking at Nissan, they suggest, is far from that suggested by sporting imagery. The fragility of JIT production systems necessitates that workers can cover for each other to the extent of being able to perform a range of standardized tasks that fall within their team's remit. However, although Wickens might present this flexibility as involving multi-skilling and job enrichment, Garrahan and Stewart suggest that in reality operators experience job enlargement and task accretion through the acquisition of a limited number of cognate tasks that result in a work pattern characterized as routine variety. The nature of job enlargement – taking on responsibility for some setting up of machinery, inspection and cleaning – combined with required flexibility, effectively eliminates downtime or porosity in the working day and contributes to work intensification. Further, such 'skills' as are acquired, being plant specific, do little to enhance the worker's value in the general labour market (or 'transfer market', to continue the sporting analogy), but rather serve to enhance their dependency on this 'exploitative' employer. In other words, the 'team' that, in managerialist eyes, resembles a sports team of talented individuals (or is presented as such), in Marxist eyes, equates with a team of homogenized, interchangeable beasts of burden, redolent of the chain-gang.

One might add to these points the potentially negative organizational effects that are likely brought about by the negative sides of the *team*, the *resource/asset*, and the *customer* images. If Nonaka and other 'knowledge organization' theorists are correct, knowledge and creative thinking require the presence of downtime to enable double-loop learning or a questioning of established practices to occur. What is downtime for the knowledge organization is 'waste' for the customer or resource.

If the positive image of *family member* is 'caring', then the negative image is the whole range of problems associated with paternalism: that it cannot be relied upon to maintain a just balance between employer and employee interests and that it does not adequately respect the moral agency of the employee. In other words, as Peter Anthony notes, paternalism, in its transformation from 'traditional' to 'costed' paternalism and finally into 'welfare management', can end up a manipulative approach to employee relations. The image of the employee effectively as a child or at best a wayward adolescent is one that denies autonomy and equality and, hence, self-respect at work.

Deconstructing negative employee images

Can anything positive be derived from the negative images of employee as *commodity*, or a *cyborg* or interchangeable cog or link in a chain-gang (an image not often publicly voiced even if, judged by patterned regularities of behaviour, comprising some management's mental picture of some subordinates)? Possibly. A cyborg, if non-human, may at least be seen to have superhuman strength and endurance, even if the intelligence resides in the machine. Certainly, that assumption underpinned Fordism, even if for the employees themselves, the non-human, alienating aspects of their jobs predominated. If one focuses on, and sees value in, the efficient, task-focused, 'Robocop' type aspect of this image then it need not be negative.

As for the other two images, while they appear to offer nothing for employees, for management there is an upside: they represent the assertion and justification of the managerial prerogative. A commodity (and note, an interchangeable unit has many of the characteristics of a commodity) has no individuality or autonomy of its own. It is defined by others' assessments of its use or exchange value. Management, as the agent of the owner, buys the labour commodity and, as buyer, gains rights of direction, of how the commodity is to be used. Management, as user of the labour commodity, defines its function and attributes value. Until this happens, the commodity is inert and valueless – indeed it lacks the attribution even of commodity status. Conceptualizing employees as commodities and management as the buyer and user of that commodity justifies managerial prerogative and regimes of control and, by extension, the value of management.

However, we could look at the other side of the commodity coin. At least these images are a bit more 'up front' and less ambiguous about the exchange in question: if the employer requires another unit of *commodity* (e.g., overtime, working through lunch), he or she must pay the going rate for it. The seller of the commodity knows up front what he or she will get out of the transaction and may even choose not to supply it. In contrast to the positive images mentioned above, there is less of the 'fear of the unknown' and social compliance that lead employees to give and give because they are never certain that they have given enough. Additionally, the commodity image denies employers or managers the smugness that often comes from feeling that 'my employees are better off because I treat them like team members/family/assets, not like commodities – they have much more freedom, they are truly empowered'. Indeed, one might deconstruct 'empowerment' along these lines and suggest that the negative side of empowerment (particularly if it is combined with 'accountability') is that it means that 'lower-downs' take on more of the responsibility and risk while 'higher-ups' still take on more of the pay.

In a more spin-savvy age, where less and less people are prepared to believe that their employers really love/value them unconditionally, and more people value the time that they can have away from thinking 'work', it is not difficult to see how the employee might increasingly want to see him or herself as a *commodity*.

Conclusion

The argument developed in this chapter is that the images of employees that commonly occur in organizations tell us a great deal about management's different underlying philosophies about appropriate ways of organizing employee groups at work. These in turn reflect emergent business strategies and patterns of organizational design. However, in contrast to Chandler's 'structure follows strategy' position, it is suggested that the recipes managers have for thinking about the sources of their competitive advantage are as likely to give rise to strategies as vice versa. Both emerge from taken-for-granted assumptions about how to survive in a capitalist world.

The contrasting nature of these images, and the associated strategies for managing people at work, reflect the paradoxes and contradictions associated with capitalist systems; in particular:

- the need for both stability and change;
- the need to both harness a valuable resource and exploit a commodity;
- the need for both the 'care' and 'control' of the workforce;
- the need to both enact and obscure the commodity status of nominally free labour.

These tensions and contradictions are encapsulated, and combined with the images of employees that have informed this chapter, so that they may be taken with you as another map that informs your strategy practice, in Figure 3.7.

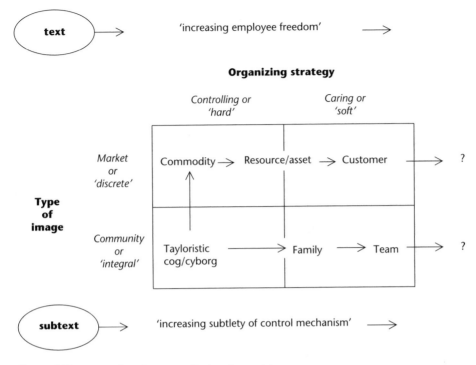

Figure 3.7 Images of employees as reflective of strategizing

The images of employees divide into those representing a discrete market transaction (commodity, resource/asset, customer) and a contractual, relatively contained relationship with the organization and those representing the all-embracing ties of community or at least the integration of the employee, as a category, into the organization's fabric (family/team member, cyborg). The modes of organizing, while superficially dichotomizing into the 'controlling' and 'caring', in fact offer two discourses. A progression from controlling to caring modes, from a managerialist perspective, may be represented as increasing employee autonomy and recognition (from 'commodity' to 'resource/asset/customer'). However, a Foucauldian reading would suggest a different story, that 'caring' is but the iron fist in the golden glove, that a move to 'caring' modes of organizing is no more than an increasingly subtle mode of control, masked in the rhetoric of the acceptable face of capitalism.

What this chapter has shown is that either/or choices of good over evil (i.e., team over commodity), or the idea that there is 'one best way' that must be integrated into a corporation as its seeks to make strategic HRM decisions are overly simplistic in these spin-savvy postmodern times. Perhaps the best that strategists can do is to use their judgement and local contextual knowledge to pick and loosely harness horses for courses. It is these complexities that evoke the image of the organization as circus. Managers as ringmasters must walk the tightrope of allowing autonomy or caring *and* controlling. They juggle the different requirements of 'core' and 'periphery' workers. They must recognize that while the lions require hard discipline and a simple exchange mechanism for things to work (i.e., one trick = one steak), the clowns must be left, more or less, to their own devices if they are to contribute to the team. They are carried insecurely on the bare back of market demand – which may seem more like attempting to tame the market lion; and the result may appear like tragi-comic clowning (e.g., Barings, Equitable Life, Marconi, Railtrack) that no amount of spin can hide. With reference to the latter, even the orchestrating ringmaster – senior management of Railtrack and the operating companies, such as Richard Branson – cannot always avoid accidents. In fact the threat of them may even be necessary if we are to continue to strive and change.

Related to this last point, I have drawn question marks at the right-hand side of Figure 3.7 in order to denote that the future will likely bring new images of organizational members. I urge you to think of what these images could be and discuss this with your peers or workmates. It is a risky business; your images may be critiqued by others and fall straight off the high wire. However, despite the current affection for being a 'customer' (and I heartily concur with the assessment in the 'Strategy as Marketing' chapter of the ultimate vacuousness of having customers drive all things), I provoke my students by saying that the best students are producers of knowledge rather than just passive consumers.

Case Box 3.1   The Dilemmas of Development

As one of the *erstwhile* 'Big Four', Arthur Andersen's (AA) roots, originating in the United States, *lay* in accountancy services, in particular, auditing.

As a transnational professional accountancy firm, its organizational structure *was* the traditional partnership, with a career structure based on the custom and practice of 'up' or 'out'. Thus, traditionally, the 'best' graduates *were* hired straight from university, intensively socialized in 'Arthur's' ways ('Simply the Best'), passed nationally accredited chartered accountants' exams and progressed up the slippery pole to partner, if all *went* well. But not all *could* reach the dizzy heights of national (let alone worldwide) partner and, traditionally, any faltering on the way to the top *was* the signal to go. For many years Andersen's employees were referred to as 'Androids'.

With the explosion of business services in the 1980s and 1990s, it was soon apparent that the growth area and high value-added side of the business was 'one-stop service', multidisciplinary consultancy. Auditing was increasingly becoming a commodity, low-margin product, but valuable in generating a large client base to whom high value-added consultancy services might be sold. In due course, the growth in the consultancy side was such that the 'Andersen Consulting' split from AA, becoming an independent firm, Accenture. Meanwhile, in the UK, AA developed its own business consulting division. *Even prior to the Enron debacle* this raised some interesting issues in relation to how to strategically manage human resources across what were now many different organizations that were once one.

1. *Should AA's auditing arm have become a learning organization as described by Marquardt and Reynolds' list of characteristics?*

2. *Multidisciplinary consultancy requires knowledge bases and commitments other than and in addition to accountancy. How would you manage the organization's need and desire to do both, paying particular attention to HRM?*
3. *Can you see how the human resource considerations might have led to the strategic decision to split Accenture from AA?*
4. *How might you have managed the relationships and transfer of knowledge between AA UK, AA UK's consulting division, and Accenture?*
5. *What alternative images of organizational members (referred to by the question marks in Figure 3.7) would you suggest for ex AA exmployees, post the firm's collapse after the Enron debacle?*

Source Material and Recommended Further Reading

Henry Mintzberg's views on strategy, which are acknowledged on many occasions in this chapter, are reviewed in H. Mintzberg et al., *Strategy Safari* (London: Prentice-Hall, 1998).

To build on my references to Derrida and deconstruction analysis, the following texts are recommended: J. Derrida, *Writing and Difference* (London: Routledge and Kegan Paul, 1978) (somewhat difficult and opaque, even if the master's, that is, Derrida's, voice); J. Culler, *On Deconstruction* (London: Routledge and Kegan Paul, 1983); and K. Gergen, 'Organisation theory in the postmodern era', in M. Reed and M. Hughes (eds), *Rethinking Organisation* (London: Sage, 1992), pp. 207–26 (a very clear and accessible account of Derrida's relevance to organizational analysis). For a deconstruction of binary terms, see S. Cummings, 'Centralization and decentralization: the never ending story of separation and betrayal', *Scandinavian Journal of Management*, 11(2), 1995, 103–17.

For those who wish to probe further into discourse analysis, see Norman Fairclough, *Language and Power* (London: Longman, 1989) which is a good starting point.

The sections on images of organizational members are drawn verbatim from my recent paper 'Representing people at work', *Organization*, 6(2), 1999, 247–64. Recently, I found a paper by Catherine Casey, published around the same time, that similarly, but from a psychoanalytic standpoint, deals with the effects of organizational cultural practices of 'family' and team' on processes of regulation, discipline and the control of employee subject selves. It is entitled ' "Come join the family": Discipline and integration in corporate organizational culture', *Human Relations*, 52(2), 1999, 155–77. A useful commentary and critique of her arguments are offered in Y. Gabriel, 'Beyond happy families: A critical reevaluation of the control-resistance-identity triangle', *Human Relations*. 52(2), 1999, 179–203.

Sources on what I have termed 'images of the marketplace' are: J. O'Neill, *The Market: Ethics, Knowledge and Politics* (London: Routledge, 1998); Paul du Gay and Graeme Salaman, 'The culture] of the customer', *Journal of Management Studies*, 29(5), (1992), 615–33; J. Atkinson and N. Meager, *New Forms of Work Organisation*, IMS Report 121 (Brighton: Institute of Manpower Studies, 1986); J. Purcell, 'Pulling up the drawbridge: high commitment management and the exclusive corporation', paper presented at the Cornell Conference, *Research and Theory in SHRM: An agenda for the 21st century*, October 1997; R. B. Reich, *The Work of Nations* (New York: Knopf, 1991) (for reference to 'symbolic analysts'). A paper that develops and updates some of Atkinson's and Purcell's themes is my own 'Flexibility: The gift wrapping of employment degradation?', in P. Sparrow and M. Marchington (eds), *Human Resource Management: The New Agenda* (London: FT/Pitman, 1998), pp. 286–95.

For work relevant to 'images of the community', I recommend Peter Anthony, *The Foundations of Management* (London: Tavistock, 1986); also Richard Warren, 'Between contract and paternalism: HRM in the community of purpose', paper presented at the second UK *Conference on Ethical Issues in Contemporary HRM*, Kingston Business School, January 1998. Then there is Edward Cadbury's classic account of paternalism in action at his plant at Bournville, *Experiments in Industrial Organisation* (London: Longman, 1912). The contrasting perceptions of teams at Nissan, Sunderland, may be explored in the managerialist, not to say triumphalist, account of the then personnel director, Peter Wickens (1987) *The Road to Nissan* (London: Macmillan, 1987) and in the Marxist critique of Philip Garrahan and Paul Stewart, *The Nissan Enigma* (London: Mansell, 1992). The original imagery of a team as beasts of burden comes from M. Parker and J. Slaughter, *Choosing Sides: Unions and the Team Concept* (Boston: Labor Notes, 1988).

There is an enormous literature on the management of employment relationships, whether from an industrial relations or HRM/personnel management perspective. From an industrial relations perspective, P. Blyton and P. Turnbull, *The Dynamics of Employee Relations*, 2nd edn (Basingstoke: Macmillan (now Palgrave), 1998), and S. Kessler and F. Bayliss, *Contemporary British Industrial Relations*, 3rd edn (Basingstoke: Macmillan (now Palgrave), 1998) are recommended. At the risk of appearing immodest, a good summary of research on personnel management and HRM up to 1995 is my book *HRM, Rhetorics and Realities* (Basingstoke: Macmillan (now Palgrave), 1995). Four books that update the debates about HRM and its relationship to strategy and performance are P. Boxall and J. Purcell, *Strategies in Human Resource Management* (Basingstoke: Palgrave, 2002); J. Storey (ed.), *Human Resource Management: A Critical Text*, 2nd edn. (London: Thomson Learning, 2001); S. Bach and K. Sisson (eds), *Personnel Management* (Oxford: Blackwell, 2000); and P. Sparrow and M. Marchington (eds), *Human Resource Management: The New Agenda* (London: FT/Pitman, 1998). Several key papers that develop the conventional debates about the relationship between HRM and strategy are, in chronological order, J. Purcell, 'The impact of corporate strategy on human resource management', in J. Storey (ed.), *New Perspectives on Human Resource Management* (London: Routledge, 1989), pp. 67–91; P. Boxall, 'Strategic human resource management: beginnings of a new theoretical sophistication?', *Human Resource Management Journal*, 2(3), 1992, 60–78; J. Purcell, 'Corporate strategy and human resource management', in J. Storey (ed.), *Human Resource Management: A Critical Text*, 1st edn (London: Routledge, 1995), pp. 63–86; P. Boxall, 'The strategic HRM debate and the resource-based view of the firm', *Human Resource Management Journal*, 6(3), 1996, 59–75; J. Purcell, 'Best practice and best fit: chimera or cul-de-sac?', *Human Resource Management Journal*, 9(3), 1999, 26–41; J. Purcell, 'The meaning of strategy in human resource management', in J. Storey (ed.), *Human Resource Management: A Critical Text*, 2nd edn (London: Thomson Learning, 2001), pp. 59–77. A useful paper that summarizes and critiques the contribution of North American positivist research to debates about the relationship between HRM and organizational performance is K. Legge 'Silver bullet or spent round? Assessing the meaning of the "high commitment management"/performance relationship', in J. Storey (ed.), (2001), op. cit., pp. 21–36.

Some interesting work has been done in applying more critical discourse and Foucauldian analysis to HRM. Notable references here are T. Keenoy, 'HRM: a case of the wolf in sheep's clothing?', *Personnel Review*, 19(2), 1990, 3–9; D.E. Guest, 'Human resource management and the American Dream', *Journal of Management Studies*, 27(4), 1990, 378–97; T. Keenoy and P. Anthony, 'HRM: metaphor, meaning and morality', in P. Blyton and P. Turnbull (eds), *Reassessing Human Resource Management* (London: Sage, 1992), pp. 233–55; B. Townley, *Reframing Human Resource Management* (London: Sage, 1994), and T. Keenoy, 'HRM as a hologram: a polemic', *Journal of Management Studies*, 36(1), (1999), 1–23.

As for references cited in the 'Reflective of strategy' section of this text (other than those already referred to here), these are P. Drucker, *The Practice of Management* (London: Mercury, 1961, first published 1954); J. Purcell and K. Sisson, (1983). 'Strategies and practice in the management of industrial relations', in G.S. Bain (ed.), *Industrial Relations in Britain* (Oxford: Blackwell, 1983), 95–120 ('constitutionalist' and 'standard modern' styles); C. Hendry and A. Pettigrew, 'The practice of human resource management', *Personnel Review*, 15(5), 1986, 3–8 ('utilitarian instrumentalism' and 'developmental humanism'); J. Storey (1987). 'Developments in the management of human resources: an interim report', *Warwick Papers in Industrial Relations*, 17, IRRU, SIBS, University of Warwick (November 1987), (first recorded use of the phrase 'hard' and 'soft' HRM); L. Baird and I. Meshoulam, 'Managing the two fits of strategic human resource management', *Academy of Management Review*, 13(1), 1988, 116–28; J. Barney, 'Firm resources and sustained competitive advantage', *Journal of Management*, 17, 1991, 99–120. When personnel management becomes termed human resource management can be found in Alan Fowler, 'When chief executives discover HRM', *Personnel Management*, 19, 1987, 1–3.

Turning to 'reflective of organizational structure', the classic work on business process re-engineering is M. Hammer and J. Champy, *Re-engineering the Corporation* (London: Nicholas Brearley, 1993). Several excellent papers critiquing the concept are K. Grint, 'Re-engineering history: social resonances and business process re-engineering', *Organization*, 1(1), 1994, 179–201; C. Grey and N. Mitev, 'Re-engineering organisations: a critical appraisal', *Personnel Review*, 24(1), 1995, 6–18; H. Willmott, 'Business process re-engineering and human resource management', *Personnel Review*, 23(3), 1994, 34–46 and H. Willmott, 'The odd couple?: Re-engineering business processes; managing human relations', *New Technology, Work and Employment*, 10(2), 1995, 89–98. Mintzberg's discussion of 'machine bureaucracy' may be found in H. Mintzberg, *The Structuring of Organisations* (Englewood Cliffs: Prentice-Hall, 1979). The classic work on 'McDonaldization' is George Ritzer, *The McDonaldization of Society*, revised edn (Thousand Oaks, CA: Pine Forge Press, 1996). For references to the auditing society, see M. Power, *The Audit Society: Rituals of Verification* (Oxford: Oxford University Press, 1997).

A useful summary of some of the debates and issues associated with 'lean' organizations may be found in K. Legge, 'Personnel management in the lean organisation', in S. Bach and K. Sisson, op. cit., pp. 43–69; and Ackroyd's and Proctor's discussion of the typical form of 'non-Japanese' lean organization in UK manufacturing may be found in S. Ackroyd and S. Proctor, 'British manufacturing organisation and workplace relations: some attributes of the new flexible firm', *British Journal of Industrial Relations*, 36(2), 1998, 163–83.

There is now a very large literature on the learning organization. First, the source of the provocative quotation from Karl Weick and Frances Wesley: K. Weick and F. Westley, 'Organizational learning: affirming an oxymoron', in S.R. Clegg, C. Hardy and W.R. Nord (eds), *Handbook of Organisational Studies* (London: Sage, 1996), pp. 440–58. Four classics on this subject are: C. Argyris and D. Schön, *Organizational Learning* (Reading, MA: Addison-Wesley 1978); P. Senge, *The Fifth Discipline* (New York: Doubleday, 1990); M. Pedler, J. Burgoyne and T. Boydell, *The Learning Company* (London: McGraw-Hill, 1991); and I. Nonaka and H. Takeuchi, *The Knowledge Creating Company* (Oxford: Oxford University Press, 1995). A useful overview is provided in M. Marquardt and A. Reynolds, *The Global Learning Organization* (Burr Ridge, IL: Irwin, 1994). Criticism of the feasibility of achieving a true learning organization in present day organizations may be found in E. Keep and H. Rainbird, 'Towards the learning organization?', in S. Bach and K. Sisson, op. cit., pp. 173–94; and in G. Salaman, 'A response to Snell: the learning organization: fact or fiction?', *Human Relations*, 54(3), 2001, 343–59. The paper to which Graeme Salaman is referring, by Robin Snell, 'Moral foundations of the learning organization', *Human Relations*, 54(3), 2001, 319–42 argues that not only is the learning organization challenging to conventional organizational structures and cultures, but it is counter to prevailing ethical systems. Work dealing explicitly with the tensions between 'care' and 'control' are T. Watson, *Management, Organisation and Employment Strategy* (London: Routledge, 1986); and M. Burawoy, *Manufacturing Consent* (Chicago: University of Chicago Press, 1979). Watson extends his arguments by way of discourse analysis in *In Search of Management* (London: Routledge, 1994). Much of this work rests on the concept of 'hegemonic' or ideological control, first discussed in the writings of the Marxist Gramsci: see A. Gramsci, *Selections from the Prison Notebooks* (London: New Left Books, 1971). Two useful papers on ideological 'concertive' control in teams are by J.R. Barker, 'Tightening the iron cage: concertive control in self-managing teams', *Administrative Science Quarterly*,

38, 1993, 408–37; and by Graham Sewell, 'The discipline of teams: the control of team-based industrial work through electronic and peer surveillance', *Administrative Science Quarterly*, 43, 1998, 397–428. A polemical critique of globalization and multinationals' manipulation of consumerism may be found in Naomi Klein, *No Logo* (London: Flamingo, 2000). A discussion of the 'Icarus paradox' may be found in Danny Miller, *The Icarus Paradox* (New York: Harper Business, 1990). The reference to Berger and Luckmann is, of course to P.L. Berger and T. Luckmann, *The Social Construction of Reality* (New York: Doubleday, 1966). The reference to Michael Foucault is from M. Foucault, *Discipline and Punish* (London: Allen Lane, 1977).

Finally, throughout this chapter there have been references to Chandler. The classic reference here is A.D. Chandler, *Strategy and Structure* (Cambridge, MA: MIT Press, 1962). In addition, Michael Porter's work has been generally referenced and can be found in M.E. Porter, *Competitive Strategy* (New York: Free Press, 1980).

The text on 'representing organizational members', including 'images of the marketplace', 'images of the community' and 'tensions and contradictions', are taken, virtually verbatim, from an earlier paper, 'Representing people at work' (reference above), with thanks to *Organisation* and Sage Publishers. I am grateful to Stephen Cummings for providing many of the figures in this chapter.

Strategic success is often attributed to having a clear intent that provides a central focus. However, relying solely on intention has its weaknesses. These weaknesses may be tempered by developing our ability to anticipate the actions of others and seeing intent as a flexible co-ordination mechanism rather than an unshakeable vision. This chapter assembles a cast of thousands including Schrodinger's Cat, the SAS, the guns at Singapore, disco cheats, Abe Lincoln and game theory to argue that strategy is thus about reconciling the paradoxical co-existence of two old adages: 'who dares wins' and 'looking before you leap'. It boils the views of these eclectic informants down to a 2 × 2 matrix: a matrix that outlines four styles of strategic development based on various blends of **intention** and **anticipation**: 'meandering', 'meditative', 'myopic', and 'manoeuvring'.

4 Strategy as Intention and Anticipation

ROBIN WENSLEY

Does intentionality matter? How does it matter? These questions have occupied center stage in research on adaptation and selection and in practitioner-oriented writings since the dawn of modern theorizing and research on management and organization. Intentionality is rooted in social-psychological theories of human behavior and purposeful action. It underlies theories of rationality in economics, strategic management, and decision sciences. It has been the foundation of management practice and the raison d'être *for the thriving enterprise of teaching and research in schools of business.*

A.Y. Lewin and H.W. Volberda

Despite 'intentionality' underlying theories of rationality in economics, strategic management and the decisions sciences, as Lewin and Volberda rightly assert, we, as strategic decision makers, rarely reflect on how it shapes strategy or on how understanding this better could make us better strategists. For example, as Karen Legge notes at the start of Chapter 3, 'Conventionally strategy is seen as a *purposeful, future orientated* activity', and one particularly useful way of 'unpacking' the twin aspects of purposefulness and future orientation is by focusing on the aspects on *intention* and *anticipation* respectively. The *Oxford English Dictionary* definition of each term is:

Intention = 'the *purpose* or goal of an action';
Anticipation = 'the action of looking forward to *something*'.

The two terms interrelate in a manner that we might represent in Figure 4.1.

My argument in this chapter is that we can see strategy and the result of the 'coming together' or interplay of human (or organizational) intention and anticipation. My aim is to demonstrate that we may become better strategists by reflecting on and better

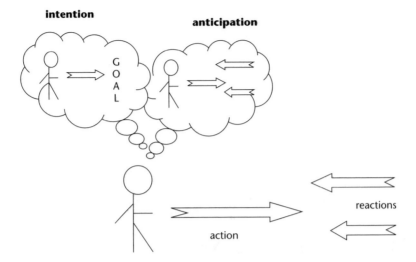

Figure 4.1 The interrelationship between intention and anticipation

understanding this interplay and how it can provide companies with an internal coherence that is at once flexible and adaptive.

My own interest in this area was stimulated by a mathematical colleague of mine
who, after a seminar to discuss modelling approaches to organizational actions and competitive market dynamics, commented that, unlike those who model phenomena or
behaviour like turbulent flow in fluids, those of us interested in arenas influenced by
human action faced issues of both intention and anticipation. Indeed, the distinction
between 'phenomena' or 'behaviour' and 'action' is useful here. The first two terms do
not necessarily reflect any sort of 'choice' or 'agency'. Fluids generally do not have a
choice as to their movement (unless they fall under the ambit of an agent). Action
indicates choice. This means that action is connected to a plurality of potential
outcomes, some consideration of different outcomes (their relative worth, probability
of achievement, and so on), and that how one chooses to act depends on *future* projections, *future* purpose and *future* aspirations. Human action also implies an element of
reaction, thus it implies some reflection on *previous* experience. This means that, to
some extent at least, we have a time line going backwards and forwards: intention and
anticipation link future outcomes back to current choices. Dealing with a modelling
context in which time moved in both directions, backwards and forwards was, as my
colleague ruefully observed, 'rather difficult'.

I do not intend or claim to resolve this little difficulty in this chapter but I do hope
to address a set of related concerns as we confront the twin issues of intention and
anticipation. In doing this, I start by looking at strategy as intention and then, having
highlighted the limitations of this approach, examine strategy as anticipation. I then
revisit intention – this time as a key means to co-ordinate organizational actions –
before summarizing the analysis. This will result in seeing strategy in terms of various
combinations of intention and anticipation, boiled down into the form of a 2 × 2
matrix (a form beloved by strategy analysts).

Strategy as Intention

The notion of strategy as intention is not itself new, after all, as already indicated, it is really linked to any concept of strategy as purposeful behaviour. Some might reasonably argue that it is indeed embedded in the old saying, and more recently the motto of the British Special Air Service (SAS) formed during the Second World War: 'Who dares wins'. The logic behind this is that the person or unit that is bold enough to act first will catch out those who ponder. Indeed, this is a view beloved by 'special forces' throughout military history or, for that matter, any smaller or more decentralized fighting force seeking to differentiate itself from a rival that it derides as sluggish or bureaucratic. Thucydides, for example, wrote of how the Athenians saw their key strength as their being 'capable of real action, first making their plans and then going forward without hesitation while their enemies have still not made up their minds'. (However, the leading Athenian general of that period, Pericles, was a little more measured claiming that: 'We combine boldness with reasoning about the business we are to take in hand, whereas for other people it is ignorance that produces courage and reasoning produces hesitation' – a statement that nicely anticipates this chapter's attempts to fruitfully link intention and anticipation.) In any case, intention links to the central assumptions of two areas that have influenced more recent strategy analysis.

The first is *agency theory*. This emphasizes the extent to which those who have decision-making powers also have discretion within a structure of both internal organizational incentives and also external constraints. While the interests in much of the work done on agency theory are different – it is often used to try and design incentive systems to ensure that managerial discretion is enacted in such a way as to represent the interests of the owners of the firm – there remains a key assumption that those who have agency are presumed also to have influence on outcomes.

Second, the role of intention is given much more direct emphasis in the concept of *strategic intent*. This term was invented by Gary Hamel and C.K. Prahalad and popularized by a paper entitled 'Strategic Intent' published in the *Harvard Business Review* in 1989. Here Hamel and Prahalad suggested that strategic intent was about 'envisioning a desired leadership position' and argued that this vision of what a company was trying to do and the consistency of purpose informed by this vision were far more important than any long-winded set of plans, policies or mission statement. Hamel and Prahalad's description of companies that were already 'good at strategic intent' drew particularly on Japanese companies. For example, they noted how Komatsu had developed a position of strength with the strategic intent of 'Encircling Caterpillar'. This intent encapsulated Komatsu's strategy of growth through tailoring its products to meet particular niches around the main Caterpillar products, niches that Caterpillar, given that its business model was based on economies of scale, could not afford to meet. Having surrounded their basic models in this way, Komatsu would then nibble away at Caterpillar's market share.

As we will argue later, there are some further complications to be considered. These include the extent to which strategic intent, as it is described above, does not really separate out either the issue of multiple intentions (after all, any individual firm is not the only purposeful actor in a competitive market), as well as the anticipation of the behaviours of others who influence the evolution of such a marketplace. But even at this stage we need to recognize two rather important caveats:

(1) What might be described as the alternative or cautious view nicely encapsulated in a further old adage: 'Look before you leap'. (Of course, we could enunciate some rather Zen-like principle that we can and indeed should always find a contrary adage when advice is being offered about acting in an inherently uncertain world, so perhaps we should not be too concerned.)

(2) We should recognize the important distinctions between different 'units of analysis', e.g., the *individual*, the *group* and the *organization*. While at the individual level, common experience for most of us would suggest that there is undoubtedly some good sense in the importance of having intention, we can even here recognize two seemingly contrary needs:

- the idea of clearly co-ordinated and focused action, and
- a willingness to take risks (or to think 'outside the box') to continue to succeed.

In a way these contrary human needs can be related to the discussion in Chapter 2, 'Strategy as Ethos', on how firms gravitate toward copying 'best practice' for reasons of 'security' and 'coherence', while they need to focus on staying ahead of the game by developing 'next practice'. As we look further at the notion of intention we will see that these two needs or issues, *co-ordination* and *risk taking*, often tend to become conflated. I begin this further look by focusing first on taking risks.

Risk taking or 'who dares wins'

In traditional decision theory we basically consider decision choices against what is termed 'the state of nature'. And we can *either* assume that the distributions of these 'states of nature' are independent of our action choices, *or* that there is some form of interaction between:

- our actions;
- those of others; and
- the outcomes of actions, as they flow into our future considerations.

For convenience, since we will consider the issue of anticipation later, we want at the moment to consider the question of choice behaviour against an independent state of nature. But can we really believe that a concerted independent action itself improves the likelihood of the desired outcome: that in some senses the prior probabilities will be altered by the nature of the action? In a simple sense this is a little difficult to believe in normal circumstances, yet we do know that action, or even observation, resolves uncertainty at the quantum level. We can demonstrate this with reference to one of quantum mechanics' most famous problems: the paradox of Schrodinger's cat.

On 7 June 1935, Erwin Schrodinger wrote to Albert Einstein to congratulate him on what is now known as the EPR paper, a famous problem in the interpretation of quantum mechanics. Soon thereafter, Schrodinger published what was to become one of the most celebrated paradoxes in quantum theory. Here a cat is placed in a box, together with a radioactive atom. If the atom decays and the Geiger counter detects an alpha particle, the hammer hits a flask of prussic acid, killing the cat. The paradox lies in the clever coupling of quantum and classical domains. Before the observer opens the box, the cat's fate is tied to the wave function of the atom, which is itself in a superposition of decayed and undecayed states. Thus, said Schrodinger, the cat must itself be in a superposition of dead and alive states before the observer opens the box, 'observes' the cat, and 'collapses' its wave function. Here indeed is an extreme example, admittedly created by moving between the quantum and everyday scale of events, of an action directly effecting the outcome! Until one observes, both probabilities (of the cat being alive or dead) coexist.

We can build upon this example by asking what you would do if you were in the position of the observer/actor (or we might say strategist)? Would you sit there and leave the cat to its own devices, knowing that it will 'get it' in the end? Or would you attempt to intervene, knowing that logically your actions could lead to the cat 'getting it'? And although the outcomes could be the same, whom would we admire most? The person who sat around waiting for the cat to get it or the person who dared to do something? Curiosity, indeed, may kill the cat.

Indeed, maybe the same is somewhat true of the SAS, which, while greatly admired, probably has a small impact on actual outcomes relative to the attention paid them. As John Newsinger observed:

> A succession of best-selling memoirs have appeared, as well as around a hundred SAS novels currently in print, some written by former SAS soldiers, plus numerous handbooks and manuals. This unprecedented publishing phenomenon vastly inflates the importance of the SAS, but obviously has a compelling appeal for a significant number of people. What this popular militarism reveals about the British national psyche in the 1980s and 1990s only time will tell.

We might speculate, however, we believe that the impacts of acts of bravery by a very small number of men such as the SAS lead to very significant outcomes. Or we might speculate that we simply admire (and perhaps aspire to be) those who dare, those who are brave enough to take their own life in their hands, to make the first strike – 'damn the torpedoes!' Faced with the, albeit mawkish, prospect that we as humans all to some extent face – that we are 'damned if we do and damned if we don't' – we prefer those who do. The West's most pervasive storyteller, Hollywood, will back me up on this (although on reflection there may be some gender bias here?).

In general, therefore, the enthusiasm for 'intent' may really be about two issues other than any necessary link to the efficacy of actions necessarily leading to preferred outcomes:

(1) Intent is perhaps seen as a means to counteract risk aversion or inert behaviour in many risky situations and thus, in itself, a positive trait or characteristic; or

(2) Intent is seen as important in the light of a recognition that in complex uncertain and interactive situations, minor intentions and actions can have a major and critical impact on outcomes as we recognize in certain other approaches such as those based on chaos and complexity theory (e.g., the length of Cleopatra's nose led to the fall of the Roman Empire).

Risk aversion and co-ordination: 'look before you leap'

In many ways the two issues described above are both aspects of a similar issue when it comes to making decisions or choices. Much as Frank Knight observed in 1921, we face problems of both, what he termed, 'risk' and 'uncertainty':

It will appear that a measurable uncertainty, or 'risk' proper, as we shall use the term, is so far different from an unmeasurable one that it is not in effect an uncertainty at all. We shall accordingly restrict the term 'uncertainty' to cases of the non-quantitative type.

We could go somewhat further and suggest that the issue of 'risk' (relating to a distribution of probabilities) is more about the first issue of risk aversion while 'uncertainty' (relating to the question of whether particular factors have any causal impact or not), relates more to the second one of minor actions but major impacts.

Subsequently, Frank Knight himself was an very much a 'look before you leap' enthusiast:

With uncertainty present, doing things, the actual execution of activity, becomes in a real sense a secondary part of life; the primary problem or function is deciding what to do and how to do it [before one acts].

However, we might take issue with Frank Knight on this particular observation. Turning Schrodinger's cat upside-down, we could argue that *uncertainties can only be resolved by action not analysis!* However, we might agree with him that while action is inevitable, this itself provides no guidance for choice.

Some, most famously Michael Porter, have argued that 'intent is not strategy' or 'bad strategy', and that the attention that has been paid to the concept since Hamel and Prahalad's 1989 paper and the subsequent emphasis upon learning from Eastern companies have been to our detriment. However, intention, given our discussion above, may not so much be a good or a bad thing as an inevitable thing. Either way, our views of intention, whether explicit or implict, influence decision making and the way that we strategize and manage. The continuing stream of 'hero manager' books about the 'visions' of strong (SAS-like?) executives such as Richard Branson or Jack Welch or Anita Roddick, is evidence that managers value intention whether it is good for them or not. And if this is the case we would do well to consider the strengths and weakness of intention when we seek a better understanding of strategy.

Case Box 4.1   Acting with Intent

As described earlier in this chapter, the Japanese industrial and construction machinery company Komatsu has been lauded for the simplicity of its strategic intent, articulated as 'Encircle Caterpillar'. More recently, Hewlett-Packard has attracted attention by paring its strategy down to one word: 'Invent'.

1. *What advantages to you think might accrue to companies like Komatsu or Hewlett-Packard through having such a clear or strong vision of their strategic intent?*
2. *Can you outline any potential disadvantages that might stem from having such a clear or strong sense of strategic intent?*

Strategy as Anticipation

In organizational practice we have to introduce 'others' into our analysis. When we are talking about others in a strategy context we are mainly considering competitors at this stage, but often, critically, there is a wider set of others certainly including both suppliers and buyers.

Once we introduce others, who themselves have agency and exhibit intent, and whose actions impact on us as indeed our actions do on them, life gets analytically much more complex. If we return to my mathematical colleague, we are now very evidently in a modelling situation in which one can only derive optimum behaviour by a form of analysis that starts from the future and works back to the present: a process known as backward iteration. (Haridimos Tsoukas, a former colleague at Warwick, makes a similar distinction between simple situations where we might be able to ascertain 'causes' of things and more complex, uncertain or human situations where we can only realistically ascertain 'reasons' for things.)

However, this poses potentially severe problems in our anticipation of others' behaviour, let alone our own, because we are just plain not good at such forms of modelling and analysis. There is consistent evidence that cognitively we find difficulty in undertaking various relatively simple reasoning tasks, particularly those that involve backward iteration. This seems to be true even when we are presented with effectively full information. John Sterman has used various versions of the classical 'beer game', which is based on a simulation of the retail and wholesale supply chain for beer, to show that given stock and demand leads and lags, participants, even with effectively full information, have great difficulty avoiding decisions to 'reorder' which themselves create further instabilities, much along the lines originally demonstrated by Jay Forrester with his early system dynamics models.

More generally, over recent decades, evidence has been building up that humans are amazingly bad at solving logical problems in terms of simple choice behaviour. This is partly demonstrated by the work of researchers such as Daniel Kahneman and Amos Tversky in experiments on decision making in businesslike contexts, but also goes much wider than this. For instance, the 'Wason selection task' is just one example from a huge body of experimental data. It involves cards with a letter on one side and a number on the other. Experimental subjects are asked which two of the following four cards they should turn over to test the hypothesis that each vowel has an odd number on the other side and that non-vowels are backed with even numbers:

E	3	4	D

People are awful at this task. The right response is the first and third card, but only about 10 per cent of normal subjects answer correctly. Cards E and 4 represent the antecedent (E) and the false consequent (4) of the rule that each vowel has an odd number on the other side.

How we interpret this, however, has proved to be highly controversial. Leda Cosmides, an evolutionary psychologist, emphasizes the way in which the specific context in which a task is presented seems to have a major impact on performance. For instance, imagine a variant of the card game above where you are at one of those discos where men must pay but women do not. Everybody has a card indicating their sex on one side (M or F), and whether they have paid (P or not-P) on the other. Which two cards (M, P, not-P or F) should you turn over to test whether the payment rule has been generally obeyed?[1]

M	P	not-P	F

With the problem recast in this way, many more people correctly pick the first and third cards. Even though the two tasks are structurally identical, somehow the new format makes the solution easier to see. Cosmides' theory is that this is because we have an ancestral cheater-detection module that evolved to identify those who go back on their promises or attempt to get in without paying when they should. This module is intrinsically suited to the second problem, but not to the first. Whereas the second format hooks into an understanding of relations with other humans, the former does not.

Others, however, have argued that the more appropriate interpretation is not one that relies on some form of evolutionary psychology but one that recognizes that the presentation of problem itself can be interpreted in different ways. Mike Oaksfield and Nick Chater, for instance, have argued strongly that the selection task should not be seen as a problem in *logic reasoning* but one in *decision choice*. As such, they argue that the specific choice of cards to turn over should be seen in terms of Bayesian informational criteria (which roughly means that we are more concerned about the additional information about the problem system as a whole generated by a particular choice) and that this can explain many of the various so-called 'irrational' results.

More recently but in rather a similar vein, Keith Stenning and Michiel van Lambalgen, in reviewing a wide range of empirical work and interpretation on the selection task, have suggested that a key issue should be much greater concern for semantics (the meaning and use of words) in understanding the ways in which the selection task is structured and understood by respondents.

To understand, therefore, the likely rationale behind the sort of choices that both ourselves and others will make can get pretty complicated! To provide some form of simplification in our analysis of the links between anticipation and intention toward strategic action, we will start from the premise that in strategy we are interested in anticipating 'their' (competitors, customers, suppliers) *collective actions* while considering 'our' *individual intent*.

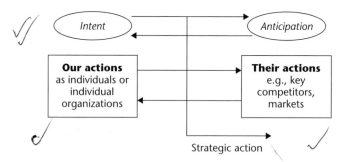

Figure 4.2   Thinking through 'our' and 'their' likely actions

Obviously our interest in 'their' actions and how much this is treated in an individual or collective manner will vary. At one extreme, when, for instance, we are considering a very anonymous and large group of, say, customers, we will resort to an analysis that treats their behaviour as a single so-called *market*, and in the simplest sense we can use the price mechanism as the key measure. Hence, we need to anticipate prices and markets. At the other extreme, we can consider the situation in which we are concerned to anticipate the behaviour of just one key *competitor.*

Game theory and anticipating prices, markets and other 'others'

The simple 'efficient' market assumption is generally traced all the way back to Adam Smith and was thus for some time seen as an immutable foundation stone of economics. It starts from the view that the current price in the market reflects a realistic evaluation of all available public information by similarly rational, self-interested and economically motivated individuals. In reasonably active markets with many buyers and sellers, it seems to be a satisfactory assumption and starting point.

Even so, there are two important caveats that quickly emerge: one relates to individuals' actual desire to act 'rationally', the other to our collective behaviour. The first caveat is fairly uncontested. By definition, access to appropriate private information may give any individual an ability to recognize situations in which the market price is inappropriate and/or subsequently seek to act 'irrationally' or politically so as to distort things.

The second caveat is more contentious. This is that markets sometimes exhibit irrational, herd-type behaviour that results in phenomena often described as 'bubbles'. Common examples quoted are Dutch tulips and the South Sea Bubble. In 1630s' Holland, a frenzy built up over an exotic bloom newly imported from the East: the tulip. Over three years, rare tulip bulbs changed hands for sums that would have bought a house in Amsterdam: a single bulb sold for more than £300,000 at today's prices. Finally, there was a horrendous crash and prices collapsed overnight, ruining thousands. Mike Dash, who is a historian with a special interest in mass hysteria, described the detailed events very effectively in his recent book *Tulipomania*. In the case of the South Sea Company, it financed its right to refund the British Government debt by way of expansion of shares. To ensure that the necessary legislation was passed, it provided various bribes to ministers and to Members of Parliament. This was apparently relatively common behaviour at the time. Initially, it succeeded in both its share placements and in acquiring the required level of debt from the previous owners but then its share price collapsed from abut £775 on 31 August to about £290 on 1 October 1720. One could quite easily see the rise and fall of dot.com stocks in a similar light.

Actually, in both the South Sea and tulip cases the evidence for irrationality (as opposed to wide variation in values that could be explained merely by considerable uncertainty) is itself subject to some debate. In particular, Peter Gerber has argued that much of the commentary in both these instances does not adequately distinguish between valuations that could be made on the basis of economic fundamentals from those that necessarily require valuations on the basis of expectations about other agents' valuations. (Those of us who are less expert in this field can, however, see that this distinction is itself pretty subtle!) Equally in the context of the much more recent concern about dot.com stocks, Higson and Briginshaw demonstrated that an analysis of value for Internet companies such as Amazon.com could produce a very wide range of results solely based on the market uncertainties. Of course, as often, it is easier to see the wood for the trees with a bit of hindsight.

All in all, the debate about market prices and irrationality is likely to continue. In the meantime, while we cannot expect market prices to resolve what remain essentially serious uncertainties, we can say that it may be unwise in any strategic analysis we undertake to assume that markets are likely to be systematically irrational.

At the other extreme from the notion of a market prices derived from anonymous, economically rational, and equally self-serving interactions between countless buyers and sellers is the notion of a very limited number, maybe only one, other participant whose behaviour we need to anticipate. This is the realm of 'game theory' – the formalized study of action in situations where the welfare of each agent in a group depends upon how other group members act.

As *Encyclopædia Britannica* explains, game theory is a branch of applied mathematics fashioned to analyse certain situations in which there is an interplay between parties that may have similar, opposed, or mixed interests. Although game theory may be used to analyse ordinary parlour games, its range of application is much wider. In fact, the Hungarian-born American mathematician John von Neumann and his colleague Oskar Morgenstern, a German-born American economist originally designed game theory, to solve problems in economics. In their book *The Theory of Games and Economic Behavior*, published in 1944, von Neumann and Morgenstern asserted that the mathematics developed for the physical sciences, which describes the workings of a disinterested nature, was a poor model for economics. They observed that economics is really more like a game in which the players anticipate one another's moves and that it therefore requires a new kind of mathematics.

Game theory may be applied in situations in which decision makers must take into account the different ways of reasoning that could be exhibited by other decision makers. By stressing strategic aspects – aspects controlled by the participants rather than by pure chance or general laws – the method both supplements and goes beyond the classical theories of probability or mechanical physics. It can and has been used, for example, to determine the formation of political coalitions or business conglomerates, the optimum price at which to sell products or services, the power of a voter or a bloc of voters, the selection of a jury, the best site for a manufacturing plant, and even the behaviour of certain species in the struggle for survival.

In a typical illustrative 'game', decision-making 'players', who each have their own goals, try to outsmart one another by anticipating each other's decisions; the game is finally resolved as a consequence of the players' decisions. In strategic management, playing such games serves as a guide for 'players' acting in other games in their working lives and as a tool for predicting the outcome of such games.

Game theory has received renewed public prominence recently with the release of the movie *A Beautiful Mind* based on the life story of John Nash, one of game theory's pioneers and a subsequent mathematics Nobel Prize winner. In a telling moment in the film (albeit a 'Hollywood version' of Nash's life) Nash, rises deep in thought from the dinner table from where his friends have been watching women to say: 'Gentleman, Adam Smith was wrong'. Game theory debriefs subsequently reflect on and prescribe 'Nash's Equilibria', that rather than simply seeking to blindly act out one's own intentions and leave the rest to chance or the market to resolve, each agent's strategy must maximize expected utility given the strategies of others. This generally requires some fruitful combination of:

- anticipation;
- political expediency;
- active collaboration;
- private knowledge sharing; and
- trust.

Game theory's potential usefulness for understanding human actions in what we might grandly call 'communities of practice' is illustrated in the 'prisoners' dilemma' case box below. And its usefulness for addressing strategic management concerns more specifically is illustrated in Case Box 4.4 at the end of this chapter. (Despite Mrs Thatcher's argument in the 1980s and early 1990s that it all comes back to the individual, these cases show that communities of practice really do matter!)

Case Box 4.2: *The Economist* on Game Theory

If you want to stay ahead of your competitors, it pays to know what they are thinking. Can management theory help?

When Square D's competitors learned of the firm's new strategy they ridiculed the idea. The plan, leaked to an industry trade journal, was to shrink the time needed to deliver its circuit boards and other customized components used in commercial buildings. At the time (the late 1980s), the typical delivery took 10–12 weeks. Square D's plan was to slash that to a week, by holding higher inventories and getting its employees to work overtime. But this seemed ludicrous in an industry that demanded customization and skilled labour. Fortunately, Square D had one thing going for it: the story was not true.

In fact, the entire tale had been fabricated by Square D to throw competitors off the scent. The firm, which has since been acquired, had discovered that customers would indeed pay a substantial premium for faster delivery, and it had devised an entirely new system of order-taking, product-design and assembly to satisfy this unmet demand. But Square D needed time both to switch to the new methods and to find distributors that could implement the new approach. Convincing competitors that it was heading in the wrong direction helped Square D gain the head-start it needed.

This kind of gamesmanship is common in the business world, and is one of the main reasons why economists often fail to be useful to businessmen. In many industries, firms bear little resemblance to the passive bodies portrayed in the traditional economics textbook. Instead managers try to anticipate the actions of others – whether they be competitors, suppliers or customers – and influence those actions to their advantage.

Part of the task is assiduous routine fact-finding. In the 1990s, firms that offer 'business intelligence' services have grown rapidly: the revenues of one, Kroll Associates, have tripled in the past three years. But it is hard for managers to create a clear picture of competitors from the fragmented images flashed before them. Information from salespeople, technical experts and the business press are sketchy, and often seem contradictory.

That is where game theory comes in. Its chief insight is simple: if a firm makes decisions based only on the current business environment, it will fail. In the real world, firms respond to threats and the environment changes. By analysing the others' potential responses, game theory adds another dimension to a firm's sleuthing. Instead of simply asking what another party is planning to do, game theory encourages managers to ask what is in the other's best interest.

This often involves the cut and thrust of competition. A well-timed investment, or price cut, can cause others to think twice before invading your patch. Only last week, for example, Boeing announced that it would make a new regional jet – a move that seems designed to undermine Airbus's attempts to design an aircraft for the same market.

But game theory is not only about intimidating competitors. In many cases, it illuminates the importance of winning people's trust. When Intel was trying to establish its chip as a standard, it had to convince PC makers that they would not be held hostage. By licensing its technology to others, it assured buyers of a competitive supply. Once Intel chips had become standard, and PCs were widely adopted, the firm stopped the practice.

However, Adam Brandenburger, an economist at Harvard Business School, argues that game theory can also do something far more powerful. Through elaborate scenarios, it can help managers imagine how their industry would evolve if they were not part of it. This makes them aware of what it is that they in particular have to offer, while reminding them of other firms' strengths.

This, Mr Brandenburger argues, is the secret of making money in many new sectors. By working together, firms can make a new sector grow more rapidly. Yet to obtain these advantages, firms must often give up some bargaining power. Striking a balance between co-operation and competition can be one of the manager's hardest tasks. The choice is often between dominating a small market or assuming a humbler role in a huge market.

By allowing Microsoft to license its operating system so that other firms could make PCs, IBM enabled the personal computer to grow far more rapidly than it would have if IBM had gone off on its own. Even though IBM itself missed many of the gains – which have been captured by Microsoft, Intel and rival PC makers – it still does a thriving business thanks to the PC market's sheer size. By contrast, Apple tried to hold on to its monopoly in the Macintosh market by refusing for many years to grant licences.

Such co-operative rivalry, which has been given the ugly name of 'co-opetition' by Ray Noorda, the founder of Novell, a software firm, crops up time and again in rapidly evolving industries. It is easy to see why Oracle, Netscape and Sun are together promoting the Java language, since the success of the network computer would create a bigger market for all three. Similarly, the growth of defined-contribution pensions – in which employers offer a range of mutual funds to their workers, and make it easy for them to manage their investments – helps several different kinds of firm, from fund houses to custody providers to providers of information systems. By collaborating, these firms can help the industry take off.

The hallmark of such industries is confusion. From one moment to the next, firms cannot tell their allies from their rivals. Should Fidelity co-operate with other mutual funds by selling them through its 'supermarket', or should it try to crush them by leaving them out? Should Microsoft try to prop up Apple, or drive it out of business?

1. *Think of a company that you are familiar with, either one you work for or know well – we shall call this company X. Concoct a radical new strategy for company X. How might this company's competitors react to this new strategy?*
2. *How could your company X take advantage of these reactions? Are there any reactions that you can think of that might put company X at a disadvantage? If so, how might you modify your new strategy for company X?*

3. *Concoct a radical new strategy which could be followed by one of X's main competitors. What systems or culture would X need to have in place in order to anticipate or effectively react to such a strategy?*
4. *Think of a collaborative effort that could be arranged between company X and another 'player' or group of players (it could be a competitor, a group of customers, the government, etc.). How would all parties collectively benefit from such a strategy?*

Source: *The Economist*, 'Business movers and shakers' (24 January 1998)

The limits of game theory

In an analytical sense, game theory can provide a very effective framework within which to investigate a whole series of contexts where the outcomes are a result of the interactions between the intermediate choices of various actors. It can ensure that we systematically model the impact of various decision rules for the actors themselves and do not assume, without defining them carefully, distortions such as information asymmetries between the actors. It can provide us with a better understanding of robust competitive strategies in many situations of direct competition (such as the so-called 'tit-for-tat' approach), as well as the impact of changes in rules and regulations.

When we come, however, to the complex, and to some extent contested, context in which strategic management operates, the benefits are perhaps a little less clear. This is perhaps for three reasons:

* First, there is the issue of the pay-off matrix. In the archetypal game theory situation, for instance, that of the prisoners' dilemma, the impact of any pair of actions by the two 'players' is specified separately for each player. In more common practical situations, considerable uncertainty (that word again) surrounds the actual nature of the pay-off matrix. Indeed, as some, such as Philip Nattermann, who are more interested in an evolutionary view of competitive markets have recognized, the so-called pay-off matrix might be better seen as the outcome from a particular 'fitness landscape'. Firms position themselves to try and achieve a higher degree of fitness with their environment but this very fitness can be influenced by interactions between the positions they choose.
* Second, there is a more complex continuum of competitive or co-operative behaviour than can easily be represented in any simplified game theory model.
* Third, it often turns out in practice that trying too hard to think about the situation 'from a competitor's viewpoint' can itself prove rather dysfunctional. For instance, as Robert Waterman argued, this sort of approach does not work because 'people get stuck in trying to carry it out'. In effect, companies that try too hard to be good players 'get hamstrung' or paralysed. This happens, he argues, for three reasons:
  ○ There is usually no single, easily identified competitor.
  ○ Business is a positive sum game: at one level firms compete fiercely, at another level they help each other. In other words, paradoxically, they often compete and collaborate. At the level of the individual this would seem to be a betrayal of trust. But in a company comprised of many different personalities and departments, all with a myriad of relationships, such duplicity is not nearly so direct or obvious.

o   Competitors are human: they are neither superhuman (i.e., all knowing and able to follow up all opportunities) nor dumb (i.e., unable to know or do very much). And, while they may not occupy either end of this spectrum, no two competitors occupy the same point in between. Through different levels of ability or concern we all have our own level – making transactions increasingly complex.

At the current state of knowledge, therefore, both game theory itself, and indeed sophisticated competitor-focused analysis, may only have limited application as the strategic context involves more players, more co-operative and competitive options, and more bounded rationality and uncertainty.

This is not to suggest some degree of anticipation is not an important component in a strategic analysis. After all, as Waterman notes above, one's competitors are not dumb and one might also argue that this is a particular, and rather colourful way of representing the notion of 'rational expectations' in economics! Hence we should hardly be surprised to discover that most sustained commercial successes seem to depend more on a whole sequence of sometimes relatively minor actions that have worked rather than one big action that no competitor could imitate or recognize.

So, given the weaknesses of relying solely on intent, we have argued for some level of anticipation in strategy – but not too much: the usual issue of getting the right balance! We now will return to the issue of intention but from rather a different perspective. Mentioned earlier was the need to recognize the question of the 'unit of analysis' and when we look at the organizational or firm as the 'unit' we note that intention in strategy also achieves other important objectives.

Revisiting the Benefits of Corporate Intention

Strategic management has always been closely linked to the art of war and the military. The introductory chapter to this book and a number of Stephen Cummings' other publications trace strategy back to its etymological roots in ancient Greek military settings. However, I do not intend to look back that far in this chapter – I only need the last couple of centuries to make a few salient points.

Among military strategists of the modern era, Carl von Clausewitz is perhaps the most widely quoted authority on the benefits of co-ordinated action, particularly when it is used to inflict the maximum force on a competitor's weakest point. Indeed it was reputed that in the 1980s, Clausewitz's nineteenth-century teachings were widely disseminated in the Boeing Aircraft Company as it faced severe competition from both established and new competitors. The intention was that all staff should understand the importance of such axioms as massing collective forces at the enemy's weakest points when involved, say, in sales meetings with actual or potential customers. In certain circumstances this, for Boeing, would clearly mean giving considerable emphasis to issues of reputation and safety relative to their competitors.

As an authority on competitive strategy, Clausewitz was undoubtedly right about the benefits of clear intent and co-ordinated action (and, subsequently, central logistics) in overwhelming 'the enemy'. However, some modifications to this overly simplistic view should be made.

First, much of the more recent interpretation of competitive military strategy has recognized, as with Liddell Hart's view of military strategy, that it is more useful to focus intention upon achieving a better state of coexistence rather than the annihilation of one's competitors. This is especially true when the nature of the competitive 'landscape' may be more appropriate to guerrilla warfare rather than large 'set-piece' battles, consequently requiring greater attention be paid to coalitions and alliances rather than simply relying on one's ability to overwhelm as a 'stand-alone' superpower. Some might well see such issues being played out yet again in the various disputes between Microsoft, its competitors and the US federal government, or in the efforts that were made in forming political alliances before military engagements took place in Afghanistan.

Second, moving back into the realm of strategic management, Fred Gluck and his co-authors have observed that:

> Strategic thinking is usually indirect and unexpected rather than head-on and predictable. Basil Henry Liddell Hart, probably the foremost thinker on military strategy in the 20th century, has written, 'To move along the line of natural expectation consolidates the opponent's balance and thus his resisting power.' 'In strategy,' says Liddell Hart, 'the longest way around is often the shortest way home.'

This viewpoint coincides with the postmodern theories of power expressed by Michel Foucault: that fighting 'the power' head on only makes that power better able to concentrate its forces and resist you. Far better to form a coalition of like-minded bodies and create your own network that works around 'the power' to gradually and quietly achieve your aims.

Both of the modifications implied in the paragraphs above suggest that there are still substantial benefits to co-ordinated action based on clear intent. But we need to be more sophisticated in terms of 'who' is being co-ordinated. In particular, we need to be more aware of who is actually 'internal' or 'external' to the organization concerned – who is 'us' and who is 'them', in other words. To prefigure some of the material from Chapter 9 'Strategy as Systems Thinking', we should be careful where we draw an organization's boundaries, as drawing this too tightly can cause us to take our eyes off of those to which we might do well to see our interests connected. And we need to be more aware of the means of co-ordination itself, developing more sophisticated and integrated information systems (see Chapter 6 'Strategy as Data plus Sense-making') to inform our intentions rather than just relying upon a simple but general unifying but inflexible and/or unquestioned ideology. The paragraphs that follow seek to build further subtlety into our understanding of intention by exploring in greater detail its role as a co-ordinating force, and its strengths and limitations in this regard.

Intention as a means of collective co-ordination and general direction setting

One of the most common justifications for an objective or a plan or clear intent within any organization is that 'it helps to know where you are trying to go'. Perhaps the two best expressions of this near-truism come from suitably famous Americans:

Abraham Lincoln: 'If we could first know whither we are tending, we could better judge what to do and how to do it.'

Casey Stengel: 'If you don't know where you're going you'll probably end up somewhere else.'

At some level the sentiment expressed above is undoubtedly true: in the case of basic logistics, for instance, where we need to co-ordinate various supplies to enable particular actions. However, as others have also observed, this logic should not be pushed too far. Robert Hayes, for instance, has suggested that the 'road map' analogy implied in this sentiment could be very misleading:

> When you are lost on a highway, a road map is very useful: but when you are lost in a swamp, whose topography is constantly changing, a road map is of little help. A simple compass which indicates the general direction to be taken and allows you to use your own ingenuity is much more valuable.

Of course, we can go further in this direction and suggest that Robert Hayes himself is being too literal. Chapter 1 of this book considered Karl Weick's famous story about the group of military trainees lost in the Alps to argue that having any map is much better then having no map! In effect, the map of the Pyrenees, although the wrong map, acted as an integrating focal point that stimulated collective intent through interaction where there previously was none. As several others have commented, tracking down the source of this story is a little more difficult. It may be, however, as Susan Blackmore would note, the difficulty in finding the original source is not very significant anyway. As she comments in the context of another urban myth:

> This is an example of an 'urban myth', a story that takes on a life of its own regardless of its truth, value or importance. [This] story is probably untrue but truth is not a necessary condition for [it to be] successful.

We can therefore argue that the very popularity of Weick's map story (as a guide to doing strategy in itself), to which Chapter 1 referred, points to its 'truth value' even if its actual origin, and subsequent 'factual-ness', is highly obscure.

So we should consider 'intent' rather more as a sense of collective co-ordination or general direction, as embodied in the compass in Robert Hayes' analogy, the map of the Pyrenees, of Weick's analogical guide, rather than as a detailed road map that we simply follow without critical reflection. Intent in this sense has elements of a general sense of organizational purpose and it is not surprising that it can be somewhat conflated with notions of 'mission' or 'culture' or 'ideology'. It therefore links quite closely to what is termed in this book 'strategy as ethos'. In this sense, some degree of common intent can have a significant impact on internal organizational effectiveness. It is motivational as well as the more obvious benefits that we have already considered in terms of co-ordination where it is appropriate. This is an approach that relates directly to that developed by Hamel and Prahalad in their original *Harvard Business Review* article but often overlooked since:

> On the one hand, strategic intent envisions a desired leadership position. At the same time strategic intent is more than simply unfettered ambition. The concept also encompasses an active process that includes: focusing the organisation's attention to the essence of winning, motivating people by communicating the value of the target, leaving room for individual and team contributions, sustaining enthusiasm by providing new operational definitions as circumstances change, and using intent consistently to guide resource allocations.

Hamel and Prahalad, however, tend to discount that the aspects of co-ordination and motivation also apply *outside of* the individual organization of the 'us'. Indeed, as one might expect given the general approach adopted to time in the analysis outlined in this chapter, it is also clear that we are all inevitably prisoners of our own historic context to some extent (for more on this, see Chapter 10, 'Strategy as Process, Power and Change'). Indeed, Hamel and Prahalad's paper has the strong feel of 'the conquering Japanese (i.e., 'them') are coming'. (Something followed up by Porter's dismissal of the 'Japanese wave having failed to overwhelm "us" because it was fundamentally flawed'.) Certainly more recently, at both the macroeconomic and the corporate level, the invincibility of the Japanese economic machine has been rather less evident. But in a strange way Hamel and Prahalad's traditional perspective on the *external* impacts of clear intent reinforces the notion of an external, subversive and rather hidden threat. Indeed, Hamel and Prahalad made much of the fact that key Japanese competitors, despite their clear intent, remained relatively invisible to their Western 'targets' during much of the competitive conflict and the building of competitive positions. Maybe it is just a rerun of the inscrutable Japanese and the guns facing the wrong way in the defence of Singapore! (Note: this example refers to the British land guns in Singapore being all fixed pointing out to sea rather across the Malay peninsula on the assumption that no army could actual make its way through the jungle there. The guns were subsequently next to useless in the course of what unfolded.) We should be aware, therefore, of both the positive and negative effects of formulating ideas about the intentions of others.

However, we should recognize that, in general, clear statements of strategic intent not only can help in mobilizing and co-ordinating internal action, they can also have significant effects on competitor behaviour. A wider literature and analysis of competitive market evolution recognizes that clear signalling of intention can be important in terms of acquiring *fellow supporters* at key stages in market development where issues remain about contested standards. It can also be important in the more traditional economic policy context of entry or expansion deterrence, where a clear signal of commitment from one competitor or a network of competitors can act as a barrier to entry (see the discussion of Porter's five forces in the introductory chapter). Such collective expressions of intent are likely to dissuade other competitors from taking the same, or even in some cases similar, action.

I conclude this section, however, by returning to the central concern with uncertainty. To make a credible commitment of intent, both within and outside of the organization, we need to make specific choices in an ambiguous situation. Of course, as we might expect there is another difficult trade-off here. We are all aware that sound advice in an uncertain situation is to keep one's options open. Now with the recent developments in 'real options theory', we are in a better position to recognize the substantial economic benefits from such a strategy in uncertain situations, although significant practical problems remain (see Case Box 4.3 below). But, as this excerpt from *The Economist* implies, it is useful to have some way of comparing the benefits of keeping options open with those that might arise from pre-empting a competitor's intent.

Finally, in this world of uncertainty, we also need to recognize that even some of the benefits of pre-emption might be somewhat illusory. While we do know that in some situations there is indeed a genuine first mover advantage, we also need to recognize, as Steven Schnaars has documented, that there are often situations in which competitors can overcome this advantage by what might be seen as more sophisticated 'imitative strategies', based on reading the market signals from the earlier entrants and improving their offerings and strategy in key areas. Hence, we could connect the argument developed in this chapter to debates about timing market entry strategies something to which a colleague at Warwick, Scott Dacko, has devoted a good deal of energy. A small list of publications is provided in the biographical notes at the end of this chapter for those who want to explore this issue further.

Case Box 4.3   *The Economist* on 'Real Options'

Real-options analysis starts by recognizing that most investment opportunities have embedded in them a series of managerial options. Take, for instance, an imaginary oil company. Its bosses believe that they have found an oil field, but they know neither how much oil it contains nor what the price of oil will be once they are ready to pump. So:

- As a first step, they could simply put enough money down to buy or lease the land and explore.
- If they do not find oil, they can cap their outlays at the costs already sunk.
- If they do strike oil, however, they might invest a bit more and put the drilling gear in place.
- But suppose the oil price then plummets. Management could put the project on hold and let its field lie fallow.
- Perhaps it could also switch to producing gas instead of oil.
- Or it could drop the project and sell the land.
- If, on the other hand, the oil price goes up, the firm is ready to pump.

Since oil prices and other factors are uncertain, in other words, the mere option to produce has value.

The logic is similar in other industries. Pharmaceutical companies, for instance, are in the business of searching for new pills, but never know which will work. So they may start researching several drugs, in the hope of striking lucky with just a few.

Options on 'real' assets behave rather like options on financial assets (puts and calls on shares or currencies, say). The similarities are such that they can, at least in theory, be valued according to the same methodology. In the case of the oil company, for instance, the cost of land corresponds to the premium (or downpayment) on a call option, and the extra investment needed to start production to its strike price (at which the option is exercised). As with financial options, the longer the option lasts before it expires and the more volatile the price of the underlying asset – in this case, oil – the more the option is worth.

There is a snag, of course: sheer complexity. Pricing financial options is daunting, but valuing real options is harder still. Their term, unlike that of financial options, is usually open-ended or undefinable. The volatility of the underlying asset can be difficult to measure or guess, especially since it is not always clear what it is – if, for example, it is yet to be invented. How can one define the appropriate benchmark asset-class in the case of a new drug for a rare disease? And there may be additional variables to consider, such as the strategic benefit of pre-empting a rival.

1. Outline a real options system that would act as a useful decision-making aid for the oil company described above.
2. What are the strengths and weaknesses of your model as a strategic decision-making tool?

Source: The Economist, 'Keeping all options open' (14 August 1999)

Strategy as Blending Intention and Anticipation: The M-Matrix

Mindful of the importance of both 2 × 2 matrices and alliteration in any strategy analysis (they, like Weick's map, while not capturing the complexity of our world, can be very useful aide-mémoires), we can consider the relationship between intention and anticipation in terms of the box diagram before drawing some conclusions. This is presented in Figure 4.3 with intention and anticipation forming the two axes. This leads to four generic approaches: meandering, myopic, meditative and manoeuvring.

In the interests of simplicity and alliteration we have somewhat conflated two slightly different issues here. Because we are considering the notion of strategy and the level of the unit of analysis as 'the organization', we have rather conflated 'intention' with 'collective action', although given the previous discussion in this chapter we would also argue that these two notions are very closely linked. Similarly, again as previously discussed, 'anticipation' is linked strongly to some notion of 'consideration' or 'thought'. However, we would not wish this simple model to suggest that we would consider the relationship between thought and action in the traditional linear fashion; we need to adopt more of a synchronic rather than a diachronic perspective. Or, in other words, to see the relations between intention and anticipation as happening simultaneously and forming a continuous feedback loop where time is a circle and impressions of the past and the future both inform the present; rather than happening in a linear causal fashion through or across a time line. This view, diagrammed in Figure 4.4, is, of course, a form of answer to the modelling question which started this chapter. It should be borne in mind when applying the M-matrix.

It would appear that 'manoeuvring' with its combining of high levels of anticipation and high levels of intention would obviously be the best of these approaches. Given the arguments I have outlined in this chapter, I would generally tend to agree with this. However, as has surfaced in the debates that I have had with the editors of

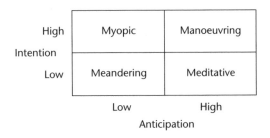

	Low	High
High Intention	Myopic	Manoeuvring
Low	Meandering	Meditative

Low   High
Anticipation

Figure 4.3 The anticipation-intention relationship or M-matrix

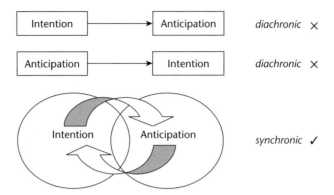

Figure 4.4 The intention-anticipation relationship as synchronic

this book, one should perhaps take the more postmodern view that there is no 'one best way'. And indeed, when one goes through the four approaches, as in the paragraphs below, one can see that the other three Ms may also have certain strengths that flesh out some of the complexities that have been discussed above. Subsequently, we would do well to learn from them too.

Meandering mode

> 'Which way should I go from here?' said Alice
> 'That depends a good deal on where you want to get to,' said the Cat.
> 'I don't much care where __' said Alice
> 'Then it doesn't matter which way you go,' said the Cat,
> '__ so long as I get somewhere,' Alice added as an explanation.
> 'Oh, you're sure to do that,' said the Cat, 'if you only walk long enough.'
> Alice's encounter with the Cheshire Cat, in Alice's Adventures in Wonderland, Lewis Carroll

If we have little intention and low anticipation, we are destined to a world in which all that happens to the organization will be seen as the impact of external forces beyond control and beyond prediction. To misquote, and develop upon, an oft-misquoted Henry Ford, here not only is history bunk but also so is the future! We become, in other words, a meanderer (a term of Greek origin named after the River Meander – a particularly winding, wandering and seemingly aimless stream). While this is of course a rather extreme characterization, it is worth considering that for some organizations it would appear that it is not so far from the truth. Ed Bowman's original article on 'Strategy and the Weather', published in the *Sloan Management Review*, certainly suggested that at least in terms of their more public pronouncements some organizations appeared to ascribe any problems that they encountered to factors totally outside of their control!

With little clear intention, and no consideration of the likely future responses of customers, suppliers or competitors, the implicit management strategy becomes one of wandering. Expressed in such terms we seem to have pretty much the antithesis of strategy as we know it, but we should be careful in this interpretation. Meandering could also allow for *serendipity*: after all we can come across new and unexpected opportunities as often by mistake as by intention. Here we have the dilemma of the notion of an emergent strategy. One that works well, at least after the event, is often one in which the opportunities that did arise, however unexpected beforehand, were able to be recognized as potentially interesting and acted upon on. This, of course, requires what many others have commented on before – the 'prepared' mind, and the prepared mind is often the open mind, even the unfocused or undirected mind. (Steve Cummings has informed me of this rather nice quotation from Thucydides in this regard: 'To face calamity with a mind as unclouded by preconceptions as may be, and quickly to react against it – that, in a city and in an individual, is real strength'.) Again, this is all sounding very Zen!

How then do we recognize what might be termed 'meandering' in a purposeful or positive manner? Perhaps by associating this approach with a 'quixotic' manner (and I mean 'quixotic' in its most literal sense derived from the character of Don Quixote)? An approach characterized by open-minded enthusiasm for whatever emerges on one's travels, an enthusiasm that others might see as naïve. Sometimes such an attitude may not be such a bad thing for the strategist.

Myopic mode   *Myopics cannot see things where they are far away*

This approach is what emerges when we have clear intentions but no anticipation, or equally no sense of history. Despite our clear intention to achieve various objectives, we are inevitably thrown off course by our inability to consider the actions of others and how these tend to change over time.

Ever since Ted Levitt's classic *Harvard Business Review* article, the issue of myopia in business or at least in marketing strategy has been seen as a central concern. Ted suggested that because firms defined the scope of their business too narrowly, without considering the ways in which what they had to offer related to the changing nature of their customer's needs, they often lost demand over time to new entrants who saw these changes and responded accordingly.

To those of us, however, who have actually suffered from myopia for most of our lives, this analysis is potentially misleading. Myopia is not so much about not looking forward as about being unable to get anything but those items very close to one into focus! It is not so much about intention as ability! However, we can say that meandering's strengths (openness to seredipity, chance and new influences) are myopia's weaknesses, and vice versa.

In the context of the nature of a future marketplace it could also be true that it may prove impossible to see the future clearly – the issue of uncertainty again. While Ted Levitt's classic question 'What business are you in?' remains a good question, we should not assume there is likely to be a single and clear answer. This is for two reasons:

(1)   The future orientation perspective implied in the framing of the question may mean having to address issues of uncertainty; and

(2)   At least in terms of the strategy implications, the question itself presumes that the key constraint for the organization is its understanding of the changing nature of its marketplace rather than, say, its ability to respond competitively to such changes.

As already suggested in the context of this analysis, a degree of myopia in strategic behaviour is probably inevitable: because analysis is generally undertaken towards achieving some sense of certainty of direction in environments where information is incomplete and the future is uncertain. And indeed in some situations myopia may be a good thing. For example, where the environment is stable and relatively certain, valuable time and resources could be wasted doing the sort of scanning and self-analysis implied in an approach based heavily on anticipating potential futures. Or in environments where competitors are 'losing their heads' engaging in numerous changes of strategy to the point where they are confusing customers and other stakeholders, keeping one's head and having an unshakeable sense of purpose could be a competitive advantage.

→ relate to act of meditate or say the act of thinking very deeply abt something

Meditative mode

In this mode we are the informed but inactive observer. We might see this as the domain of mystics, but it is also a criticism levelled at academics (and, to a lesser extent, consultants)! However, just as myopia implies seeing the future, and in particular anticipating the actions of competitors, customers and suppliers, in a fuzzy and imprecise manner rather than not at all, the meditative mode should not just be seen as a process of reflection without *any* purpose. In any practice, the very domain in which one's reflection is focused at least implicitly defines a purpose, however broadly. Indeed, borrowing a term from Chapter 2, 'Strategy as Ethos', one always has a *telos* even if one may not be able to articulate this at a particular point in time.

Just as with the analysis of myopia, there are two critical issues in this domain. First, how do we ensure that the process of reflection or anticipation does not continue beyond its usefulness? This problem of 'defining a "stopping rule"', is actually a rather generic one in a number of areas. The answer is difficult because we encounter a logical contradiction: we can only value any analysis when we have completed it: we cannot anticipate its value beforehand so we can work out the trade-off between the costs and the benefits. Much like the apocryphal PC user who is left staring at the hourglass symbol on their screen trying in a vain attempt to ascertain whether the powder is flowing from the upper to the lower chamber and know how long the program is going to take to load: we only really know when it has finished!

The second issue revolves more around the question of not so much the cost as the benefit of 'thinking broadly' or seemingly without clear intent. Much emphasis is given nowadays to notions such as 'thinking outside the box', yet another way of representing this is, of course, to encourage thinking about issues which are initially seen as irrelevant to the problem at hand. After all, the 'box' is in many ways defined by what is seen as most important and appropriate to the issue to be addressed. In terms of anticipation, this is nicely illustrated by the follow-up to the original Rand studies using the Delphi technique to look at technology futures. The most obvious result in retrospect was that the most significant error had been to leave certain stakeholders out of the original membership of the panel. Of course the problem was that they were not recognized as stakeholders when the panels were constituted but only as such ten to fifteen years later.

There is a range of research available now that indicates the importance of taking a meditative approach to strategy in certain situations. Knowledge management gurus such as Ikujiro Nonaka argue for being less myopic about efficiency being our goal and building slack into a workplace to allow knowledge and thinking the 'space' to emerge. Innovation researchers recognize the advantages of 'free association' or solving problems through 'disassociative thinking' (see Chapter 7, 'Strategy as Creativity').

Similarly, educationalists have long argued that children need time away from the standard curriculum in order to develop their creative abilities. This is why it is called 're-creational time'.

And we can find many examples of companies that have benefited from introspection at certain points of their life cycle. After several years of misguided 'thrashing about' in the doldrums, Apple Computers had to meditate long and hard over what its competitive advantage could and should be before beginning to resurrect itself. And Nike, in order to fully understand the level of hatred directed at its operations in developing countries and the complexity of changing its strategy to satisfy a new mix of stakeholders, had to enter a similar mode before formulating and implementing a coherent response.

Manoeuvring mode

Manoeuvre:
1. *To perform manoeuvres or evolutions; to make movements of changes in the disposition of troops, vessels, etc.*
2. *To employ strategem, to manage by artifice, to scheme. To contrive to get.*
3. *To drive or entice* into *or out of* by manoeuvring; *to make (one's way) into by manoeuvring.*

Oxford English Dictionary

Although originally not convinced of this term in this position in the M-matrix, I have grown to like it, particularly when one considers the definitions, listed above, and the etymology of manoeuvre. It comes from the French *manœuvre*, from the old French *maneuvre* (meaning work done by hand), and from the Latin *manu* (to operate or work by hand). Of course, this is also the root of our word *management*. However, it seems to me that there is a subtle difference between management and manoeuvring:

Management – being 'to move or steer by an act of control'; and
Manoeuvring – being to handle or direct with a degree of skill, dexterity, artifice and sensitivity to the actions of others.

The manoeuvring mode of the M-matrix encapsulates strategic action in which intention and anticipation are both adroitly applied to the choices that have to be made. The *Oxford English Dictionary* definitions remind us of the central importance of skill, strategy and action over time, all of which would seem to add up to an approach to strategy that would, in most instances, be highly desirable. However, as always, there remains a question of proportion and balance. I have noted below two potentially negative conditions for manoeuvrers to be wary of falling into.

First, in the field of marketing strategy, Peter Leeflang and Dick Wittink argue that there is evidence of what might be termed 'over-competition', that firms can overreact to competitive moves when there is little likelihood that customer behaviour would actually respond. This relates back to Waterman's ideas that too much competitor-sensing activity can hamstring a company, leading to 'analysis paralysis' as it is often called. We can use some sporting examples to draw a useful 'memento' that may guide us away from being stymied in this way. In sports such as motor racing, cricket or baseball, where the environment is both structured and uncertain (much like business) and speed of reaction is key, the brains of top competitors do not have time to think (good sports people will often equate bad form to 'thinking too much' and good form to 'being in the zone' – that is, acting without thinking). However, it has also recently been proven that they do not physically have time enough to even act or react. They seem to succeed by combining a predetermined *intent*, honed through the combination of a clear sense of their abilities and what we might call their style, ethos or œuvre (i.e., 'body of work'), with lots of practice in 'match-like' circumstances. This puts them in position, or sets them up, to *anticipate* what they need to do as things unfold. Indeed, as John McGee, the author of Chapter 5, is fond of telling me, the reason why the England rugby team is so good at the moment is that it goes out on the field with a clear intent, but is still able to be flexible, quickly question this intent, and act accordingly should it anticipate that an opponent's actions are about to stymie its objectives.

The second potentially negative condition relates to the way in which manoeuvring carried to an extreme may result in a company being seen as overly scheming or Machiavellian, as we Europeans might say, or not a 'straight shooter', to use terminology more familiar to Americans. This type of reputation is one from which most organizations will eventually suffer.

However, there is evidence that contradicts even these seemingly reasonable provisos. Bruce Clark and Dave Montgomery have argued that such 'paranoia', be it analytical or political, can actually help improve firm performance! Either way, given contradictory evidence and a complex and uncertain world, one would do well to be aware, as with the previous three images put forward here, of both the potential strengths and weaknesses of manoeuvring, rather than attempt to ascertain whether it is generally good or not.

Overall this analysis would suggest that while intention serves a number of useful purposes, one should consider tempering intention with anticipation. However, both can be carried too far. As with many things, a bit of critical thinking and moderation is required. The key ability with regard to strategy as intention and anticipation is to be able to tell the difference in practice between meandering and manoeuvring! This is not to say one is good and the other bad. Rather, the exercise is better seen as analysing and discussing whether it is a good thing for a company to be meandering right now. Should it be more myopic? Is this a time where it would benefit from being more meditative? And so on.

Or indeed, one may take on board the notion of postmodern fragmentation expressed in Chapter 1 here, or in the Chapter 2, 'Strategy as Ethos', last case study, or the later themes of 'Strategy as Organizing', to ask whether different parts of a company should be occupying different segments of the M-matrix. One could use traditional models such as the Boston Consultancy 'Growth-Share Matrix' to debate whether:

- those running a high-growth low-share product or 'question mark' should be meditative in order to think long and hard about how to turn that product into a star;
- those running a high-growth high-share product or 'star' should be myopically focused on running to get the most out of that product;
- those running a low-growth high-share product or 'cash cow' should be manoeuvring to get the most out of that product; and

- those running a low-growth low-share product or 'dog' should be purposefully meandering in order to dream up new ways of selling that product.

If this fragmentation or dentralization of focus is the case, then the challenge becomes the fruitful orchestration or networking of these different modes and models. However, while I have anticipated these themes: fragmentation, orchestration and networking; exploring them further is more the intention of the chapters that follow.

Case Box 4.4   A Type of Prisoners' Dilemma – 'Customers – Those Bastards!'

You are the managing director of 'Mother's Preference' a manufacturer of baby furniture, prams and child restraints. The 'Target' chain of discount stores is your largest customer taking 30 per cent of your sales, worth about AU$19 million in contribution to your total margin per annum. Louis is Target's new 23-year-old nursery buyer and he is determined to make his mark and progress quickly up the company. You are about to go into session to draw up the contract for next year's order from Target.

In a stagnant market you hold about 25 per cent total market share. Your closest competitor, 'Mother's Hope' holds a similar share. Two or three other smaller competitors have around 10–12 per cent each. Both you and Mother's Hope have well-established brand names and similar product ranges that are sold exclusively through retail outlets. Although you have active advertising pro-grammes, the most important influences on the buying decision are 'point-of-sale' and 'word-of-mouth'. Due to the 'top-of-mind' nature of the two major brands, the large chain and department stores tend to use one or other of you as a 'loss-leading' traffic generator on the front of their catalogues (i.e., to lure customers into the store in the hope that they buy other, higher margin items while picking up their 'cheap' pushchair or child-seat).

After each major promotion your phone always runs hot as other buyers ring to demand to know:

'How the hell can those bastards at Target/Big W/Baby Co./K Mart/etc. afford to offer those prices? You must have given them a sweet discount. So you better give it to us or else.'

Despite your generally truthful assertions to the contrary, you are rarely believed and never sympathized with, and all of your customers continue to demand preferential discounts in a downward spiral as they claim that 'there's no bloody margin in your product!'

A couple of years ago you were the clear market leader, but Mother's Hope has recently gained ground by taking share from the lesser brands. Your 'moles' suggest that this has been achieved by significant discounting cleverly disguised as either 'contribution to advertising', 'consignment stock', 'volume rebates', 'early payment discounts' or 'payments for buyers to visit supply factories in Taiwan' (via Hong Kong for shopping and/or hours of pleasure – depending on the buyer). But when you had the opportunity to confront the MD of Mother's Hope about this, he vehemently denied any such underhand behaviour.

'So, here's the deal', says Louis. 'For the supply contract next year I need a 15 per cent reduction in your delivered price across each of the three major product groupings. Oh, and by the way, my assistant is outlining the exact same proposal to your chief competitor across the hall.'

At this point you start to wail about the effects this will have on your children and the children of the employees you will be compelled to 'retrench' with one day's pay. But Louis is unrepentant. He offers three possibilities:

(1) 'If one of you gives me the reduction and the other doesn't, then the one who does gets all the business' (which you currently split with Mother's Hope 50/50 in all the product categories).
(2) 'If you both give me the discount I'll leave the share split as it is for next year.'
(3) 'If neither of you gives me the discount I am forced to leave it as it is for next year, but I will begin to look for some other suppliers who we can work with.'

You are *pretty* sure that this last point is a bluff. He could not afford to de-list both of you. Could he? However, he *can* easily afford to de-list one of you (although he would probably prefer not to if he was honest).

'I will not negotiate any other price, and here, in writing, is my contractual commitment to go by the decisions that you and your competitor make. Decide what you will do with *furniture* first; *prams and pushchairs* second; and *child restraints* last. I will send my assistant for your first decision (on furniture) in 15 minutes. He will let you know what your competitor has decided on this category. Then we will do the same thing for the second and then the third categories.'

You had been expecting something like this from Target and had roughly worked out the losses/gains based on various combinations of price reduction and percentage loss of share of the Target account. Below is your best shot quick calculation for the alternatives that Louis has laid down. The figure in the last column relating to the position should you offer the discount and Mother's Hope does not (thus leaving you to fulfil all of Target's needs) includes the advantages to be gained through greater economies of scale.

Product category	Current contribution to margins	15% reduction with half Target account	15% reduction with all Target account
Furniture	5	3	8
Prams/pushchairs	5	3	8
Child restraints	9	5	14
Totals	19	11	30

Although it is technically illegal, it is not unknown for you to discuss issues of pricing etc. with competitors. After all you do sit on standards committees together in an attempt to protect the Australian mother from 'unscrupulous operators', and an 'orderly' market can only be a good thing for mothers. There may (or may not) be an opportunity for one of your number to be in the toilets at the same time as one of theirs . . .

1. *Assuming you can get no further information, what would your overall inten-tion be for this decision-making process?*
2. *Assuming you can get no further information, what would your first decision on furniture be?*
3. *What then would your strategy be as the rest of the decision-making process unfolds?*
4. *What does a 'prisoners' dilemma' exercise such as this teach us about strategy?*

This case is based on a true story (names have been disguised). It was 'lived' and written up by Chris Smith, © Chris Smith. Chris is also the author of Chapter 12 'Strategy as Numbers'.

Note

1 The logic is basically defined by the Cosmides version. Here it is much more obvious that one is mainly interested in those who haven't paid and those who are male hence not inter-ested in females or payers. In the case of the pure form the key issue is that vowels are much less common than non-vowels.

Source Material and Recommended Further Reading

Current perspectives on the problems of 'mathematical' modelling of market-based systems that allow for the actions of a number of agents tend to fall broadly into two categories. One focuses on the overall process as one of co-evolution and this is summarized in two papers co-authored by Arie Lewin: Arie Y. Lewin, Chris P. Long and Timothy N. Carroll, 'The Coevolution of New Organizational Forms', *Organization Science*, 7(5), 1999; and Arie Y. Lewin, and Henk W. Volberda, 'Prolegomena on Coevolution: A Framework for Research on Strategy and New Organ-izational Forms', *Organizational Science*, 10(5), Sept.–Oct. 1999, 519–34. The later paper is where the quotation at the start of the chapter is taken from. The other links to a wider set of methods that go under the title of agent-based modelling. See L. Tesfatsion, 'Guest Editorial: Agent-Based Modelling of Evolutionary Economic Systems', *IEEE Transactions on Evolutionary Computation*, 5(5), 2001, and also her excellent website ⟨http://www.econ.iastate.edu/tesfatsi/ace.htm⟩. The question of time 'reversibility' also links to more general issues related to time; see Paul Davies, *About Time: Einstein's Unfinished Revolution* (Harmondsworth: Penguin Books, 1996), as well as our under-standing of interactive circular processes, where any question about causality is more 'chicken or egg' than linear. See, for instance, Michael Gibbons, Camille Limoges, Helga Nowotny, Simon Schwartzman, Peter Scott, and Martin Trow, *The New Production of Knowledge: The Dynamics of Science and Research in Contemporary Societies* (London: Sage, 1994) on Mode 2 rather than Mode 1 knowledge production.

John Newsinger's book on the SAS in entitled *Dangerous Men: The SAS and Popular Culture* (London: Pluto Press, 1996). The quotation comes from a note he published entitled 'Who Dares . . .', *History Today*, 48(12), 1998, 40.

The issue of risk and uncertainty, which we attribute to Frank Knight (*Risk, Uncertainty and Profit*, Chicago, 1921), remains a key issue in more recent economic thought (see C. Camerer and M. Weber, 'Recent Developments in Modelling Preferences: Uncertainty and Ambiguity', *Journal of Risk and Uncertainty*, 1992, 325–70; and R. Langlois, M. Cosgel, and F. Knight, 'On Risk, Uncertainty, and the Firm: A New Interpretation', *Economic Inquiry*, 1993, 456–65). Giddens even chooses to relate his notions of increasing manufactured risk (i.e., due to human agency and organization) as compared to external risk, to Knight's notions of uncertainty and risk respec-tively (A. Giddens, *The Director's Lectures*, Runaway World: The Reith Lectures Revisited, Lecture

2: 17, November 1999, LSE). While Runde notes that Knight confounds trials and outcomes, he also recognizes that much of the distinction between risk and uncertainty can be retained (J. Runde, 'A Clarification of Frank Knight's Discussion of the Meaning of Risk and Uncertainty', *Cambridge Journal of Economics*, 22, 1998, 539–46.

Although Frank Knight's distinction was between risk when the distribution of probabilities for events is known and uncertainty when it is not, others, as we have noted in this chapter, have linked the issue of uncertainty directly with the concept of causal ambiguity that is central to much strategic analysis about the sustainability of competitive advantage. See J.G. March, 'Bounded Rationality, Ambiguity and the Engineering of Choice', *Bell Journal of Economics*, 9(2), Autumn 1978, 587–609; and R. Reed and R.J. DeFillippi, 'Causal Ambiguity Barriers to Imitation and Sustainable Competitive Advantage', *Academy of Management Review*, 15(1), 1990, 88–102. More recently, Alicia Juarrero in *Dynamics in Action: Intentional Behavior as a Complex System* (Cambridge, MA: MIT Press, 2002), has gone much further and suggested that when we consider the impact of intention in the complex social world, we need to revisit our fundamental conventions about the nature of causality itself. In passing, she also notes, consistent with the perspective in this chapter that we need to reframe our view of 'uncertainty, which is, in its very form a negative word (p. 258).

The overall approach also leads to the emphasis in decision making on understanding the differing problem structures of the various participants. When dealing with a few participants, it would seem appropriate to make an explicit attempt to model such differing structures individually as in the work by Axelrod, who applied cognitive mapping techniques to group decision-making situations such as the British Cabinet (R. Axelrod, 'Decision for Neoimperialism: The Deliberations of the British Eastern Committee in 1918', in *The Structure of Decision: Cognitive Maps of Political Elites* (Princeton, NJ: Princeton University Press, 1976). Such an approach has also been recommended in attempts to improve communication and understanding in decision-making groups such as boards of directors (see C.R. Schwenk, 'The Cognitive Perspective on Strategic Decision Making', *Journal of Management Studies*, 25(1), 1988, 43–55 and C. Eden and J.C. Spender (eds), *Managerial and Organisational Cognition* (London: Sage, 1998).

Schrodinger's cat remains a confusing dilemma to many. The description used here is taken from ⟨http://www.lassp.cornell.edu/~ardlouis/dissipative/Schrcat.html⟩ and E. Schroedinger, *Naturwiss* (23, 1935, 807), translated into English in J.A. Wheeler and W.H. Zurek (eds), *Quantum Theory and Measurement* (Princeton, NJ: Princeton University Press, 1983). It is difficult perhaps because it is designed to confront our common-sense views with the apparent fact that at least at the particle or quantum level we are dealing with a situation in which not only are we uncertain about the state of the cat, but also there is really no such thing as the objective state of the cat. See, for instance, T. Lawson, 'Probability and Uncertainty in Economic Analysis', *Journal of Post Keynesian Economics*, 11, 1988, 38–65, who categorizes views on probability according to whether they are quantifiable or non-quantifiable and whether they are subjective or objective. Others, however, such as Paul Budnik (from ⟨http://www.mtnmath.com/faq/meas-qm-faq-3.html⟩ see the illustration as particularly elegant:

> When and how does the fog bank of microscopic possibilities transform itself to the blurred picture we have of a definite macroscopic state? That is the measurement problem and Schrodinger's cat is a simple and elegant explanations of that problem.

The reference to the discovery of analogous behaviour in the field of superconductivity comes from ⟨http://physicsweb.org/article/news/4/7/2⟩.

There has been much interest in the application of approaches from chaos and complexity. The most illuminating of the more popular and general books are Mitchell Waldrop, *Complexity* (Harmondsworth: Penguin Books, 1994) and Jack Cohen and Ian Stewart, *The Collapse of Chaos: Discovering Simplicity in a Complex World* (X2 Penguin Books, 1995). From a more managerial or policy perspective, Robert Alexrod and Michael Cohen, *Harnessing Complexity* (New York: Free Press, 2000) is useful, while Robert Alexrod, *The Complexity of Cooperation: Agent-Based Models of Competition and Collaboration* (Princeton, NJ: Princeton University Press, 2001) links to a number of themes in this chapter. Finally, a very thoughtful book linking the ideas back to social science is David Byrne, *Complexity Theory and the Social Sciences: An Introduction* (London: Routledge, 1998).

The issue of interpretation of apparent biases in decision making involves a range of contributors such as the original work by A. Tversky and D. Kahneman, 'Judgement under Uncertainty Heuristics & Biases', *Science*, 185, September 1974, 1124–31. Sterman's experiments with the beer game are reported in J. Sterman, 'Misperceptions of Feedback in Dynamic Decision Making', *Organizational Behavior and Human Decision Processes*, 43(3), 1989, 301–35. The original book on industrial dynamics was Jay W. Forrester, *Industrial Dynamics* (Cambridge, MA: MIT Press, 1961). Cosmides' perspective in evolutionary psychology is to be found in L. Cosmides, 'The Logic of Social Exchange: Has Natural Selection Shaped how Humans Reason? Studies with the Wason Selection Task', *Cognition*, 31, 1989, 187–276, while the Bayesian learning view is covered in M.R. Oaksford and N.C. Chater, 'A Rational Analysis of the Selection Task as Optimal Data Selection', *Psychological Review*, 101, 1994, 608–31. The review by K. Stenning and M. van Lambalgen, 'Is Psychology Hard or Impossible? Reflections on the Conditional', is a chapter in J. Gerbrandy, M. Marx, M. de Rijke, and Y. Venema (eds), *Liber Amicorum for Johan van Bentham's 50th Birthday* (Amsterdam: Amsterdam University, 1999).

The issues of market efficiency are widely discussed. See, for instance, *Principles of Corporate Finance* by Richard A. Brealey and Stewart C. Myers, 6th edn (London: McGraw-Hill, 2000). Some of the anomalies such as the so-called 'small-firm' effect can be linked backed to issues of uncertainty (see R.A. Olsen and G.H. Troughton, 'Are Risk Premium Anomalies Caused by Ambiguity?', *Financial Analysts Journal*, March–April 2000, 24–31). On the question of market bubbles, as described colourfully by Mike Dash in his book *Tulipomania* (London: Weidenfeld, 1999), the evidence is more mixed, and in particular critically examined, by Peter M. Gerber in *Famous First Bubbles: The Fundamentals of Early Manias* (Cambridge MA, MIT Press, 2000). Robert Shiller's *Irrational Exuberance* (Princeton, NJ: Princeton University Press, 2000) provides a cautionary *ex ante* analysis of the more recent dot.com 'mania'. The recent work on valuing Amazon.com, before the dot.com crash is to be found in Chris Higson and John Briginshaw, 'Valuing Internet Business', *Business Strategy Review*, 11(1), 2000 and that about valuation more generally afterwards in T.M. Koller, 'Valuing Dot-coms after the Fall', *The McKinsey Quarterly*, 2, 2001.

The original book by von Neumann and Morgenstern was *Theory of Games and Economic Behavior* (Princeton, NJ: Princeton University Press, 1944). Sylvia Nasar's book, *A Beautiful Mind* (London: Faber and Faber, 1998), not only provided the basis for the film of the same title but also much more background on John Nash and the development of game theory. However, the actual scene from the film in which Nash claims to contradict Adam Smith may be somewhat apocryphal: in her book, Nasar actually refers to the A. Dixit and B. Nalebuff key text *Thinking Strategically: The Competitive Edge in Business, Politics, and Everyday Life* (New York: W.W. Norton), first published in 1991, for her assertion that 'the Prisoners' Dilemma contradicts Adam Smith's metaphor of the invisible hand'. Two caveats need to be recognized: first actually Adam Smith himself only gave a very minor role to the 'invisible hand' in his analysis of the political economy (see J. Tobin, 'The Invisible Hand in Modern Macroeconomics', in M. Fry (ed.), *Adam Smith's Legacy: His Place in the Development of Modern Economics* (London: Routledge, 1992)) and, second, the whole notion of the pay-off structure in the prisoners' dilemma does not so much contradict the 'invisible hand' as conflate two different units of analysis within the political economy. Indeed, Adam Smith himself gave much more emphasis to his concerns about the extent to which a few influential players in a market economy could organize things so that they all benefited considerably but at a wider cost to society as whole: the prisoners' dilemma says nothing about the wider issues of the value of truth, equity and justice; who loses if the two players collude!

Game theory is covered in a range of economic texts such as David M. Kreps, *Game Theory and Economic Modelling* (Oxford: Clarendon Press, 1990) and a recent review is to be found in Kalyan Chatterjee and William F. Samuelson (eds), *Game Theory and Business Applications* (Dordrecht: Kluwer Academic, 2001). However, game theory still seems rather bedevilled by experimental anomalies when it comes to asymmetric pay-offs, for instance see J.K. Goeree and C.A. Holt, 'Ten Little Treasures of Game Theory and Ten Intuitive Contradictions', *American Economic Review*, 91(5), December 2001, 1402–22. As the chapter also indicates, there is a lot of difference between the strict and sometimes complex mathematics of academic game theory and the much more general approach often suggested of thinking through the potential strategies for other players. Kesten Green has recently tried to test the relative efficacy of these two approaches in a series of scenarios, and concludes that the more generic role-playing approach is more effective than analytical game theory. Scott Armstrong, in commenting on the analysis, also suggests that, if anything, the experimental treatment is biased in favour of game theory. See K. Green, 'Forecasting Decisions in Conflict Situations: A Comparison of Game Theory, Role-playing, and Unaided Judgement', and S. Armstrong, 'Assessing Game Theory, Role Playing, and Unaided Judgment', both forthcoming in *International Journal of Forecasting*, and available at Armstrong's personal website: ⟨http://www-marketing.wharton.upenn.edu/people/faculty/armstrong.html⟩.

The article cited by Philip Nattermann is 'Best Practice Does Not Equal Best Strategy', *The McKinsey Quarterly*, 2, 2000, 22–31; and the book by Robert Waterman is *The Renewal Factor* (London: Bantam Books, 1988). Michael Porter's work can be found in M.E. Porter, *Competitive Strategy* (New York: Free Press, 1980).

Herbert Simon was central in the development of both the notions of rational expectations and bounded rationality. See, particularly, H.A. Simon, 'On How to Decide What to Do', *Bell Journal of Economics*, 9(2), Autumn 1978, 494–508 and 'Rational Decision Making in Business Organizations', *American Economic Review*, September 1979. The first major paper on rational expectations was, however, by one of Simon's co-workers (see J.F. Muth, 'Rational Expectations and the Theory of Price Movements', *Econometrica*, July 1961). Bounded rationality approaches have been developed further (see, for instance, C.A. Tisdell, *Bounded Rationality and Economic Evolution: A Contribution to Decision Making* (Cheltenham: Edward Elgar, 1996). Overall, it has become a major area in economics and further analysis is rather outside the scope of this chapter. In a strict sense a 'rational expectations' perspective actually implies something more than competitors just not being 'dumb' or superhuman – but Waterman's way of expressing it is entirely consistent with more analytical assumption that they are as well informed as the particular firm.

As previously referenced in Chapter 1, Stephen Cummings, *Recreating Strategy* (London: Sage, 2002), traces the roots of strategy back to the Greek military context. The general field of military strategy is also really outside the remit of this chapter, but Frederick W. Gluck, Stephen P. Kaufman, and A. Steven Walleck, 'The Evolution of Strategic Management', *The McKinsey Quarterly*, 3, 2000, has some interesting observations. The classical texts are C. von Clausewitz, *On War* (London: Routledge and Kegan Paul, 1968); and B.H. Liddell Hart, *Strategy*, 2nd edn (New York: Praeger, 1967). Writings by Michel Foucault on issues of power are legion but an interesting perspective is provided by Barbara Townley in *Reframing Human Resource Management: Power, Ethics and the Subject at Work* (London: Sage, 1994).

The key article on strategic intent is Gary Hamel and C.K. Prahalad, 'Strategic Intent', *Harvard Business Review*, May–June 1989, 63–76, although since then Gary Hamel, particularly, has moved the notion of intent further in the direction of espousing the power of revolutionary leadership in *Leading the Revolution* (Cambridge, MA: Harvard Business School Press, 2000). Robert Hayes's rather more prosaic view on these matters is to be found in 'Strategic Planning – Forward in Reverse?', *Harvard Business Review*, Nov.–Dec. 1985, 111–19. Susan Blackmore, *The Meme*

Machine (Oxford: Oxford University Press, 1999), introduces an analysis of memetics that might suggest a whole set of questions for the propagation of managerial fads and fashions as initially described in E. Abrahamson, 'Managerial Fads and Fashions: The Diffusion and Rejection of Innovations', *Academy of Management Review*, 16(3), 1991, 586–612.

Schnaars provides a range of practical advice with examples in *Managing Imitation Strategies: How Later Entrants Seize Markets from Pioneers* (New York: Free Press, 1994).

The real options approach is covered in general by A. Dixit and R. Pindyck in 'The Options Approach to Capital Investment', *Harvard Business Review*, 73(3), 1995, 105–15, and in more detail in Lenos Trigeorgis (ed.), *Real Options and Business Strategy: Applications to Decision-making* (London: Risk: 1999). The knowledge management approach can be found in I. Nonaka and H. Takeuchi, *The Knowledge Creating Company: How Japanese Companies Create the Dynamics of Innovation* (New York: Oxford University Press, 1995).

The distinction between a diachronic and a synchronic perspective was initially outlined by Jung (see Carl Gustav Jung, *Synchronicity: An Acausal Connecting Principle* (translated by R.F.C. Hull, (Princeton, NJ: Princeton University Press, 1973)). The classical Ted Levitt article is 'Marketing Myopia', *Harvard Business Review*, 38(4), 1960, 45–56, but it is interesting to note that K. Simmonds, 'Removing the Chains from Product Strategy', *Journal of Management Studies*, 1968, 29–40, recognizes many of the problems with the oversimplistic application of the 'myopic' approach but has been much less referenced. Ed Bowman's paper is 'Strategy and the Weather', *Sloan Management Review*, Winter 1976, 49–62. A useful historic paper on the Delphi technique is A.R. Fusfeld and R.N. Foster, 'The Delphi Technique: Survey and Comment', *Business Horizons*, June 1971, 63–74. The knowledge management perspective is well covered in Ikujiro Nonaka, *The Knowledge-creating Company: How Japanese Companies Create the Dynamics* (Oxford: Oxford University Press, 1995).

In terms of competitive responses the original P.S.H. Leeflang and D.R. Wittink paper was 'Diagnosing Competition: Developments and Findings', in G. Laurent, G.L. Lilien and B. Pras (eds), *Research Traditions in Marketing* (Norwell, MA: Kluwer Academic, 1993). The more recent work on the potential advantages of 'paranoia' in competitive behaviour is to be found in B.H. Clark and D.B. Montgomery, 'Managerial Identification of Competitors', *Journal of Marketing*, 63, July, 1999, 67–83; and B.H. Clark and D.B. Montgomery, 'Perceiving Competitive Reactions: The Value of Accuracy (and Paranoia)', *Marketing Letters*, 7(2), March 1996. The issue of how to treat competitive reactions, both in analysis and in practice, however, remains contentious. For instance, a recent empirical paper suggests that non-reaction is the most common response (J.B. Steenkamp, V.R. Nijs, D.M. Hanssens and M.G. Dekimpe, 'Competitive Reactions and Cross-Sales Effects of Advertising and Promotion', Working Paper, September 2001), while Shugan argues that in a number of cases what he calls 'monopoly models', that is those that ignore competitive response, may actually be more appropriate and robust from an analytical perspective. See S. Shugan, 'Marketing Science, Models, Monopoly Models and Why We Need Them: An Editorial', *Marketing Science*, 2002 (forthcoming) and available at ⟨http://bear.cba.ufl.edu/centers/MKS/general/editorial0402.htm⟩.

People used to debate whether strategy drove structure or structure drove strategy. Now we recognize that it is not an either/or choice. Strategies and views of structure influence one another. Thus, as images of organizations change, so the way we think strategy must change too. It is increasingly less useful to think in terms of images of stand-alone corporate entities, hierarchical triangles and generic linear value chains. Subsequently, conventional modes of control are less useful. This chapter picks up on the theme of 'organizational fragmentation' discussed in Chapter 1 and touched on in Chapters 2 to 4, to paint a picture of organizations as webs or constellations of knowledge. However, despite the decentralization inherent in this, these constellations still require strategic co-ordination. But the strategist in this world of networks must use a lighter and more skilful touch. They must be less a planner, director, organizer and controller and more an 'orchestrator'. However, with the emphasis on individualized constellations or networks rather than a generic organizational shape, there is no 'one-best' style of orchestrating. This chapter outlines four styles of strategy as **orchestrating knowledge**: the trainer, the mentor, the leader and the lion tamer. What type of orchestrator, or combination of types, will you become?

5 Strategy as Orchestrating Knowledge

JOHN McGEE

[The great strategos Pericles] proved that rhetoric, in Plato's phrase, is the art of working upon the souls of men by words, and that its chief business is the knowledge of characters and passions which are, so to speak, the strings and stops of the soul and require a most skilful and delicate touch.

Plutarch, Life of Pericles, 15

Our view of the firm has been developed through a stream of writers such as Marshall, Coase, Williamson, Penrose and many others reaching back into the nineteenth century. It has been refined and further defined in the modern writings of industrial organization and industrial economics, and has been conditioned but not fundamentally challenged in other modern writings. The core of this thinking holds that the 'vertical integration' that represents the firm's activities (or value chain) exists because the transactions costs of managing it are less than the costs of maintaining the same relationships through market contracting costs. In other words, the planned economy of the firm is more efficient than the 'disintegrated' market economy. But it is more than efficient; it is also more effective strategically and exhibits characteristics that economists have termed 'progressiveness'. Thus the modern firm is held to be a triumph of static efficiency and dynamic progressiveness. The legal constitution of the 'limited' company and advantages accruing from tax treatment of corporate income has served and continues to serve to tip the balance towards the planned economy of the firm and its characteristics of vertical integration. The ability of the owners (the shareholders) to risk their capital under relatively controlled conditions enables dynamic efficiencies in terms of more 'effective' resource allocation over time and a general increase in the level of private investment.

Strategic management has grown and developed as a field of study within this paradigm of the firm. The economic dimension of the field has focused on the scope (range of activities) of the firm as a key defining characteristic and follows in the footsteps of economists in asserting that internalization can increase shareholder value by the perception, pursuit and capture of 'synergies' from further horizontal and vertical integration. Williamson's approach through transaction cost economics provides the definitive explanation. The reason why the planned economy of the firm works arises from the existence of some tacit, implicit knowledge of how to organize and manage the range of activities within the scope of the firm. Thus, the vertically integrated value chain contains firm-specific assets supported by highly orchestrated vertical linkages with suppliers and buyers. The tacit knowledge within the firm enables the serial connection of the elements within the vertical chain. This is different from those technological economies that are explicit and codifiable – as for example in steel making where the integration of the sequential activities of steel ingot production and rolling mills removes the need and the cost to reheat steel ingots. This results in vertical integration as an industry phenomenon but not as an idiosyncratic phenomenon at the firm level. It also enables us to explain corporate overheads as 'service' activities that add value to the stream of production activities because the simultaneity and proximity of the service delivery to operational activities are more efficient. The way in which the firm orchestrates and delivers these services are also highly idiosyncratic and tacit in nature and provides distinctiveness between firms that otherwise compete on similar economic terms. Thus we see and understand that a Procter & Gamble can be and is very different from a Unilever despite their presence in similar, even identical, product markets.

All this analysis is Williamsonian in character. In his language the make-or-buy decision hinges on the extent to which transactions become more idiosyncratic – as already specialized human skills and physical assets are increasingly dedicated to a single use, then greater value is obtained by making internally. Where knowledge idiosyncrasy is low then the cost savings from the commoditization of knowledge by external suppliers will prevail. Idiosyncratic, often tacit, knowledge embodied in highly specific assets is often known as organizational capital or more colloquially as the 'corporate glue'. The nature of this 'corporate glue' is changing and with it is changing the relationships between buyers and suppliers and between firms and their industries. This is not to challenge the fundamental proposition that the trade-off between transaction costs and market contracting costs mediates the firm's boundaries. But the way in which these costs arise and the outcomes of the trade-offs are changing with far-reaching consequences.

Knowledge-led Strategies

The language of competitive advantage and core competences, or more generally that of the market-based view and the resource-based view, holds that the basis of value creation is the creation of distinctive and idiosyncratic assets and capabilities that can be translated into a product/service bundle which has unique value to the customer.

The essence of the argument is that rents available to firms are rooted in temporary monopolies of knowledge held within the firm, that knowledge being unique and inimitable at least for a period. Such knowledge is by definition tacit and implicit otherwise it would be copied or it must have some other form of legal protection such as a patent or a trademark (ignoring barriers to imitation erected by illegal activities). Thus a 'conventional' view of strategic advantage asserts that value to the customer arises from the kind of product distinctiveness that adds to the customers' returns without adding to their risks.

Another view of value to the customer pays direct attention to the risk in the return risk calculation. Products may not obviously be 'better' but they may be a safer bet because of their origin (the brand name effect). This effect also has roots in the ability of the firm to maintain a broader and more effective scope of operations by virtue of its ability to create linkages and interactions between the varieties of different activities. Again this is a story of idiosyncratic knowledge manifested in the different ways in which otherwise similar firms appear to conduct their affairs.

Knowledge: demand and supply

What is changing is that the tacit, idiosyncratic knowledge that sustains the firm is increasingly being made explicit, being appropriated by others, being diffused and replicated, and is becoming industrialized (i.e. being produced in large volumes at lower cost). If the tacit-knowledge base of the firm were to become substitutable by external knowledge providers then the nature of the firm changes because its vertical integration and diversification patterns will become unsustainable, first eroding and then being replaced by different patterns. As knowledge changes, proprietary links give way to markets under labels such as outsourcing, deconstruction and the hollowing-out of the corporation.

The market for knowledge has grown dramatically over the past 25–30 years. Not only has trade developed at a rapid and sustained pace but also the pattern of consumption has moved towards more knowledge-intensive products and away from industrial commodities. Product complexity has grown and along with it the varieties of knowledge that are required to be incorporated within products and services. As the market has grown so also on the supply side there have been the changes that one would anticipate from industrial history. As knowledge production has grown in response to the market, it has become more specialized and more diverse in its sources. It has moved from being a cottage industry to being an industrialized activity. 'Pieces of knowledge' are initially created and appropriated for use by individuals or individual firms. As the market grows and as experience with this form of knowledge develops, this knowledge progressively becomes codifiable and thus explicit. It then diffuses by moving away from its original appropriators to those who can replicate it and find markets for it. More capital-intensive processes then follow simple replication of this kind and by combination with other pieces of knowledge to create new packages of knowledge that themselves will have markets.

Thus a firm might initially create its own computer facilities to provide administrative data and support services but find eventually that what it originally knew and developed has become outmoded by rapid developments elsewhere sponsored by those with a more direct investment in this as core knowledge. At this point an outsourcing decision could be made and the firm's scope of activities would be reduced with consequences for the ways in which its remaining assets are co-ordinated and directed.

The role of disintermediation

This tale would not be so important were it not being repeated so often. Clearly, firms adjust their scope at the margin to changed circumstances in just this way. The serial decisions about make versus buy reflect changing economic circumstances and shifts in relative costs. The point now is that there has been a wholesale change in the nature of knowledge investment and production leading to a fundamental change in the structure of supply and demand for knowledge. What was previously idiosyncratic can either be bought on the open market or can be substituted by something better.

Quinn describes these pervasive changes in six distinct phases. The first sees the appearance of *new economies of scale*. This enables the capture of key activities by large organizations leading to the demise of smaller enterprises that lack capital and expertise. In the course of time the emergence of networks of provision enables smaller enterprises to act as feeder systems for the larger.

The second phase sees the emergence of new *economies of scope* where the same technologies that created the economies of scale (or the supporting technologies that are necessary to implement the larger-scale technologies) allow the handling of more data, more output functions, or more customers without corresponding cost increases. These are so powerful that those competitors with narrow scope can find it difficult to respond to the lower costs of the broader-based innovators. The new scale and scope economies seem to favour the big battalions. This increased complexity requires new forms of management often through information systems and computerization, which is specialized and distinctive in itself with some degree of co-specialization with the scope of the firm. At this stage we have the conventional picture of the large corporation buttressed by impregnable economies of scale and scope.

However, changes in the fundamental conditions of demand and supply of knowledge can lead to the next phase – disintermediation. Disintermediation is the process by which proprietary links within the firm give way to the co-ordination mechanisms of markets. Firms can replace elements of their value chain by outsourcing (buying rather than making). But there are also opportunities for collaboration with (potential) suppliers who have acquired greater skills and knowledge than their own clients. Both of these developments undermine the traditional vertical integration of the firm, replacing it with a flexible mix of open markets and partnerships. This is not an inevitable process and it is possible to misread the trade-off between access to superior external knowledge against internal customization ability. There often follows a restructuring of existing industries and changes in the nature of barriers to entry.

Disintermediation refers to the piecemeal replacement of internal activities by external provision. Where this replacement is systematic and extensive it is known as *deconstruction* – the process of systematically undermining fundamental concepts (in this case the logic of vertical integration). As deconstruction takes hold we enter a phase of *deregulation* in which new competitors with new knowledge make cross-competition more possible. Policy makers find that market forces coupled with regulation can become effective in controlling what were hitherto publicly owned monopolies. This in turn leads to further restructuring and major changes in barriers to entry.

Finally, there are rounds of *redispersion and redecentralization*. After centralization and disintermediation there is often a reassertion of the need for more localized and personalized contact and new forms of broking, selling, and agencies emerge. For example, *The Economist*, in its survey of e-management, observes that the Internet is the 'greatest force for commoditization ever invented'. It cuts the costs of routine transactions but at the same time offers new ways of reaching those customers, monitoring their activities, and building new relationships with them. In summary, it is commonplace to observe that the systematic accretion of knowledge and its diffusion around the world have had the effect of forcing a restructuring of industries and even whole economies even to the extent, as Quinn claims, that the entire US economy has been fundamentally changed.

What does this mean for the strategist? First, the notion that advantage derives simply from the possession of unique but codifiable and explicit knowledge has been under pressure for a long time. Where such knowledge exists and results in value it is generally because intellectual property rights protect it. Second, there is now a growing realization that the traditional forms of tacit knowledge, 'corporate glue', are eroding and – depending on which commentators you read – are eroding quickly. The strategist needs to understand the ways in which this erosion or deconstruction is taking place, the defensive moves that can be made, and the strategic principles behind new combinations of knowledge that might be effective.

Deconstructing the value chain

The Boston Consulting Group argument about the revolution in the economics of information, as articulated by Carl Stern, runs as follows:

> Information has always been the glue that held value chains together. The cost of getting sufficiently rich information to suppliers, channels, and customers made proprietary information systems and dedicated assets a necessity, and gave vertical integration its leverage. That glue is now melting. Universal connectivity and common communication standards are enabling the open and virtually cost-free exchange of information of all kinds. Companies share product designs, CAD/CAM parameters, logistics information, and financial data with equal ease both inside and outside the corporation. New intermediaries are emerging to support interconnection, facilitate comparison, guarantee performance, and make markets. Searching and switching are vastly easier than they used to be.

The open standards and the universal connectivity inherent in information technology enable knowledge modules to be 'snapped together' (like LEGO) without any expensive customization or re-working. Thus, knowledge production can be outsourced with minimal risk.

The change in the economics of information and knowledge is the key to understanding why and how industries are restructuring and how firms are refocusing their strategies and their value chains. These shifts in the economics of knowledge can be summarized as:

(1) a huge growth in knowledge and its incorporation in products, and its systematic diffusion across the world;
(2) development of specialization in the supply of knowledge;

(3)   knowledge becomes a tradable good and markets emerge undermining the specialized, proprietary knowledge held within and protected by companies;

(4)   a progressive and accelerating shift from data mechanics to information and knowledge management;

(5)   emergence of new specialized, intermediaries.

Having acknowledged the international division of labour in knowledge, there are further assumptions to specify about the new economy. The first is that knowledge-based activities (Quinn limited his argument to knowledge-intensive service activities) are significant elements in most value chains and that these are significant in size and critical for competitive advantage. The second is that the pressures of competition mean that simple technical efficiency is not enough. There are opportunity costs of not buying from the most efficient suppliers and outsourcing becomes not only attractive but also necessary. Third, and most important, firms need to focus their strategic investments and their management attention on those knowledge-intensive activities that form the basis for sustainable competitive advantage. This means that it is no longer sufficient to maintain a portfolio of competences in which most of the competences (or assets competences) are at best only co-specialized with the core competences. Historically firms have invested capital in those journeyman competences that were required to bring the truly distinctive assets, the core competences, to market. Now, however, they do have the prospect of replacing them with lower cost or more effective substitutes from external suppliers.

The construction of new value chains

Three new business models develop from this: the new competitor; the deconstruction model – the substitution of hierarchies by markets; and the reconstruction model – a rethinking of the nature of the corporate glue which defines the scope of the firm and the nature of its identity.

With the emergence of the Internet it is easy to see the new competitors that mount direct attacks on established businesses by splitting the information flows from the physical flows (see Figure 5.1). Amazon.com is an example in the form of a start-up company. The business model is not simply the replacement of an expensive (for the customer) shopping process by cheap electronic means but also an approach of differentiation aimed at turning a direct online bookseller into a virtual focal point. Egg's approach to online financial services is much the same. In both cases the very high fixed costs of online selling are defrayed not just by high volumes but also by the economies of scope that follow from diversification channelled through the online shopping point. Philip Evans and Thomas Wurster make the same point with an example about separating the information-rich part from the commodity part in their well-known book about deconstruction and being 'blown to bits'.

The deconstruction model with multiple points of disintermediation (see Figure 5.2) stems from the need to focus the firm's attention on those few, typically knowledge-based activities that underpin long-term competitive advantage. To do this the firm has to redefine its remaining capabilities as activities which can be bought in from 'best-in-class' suppliers. This applies equally to overhead 'services' as much as it does elsewhere in the value chain. In this way the firm becomes less vertically integrated in the conventional way – it has to deny the old saying that 'what it does not own it cannot

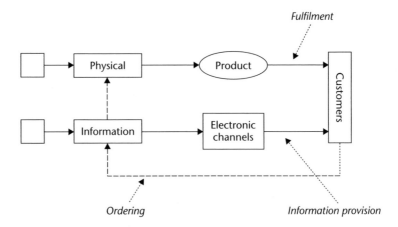

Figure 5.1   The new competitive model

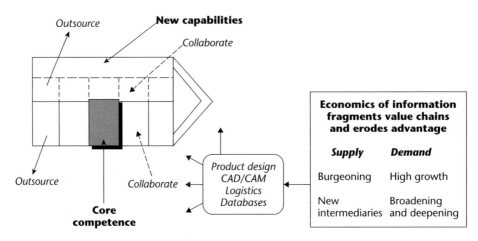

Figure 5.2   The deconstruction model: disintermediating

command'. However, it does maintain its control of the value chain and of the advantages accruing to the customer by actively reinforcing the core competences that it has retained (more on this below) and by investing in the management of its outsourcing so as to maintain its bargaining power with its (new) suppliers and partners.

In this deconstructing world, there is a battle for control of the supply chain – a battle for ownership and control of competitive advantage. One mode of operation occurs when integration gives way to *orchestration*. Successful orchestrators possess powerful brands and other core competences that give them competitive advantage by virtue of which they can control the terms of supply (see Figure 5.3). Nike and Hewlett-Packard are examples of this mode. In Williamsonian terms the orchestrators retain sufficient idiosyncratic capital to preserve some degree of vertical integration sufficient to exercise power throughout the supply chain. But control over the supply chain depends on the location of knowledge in the chain. Those players who focus

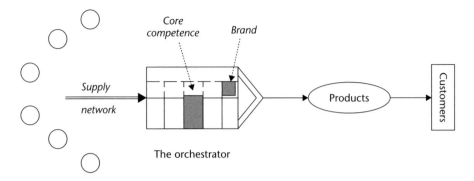

Figure 5.3   The deconstruction model: orchestrating downstream

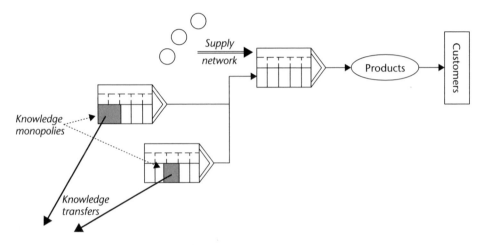

Figure 5.4   The deconstruction model: orchestrating upstream

on a specific value-added step have incentives for scale and scope effects with the possibility of wresting control from the traditional integrated players (see Figure 5.5). Intel and Microsoft did this to IBM because IBM was not able to control the IBM standard for PCs. Instead Intel's microprocessor technology and Microsoft's software represented the key knowledge assets which then dominated the supply chain. In the extreme case, the integrated firms deconstruct entirely with each value-added step in the supply chain becoming a business in its own right. Competition is then fragmented, products become near-commodities, and rents are minimal and transitory.

The 'reconstruction model' has two elements. The first applies existing core competences into other value chains to establish new economies of scale there and in doing so creating new economies of scope (see Figure 5.4). This is familiar in that it replicates familiar processes of related diversification. But it is different in that it represents an attempt to dominate other apparently related supply chains with existing knowledge-based competences. In this process, the nature of scope has changed from product-market relatedness to knowledge (or resource) relatedness. In this resource-based view of the corporate portfolio, competition is as much a competition for

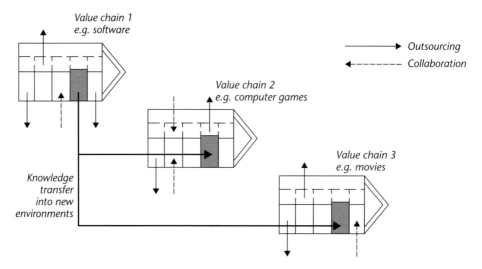

Figure 5.5   The reconstruction model: knowledge transfer

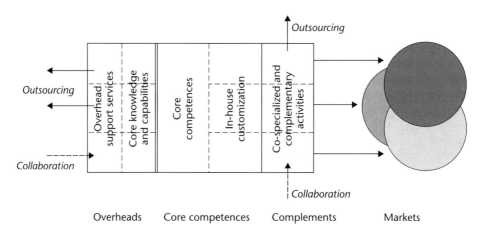

Figure 5.6   The reconstruction model: the composite new value chain

competences and for knowledge as its more familiar application to products. Evans and Wurster have dubbed this the 'rewiring' of the firm in which knowledge-based competences have become the controlling element in multiple supply chains through several highly focused (i.e. short) value chains (see Figure 5.6). The second element is the creation of a new set of corporate-level capabilities whose purpose is to identify and manage the set of collaborative relationships that make up the web of partners and strategic suppliers.

Indeed, the vertical integration metaphor of the value chain gives way to the language of the value web (see Figure 5.7). The centre of the web contains the new corporate glue (idiosyncratic knowledge) that maintains the new style of portfolio positions across value chains and across industries and orchestrates strategic linkages so as to retain

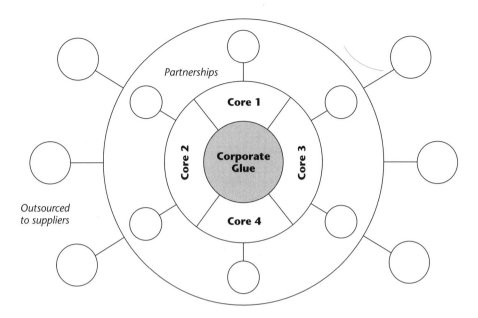

Figure 5.7   The value web

control over the traditional value chains. The points of leverage for this core compe-tence are the specific knowledge-based assets that are applied across different indus-tries. In this new game companies can develop a much higher degree of focus in applying their strategies through their knowledge-based assets rather than through trad-itional product–market strategies.

In general, the focus of strategic thinking has shifted from domination of markets and of supply chains through a vertically integrated set of activities to an assertion of leading positions in key intellectual assets coupled with new thinking at the corporate centre about knowledge management, risk assessment, and the management of infor-mation and knowledge. The focus has shifted from products and product classes to activities, knowledge and competences.

Case Box 5.1   Deconstructing and Reconfiguring the Value Chain

Levi-Strauss is a great brand and it makes great jeans. But then so do a lot of other companies nowadays. In order to continue to be at the forefront of casual-wear and related products, Levi-Strauss is rethinking the value chain. Using the traditional linear input–process–output view of adding value, clothes' manufac-turers take inputs such as fabrics and fixtures, use the company's information systems and knowledge to subject these inputs to value-adding processes (such as design and assembly), and then distribute outputs to customers who pay for the finished product and then go on their way. Levi has attempted to deconstruct these assumptions and look at ways in which it can *involve* its customers in the value-adding process so that they become part of the 'Levi's community'.

Flagship stores, such as those in San Francisco and London, now contain 'Levi's customization area'. Here customers can photograph themselves and input these images into computer terminals that allow them to see what various outfits from the Levi's range would look like on them. Then they can become part of the value-adding design team by testing out how customized alterations (different cuts, or washes, or buttons, or pockets, or rips, or stitching, or patches and so on) would look on them. Finished designs can then be taken to an in-house construction team that works with the customer to develop what is wanted. Information on individual customers can be kept for return visits and aggregated to provide insights into popular trends.

Moreover, the London store has been refurbished into a combined store and club/arts venue. It incorporates a 'chill-out' area, Internet stations, plasma screens, ISDN links, a suspended two-tier DJ booth designed by DJ Paul Oakenfold, and a record outlet called Vinyl Addiction. It can be transformed into a 500-capacity venue with facilities to host club nights, live music, fashion shows, film screenings, comedy nights and exhibitions. It can create and sustain 'value' in many more ways than the traditional, 'go in–browse–buy–leave' store.

Land Rover UK has attempted to achieve similar aims with its Land Rover Club. In order to stay involved with Land Rover drivers and keep adding value after a Land Rover is purchased, the club seeks to link interested Land Rover customers to one another. Drivers are provided with free off-road driving lessons, invited to off-road rallies, other special events and 'adventures' (you can see these at <http://www.landrover.co.uk/index.asp>), kept informed of news with respect to Land Rover, off-roading and other related spheres of interest, and involved in forums where they can provide ongoing feedback and raise any ideas or concerns. The idea behind the club is to build on Land Rover's brand values and foster the idea that when one bought a Land Rover they were getting something far more valuable than a collection of parts and technology assembled into a truck. The concept is now being adopted in other parts of Land Rover's global network.

1. *How would you draw Levi's and Land Rover's value-adding processes described in the case above?*
2. *What advantages might Levi and Land Rover accrue by conceptualizing their value-adding processes in these ways?*

This case is co-written by Stephen Cummings and John McGee.

Knowledge-led Strategy and the Corporate Centre as 'Orchestrator'

Traditional microeconomics is unhelpful regarding the internal organization of the firm and in particular regarding the role of the corporate centre. The economic argument for multi-business firms centres on the benefits of relatedness between the resources that underpin a multi-business structure. But the apparent simplicity and clarity of that argument are not matched by unambiguous support from empirical studies. There has been a long and still unresolved debate about the performance benefits of related business structures. The protagonists of relatedness might be ahead on points but there is a disturbing amount of empirical evidence that the largest firms, almost all of them multi-business, have been value destroyers over considerable periods. Does this mean that the economic logic of relatedness is wrong-headed? Does it perhaps mean that there has been a failure of corporate governance with too much discretion for the pursuit of managerial objectives? Does it mean that the case for related diversification is subverted by managerial individualism that results in relatedness not being exploited? What implications might this have for the role of stakeholders and for social responsibility and environmental sustainability? The traditional portrayal in textbooks of the corporate centre is as a rational allocator of resources between competing ends, as the architect of organization structure, and as the location of eventual command and control. This is perhaps too simplistic because it says nothing about stakeholders other than shareholders (and is none too explicit about these also). It is silent on the great issues of social costs that are highly significant in the way in which the corporation mediates its relationships with its environment. It gives some guidance on the nature of scope decisions but is limited in its analysis of risk and of strategic decisions such as diversification, alliances and outsourcing.

In their review of the academic literature on the nature of corporate headquarters, Ewan Ferlie and Andrew Pettigrew pointed to the major changes in HQs, including the widespread reports of downsizing, a trend towards decentralization and flatter structures even towards polycentric structures, and the development of more elaborate processes and systems for controlling large organizations. Taken together, these suggest a contemporary shift away from formal, hierarchic mechanisms of communication and control to more flexible and less formal ways of managing headquarters–business relationships. Recent literature on multinational enterprises also indicates that more sophisticated styles of management are emerging in the context of global competition. In particular, corporate level mental maps are paying attention to knowledge management and organizational learning as businesses make new and radical responses to new market conditions and to changed contexts for businesses.

Christopher Bartlett and Sumantra Ghoshal suggest that a structural solution might be a transnational form of organization in which companies need to develop competence in global competitiveness, multinational flexibility and worldwide learning simultaneously. In terms of managerial processes and systems organizations appear to be moving from reliance on formal information and strategic planning systems to more informal and flexible systems based on interpersonal communications and relationships. Writers such as Bartlett and Ghoshal portray a shift from hierarchy, rules and procedures and formal goal-setting to devices such as liaison roles, staff transfers, and the use of integrating roles and departments and socialization into a common managerial culture. The ideas embodied in organizational learning are important for companies that are trying to redraw their mental maps. The move to flatter, more informal structures requires a managerial mindset conducive to information sharing and to the diffusion of knowledge and expertise from individual or localized domains into the wider corporate resource pool.

The domains of activity at the corporate centre

The mental map that the headquarters has of its corporate and external environment can be thought of as deriving principally from its perceptions of four information domains.

- The *strategic domain* is made up of perceptions about the nature of the strategic landscape. These are based on information about what other, competing parents are up to, what the overall corporate positioning is in terms of performance benchmarks and corporate image (as reflected in the opinions of key external observers such as the city, shareholders and so on), and what constitutes value in the parenting context.
- The *business domain* is made up of perceptions about individual businesses regarding the nature of the competitive environment for each business, the resources required for competitive positioning by each business in its competitive context, the resource base that exists within each business, and the performance of each business.
- The *organizational domain* is made up of perceptions about the formal structural arrangements (e.g. centralization, decentralization), and the formal and informal processes that exist for communication, co-ordination and control through the organization.
- The *knowledge domain* is made up of perceptions about the value of the knowledge and competence base that exists in each of the businesses, and how the overall corporate knowledge and competence pool looks.

The way that the headquarters relates to each business and its role in co-ordinating collaboration across businesses is an important determinant of headquarters' success. There are two interrelated strands of thinking that are particularly useful for enabling us to better understand patterns of 'successful headquarters' behaviours'. The first strand is concerned with the understanding of headquarters' behaviours and characteristics as they relate to the external strategic domain (portfolio design, acquisition and globalization strategies and so on). The second strand focuses on the headquarters–business relationships (the internal business domain) and is concerned with characterizing the types of relationships that exist and understanding how various headquarters–business interactions work. Both of these strands together are important in addressing the question of how the headquarters can add value. The central management imperative in this context is about obtaining the optimal 'value creating arrangement' where there is effective utilization of resources and competences (the knowledge domain) for sustained viability and competitive success and resources and competences (business and corporate) are developed and utilized effectively (the organizational domain) to achieve a desired and feasible balance between the individual interests of the constituent businesses and those of the headquarters.

The value-creation process at headquarters is concerned with figuring out how the collective corporate competence and resource base can be developed and leveraged most effectively given the extant strategic and business contexts. In order to be effective in this respect, it is essential that the operative (internal) mental map is congruent with the contemporaneous extant environment. This requires the headquarters staff to engage in a continuous cycle of knowledge acquisition and learning in order to develop a comprehensive stock of knowledge on which to base action, and to create an organizational environment (structures and relationships) that is conducive to the effective development and exploitation of corporate-wide resources and competences.

A transactions analysis model

The questions that emerge from this discussion concern the changing role of HQs as the nature of organizations change. Some of the concerns are about structures, some

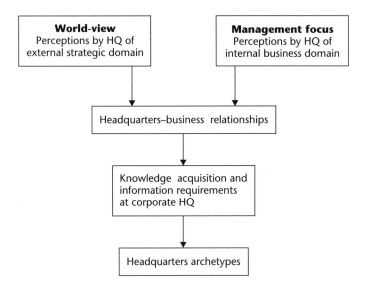

Figure 5.8   Knowledge, information and corporate headquarters: the basic model

are about control, much is about style, but all of it raises the issue of the information required at the centre. Fundamentally, there exists the dilemma of command and control versus information and guidance, a dilemma that also arises from the tensions of formality versus informality or tight versus loose systems. Yasmin Merali and I have analysed the transactions that take place between HQs and their businesses in order to obtain a portrayal of information needs and learning characteristics. Just as any other organizational unit, the HQ (or corporate centre) displays path dependency and creates knowledge and competence bundles that are ingredients in the wider learning and knowledge networks within the firm. In this view the centre manages and leverages knowledge and it can adopt roles of orchestration, coaching, learning, and advising. Merali and McGee deploy a simple model of the role of the corporate centre in order to generate a set of HQ archetypes. Their model asserts that the knowledge base at the centre and its information management requirements are shaped by two fundamental perceptions held within headquarters of its role and purpose. The first is its degree of proactivity in responding to and managing the external environment. This is akin to the German notion of *Weltanschauung*, which has a very deep sense of philosophical purpose. The model uses the simple label of 'external view'. The second is its perception of how members of the organization relate to each other both formally and informally. This is a concept of self-management simply labelled as 'management focus'. These two independent variables transmit their effects through the HQ–business relationship. This relationship then becomes central to the way in which HQ acquires knowledge acting as a filter for what enters the HQ knowledge base. Whether formalized or not, the knowledge base is an inherent structural characteristic of HQ. Explicit in each archetype of HQ is a perception of the channels of communication within the company: each archetype and each HQ–business relationship has a 'bandwidth' and an 'integrity rating' associated with its value as an information conduit for the centre's knowledge acquisition activity. Figure 5.8 illustrates the model.

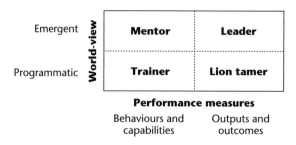

Figure 5.9   Headquarters archetypes

Archetypes of behaviour at the corporate centre

Figure 5.9 shows the four headquarters archetypes. The two dimensions used to define the scripts were *external views* and *management focus*. *Management focus* is a dimension whose extremes are defined respectively as *capability focus* and *product focus*:

- A *capability focus* exists when management engagement and concern are focused predominantly on the capabilities and competences of the business. This is the tradition of the resource-based view.
- A *product focus* exists when management engagement and concern are focused predominantly on the product/output of the business. This is the market-based view.

The *external view* (or *Weltanschauung*) is a dimension whose extremes are defined respectively as *programmatic* and *emergent*.

- A *programmatic view* exists when the relationship is acted out according to a mindset where the world is largely 'anticipated' and 'planned for', and actions and behaviours are designed to deliver explicit outcomes.
- An *emergent view* exists when the relationship is acted out in a dynamic, interactive mode predicated on a mindset where the world is viewed as uncertain and 'shaping', but also 'shapable'.

The *archetypes* that resulted were named *lion tamer, trainer, leader* and *mentor*. These archetypes are 'pure' and fictional, each operating exclusively within a single paradigm. Nonetheless, they represent useful analogues, and together a useful 'map', to help our understanding of the enactment of headquarters scripts.

The characteristics of significance that are associated with each archetype are expressed in terms of learning styles (see Figure 5.10) and concepts of single-loop and double-loop learning.

The *lion tamer* is internally focused, and concerned almost exclusively with short-term output measures for the business. *Lion tamers* tend to adopt a programmatic style of management where the locus of control is unashamedly centralized, with linear communications. They excel at efficiency-oriented resource management. The communication channel is typically a vertical command-and-control conduit, and there are no resources allocated to horizontal co-ordination between businesses. This style encourages the individual business to develop a conformance orientation and HQ has a very strong regulation competence reflected in good housekeeping and strong hygiene characteristics. A company such as Hanson, as a 'British-style' financially oriented con-

	Mentor	**Leader**	**Trainer**	**Lion tamer**
Focus	external	external	internal	internal
Time horizon	long-term	medium- to long-term	long-term	short-term
Locus of control	embedded in relationships	discrete, delegated	centrally managed	discrete, central
Performance orientation and learning styles	• cross-boundary learning • innovation networks • double-loop learning • knowledge diffusion and organizational competence	• effectiveness orientation • directed operational networks • self-concept enhancement • disciplined creativity • co-ordination competences	• discrete individual competences • task-related training • centralized innovation • single-loop learning	• efficiency orientation • linear communication • conformance orientation • regulation competence

Figure 5.10   Characteristics of the headquarters archetypes

glomerate, applies a management methodology that is simple and direct along these lines. For example:

(1)   it acts swiftly to eradicate weaknesses and weak operations;
(2)   post-acquisition management follows a highly developed model;
(3)   values and routines applied to new situations have been tried and tested previously, and management is committed.

The *trainer* also tends to be internally focused, but is concerned with the development of specific competences over the long term. The locus of control is centrally distributed, according to a programmatic schema. *Trainers* have a very deep commitment to training and development of the businesses in keeping with the centrally determined blueprint. In other words, they are very good at equipping individual businesses to do what they do well and to engage in continuous improvement. As we will see later, the culture here is conducive to programmed, incremental learning, with innovations being centrally led, of a programmatic nature. Companies such as Unilever display many of the characteristics of this archetype. According to Robert Hellar, Unilever allows people to take initiatives without fear of failure or fear of the consequences of failure. Its ethos has always been decentralization combined with the extensive training of managers to run their businesses in the 'Unilever way'.

The *leader* has an external focus and is concerned with outputs and performance measures over the medium term. *Leaders* excel at efficacy-oriented resource management, and are concerned with issues of flexibility and responsiveness in relation to the threats and opportunities that they perceive in the external environment. They operate by way of directed operational/tactical networks, oriented towards achieving specific performance targets (e.g. exploiting economies of scale and scope). The locus of control is 'centrally' decentralized, being formally proscribed and delegated by the centre to discrete business entities. The business culture is one of focused achievement and disciplined creativity where the focus and the discipline are encouraged and led from the

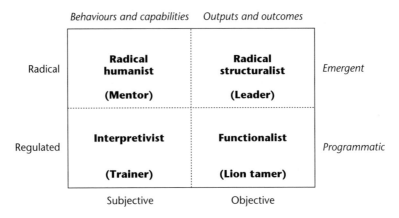

Figure 5.11   The headquarters archetypes in Burrell-Morgan language

centre. This style encourages the individual businesses to continually enhance their self-concept (by way of recognized achievement) and to develop very strong co-ordination competences. The ethos of companies such as Shell shows some of the characteristics of this archetype. Shell became famous for its high degree of decentralization and its extensive reliance on matrix management. Recent reorganizations have sought to keep the strengths associated with this approach while increasing flexibility and responsiveness by removing the bureaucratic clutter that often comes with the application of matrix management. Similarly, for ABB a significant part of its strategy is the use of middle-level managers as resource providers and informative bastions. And Sam Walton at Wal-Mart not only instilled a vision but also excelled at motivating employees, whom he called 'associates' or 'partners'.

The *mentor* has an external focus and is concerned with the development of organizational capabilities over the long term. The emphasis is on knowledge diffusion and the development of organizational capabilities. Accordingly the *mentor* will commit significant resources to facilitate co-ordination across businesses to enable cross-boundary learning and innovation networks. The locus of control is diffuse and tends to be embedded in relationships. As shown later in this chapter, this provides an environment that is conducive to the diffusion of tacit knowledge through collaborative mechanisms. Like the *leader*, the *mentor* is enacting the relationship in an emergent mode. However, in the case of the *leader* the dominant set of emergent perceptions shaping business activity are those of the headquarters in relation to performance in the external environment, but for the *mentor* activity is shaped dynamically by the emergent perceptions of the both actors. Companies such as Canon show many of the characteristics of this archetype. Canon – like some other Japanese companies – has concentrated on making matrix management work. It has three main co-ordination committees that transfer and implement knowledge and capabilities in the areas of technology, manufacturing and marketing.

The four archetypes are quite distinctive. Describing them using Gibson Burrell and Gareth Morgan's scheme (which defines paradigms along objective–subjective and regulation–radical change dimensions), it can be seen that each archetype maps directly onto a single paradigm within Burrell and Morgan's schema (see Figure 5.11):

ARCHETYPE	Shared model	Feedback information	Dominant control instrument	Communications systems
Lion tamer	operational efficiency	efficiency data	preset internal targets	formal, linear, hierarchically operated
Leader	economic performance	performance figures and targets	external performance	formal, lateral, and hierarchical linkage structures
Trainer	competence matrix	discrete task-related competence measures	formal standards and protocols	formal, functional and process integration
Mentor	transformational capability	progress and positioning indicators	empowerment	formal and informal information networking

Figure 5.12 Information characteristics of the headquarters archetypes

- The *lion tamer* sits comfortably within the *functionalist* paradigm having a predominantly objectivist view of the world coupled with a need to maintain stability.
- The *trainer* has a more subjectivist viewpoint and is concerned with standardization, so it sits comfortably in the *interpretivist* quadrant.
- The *leader*, like the *lion tamer*, has an objectivist viewpoint but has a very strong concern for the radical change of structural realities and so it sits squarely in the *radical structuralist* quadrant.
- And finally the *mentor* has a subjectivist viewpoint, is concerned with fast changing but subjectively framed realities and can be classified quite neatly as a *radical humanist*.

The corporate *external view* acts as a filter for viewing the world, and determines the type of information that is considered to be relevant for making sense of the environment. The *management focus* variable provides the internal filter by which sense is made of external information. The information matrix in Figure 5.12 provides a schematic representation of the types of information that underpin and characterize the enactment of each archetype. The *shared model* for a given archetype characterizes the dominant headquarters' perception about what constitutes the ultimate set of values that all meaningful endeavour is designed to satisfy (i.e. the ultimate 'pay off' towards which the script is directed). *Feedback information* is the type of information that is used by the headquarters to monitor what is happening within the business context. In particular this information is used to assess the congruence between the business's endeavours and the headquarters' perception of the shared model. *Dominant control instrument* characterizes the means (or instruments) employed by the headquarters to shape the business' endeavours. *Communication system* characteristics reflect the communications infrastructures that are necessary for the enactment of the archetype.

The *lion tamer*, with its focus on operational efficiency, will employ systems that provide financial data about the business, and evaluate individual output against preset internal targets, using financial reward mechanisms to reinforce 'appropriate' business behaviour. The communication infrastructure is characterized by formal protocols for linear communication through functional hierarchies.

The *leader*, with its focus on economic performance through process efficacy, will employ systems that provide performance figures about the business and evaluate individual business performance against external benchmarks, using 'best practice' transfer mechanisms to implant 'appropriate' business behaviour. The communication structure is predominantly formal in style, characterized by vertical control channels with transverse integration linkages (or networks) between businesses for purposes of tactical and operational co-ordination.

The *trainer*, with its focus on internal effectiveness based on business competence, will employ discrete, function-/task-related competence measures to monitor business performance, using formal standards and protocols to orchestrate the development of specific competences in individual businesses so that these map on to the headquarters' blueprint of the corporate competence matrix in a complementary fashion alongside the other businesses in the portfolio. The communications structure will tend to reflect the matrix structure with formal function/process integration.

The *mentor*, with its focus on developing capabilities that can both generate and survive discontinuities in the competitive and strategic contexts, will employ progress and positioning indicators to assess the nature and value of the capabilities being developed by the individual businesses and to learn about the mode in which these capabilities are leveraged by the businesses. The *mentor* is concerned with aspects of effective organizational learning, and perceives the headquarters–business relationship as one within which a learning partnership exists. Accordingly, it reinforces 'appropriate' business behaviour through continued empowerment of the business within the relationship context. The communications structure is organic, characterized by a fusion of formal and informal communications (and relationship) networks linking the individual business with each other and the headquarters.

Knowledge management at the corporate centre

Following M. Boisot's approach to organizational learning, the archetypes follow in cumulative fashion the stages of knowledge management. Thus the *lion tamer* is competent at scanning the environment to obtain information to identify problems and opportunities. The *leader* is, in addition, good at codifying knowledge, making knowledge explicit so that it can be communicated readily. The *trainer* is further noted for its ability to diffuse and spread knowledge around the organization. The *mentor* adds to all this with skills at knowledge absorption, the ability to internalize knowledge and create deeper understandings. The more complex the organization, the greater is the degree of sophistication on the use of knowledge in order to create organizational learning.

The nature of knowledge itself (the theme of this chapter) conditions the way in which organizations *can* behave. The nature of knowledge can be captured in part in terms of codifiability and appropriability. Codifiability refers to the degree to which knowledge is explicit and can therefore be captured in terms of routines or specifications. Appropriability is the extent to which knowledge can be captured, adapted and turned to advantage. Where codifiability and appropriability are low (see Figure 5.13), the HQ can only promote learning through informal networking because formal

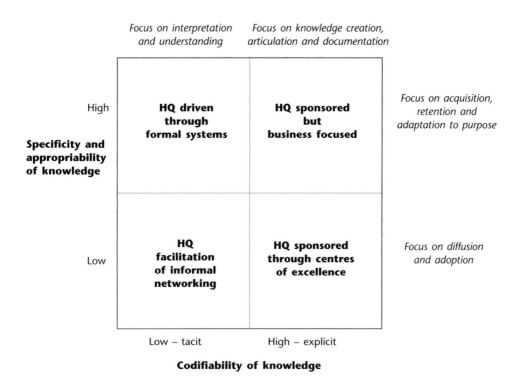

Focus on interpretation and understanding   *Focus on knowledge creation, articulation and documentation*

Focus on acquisition, retention and adaptation to purpose

HQ driven through formal systems	**HQ sponsored but business focused**	
HQ facilitation of informal networking	**HQ sponsored through centres of excellence**	

Specificity and appropriability of knowledge — High / Low

Focus on diffusion and adoption

Low – tacit   High – explicit

Codifiability of knowledge

Figure 5.13   Impact of knowledge management at the corporate centre

systems and processes cannot cope with imprecision. Where these regimes are high in explicit knowledge and the ability to capture it, then the HQ can focus on knowledge creation, articulation and documentation but will require the businesses to acquire the knowledge and adapt it for their own purposes.

As the appropriability regime becomes weaker, the businesses have to operate through less well-defined processes of knowledge diffusion. In this case the HQ would wish to sponsor knowledge through centres of excellence. Where knowledge is very tacit in character but the appropriability is high, then the role of HQ is to provide interpretation of 'fuzzy' knowledge and to promote understanding through formal systems. This approach provides extra dimensions to our understanding of the behaviour of corporate centres. The *trainer* needs to operate in an environment where knowledge can be readily codified, so training is possible. The *leader*'s style of behaviour is appropriate to a regime of high appropriability of knowledge so that adaptation to purpose can be driven from the top. The *mentor*, of course, operates in environments where knowledge is fuzzy, not malleable, probably unknowable, and therefore not appropriable. Hence, the need for informal networking and the fostering of learning approaches across the organization. The *lion tamer* lives in a simplistic world probably off the map to the top right-hand side where, with a little effort, everything is thought to be known.

The Merali and McGee approach goes on to articulate the changes needed and the migration path required when corporate characteristics have to change in response to changing circumstances. It suggests that migration requires a change in fundamental perceptions underpinning the headquarters' self-script resulting in changes in its primary focus, values, aspirations, behaviours, structures, attitudes and relationship scripts. These are essentially the challenges faced by the corporate centre in responding to the restructuring of industries and the refocusing of companies following the revolution in the economics of information.

Conclusion

The implications of the changes in the economics of information and knowledge are profound and far-reaching:

(1) *The traditional (product-based) definitions of industries will become obsolete, as therefore will all the conventional categorizations of competitors, suppliers and buyers.* Increasingly our units of analysis will be activity and knowledge-based rather than product-based.

(2) *Firm strategies will become much more focused with complementary and co-specialized assets outsourced to 'best-in-class' suppliers.* Traditional value chains will be broken up through outsourcing of those activities in which outside providers have advantages arising from their specialized knowledge.

(3) *Competitive advantage will increasingly be based on knowledge-based individual activity or layer in the value chain and advantage arising from integration across the individual elements of the value chain will become less relevant.* Traditional integration *down* the value chain will increasingly be seen as less valuable and useful than integration of knowledge-based activities across value chains.

(4) *Horizontal strategy will become essential in order to gain economies of scope – to put it another way: economies of scope will become available across apparently unrelated industries and product classes.* The entire debate about synergies will move from product-relatedness to knowledge-relatedness.

(5) *Intermediaries will become 'flashpoints' in the value chain, being subject to disintermediation yet also the potential locus for highly focused competences.* Certain companies will take 'leadership' roles in their speed of deconstruction and insight into the possibilities for orchestration. Around these companies will flow the battles for control of the 'old value chains' and the 'new value webs'.

(6) *Corporate headquarters will go through radical reappraisals to foster greater informality and flexibility and to stage-manage the learning and knowledge management of the company.* Such major changes as detailed in *(1)–(5)* above will have to be fostered by corporate headquarters taking much more explicit roles as strategists through brokering knowledge and fostering organizational learning.

(7) *Information processes and knowledge networks that underpin organizational learning will become essential and distinctive elements in the relationships between corporate headquarters and their businesses.* The management of knowledge requires specific capabilities in information processing and in the understanding of how internal networks can act as repositories for knowledge and as agents for knowledge transfer.

These changes will in many ways increase competition. Traditional brands will become vulnerable. Customers will have more choice. Proprietary knowledge will not last as long. However, the new competition may be complex in character and new pockets of proprietary information will emerge. Boundaries of companies will become more permeable and ownership will no longer be a condition for effective control or co-ordination. As Carl Stern from the Boston Consulting Group puts it 'the attacker has the advantage. Incumbents are under threat . . .'. We will need a replacement for the value chain, and, subsequently, more strategists as orchestrators rather than as planners, directors and controllers!

Case Box 5.2   The Role of Headquarters: The Case of ABB and Percy Barnevik (former CEO of ABB)

The Economist on Barnevik and ABB

'By trusting in multiculturalism and decentralisation, Percy Barnevik has created a world beater. Could the firm hang together without him?'

If Europe has a management superstar it is Percy Barnevik, boss of ABB Asea Brown Boveri, an electrical engineering giant. A tall, bearded and fast-talking Swede who has the restless manner of a man over-endowed with energy, Mr. Barnevik has won almost every honour bestowed upon his profession, from 'emerging markets CEO of the year' to (twice) boss of Europe's most respected company. His name is dropped by management theorists and by the *Harvard Business Review* almost as frequently as that of Jack Welch of America's General Electric. And the gap is closing fast. 'Our greatest rival is no longer GE,' confesses one Japanese competitor. 'The one we have to be most on guard against is ABB.'

For once, the hyperbole is largely warranted. There are several reasons to praise Mr. Barnevik. One is that he has shown how a company can be big and small at the same time: ABB consists of 1,300 separate companies divided into 5,000 profit centres. He has also pioneered such fashionable practices as internal benchmarking, centres of excellence and corporate parenting. But perhaps his most striking idea is the 'multicultural multinational'.

Not long ago, pundits held that globalisation would erase national differences and homogenise consumer tastes. Mr. Barnevik's view is more nuanced. He argues that purely national companies have little chance of thriving as governments deregulate and as the cost of travel and information plummets. But he stresses that companies need to keep deep roots in local markets, because markets will continue to differ. His answer is a cosmopolitan conglomerate diverse enough to respond to local tastes but united enough to amount to more than the sum of its parts.

ABB was born with such diversity. In 1988 Mr. Barnevik fashioned the organisation from two century-old companies: ASEA, the Swedish engineering group which he ran from 1980, and Brown Boveri, an equally proud Swiss competitor. Since then, the company has been involved in more than 100 acquisitions and joint ventures, expanding into Eastern Europe and Asia, and adding (after many lay-offs) 18,000 workers in 40 different countries.

This makes for an impressive array of dots on the map. But how do you join them up? Remember, for instance, the recent national rivalry between different parts of Royal Dutch Shell, another multicultural multinational, over its oilrig fiasco. That is where Mr. Barnevik has been particularly successful. He forces all employees to read his 'bible', a short booklet on the company's aims and values. He made English his firm's official language, although only a third of the employees speak it as their mother tongue (Mr. Barnevik himself has a strong Swedish accent). He moved ABB's headquarters to Zurich so that the merger would not look like a Swedish takeover. But he keeps the headquarters staff small (currently 171 people from 19 different countries) in order to avoid the impression that ABB is now a Swiss company. In making cuts, he has made sure that the burden is spread fairly evenly. Indeed, the most common criticism is that he treats his native Sweden rather too harshly; he once needed a bodyguard there to protect him from angry former employees.

Mr. Barnevik's leadership style is not risk-free. He has always relied on speed to pre-empt nationalistic passions, either within the company or in national parliaments. Merging ASEA and Brown Boveri took a mere six weeks, and Mr. Barnevik has been adding companies ever since.

Some critics say that this relentless expansion has prevented ABB from putting down any deep common roots, and that it runs on nothing more substantial than the adrenalin of permanent revolution. This, remember, is a company with a small core and only a thin layer of managers to supervise a myriad of subsidiaries and profit centres. ABB's retort is that its identity is buttressed not only by its possession of a coordinating executive committee (with members from eight countries) but also by an elite cadre of 500 global managers, a Praetorian Guard that Mr. Barnevik selects carefully, paying particular attention to the cultural sensitivity of its members, and to their spouses' willingness to move. He shifts them through a series of foreign assignments, and takes a close interest in their careers. Worth more than their weight in gold, according to Mr. Barnevik, their job is to knit the organisation together, to transfer expertise around the world, and to expose the company's leadership to differing perspectives.

In the end, however, a lot of ABB's corporate glue comes down to Mr. Barnevik's own relentlessness. ABBers around the world speak reverently about his ability to get by on four hours' sleep a night and his familiarity with every nook and cranny of the organisation. He reckons he speaks personally to 5,500 of his employees every year. He spends only a couple of days a week at headquarters (often Saturday and Sunday); much of the rest of the time he is in an airborne office in a corporate jet.

'So what?' one of ABB's many happy shareholders might ask, adding that it is difficult to imagine Mr. Barnevik sitting still anywhere. But ABB's current structure – and indeed the modern management fashion which Mr. Barnevik has done so much to influence – has thrust an awesome amount of responsibility to the very top of the organisation. The more global it has grown, the more it has relied on a strong leader to hold it together. The bigger test of Mr. Barnevik's skills may be not how well the company performs while he is still in charge, but what happens to it after his departure.

Time Magazine *on Barnevik*

'. . . Barnevik (is) analytical, quick, blunt and, above all, global. As chairman of ABB Asea Brown Boveri, the world's largest electrical engineering group,

Barnevik, 57, presides over a $36 billion federation of more than 1,000 compa-nies with 217,000 employees in 140 countries. Zurich-based ABB is the biggest single investor in Eastern Europe and the former Soviet Union, a Western pioneer in India and an aggressive player in East Asia and Latin America. For three years running it was voted 'Europe's most respected company' in a poll of executives by *The Financial Times* newspaper. The structure Barnevik devised to run this globe-girdling behemoth 'has become the new prototype for the post-industrial-age corporation,' says Manfred Kets de Vries of the INSEAD business school outside Paris.

'The champion of globalisation started life in a provincial setting: the isolated west coast of Sweden. Educated as an economist, Barnevik left a management-consulting job to help a troubled Swedish steel company. Success there led to the CEO spot at Asea, a large electrical engineering firm then in decline. Barnevik carried out a radical and initially painful shake-up, dubbed "Percy's reign of terror". He completed the ABB merger, Europe's biggest cross-border deal in six weeks, following a key Barnevik rule: act fast, even at the risk of making mis-takes. Or as the ABB "bible" he inspired puts it, "Not to take action is the only nonacceptable behavior".'

Barnevik on Barnevik's Management Style

On his organizing principles
'The only way to structure a complex, global organization is to make it as simple and local as possible. ABB is complicated from where I sit. But on the ground, where the real work gets done, all of our operations must function as closely as possible to stand-alone operations. Our managers need well-defined sets of responsibilities, clear accountability, and maximum degrees of freedom to execute.

'We are fervent believers in decentralization. When we structure local operations, we always push to create separate legal entities. Separate companies allow you to create real balance sheets with real responsibility for cash flow and dividends. With real balance sheets, managers inherit results from year to year through changes in equity.'

'ABB is a huge enterprise. But the work of most of our people is organized in small units with P&L responsibility and meaningful autonomy. Our operations are divided into nearly 1,200 companies with an average of 200 employees. These companies are divided into 4,500 profit centres with an average of 50 employees.' (iii)

On the organization structure
'ABB is an organization with three internal contradictions. We want to be global and local, big and small, radically decentralized with centralized reporting and control. If we resolve those contradictions, we create real organizational advantage.

'That's where the matrix comes in. The matrix is the framework through which we organize our activities. It allows us to optimize our business globally and maximize performance in every country in which we operate. Some people resist it. They say the matrix is too rigid, too simplistic. But what choice do you have? To say you don't like a matrix is like saying you don't like factories or you don't like breathing. It's a fact of life. If you deny the formal matrix, you wind up with an informal one – and that's much harder to reckon with. As we learn to master the matrix, we get a truly multidomestic organization.' (iv)

On the difficulty of managing the transition into ABB
'It does require a huge mental change, especially for country managers. Remember, we've built ABB through acquisitions and restructurings. Thirty of the companies we've bought had been around for more than 100 years. Many of them were industry leaders in their countries, national monuments. Now they've got BA managers playing a big role in the direction of their operations. We have to convince country managers that they benefit by being part of this federation, that they gain more than they lose when they give up some autonomy.' (v)

On creating a culture: why the 13 members of the Group Executive Management Team meet every three weeks for one day
'Sitting in one room are the senior managers collectively responsible for ABB's global strategy and performance. These same managers individually monitor business segments, countries, and staff functions. So when we make a decision-snap, it's covered. The members of the executive committee communicate to their direct reports, the BA managers and the country managers, and the implementation process is under way.' (vi)

On diversity
'We can't have managers who are 'un-French' managing in France because 95% of them are dealing every day with French customers, French colleagues, French suppliers. That's why global managers need humility. A global manager respects a formal German manager – Herr Doktor and all that – because that manager may be an outstanding performer in the German context.' (vii)

On building a culture of trust and exchange
'Sharing expertise does not happen automatically. It takes a trust, it takes familiarity. People need to spend time together, to get to know and understand each other. People must also see a payoff for themselves. I never expect our operations to co-ordinate unless all sides get real benefits. We have to demonstrate that sharing pays – that contributing one idea gets you 24 in return.' (viii)

On selecting top managers for ABB
'We sought people capable of becoming superstars – tough-skinned individuals who were fast on their feet, had good technical and commercial backgrounds, and had demonstrated the ability to lead others . . . For the merger to work it is essential that we have managers who are open, generous, and capable of thinking in group terms.' (ix)

On decision-making
'Nothing is worse than procrastination . . . When I look at ten decisions I regret, there will be nine of them where I delayed . . . Better roughly and quickly than carefully and slowly.'

'Take the initiative and decide – even if it turns out to be the wrong thing. The only thing we cannot accept is people who do nothing.'

[To emphasize the point Barnevik banned the phrase 'I think' at meetings: 'either you know or you don't'] (x)

On managers
'Global managers are made, not born. . . . you rotate people around the world. There is no substitute for line experience in three or four countries . . . you encourage people to work in mixed-nationality teams. You *force* them to create personal alliances across borders . . . You have to force people into these situations.' (xi)

On information used by the executive committee
'We look for early signs that businesses are becoming more or less healthy. . . . I stop to study trends that catch my eye. . . . (I don't) start giving orders. But I want to have informed dialogues with the appropriate executives.' (xii)

On communications
'You don't inform, you overinform.' (xiii)

On the role of headquarters
'We operate as lean as humanly possible. It's no accident that there are only 100 people at ABB headquarters in Zurich. The closer we get to top management, the tougher we have to be with head count. I believe you can go into any traditionally centralized corporation and cut its headquarters staff by 90% in one year. You spin off 30% of the staff into free-standing service centres that perform real work – treasury functions, legal services – and charge for it. You decentralize 30% of the staff – human resources, for example – by pushing them into the line organization. Then 30% disappears through head count reductions.' (xiv)

1. *How does ABB's organization work? What are the key roles of managers at the country level? At the business area (BA) level? At the front line and the business unit level?*
2. *What role does headquarters play in getting this organization to work? Which of the four archetypes of headquarters as orchestrator is most like ABB? Or does ABB have its own particular blend of these archetypes?*
3. *How is ABB's approach to orchestration informed by the ethos imparted by Barnevik?*
4. *What are the strengths and weaknesses of ABB's particular approach to orchestration?*

(i) *The Economist*, 6 January 1996; (ii) Jay Branegan, *Time*, 24 February 1997, p. 34; (iii) William Taylor, 'The Logic of Global Business: an Interview with ABB's Percy Barnevik', *Harvard Business Review*, March–April 1991, reprint no. 91201, p. 99; (iv) see Taylor, above, pp. 95–6; (v) see Taylor, above, p. 98; (vi) see Taylor, above, p. 100; (vii) see Taylor, above, p. 95; (viii) see Taylor, above, p. 97; (ix) Jules Arbose, 'ABB: The New Energy Powerhouse', *International Management*, June 1988; (x) Jonathan Kapstein and Stanley Reed, 'Preaching the Euro-Gospel: ABB Redefines Multinationalism', *Business Week*, 23 July 1990, p. 36; (xi) see Taylor, above, p. 95; (xii) see Taylor, above, p. 100; (xiii) see Taylor, above, p. 104; (xiv) see Taylor, above, p. 99.

Source Material and Recommended Further Reading

The genesis of economists' thinking about the nature of the firm is often attributed to Alfred Marshall whose *Principles of Economics*, first published in 1890 (London: Macmillan) is still very readable. The 'modern' era was heralded by Richard Coase who in his seminal article on the 'Nature of the Firm', in 1937 in *Economica* (386–405), described the firm as the organizational arena in which resources were allocated by direct orders outside the marketplace. The field of strategic management began to take shape in the 1970s and Oliver Williamson was one of its earliest and most influential theorists through his two books *The Economic Institutions of Capitalism* (New York: Free Press, 1985) and *Economic Organization: Firms, Markets, and Policy Control* (Brighton: Wheatsheaf, 1986). He introduced the idea of transactions cost economics seeing the firm (as a transaction cost economizer) and the market as optional and alternative governance structures guiding the allocation of resources.

The giant corporation had long been known but Alfred Chandler, the Harvard historian whose work has underpinned much of the development of strategic management, expressed its formal logic in terms of economies of scale and scope in his *Harvard Business Review* paper 'The Enduring Logic of Industrial Success' (March–April 1990, 130–40). Intellectual challenges to the hegemony of giantism soon began to emerge. James Brian Quinn explored the interplay between the advancement and the specialization of knowledge and the make or buy decisions of service firms in his 1992 book *The Intelligent Enterprise* (New York: Free Press). Various authors have taken this argument into manufacturing firms, notably Evans and Wurster in their 1997 *Harvard Business Review* paper 'Strategy and the New Economics of Information' (Sept.–Oct., 70–82), and their later book *Blown to Bits: How the New Economics of Information Transform Strategy* (Boston: Harvard Business School Press, 1999). Both of these authors base their views on their Boston Consulting Group experience but the Boston Consulting Group has also published their approach directly in *Perspectives: The Deconstruction of Value Chains* written by Carl Stern (September 1998).

More recent challenges to accepted thinking have developed out of the growth of virtual networks (e.g. fax systems and WINTEL computer systems). These have reawakened interest in the economics of networks and the implications for competition. Brian Arthur has captured the essence of 'network economies of scale' in his *Harvard Business Review* paper 'Increasing Returns and the New World of Business' (July–Aug., 1996, 100–9). Carl Shapiro and Hal Varian have written a very readable summation of these 'new rules' in *Information Rules: A Strategic Guide to the Network Economy* (Boston: Harvard Business School Press, 1999).

The nature of social responsibility and its incorporation into the subject of strategic management and its impact on managerial mindsets is summarized in Jorg Andriof's doctoral thesis *Managing Social Risk through Stakeholder Partnership Building* published by Warwick University in 2000.

The role of corporate headquarters in multi-business firms has attracted much attention in the 1990s. Ewan Ferlie and Andrew Pettigrew have written one of the few literature reviews on the subject: this is to be found in the *Journal of Management Studies* as 'The Nature and Transformation of Corporate Headquarters: A Review of Recent Literature and a Research Agenda' (33(4), 1996, 495–523). Chris Bartlett and Sumantra Ghoshal wrote a very widely read book on the way in which multinationals approached this problem, *Managing Across Borders* (London: Hutchinson, 1989). Later they extended their thinking into a broader critique of the multidivisional form (M-form) in a paper 'Beyond the M-form: Toward a Managerial Theory of the Firm' (*Strategic Management Journal*, 14, 1993, Special Issue, 23–46). Bill Starbuck is one of many who have criticized the value of formal, top-down strategic planning and he offers an interesting alternative 'Strategizing in the Real World' (*International Journal of Technology Management*, 8(1/2), 1992, 77–85). Gibson Burrell and Gareth Morgans' schema is described in *Sociological Paradigms and Organisational Analysis* (London: Heinemann, 1979).

The basis for the second part of this chapter derives from an information-based approach to the design and management of HQ processes which is developed in two papers by Yasmin Merali and John McGee. The first is 'Information Competences and Knowledge Creation at the Corporate Centre', in Gary Hamel, C.K. Prahalad, Howard Thomas and Don O'Neal (eds), *Strategic Flexibility: Managing in a Turbulent Environment* (Chichester: Wiley, 1998, pp. 195–218).

The second is 'Planning the Migration: Rewriting the Script for the Corporate Centre', in Michael A. Hitt, Joan E. Rican I Costa and Robert D. Nixon (eds), *New Managerial Mindsets: Organizational Transformation and Strategy Implementation* (Chichester: Wiley, 1998). Their approach relates to the original work by Berne in 1961 on *Transactions Analysis in Psychotherapy* (New York: Grove Press). In this view the transactions undertaken by the centre with its subsidiaries are influenced by the perceptions of the business of itself in relation to the headquarters and vice versa. These perceptions when expressed formally are analogous to the so-called *scripts* referred to by the adherents of *transactions analysis*.

An information approach requires some concepts of organisational learning. The approach in this chapter is based on Ashby's seminal paper on 'Adaptiveness and Equilibrium' (*Journal of Mental Science*, 86, 1940, 478–83), and also on his much later book *An Introduction to Cybernetics* (London: Chapman and Hall, 1956). Chris Argyris' and Donald Schön's book *Organizational Learning* (Reading MA: Addison-Wesley, 1978) is also fundamental to any appreciation of how corporations develop over time. Max Boisot's recent organizational learning model is fundamental to the approach adopted in this chapter where knowledge is, in sequence, scanned (obtained), created, codified, diffused, and absorbed. This is described in M. Boisot *Information and Organizations: The Manager as Anthropologist* (London: Collins, 1987).

The companies used as headquarters archetypes are described in various case studies. See, for example, 'Canon: Competing on Capabilities', in B. de Wit and R. Meyer (eds), *Strategy: Process, Content, Context* (London: ITP, 1998, pp. 1038–53). Robert Hellars' wide-ranging book *In Search of European Excellence* (London: HarperCollins, 1998) contains an extensive discussion of Unilever and a good description of financially oriented conglomerates including Hanson plc.

Also referred to in this chapter were 'A Survey of E-Management' (*The Economist*, 18 November 2000), and E. Penrose's *The Theory of the Growth of the Firm* (London: Basil Blackwell, 1959).

'Information' used to be viewed by many as a minor issue that only concerned 'technical people' at the operational or day-to-day level of the organization. Then IT became fashionable and was quickly elevated to the point where it became something of a Holy Grail that unquestioningly drove organizations' strategic choices. This chapter suggests that neither extreme is useful. The first neglects the benefits that can spring from aligning information systems with corporate strategy. The second promotes approaches such as business process re-engineering that are overly driven by new technologies, efficiency, revolution and generic one-size-fits-all solutions, approaches that neglect the nature of human beings and their relationships with technology and how these relationships add up to more than just information or data. This chapter advocates an alternative image, one that embraces the importance of the efficiency and other gains offered by technological change, but which does not override the unique, organic and embedded nature of organizational knowledge and wisdom. This image sees strategy as **data plus sense-making**. The frameworks and examples that the authors provide using this image will aid your ability to utilize information and knowledge to orchestrate fragmenting organizations (Chapter 5) while building upon an organization's particular intentions (Chapter 4) and emergent ethos (Chapter 2).

6 Strategy as Data Plus Sense-Making

BOB GALLIERS AND SUE NEWELL

Where is the wisdom we have lost in knowledge?
Where is the knowledge we have lost in information?

T.S. Eliot, The Rock *(1952)*

Few would surely argue that the strategic management of data, information and knowledge and the associated information technology (that together encompass the information systems (IS) strategy of an organization), represent a major strategic challenge and opportunity for organizations as we enter the new millennium. We talk glibly of 'the information age', of 'the networked society', of 'globalization', of 'the knowledge economy' – each in their own way enabled and facilitated by information technology (IT), but we rarely strategize about these issues. For example, the market for IT products and services can be measured in tens of billions of whatever currency you can think of. It is estimated that companies in the developed world spend something in the region of 2 per cent of turnover annually on hardware and software alone. The costs associated with staff development, maintenance and managing the change associated with the implementation and ongoing operation of IT-based systems would doubtless more than double that figure.

And while attitudes differ – with some seeing the advent of this 'brave new world' as being nothing other than a boon, while others mutter their discontent at the spiralling costs involved, at 'techies' who fail to understand the subtleties of organizational life, at the disruption, at the invasion of privacy, etc. – there is little doubt that IT is here to stay. More than that, the impact of IT will be felt increasingly as its power and reach continue to outstrip even the wildest of predictions. And this impact is to be felt by the individual, by organizations, by national governments, and by society as a whole. What more need we say to argue that this is a topic worthy of our attention in any strategy discourse?

Funny then, that IT/IS strategy barely rates a mention in most MBA strategy courses. Funny that it often appears as an optional course only in many an MBA curriculum. Funny that many firms rush, lemming-like, to avoid the pain of managing their information resource and the related technologies by outsourcing their IT or information services departments. Funny that we reel from one IT bandwagon, one fad (e.g., business process re-engineering, enterprise resource planning systems, knowledge management systems), to the next – with apparent abandon – often to rue the consequences later. Funny that we simultaneously revel in, and yet revile the industry that plies us with solution after solution, without even asking the crucial question: 'why?'

The aim of this chapter is to outline the images that emerge by analysing the key issues that appear to be related to IS strategizing: about the management of organizational data, information, knowledge, wisdom and their relation to IT. This chapter also seeks to build on the notion developed in Chapter 5 – that organizations are becoming increasingly fragmented – and to outline some frameworks that can help incorporate information strategies that can orchestrate such networks.

This is not a technologically oriented, nor indeed a technologically deterministic treatment of the topic. Rather, it deals with developments in our thinking and practice as regards information systems (IS), from a strategy – or rather, strategizing perspective. It also provides a critical commentary on some of the more trite treatments of the topic, which have appeared in the popular media, and provides some clarification of the terms that are currently in use – and which often cause confusion.

The chapter is organized as follows. First, we provide a brief history of the manner in which IS strategy has developed since the early days of commercial data processing up to the 1990s. Second, we take a look at some of the key concepts and frameworks that have underpinned much of IS strategy theory during this period. We then proceed to consider some of the more recent developments and new thinking in the field that have emerged over the past decade or so with a view to pointing out future directions and current concerns. Interspersed in these sections are several illustrations and mini cases, designed to clarify and reinforce key lessons to be drawn from the text.

To pre-empt the conclusions that we draw in this chapter, we argue that the current emphasis on the strategic importance of knowledge is not necessarily best met through the development of ever-more sophisticated IT solutions that can encourage the sharing, creation and storage of knowledge. Rather, we argue that we need to go 'back to the future' and recognize that IT systems can only ever be tools for the processing and communication of data or information. It is the intelligent receiver (user) of these data who will use his/her knowledge to interpret and make sense of the data in a specific context and for a particular purpose. The emphasis is, then, on the strategic use of data through ensuring that individuals will make sense or meaning of these data, based on their existing knowledge of the business strategy and the particular context in which the business is operating. We conclude, inspired by Eliot's quote with which this chapter began and in keeping with the spirit of this book, by asking you to produce the future of strategy. If the 1950s and 1960s were associated with management data systems, the 1970s, 1980s and 1990s with information systems, and the late 1990s and early 2000s with knowledge management, what might the future hold?

Some Background History: From Data Processing to Competitive Advantage

Figure 6.1 provides a simplified model within which to situate the changes in IS strategy since the 1960s when the first computers became commercially available. This suggests that there have been four phases that have differed in terms of the degree to which the IS strategy has been driven as a 'top-down' versus a 'bottom-up' process and the extent to which the strategy has been based on short-term problem-solving versus longer-term strategic goal setting. The model suggests that we have seen the focus shift away from and back to IT itself, and from matters of efficiency, to matters of effectiveness and competitiveness. While such a stylized view certainly oversimplifies developments, it helps in providing a brief summary of the changes that have taken place over this time period from the 1960s to the 1990s.

The model indicates that, in the early years of commercial computing, IS strategy was, for the most part at least, *isolated* from the rest of the business. The focus was on issues of the day and on the efficient utilization of the technology for mainly operational purposes. There followed a period where formal, 'top-down', business-driven strategies were the norm, with the emphasis being more on *effectiveness*. Such strategies took as read the existing business imperatives and attempted to identify IT applications based on those objectives and concerns. Over time, strategies became more forward-looking, bearing in mind the need to invest in IT and to develop IS that would stand the test of time. Such strategies were therefore essentially *prospective* in nature. A move to the *proactive* use of IT to create competitive advantage, applying Porterian concepts, emerged during the 1990s and was supplemented by the BPR (business process redesign) movement, which aimed to automate streamlined processes in line with customer requirements. Below we outline developments during these different 'periods' in more detail.

Operational efficiency (the isolated period)

In the beginning, there was . . . 'ad hocracy'. And here we mean the 1960s and early 1970s. In these early days of commercial computing, little strategic thought was given by senior managers to the use to which IT could be put in their organization, other than to think in terms of improving operational efficiency or attempting to cut costs. It was therefore left to their lower level IT colleagues to develop and implement what was thought to be necessary so far as computing was concerned. Targets for computerization (automation by another word) were simple production processes and record keeping – such as accounting systems. Little, if any, thought was given to the impact of the 'new' technology to ongoing operations, little concern was expressed over the kind of skills that might be required to get the best out of the investment, and most developments or acquisitions were undertaken on a piecemeal basis. What little management of IS there was tended to be considered to be the province of what we now

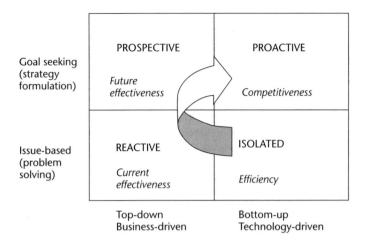

Figure 6.1   Tracing the developments in informations systems strategy

often call the IT department and its management – known as the DP (data processing) department in those days. In short, there was little planning for IS, and IS strategy would have been considered – in this period at least – to be an oxymoron!

Current effectiveness (the reactive period)

Increasingly, however, senior management became concerned that DP was not delivering the promised efficiency gains, or focusing on key business concerns and imperatives. From the days when DP was seen as almost entirely the province of the technologist, we gradually saw the emergence of business-driven IS planning approaches. One such was IBM's business systems planning (BSP) methodology – a service provided by IBM to its customers which was meant not only to identify how the organization could harness IT to meet business needs, but also of course to demonstrate the need for more computing. In a nutshell, the BSP methodology was developed to identify key business processes and their associated information and IT requirements. A comparison with the data output from existing systems would then lead to the identification of additional required applications – and, in particular, additional IT (i.e. computer hardware and software). It is during this era that we were first introduced to the idea that IS/IT and business needed to be aligned, and this is an issue that has remained with us ever since – of which more later. At this time the mainframe computer was king. Organizations had to rely on mainframe technology with so-called 'dumb' terminals on employees' desks, usually providing periodic output for control purposes. This was commonly known as 'batch processing', as data were processed in batches rather than on a continuous, real-time basis. For example, weekly or monthly management reports (so-called management information systems, or MIS) would be produced on reams of paper, and usually required much additional human analysis to provide anything meaningful. Such MIS output was often of limited use and would commonly be most evident as a door stop!

Future effectiveness (the prospective period)

The advent of database technology in the late 1970s and 1980s not only led – eventually at any rate – to the ability of managers to query the database in order to obtain answers to specific questions (so-called executive information systems, or EIS), but also to a major rethink of IS strategy. The thought here was that rather than identifying particular IS applications, organizations would simply have to identify key data entities with which they were dealing (e.g., customer, product) and their attributes (e.g., name, address, product code, size). These could then be mapped to demonstrate their linkages as a precursor to database design. A champion of this approach was James Martin, who had been an executive with IBM. What might be called a 'garbage can' approach to database design thus appeared on the scene. It was thought that organizations would no longer have to concern themselves with issues of prioritizing information requirements associated with particular managers or processes. Rather, the database would enable the delivery of whatever information was required, wherever and whenever needed. In some cases, the error in this line of reasoning (given the technological limitations at the time) was not realized until after the invoice had been received for the massively increased computing power necessary to run the resultant database.

In some ways this era may be seen to have spawned the so-called critical success factor (CSF) approach – an approach developed by Jack Rockart at Massachusetts Institute of Technology (MIT). Under the guise of executives defining for themselves their own, critical data needs, the approach was quickly pounced upon by executives and consultants alike since it facilitated prioritization of IS developments. The approach was welcomed as it brought an element of control back to harassed executives who had seen their IS/IT budgets expanding at a time when they were being promised increased computing power for their limited financial resources – and were becoming increasingly concerned about budget overspends. In outline, the approach centred on the identification of key objectives for the organization or business unit concerned, followed by the identification of key management processes necessary to enable the achievement of the stated objectives. Critical success factors (CSFs) associated with these processes were then identified as a means of identifying the data that had to be made available for executives to manage and control the processes within their sphere of responsibility. Various approaches utilized the CSF concept, including another IBM methodology – programme quality management (PQM). And many still incorporate it to this day.

Competitiveness (the proactive period)

As we moved into the 1980s, Michael Porter and colleagues, such as Warren McFarlan, at Harvard Business School had an enormous impact on thinking regarding the competitive advantages to be gained from the astute use of IT by firms. Utilizing such models as the five-forces and value chain, Porter and his colleagues demonstrated how IT, and the information it could produce, could provide added value to goods and services, could retard competition from both traditional rivals and new entrants, and could be used to leverage relationships with suppliers and customers alike. A considerable amount of consultancy activity was spawned by this kind of thinking, and a great deal of literature was written on the topic throughout the 1980s and into the 1990s.

In line with this, there emerged in the 1990s another approach to the strategic utilization of IT, but this time focusing more on internal processes. The movement was championed by the likes of Michael Hammer and Tom Davenport and became known as business process redesign, or simply, BPR. The basis for their argument was that the mere computerization of a messy situation will lead to nothing more than a computerized mess, which is probably not where one wants to end up! They argued for a clean slate approach that identified and streamlined the key business processes. The trick was then to identify how IT could support these processes to improve efficiency and cut costs. This involved automating certain processes and almost always involved getting rid of middle management (downsizing) who were now deemed to be surplus to requirements given the streamlined processes. In addition, it was argued, by focusing on customer requirements, the processes would lead to improved effectiveness.

While success rates were reported as being quite low, and while the advocates of the process were at pains to warn organizations of the risks involved (while talking up the potential gains, it has to be said), BPR was big business and was attempted by most major corporations in the English-speaking world. For example, in 1995, the market for BPR services was estimated to be in excess of $50 billion. By 1996, however, the bubble had begun to burst with one of the founding fathers of the movement, Tom Davenport, finally recognizing the loss of considerable organizational knowledge through the swathes of redundancies brought about by the downsizing strategies which accompanied many BPR efforts. BPR had become, in his words, 'the fad that forgot people'.

In some respects, then, we had come full circle. When we first began to think of IS planning and strategy, the focus was primarily on the technology itself, since managerial concerns for computing were mainly on matters of operational efficiency. We then entered an era during which business-driven approaches were prevalent, with concern shifting to matters of effectiveness, and prioritization. As we entered the 1980s and into the 1990s, the focus shifted to IT for competitive advantage, and subsequently BPR. In this era attention shifted once more to a concern for how the technology could be harnessed proactively to increase competitiveness, formerly through an analysis of the competitive environment, and latterly through an analysis of internal processes. In other respects, much of current thinking and IS strategizing attempts to incorporate aspects of each of the four phases. Current issues need to be dealt with at the same time as future requirements. Current business imperatives need to be supported by IS, while at the same time, we look for innovative uses of IT that might change the nature of, or at least add value to, the goods and services we offer.

Throughout the whole period, however, approaches to IS strategy might reasonably be characterized as being based on a rational and deliberate paradigm, as illustrated in Figure 6.2. Here, we see many of the approaches in common usage focusing on a deliberate, single outcome of profit maximization, based on a rational analysis of what are deemed to be business imperatives. Little attention has been paid to more emergent, pluralistic and innovative strategizing. In addition, there has been a tendency, certainly in practice, to assume the equivalence of data, information and knowledge. Latterly, however, both tendencies have been brought into question, as we shall see later.

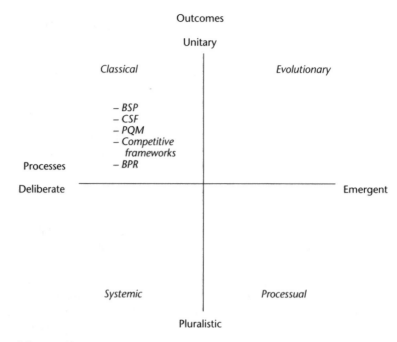

Figure 6.2   Locating common information systems strategy approaches
Source: Based on Whittington (1993).

From Localized Exploitation to Business Scope Redefinition

A related but somewhat different framework developed to capture the changes in the nature of IS strategic thinking was identified during a major research programme that was co-ordinated by Massachusetts Institute of Technology (MIT) under the title *Management in the 1990s*. The programme was funded by major corporations from both sides of the Atlantic and sought to uncover means by which IT could be harnessed to provide truly significant advances in terms of business performance. One of the resultant frameworks is reproduced here as Figure 6.3. A conclusion that the research team drew was that many companies were obtaining only relatively low business benefits from their investment in and application of IT because very few were actually attempting any business transformation (i.e. most companies were operating at levels 1 and 2 of this framework). Such evolutionary approaches, the researchers argued, would not deliver the requisite order of magnitude improvements being sought, and that they deemed to be necessary, in highly competitive markets. This could only occur by way of revolutionary change of the style put forward by the BPR advocates. 'Don't automate, obliterate' was the uncompromising title of one famous article by Michael Hammer which appeared in *Harvard Business Review*. But, as we have seen, BPR focused for the most part on internal process redesign. The MIT team extended the focus of BPR, in much the same way as the Porterian school had done with the value chain concept, to include what they termed 'business network redesign'. In other words, extending the process analysis to ensure electronic links along the value chain, to

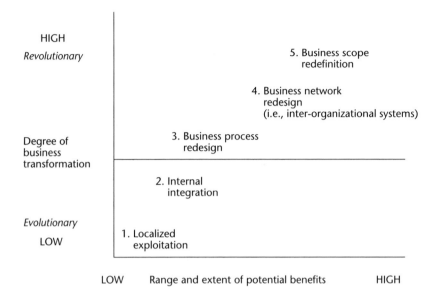

HIGH
Revolutionary

5. Business scope
redefinition

4. Business network
redesign
(i.e., inter-organizational systems)

Degree of
business
transformation

3. Business process
redesign

2. Internal
integration

Evolutionary

LOW

1. Localized
exploitation

LOW   Range and extent of potential benefits   HIGH

Figure 6.3   The MIT 'Management in the 1990s' programme: revolutionary change on the back of IT leads to major business benefits
Source: Venkatraman, N. (1991). IT-induced business reconfiguration. *In The Corporation of the 1990s: Information Technology and Organization Transformation* (ed. M. S. Scott Morton), New York: Oxford University Press.

include suppliers and customers to form electronically mediated strategic alliances. At that stage, this would have involved utilizing electronic data interchange (EDI) technology. Nowadays, the worldwide web (WWW) and the Internet would be used.

The conclusion from this MIT work was that truly significant business benefits would emerge from redefining the very scope of the business by utilizing the full power of IT to create new products and services (stage 5 in Figure 6.3). Examples that have entered the mythology of strategic IS include the Apollo and Sabre airline reservation systems of United Airlines and American Airlines. These systems were introduced initially with a view to increasing the efficiency of the reservation process. After all, the value of an empty seat on an aircraft after take-off is zero. The systems underwent various enhancements and, somewhat serendipitously, provided American Airlines and United Airlines with what their competitors viewed as being an unfair advantage. The enhancements included making data on flights and seat availability, prices, etc., available in real-time to travel agents. American Airlines and United Airlines were required to list other airlines' flights too, but these were listed after their own flights. The outcome? Travel agents filled up American Airlines or United Airlines flights first before bothering to look at alternatives.

Max Hopper, CEO of American Airlines, has been quoted as saying that he would have preferred to have his fleet grounded than his airline reservation system crash. The reason? Greater profitability from the reservation system than from running the largest passenger airline fleet in the world! This is because the system has been leased to many other major airlines the world over.

A similar system was introduced by Thompson Holidays in the United Kingdom. Called TOPS, this system provided the package holiday company with a distinct advantage over its rivals, which were reliant on telephone or postal bookings for the most

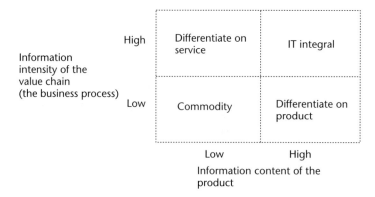

Figure 6.4 Applying the 'information intensity' matrix

part. This was so particularly during the price war that took place in the mid-1980s. Why? Access to Thompson was facilitated by the TOPS software. Access to their rivals was often difficult due to busy telephone lines and postal delays. Thompson stole a major share of the market as a result.

While Figure 6.3 stresses only the revolutionary potential of IT, it is clear that it is not always sensible to revolutionize. A means of deciding whether there is potential strategic advantage to be gained from providing added value services based on information is provided by the so-called 'information intensity matrix'. This is illustrated in Figure 6.4.

Here, we are asked to consider the extent to which information forms a critical part of the value chain activities and of the product itself. In situations where this 'information intensity' is high, it can be concluded that IT is integral to the delivery of goods and services. Where it is low, the potential use of IT is more limited. Competing on the basis of providing additional information in terms of the product itself or in relation to value-chain processes can also be considered utilizing this framework. So, consider the VBA case, the Alsmeer flower auction, just outside of Amsterdam's Schiphol airport, included in Case Box 6.1. Here, added value information is provided both in relation to the business processes (e.g., in terms of demand patterns and billing) and to the products themselves (e.g., quality, colour, perfume). The case of VBA also illustrates how IT has been utilized to improve competitiveness through business scope redefinition.

Case Box 6.1 VBA – The Aalsmeer Flower Auction

You are about to land at Amsterdam's Schipol airport. As you survey the flat Dutch landscape below, your eye catches sight of what seems like row upon row of low lying buildings, covering an area of what must be the equivalent of 100 football fields. If you have ever experienced this sight and wondered what was housed in those buildings, it is VBA – the Aalsmeer flower auction. Buy a bunch of flowers anywhere in the world, in San Francisco, London, Singapore or Tokyo, and it is likely that they passed through VBA but a day or two before. VBA has virtually cornered the world's flower auction market, as a result of its astute use of IT to provide not only an efficient service, but one that adds value to both growers and buyers alike. How does it work?

First, the blooms are sent to VBA to be auctioned. There, they are graded for quality, perfume, colour, etc. and are placed in lots onto carts, somewhat similar to the golf carts that are familiar on many golf courses. The carts are guided into the auction rooms before hundreds of buyers sitting in a tiered horse shoe-shaped 'theatre'. Each has a console immediately in front of them, which they activate to make a bid. On the wall in front of all the buyers is a giant clock that is used to 'count down' the price of each lot. Remember that in a Dutch auction, the price starts at a high point and is counted down. It is the first bidder who purchases the lot.

Once the bid has been made, the carts are automatically dispatched to the buyer's loading bay and, while the auction continues, invoices are automatically prepared. In this way, once the auction is over, the buyers can settle their accounts and return to their loading bay to find all of their purchases already loaded for transport. Speed of transaction is of the essence of course, since the blooms have a finite life. And the Dutch auction system – and the IT employed by VBA – is particularly effective in this regard. But there is more to the VBA service than mere efficiency. Information is provided to both growers and buyers alike. And it is this additional information that sets VBA's level of service apart from its competition. For example, growers obtain information on demand trends so that they can bring on their blooms faster or slower to meet demand and get the best price. Buyers rely on VBA's expertise in grading the blooms and in providing information on varying demand the world over.

Thus, VBA not only provides an efficient auction service, it also provides added value services to its customers in the form of information – and this is enabled by the IT systems it has employed. While the IT systems can be readily and easily copied by the competition, the expertise and goodwill VBA has built up over the years mean that they have been able to sustain their advantage.

1. *How would you describe the IT system developed by VBA: isolated, reactive, prospective or proactive? Justify your answer in terms of the model in Figure 6.1.*
2. *Where would you place the VBA example on the MIT model depicting the degree of business transformation (Figure 6.3)?*
3. *Apply the information intensity matrix (Figure 6.4) to VBA. What do you conclude from this?*
4. *Explore the possibilities for further encouraging business transformation using IT in the VBA case.*

Distinguishing the Elements of an IS/IT Strategy

Much of this MIT work suggests that the key issue is to align the IS strategy with the business strategy, as do approaches such as BSP, CSF and PQM. However, there is quite a conceptual gap between a business strategy and the necessary IT infrastructure to

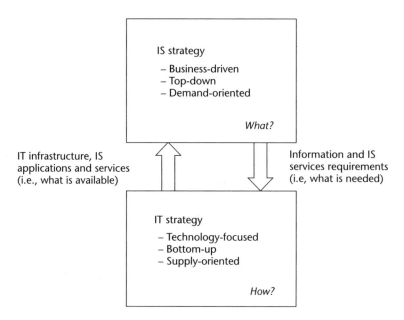

Figure 6.5   Earl's distinction between information systems and information technology strategy

support such a strategy. This is demonstrated by Michael Earl in his distinction between the components of an IS as against an IT strategy. He argues that the former is essentially concerned with *what* information is required, while the latter is concerned with *how* IT might be used to provide that information. The distinction is illustrated in Figure 6.5.

Note that Earl proposes that the IS strategy is essentially business-led and demand-driven. In other words, it can be seen as a 'top-down' process, feeding off the business strategy. Further, he argues that IS strategy should be the concern of the business executive – not IT. Conversely, in his terms, the IT strategy is seen as being more technologically and supply-driven, in that it depends in part on the *existing* technological infrastructure (i.e., what is feasible, from a technological standpoint, within the current planning horizon). It is much more within the province of the IT director, therefore. Earl's distinction also brings with it some implications for the concept of alignment. For example, IS strategy is viewed here as being ongoing and processual – it is about strategizing in other words. Conversely, the IT strategy is (relatively) fixed. This makes alignment difficult – but more on this later. Earl developed this line of thinking further by adding another component to IS and IT strategy, namely information management (IM) strategy.

Having asked the 'what?' and the 'how?' questions, the IM strategy, in Earl's formulation, asks the question 'wherefore'? Or, in other words, 'why?' Why this particular strategy as against any other?

Galliers, building on this earlier work of Earl, produced a more comprehensive framework for IS strategy, to incorporate each of Earl's components. This is depicted in Figure 6.6. Galliers's framework also included the questions related to:

Figure 6.6 Components of IS strategy

(1) 'what?' (the information strategy);
(2) 'how?' (the IT strategy); and
(3) 'why?' (the business strategy).

But it added the additional question – 'who?' Moreover, it considered issues related to implementing the strategy and the attendant management of change issues.

In terms of the 'who?' question, the model emphasizes the importance of developing an integrated information services strategy, considering the organizational arrangements for the provision of IS services. In particular, a key question here is whether to outsource the IT provision – a strategy that became particularly popular in the 1980s and into the 1990s. IT outsourcing refers to the 'significant contribution by external vendors in the physical and/or human resources associated with the entire or specific components of the IT infrastructure in the user organization' (Loh and Venkatraman, 1994: p. 264). So, with IT and IT services outsourced, a firm has to rely on a third party to integrate IT into its business strategy. It can be argued that IT outsourcing gained momentum as a result of two major factors. The first related to top executives' growing frustration with the apparent inability of IT *management* (our emphasis) to deliver promised business benefits and so shareholder value. The second related to the argument posed by Prahalad and Hamel for organizations to focus on what they called their core competence. Almost by definition in most industries then, IT would not have been seen as core, and has therefore been outsourced in many companies. The downside? Relying on third parties to provide IT services, firms' ability to differentiate themselves from their competition on the back of IT and their ability to integrate their IS and business strategies have both been seriously eroded.

The second additional element in the Galliers model is the explicit recognition of the importance of managing the change process. He had become very much aware from empirical research and consultancy assignments that the outcome of many IS strategy projects was what might be termed 'shelfware', in that little IS *implementation* occurred as a result of such projects, with plans often collecting dust on the office shelf. In addition, it appeared that few lessons had been learnt from the mainstream literature on strategizing. This was particularly in relation to the consideration of implementation and change management issues from the start (see Chapter 10, 'Strategy as Process, Power and Change' for more on this). Additionally, he was very much aware of the *emergent* quality of strategies and strategizing and, drawing on systems theory (see Chapter 9, 'Strategy as Systems Thinking'), the need to monitor and learn from the unintended consequences of strategic decisions (see Chapter 4, 'Strategy as Intention and Anticipation'). The model incorporated change management and ongoing review and feedback (see Figure 6.6).

The suggestion is that this framework can be used in analysing IS/IT strategies in organizations by considering the extent to which each of the components is in place. This may provide an insight into the orientation of any particular organization towards IS strategy. For example, does the organization emphasize IT strategy (the how?) to the detriment of identifying strategic information requirements (the what?)? Or does the organization consider implementation and change management issues as part of their strategizing? In addition, however, it suggests that each component of the IS strategy is mutually dependent on each other component. So, for example, questions can be asked as to whether strategic decisions regarding the organization of IS services (e.g., whether they should be centralized or distributed; whether to outsource or not) are considered as an integral part of the IS strategy, or whether they are considered in isolation. Similarly, questions can be asked, not only in relation to the extent to which required information is identified in line with the existing business strategy, but also if information is available that can actually question whether the strategy is appropriate or not, given changing business circumstances, and as a consequence of the ongoing assessment and review of outcomes. This is the 'why'? question that appears in Figure 6.6. An illustration of how the Galliers model can be applied is provided in Case Box 6.2.

Case Box 6.2   Ebank

Ebank has around 70,000 employees and operates in approximately 70 countries worldwide. It has its headquarters in Europe. Ebank was formed from a merger of two banks from the same country and has subsequently grown through the acquisition of banks in the various countries in which it now operates. Its structure is highly decentralized. A problem arose in Ebank when a key global client transferred its business to another bank. The client moved because it was dissatisfied that the procedures and services provided by Ebank were not consistent across the countries in which it operated. Ebank responded with the definition of a new business strategy that aimed to create 'The Networked Bank'.

The main way in which this strategy was to be achieved was through developing an intranet (an IT – 'how?' – solution) that would connect the various departments and units across its global operations. The idea was that this intranet would create a network across the bank so that knowledge and information could be shared more effectively across functions and geographical regions. It was assumed that this would lead to the sharing of 'best practices', which in turn would stimulate the integration of services and procedures.

Unfortunately, the actual impact of Ebank's strategy was exactly the opposite to that which had been intended. During the 18-month life of the pilot intranet project, more than 150 independent intranets had been set up by individual departments in individual countries. These intranets made communication between departments and functions more, rather than less, difficult. Moreover, even within an individual department, the intranet was used for little more than basic data sharing. For example, the most common use of one of the more sophisticated intranets that had been set up was to find the company bus timetable (to provide information on the company bus that circulated between Ebank's three headquarters buildings every 20 minutes)!

A key problem in this case, then, was that the existing structure and culture of Ebank (based on decentralization and autonomy) were not conducive to the stated strategy of developing common 'best practices'. Yet there had been no attempt to manage the change process and develop some common understanding. Instead the assumption was that the adoption of IT (in this case intranet technology) would drive through the stated business strategy of developing common procedures and services to accommodate the needs of global customers.

1. *Using the Galliers model of IS strategy (Figure 6.6), explore the reasons why Ebank failed to implement its intended business strategy.*
2. *Use the same model to identify what Ebank might have done to improve its chances of fulfilling its stated strategy.*

The identity of the bank has been kept confidential at its request.

Stages of Growth – Recognizing Organizational Limitations in Respect of IS/IT Strategy

Deciding on an appropriate strategy depends, in part at least, on an organization's ability to pull it off. As can be seen from Figure 6.7, there are occasions when it may well be advisable – notwithstanding the arguments of those that follow the revolutionary change school of thought – to follow a more conservative line. For example if, following an analysis of the information intensity of an organization's business processes and products and/or services (see Figure 6.4), the opportunities for value added by way of information are limited, a more evolutionary approach would appear to be called for. In addition, however, if the opportunities are there, but the capability is limited, then such an aggressive approach may well present too great a risk without outside assistance or the further development of internal human and technological resources.

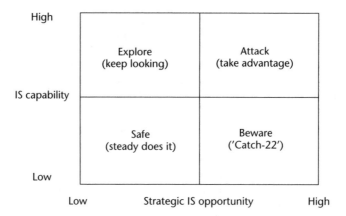

Figure 6.7 When – and when not – to pursue an aggressive business strategy based on the strategic application of information technology

The problem is that many organizations find themselves in the 'catch-22' position of the lower right-hand quadrant of Figure 6.7. In a sense, they are damned if they do, and they are damned if they don't. In such circumstances they have to beware of the aggressive strategies of a competition that might well have greater IS capability than themselves. In response, they may well attempt a similar strategy themselves, but fail in the attempt due to their lack of internal IS resources – human as well as technical. Should they decide the risk is too great and do little in response, they are likewise open to attack. But, how might an organization evaluate their current IS capability? Well, one approach is to assess their current IS strategy using the framework illustrated in Figure 6.6. But this provides an overview only. A more detailed positioning framework is provided in Figure 6.8. This is based on a combination of the so-called 'stages of growth' thesis first enunciated by Dick Nolan, of Harvard Business School, and on the well-known McKinsey '7-S framework'.

Nolan's Stages model has its roots in Greiner's earlier work on organizational change as a series of evolutionary and revolutionary phases. It essentially posits that firms will grow in maturity through recognizable 'stages' in terms of their management and use of IT. Nolan first formulated a four-stage model but later extended this to six stages to take account of the database technology that was becoming available at the time. This technology enabled firms to integrate their systems across functions and business units in a manner that had previously been impossible (see the second stage of the MIT model in Figure 6.3). His six stages were:

I. Initiation
II. Contagion
III. Control
IV. Integration
V. Data administration
VI. Maturity

The story unfolds as follows:

- First, organizations are relatively unaware of the capabilities and potential uses of new and emerging IT (stage I).
- But once they have a few adherents there is a kind of 'me too' mentality that sweeps through the organization and demand increases almost exponentially (stage II).
- As a result, management becomes increasingly concerned that things – and especially budgets – are getting out of control, and they therefore impose tighter controls on IS/IT expenditure (stage III).
- As management becomes increasingly aware that the looked-for business benefits from the IT investment are escaping them because of lack of compatibility between different systems and a lack of information flow across processes and functions, further investment occurs in technologies that enable greater systems integration (stage IV).
- This stage leads into one during which greater efforts are expended in ensuring that the data that are being shared are consistent (e.g., in terms of definition and interpretation) across the organization (stage V).
- The final stage of maturity is reached once integration is complete and compatibility is assured (stage VI).

As is implied by the above, patterns of expenditure on IS/IT give a clue as to which stage an organization has reached. Expenditure accelerates during stages II and IV/V and tapers off in stages III and VI – thus following a kind of double-S curve.

While Nolan's model has been criticized in academic circles for its lack of conceptual underpinnings and its failure to provide an accurate prediction of growth empirically, it nonetheless was highly popular and used extensively by many major corporations in the English-speaking world. Indeed, it spawned a consultancy company – Nolan Norton & Co. – that was eventually taken over by KPMG. Notwithstanding, it clearly had its limitations, particularly in relation to its technological focus, and an extended 'stages model' was developed by Bob Galliers and Tony Sutherland, following case study research in both Europe and Australia. This model, depicted here as Figure 6.8, focused on broader IM issues and, as already indicated, borrowed the earlier mentioned '7-S framework' which was in widespread circulation at the time.

The framework is difficult to take in at first glance and so an example of its application is provided in Case Box 6.3. Essentially, however, it parallels the Nolan model in terms of the six stages of growth, but renames them, as follows:

I.	Adhocracy	instead of	I.	Initiation
II.	Starting the foundations	instead of	II.	Contagion
III.	Centralized dictatorship	instead of	III.	Control
IV.	Democratic dialectic and co-operation	instead of	IV.	Integration
V.	Entrepreneurial opportunity	instead of	V.	Data administration
VI.	Integrated harmonious relationships	instead of	VI.	Maturity

Referring to the account of the developments in thinking and practice with respect to IS strategy earlier in this chapter, we can trace this development through the six stages of strategy growth. We can see, for example, that IS strategy develops from what

Stage / Element	I	II	III	IV	V	VI
Strategy	Acquisition of IT (services)	Audit of IT provision	Top-down analysis	Integration, co-ordination	Competitive advantage	Interactive planning, collaboration
Structure	Informal	Finance controlled	Centralized IS department	Information centre	SBU coalition	Co-ordinated solutions
Systems	Ad-hoc operational, accounting	Gaps/duplication large backlog, heavy maintenance	Uncontrolled end-user computing versus centralized systems	Decentralized approach, some executive information systems	Co-ordinated centralized and decentralized IS, some strategic IS	Inter-organizational systems, IS/IT-based products and services
Staff	Programmers, contractors	Systems analysts, data manager	IS planners, IS manager, database specialists	Business analysts, information resource manager	Business and IS planners integrated	IS/IT director (board level)
Style	Unaware	'Don't bother me (I'm too busy)'	Abrogation, delegation	Partnership, benefits management	Individualistic (product champions)	Multidisciplinary teams (key themes)
Skills	Individual, technical, low-level	Systems development methodology, cost-benefit analysis	IS awareness, project management	IS/business awareness	Entrepreneurial marketing	Lateral thinking (IT/IS potential)
Shared values	Naivety	Confusion	Senior management concern, IS defence	Co-operation	Opportunistic	Strategy making and implementation

Figure 6.8 An extended 'stages of growth' model
Source: Amended from Galliers and Sutherland (1991); elements from Pascale and Athos (1981).

is little more than the acquisition of IS products and services on more or less an ad hoc basis, through to top-down, business-led planning (see Earl's model) and on to competitive advantage. The sixth stage is characterized by a strategy which integrates IS considerations into the business strategy itself. Similarly, we can trace developments in the kind of staff and skills that are available to the organization (whether in-house or through a sourcing arrangement). Managerial attitudes towards the strategic aspects of IS/IT can also be traced. From the bewilderment and confusion of the early stages of growth (stages I and II), there has been a tendency for management to adopt the somewhat negative and adversarial stance associated with stage III. This has tended to be as a result of past disappointments and concerns over spiralling IT expenditure – with sometimes little in the way of business benefits in return. The latter stages are characterized by a more positive, but informed perspective. More specifically, with growing co-operation and a realization that greater integration across functions and business units is called for, a more concerted approach towards integration is evident in stage IV. A more outward-facing perspective characterizes stages V and VI, with an entrepreneurialist and opportunistic stance being in evidence.

The foregoing might unwittingly give the sense that all this development is pre-ordained and is followed in every instance. This is far from being the case. The model is no more than a model – a positioning framework. It has been found to be useful in enabling useful *questions* to be asked as to the current state of play with respect to the management of IS in organizations, and managerial attitudes towards IS/IT. It does not purport to provide any *answers*. It is an aid to sense-making and, used judiciously, it can be of assistance in gaining a shared appreciation of key IS management issues on the part of management teams. It is a subjective measure, and opinions will sometimes diverge, but it at least provides a kind of benchmark against which to assess matters, and to begin to understand why certain views are held by some and not others.

Case Box 6.3 'Midlands Chemicals PLC'

With its headquarters located in the centre of England, this company has been involved in the chemical industry since the late nineteenth century. It is a major international player in its particular niche market, and now holds fourth place by annual turnover in world terms. Major competitors are located in the USA and China.

'Joe Taylor', the newly appointed CEO, has recently been headhunted from the US competitor, and has been impressed by articles that indicate that competitive advantage can be gained from the astute use of IT. So much so that his first senior appointment was 'Chris Mayday' as chief information officer or CIO (i.e., IT director) as a full member of the board. Joe's mind is very much focused on competitive advantage of late as a result of the troubling news that Midlands has fallen from third to fourth place in the world rankings – overtaken by one of its two major Chinese competitors.

Chris had come to Midlands with glowing references from his previous appointments. He was considered by many in the industry, and in the media, as being in line for a CEO position, thanks to the turnaround he was able to achieve at his previous company. Note the use of the past tense in the previous sentence, however! Things had not progressed particularly well since his appointment at Midlands. The board had given him a free hand, but little had apparently been achieved. Other board members failed to be impressed with him or with IT. What had this to do with chemicals? Hadn't they managed well enough without IT up till now? And what language did Chris speak anyhow? It certainly was not English!

Troubled by the lack of progress and by the board's general antagonism towards Chris and his initiatives, Joe invited an IS strategy expert – 'Guy Mooney' – to come and assist the Midlands board in taking stock of the situation and in coming up with a realizable strategy. Following a briefing session during which Guy explained his approach, a one and a half day 'retreat' was arranged, with all board members required to attend.

Things did not start auspiciously. First, it was obvious that few board members were looking forward to being away from their respective duties for 'a full day and a half'. Second, it appeared to Guy that relationships among the board were not as good as they might be. Team spirit and mutual co-operation did not appear to be on their agenda. Third, Chris appeared to be in a beleaguered position, almost ostracized from the rest of the group. He cut a lonely figure, drinking his coffee in the corner prior to the meeting getting under way. And finally, as if all this was not bad enough – and despite the briefing session – the meeting was introduced by Joe with the comment that Guy was an expert who

Stage Element	I	II	III	IV	V	VI
Strategy		Provision	Top-down analysis	Integration, co-ordination	Competitive advantage	Interactive planning, collaboration
Structure				Information Centre	SBU coalition	Co-ordinated solutions
Systems			Uncontrolled end-user computing versus centralized systems	Decentralized approach, some executive information systems	Co-ordinated centralized and decentralized IS, some strategic IS	Inter-organizational systems, IS/IT-based products and services
Staff			IS planners, IS manager, database specialist	Business analysts, information resource manager	Business and IS planners integrated	
Style			Abrogation, delegation	Partnership, benefits management	Individualistic (product champions)	Multidisciplinary teams (key themes)
Skills		Systems development methodology, cost-benefit analysis	IS awareness, project management	IS/business awareness	Entrepreneurial marketing	Lateral thinking (IT/IS potential)
Shared values			Senior management concern, IS defence	Co-operation	Opportunistic	Strategy making and implementation

Figure 6.9 An extended 'stages of growth' model applied to Midland Chemicals

was going to tell them what was wrong and what their strategy ought to be. Guy had been at pains to explain that his role was one of facilitation, and that any resultant decisions were to be the board's, not his.

After an uncertain start, and a quickly arranged coffee break, Guy was able to get the board to agree on the process by which they would take stock of the situation. During the break, he managed to get the ear of Joe, Chris and another board member, Judy, who had appeared more ready to listen than most. With their help, the meeting got underway. Guy explained that Midlands would have somehow to take things more seriously than before and that IS strategy really was a matter for the board, as a whole. He introduced the extended stages model and was able to ask questions that led the board to come to some level of agreement (sometimes after heated debate) as to where things stood at that point in time. A summary of their conclusions is provided above in Figure 6.9.

So, what did this analysis mean for Midlands Chemicals? First, there was immediate recognition on the part of the CEO and the board that any appointment of a CIO as a member of the board would not necessarily lead to improved management of IS/IT. A CIO at board level may be a necessary appointment, but it isn't sufficient. The Midlands board had simply left responsibility for IS strategy to Chris alone and had not taken shared responsibility for either the formulation or implementation of that strategy. Indeed, some had withheld co-operation, either through apathy or antagonism.

A joke had circulated in the US during the 1990s that the title CIO had come to stand for 'career is over', given the large number of CIOs who had lost their jobs. One of the root causes of this high mortality rate was that many, like Chris, had been left to effect change alone. And when that change did not occur, or did not occur fast enough, they paid the price. They were made the scapegoat. Had not Joe and his fellow board members come to realize in time that they were beginning to scapegoat Chris, doubtless his career was about to end too.

Additionally, they realized that their desire to compete more aggressively on the back of IS/IT was likely to be doomed from the outset given their low capability. They needed to advance to around stage IV of the framework in order to have the necessary platform to succeed with such a strategy. This implied improvements in their skill base, changed attitudes and a more business-driven IS strategy. The board therefore initiated a number of projects, each championed by at least one of their number, and accountable to the CEO, with a view to bringing about the required change. In some instances the projects were a joint initiative between the CIO and another board member. For example, improving the skill base was the joint responsibility of Chris and the HR director. The team responsible for the revised IS strategy was jointly headed by Chris and the marketing director.

1. *What can we learn from the Midlands Chemicals case in terms of applying the extended stages model?*
2. *What are the limitations of the model when applied in this case? More generally?*
3. *Imagine a company that appeared to be positioned in stages V and VI. What next? What other models introduced thus far in this chapter might be employed to good effect?*

Note: (The identity of the company has been kept confidential at its request.)

It should be noted again that the extended stages model is a positioning framework only. It should be seen as a means of facilitating shared understanding as a result of posing a series of questions in relation to aspects of IS management, based on the 7-Ss. It certainly does not provide any answers. And shared understanding does not necessarily mean consensus. There may still be conflicting opinions being expressed in relation to an organization's position on the framework. But by discussing these different opinions, there can be growing understanding as to why it is those opinions are held.

Moreover, there is no God-given right for organizations to move inexorably through the stages towards stage VI. In the case of Midlands Chemicals, it had become stuck around stage II for quite a number of years. Indeed, some companies have realized that they have moved 'backwards' on occasion. A series of discussions as to why movement has or has not occurred may provide further insight. It is also the case that different parts of the organization may present a different profile one from another. In the Midlands Chemicals case, the profile presented above represented the view of the board about the situation generally. Later, the framework was discussed within different locations, business units and functions, and sometimes quite different profiles emerged. As a result, assessments could be made as to the reasons for these different perspectives. Questions were asked whether these differences were harmful and needed to be dealt with, or whether the company could live with them.

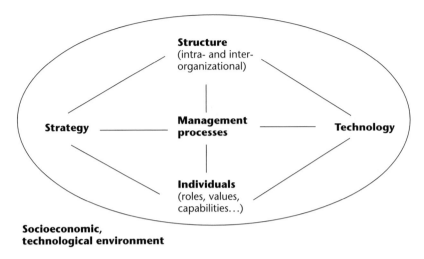

Figure 6.10   The MIT 'Model of Strategic Change and Fit'

Organizations will not find themselves at a particular stage with respect to all the elements, but some will lag 'behind' while others will be further 'ahead'. Again assessments can be made as to what these differences mean in terms of strategic directions and imperatives. Further, it will seldom be the case that an organization's profile will fit neatly into the stages: there will be elements that exhibit characteristics of more than one stage. This is an imprecise 'science'. However, it may prove useful to map the implied profile of a proposed strategy and contrast this with the existing situation. If there is considerable distance between the two, an assessment of the risks involved in attempting the proposed strategy can be made. In the Midlands Chemicals case, the intended strategy implied reaching stage VI within months. The board came to the conclusion that this was infeasible and scaled down their expectations to aim initially for stage IV, from which base stage VI could more feasibly be attained.

As a result of these kinds of deliberations using the extended stages model, the shared understanding reached should lead to the identification of change projects designed to move the organization to the desired location on the framework. This was the case with Midlands Chemicals in relation to the IS strategy itself and the HR initiatives.

The State of IS Strategy Thinking in the 1990s

As we have seen, the field of IS/IT strategy had come some distance in the latter part of the twentieth century. From a relatively isolated and narrow, technologically oriented activity, it had become much more business-oriented and competitively minded. There had been increasing realization, too, that the management of change and people issues are a significant – perhaps the key – aspect of the rubric. In some respects, though, IS/IT strategy has not come very far at all. We could infer this from Figure 6.2. In addition, we could argue that it has reached a point at which current thinking might also reasonably be summarized by another model arising from the MIT *Management in the 1990s* research. This appears as Figure 6.10.

For example, we had learnt our lessons from the many BPR failures that IS strategy and change were more, much more, than focusing on business processes and technology alone. People mattered, and their capabilities and knowledge had to be nurtured. Information systems needed to be seen as social systems, admittedly with an increasingly technological component, but not technological systems *per se*. The importance of all of these aspects of an IS strategy is illustrated in the AirCo case described in Case Box 6.4.

Case Box 6.4 AirCo

AirCo had 356 aircraft in 1999, operating over one thousand flights a day and flying 45 million passengers in 1998–99. It had approximately 64,000 staff worldwide, 80 per cent of them based in Europe. The issue confronting AirCo was that many of its central departments were housed in different buildings with consequent inefficiencies and complex communications. A new headquarters was therefore planned, presenting an opportunity to upgrade systems, utilizing the very best in IT. A project team was set up, with a representative from each of the departments affected by the proposed move. The initial major objective was to save money through streamlining procedures, reducing paper usage and reducing head count. The project was perceived by the project team as representing not only an opportunity to save money but also as an opportunity to improve communications across departmental boundaries and to stimulate innovative thinking. The scope for the project was thus expanded to include new ways of working, streamlined procedures and extensive training for all those involved in the move. More importantly perhaps, the project team recognized the importance of encouraging widespread participation in the project. In this way, the very process of preparing for the move set the tone for the new working environment with knowledge sharing and knowledge creation being encouraged and rewarded.

IT was used extensively in the new headquarters, including an intranet, to facilitate communication across the group. However, the building was also designed to enable informal meetings to take place – with coffee bars and meeting places located on either side of a main thoroughfare. Individuals did not have fixed offices, but were rather encouraged to 'hot desk' to facilitate interaction across a wider range of people. In this way, the IT was seen to complement, rather than supplant, face-to-face communication.

1. Consider the AirCo case in relation to *the MIT model of strategic change and fit (Figure 6.10). What do you see as the key elements in the approach adopted that made the project a success?*
2. Compare the introduction of IT in AirCo, with the introduction of IT in the Ebank case discussed earlier. What are the key differences that help to explain the differential success of the two projects?

Note: (The identity of the company has been kept confidential at its request.)

While this MIT model moves us well beyond the technical focus of earlier IS strategy models, the similarities between this model and Leavitt's 'diamond' of the mid-1960s should be noted. Harold Leavitt suggested that organizations could be viewed as complex systems, consisting of four interacting variables – objectives, structure, technology and people. These variables clearly bear a remarkable similarity to those identified in the MIT model. IS strategy had indeed come a long way, but it also still has a very long way to go to catch up with other strategy discourse. This is illustrated in the penultimate section of this chapter on recent developments and new thinking, which illustrates some prevailing myths about the potential of IT that continue to be promoted in the twenty-first century.

Recent Developments and New Thinking

There have of course been many developments in IT in recent years – the worldwide web (www) and the Internet, for example. In this section of the chapter, recent developments in IT will be considered in relation to various strategy issues. Specifically, we will argue that, despite developments in thinking about IS strategy, as discussed above, many myths about IT continue to be promulgated:

* myths about how to strategically develop IT;
* myths about how to use IT to support knowledge management; and
* myths about IT and competitive advantage.

Myths about how to strategically develop IT

There are essentially two related elements to this myth:

(i)   that IT systems should align with the business strategy; and
(ii) that IT systems should be rationally planned.

First, as noted earlier in this chapter, a central tenet of much of the theory and practice of IS/IT strategy has been the concept of alignment. Intuitively appealing, alignment has been a taken-for-granted concept that has remained largely unchallenged. The problem is how to align IT, which is relatively fixed, with the business strategy, which needs to be incessantly modified in line with changes in the external environment. Earl's distinction between IS strategy and IT strategy (Figure 6.4) is very helpful in terms of demarcating the two terms, as we have seen. However, the distinction does not help to overcome a key issue with respect to alignment. That issue concerns the fact that, for the great majority of organizations, their information needs are in constant flux. Of course, there is a subset of information requirements that remains reasonably constant over time, but with fast-changing competitive environments, that subset is by no means representative of the totality. Conversely, organizations are investing in IT that will remain with them for quite some time, and will have to serve the test of time. In other words, IT decisions, while they may be cumulative, are one-off and fixed notwithstanding. The question of alignment is therefore vexed: changing information requirements and (relatively) unchanging technology. Increasingly, too, alignment is required along the (virtual) value chain – with electronic links to suppliers and customers alike. And with the open nature of the Internet, and with new customers and sources emerging constantly, this can complicate matters enormously. 'Alignment with whom?' becomes a significant and increasingly difficult question to answer.

Second, as we have seen, most of the approaches to IT development suggest an objective rational analysis of present IT needs as if one was starting with a blank sheet of paper. For example, the *revolutionary* or 'radical' approach championed by the MIT team, or as articulated by the advocates of the BPR approach, both start from the premise that a rational analysis of IT needs should be undertaken. Indeed, the notion of alignment suggests that developing IS strategy is a rational and deliberate activity.

There is an increasingly strong school of thought surrounding the *emergent* nature of IS strategy and of strategic IS; about the importance of allowing strategies to emerge and grow organically over time. Moreover, many of the successful IT systems that have been developed, for example the Apollo and Sabre airline reservation systems mentioned earlier, have emerged through a process of gradual enhancement and improvisation. Ciborra uses the terms tinkering and bricolage to signify the bubbling up of innovative ideas within organizations. The AirCo example provides a useful illustration of this bricolage. What started as a mere cost-saving exercise developed into something much more comprehensive, through involving employees in the process of considering how they might work differently in the new headquarters building, and through readapting to and learning in the new working environment.

This analysis suggests that no amount of rational planning can ever hope to create an IT system that aligns with the business strategy, even in the short term. IT system development is thus best considered as an interactive process, which is constantly ongoing and emergent as new information needs arise and new opportunities are identified.

Myths about how to use IT to support knowledge management

'Knowledge management' is one of the latest fads to flash before the eyes of managers. The emergence of this concept followed the 'discovery' that knowledge is perhaps *the* key resource of organizations, allowing them to innovate and compete. Perhaps ironically, this recognition occurred at about the same time as the BPR revolution, when much valuable knowledge passed through companies' back doors along with legions of middle-ranking executives made redundant in the name of efficiency – often as a direct result of BPR initiatives (see Chapter 7, 'Strategy as Creativity' for more on this).

'Enterprise resource planning' or ERP systems were subsequently developed, and these were supposedly more in tune with this recognition of the importance of organizational knowledge. ERP systems have been diffused and adopted widely during the late 1990s and early 2000s, sold on the premise that they will assist in integrating knowledge about business processes across functions, business units and locations in order to improve efficiency. Importantly, ERP systems are promoted as systems to transfer 'best practice' knowledge. Thus, a key feature of ERP systems is that they have built-in processes so that a company adopting an ERP system is forced to adapt the organization and the processes to the exigencies of ERP software. These in-built processes are, supposedly, based on 'best practice' industry models. In this instance, then, IT has been a force for standardization, thus *speeding* competitive convergence, given that the model remains more or less constant irrespective of the company implementing the ERP system. The myth is thus created that by adopting an ERP system a company will also be transferring to itself the 'best practice' industry knowledge of how best to organize various processes.

It is clear to see the appeal of 'best practice' solutions – it is the holy grail of management to be able to capture what is 'best' elsewhere and copy this to become similarly successful. However, the assumption that there is something such as a generic 'best practice' is highly questionable in our fragmenting world, as described in Chapter 2, 'Strategy as Ethos' and illustrated in the examples in the case box at the end of this chapter.

Continuing with the myths created about ERP systems, it is interesting to consider such systems in relation to the earlier discussion about alignment. Thus, ERP systems are sold partly on the basis of the need to replace 'legacy systems', which have become outdated and which no longer align with business goals. Presumably, however, in time, ERP systems themselves will be a legacy! Moreover, by advocating the copying of 'best practices' to improve efficiency, companies are, potentially at least, running the risk of reducing their capacity to create new knowledge and so innovate and creatively respond to the ever-changing environment – the key concern for any business strategy, surely. Another way of putting this might be to think of the issue in terms of the age-old dilemma between efficiency and innovation, or between exploitation and exploration (see Chapter 8, 'Strategy as Exploration and Interconnection').

To illustrate, we can pick up on the cookery examples used at the end of Chapter 1. I may decide that, rather than learn to cook myself, I will use ready-made meals that simply need to be put in the oven or microwave and reheated. In doing this, I am exploiting someone else's knowledge, reusing their hard gained 'best practice' knowledge and skill as to how to actually make a particular dish such as lasagne. But this choice will mean that I do not learn to cook lasagne myself, never mind learn how to create something unique. Similarly, if a consultant is told that she/he must use existing solutions to solve clients' problems then she/he is exploiting existing solutions but at the expense of being able to create unique solutions later on.

The above distinction between efficiency and innovation is important in attempting to understand the role that IT can play in an IS strategy that seeks to harness the increasing power of the technology while facilitating innovation and knowledge creation in organizations – especially those that operate on a global basis. IS strategy, as we have seen, attempts to square the circle between *efficiency*, *effectiveness* and *competitiveness*. Competitiveness increasingly relies on constant innovation for it to be sustained. If IT (e.g., ERP systems) has been a force for competitive convergence and standardization, then how can we claim that such IT as this provides firms with new means of competing?

These problems and myths surrounding ERP systems can be related to more general myths that have emerged about knowledge management and IT systems. Most importantly, the myth has been created that suggests that IT systems can store and transfer *knowledge*, thus supporting and facilitating *knowledge exploitation* (the reuse of knowledge across time and space, for example by the transfer of 'best practices') *and knowledge creation*. The software solutions that were peddled as executive information systems or mere database systems but a few years ago have been metamorphosized by marketing people into the knowledge management systems of today. These systems are based on the view that knowledge is 'out there' to be harvested or mined – utilizing IT of course! We beg to differ.

To comprehend our argument more fully it is perhaps useful to go back to basics and understand the distinction between data, information and knowledge – terms that

Table 6.1   Key characteristics of data, information and knowledge

	Data	**Information**	**Knowledge**
is . . .	Explicit and prescriptive	Interpreted and adaptive	Tacit/embedded and seminal
is about . . .	Exploiting	Exploring	Creating
its aim is to . . .	Use	Build/construct	Rebuild/reconstruct
the approach . . .	Follow old recipes	Amend old recipes	Develop new recipes
learning? . . .	No learning	Single-loop learning*	Double-loop learning*
encourages . . .	Direction	Communication	Sense-making
criterion . . .	Efficiency	Effectiveness	Innovation/redundancy
set-up is . . .	Predetermined	Constrained	Flexible
system type . . .	Technical	Socio-technical	Social networks
context focus?	Context-free	Outer context	Inner context

Note: * The concepts of single and double loop learning are defined at the beginning of Chapter 9, 'Strategy as Systems Thinking'.
Source: Adapted from Galliers and Newell (2001).

tend to be used synonymously in everyday parlance. Data become informative for a particular purpose to human beings by them interpreting the world about them through their own individual lenses, and by applying their memory and personal knowledge to each new situation they confront. This is the way in which we innovate and adapt. Data are context-free and can be interpreted in many different ways for different purposes. The results of any election in any country will doubtless be interpreted in different ways by the victor and the vanquished! So-called information technology (IT) processes data, not information and certainly not knowledge therefore. We should, as a result, revert to the original terms used in the 1960s and 1970s and call computer-based systems by their former name, that is, data processing or DP systems. Individuals inform themselves in order to undertake some particular task or make a particular decision. Information is therefore context dependent, and information systems (IS) must include human beings and the act of interpretation for the term to be at all meaningful. This act of interpretation depends upon an individual's knowledge. Knowledge is tacit and embedded. It is individuals' 'justified belief'[1] that allows them to interpret data and take action in the world around them. It enables us to make sense of the data we capture. The distinction between the terms is made clearer in Table 6.1.

This characterization of knowledge or, rather, *knowing* suggests that knowledge sharing is facilitated through discourse and dialogue. Thus, the emphasis is on developing 'communities of practice' (a term introduced by Brown and Duguid and already mentioned in Chapter 4, 'Strategy as Intention and Anticipation'), and on project teams where individuals interact over time to develop a shared understanding that can lead to innovation and creativity. IT systems can support, at least partially, this dialogue. But IT systems cannot store or transfer knowledge *per se*. IT systems store and transfer data that will be interpreted in each context by individuals making sense of these data based on their personal knowledge or their wisdom gained from past experiences.

Myths about IT and competitive advantage

Undoubtedly, the growth and impact of the Internet have been the most noticeable development in IT in recent years, spawning so-called dot.com companies and a considerable degree of hyperbole concerning e-business. Subsequently, the myth that such developments in IT fundamentally would change the basis of competition quickly became widespread.

In a compelling *Harvard Business Review* article published in 2001, however, Michael Porter argues with some vigour that firms should view the Internet as a complement to, rather than something that cannibalizes, more traditional forms of organization and organizational IT. While some have argued that 'the Internet renders strategy obsolete . . . the opposite is true . . . it is more important than ever for companies to distinguish themselves through strategy'.

His argument echoes what he was saying 20 years ago: it is not the technology (in this case the Internet) itself that will create competitive advantage but the *uses* to which it is put that may do so. As ever, he sees the two fundamental factors that will ultimately determine profitability as being industry structure and sustainable competitive advantage. The former determines the profitability of the average competitor. The latter allows a firm to outperform the average competitor (refer to Chapter 1 for a brief summary of Porter's key arguments).

Porter goes on to argue that, while the Internet has created new companies and even industries (e.g., on-line auctions and financial institutions), its impact will be felt most in enabling 'the reconfiguration of existing industries that had been constrained by high costs for communicating, gathering information, or accomplishing transactions'. He gives, as examples, distance learning programmes, catalogue retailers and automated fulfilment centres, and argues that the Internet 'only changes the front end of the process'.

Hence Porter sticks to his guns with respect to his five-forces analysis. They 'still determine profitability even if suppliers, channels, substitutes, or competitors change'. However, because the impact of each force varies from industry to industry, he argues that it would not be appropriate to attempt to draw any general conclusions regarding the Internet's impact on long-term profitability. He does point to some general trends, though, and he notes the following:

- IT tends to bolster *buyer bargaining power* by providing easier access to information on products and services.
- IT reduces *barriers to entry* by circumventing existing channels, and creates *substitute* products and services.
- *Rivalry* intensifies as a result of the open nature of the Internet and the resultant difficulties firms confront in retaining proprietary offerings.
- *Rivalry* also intensifies as a result of the global reach of the new technology.
- Finally, he argues that the Internet's tendency to reduce variable costs leads to pressure to engage in price competition.

'The great paradox of the Internet', Porter explains, 'is that its very benefits – making information widely available; reducing the difficulty of purchasing, marketing, and distribution; allowing buyers and sellers to find and attract business with one another more easily – also make it more difficult for companies to capture those benefits as profits.'

As a result of this analysis, Porter foresees greater competition due to increased numbers of competitors and pressure on prices, exacerbated by growing customer power. With the average profitability of most industries falling, the need for individual firms 'to set themselves apart from the pack' grows considerably. This leads to the conclusion that advantages must be gained in terms of cost and price – through improved operational efficiency and effectiveness, and through strategic positioning, through doing things differently from the competition. 'The Internet affects operational effectiveness and strategic positioning in very different ways. It makes it harder for companies to sustain competitive advantages, but it opens new opportunities for achieving or strengthening a distinctive strategic positioning'. However, Porter's 'six principles of strategic positioning', listed below remain fundamental.

(1) *Set the right goal* – superior long-term return on investment.
(2) *Deliver a value proposition* – a differentiated set of benefits for one's customers.
(3) *Provide a distinctive value chain* – a different set of activities than those of the competition.
(4) *Make trade-offs* – forgoing some product features or services in order to be unique in others.
(5) *Ensure fit* – making strategic choices throughout the value chain that are interdependent.
(6) *Ensure continuity of direction* – defining a distinctive value proposition and sticking with it, even if it means forgoing certain opportunities.

It should be clear from the foregoing that Porter is arguing that the Internet has not altered the basic principles of competitive advantage. His 2001 article concludes that:

> In our quest to see how the Internet is different, we have failed to see how the Internet is the same. While a new means of conducting business has become available, the fundamentals of competition remain unchanged, The next stage of the Internet's evolution will involve a shift in thinking from e-business to business, from e-strategy to strategy. Only by integrating the Internet into overall strategy will this powerful new technology become an equally powerful force for competitive advantage.

Porter consequently sees competitive advantage as being gained by those companies that can *integrate* uses of the Internet with traditional means of doing business. He argues that it is easier for 'traditional' companies to do this than for dot.coms to adopt and integrate traditional approaches. But the traditional strengths of any company remain the same, with or without the Internet, for example, unique products, superior knowledge of products and customers, strong personal service and relationships. The key for the future may well be developing the ability to embrace the beneficial aspects of IT to develop a company's competitive advantage without letting that IT (which is in itself easily copied) erode or become *the* competitive advantage.

Conclusion

What does all this mean for IS strategy in general and for the use of information and knowledge in strategy formulation and implementation in general? We hesitate to propose a framework that captures all of the above – and, indeed, the very concept of a framework might be seen to be antithetical to the arguments we have propounded in this chapter. Having said that, the spirit of this book is that frameworks do help with respect to sense making, and are useful in providing some sort of grounding against which informed debate and communication might take place. It is in this spirit that we put forward the following.

Figure 6.11 builds on Figure 6.6, but is an attempt to incorporate some of the more recent thinking that we have just introduced. This model introduces the concept of an information architecture in an attempt to connote an enabling socio-technical environment for both the exploitation of knowledge (efficiency) and the exploration of knowledge (innovation).

The concept of an information infrastructure has developed in response to the need for greater flexibility, given changing information requirements. In the 1980s and into the 1990s, the term information infrastructure usually connoted the standardization of corporate IT, systems and data with a view to reconciling centralized processing with distributed applications. Increasingly, however, the concept has come to mean not just data and systems, but the human infrastructure (roles, skills, capabilities, viewpoints, etc.), as depicted in Figure 6.11 – and this is where knowledge creation and sharing play an important role. Star and Ruhleder unbundle the concept still further by talking of infrastructures in terms of, for example, their embeddedness, transparency, reach, links with conventions of practice, and installed base. Infrastructures are thus seen as being heterogeneous and socio-technical in nature.

Information systems strategy, incorporating an information architecture strategy, as depicted here, is meant to be interpreted as being a part, albeit an increasingly important part, of a *collaborative* business strategy. Collaborative, because the focus will be not just in relation to internal matters, but will also, crucially, involve partner organizations, such as customers, suppliers and those organizations, for example, with whom sourcing arrangements are in place (see Case Box 5.1 on Levi's and Land Rover's 'value webs' in Chapter 5). The implication here is that the very boundary of an organization will become increasingly porous and debatable.

Strategy, especially IS strategy, needs therefore to take this into account given the virtual nature of many collaborative arrangements. IS strategy, therefore, in addition to the more deliberate, designed and codified IT 'solutions' that have conventionally been implemented, should also be seen as being:

- ongoing and processual;
- crucially dependent on learning from 'below' as well as from outside or above;
- crucially dependent on tinkering and improvisation; and
- ready to learn from or respond to the emergent and unintended consequences of strategic decisions as has been outlined in Chapter 4, 'Strategy as Intention and Anticipation'.

Figure 6.11 incorporates the kind of embedded, socio-technical characteristics of information architectures – architectures that provide the kind of environment in which knowledge sharing and knowledge creation may be fostered. Strategic information, therefore, not only supports existing strategic processes, but also questions the kind of taken-for-granted assumptions on which they may be based. IT is there too. Not as *the* answer, not as a 'solution', but as a means of capturing data that may be interpreted in a purposeful, knowledgeable or wise manner, so as to make sense of phenomena in unique and individualized circumstances. And if you have found these frameworks

Figure 6.11   Towards a more inclusive framework for information systems strategizing

useful, then the ideas put forward in Chris Bilton et al.'s chapter, which follows, should inspire you further toward developing your own 'architectural' models for understanding, developing, configuring and reconfiguring the flow of information, knowledge and wisdom throughout organizations as they develop their strategies for the future.

Case Box 6.5   Examples of Strategy as Data plus Sense-making

A.   A global clothing manufacturer's Italian subsidiary adopted an ERP system's human resource module, which required automated recruiting and selection procedures. However, this proved counterproductive as informal, face-to-face recruitment was the accepted norm in this region. Recruiting performance actually declined until the automated parts of the new module were bypassed and personal interviewing was revived.

B.   Similarly, an international bank introduced a standard system for mortgage application processing, based on customers submitting their applications electronically. While this system worked well in certain countries where the bank operated, in others it actually slowed down the application process because customers did not have access to the Internet.

C.   Josephine Green, Director of Trends and Strategy at Philips and a regular guest speaker at WBS, likes to tell the story of how many consumer electronics companies started to use Italy as a launch pad/test market for new technology products after their data showed them that Italians adopted mobile phones incredibly quickly. This data, they presumed, indicated that Italians were unusually adaptive and receptive to new technology. But, several failed initiatives later, this was discovered not necessarily to be the case. If somebody had stopped to think about the context, Josephine says, they might have figured out that the Italians, generally speaking, do not so much love new technology more than the rest of the world does – they simply love fashion and they love to communicate. (As spending even a small amount of time in Italy would tell you.) Mobile phones had enabled them to express both of these loves at once.

D.   For a long time a well-known European manufacturer of home ware did not know what to make of the sales data from some of their new American branches. This data showed unusually low sales of their drinking glasses and unusually high sales of their vases. Can you figure out any reasons to account for this data?

1.   *Can you think of any further examples where the 'blind' collection of data and the implementation of global 'best practice' may be dubious?*
2.   *What do these examples tell you about the general idea of 'best practice' based on information technology?*
3.   *What are the pros and cons of ERP systems?*
4.   *Is it the case that efficiency will necessarily be gained at the expense of knowledge creation or innovation?*
5.   *Reflecting back on this chapter and on Table 6.1 in particular, what do you think the key characteristics of wisdom, as a development upon knowledge, information and data, would be?*
6.   *Could a computer figure out the question posed in the fourth example above on its own? How would you go about developing a 'wisdom system' that could answer this question? How could this system inform the development of an organization's strategy?*

This case is written by Stephen Cummings, Bob Galliers and Sue Newell. With special thanks to Josephine Green.

Note

1 Nonaka and Takeuchi, after Plato, talk of knowledge as 'justified true belief'. Given our emphasis on the process of applying knowledge to data in order to make informed judgements about 'the real world', we would drop the word 'true' in our definition.

Source Material and Recommended Further Reading

The notion of sense-making is taken from the work of Karl Weick; Peter Checkland also talks about information as 'data plus meaning'. 'Back to the Future' was an article written by Galliers and Newell (2001) that argued that so-called knowledge management systems are a misconception. A good source of Leavitt's work can be found in Narold Leavitt, *Managerial Psychology* (Chicago: Chicago University Press, 1972).

PQM was a further refinement of the BSP and CSF approaches. Again, essential business processes were identified in line with business objectives. These processes were assessed in terms of the number of CSFs impacting on them, and the quality (and cost) of the IT-based information systems in place to support them. Further necessary developments were identified on the basis of criticality (in business terms) and performance (both business and technological; current and future).

The *Journal of Strategic Information Systems* (Elsevier) has, from 1991 onwards, provided much rich material, including case studies, on the general topic of information systems strategy.

The more avant-garde conceptions of IS strategy, which emphasize the emergent nature of IS strategizing, can be found in C.U. Ciborra, 'From Thinking to Tinkering: The Grassroots of IT and Strategy', in C.U. Ciborra and T. Jelassi (eds), *Strategic Information Systems: A European Perspective* (Chichester: Wiley, 1994). See also C.U. Ciborra et al., *From Control to Drift: The Dynamics of Corporate Information Infrastructures* (Oxford: Oxford University Press 2000), for a development of the notion of Information Architecture as a socio-technical concept.

Michael Earl's work on IS strategy builds on mainstream thinking and practice in the IS strategy field. See, for example, M.J. Earl, *Management Strategies for Information Technology*. (London: Prentice Hall, 1989); M.J. Earl, 'Experiences in Strategic Information Systems Planning', *MIS Quarterly*, 17(1), 1993, 1–24; and M.J. Earl (ed.), *Information Management: The Organizational Dimension* (Oxford: Oxford University Press, 1996).

Michael Porter reflects on the impact of the Internet on his earlier analysis of strategic forces in M.E. Porter, 'Strategy and the Internet', *Harvard Business Review*, 79(3), March 2001, 63–78.

Tom Davenport provides a rich source of material on BPR. In particular, see T.H. Davenport, *Process Innovation. Re-engineering Work through Information Technology* (Boston: Harvard Business School Press, 1993); and T.H. Davenport, 'Why Re-engineering Failed: The Fad that Forgot People', *Fast Company*, Premier Issue, 1996, 70–74. The former provides an account of the promise of BPR, while the latter is a more serious reflection on its failings. See also R.D. Galliers and J.A. Swan, 'Information Systems and Strategic Change: A Critical Review of Business Process Re-engineering', in W.L. Currie and R.D. Galliers (eds), *Rethinking Management Information Systems* (Oxford: Oxford University Press, 1999), pp. 361–87.

A holistic perspective, and a number of case studies, on the topic of organizational transformation and IT are provided by R.D. Galliers and W.R.J. Baets (eds), *Information Technology and Organizational Transformation: Innovation for the 21st Century Organization* (Chichester: Wiley 1998). See also C. Sauer, P.W. Yetton, et al., *Steps to the Future: Fresh Thinking on the Management of IT-Based Organizational Transformation* (San Francisco: Jossey-Bass, 1997).

A wide range of IS strategy issues is treated in L. Willcocks, D. Feeny and G. Islei (eds), *Managing Information Technology as a Strategic Resource* (Maidenhead: McGraw-Hill, 1997). See also R.D. Galliers, D.E. Leidner and B.S.H. Baker (eds), *Strategic Information Management: Challenges and Strategies in Managing Information Systems*, 2nd edn (Oxford: Butterworth-Heinemann, 1999). The third edition of this course text is due to be published in 2002. Both editions provide a detailed treatment of the 'stages of growth' model used in the Midlands Chemicals case.

The topic of knowledge management, and more particularly, knowledge creation, is dealt with in G. Von Krogh, K. Ichijo and L. Nonaka, *Enabling Knowledge Creation: How to Unlock the Mystery of Tacit Knowledge and Release the Power of Innovation* (New York: Oxford University Press, 2000). See also R.D. Galliers and S. Newell, *Back to the Future: From Knowledge Management to Data Management*, Information Systems Department Working Paper, No. 92 (London: London School of Economics, 2001) for more detail on the distinction between data, information and knowledge.

As for the other references relevant to the concepts covered in this chapter, they are as follows. J.S. Brown and P. Duguid, 'Organizational Learning and Communities of Practice: Toward a Unified View of Working, Learning and Innovation', *Organization Science*, 2(1), 1991, 40–57;

P.B. Checkland, *Systems Thinking, Systems Practice* (Chichester: Wiley 1999); R.D. Galliers, 'Strategic Information Systems Planning: Myths, Reality and Guidelines for Successful Implementation', *European Journal of Information Systems*, I(1), 1991, 55–64. R.D. Galliers, 'Beyond Competitive Advantage', *Journal of Strategic Information Systems*, 3, 1993; M. Hammer, 'Don't Automate, Obliterate', *Harvard Business Review*, 68(4), July–August 1990, 104–12; F.W. McFarlan, 'Information Technology Changes the Way You Compete', *Harvard Business Review*, 62(3), May–June 1984, 98–102. H. Mintzberg and J.A. Waters, 'On Strategies, Deliberate and Emergent', *Strategic Management Journal*, 6, 1985, 257–72. R.L. Nolan, 'Managing the Crises in Data Processing', *Harvard Business Review*, 57(2), March–April 1979; I. Nonaka and H. Takeuchi, *The Knowledge-Creating Company* (New York: Oxford University Press, 1995); R. Pascale and A.G. Athos, *The Art of Japanese Management* (Harmondsworth: Penguin, 1981); M.E. Porter and V.E. Millar, 'How Information Gives You Competitive Advantage', *Harvard Business Review*, 62(4), July–August 1984, 149–60, C.K. Prahalad and G. Hamel, 'The Core Competence of the Corporation', *Harvard Business Review*, 68(3), May–June 1990, 79–91; J.F. Rayport and J.J. Sviokla, 'Exploiting the Virtual Value Chain', *Harvard Business Review*, 73(6), November–December 1995, 75–85; M.S. Scott Morton (ed.), *The Corporation of the 1990s: IT and Organizational Transformation* (New York: Oxford University Press 1991); S.L. Star and K. Ruhleder, 'Steps Towards an Ecology of Infrastructure: Design and Access to Large Information Spaces', *Information Systems Research*, 7(1), 1996, 111–34. R. Whittington, *What is Strategy? And Does it Matter?* (London: Routledge, 1993). The article by Loh and Venkatraman was a chapter in R.D. Galliers and B.S.H. Baker (eds), *Strategic Information Management: Challenges and Strategies in Managing Information Systems* (Oxford: Butterworth-Heinemann, 1994) and first appeared in *Journal of Management Information Systems*, 9(1), 1992, pp. 7–24.

'Strategy as **creativity**' is in three parts. First, we offer up some historical reasons why management and strategy have not been particularly creative domains. Next, at a practical level, we discuss how people traditionally concerned with business strategy have never really embraced creativity, only ever taking to the buzzwords that are seen to represent it in the most superficial ways; and how the prejudice against 'management' by people in the creative industries has led them to not engage with debates about strategic direction. To address the 'double-miss', the third part of this chapter puts the strategy ball back in the court of a group of young people engaged in the creative industries. They are encouraged to envisage new organizational shapes and subsequently, new images of what strategy could be. Creative (but highly disciplined) chaos ensues and pretty soon you can't see the hierarchical triangles for the ray-guns, cookbooks, dodgem circuits, knitting needles, tumbleweeds and placentas. What they come up with seems to reinforce the view advanced in Chapter 1, that if we wish to think strategy differently, we should 'shake hands' with those who have already been initiated into the field strategy and what are conventionally seen as its contributing disciplines.

7 Strategy as Creativity

CHRIS BILTON, STEPHEN CUMMINGS AND DAVID WILSON

'It is obvious', says Hadamard, 'that invention or discovery takes place by combining ideas. The Latin verb cogito for "to think" etymologically means "to shake together".' . . . The creative act, by connecting previously unrelated dimensions of experience is an act of liberation – the defeat of habit by originality.'

Arthur Koestler

Strategy people should be the ones with the longest arms (so they can make the biggest, most inclusive circles).

Robin Wensley

Historical Limits
Stephen Cummings

By any measure 'management' and 'strategy', are not particularly creative fields. And it is easy to understand why by applying Arthur Koestler's reasoning that creativity must come from combining different, seemingly unrelated, dimensions of experience.

There are a number of ways that we illustrate management and strategy's lack of creative invention. Here are two of the most effective.

Most consider that management, as a stand-alone subject, began around the turn of the twentieth century. In the first decade of that century the most popular management theory was F.W. Taylor's 'scientific management'. In the last decade it was Michael

Hammer's 'business process reengineering' (BPR). Consider the following pairs of statements taken from either Taylor or Hammer's work. One of each pair is from Taylor, the other from Hammer. Can you guess which are which? (Answers are provided at the end of this chapter's reading list.)

(1)   A: 'Tradition counts for nothing. [This approach is] a new beginning. Managers must throw out their old notions about how businesses should be organized and run.'
      B: 'The defective systems of management which are in common use [must be substituted].'

(2)   A: '[This approach] is so much more efficient than the old [ways].'
      B: '[This approach] means doing more with less.'

(3)   A: '[This approach] must come from the top of the organization [because] people near the front lines lack . . . broad perspective . . . Their expertise is largely confined to the individual functions and departments that they inhabit. They may see very clearly . . . the narrow problems from which their departments suffer, but it is difficult for them to see a process as a whole.'
      B: 'All of the planning which under the old system was done by [people near the front lines], as a result of his personal experience, must of necessity under [this approach] be done by management in accordance with the laws of science. Because even if [he] was well suited to the development and use [of this approach], it would be physically impossible for him to work at his machine and at a desk at the same time.'

(4)   A: 'The fundamental principles of [this approach] are applicable to all kinds of human activities . . . whenever these principles are correctly applied, results must follow which are truly outstanding.'
      B: '[This approach] applies to any organization in which work is performed . . . [It is] the single best hope for restoring the competitive vigor of American businesses.'

(5)   A: 'Fundamentally, [this approach] is about reversing the industrial revolution . . . We need something entirely different [this approach] is to the next revolution of business what the specialization of labor was to the last.'
      B: 'In its essence, [this approach] involves a complete mental revolution.'

Despite Taylor writing at the beginning of the twentieth century and Hammer at the end, it is often hard to see the difference because the underlying assumptions, or habits, haven't been challenged. Both argue for throwing away all that has gone before, because the new ideas they have to offer are more efficient. Both talk in terms of a hierarchical system of relationships, with those at the top having a better view and thus best placed to make key decisions. Both offer their theory as the new universal 'best way'. And both subsequently urge a revolution that will see their ideas save us all. While Hammer seeks to overcome Adam Smith's taking apart and simplification of work tasks into 'meaninglessly thin slices', he appears to 'replace' this with the taking apart and simplification of processes. The universal means and end of increased performative efficiency, a measure of machine performance developed in the nineteenth century and then applied to human affairs as it was decided that humans and machines were analogues, are not questioned. After one hundred years of feverish 'development' in management studies, nothing much has changed.

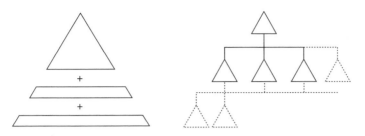

Figure 7.1 Organizational development constrained by triangular views

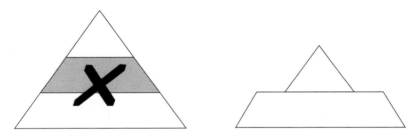

Figure 7.2 The general impact of BPR

Our second illustration is graphic. Ask anyone to draw 'an organization'. The vast majority of people still draw the same thing as would have been drawn a century ago. A hierarchical triangle of boxes connected by lines. Why does this matter? First, seeing organizations in this way reinforces many of the habits with regard to strategy discussed in Chapter 1. Ask the person who has drawn the triangle of organization where strategy comes from and they will generally point to the apex. A few might say from the bottom-up. In other words, the generic triangular view reinforces the either/or choices about strategy that we are trying to go beyond in this book.

Another problem caused by seeing organizations in terms of triangular charts is that it seems to influence our notions of managing strategic change. Seeing all organizations in terms of the same hierarchical triangle has meant that most of the recent big theories of change have been seen in these same generic terms and, subsequently, as about either adding or subtracting from the layers of these hierarchies.

Thus, 'organizational development' up until the 1990s generally meant either 'adding more layers' or creating more subsidiary triangles.

Then a revolution occurred in the 1990s. This sort of accretion was associated with inefficient waste by BPR and 'rightsizing' (which generally means downsizing). The suggested remedy was 'delayering' or 'flattening the triangle' (effectively the same thing) or, in BPR terms removing the 'middle management' layer (refer back to Chapter 6, 'Strategy as Data Plus Sense-Making' for more on this).

It is true that it was difficult to measure what middle managers actually did. Lower level employees contributed because they interacted with the outside world and produced outputs, and you could not sack too many senior executives. However, many firms who had been BPRed soon found that they had lost something (even if they may not have been able to measure what it was exactly). If strategy happens top-down *and* bottom-up (rather than either/or), then good middle managers are imperative, a crucial lynchpin. They pick out and sponsor those opportunistic initiatives taken on 'the ground' that can be connected to the organization's strategic trajectory (if it is all bottom-up emergence then it is all 'animation' and no 'orientation' – see Chapter 1). And they make sure that 'pie in the sky' plans turn into actions or get knocked back 'upstairs' if they cannot be implemented (if it is all top-down planning then it is just all 'orientation'). Organizations, it turns out, needed good middle mangers more than ever. And so, after adding a whole load into organizations in the 1970s and 1980s and throwing a whole load out in the 1990s, back they now come (although they are now given grander titles like 'corporate knowledge officer', 'chief quality manager' or 'information manager').

But these limited ways of looking and the ensuing over-simplistic or overgeneric strategic solutions that they encourage need not apply. There are other ways of drawing organization and thinking strategy that do not get stuck on the same habits and generic either/or choices. An interesting thing that we have found with the drawing organization exercise mentioned above (and explored further in Case Box 7.1) is that people not trained in management or strategy are more likely not to draw hierarchical triangles.[1] One reason for this is that people without management backgrounds have not had their habits or predispositions shaped as to what organization and strategy are to the same extent. And one can see these predispositions by looking at what is considered to be the history of management, something generally taught at the outset of any management course.

A brief history of strategy and management

In the 1950s, when management was considered worthy enough to be incorporated into most universities, attention was paid to writing up its history. To provide a lens with which to look into the past, it was decided that management was, in keeping with the newly formed American Management Association (AMA) definition of management's 'universal basic functions', as:

(1) planning;
(2) organizing (effectively the division and ordering of labour); and
(3) controlling.

These functions corresponded to an understanding that management was about improving efficiency and the triangular hierarchy form. No wonder that, looking with

---

[1]   This chapter is written in a polemic style in order to provoke the reader into thinking about the lack of creativity generally exhibited in the fields of management and strategy. However, this is not meant to imply that interesting and challenging currents are not bubbling under the mainstream. For example, as we left the twentieth century, Ikujiro Nonaka's excellent works on the 'knowledge organization' were beginning to gain ground against conventional Western perceptions. Nonaka and colleagues employed an organic approach that placed learning above efficiency, and argued, therefore, for the creation of 'ba' space in organizations to enable people to have time to think creatively rather than simply seeking to improve efficiency. Many of his ideas echo the philosophical arguments developed in Koestler's much earlier *The Act of Creation*, quoted at the head of this chapter. However, even with Nonaka's work, the diagrammatic perspective is one that follows management conceptions in terms of reducing and synthesizing organic behaviour into generic rather than individualized functions. See the list at the end of the chapter for further reading in this regard.

this lens, historians identified Taylor and Henri Fayol as management's 'founding fathers'. Alfred Chandler's influential thesis showing how the 'visible hand' of organization came into being by *more efficiently* fulfilling the market's ordering functions, similarly led to organization being defined in the manner that we are attempting to see beyond here. In Chandler's words, the object of his histories was 'easily defined, it has two specific characteristics: it contains many distinct operating units and it is managed by a hierarchy of salaried executives' (see Chapter 1 for Chandler's accompanying illustration). Luther Gulick, writing in the same period, summed up the corresponding purpose of management succinctly: 'whether public or private, the basic "good" is efficiency'.

Mooney's history of organization since 'time began' similarly found that 'the formal principles' of organization were:

(1)   scalar hierarchy; ✓

(2)   the functional division of labour; and

(3)   co-ordination. ✓

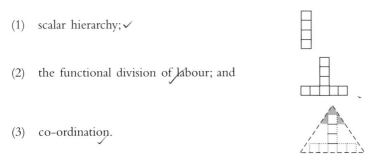

Mooney claimed that these principles were universal and, consequently, would hold true in the future. Thus, in the words of one collection of historical works in management: 'The principal directions in which management will develop have already been pointed out by its pioneer thinkers. They present it with vision and with an authority that is beyond challenge.' One can see how this historical perspective (which, because it has not been challenged, continues to be redoubled in every management text) might limit our ability to think otherwise for the future.

The problem with this history

Management and strategy are not the only fields that have found themselves constrained by historical habits and predispositions about what they should be aiming for. In the past twenty years fields as diverse as art, architecture, physics and medicine have all begun to critically examine their incremental, rather than creative, development in this respect. How have they responded? Partly, at least, by trying to incorporate or connect to other approaches so as to take a more eclectic or postmodern approach to problem solving. But this has not happened to the same extent in management. Why? Again, historical assumptions may be to blame.

When one reads the history of art or architecture, for example, one learns of many styles and ends. Thus, these fields have, in Koestler's words, more unrelated dimensions to connect. When management's historians looked beyond the likes of Taylor and the American railroad companies, in order to grant their fledgling field greater *gravitas*, they tended to write up the pre-modern past in very modern terms. Subsequently, the Egyptian pyramids, for example, are typically discussed because a large group of people were 'ordered towards a common goal', and labour was 'broken down, standardized and specialized'. The world's best selling OB text describes the 'breakthrough' represented by the pyramids thus: 'someone had to *plan* what was to be done, *organize* people and materials to do it, lead and *direct* the workers, and impose *controls* to ensure that everything was done as planned'. But to categorize and discuss the building of pyramids only in these modern terms is to overlook any different dimensions. If one stops to think, perhaps the most remarkable thing about the building of the pyramids is why they were built? What unique beliefs possessed people to create them? But management and strategy, as we have constituted them, do not enter into discussions about particular values or traditional ends.

This is problematic on two counts. First, it is historically 'dodgy' in that it requires putting words in the mouths of people that they did not use themselves. Most ancient civilizations, for example, did not have a word that equated to our notion of 'efficiency' (Mooney admitted that ancient people did not speak in his modern terms, but got around the problem by claiming: 'That the great organizers of history applied these principles unconsciously proves only that their technique was inherent in their genius'). Second, and more worrying from a creativity standpoint, with such a narrow historical view, alternative dimensions that could be combined will not be recognized. Indeed, upon reflection, we should be a little disappointed that the Egyptians who have offered us so much that is different from how we live today on which to ponder, can here only offer us a more simplified versions of what we already assume. This does not give us much that is different to 'shake together' to borrow Arthur Koestler's phrase. It is hardly the 'increasing ocean of mutually incompatible alternatives, forcing others into greater articulation', that Paul Feyerabend recommended in Chapter 1 of this book. Hence, management academics have rather short un-inclusive arms. And if strategy is a subset of management, then strategists look like Daleks.

Thinking beyond our historical limits

How might we think beyond these historical limits? We believe that one way is to learn from people who are less influenced by the habits of management and strategy. The University of Warwick runs a post-experience MA in Creative and Media Enterprises which seeks, among other things, to enable people from the creative enterprises to interact with management and business interests in more fruitful ways. One of the biggest problems that programme director Chris Bilton has identified in this regard is that at a time when it is increasingly imperative that creative arts organizations connect with business concerns, most people from creative backgrounds think that management and strategy has nothing to do with them. These things are, they assume, all about economics, efficiency and hierarchy – or what they see as the opposite of being creative.

In an attempt to rectify this preconception Chris has sought to involve several people from Warwick Business School, including David Wilson and myself, in the MA's programme. As we have become involved we have found ourselves learning more than we teach, as Chris's students consistently highlight what the students and the executives that we generally interact with often lack – an eclectic and creative disposition. The relationship has subsequently become reciprocal as we have sought to use Chris's students as guest speakers on MBA and undergraduate programmes and to develop an MBA elective on creative thinking run by Chris and his colleagues. In so doing, what we are attempting to rectify is an unhelpful 'double miss'. At a time when companies want to be more creative, truly creative people do not feel they connect to them (so companies are left to 'hire in' unbounded creativity exercises such as juggling and sand-castle building, things that do very little to substantially change mindsets 'on the job'). And, at a time when people in creative industries need to engage with business they are not engaging, which leaves people from traditional management backgrounds to run things, often to the long-term detriment of creative organizations' capacity to create.

In seeking to join these currently poorly connected realms of creative thinking and strategy, the remainder of this chapter is structured as follows. Drawing on his experience as the head of Warwick Business School's Centre for Corporate Strategy and Change, David Wilson discusses why 'strategy' and people from the 'creative industries' (or 'creatives' as the are often called) have not mixed well in the past, and the implications of this. In the following section, Chris discusses why 'creatives' can be just as insular, usually to their own detriment. In the final section we attempt to conclude this discussion by following the leads of our MA students as they confront and connect the realms of strategy and creativity.

Case Box 7.1 Drawing Organization

A recent article in *The Guardian* newspaper on a new book called *Experimental Houses* begins as follows:

'Why don't people live in radical, experimental houses? Answer: Ask a five year old child to draw a house. Whether from a rich or poor background, whether born in a council flat in Glasgow or a mock Tudor mansion in Weybridge, the result will almost always be the same. A funny little box-like house with a patched roof, smoking chimney, centrally placed door, a window on either side downstairs and two windows more or less symmetrically arranged above them.'

The same idea can be applied with our perceptions of organization (albeit not to young children – our understanding of 'organization' is seemingly more 'learned' and less 'primal' than 'house').

Pictionary, a board game popular in the 1980s and 1990s, is also a good way of illustrating how historical learnings stay with us. The object of the game is to draw things without using words in order to enable your partner or team to guess the word as quickly as possible. Try drawing 'an organization' in such a way that your work colleagues, fellow students, friends or family members can promptly guess what you are trying to express. Although we think we live in caring, soft, post-bureaucratic times, the fastest way to get people to think an organization is still to reproduce something like the boxes-and-lines triangular hierarchy that Chandler's histories took as their object.

However, there do seem to be some differences according to different backgrounds. A few years ago, when I had opportunity to be concurrently teaching undergraduate courses in organization studies towards a business degree and ancient history towards an arts degree, I gave out a blank sheet of paper to each student from each class and asked them to draw, without words, 'an organization'. While most from both classes drew organization in terms of the boxes-

and-lines triangle without any direct reference to people (not even a stick figure), the percentage for the arts students was significantly less (business students = 49/73 or 67 per cent; arts students 18/33 or 55 per cent). The balance, 24 business students and 15 arts, drew a variety of people interacting or 'flow diagrams'. Some even drew funny little box-like houses.

1. *Why do most people still see the boxes-and-lines triangle when thinking organizations?*
2. *Why do you think the arts students might be less likely to see in terms of the triangle?*
3. *How might this view of what an organization is influence our views of what strategy is?*
4. *How might management and strategy be thought differently if, for example, most people drew a house rather than a boxes and lines scalar hierarchy to describe an organization?*

Elements of this case are abstracted from 'Beautiful Strangeness', by Jonathan Glancy in *The Guardian* (4 November 2000), and 'The Organizational Advantages of Double Vision', by Stephen Cummings in the *Proceedings of the 1992 ANZAM Conference*, Sydney. A version of this case first appeared in the book *ReCreating Strategy* by Stephen Cummings (London: Sage Publications, 2002)

'Them and Us' 1: Why Strategy and 'Creatives' Do Not Mix – The Management Mindset
David Wilson

'A person who, seeing farther and probing deeper than other people, . . . has energy enough to give effect to this extra vision.'

George Bernard Shaw's definition of the creative genius

Despite the colourful metaphors and analogies in management disciplines (some of which use the word creativity itself, or refer to it by supposed similes such as innovation, improvisation and novelty), it is very hard to see that this is other than window dressing, largely for the benefit for those in 'innovation' management (or perhaps more generally management training and research). Ironically, such talk of creativity in management also has virtually no connections with those who work in creative enterprises (such as musicians, artists and poets). There remains a mutual distrust between those in the 'creative' industries and management, which Chris Bilton explores in more detail in the next section. Even within the realms of management theory and practice, it is hard to see where notions of creativity have had any substantial influence at all in the world of mainstream management. I argue that there is largely a myth of creativity in management generally and that sub-disciplines of management, such as strategy, have also consistently avoided engagement with notions of creativity other than the lip service referred to above.

The word itself certainly has impeccable etymological credentials. 'Creativity' originates from the Latin verb *creare*, which means *to make or produce* and, specifically, the divine creation of the world. The meaning here is both on a past event (the creation of the world) and the creation (by God) of the world and its creatures. I hesitate only slightly to draw the comparison here between modern-day strategists and their (some-times assumed) God-like status in the management disciplines!

The *Oxford English Dictionary*, however, comes to our rescue by distinguishing *the* Creator and *a* creator (someone who brings something into existence), which as we shall see becomes a modern meaning of the word in management theory. During the sixteenth century the meaning of the word *created* was widened to denote both future and present acts. For example, we see reference to individuals. Raymond Williams in his wide-ranging study of *Key Words* gives the example of such usage as 'the King's Grace created him Duke'.

During the eighteenth century, the word *creative* becomes used to denote a specific human faculty, especially associated with art, and *creativity*, finally, is a twentieth-century term very much concerned with concepts such as the future and becoming. The shift from divine act to humans fashioning their futures (to an extent at least), with a view to what they want to become, is delineated in the shift from created to creativity. This shift occurred during the period of Renaissance humanism and permeates manage-ment theory and practice.

Yet this apparent autonomy has remained bounded in management theory and, more particularly, in the field of strategy. For example, strategic management uses almost a full range of levels of analysis – from individual to global perspectives – yet manages to homogenize them into one rather dull, deterministic approach! Cameron Ford notes that management theory has rather avoided embracing creativity, preferring the term innovation instead. Ford argues that, in terms of the specialization of academic disci-plines, psychologists have been the scholars most interested in creativity. This is true, but the problem is that even the psychologists are interested in predominantly one aspect of creativity, that of identifying the characteristics and traits of creative individ-uals (however defined). The challenge for strategists is to analyse and assess creative processes as well as creative contexts in which creativity might be fostered and encour-aged to help their organizational concerns.

Common creativity metaphors in strategy and their limitations

Thus far, however, empirical evidence and theoretical approaches in strategy are dis-appointing. Common metaphors that are related to fostering innovation and creativ-ity are those of improvisation and jazz music.

Scholars such as Kathleen Eisenhardt have attempted to use sports analogies, and in her case using bicycle racing (road racing such as the Tour de France) as a metaphor. Closer inspection of the sports metaphor reveals that really we are talking the same rather deterministic model. The dependent variable is 'performance' and the inde-pendent variables become 'teamwork' so that the individual winner can emerge (build-ing on strong teamwork). Teamwork is thus all about collective control toward these goals (also re-read the deconstruction of the 'team' metaphor in Chapter 3, 'Strategy as Organizing'!).

Well, it is true that there have been few winners of the Tour de France who have not also had the support of a strong team. But it is equally true that stage racing in professional cycling is one of the most structured and least creative of sports (I speak from the experience of having been a racing cyclist for many years and as a fanatical follower of professional racing today). Tactics are determined in advance. It is clear which teams will help other teams and which will not. Riders are specialists (climbers, sprinters and what the French call *rouleurs* – roughly translated as those who can ride brutally fast for long periods of time mostly on the flat and are thus good time trialists). They combine these specialisms in exactly the same way we might see functional interdependence in commercial organizations (J.D. Mooney would have been pleased to see this as further evidence of the universality of his definition of organization). Cycle racing is perhaps more colourful, but is equally deterministic in the final analysis as the top-down rational planning view of strategic management that stems from Mooney and Chandler's definition of organization.

Improvisation and jazz I will explore together since, to a large extent, they share the same metaphor – that of abandoning formal structures in the hope that something creative will emerge. The idea, as Teresa Amabile and her co-authors argue, is 'the production of novel and useful ideas in any domain'. Well, it is true that some of the most innovative and creative music (and drama) has been produced when players improvise. *Commedia-delle-Arte*, for example in the field of drama and long improvisation sessions by musicians such as Miles Davis have all produced work of outstanding creativity. But here we must ask a number of questions about the direct application of the improvisation metaphor. First, it is mostly the case that those who can improvise well are also those musicians and actors who are most talented and innovative in the first place. What they play, therefore, sounds good. It would in any context. Second, the majority of improvisation revolves around structured routines which actors and musicians already know in advance. They may apply such routines in ways that are different, but they are nevertheless routines which are recognizable, even to uninformed listeners if they listen enough times to the performance!

Mary Jo Hatch writes about jazz improvisation in this way (and, unlike many writers who use the improvisation metaphor, she is informed – her partner is a jazz drummer). She characterizes the ways in which musicians improvise, taking first the original melody and then working around the tune and developing it (nevertheless still with the original tune recognizable). This original melody becomes the 'head', from which a range of improvised passages might proceed and develop. To reconcile the piece, the musicians return eventually to the original melody and end the music. What she shows is how structured the process of improvisation really is.

Strategic managers and their creative limitations

I have discussed the above points on many occasions with senior managers, themselves charged with injecting innovation into strategic thinking in their organizations. They asked me to run a few sessions on improvisation. No actor, but a musician, I was able to take them through some steps in the improvisation process. The managers came from a wide range of organizations from both the public and the private sectors. The results were interesting and revealed a lot to me about the limits which individuals self-impose in this process.

'True' improvisation means altering both the structure and the process of musical melodies and tempos. I began by identifying a melody which all could identify. It happened to be Paul McCartney's *Yesterday*, but any well-known melody would have sufficed. I then played the song, keeping tempo and melody as they are on the original record. Some listeners looked interested, others bored by what they foresaw as some silly behavioural experiment. I then changed the tempo (the beat) playing the same notes in the original sequence of the melody, but altering the timing patterns. The song began to sound a little strange, but the original melody was still recognizable. I then altered the timing even further, putting multiple time signatures into the song, but still retaining the original notes of the song in the same sequence as they had been written originally. All were listening intently now. Finally, I changed both the time signatures and the sequences of the song. It was unrecognizable as the original song, but used only its original notes and no additions.

Discomfort among the managers was intense. Losing the tempo meant they had to listen harder to retain the melody. Losing both melody and tempo resulted in most of the audience experiencing high levels of discomfort and many gave up the struggle to keep listening. However, a return to the original tempo and melody produced noticeable signs of relief and increased levels of attention from the managers.

The limits that these managers reached were met quite soon into the improvisation process. A loss of recognizable structures (the melody line) and processes (the sequence of the notes) meant nearly all experienced severe discomfort. We discussed this experience at length, concluding that what at least this set of managers understood as improvisation was, in fact, placing variation in only one aspect of a multivariate process. As Greg Oldham and Anne Cummings argue, creativity is about combining both the original and the novel, but that most individuals experience severe tensions in trying to achieve both of these.

Other critiques with respect to the limits of creative thinking in management and strategy can be drawn from a combination of my experience and from the literature on creativity in organizations.

My first, experiential, example comes from time I spent researching advertising agencies as part of a larger project looking at innovation in organizations. What was striking about these agencies was that the term 'creatives' was ubiquitously used to describe those individuals who designed and developed advertising ideas. From a strategic management perspective, these individuals were the 'core competence' and the 'key strategic resource' of the firm. Yet in all cases, those managers responsible for organizational strategy would go to great lengths to ensure the 'creatives' were excluded from strategy formulation. After all, what do these individuals know about strategic management and what value did their voice have? In one agency, the 'creatives' had been put together in one part of the building, isolated from the rest of the organization and only given work to do, rather than be consulted about wider organizational issues.

Relatedly, a second striking set of limits that may be seen in the literature on creativity (especially as it may apply to management) is the astounding levels of normativism extant across a wide range of literatures. Searching through the top journals in the fields of management and strategy reveals a curiously unified set of underlying assumptions. Creativity is assumed by the majority of authors to have solely positive effects or influences in organizations. For example, it liberates individuals, enhances commitment and underpins innovative strategic decision making. Special issues of scholarly journals on improvisation, innovation and creativity reveal a remarkable coherence toward this normativism. Even in the wider realms of social science (such as in the work of Jean Baudrillard), creativity is firmly placed as both a positive and a desirable aspect of social organization (and, indeed, individuals). What, one might ask, of 'creative accounting' as a positive aspect of organization? Or 'creative defences' in law?

Subsequently, the management mindset, especially as reflected in strategic management, clings with some determination to the 'normal', using the word creative as either a term of disparagement or diluting its meaning into common parlance (so we see the trivialization of the term creative or we see its application to jobs that may be artistic, but are repetitive and certainly not novel). An academic colleague (Jaan Grunberg), while on study leave at Warwick Business School, collected the following data that give some indication of the trivialization of the concept of creativity in practice. Using the local telephone book, he identified nearly twenty organizations ranging from 'Create & Co' to 'Creative Windows and Conservatories'. One might legitimately ask if the company 'Creative Financial Services and Will Writing Centre' should be included in the normatively good category!

Further analysis revealed that the majority of companies using the term creative in their title denote organizations which deal with *technologies* that may be used in expressive ways, either as corporate communication or as expressing personal image (e.g., 'Creative Resources, Photo Design and Print'; 'Creative Fragrances Ltd'). It is also revealing how many companies begin their name with the word 'creative' (157 in the UK in 1999), rather than innovative (25 in the UK in 1999), using *OneSource* data base. The companies calling themselves 'innovative' fell into no discernible pattern, covering a wide range of industries. With the companies calling themselves 'creative', it was easier to find patterns concentrating largely on advertising and market research (20 companies), printing (14 companies) or business and computer services (36 companies). Between 1993 and 1999 there was also strong evidence of companies changing their name to include the word 'creative' in their title. Examples are Creative Direction Consultants Limited (previously Rychent Ltd) and Creative Labs (UK) Ltd (previously MPC Distribution Ltd).

While creativity has increasingly become a buzzword in strategic management, examples like those listed above which attest to the way it has been implemented indicate that it has been a fairly meagre form of creative thinking that has become widespread. While we, as strategists and managers, would like to think that we too are now 'creatives', perhaps we are just kidding ourselves? Case Box 7.2 on the dissemination of 'scenario planning' as a creative thinking tool illustrates these limits further and gives some indication as to where we might look if we really want to get some creativity into strategy.

Case Box 7.2 Scenario Development

Scenario development is an integral part of scenario planning. Whereas scenario planning focuses on imagining a series of multiple futures to which contingent strategies are then attached, scenario development is more about the process of imagining how different (and in which ways) the future might be.

Scenario planning in commercial organizations is usually argued to originate with the work of Shell strategists (especially Pierre Wack) who took the then unusual step of looking forward and imagining how things might be very different in the industry. The argument is that such a technique enabled Shell to foresee (in the 1960s) the possibility of a severe price increase in crude oil coupled with shortages of supply resulting from the Asian crisis (in the early 1990s). Shell was able to weather this crisis better than its competitors since it had designed a contingent strategy to deal with such eventualities. The competition had not.

Mechanical though it sounds, planning is only a part of the process. The major part of using scenarios rests in the creation of plausible futures. This is scenario development. One way of thinking about this is to view scenario development as addressing degrees of uncertainty that organizations face. For example, there are uncertainties that are fairly certain (within limits). Demographic trends fall into this category. We can predict the number of people in various age bands that will populate the world 20 or more years hence, other factors being equal. Then, there are uncertainties which are much more uncertain. The effects of wars, terrorist activity on trade systems, or the difficulties in assessing the prob- ability of links between variables (such as the relative wealth of countries that adopt the Euro) are examples. Finally, and for philosophical purposes in the main, there are those uncertainties that we do not yet know about. We cannot know what we do not yet know. In practice, most managers have to deal with the former different levels of uncertainty where ambiguity increases as pre- dictability decreases. This means developing scenarios of plausible futures based upon often highly uncertain futures.

Work with managers from all sectors and from a variety of manufacturing and service industries reveals that managers are generally very conservative when it comes to developing scenarios. The evidence we have collected suggests that they tend to proceed on the basis of first constructing relatively fixed parame- ters and then working upon a number of scenarios. For example, they often assume relative constancy in what their organization does and the structures and processes it has in place to achieve this. They then, typically, will develop a scen- ario where existing processes are replaced by more technologically advanced solutions. Communications and interactions through web-based technologies and so-called 'e-business solutions' are often typical of this incremental rather than radical thinking. Also typical is a view that strives to increase the efficient exploitation of new inventions, technologies and organizational environments. Efficiency is defined from the present state of the organization and new tech- nologies (for example) are to be imported as they emerge. Such scenario devel- opment is incremental and is heavily 'topic'-centred focusing for example upon increasing globalization, information technology, knowledge-based competition and so on.

Asking the same questions of those not in such organizations elicits a different response. For example, after three years of developing scenarios with groups of creative and media studies students it is clear that they come up with much more creative scenarios, if we measure creativity as an ability to see further, deeper and without an embedded set of values or paradigms.

Consistently, these students (who, in the main, were running their own busi- nesses in various media activities) began their scenario development by aban- doning the notion that their current organization was inherently adaptable to future changes, or was necessary in its current form. Here was a key difference. Managers in traditional organizations relied heavily on *adaptability* – where specific changes in the environment elicit changes in the organization, however inefficiently. Media students rarely picture the future this way preferring instead to abandon any fixed points. They talk in terms of temporary, *easily disposable* organizations that, rather like butterflies, shine for a short moment, are successful and then are gone. There is no notion here of long-term survival and adapt- ability. They were also not as constrained as managers in traditional industries by sticking to the same line of business. A magazine publisher could become a music distributor and a theatre company could disband and reform as a consultancy. A key theme in developing scenarios was not just the extent and scale of the projected changes their organizations would likely face, but was also the transferability of knowledge and skills learned in one organization to a totally different set of circumstances. Media students had fewer problems in starting from the idea that total cessation of current activities was a distinct possibility and also had 'wilder' scenarios (such as abandoning planet Earth and investing in a music 'business' on some other inhabitable planet).

There is, as Jim March reminds us, a fine line between lunacy and genius but it is nevertheless true that the impact and influence of different ways of thinking about the future will be enormous on current organizational activities and processes. These differences are worth debating and exploring, since the dominance of one over the other will certainly affect the way we live in the future and the values to which we adhere. The following questions focus on these points.

1. *Why might it be that the media students came up with scenarios that were far less constrained and perhaps more groundbreaking?*
2. *What effect might thinking through the scenarios developed by the 'traditional' managers listed above have on their organizations?*
3. *What effect might thinking through the scenarios developed by the media students listed above have on their organizations? What effect might they have on the 'traditional' managers' organizations?*
4. *Are the scenarios dreamt up by the 'creatives' unstructured or are they just structured in different ways?*

The content of Case Box 7.2 would appear to suggest that there is much to be gained by an exchange of ideas between 'traditional' managers and 'creatives'. However, in the next section, Chris Bilton explores why 'creatives' and their prejudices have resisted such a potentially fruitful exchange.

'Them and Us' 2: Why Strategy and 'Creatives' Do Not Mix – Creative Prejudices
Chris Bilton

> *'When bank managers get together they talk about creativity, when arts managers get together they talk about business plans.'*
>
> *(After Oscar Wilde)*

Two years ago when I began talking about marketing and markets to a financially beleaguered singer-songwriter, his immediate response was 'you're beginning to sound like one of them'. The musician's 'them and us' mental map of the creative industries is replicated in many sectors, including advertising, music, television, film, publishing and the performing arts. Further discussion reveals that this map is actually based upon a mutual misunderstanding of the nature of creativity and the nature of management.

There is clearly a palpable tension between 'creatives' and 'suits'[1]. As David Wilson has already noted, this mutual suspicion is based on a polarized view of the worlds of creativity and management. On the one hand, creativity is wild and undisciplined, on the other hand management is linear and bureaucratic. We have already discussed the myth of creativity in the management realm. Now let us turn to the myth of management in the creative industries.

In the United Kingdom, a top-down model of bureaucratic management that was imported and evangelized across of the cultural sector during the 1980s and 1990s has reinforced the idea that management is opposed to creativity. At precisely the point where many managers outside of the cultural sector were beginning to question the purpose and meaning of strategic planning, drawing on many of the sorts of arguments set out in this book, artists and cultural bureaucrats were moving in the opposite direction.

In the public sector, the growing emphasis on financial and managerial controls in the arts over the past twenty years was part of a general trend towards increased political and financial accountability. This shift may have stemmed from a political reaction against the perceived financial indulgences and political unpredictability of publicly funded and managed organizations in the 1960s and 1970s. In the new mythology, these and other problems of the arts came to be labelled as 'mismanagement' (the possibility that certain problems might arise when arts organizations are 'over-managed' was not addressed).

The solution was a 'new managerialism', imposed from above by the sticks and carrots of government funding through the 1980s and 1990s. The instruments of the new managerialism included Audit Commission reports, consultants and accountants bought in from the private sector, sponsorship and sponsorship incentive schemes, the shift from open-ended revenue funding to a variety of quasi-contractual project funds and incentive schemes, and the 1993 National Arts and Media Strategy. Artists and arts organizations complained that creative work was taking second place to a variety of administrative tasks imposed by their funders, from evaluation reports and audience monitoring to the lengthy process of applying for funding itself.

Specialist training and education programmes developed to cope with the new financial and managerial pressures. 'Arts management' emerged both as a profession and as a specialism in higher education. The number of arts management courses in British universities mushroomed throughout the 1990s. Where in the past artists might have worked out their own systems for managing and budgeting, such ad hoc systems were no longer compatible with the demands of the arts funding system. A new generation of professional arts managers emerged, well versed in the orthodoxies of financial management, marketing and the niceties of British cultural policy, but with relatively little direct experience of artists or arts practice. The semantic shift from the more modest notion of 'arts administration' to the grander title of 'arts management' implied a new, more confident and controlling approach. The new cadre of managers, educated to higher degree level, expected to enter at the mid-point in the organizational pyramid, as junior managers and administrative assistants, not to work their way up from front-line creative positions as many of their predecessors had done.

In the commercial sector, the increasingly corporate centralization of the creative industries through technological convergence and economic mergers has led to a similar centralization of decision making and financial control. 'Independent' creative enterprises, and individual creators such as our musician, are forced to the bottom of the strategic pyramid; the planning process has been delegated upstream to remote corporate headquarters. The geographical and mental remoteness from the production process is offset by a reining in of operational activities according to the big picture of corporate strategy; without any sector-specific knowledge of the businesses they are managing, the new managers speak only the neutral language of financial controls, emerging markets and corporate objectives.

If we were to draw a picture of the new managerialism, we might observe a retreat into hierarchy, with senior managers and managerial functions increasingly separated out and remote from the creative, operational underbelly of the organization. As the senior administration of arts organizations became increasingly top-heavy, new job titles emerged. Where once the artistic director reigned supreme, they were now part of a pyramid of artistic, financial, marketing and managerial functions, all answerable to a chief executive or board.

Meanwhile, some artists responded by retreating into a kind of petulant 'anti-managerialism' at the base of the managerial pyramid (or even outside it), claiming that their creativity was incompatible with the more mundane aspects of organizational life, demanding special exemptions and privileges in a pure world of creative irresponsibility and creative destruction. The result was an extreme polarization of creators and managers, with a clear line dividing the pyramid in two. The disconnection between the artists or 'creatives' at the base of the pyramid, and the managers upstairs was reflected in lifestyle, language, and career paths. Artists were either self-taught, or else they came through education programmes which excluded managerial studies. (With a few notable exceptions. Goldsmiths College was one of the first fine arts degree courses to take marketing and management as serious parts of an artist's work. Not surprisingly, Goldsmiths' graduates have been very successful in the commercial British art market, from Damien Hirst and the Young British Artists to the nominees for the 2000 Turner Prize.) The disconnection of arts management education programmes from arts practice and the tendency of arts management graduates to come in halfway up the organizational pyramid have already been noted. Given the separate career paths for artists and arts managers, it is not surprising that a degree of mutual suspicion and stereotyping has developed.

Exploring the divide

There are personal benefits and organizational disadvantages on both sides of this divide. For artists, the mythology of individual artistic genius grants certain exemptions from organizational norms and regulations. Eccentric approaches to communication, financial management or timekeeping may be tolerated, even expected. The creative process is granted a privileged position in a chaotic, unmapped territory outside and away from the managerial boardroom. Up to a point, the licence granted to creative people and processes is tactically convenient. The artist's assumed naivety in organizational matters may nevertheless disguise a shrewd understanding of just how far the boundaries can be stretched.

For managers, their position on the pyramid allows them to stand above the messiness and unpredictability of the creative process and maintain the illusion of control and omniscience unperturbed by the creative ferment that lies beneath. These roles translate into marketable stereotypes. If a conventional firm needs to develop the creativity of its sales force, they bring in the Royal Shakespeare Company (although often nothing much changes as the underlying structure of these organizations is not greatly affected by the Bard's intervention). If an arts organization needs a financial makeover, they call in PriceWaterhouseCoopers.

These organizational divisions between creators and managers are reinforced by other stereotypes in the creative industries, including gender roles. Arts management courses attract large numbers of female students, and arts management and administration have attracted a relatively high proportion of women in relatively senior positions. However, if the senior administrator is a woman, all too often the artistic director is a man and men continue to outnumber women in creative professions for all the usual reasons. Here the stereotypes of disorganized creator and omniscient manager take on a Freudian dimension, with the boy-child's artistic ego protected from reality by the indulgent and controlling mother.

At organizational level, the separation between creative mavericks and 'suits' is more pernicious. Even the most cursory analysis of any creative project, or a quick scan of the creativity literature, will reveal that structures, limits, routines and boundaries are as much part of the process as spontaneous indiscipline. The myth of genius remains a myth, useful in the branding of artists and products, but only a very partial representation of the mental and organizational processes of cultural production. Similarly any thoughtful definition of management will reveal that it contains elements of creativity and imagination as well as bureaucratic control. The myth of management referred to at the beginning of this section propagates an idea of management and an image of strategy as top-down bureaucratic planning, inflexible systems and blueprints, and specialist 'expert' knowledge, disconnected from the mess of creativity below. The recent history of cultural organizations has reinforced this myth by separating out artists from managers and encouraging both to play to their worst instincts.

Ironically the myth of strategic management has resulted not in management by experts but in a rather banal, instrumental version of management that insulates experts from organizational reality. Working from the top of the pyramid downwards, managers and their subordinates focus on the mechanics of managerial process, not on the overriding objectives of stimulating and responding to organizational change. Anybody who has worked in an arts organization, especially a funded arts organization, is struck by the sheer quantity of paperwork which feeds the machinery of management outside the organization, rather than addressing the real issues and problems within: five-year business plans, mission statements and action plans, evaluation reports, strategic plans and endless application forms are generated for the funder's benefit, not for internal use, and bear only a passing, semi-fictional relationship to the real plans and aspirations of the organization itself.

This mythical view of strategic management perpetuates a management style that is short-sighted, cumbersome and utterly ill suited to the particular managerial challenges of the creative industries. Dealing with intangible assets, high levels of risk and supply chain dependency, unpredictable markets and processes, managers in the creative industries need to be more flexible and innovative than most. A Weberian iron cage of bureaucracy, imported best (or worst) practice style, from the public sector and from the dying days of manufacturing industry, are clearly not the only tools for the job.

In any event, the application of the strategic planning pyramid to the cultural sector has been a rather half-hearted affair. The Arts Council's National Arts and Media Strategy (eventually published in 1993) grew out of a year-long round of consultations and consultative documents, and was preceded by a much-heralded but rather cosmetic restructuring of the arts funding system. Intended to provide a policy framework not just for the Arts Council but for regional, local and commercial sector partners, the document's attempt to impose a coherent strategic direction on the many possibilities thrown up during the consultation ended, reassuringly, in failure. Even those who began by criticizing the Arts Council for imposing its vision on the rest of us were forced to concede that the vision was indeed a rather blurred one, riddled with contradictions. (In the end the criticism in some quarters was that the document had not been strategic enough!) It was not, however, a waste of time. For those who took part, the consultation process, through rowdy public meetings, provocative and opinionated proposals and counter-blasts, forced the arts community to think seriously about what it was doing and why. The fact that this consultation was seen only as a means to an end, not a strategic process in its own right, indicates another aspect of the myth of management in the cultural sector. Strategy is seen to consist only of the plan not the planning, the blueprint, not the rough drafts which precede and follow it.

The same phenomenon can also be seen with regard to business ethics, another difficult area to 'tie down'. In March 2001, a spokesperson for the campaign for an oath to set global ethical standards for scientists announced that they were 'dropping the future pursuit of it'. It was not so much stalled by a lack of interest or a failure to see it as an important issue that had stalled it, as by the inability of the many bodies concerned to agree the wording of a common code. However, as one executive director of a leading scientific research society said: 'I'm sceptical about the practicality of an oath that can be widely applied, but the spirit of the discussions that led toward the oath may be more important than the oath itself.' (It would be worth relating this example to Case Box 2.3 in Chapter 2, 'Strategy as Ethos'.)

Interestingly, and insightfully given our discussion here, many publicly funded arts organizations have developed a kind of managerial sub-culture, which appears to be more flexible and pragmatic than the limited top-down approach outlined above. While going through the correct procedural motions, speaking the language of fiscal propriety and managerial accountability, these organizations have followed their own agendas of creative experiment or social purpose. The 'official' strategy has conformed to the demands of the system in order to play the system, but the 'real' strategy is more closely aligned to the unpredictable and divergent quality of the creative process than to any strategic blueprint. As with any form of strategic 'decoupling', there are problems with this dual approach. The unofficial strategy is not properly scrutinized or acknowledged, and the official, 'fake' strategy tends to be what the stakeholders identify with and buy into, often mistakenly. Arts organizations have many years' experience of developing semi-fictional business plans for external consumption; this is what they have been asked for. The problem comes when they have to produce a real long-term plan and be held accountable to it. The over-optimistic projections and subsequent fallout from numerous National Lottery-funded capital projects suggest that arts organizations have become so accustomed to the 'decoupled', semi-fictional version of strategy, that they have started to believe their own propaganda.

Nevertheless, this tendency in some artistic organizations to develop an alternative strategy inside the shell of the official, expected and preconditioned model, suggests a possible alternative. Like the proverbial thin man in a fat man's body, when it comes to creative organizations every pyramid might conceal a different, more interesting and imaginative model of organization and image of strategy, waiting to get out. It is like the combination of pre-modern, individual 'inside-out' perspective, and the modern hierarchical triangle discussed in Chapter 1.

New connections?

It was with this possibility of joining this historical polarization in mind that we asked our students on the MA in Creative and Media Enterprises to draw alternative, individualized rather than generic, 'images' of organization and strategy – either a creative business they had worked for, or one they knew or admired. The MA in Creative and Media Enterprises was set up to target students who wanted to set up or manage small enterprises in the commercial creative industries. Most of them had some kind of experience of working in the cultural sector, broadly termed. Each intake is very culturally diverse with students from the UK, continental Europe and Asia, and, with only one or two exceptions, students did not have a background in management or business studies. (They contributed some of the creative scenarios mentioned in the case box in the previous section of this chapter.) The images could take any form they chose. The results of the exercise are discussed in the next section. Contrary to the myth of management, some of these images indicate that talking about strategy does not have to be an uncreative process, nor does it have to mean 'sounding like one of *them*'.

Shaken and Stirred: Creatives Confront Strategy

The creator is an artist and cannot follow the same path as a businessman. When a creator invents, it is not a unified or rational process. But the management side is very rational, organised and result-oriented. So the two sides sometimes clash. It is from this type of contradiction that you create real progress, real invention and, finally, real success.

Bernard Arnault, CEO Louis Vuitton MH

Creative drawing

One of the things that we have been doing over the past few years to try and rectify the 'miss' between 'management things' and 'creative things' described above, is to run sessions for MA in Creative and Media Studies students to 'deconstruct' the premises about management that they may have bought into. To argue that management, organization and strategy can be about more than efficiency and triangles, we ask each student to freehand a 'picture' or map of their organization as they understand it – not in what they understand to be managerial terms. The results are particular scribblings that reflect local understandings and unique 'geographies' in order to express particular ends. These creatives draw their organizations as anything from knitting needles and ray-guns, undersea worlds and train sets (see Plate 7.1 for some examples). These then provide maps or pictures that can be put before the rest of the group like a map (not unlike that used by the Hungarian detachment in the Alps in Chapter 1) in order to explain how they see their organization's particular orientation.

These pictures or maps can then inspire *mapping* in particular ways. What generally happens during these presentations is that other members of the group upon seeing a particular image can say, for example, that 'it's all very well running a gallery like this

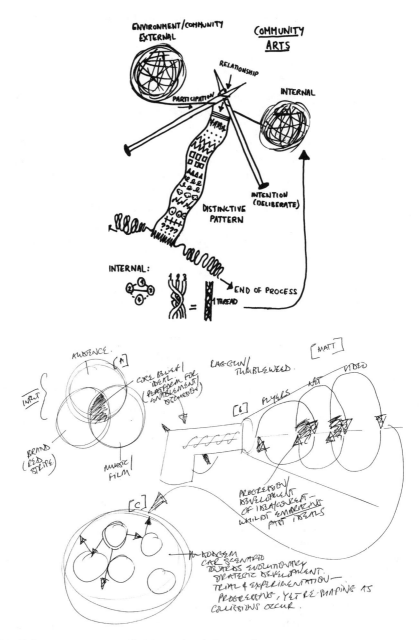

Plate 7.1   The organization as knitting, and as dodgems and a ray-gun

train on that set of tracks, but, given the type of gallery you're describing, we need some people looking at developing some new tracks here and here for the future'. Or, 'sure but we've got to be careful that we don't end up pulling too many carriages and slowing the whole thing down'. Or, 'if that ray gun is to be effective, then it has to shoot an increasingly wider beam, but not too wide'. These contributors can also draw what they mean on to the 'map', gradually forcing one another to greater levels of articulation. Before they realize it, these people are connecting into strategy issues, but in an individualized, interactive, and hence more creative and meaningful, way.

These individual pictures at once animate and orient a particular group of people in ways that a generic triangle or organization chart can never do. Indeed, we now use examples such as these to inspire MBAs and people on executive programmes to draw their organizations creatively and individualistically, and to use these drawings as a basis for thinking differently about strategy for these organizations. If this all seems a bit too far-fetched for you and your organization, then we recommend moving's on to Chapter 9, 'Strategy as Systems Thinking', which offers some more structured approaches to redrawing organization and strategy. However, if you are comfortable with this level of creative thinking, then the sub-section that follows this 'pushes the boat out' even further.

Creative discussions

Beyond the students drawing their own images we like to open up the discussion in order to reflect on and begin to understand why the 'creatives' have drawn what they have and to reflect on the future of strategy in the light of what they have drawn. We can think of no better way to end this chapter than by incorporating as much of this dialogue as space allows. It points out some interesting pathways that will hopefully inspire you to think further outside of the conventional strategy box (a character key is provided in 'Source Material and Recommended Further Reading' at the end of the chapter):

MJ: I just wanted to ask, if BPR seems to have been 'dead' for quite a while already what's next?

SC: Nobody's quite sure, there's knowledge management, but it's not as universal as BPR. There's a lot of appropriation by management of all sorts of things ranging from 'holding hands' to acupuncture. But it's mostly appropriation because the people selling it really don't have a background in the traditions of these things. I think we're hoping that the fact that there isn't an obvious successor to BPR might be a sign of the times – perhaps things can be less 'one best way' and more open to individualistic approaches. And, to that end, it's people like you guys we probably should look. To people with backgrounds in other traditions that may have personal favourite images that can more knowledgeably inform different ways of thinking organization and strategy. We were hoping that you might tell us where strategy could go.

MJ: Well, in the organizations where I worked it was never really like that [the triangle]. It was more like two triangles stuck together. Or a diamond. And strategy happened (or was joined?) in the middle. With ideas being gathered in and then going back out.

DW: This may be related to what's happening in the field of knowledge management, where the role of middle management is becoming conceptualized as useful [rather than a barrier to creativity and change as was perceived by BPR pundits]. There are some discernible strategies emerging toward 're-layering' – putting middle managers back into the firm as useful intangible knowledge and communication assets.

CB: The way we used to generate dialogue [in staging theatre] sometimes, by prompting and feeding off one another, could actually be related to the way that strategy happened. Ideas would be tossed in, create an effect and then come back out in ways that would partly reflect the person's character and partly what had prompted them. Then each interaction would spark off other interactions.

MH: It's kind of like what I was thinking about. I don't agree with these triangles. I was thinking that organizations, or at least the ones that I know, are kind of like tumbleweeds. They tumble through the environment and some things attach to them and move to the centre of the organization and other things get spun off as it moves. If you were to think about strategy according to this image, then it would be at the middle – like with MJ's diamond. But also it would be like what Chris said, it would always be about picking up and bouncing off things that were happening around you as you take a particular course.

Actually, I was thinking about this last week. But now I'm thinking maybe there could be a bit more to it. I was thinking of how we did this job for Red Stripe [a Jamaican beer]. We were trying to create ideas that would help raise awareness. We had it so that there would be media and arts and film people, people from different spheres, kind of in this arena [draws it as he talks it]. We played movies and stuff, so there were ideas entering this arena from the outside and then things were being 'bounced around'.

It's like dodgem cars, but if you were looking from above it would look like this (see the bottom of Plate 7.1). So what's happening is that different people are bumping into each other and getting something from that. Like, I don't know, a bit of different colour from the other's paint palate.

SC: Maybe like a different sort of momentum from the knocks or 'prompts' from other cars, a bit like what Chris was saying about the theatre prompting.

DW: The 'collisions' also imply a slowing down or cessation of momentum. There are immediate parallels here with institution theory in strategic management.

SC: And with the idea that often a jolt is needed to make someone question an established logic.

MH: Yeah, maybe like that. Anyway, so there's all these creative ideas being generated in this arena but then you need some way to think about how you get this strategy out there. So I thought of a ray-gun. Then it's a matter of thinking about how you can increase the loop or the frequency of the gun with increasing loops so that the image is hitting an increasing range of people.

N: I'm involved in an organization that manages public events in Thailand. So it's like the [Roman] 'arena' idea and you have an inner and outer wall through which life comes in – supplies that you need to do what we do. There are different gateways. Hopefully you arrange it so what you need comes in and what you don't doesn't. I thought it was like a foetus. Within this is an ocean, so that things are fluid. Within the ocean are different parts of the organization afloat. They are different shapes – because they are different. They do different things but some, like accounting or finance think like this, like a triangle, because they have to and you need them. But they all do their jobs and the water passes things between them.

SC: I always thought it was interesting about Thailand that there weren't many straight lines there. Maybe I'm grasping at straws but you see it in the Thai language, when it's written down. No straight lines. You can see this [the curve rather than the straight line] in Thai architecture too.

M: The idea I had, it's hexagonal. A collection of these, a collection of cells, like a honeycomb. And the bees just set about doing what they do. They don't plan it. They just seem to know what they are doing and they work in with everyone else to fill whatever cell needs filling. So it's a very flat structure. You have a queen at the 'top'. Like a parenthesis on its side. And you wouldn't want to be the queen if that's what we'd equate to a strategic manager, because she doesn't really interact with the outside world and its actually not her that really makes things happen or makes the strategy – it's the bees that are out there working.

DW: Although in a way I guess it all 'goes through' the queen.

M: Perhaps there has to be a focal point, even if this is not where the strategy actually comes from. The strategy comes from all the interactions, the doing of what gets done.

DW: The 'queen' is a paradox since she may be considered in many ways inferior to the worker bees. The queen and workers are interdependent, but she is imprisoned within the hive. It is also fascinating how, despite high competition for pollen, the various bees don't compete along the lines suggested by economic principles.

E: I thought that strategy comes from something like reading a [cook]book like the *Larousse Gastronomic*. It's very rich, full of tradition. You have to buy into that. You can't just say anything goes. But the tradition is alive and while there are recipes it's up to you to interpret them and it doesn't make you afraid to experiment a bit and reflect your own personality.

DW: It's like the idea of the reader (or in this case the manager) as the author. A lot of this notion of the author is now entering management and organization studies. The idea of challenging the 'author-ity' traditionally claimed by management is inextricably bound up in these debates.

E: But those debates are so old in the art world! I also thought that while the interaction with a cookbook is a good metaphor for how things (or in this case strategies) get formed, *Larousse* is a nicer model than, say, Delia Smith.

CB: Why?

E: Because with Delia it's so straightforward. 'This is the best way to make eggs, so you must do it like I show you (in excruciating detail) and then everyone will make eggs well'.

SC: It's like best practice. But the problem is that most people have different preferences or traditions of how they prefer things or what suits them best.

E: Yes. Even with toast you get the impression that there's a 'Delia Way' and this is how you should have it.

SC: But in 'real life' everybody has his or her own way with toast. We talk [see Chapter 12] about how you can learn a lot about a person's or an organization's ethos from three anecdotes about them. Perhaps you can do it with the toast image – the three things that a person does with toast in the morning. Or to extend the metaphor, how an organization would treat toast if they were a person. It's interesting how we could believe in Best Practice for something as complex as managing people and yet the idea of Best Practice for managing a piece of toast seems absurd.

E: Not with *Larousse* though. Because there's this combination of tradition in a discipline but with an inventive idiosyncratic style. You are inspired but you don't want to copy him – well only in the sense of working with the traditions but toward developing your own individual style of cooking. Or your own individual strategy I mean.

CB: With Delia you have to have all the correct ingredients for the plan before you can begin. If you don't have the correct herb forget it. Perhaps with *Larousse* you feel more comfortable to make do, to work with what you've got. If you haven't got this then maybe that will work – it might be different, but that might turn out to be good, within the broad traditions of how things or flavours go together. Maybe this is how strategy unfolds? Organizations can't wait until they have everything lined up – the pot is already boiling.

SC: But there probably is a place for the Delias too. Delia is a very efficient manager of a kitchen – a good approach with trainees. It's hard to imagine her creating many new recipes or having a Michelin starred restaurant, but she would run a great school canteen. She's a manager in the classic sense of the manager as an administrator. *Larousse*, though, is a 'professional'.

DW: This may be part of the problem – the replacement or superseding of different professional traditions with managerial administration to the detriment of difference. Actually, the difficulty may lie in polarizing professions versus management. This sets up an either-or in which management seeks to gain the administrative upper hand. Professions are assumed by many managers to be difficult to handle or measure the performance of and likely to misunderstand key organizational principles. Hence, management takes it upon itself to inform the professions of organizational best practice and subsequently 'normalizes' them.

Conclusion

This chapter, looking at strategy as creativity, has built upon the themes outlined at the end of Chapter 1 to suggest that strategy can only come about by the combining of different ideas and dimensions in the light of particular problems or situations. This chapter's logic has also graphically illustrated that our conventional images of strategy should not be the be all and end all, particularly if we want to continue to think creatively. Strategy can be thought in terms of diamonds, tumbleweeds, dodgems, rayguns, knitting, developing dialogue, Thai architecture, beehives, cookery or even a piece of toast. In fact, anything that helps people communicate what they think is important to achieve.

But the images that have been discussed here really only scratch the surface of how strategy could be seen. So, what would you add? What might your, or your group's, images of strategy and organization, be and how could you use these images to think creatively about strategy in your organization?

Case Box 7.3   Folkdevils United

With four years' experience as a 'coolhunter' (young people picked out by companies to tell them what will be cool next year), Matt Hardisty was looking for a new challenge, one that would allow him to explore his interest in the creativity beginning to be showcased over the Internet. He took a year out to do the MA in Creative and Media Enterprises at Warwick during which time *folkdevil.com* was born. Matt was awarded a distinction for his Master's and while continuing to guide *folkdevil*'s organic growth has joined *Naked Communications* as a strategist. Quick to spot *Naked* and *folkdevil*'s rapid development, *Campaign* magazine listed Matt as one of its key 'faces to watch' in 2001. Matt explains the symbiotic relationship between the styles of thinking that *Naked* and *folkdevil* promotes:

> Configuring yourself to sell things used to be about defining a demographic or target segment developing something that provided the general function that that group wanted – then using economies of scale to reduce costs and then pushing the product on to them through one or two static channels. But Britain's cities have actually been awash with a new mode of marketing for quite some time. The division between the traditional creative disciplines of music, clothing and art are dissolving for branded 'association'. Age is no longer considered to be such a big measure, as the word 'youth' becomes blurred as we progress to targeting by 'lifestyle'. Brands have become 'cultures', creating immersive environments through which consumers can experience a brand's values. There has been an explosion in new, innovative types of channels. And this diminishing of traditional boundaries has led to a new creative fusion. Beyond bland 'sponsorship' and 'promotional activities', new processes of 'promotional symbiosis' have evolved whereby particular relationships are developed by networking together a blend of micro and macro channels in order to convey a particular set of values or 'mythology' about a brand. An example of this new phenomenon can be seen in the fashion brand, skim.com. The label's clothing features a unique e-mail address on each garment facilitating passersby to contact the wearer in an attempt to traverse the on- and the off-line realms and this helps build a particular sense of what *skim is* about.

'It's all about how hard you push the boundaries', Matt explains. 'And what we try and do at *Naked is* to help our clients think of themselves as not contained within traditional boundaries or channels. We network a web of channels into a dynamic family that helps develop a complex relationship with customers to convey a sense of something truly different in order to capture people's attention.' Matt draws the following figures to convey the concept.

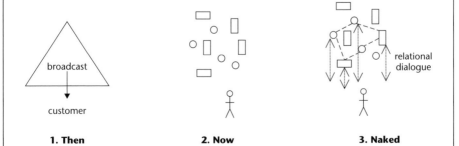

1. Then   2. Now   3. Naked

One of Matt's latest projects for *Naked* involved connecting Reebok, local radio stations, skateboarding and bmx communities, various DJs, and people who wanted to have a laugh playing football, for 'The Sofa Games'. Inspired by Reebok's recent ads featuring underactive people being eaten by sofas, this involved temporarily transforming an urban area of Dublin into a playground featuring old sofas as goals for five-a-side football and 'urban furniture' for skateboarders and bmx-ers, surrounded by 'chill-out' lounges serving drinks and food, all 'cushioned by an Irish backdrop of progressive nu-skool beats'.

This way of 'connecting' and building links or a 'relational dialogue' is very similar to that which inspires Matt's work with *folkdevil*. Here, partners are helped to think of their organizations differently: not as isolated fragments or separated stand alone monoliths, but independent local units that are at the same time interconnected across traditional boundaries with other like-minded customers and organizations (Matt claims that the distinction between 'customer' and 'company' and 'competitor' is becoming increasingly irrelevant as things fragment):

> The Internet is enabling a new entrepreneurial spirit to emerge. No longer marginalized to the classifieds, fly-posting or word-of-mouth communication, new local start-ups can now focus on particular niche characteristics and personal identities and then extend beyond their immediate geography and embrace a 'global' audience. But for all the cries of an emerging egalitarian environment (coupled with IBM's visions of 'Mom and Pop' stores selling olive oil from remote parts of Italy to 'cash rich, time poor' consumers in urban areas), the reality is that while these 'Folkdevils' [Matt's word for these new little 'global' players] are good at producing innovative content, they are bad at consolidating this into a viable ongoing organization. These independent enterprises behave like a quasi-cottage industry – 'folksy', which is good, but also introverted and detached. A cross-cutting collaborative network promoting independent talent is needed. To allow 'folkdevils' to progress beyond 'contacts' and facilitate business on a global basis, a new empathetic resource is needed to enable their dreams to become a reality – a 'virtual cultural intermediary' – to compensate for the increasing fragmentation in the workplace, and a means through which productive exchange can take place. That's where *folkdevil.com* comes in.

One way that *folkdevil.com* 'comes in' is through an individualized mapping technique. Matt explains this while free-handing a configuration of identities that he has been working on recently:

> Here you've got a radio station, a ticket seller, a record label, an info-website and a couple of clothing labels – they share what we call the same 'tribal frequency,' so they benefit by linking their marketing spends and subsequently developing a collective brand equity. But they all stay independent, which is what they're into it for. Collectively they hook into other Internet sites and channels that help convey their 'tribal freq', while these sites and channels also gain by association while staying independent and creative. Drawing things in this way helps them see how they can change with the new environment, keeping what they like about their histories – their independence and creativity – and growing for the future.

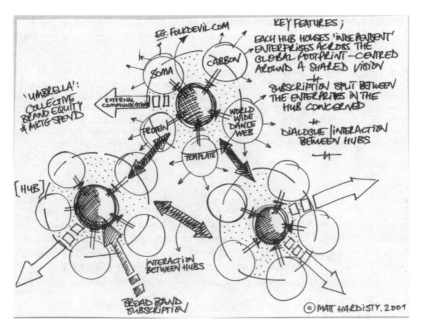

The recently launched 'Reading Room Media Network' provides an example of the independent/co-joined model that Matt and *folkdevil* help develop. The Reading Room Media Network's organic sites are a showcase for independent British talent, from record labels to film makers, while also providing credible content for the astute cultural consumer. Not only do the sites provide independent lifestyle brands (with little budget) with the ability to reach larger audiences, but allow a marketer wishing to target a 'fibre-optic' audience the chance to communicate in a credible fashion across a previously elusive network of channels.

Matt believes that these united folkdevils are breathing a breath of fresh air into business: 'They are stamping out the earlier apathy of Generation X and the British condition of it being a crime to take anything too seriously.' Moreover, more traditional businesses must similarly rethink the way they perceive themselves as being configured. 'There is now a real need for many organizations to fragment and focus on particular vibes while sharing information and ideas about their often-common customers, and begin to collaborate and co-evolve in order to exploit the new opportunities presented by the multimedia economy,' says Matt. 'With central "sites" holding independent people together as a fluid entity,' he explains, 'the idea is that enterprises within the ecosystem can benefit from shared traffic across different ecosystems in a globally networked environment. So that they can grow without becoming the sort of monolithic corporations that by their nature dull the things that the people who started these enterprises are passionate about: creativity and independence.'

1. *Can what* Naked *and* folkdevil *do be captured with hierarchical triangles and straight lines?*
2. *What does the individualized mapping approach allow* folkdevil *to do for its partners?*

3. What folkdevil *is doing is all very well for so-called youth projects but in what ways might what is going on here also be relevant for bigger and more established companies?*

This case was written in January 2001 and updated in February 2002. With special thanks to Matt Hardisty and the good people at *Naked.* Further resources on this emerging phenomenon can be found at ⟨www.folkdevil.com⟩, with additional examples of community-sustained 'independence' available at the San Francisco-based sites ⟨www.skinny.com⟩ and ⟨www.betalounge.com⟩, and the Toronto-based ⟨www.2Kool4Radio.com⟩. If it's still up, The Sofa Games can been seen at ⟨www.sofagames.ie⟩. Comments may be directed to matt@nakedcomms.com. An earlier version of this case was first published in S. Cummings, *ReCreating Strategy* (London: Sage Publications, 2002)

Note

1 The use of such terms in London's media industries is often ironic, playful and self-deprecatory rather than pejorative. Nevertheless, 'creative and suits' are frequently referenced (often literally, for example in the dress codes of an advertising agency) as a self-conscious playing out of roles. It is this retreat into 'mythical' roles which concerns us here; it is certainly not the authors' intention to perpetuate stereotypical views of managers and artists – quite the opposite in fact.

Source Material and Recommended Further Reading

The quotation from Arthur Koestler at the head of this chapter is taken from the brilliant *The Act of Creation* (London: Hutchinson, 1976), probably still the best philosophical assessment of creation available. The quote from Robin Wensley is just something he said in the department. The limited history of management and strategy, and some of the other themes addressed in the early and later parts of this chapter, are given a fuller treatment in S. Cummings, *ReCreating Strategy* (London: Sage, 2002).

F.W. Taylor's *Principles of Scientific Management* was first published in 1911 (New York: Harper). It was reissued in 1947 as *Scientific Management* by the same publisher to tap into the renewed demand for 'Management' after the Second World War. The excerpts from Michel Hammer are taken from M. Hammer and J. Champy, *Reengineering the Corporation: A Manifesto for Business Revolution* (London: Brealy, 1994).

Luther Gulick's work on efficiency dates back to his work with Urwick – see L. Gulick and L. Urwick, *Papers on the Administration* (Free Press: New York, 1937).

Ikujiro Nonaka has authored and co-authored many books and articles on the importance of knowledge in organizations. However, a good introduction to these ideas is provided in 'SECI, Ba and Leadership: A Unified Model of Dynamic Knowledge Creation', which illustrates Nonaka's diagrammatic syntheses of organic thought processes (I. Nonaka et al., *Long Range Planning*, 33, 2000, 5–34). Also worth consulting in this regard are Max Boisot's books: *Information Space: A Framework for Learning in Organizations* (London: Routledge, 1995); and *Knowledge Assets: Securing Competitive Advantage in the Information Economy* (Oxford: Oxford University Press, 1998).

Good examples of the limited history generally taken on board by students of management and strategy maybe be found in C.S. George's *The History of Management Thought* (Englewood Cliffs, NJ: Prentice-Hall, 1968); Daniel Wren's *The Evolution of Management Thought* (New York, Wiley, 1972 and 1994); or Stephen Robbins' best-selling textbook *Management* (Englewood Cliffs, NJ: Prentice-Hall, 1983).

The formation of the AMA is described, with first-hand knowledge, in L.A. Appley, *Management at Mid-century* (New York: American Management Association, 1954). For research 'confirming' the acceptance of the essential elements of management, see J.F. Mee, *A History of Twentieth Century Management Thought* (Ann Arbor, MI: University Microfilms Inc., 1963).

J.D. Mooney's views are taken from *Onward Industry: The Principles of Organization* (New York: Harper & Row, 1947). A.D. Chandler's presuppositions about what his history was investigating can be seen in *Strategy and Structure: Chapters in the History of the Industrial Enterprise* (Cambridge, MA: MIT Press, 1962); and *The Visible Hand: The Managerial Revolution in American Business* (Cambridge, MA: Harvard University Press, 1977).

Kathleen Eisenhardt has many articles on flexibility and teamwork. The bicycle racing analogy came from a keynote address she gave to the Colloquium of the European Group for Organization Studies, Maastricht, the Nethertands, 1996, but the concepts in use can be found in S. Brown and K. Eisenhardt 'Product Development: Past Research, Present Findings and Future Directions', *Academy of Management Review*, 20, 2, 1995, 343–78.

Mary Jo Hatch's work is best explored in her book: Mary Jo Hatch, *Organization Theory: Modern Symbolic and Postmodern Perspectives* (London: Oxford University Press, 1997).

Jim March's comment on the fine line between lunacy and genius can be found in: Jane G. March, *The Pursuit of Organizational Intelligence* (Oxford: Blackwell, 1999).

To build on some of the ideas and references to creativity in management the following references will be useful. Steven Feldman (1990) identifies some links between symbolism and politics that are forged by story-telling and cultural creativity in *Human Relations* (43 (9), 809–28). This chapter has not really focused on these aspects of creativity and Feldman's article is, therefore, a useful addition. Cameron Ford's work is, however, more mainstream in that it links creativity directly to innovation. This can be read in 'A Theory of Individual Creative Actions in Multiple Social Domains', *Academy of Management Review*, 21(4), 1996, 1112–42. Typical of many authors in management theory, Ford's main conceptual lens revolves around innovation and he uses creativity (or more strictly creative acts and leaps in thinking) more in the way of an addendum to innovation. He notes in the same article that the *Academy of Management Review*'s subject index entry for creativity reads 'see Innovation'! Teresa Amabile and her co-authors (Conti, Coon, Lazenby and Herron) take a similarly conservative view of creativity, arguing that it equates at least in part to having good ideas. This is outlined in 'Assessing the Work Environment for Creativity', *Academy of Management Journal*, 39, 1996, 1154–84. However, the strength of Amabile et al.'s work is that they directly address the question of the contexts in which such new ideas can emerge. They assessed perceived work environments which, although very skewed toward a psychological analysis of the workplace, nevertheless reveal key factors such as the encouragement of creativity, high levels of autonomy, having resources for example which positively correlate with the emergence of new and innovative ideas.

Richard Woodman (along with Sawyer and Griffin) takes an interactionist approach to the same question posed by Amabile and her colleagues. In 'Toward a Theory of Organizational Creativity', *Academy of Management Review*, 18(2), 1993, 293–321, they take the view that creativity is 'doing something for the first time anywhere or creating new knowledge' (p. 293). Again, they focus upon the availability of slack resources, open information flows and organic organizational structures such as networks or matrices, as conducive to creativity. The work of Greg Oldham and Anne Cummings is also in this vein, 'Employee Creativity: Personal and Contextual Factors at Work', *Academy of Management Journal*, 39, 1996, 607–34.

There is a great deal of similarity between creativity and what has become known in management theory as 'knowledge management'. The prevailing hypotheses in this context argue largely that tacit knowledge helps foster creativity which, in turn, underpins innovation (note the subsuming of creativity to innovation once again). The work of Dorothy Leonard and Sylvia

Sensiper is typical. In 'The Role of Tacit Knowledge in Group Innovation', *California Management Review*, 40(3), 1998, 112–32, they argue that tacit knowledge and creativity are inter-linked (again through the process of innovation). Tacit knowledge is that which cannot be codified entirely and hence remains subjective and largely experiential. It is the ability of individuals to communicate and to utilize this tacit knowledge which underpins creative and innovative actions. As Leonard and Sensiper argue, 'the creativity necessary for innovation derives not only from obvious and visible expertise, but from invisible reservoirs of experience' (p. 127).

On a more philosophical note, the dilemma between potentiality and actuality in creativity is well captured in an article by Almer J. Mandt in a little-known journal called *The Modern Schoolman* (LIX, March 1982). He writes of Aristotle, Hegel and Whitehead on creativity. Drawing on the different interpretations of the philosophers Aristotle, Whitehead and Hegel, Mandt argues that the Aristotelian view of creativity focused largely on its actuality – its being as an actual thing. For Hegel and Whitehead (not often considered together as being similar) creativity is far more about the process of becoming – focused upon how individuals create and re-create themselves and their interpretive 'reality'. In terms of strategy, potentiality could be taken to be the resource base and the capacity for creativity in all aspects of organization (people, processes and context) while actuality refers to implementation (putting it into practice). Both Hegel and Whitehead would (as strategists) likely emphasize the capacity and resource-based view (including tacit knowledge) while Aristotle would emphasize the actuality – what happens and exists when creative strategies are put in place and implemented? The distinction is more than just the domain of philosophers and of interest to scholars interested in metaphysics. Managers, in organizations of all kinds, are faced with the ambiguities and uncertainties that emanate from having to 'do' something yet at the same time they are expected to balance 'universals' (such as structures, concepts and ideas) with 'bare particulars' (impressions, feelings and senses). In commercial organizations, they are also expected to be successful and make profit from such strategic actions. For those interested in pursuing the philosophical investigation, an earlier article by Berndtson, 'A Theory of Radical Creativity', *Modern Schoolman*, 53, November 1975, 1–18, would be rewarding reading.

Other philosophers also mirror some of the key debates in organizational strategy. In the debate between 'planned' and 'emergent strategies', the philosophy of Gilles Deleuze and Félix Guattari, *A Thousand Plateaux: Capitalism and Schizophrenia* (London: Athlone, 1988) is revealing. Finding its source in French intellectual tradition, this work questions creativity as some element of development toward some predetermined purpose and, ultimately, achieving some unanimity of order (such as that proposed by historian Francis Fukuyama in *The End of History and the Last Man* (Harmondsworth: Penguin, 1992)). Rather, the French view is that creativity is an 'involution' whereby creativity (through art, for example) is not only an emergent process but is also likely to produce an outcome (in the language of strategic management), which was neither intended by the artist, nor perceived in the same way as the artist (as subject) intended (see also Robin Wensley's chapter 'Strategy as Intention and Anticipation', this volume). So 'creative' strategies may not be imbued with intention of order and producing something and, at the same time, what is produced in terms of a decision 'outcomes' may not represent the original intention of the strategist, since in their becoming they are transformed and perceived differently by those upon whom strategic decisions impinge.

Finally, Raymond Williams in his book *Key Words* (London: Flamingo, 1983), notes how the meaning of the word creativity has changed dramatically in terms of temporality from denoting a divine action in the past, to a potential (creative) production or human action in the future. Williams also points to the trivialization of the word, particularly in popular management-speak and in industries such as advertising where he notes that advertising professionals, who describe themselves as creative, actually carry out basically repetitive tasks. It is also a fruitful exploration to compare the emergence of creativity alongside the emergence of concepts such as 'charisma', which was also to produce novelty by the bearer of charisma inverting 'all value hierarchies and overthrowing custom, law and tradition (see Max Weber, *Economy and Society* (New York: Bedminster, 1968)).

For a critique of the 'new managerialism', see Mike Power, 'The Audit Society', in Peter Miller and Anthony G. Hopwood (eds), *Accounting as Social and Institutional Practice* (Cambridge: Cambridge University Press, 1994); and Jim McGuigan, *Culture and the Public Sphere* (London: Routledge, 1996), pp. 59–67.

For a critique of the 'myth of genius', see Robert W. Weisberg, *Creativity: Beyond the Myth of Genius* (New York: Freeman, 1993). Margaret Boden provides a useful summary of some of the myths and counter-myths in the opening chapter of *Dimensions of Creativity* (Cambridge, MA: MIT Press, 1994). Boden emphasizes the importance of boundaries in the creative process. For a more pragmatic, less theoretical treatment of the creativity question, see Winston Fletcher, *Tantrums and Talent: How to Get the Best from Creative People* (Henley on Thames: Admap, 1999). In the management literature, Teresa Amabile and Rosabeth Moss Kantor both provide a helpful discussion of how creativity can be 'managed' (or not) in organizations. See Teresa M. Amabile, 'How to Kill Creativity', in *Harvard Business Review on Breakthrough Thinking* (Harvard, MA: Harvard Business School Press, 1999); and Rosabeth Moss Kantor, 'When a Thousand Flowers Bloom', in *Research in Organizational Behaviour*, 10, 1988, 123–67.

Freudian theories of creativity are analysed by Anthony Storr in *The Dynamics of Creation* (London: Secker and Warburg, 1972). For the place of women in the cultural industries, see Gillian Swanson and Patricia Wise, *Going for Broke: Women's Participation in the Arts and Cultural Industries* (Brisbane: Australian Key Centre for Cultural and Media Policy, Griffith University, 1998). See also Danielle Cliche, Ritva Mitchell and Andreas Johannes Wiesand (eds), *Pyramid or Pillars: Unveiling the Status of Women in Arts and Media Professions in Europe* (Bonn: ARCult Media, 2000).

Statistics on employment and training in the creative industries in Britain come from Andy Feist and Jane O'Brien, *Employment in the Arts and Cultural Industries: an Analysis of the 1991 Census* (London: Arts Council of England, 1995).

There have been many sociological studies of the tensions between 'creatives' and 'suits' within organizations, notably from the 'new institutionalist' school of American sociologists including Paul DiMaggio and Walter W. Powell. See for example, Walter W. Powell and Rebeca Jo Friedkin, 'Organisational Factors in Public Television Decision-making', in Paul J. DiMaggio (ed.), *Non-Profit Enterprise in the Arts: Studies in Mission and Constraint* (New York: Oxford University Press, 1986), pp. 245–69. For a contemporary variation on the theme, see also John Seabrook, *Nobrow: The Culture of Marketing, the Marketing of Culture* (London: Methuen, 2000).

The quotation at the head of the 'Shaken and Stirred' section by Bernard Arnault is taken from 'Capitalist du jour', by Anthony Sibillin (*EuroBusiness*, 2(8), January 2001, 56–66). Special thanks to Silviya Svejenova from IESE in Spain for bringing this to our attention.

A more structured approach to drawing organization, and thus thinking strategy, differently is provided by Henry Mintzberg's, 'Organigraphs: Drawing how Companies Really Work', *Harvard Business Review*, September–October 1999.

Answers to Taylor versus Hammer statements: 1A Hammer; 1B Taylor; 2A Taylor; 2B Hammer; 3A Taylor; 3B Hammer; 4A Taylor; 4B Hammer; 5A Hammer; 5B Taylor.

The 'alternative' views of organization and strategy shown in Plate 7.1 are drawn by Stacey Arnold (top) and Matt Hardisty (bottom). Many thanks to them.

Character key for the discussion in the 'Shaken and Stirred' section is as follows: CB = Chris Bilton; DW = David Wilson; E = Emma Chetcuti; M = Marie Brennan; MH = Matt Hardisty; MJ = Yu-Jeong 'MJ' Mun; N = Kewalin 'Nim' Khunawong; SC = Stephen Cummings.

*With organizations fragmenting into networks and clever firms recognizing that because they can no longer be all things to all people they must maintain particular identities within different segments (Chapter 1 and 2), the ability to successfully create (Chapter 7) and orchestrate (Chapter 5) and communicate between (Chapter 6) different elements has become an increasingly important strategic skill. Within the conventional strategy literature, interconnection has generally been addressed within the sub-field of mergers and acquisitions (M&As). This has tended to use the image of 'warfare' and the frameworks of microeconomics to explain corporate behaviour in this regard. This chapter argues that this traditional language lacks the richness to convey the organic and emotional aspects of why and how firms actually connect and how these connections may succeed or fail, and proposes a new image: **exploration**. This analogy, and different famous explorers and expeditions, are used to develop a greater appreciation of M&A and how the strategist may manage **interconnection** more effectively.*

8 Strategy as Exploration and Interconnection

DUNCAN ANGWIN

The unknown always passes for the marvellous.
Tacitus, Agricola *(c. AD 98)*

The eye altering alters all.
William Blake, The Mental Traveller *(1800–1810)*

Mergers and acquisitions (M&As) are grand statements of strategy. When acquisitions are completed, they represent strategic revitalization for the acquirer and frequently corporate death, or an ignominious process of wasting away, for the acquired. The stakes in such deals, which can reach gargantuan proportions, are high for all stakeholders and lead frequently to extreme tensions and conflicts. It is no small surprise then that in these situations the language of war dominates negotiations:

- opposing sides 'manoeuvre for advantage';
- 'war rooms' are used for planning the campaign; and
- tactics are couched in terms of 'keeping the powder dry' for last minute 'assaults' on winning the hearts and minds of a complex array of stakeholders.

The warfare analogy, popularized in the films *Wall Street* and *Barbarians at the Gate*, views the eventual acquisition as the 'conclusion of a battle', with a victor and a vanquished. The hero of the hour is the acquirer's all-conquering CEO. It is he or she who has led forces in the most effective way in the clash of competing visions for the future of the target business. However, hostile takeovers are but a very small minority of all deals transacted. The analogy with open warfare, while attractive to the world's media, is therefore too extreme for the majority of acquisitions, where there is always some posturing but where both sides ultimately want to come to agreement.

Beyond the language of warfare, the dominant conceptual frameworks of the M&A terrain have been formed from the perspectives of economics and finance. These two disciplines have provided narrow views of the phenomenon in terms of overly rationalist explanations of why M&As take place and limited approaches to M&A performance. More recently, the disappointing insights provided by these fields on M&A performance have encouraged those within the 'organizational behaviour' field to focus upon human issues in the post-acquisition phase.

While these three perspectives and the language of war now make up the conventional map of M&A, I want to suggest that 'exploration' offers a richer language and analogy for M&A. This chapter aims to show, through analogy with *exploration and explorers*, fresh perspectives upon the M&A field and to give further insight into strategy. Exploration still retains the element of M&A as drama, as heroic life and death struggle over unknown futures, but it reduces the over-emphasis on a military image of conflict and destruction and rational context-free or predictable choices. Exploration focuses attention upon reaching into the unknown, extending boundaries of knowledge, experience and ownership. Explorers show heroism in risking life and limb for the dazzling potential of alluring possibilities. Rather than conflict, M&A in these terms is about *the race* between potential acquirers: to participate, to be first, and to continue to explore. In the recent mega-merger boom, where the global geography of business is increasingly warped and weaved, connected and interconnected, the analogy with exploration resonates with corporate giants in their race to acquire and redefine global industries. In striving to dominate new territory, vast gains are predicted for leading acquirers, while those left behind may dwindle and perish in the cold winds of increasing competition. With each megadeal, part of the global competitive landscape is recreated.

Rather like the changing boundaries brought about by the process of exploration, M&As in practice are a shifting montage of changing emphases and values. However, to focus only on the notion of *exploration* for insight into M&A would be to fall into the same trap as the other traditional perspectives mentioned above, of missing the vital importance of *interconnectedness*. As I shall argue, the pressure for M&As to perform in the Anglo-American system has led to an over-emphasis upon narrow financial and economic perspectives at the expense of other, often human, issues and an almost total blindness to other critical linkages. Interconnection is a vital component in understanding the M&A process and an equally critical facet of Strategy. Figure 8.1 outlines the emphases of conventional views of M&A and the richer picture provided by the exploration analogy.

In order to convey our rich exploration and interconnectedness perspective on M&A, and in keeping with the visual mapping emphasis of this book, I shall draw upon the illustration 'Treasure Island' and its corresponding key (Plates 8.1).

Immediately the eye is drawn to the heroic quality and strong narrative feel of the illustration as a group of explorers make landfall on an island where there is believed to be treasure. While this heroic focus upon the explorers is a core element in our rich portrayal, we wish to draw out the importance of the process of exploration, embedded in a rich multi-level set of shifting contextual influences. All interconnect in various ways and shape the human enactment of exploring for treasure. This chapter

Plate 8.1 The mergers and acquisitions 'Treasure Island' (replete with hidden dangers)
Source: Illustration by Richard Barrett. © Richard Barrett.

Treasure Island in a Sea of opportunity

Outer circle
- Arbitrage vulture
- Clouds of economic recession
- Competitor galleons
- Distant financial markets
- Investing hawks and doves
- Lightning share price plunge
- Political sea monsters
- Sun's media interest

Island perimeter
- Due diligence corals
- Lured or fleeing natives?
- Legislative reefs
- Rocks of bad publicity

The explorers
- Cannon balls – cash and equity
- Crude map of certainty – 'X marks the spot'
- Flag of intention
- Prepared for action

On the island
- Blizzards of minutiae
- Downsizing wastelands
- Fool's gold
- Friendly natives?
- Gulf of misunderstanding
- Jaws of reporting
- Jungle of misrepresentation
- Mountainous communications pass
- Mountains of debt
- Peeks of optimism
- Pyramid of unfamiliar knowledge
- Quicksands of uncertainty
- Rift valley of retrenchment
- Snake of suspicion
- Stone idols of hidden beliefs
- Swamps of despondency
- Volcanic customer(s)
- Whirlpool of rumours

Beware of invisibles
- Intractable IT fever
- Lethargy sickness
- Morale virus
- Redundancy plague

Plate 8.1 (continued)

Conventional views of M&A	Exploration
Simplified and rational motives	Complexity of motives
Focus on signing the deal	Focus on the process
Traditional emphasis upon numerical and contractual issues	Emphasis upon human qualities and interactions
Fragmentation of issues	Interconnection of issues and levels of analysis
Single performance outcomes post-deal	Multiple outcomes post-possession
Deal as an end in itself	Possession marking the beginning of further exploration Expedition as legitimating further exploration

Figure 8.1   The different emphases of conventional and exploration analogies of M&A

is structured around seven themes arising from the exploration process, highlighted by this illustration.

(1)   First, the explorers in the foreground raise the issue of 'why are they there?'. There has clearly been some sort of planning as they are holding a crude map of the island and they can also see half-hidden treasure on the shore, lush vegetation and shrouded peaks. The first section of this chapter thus asks *what motivates explorers* examining parallels with the motivations behind M&As. Often it is simply that the unknown passes for the marvellous, to borrow Tacitus's words.

(2)   The explorers are clearly well equipped with substantial armaments and a map. How did they manage to get into such a position? Section two examines the *launching of an expedition*. This is where arguing the case for an expedition or acquisition requires a legitimising rationale or vision, often based on the promise of riches. The exploration analogy highlights how tantalizing promises can overwhelm rationality. The eye altering, can indeed as Blake said, alter all.

(3)   Our explorers are in the early stages of their expedition, but are already encountering and anticipating significant obstacles. Gathering storm clouds may be an economic downturn, with lightning representing volatility in stock markets. Sea monsters may be political uncertainty and in the distance there are competitors' galleons. Previous explorers have sunk on legislative and regulatory reefs, and it is not clear the type of welcome that foreigners will receive. When expeditions are under way, explorers and acquirers, alike, battle the elements. With regard to M&A, there is a considerable literature on how to carry out the technical aspects of a deal. However, as the exploration analogy in section three will show, the processual dynamic, in terms of different *styles of exploring*, of working with or against the elements in different ways, is missing. In this section I suggest a typology of different styles for acquirers. Depending on the context, different styles can lead to success or failure in terms of possessing what the explorer is seeking. If the explorer/acquirer has an ego (and all do), 'failure' will generally lead him or her to mount another expedition, and (less often) question and change his or her style. Success, on the other hand, leads to possession and also further expeditions.

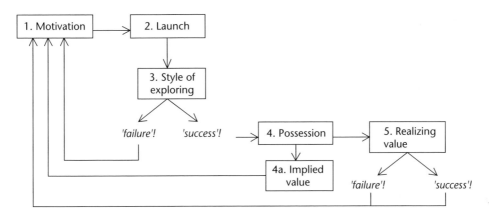

Figure 8.2   The perpetual exploration/acquisition cycle

(4) For our explorers, once through the legislative and due diligence reefs, it seems only a short leap to the shore to embed a flag and claim ownership over the island. However, there is so much that is not known or anticipated, that this exercise can only be symbolic and not reflect real understanding of the risks and opportunities that lie ahead. In section four, on *possession and a hero's welcome*, I show the symbolic importance of planting the flag, and how it can easily be seen as the end point in the acquisition process, with the emphasis placed on 'implying value' and moving on to the next mission rather than actually realizing value.

(5) 'Treasure Island' is replete with challenges for our explorers and section five looks at attempts to *search for gold* or realize value. Poor outcomes suggest that there are structural difficulties in exploration and M&A alike that lead to the destruction of value. The nature of the acquisition process itself, the deal-centredness that leads to inflated expectations, and implementation difficulties, all contribute to disappointing results. This begs the question of whether gold ever existed. As with many expeditions, the intended results may have been disappointing but with hindsight considerable rewards may have occurred from surprising discoveries. Similarly with M&A, intentions may not be fully achieved, but there can be significant unintended benefits, where companies have the eyes to see and the ability to learn.

(6) The previous sections describe a sequence of exploration steps. In section six I view this *exploration cycle* as self-perpetuating. Failure to seal the deal often hastens the quest to find other targets for fear that others will get there first too. Failure to extract value post-acquisition will also build motivation to find richer seams. Even a completed expedition, or M&A deal, which represents concrete success for many stakeholders is not merely an end. This outcome legitimates further exploration or deal making and so the cycles are connected: event completion provides both further motivation and 'capital' for making further expeditions or deals (this cycle is depicted in Figure 8.2). However, 'deal doing' capital ebbs away as memories fade fast. The cycle of expedition or deal making must be repeated quickly to maintain its worth. And with shortening time horizons, companies or explorers often race to make deals and pronounce their successes before value can be properly extracted, all of which can lead to overstretch and an eventual hasty demise.

(7)   Finally, I look at the broad implications of exploration in *redrawing boundaries*. Acquirers are now acting on international and global scales and redrawing industry boundaries. In so doing, boundaries and barriers in business, geography and even time, are being fundamentally altered. However, these boundaries are being redrawn based upon a narrow set of commercial dimensions. These subsume many other connected non-commercial dimensions, which will continue to influence business in unanticipated ways. As a consequence, new challenges will emerge constantly. As old boundaries fade, new ones emerge at different levels and with different complexions, and to tackle them, new breeds of explorer will be needed.

Why Explore?

Explorers

> *Zipangu is an island in the eastern ocean . . . its inhabitants are handsome, fair skinned and civilised in their manners. They have gold in the greatest abundance, their supplies being inexhaustible.*

Marco Polo

Marco Polo's journey inspired generations of explorers. His *inspirational depictions*, of golden pagodas, teeming cities, wharves and markets thronged with merchants; cargoes of gold, spices, jewels; the palaces and hunting parties of the Great Khan Kublai, were accounts which were translated and copied over and over by medieval scholars. European artists reinforced this literary vision, even though they had little idea of the ethnic or architectural features of the Far East, depicting the Great Khan as King Arthur or Charlemagne, and fortresses as Tintagel or Carcassonne. One avid reader was Christopher Columbus who made copious notes in the margins of a translation. In particular he focused upon the rewards, such as natural wealth and rich artefacts, allusions to ethnological features and anything that accentuated the difficulties and lengths of the overland journey to the East.

There is no doubt, therefore, that *commercial rewards* are important incentives for exploration. For the Iberian explorers of the fifteenth and sixteenth centuries, the principal sources of wealth were land and labour. The quickest and socially most acceptable way for personal advancement was by seizing land with a docile peasantry. As the opportunities in Spain and Portugal were limited, new territories held much promise.

Commercial incentives, however, are arguably not the most important motives. *Ideological and political beliefs*, such as the drive for religious conversions, played an important role in much exploration. Vasco da Gama went in search of Christians and spices. Bernal Diaz, in his conquest of Peru went, 'to serve God and His Majesty, to give light to those who were in darkness, and to grow rich, as all men desire to do'. For Columbus, his professed goals were to hasten the conversion of the world to Christianity. Indeed, as early as his first voyage, he suggested that all profits from his enterprise should be used for the Christian re-conquest of Jerusalem from the Muslims. Nearly all early explorers reiterated the desire to spread Christianity, a religiosity that held extraordinary power in medieval and early modern Europe and touched virtually every aspect of human life.

Personal fame and reputation are also of great importance. When Cortes scuttled his boats at Vera Cruz, in preparation for marching into Mexico against the Aztecs at Teotihuacan, he made many comparisons with brave deeds done by Roman heroes.

Reputation was clearly in Diaz's mind in Peru when speaking to his followers, 'my descendants can say "my father came to discover and conqueror these lands"'. Although on a 'no-win, no-fee basis', Columbus managed to extract considerable promises of status from the Spanish sovereigns. He was to be appointed Admiral of the Ocean Sea with all rights and prerogatives to pass to his heirs in perpetuity. In addition he was to be made viceroy and governor of the lands with the right to appoint administrators and justices.

With such rewards on offer, *personal rivalries* are commonplace. While they can produce negative behaviours, the existence of rivals helps define goals, maintains and sustains 'the race'. The more recent example of Scott and Shackleton is now legendary in this regard.

Apart from beckoning riches and visions of personal gain, perhaps the most important personal motivator is the 'need to explore'. Most explorers' sense of self-worth hinges on being able to continue exploring, so a further motivator is the *completed expedition as legitimator* of further such activity. This explains Christopher Columbus' need to make successive voyages, four in all, across to the New World, despite failing health and a dwindling reputation.

Failure to achieve the stated aims of an expedition has a personal cost in reducing the capacity of an explorer to act as an explorer. Reputation is diminished as the public regard failure with social embarrassment. The reduction in reputational capital hinders the raising of funds and support for further expeditions. The explorer's mandate to act declines rapidly and the fear of a fading reputation provides a driver for greater exploits to maintain worth in investors' eyes. As a consequence, history is strewn with examples of explorers making renewed efforts to recover from setbacks. Shackleton continued to strive for the South Pole despite nearly dying from appalling physical hardship, suffering chronic asthma (which he concealed), and being bedevilled by inadequate finance. More recently, Ranulph Fiennes has lost several body parts in repeated attempts to walk unaided to the Pole.

Many of our examples of key explorers are from the Iberian Peninsula and we should ask why there was a Renaissance there in exploration, in particular, at that time. One reason was that the Moors had recently been driven from Spain with the fall of Granada in 1492, and the enthusiasms and ambitions generated by war needed an outlet. Such *contextual pressures* for exploration are also common in other times, with John Barrow, the 'father of Arctic Exploration', explaining that the expeditions to the North Pole were a way of occupying the Royal Navy as they were beginning to stagnate after Napoleon's defeat. There was a possibility of commercial profit, but more compelling were national pride and the quest for scientific knowledge. More recently, the race to put the first man on the moon can be seen as an important push by President Kennedy to build national pride and proclaim global technological mastery over a threatening Soviet space programme.

Here the explorer image shows a multitude of motives. There are general convictions of a religious/moral nature, a wish for personal glory and recognition, the desire to exploit commercial gain for king, country and personal wealth, and perhaps most important, the insatiable *need* to explore itself. In addition, these motives are all intertwined to varying degrees so that it would be rare for an explorer to have a singular motivation.

While so much about explorers is expressed in heroic and individual terms, it is also important to recognize that there are also contextual pressures to cause exploration. Those in authority incentivized exploration to extend geographic, knowledge, cultural and religious boundaries as well as to employ under-utilized resources.

Exploration was encouraged as a means of occupying armed forces in peacetime, extending territory for religious and commercial fealty, boosting national pride and finding answers to scientific questions. Commercial investors also played an important role in facilitating exploration for the identification of potential commercial opportunities. These contextual pressures all influence the potential explorer in facilitating or constraining their activities, and indeed may give rise to the existence of more explorers at some times than others. For a full understanding of why explorers explore, we therefore have to consider interconnected personal motivations and external contextual pressures.

Acquirers

Traditional M&A literature tends to confuse motivations for deals with the need to legitimate the activity and thus adopts a narrow set of rational explanations grounded in economic and financial explanation. The analogy with exploration and explorers brings a broader appreciation of motivations and reveals, through interconnectedness, a greater complexity than acknowledged currently in the M&A literature.

Parallels can be drawn with the motivations behind exploration, described above, and M&A. At the personal level, *commercial reward* is an important, but understated, motivator of top management. It is well known that top management benefit from the increased size of the group over time as larger companies generally pay higher salaries and give better benefits than smaller firms. In addition, benefits can be tied to deals in terms of the granting of share options and various forms of golden handcuffs and parachutes, which can also provide substantial personal gain.

At the firm level, most M&A is undertaken to generate *commercial rewards* for the firm and its stakeholders. These commercial rewards can take many forms such as increasing sales, gaining entry into new markets, acquiring new capabilities, competencies and assets, improving operating efficiency and reducing the cost base, increasing bargaining power through the value chain. All these commercial gains are aimed at improving a firm's competitive position and increasing overall returns to shareholders, by raising profits and building a stronger position in the financial markets.

Linked with commercial reward is increase in *personal fame and reputation*. The success of a takeover undoubtedly reflects positively upon the person of the acquiring CEO, and a track record in achieving stated takeover goals has tremendous cachet among business leaders, investors and media. Implicit in linking a CEO's ability to close M&A deals is the image of CEO as 'hero'. This embodies noble qualities, eagerly seized upon by the media, such as heroism, virility and status. It also encompasses other ignoble motivational reasons of personal ego, insatiable greed and even malevolence. *Personal rivalries* are not uncommon, with competitions to see who can make the biggest acquisition, a charge made of Robert Maxwell's attempts to out-acquire Rupert Murdoch. More vindictively, there are instances of acquiring CEOs 'paying back' acquired CEOs for past rivalries or conflicts. Deals can also be done purely for reasons of self-preservation. Such deals are designed to disguise corporate decline and give the illusion of success, suggesting that top management are 'on the ball' and not 'out of touch'.

While no-one would suggest that corporate M&As are carried out on religious grounds, the potential acquirer is fighting to impose *ideological and political beliefs* – a certain world view or paradigm about how business should be run. Many acquirers, through offer documents and the media, make strong cases for their own past successes playing a crucial role in enhancing the new group's future performance. In Granada's hostile takeover of Trust House Forte, the CEO of Granada, Gerry Robinson, pointed to its sustained out-performance of the FTSE All-Share index, which was largely achieved by his management's ability to restructure businesses for greater efficiency. This suggested strongly that these particular skills could be brought to bear upon Trust House Forte to achieve similar performance gains. Rather like religious conviction, it is largely assumed that past success formulas in the acquirer are transferable to the acquired business, and, critically, these deeply held beliefs are rarely questioned closely.

At the international level these corporate assumptions, or 'business religion', are thrown into sharp relief. Many cross-border deals have resulted in significant resistance from the target companies and their societies, perceiving the deal as a form of territorial invasion and the erosion of social values. When Nestlé announced its hostile bid for Rowntree, the Swiss were astonished by the depth of local reaction and resistance to the deal, symbolized by workers marching on London, questions being asked in the House of Commons, and the tabloids exclaiming, 'Stop the Swiss from stealing our Smarties'. In the takeover of Mannesman, by Vodafone, considerable resistance was experienced at the outset with deep-rooted concerns being voiced about whether this was the beginnings of an Anglo–American invasion.

Politicians, trade unions and the working population feared the change that would come with such bids. In their eyes, the social market economy had been strongly associated with the postwar economic miracle. As Jürgen Ruttgers, leader of CDU in the North Rhine Westphalia remarked, 'an unfriendly takeover does not fit with the rules of the social economics which have been very successful for 50 years'. 'We should hold onto our culture and that implies our business culture as well.' This concern is not surprising given important differences in assumptions upon which businesses are based in both countries, with the Anglo–American business system reifying the profit motive over all else, whereas in Germany, and indeed in other continental European models, the importance of the contribution and role of business to wider society is stressed. This tension, of M&A imposing a socioeconomic paradigm, is at the heart of the current debate over European takeover legislation amendments: whether hostile deals improve European competitiveness through restructuring or whether they are corrosive of social, cultural and business fabric.

A further important motivator is the M&A *deal as legitimator* of further similar action. Successfully closing an M&A deal paves the way for future deals as it shows a CEO's capacity for substantial tangible achievement, ability to make big strategic decisions and resonates with the image of CEO as heroic figure. It is evidence that the CEO is able to act in a manner befitting a CEO. Carrying out M&As is a self-legitimating and self-reinforcing cycle, and there is nothing like 'success' to breed 'success'.

The other side of the coin is failure to conclude deals or missing opportunities. If acquiring CEOs fail in their attempts at takeover, the markets generally begin to doubt their veracity as leader. The CEO and his company's standing can falter and support for further M&A activity dwindle. The social capital of the CEO is damaged. A good example of this is the fate of Jan Leschley, who led SmithKline Beecham (SKB) into merger talks with Glaxo. The talks failed, much to the bitter disappointment of investors, and SKB's share price fell. From then onwards, Jan Leschley's days were numbered.

M&As occur in waves and we are currently seeing the ebbing of the largest wave in history. As with explorers, there are *contextual pressures* upon companies and their

CEOs to engage in M&A activity. Changes in the macro-environment through technological innovation, de-regulation of sectors, liberalization of countries, macro-economic conditions, political influences, and globalization pressures, throw up both opportunities and threats for the strategic advantage of business. M&A offer a rapid method for responding to such macro-environmental shifts on a scale that makes a strategic difference.

Pressures upon the company can come from most aspects of its business, but perhaps is most keenly felt from the commercial and financial markets. Loss, or potential loss, of market share, the threat of falling profits, or the fear of becoming a takeover target, can drive a company into M&A activity. One of the explanations for the current wave of mergers in the pharmaceutical industry has been the problem of patent expiries threatening to erode company market power. In the banking sector, the fear of merging competitors altering the competitive balance in the industry has driven smaller players to merge to maintain critical mass. In the United Kingdom this can be seen in the recent merger frenzy between Royal Bank of Scotland taking over National Westminster Bank, and the subsequent pressure upon Bank of Scotland, which missed out on that merger, to merge with the Halifax Building Society to create a credible fourth force in UK banking.

Another strong voice in economies such as the Anglo-American system, is the power of the stock market to influence company behaviour. In M&A terms, markets can build an acquisition rating into a company's shares based upon the scale and pace of their acquisition activity. While this may serve to raise share values, the converse is the threat that the stock market can rapidly downgrade shares if acquisition expectations are not maintained. This can threaten a company and its management team's future. No small wonder then that examples abound of companies leaping into M&A deals on the flimsiest of commercial rationales to satisfy the stock markets.

With the health and welfare of the public company in the hands of financial markets, a critical issue for top management is to satisfy stock market expectations. This can lead to significant tensions between stock market and industry psychologies. For example, the direct influence of a stock market upon a merger was the downgrading of SmithKline Beecham's shares as the stock market took the view that their post-merger integration was not proceeding as rapidly as at Ciba-Gigy, a supposedly comparable merger in the US. This was despite SmithKline Beecham's protestations that the integrations were not comparable as they were designed to achieve different outcomes and required quite different time scales.

The M&A literature emphasizes rational financial and economic explanations for CEO motives. This helps to conceal the reality, that no CEO is likely to say publicly that he did a deal to get at another CEO, to make himself even richer, that it was gut feel, or that analysts had basically told him to do one. However, as with explorers, top managers' motivations for M&A are complex and interconnected. They may embark upon M&As through personal convictions on how businesses should be run, a wish for personal glory, recognition and wealth, and a need to do deals. There are also pressures upon them to satisfy financial markets and to react to changing commercial and macro-environmental pressures. The reality is that in most situations, the motivations behind M&As will be interconnected to the extent that it may be difficult to discern single reasons for action. In addition, a practical issue is the need for significant support from a variety of sources to enable the expedition or bid to take place. As a consequence, considerable effort is put into providing convincing rationale for the expedition or bid, and this strongly flavours the picture released for public consumption. The next section examines how support is raised for expeditions and M&A deals.

Case Box 8.1   Different Motivations for Guyana

Spain's European neighbours watched, jealously, as the riches of her imperial domain in Latin America was brought home in treasure galleons. Apart from un-officially condoning acts of piracy on these ships, and raids on Spanish colonial territory, they also strove to find riches of their own. In Guyana, the English sent expeditions rushing *up* the rivers to penetrate the interior where, they hoped, 'El Dorados' would be for the taking. The Dutch, however, had a different agenda. They settled along the coast, dug in for the long term and set about the less exotic task of clearing large areas of land that were turned into plantations.

1. *Why might the Dutch adopt a different approach to the English in exploring or acquiring Guyana?*
2. *What were the different outcomes?*

Launching the Expedition

Explorers

Getting support for an expedition is critical and there is no doubt that timing and the nature of the vision are fundamental to the level of support received. The *vision*, or promise, has to be a compelling image that can be communicated and captures sponsor imagination. Although going into the unknown, the vision requires a *rationale* that gives weight to the expedition's plausibility and reduces perceptions of risk, shows that it can be done, stresses the importance of timing and indicates compelling future benefits.

Winning over investors with a compelling *vision* is critical for explorers. This is achieved through personality, tremendous dedication to goals, and presenting fascinating images of new, exciting and exotic worlds. Columbus was described as being of daring manner, with great powers of persuasion and extraordinary dedication to his goals. Scott of the Antarctic had similar dedication and was a fine presenter and writer whose book, *The Voyage of the Discovery*, captured the siren beauty of Antarctica. Shackleton had an easy charismatic rapport, which won many supporters, although he needed a ghost writer to emulate Scott's literary talent.

Early on, the media and explorers alike recognized the enormous public interest in exploration. The public was intoxicated by exciting reports of heroic and dangerous struggles to master nature. Explorers were paid considerable sums of money for diaries and journals of their expeditions. Where the British navy was involved, all such material was immediately embargoed when vessels returned to harbour. Nevertheless, many accounts were smuggled off ship in a variety of ways so that Cook's voyages, for instance, rapidly became public knowledge. It is in the interests of the explorer and media alike to create heroes and myths as this is popular with the hero-seeking public. The images created of exploration and explorers themselves are specifically designed for the consumption of select audiences. This continues to be exploited today with contemporary explorers such as Chris Bonington, Michael Swann and Ranulph Fiennes all able to generate considerable income from their abilities as after-dinner speakers. Popularizing previous exploits is a critical iterative link, in the exploration cycle, in funding new ventures.

All explorers have to convince backers to part with considerable sums and in this regard the explorers are as tenacious as in their expeditions. This requires a wide range of tactics in terms of how to win over different stakeholder groups. Columbus achieved sponsorship through his rich Genoese mercantile connections, by marriage into a family of nobility and, critically, to achieve status and honours, through royal favour. Indeed he is notable for his incessant courting of the Portuguese and Spanish kings and queens. To win over the latter, Columbus was able to put together a rich and influential band of supporters, which can 'be put down to his own personal qualities, his powers of persuasion, deep-seated convictions and a driving ambition'.

Central to the art of persuading investors to back an expedition is a convincing rationale, which includes the practical consideration of whether the expedition can be executed in practice. The language of rationales is designed to suit those in political and spiritual power at the time as well as the investors of the day. In the time of Columbus, it was obligatory to stress that converting pagans to the Roman Catholic faith was a prime reason for exploration. In addition, Columbus could stress the untold wealth, which could be tapped in Asia for the benefit of the Spanish throne, as well as a more rapid and less fraught passage by sea than by land. Against these limitless but distant rewards were obvious, and close at hand, practical obstacles. To convince the court of Portugal, Columbus needed to demonstrate to his backers that a voyage west-wards to Asia was viable. At this time, the vast majority of voyages hugged the coast-line, so a journey out into the Atlantic seemed implausible in terms of navigation and supplies. Columbus had to demonstrate that it was not only possible but also practical. He achieved this by adopting, deliberately, the erroneous notions that the continent of Asia stretched some 30 degrees farther to the east than it really did and that Japan lay 1,500 miles to the east of the Asian continent. Following this logic, the open ocean between Europe and Asia shrank to a manageable size with hospitable islands along the way. On this basis the distance from the Canaries to Japan was just 2,400 nautical miles rather than the real distance of 10,600 miles.

The acquirers

Similarly with M&A, the board of the acquirer has to gain public support for its intended action. Critical to success are a *vision* or promise, that is compelling, can be communicated and captures stakeholders' imagination. This requires a *rationale* that gives weight to the deal's plausibility, indicates compelling future benefits, and suggests appropriate timing, when the markets are receptive to such a deal.

Tremendous efforts are necessary to gain support from stakeholders. The main investors are often a highly varied group of institutions including pension and mutual funds, investment vehicles, banks, corporates, wealthy individuals and arbitrageurs, each with very different agendas in terms of investment horizons, risk profiles and respon-sibilities to their own shareholders. Major opinion formers such as analysts and the media require very careful courting in the lead up to a deal. One of the big surprises to most top management embarking upon M&A, for the first time, is the sheer physicality of the exercise. Considerable time is consumed in vital face-to-face, opinion-forming meetings, where the personal characteristics and conviction of the CEO in particular are a critical success factor. The demands of this role are such that CEOs often have to neglect the running of their own business. Rather like wooing the kings and queens of Spain, CEOs need to win over powerful investors, by convincing them of the practicality of doing the deal and getting them to believe in the vision for the future.

In M&A terms, acquirers also need to demonstrate that a deal is do-able. This may be an issue of timing in macroeconomic terms and the outlook for the market value of shares and debt and market sentiment about deals of this nature – if you like, the elements, like the trade winds, need to be favourable. Where non-standard financing is required (such as highly leveraged deals), timing and sentiment are particularly important. When junk bond finance and highly leveraged deals first appeared during the 1980s, the bids did get away but often rapidly ran into problems stemming from wildly optimistic predictions about how the deal would support the debt. With the wisdom of hindsight this appears the financial equivalent of Columbus moving continents closer together. This also illustrates the power and persuasiveness of an apparently coherent financial rationale. In many deals, a structure that shows that the intended financial structure is supportable is an important plank, or even the keel, in the vessel of persuasion. Committed support from key investors also needs to be demonstrated, often to persuade others to follow.

Part of the 'do-ability' of the deal is an underlying rationale, which will demonstrate that the resulting entity will be worth more than the two companies apart (or the deal would not be done). A myriad of rational motives are often given for how this will work; in *economic terms*, economies of scale will allow efficiency gains through cost reductions; complementary activities and resources may be shared to add value; greater scale may enhance power in the market and/or over suppliers, allowing more value to be extracted for the firm. Such enhanced power along the value chain may also result in indirectly improving the competitive balance with competitors; in *financial terms*, the increased size of the firm may allow borrowing at lower cost and lead to higher debt capacity. A portfolio effect can reduce commercial risk and may also have a beneficial effect upon the share price (where acquisition smooths a cyclical cashflow for instance, although conglomerate behaviour is likely to have an adverse affect). There can be tax advantages where there are unused tax shields or where there is a tax exposure that needs shielding; in *managerial* terms there is an argument for the acquiring management being better able to exploit the resources of the acquired firm than the current management. On this basis the acquisition target is portrayed as undervalued with its current management and the acquiring management hold out the prospect of an upward revaluation. This notion of managers competing for the right to control scarce assets is central to the market for corporate control theory.

It is worth noting that the rational language of finance and economics is an efficient means for communicating with investors. The Anglo-American business model embodies respect for profit, values technical procedures and regards the free market as an article of faith. Any business leader who repudiates these standards risks losing credibility in the face of auditors, customers, financial markets and governmental regulators, all of whom can influence success. Here, where the relationship between a business and its shareholders is diffuse and the latter are easily influenced by promises of increased returns, businesses are forced to focus upon maximizing return on investment and share price performance. In other countries, however, where there is highly interlinked shareholding and close interventionist relationships, espoused rationales take on a different complexion. In parallel with the explorers then, acquirers need to be masters of communicating acceptable rationales. In this sense, the language of economics and finance in the Anglo-American system is perhaps as much an ideology to normalize existing structures as religious conviction was to the Iberian explorers of the fifteenth and sixteenth centuries.

As with explorers, the language of the rationale is designed to suit the investors of the day. In Anglo-American markets in particular, a rationale is expected that hinges upon increasing shareholder value and it is not surprising then that offer documents are predicated upon this mantra. However, as shown above, this may simply be a rationalization, of the real underlying motives, for public consumption. From my own experience in writing such documents and speaking with the CEOs concerned, actual motives are complex and can be unpublishable. In the words of one CEO having recently launched a bid, 'Why do you think we paid a fortune to management consultants – it was to formulate a convincing rationale for the deal we wanted that we could present to the markets'. In many cases boards are more opportunistic than they would dare to admit, and often find that they need to make decisions about uncertainty, where indecision may be more expensive than not acting. In the words of Jürgen Schrempp, the current CEO of embattled DaimlerChrysler, 'You cannot always select the timing. If you do that, and sit back and wait another year or two, somebody else will act and you are defeated.' However, prior to a deal, it is not at all helpful to confidence levels in the acquirer and its board for them to proclaim that the deal is opportunistic, or that they just do not know whether it will all work out. This is not to say that deals, which are not entirely true to their espoused rationales, are therefore bad, but that a convincing rationale is critical to the socially constructed hurdle process that needs to be navigated to allow market-based deals to take place.

Inevitably, this singularity masks a complex interconnected array of mixed conscious and unconscious motives and partial legitimating rationales. It is for this reason that the many surveys that abound upon reasons why companies embark upon M&As are seriously flawed. They generally seize upon singular publicly accepted rationales and ignore critical issues such as multiple interconnected motives; external pressures to act; actions that may be the outcome of internal political processes upon which a rationale is really just a gloss; the inevitable human condition which does not sit well with neat legitimate explanation.

Styles of Exploring

Explorers

With backing in place, the expedition begins and the race is on. Tales abound of suffering appalling hardships as a result of a capricious environment. Sudden onsets of snow and ice blizzards, crevasses, plunging or soaring temperatures, tempestuous or becalming seas, threaten the very lives of all in the self-contained expedition.

To the observer, whether the explorer achieves the goal can be a nail-biting experience. For Antarctic explorers the process of attrition is all too apparent with dwindling supplies of fuel, the need to kill dogs and ponies to feed the remaining animals,

Conquered the territory?

	No	Yes
No	Bellingshausen *(the viewer)*	Scott *(the assumer)*
Yes	Shackleton *(the reflector)*	Amundsen *(the informed)*

Gained from the effort?

Figure 8.3   An explorer typology

and the onset of serious illnesses and incapacities such as scurvy, frostbite and snow blindness.

Explorers embody as many different approaches to exploring as they have beliefs and motives. In the race for the South Pole, four very distinctive types of individual battled to claim success; Bellingshausen, Scott, Shackleton and Amundsen. In Figure 8.3 I suggest that these explorers can be distinguished in terms of whether they achieved the goal of reaching the South Pole, by planting the flag, and whether they gained personally from the effort.

Bellingshausen, of the Imperial Russian Navy, on 27 January 1820, has the honour, although not widely known, of being the first to establish that the 'southern continent' existed, although numerous explorers, from Captain Cook in 1773, who circumnavigated the continent without seeing it, to Henrik Bull in 1895 who, with his men, were the first to make a confirmed landing, all contributed to changing the boundaries of challenge and defining the goal. Bellingshausen had nothing further to do with the southern continent and his thorough work 'sank little noticed after his return'. This did not preclude later success in other areas, however, and Bellingshausen achieved the status of admiral and Governor of Kronstadt and, in 1949, the Hakluyt Society reprinted his narrative.

Scott's expeditions were well funded, some taking two years to prepare. He assumed that British naval methods would be superior to others in their quest and only superficially absorbed foreign equipment improvements rather than the underlying approaches. He scorned the use of sledge dogs, ideal for the cold, and compounded the error with the use of ponies. Ponies could not be fed on seal or penguin meat, meaning that appropriate food had to be transported and they stumbled through snow and sweated constantly or froze. All but one pony died and the disastrous consequence of this decision was that the main supply camp was not located as far south as intended. Scott assumed that the weather would be better than it was and did not build any margins for error in terms of the distance between supply depots. He had fine conceptions of facing hardships and danger with their own unaided efforts and so his team man-hauled 700 pound sledges all the way, which was seen as 'a fine thing' and would 'disprove the supposed decadence of the British race'. Their supplies were inadequate, and all suffered malnutrition, scurvy and exposure. Scott managed to reach the South

Pole on 18 January 1912, only to find that Amundsen had arrived first, and then faced 800 miles of dragging sledges on the return journey. The tragedy was that they would have reached the one-ton depot on their return if it had been placed where they originally intended.

Shackleton originally managed to serve under Scott through the use of his considerable charm. He had excellent experience in sail and steam, an outgoing personality and a natural leader's ability to get men working together. Bedevilled by inadequate finance, poor standing due to his brother being implicated in the theft of the Irish coronation regalia and his irregular use of expedition loans, Shackleton had a continuous battle for funding and a lack of time. This meant using a 40-year-old ship and preparing expeditions in seven months. Like Scott, Shackleton also assumed British naval superiority in techniques, but later learned that these were mistakes. Shackleton's race for the pole got him to within 97 miles. The expedition had inadequate clothing and was malnourished, but in a letter to his wife, Shackleton wrote, 'It is better to be a live donkey than a dead lion.' This was probably the bravest and hardest decision Shackleton ever made. His refusal to risk his own life and those of others beyond a certain point, and his clear judgement as to where that point lay, were among his most admirable qualities. Shackleton was a brilliant calculator of risk and did not let emotions disturb his judgement.

Amundsen was the first to the South Pole and this was through tremendous organizational skills, logical thinking and strong focus. Amundsen was a professional explorer in a way that Scott and Shackleton were not. His success lay in methodical analysis and the adoption of relevant experience and skills from whatever source, meticulous planning and a reliance on hand-picked small teams rather than large heterogeneous and heavily resourced parties. In his successful race to the Pole, Amundsen had impressively fast-moving dog and ski specialists and set large margins of safety at every point, unlike Scott. In a series of rapid forays over a two-month period, his eight men and fifty dogs moved three times the weight of supplies further than Scott had moved a ton in a single month-long march with thirteen men and eight ponies. Amundsen used Eskimo furs to retain warmth and to avoid sweating whereas Scott used man-made clothes. Details counted, and while Scott's fuel supplies evaporated or leaked away through leather washers that perished in the cold, Amundsen used hermetically sealed containers. His dried rations included plenty of fresh meat that prevented scurvy and indeed, his men had put on weight by their return to base. Amundsen's team and twelve surviving dogs had covered over 1,600 miles in 99 days.

Acquirers

Living through a takeover can seem the corporate equivalent of the explorers battling against the extremes of volatile environments. The external environment will not remain static while the deal is being wrought, and indeed, macroeconomic influences are easily capable of undermining rationales. Whilst the world changes, the companies and their CEOs are also preoccupied with battling in the media, in a war of words and images for support of their position. Endless talks with diverse investors to persuade them of the merits of their strategy are critical uncertainties and in this regard investors can seem very capricious (see Case Box 8.2). Competitors will seize the initiative to take strategic offensives just as the deal-doing parties' eyes are off the commercial football. Employees may begin to falter as the uncertainty surrounding M&A

erodes confidence about their position in the future. The whole company and its top management come under intense scrutiny from a multitude of perspectives and, rather like explorers being battered by the elements, top management have to cope with unexpected blizzards, such as lambasting by the media, political interference at the national and regional level, sudden volatility in financial markets, competitor inroads, disruptive action from unions and employees, and mounting influence from pressure groups. In this environment, small actions and signs can have a disproportionately substantial affect upon outcome.

While acquirers do not go through such physical torment, the nail-biting nature of acquisition is all too real and the psychological toll substantial. The outcome is generally not known until the last moment and in the closing stages of the deal, it is not unusual for negotiations to go on all night. In the words of one CEO, 'we worked with eyeballs out on stalks'. Right up to the close then, both companies do their absolute utmost to achieve their ends − it is about corporate life and death.

In common with the polar explorers, we can perceive distinct approaches to acquisitions. A Bellingshausen in M&A terms would be a CEO who bids for a company and puts it into play. This may also be the first act in a subsequent wave of consolidation in an industry sector. Perhaps through pitching the original offer too low, through poor judgement or lack of resources, the door is left open for other bidders to enter and it is they who ultimately gain control. The Bellingshausen CEO effectively defines an acquisition arena by spotting the opportunity but does not benefit from his foresight and is quickly forgotten. Often these players become written out of the industry in which they precipitate the round of consolidation. An example might be the hostile failed bid by Jacob Suchard for Rowntree in 1988. Jacob Suchard had global ambitions but was substantially smaller than rivals such as Mars and Nestlé. The company was heavily dependent upon dramatic fluctuations in its coffee business, and in confectionery, it was largely exposed to low margin block chocolate. Geographically Jacob Suchard had a negligible exposure to the UK market, where Rowntree was a major obstacle to entry, and the latter was also making inroads into continental Europe. These company-specific pressures and an industry where declining returns in block and boxed chocolates were putting pressure on firms' returns, prompted Suchard to take the initiative and launch a 'dawn raid' on Rowntree shares, acquiring a 14.9 per cent stake. Nestlé subsequently entered the fray and ultimately outbid Suchard with a £2.62 billion bid which Rowntree's board accepted. Shortly after the deal in 1990, Jacob Suchard reported a 10 per cent drop in consolidated net earnings and Klaus Jacobs decided to sell his controlling stake. On 22 June, Philip Morris bought Jacob Suchard for $3.8 billion. Rather like Bellingshausen, Suchard opened the door to acquisition in the lucrative countlines sector of the confectionery industry, but was unable to gain commercial advantage from this move (although it did gain financially from selling its stake). It subsequently found its competitive position eroded as a consequence and ended up being acquired itself.

The well-resourced bidder who intends to win the M&A contest at all costs, can be characterized as a Scott of the Antarctic. Such a bidder is imbued with the thrill of the chase to the extent of losing touch with the reality of the challenge, in both cost and the practicalities of implementation. Indeed, previous poor experiences may make this bidder relatively unattractive to target companies and require substantial overpayment for the deal to close. The consequence is that the acquisition is made, but never fulfils the dream. Indeed, in extreme cases a mountain of debt and overextended management may result in disaster for the acquired company. Overzealous attempts to reduce debt may mean that critical strategic assets are emasculated and the means of sustained recovery are lost. In addition, the acquisition can have disastrous effects upon the acquirer itself, as it is pulled down by the weight of its own acquisition. This is a classic case of 'being first and coming last'.

An example of Scott's approach might be the ill-fated acquisition of Digital Equipment by Compaq, in 1998. Eckhard Pfeiffer, Compaq's CEO, masterminded the deal and, like Scott, was widely revered, being described by Forbes as 'exceptional' when Compaq was crowned company of the year. The Digital deal was for $9 billion and was the biggest acquisition in the history of the computer industry. While the goal was achieved, as the acquisition went through with a 20 per cent premium, the post-acquisition integration froze. Uncertainty among staff rose, geographic distance preserved cultural differences and where cultures did meet, they clashed. Fifteen thousand staff were laid off, and the poor atmosphere was compounded by significant levels of senior resignations. At the same time as these integration problems flared up, the external environment eroded Compaq's competitive advantage. Its meticulous forecast-based PC manufacturing system, which sold through hard won networks, was eclipsed. The rise of sub-$1,000 PC spelt the end of 30 per cent gross margins which had supported its distribution chain, and Dell's direct to consumer model left Compaq in a situation of channel conflict; unable to continue as it had, but also unable to adopt Dell's approach. The combination of poor acquisition integration and deteriorating competitive position in the markets caused Compaq to lose more money than in all its previous history; around $2 billion since the merger. Its share price halved, and like Scott of the Antarctic, Eckhard Pfeiffer was fired by the board. The target had been achieved, but the implementation, against the elements, was hell, in which Compaq was severely damaged and the leader expunged.

Shackletons in the M&A world are quick to perceive acquisition opportunities and indeed may be opportunist in this respect. However, they are shrewdly aware of the value of these targets and know when to pull out of the contest. They may also not have the resources of rival bidders and will not overextend themselves in a competitive bidding situation. The motto is 'survive to explore another day'. An example of a Shackleton might be Peter Burt, CEO of Bank of Scotland (BoS). In late 1999 he perceived an opportunity to bid for National Westminster Bank (NatWest), which had displayed 31 chequered years of performance and had served up fresh disappointments with monotonous regularity. The forays into North America and into investment banking came to grief, and although there were improvements in the retail banking side shortly before the bid, and investors were impressed with the new management team, they 'underestimated the emotional weight of history bearing down on them'.

Peter Burt's surprise hostile bid shocked the City of London, and was described as a 'braveheart initiative' in the Scottish press and greeted with a wave of national euphoria. However, after two months, Royal Bank of Scotland (RBS) joined the fray. Because the bids were hostile, the asymmetry between the amounts of information known between sellers and buyers increases the risk of overpayment. There was an auction and considerable temptation to make extravagant promises to justify increased offers. Although the offers were very similar in financial terms, the visions behind them were quite different. Similar to Shackleton's style, BoS was the more conservative of the two offers, stating they would slim down and simplify NatWest whereas RBS was far more ambitious claiming it would create a new force in banking. Years of poor performance and the frustration of institutional shareholders with NatWest 'messing them around' probably contributed to support for the more ambitious bid. Perhaps as a reflection of the City's scepticism about whether any bank integration would be able to achieve promised returns, BoS's share price rose substantially after losing the contest.

Shortly afterwards, Peter Burt proposed a zero premium merger with Abbey National. Again the opportunity had been spotted, but the approach was conservative. LloydsTSB stepped in with a £19 billion bid and shareholders clearly preferred cash. (In the event, however, the takeover panel ruled against the deals on competition grounds.) Finally, in a further surprise announcement just two months later, persistence paid off with the launch of zero-premium merger talks with the Halifax. Analysts regarded this £27.7 billion merger to have compelling industrial logic. The combined group would move into the premier division of British banks and be a credible competitor to the 'big four'. In the words of one of BoS's top five shareholders, BoS 'has got to a size where it now needs to do a deal. This is an elegant solution and a neat way out for Peter Burt.' Long regarded as one of the best-managed banks, this sequence of moves and counter-moves along an acquisition trail shows the ability to spot opportunities, to persist, and ultimately move the bank into the premier league.

The Amundsens of M&A are those that plan their expeditions meticulously and then launch them with considerable rapidity and efficiency. Their bids are sufficiently fully and well planned to deter competition and yet leave some room for further manoeuvre. These bidders do not overpay and know that their resources and skills are more than adequate for doing the deal and integrating the business. An example might be the hostile bid by Granada Group for Trust House Forte which is described in greater detail in Case Box 8.2.

Case Box 8.2 Trust House Forte Versus Granada Group

Granada Group PLC's CEO, Gerry Robinson, had spent considerable time planning his move on Forte, personally visiting its hotels and roadside Little Chef restaurants to assess room for improvement in management, use of resources and potential for synergies. On 22 November 1995, Granada launched a £3.28 billion hostile bid for Trust House Forte PLC. The bid represented a 23 per cent premium on Forte's share price and was widely regarded as rather high for a company where growth had been rather slow.

The timing of the bid was formidable as Forte had been undergoing some restructuring and had little to show for its work, and the hotel sector was just coming out of a depression. In addition, the actual moment of the offer was when Rocco Forte had a day's holiday shooting on the moors. The image of a part-time aristocratic top manager heading a large lacklustre business was seized upon by the media and proved very difficult for Rocco Forte to shake off. Gerry Robinson in comparison was the darling of the City with a 'rags to riches' story of achievement, based upon turning Granada into a strong cash generator and one of the largest and most profitable companies in Britain.

Unfortunately for Rocco Forte, the Granada team made the most of apparent management failings at Forte Group, alluding to a complacent aristocratic management dynasty, badly out of touch with its shareholders. The comparison of the two companies' performance over the five-year period pre-bid was also salutatory. Granada's share price had outperformed the FTA All Share Index by 156 per cent, whereas Forte's had under-performed by 40 per cent; Granada's operating profit had risen by 341 per cent whereas Forte's had fallen by 11 per cent. The message was clear; funds invested in Granada five years earlier would have performed far better than those placed with Forte. The implication was that Forte under Granada management could only have a greatly improved future.

Granada and its management team offered a stark contrast. Gerry Robinson, the ninth of 10 sons, was a rags to riches story. His turnaround of Granada and its meteoric growth, with a share price that had outperformed the FT All Share index by 156 per cent over a five-year period, made him the darling of the City. The bid was also timed just after a Granada announcement that they had increased pre-tax profits by 32 per cent to £351 million on a 14 per cent rise in turnover to £2.38 billion (year to September). Significantly, when Forte's defence document coincided with Gerry Robinson taking a holiday in Ireland, it barely received mention in the media.

The Granada offer was a model of clarity and rested primarily upon a comparison of the two companies' performance from which conclusions about the quality of management teams was to be inferred. With the disparity in achievement clear to all, and Rocco Forte's wrong footing at the very beginning, City sentiment was that this was a done deal.

To many people's surprise, Rocco Forte led a spirited defence, referred to as 'showing imagination and vision'. Indeed a competitor is actually on record as saying he 'was both surprised and impressed with the strength and speed of Forte's response' (Gavin Simonds, Joint MD, Inter-Continental Hotel Group). Part of the defence was to refocus attention upon the nature of Granada. In an internal memo this showed that Granada's growth had been achieved by acquisition rather than organically, and that the consequence of their history was to have a rather 'mixed collection of businesses' 'where there is no clear logic about how these businesses benefit from being looped together'. This was then argued externally and in so doing, the Forte Group was censured by the takeover panel for using the 'C' word – for implying that Granada was a 'conglomerate'. At the same time, Rocco Forte engaged in classic defence measures including a round of asset disposals (he was allowed to sell up to 10 per cent), the initiation of a £500 million share buy-back scheme, and raising the dividends. The major coup for Rocco Forte was an agreement to sell the roadside restaurant and hotel business to Whitbread for £1.05 billion on the assumption that the Granada bid would fail. This was virtually a demerger and would have greatly changed the nature of the Forte Group.

On 9 January 1996, Granada raised its offer for the Forte Group from £3.3 billion to £3.8 billion. Although Rocco Forte's spirited defence recaptured much of the lost ground, and won him admiration to the extent that some even predicted the Forte Group would survive, at the eleventh hour their biggest institutional shareholder, Mercury Asset Management, which held a crucial 14.4 per cent stake, changed sides.

A BBC documentary on the takeover is graphic in showing the tremendous emotional and physical strains placed upon the Forte Group's management team by the deal and in particular upon Rocco Forte himself. What came as a clear surprise to the Forte team was the huge amount of time and effort required personally visiting and winning over investors. Despite intensive campaigning which received praise, neither side was sure on how key institutions such as MAM would vote, right up until the very last moment. However, the clarity of Granada's vision and a well-pitched offer were sufficient, despite Rocco Forte's spirited defence, for the final bid of £3.8 billion to succeed. The subsequent integration of the two businesses was heralded as a success.

1. *What were the different perspectives of Robinson and Forte on the reasons for this takeover bid?*
2. *Why was this a hostile acquisition?*
3. *Why was Robinson's timing so impressive?*
4. *Why did the bid succeed?*

Possession and a Hero's Welcome

Explorers

Exploration is a form of conquest and ownership. The first symbolic action of an explorer reaching his destination is to firmly plant a flag on the new territory to indicate possession and presence. While the first man on the moon spoke of one giant step for mankind, the flag planted was American with strong overtones of technological mastery over other competing nations.

Great store is placed upon the act of flag planting as it symbolizes the conquest of the unknown and the end to a great journey. It is as if a veil of secrecy has been lifted and certainty over the existence of territory, its ownership and control are established. With justification, explorers are proud of their achievements. They are the first to succeed, often where others have failed, and have frequently risked life and limb. The achievement is clearly defined and easily communicated to sponsors and the outside world. The explorer is perceived to have superhuman qualities and even the natives may regard them as gods (Cortes, for example, was identified with Quezalcóatl). This reflects well on their nation, and explorers are frequently rewarded with medals, titles and the adoration of their country. In addition, with taking possession, the hyperbole used to sell the concept of the expedition now begins to be taken for granted. After all, conquering the unknown was the great adventure, and, just as the unknown always passes for the marvellous, the revealed can be taken for granted, seeming ordinary and lacking in excitement or adventure.

With this conquest comes the 'inalienable right' to exploit and develop in any way the conqueror sees fit. However, while many early explorers suggested that they would exploit and develop the territories they had opened, and indeed many such as Columbus tried, they were more likely to remain explorers through and through and soon be looking to extend other boundaries. Indeed, pushing boundaries maintained the heroic image, while exploitation risked tarnishing this image. In Columbus' case, he returned repeatedly to Spain where he strove to raise funds to support his four voyages across the Great Sea. The lure of the great adventure eclipsed the ordinary ways needed for administration. In this way explorers remain in the cycle of exploration serving to legitimate further exploration.

Acquirers

In common with explorers planting the flag, the signing of the deal and press announcements feel like a victory. It is of little surprise that the acquirers feel like conquering heroes. Planting the flag is often seen in a rapid change of symbols at the acquired business, with wholesale replacement of logos, badges, crests and with receptionists being drilled in a new corporate greeting, all announcing that the acquired company's identity has changed.

The communication of the acquisition to the media and investors is easy to achieve and can have a very significant impact upon business, communities and in some cases, countries. For larger deals, an acquisition can significantly alter the competitive balance in an industry and in some cases redefine whole industries. The power to affect so many stakeholders reflects positively upon the image of CEO as a superhuman figure. In common with explorers, those CEOs engaged in the biggest and most frequent deals are often praised and rewarded for the growth of their businesses by acquisition (e.g., Lord Hanson), although they may not be heroes in the eyes of the acquired.

Once companies are acquired, CEOs rarely become heavily involved in the integration of the businesses, passing them rapidly to more junior members of management while they move onto other more prestigious matters such as further potential deals. The reasons are clear to see. A reputation for successfully completing deals needs continuous feeding. Making acquisitions is generally seen as a legitimate and worthy activity of the CEO, it reinforces their heroic image and is also addictive in the same way that explorers yearn to explore. Post-acquisition integration is widely perceived to be of lesser importance than concluding a deal and, in the past, has used less senior executives. Indeed, this is often where the 'ball gets dropped' and a gap develops in the acquisition process. Where the integration does proceed, it is a task that goes largely unnoticed if done well, but if it goes badly it attracts considerable attention.

As in the days of the Empire, where planting the flag allowed large tracts of the world to suddenly be owned from afar, in corporate terms, acquirers are quick to give the impression that new ownership and rapid symbolic changes represent the end of the story. After receiving a brief flurry of accolades from the media, the acquirer is quick to portray the subsequent management of the new territory as 'business as usual'. Substantial efforts are made to shield the running of the new acquisition from the public eye and indeed further deals and strategic initiatives may be taken to deflect media attention from how the integration of the acquired business is faring. This is often for good reason. The reality of post-acquisition integration can be substantially different from business as usual.

Searching for Gold

Explorers

With the territory in possession, the search for gold begins. Initially the explorers need evidence to support their claims for the huge potential of the newly possessed land. Gold was a universally understood proof of untold wealth, although precious stones, spices and silks also aided this purpose. The critical importance of returning with evidence of boundless potential, not only to appease backers of the current expedition but also to ingratiate the explorer with kings and queens for status and further patronage, can be seen in the frantic efforts of explorers to collect this sort of evidence.

Within hours of Columbus setting foot on the New World, he recorded in his journal that natives were wearing gold and that he was already enquiring where there were goldfields. The sequence of his journeys among the Caribbean islands was driven by trying to find gold mines, and his journal and letters to the king and queen are full of the exaggerated mention of gold. The imagery of limitless gold set an agenda for European exploration and exploitation for centuries to come. This was later reinforced by Pizarro's audacious capture of the Inca king himself, allowing him to extort a huge chamber filled with gold as ransom.

Lured by the promise of wealth beyond their wildest dreams, all manner of prospectors may appear to find fortune. In more habitable areas these prospectors may have military and religious overtones to take control or suppress local inhabitants to their wills. In more hostile environments the prospectors may be purely commercial as in the whalers and sealers of Antarctica. In both cases the prospectors may have been lured by tales of certain types of wealth but unlike the initial explorers, they are often forced to live with a dream that might be some way distant from actual 'reality'. This 'reality' was frequently far from the initial explorer's own set of espoused values and understandings, and often resulted in atrocities borne out of misunderstandings.

At the time of Columbus, the relations between Spaniards and the native population were very bad, due to the sharp difference between Columbus' exaggerated promises of wealth, and the actual scarcity of gold. The disappointment among the Spaniards led to uprisings among Columbus' own party, but among the native Amerindians there were very substantial massacres, some seven million in all, partly through the frustration at not being able to satisfy the Spanish appetite for gold.

In attempting to extract value from their new territories, the Spanish imposed their complex administrative and religious systems. This culture was at complete odds with the indigenous ways of life and forced natives into a paradox of reconciling their own systems and beliefs, fashioned to fit their environment, with those brought from a completely different context. This is most clearly seen in the imposition of the Roman Catholic faith. The Spanish were brutal in decapitating the pyramids of indigenous peoples and crowning them with their own churches. While on the face of it this represented 'conversion', for generations the natives came to the churches to worship the 'holy stones' taken from the original pyramids and set into the walls of the churches. Collecting natives together into settlements for administrative and religious purposes, while fitting with the Spanish conception of how natives should behave under Spanish control, was disastrous where the people were semi-nomadic as periodic movements were crucial for finding new areas to cultivate and to allow current areas to recover. Population concentrations also assisted in the spread of European diseases. As a consequence the natives were resistant to adopting Spanish ways and perceived to be difficult to handle. In addition, the Spanish found the physical environment very uncomfortable and large numbers succumbed to disease. Frustration over the lack of gold, the awkwardness of the natives and an unpleasant environment led to terrible tragedies, powerfully depicted in Diego Rivera's frescos in Mexico City's National Palace, showing the torture, hanging and reverse crucifixion of Amerindians as a sub-human species.

Misinterpretation of native reactions to initial overtures and explorer initiatives abound. The early European explorers of the Pacific islands were welcomed initially with open arms and shown munificent hospitality. This was interpreted as a sign of friendship and encouraging a return visit. However, as Captain Cook discovered, fatally, on his return visit to Hawaii, the natives were subsequently hostile. The reason for this change was that the island's eco-system was fragile, and in order to protect it, the native provided bountifully on first visits so as not to offend visitors and more particularly in the hope that they would not need to return.

While explorers might be able to provide some evidence of the promise of their discoveries, actually delivering fully on the promise is decidedly rare. Despite Columbus' ability to return to Spain with sufficient gold to impress, and Pizarro having a room filled with gold, Columbus' followers were never able to deliver the promise of finding substantial gold mines, and Pizarro, and subsequent conquistadors, never found legendary cities of gold, despite numerous attempts.

The irony is that, despite the great motivation for gold, the Americas do not contain large quantities of this precious metal. The explorers had seen what they wanted to see, and the Spanish had imposed their wishes and priorities upon an unknown territory. Perhaps it is not surprising that they were largely frustrated in this quest. What the Americas are rich in is silver, of which vast quantities were discovered in Mexico, Bolivia and Peru after the conquistadors had died. Of equally profound significance was the discovery of crops such as maize, potatoes and tobacco, which have come to have global significance. At the same time there was also a rich flow of European crops, animals, customs, religion and language into the Americas. However, all of these benefits took a long time to come about and, although of immense significance, bear little resemblance to the original claims of the explorers.

Acquirers

Just as explorers needed gold to justify their endeavours, so acquirers need evidence to show that the deal was worthwhile. This needs to be in a form acceptable to the financial markets and the results need to be rapid. This explains the considerable emphasis placed upon quick wins, and the perceived need for visible, high-profile actions, which generate tangible results. As a consequence, attention is focused upon low-risk, high-profile activities such as the sell-off of non-core and duplicate assets (often agreed before the deal is signed), and cost-reduction activities (such as reducing head count), even though these may be against the spirit and purpose of the deal.

Managers involved in post-acquisition implementation, rather like the followers of explorers, may approach the new acquisition with a distorted view of how value is to be achieved, based on the necessary hype surrounding the deal. Acquiring managers will also have their own personal agendas and will be looking for ways to expand their influence and empires. The shock troops of integration, the finance department, are likely to bombard new acquisitions with parent rules and procedures to establish control. In addition, overpayment will force attention upon the need to recoup substantial acquisition premiums. Depending upon how strongly this message is conveyed, the main purposes of the acquisition may become subverted by those who believe they are being directly assessed by how much cost they can take out of a business.

The psychological shock waves of the deal and the need to find 'gold' can lead to a bitter culture clash, particularly if the acquirer has a very different culture to those acquired, and adopts a conquering hero attitude. Indigenous employees will struggle to retain vestiges of their former ways of operating and this, *in extremis*, may manifest itself in strikes, dysfunctionality, absenteeism, resignations and the loss of key client relationships. In these situations there are often significant declines in performance. A recent example of this problem was experienced by Compaq in its acquisition of Tandem computers, where substantial numbers of key employees left in the integration turmoil that followed the deal. Small wonder then that the natives may turn hostile or leave, when post-acquisition reality turns out to be quite different than that promised. Carnage can result and gold may still not be discovered.

Case Box 8.3   A Merger in 'Adland'

Two of Australia's best known advertising agencies, Mojo and Monahan Dayman Adams (MDA), merged to form Mojo MDA. Mojo brought with it a reputation as the most dynamic 'boutique' agency in Australia, while MDA was larger, more established and more low-key. A well-known advertising man, described the merger as being akin to the Beatles combining with the post office.

Mojo's offices were in Paddington, a suburb of Sydney. The entrance was by way of a long, narrow, paved drive-way lined with ferns, which then opened out into a large courtyard with willow trees and a fernery. The offices surrounded this courtyard. Those on the ground floor opened on to it, while those on the upper level opened on to a wisteria-covered balcony that overlooked it. MDA's offices were quite different, located in the concrete and glass high-rise area of North Sydney.

The agencies had also brought to the merger quite different staffing structures. Mojo's practice was to employ mainly highly paid senior staff who were given a high level of independence. They operated with a flat organizational structure of few hierarchical levels. This arrangement has been described as being 'like freelancing under the umbrella of a company with the bonus of the companionship of like minds'. MDA had a much more traditional pyramid structure of a few senior staff supported by large numbers spread over several hierarchical levels.

Mojo had a reputation for being under-managed. For example, no one holding a position in the company had a clear job description specifying the duties and responsibilities for that position: there was no such thing as formal meetings; and written memoranda were just not an acceptable practice. Some people, including many in Mojo, interpreted 'under-managed' to mean poorly managed. Consequently one of the attractions of the merger with MDA for such people was that MDA had a reputation as a well-organized 'professional' company. For MDA, the parallel attraction was the highly regarded skills of Mojo's creative staff. Together they constituted the largest Australian-owned agency. Size was also a major consideration in the merger. Both agencies were proud of their independence from foreign ownership and wished to maintain this situation while also enlarging to a size where they felt they could successfully take on the advertising giants of New York and London.

Mojo MDA was building a new office at Cremorne that would house all its staff, but until that was completed it was decided that all creative staff (copywriters, art directors and production staff) would move to Paddington while all management staff (the 'suits') would be located at the North Sydney offices. One of the Mojo people required to move was its finance director, Mike Thorley, who moved to North Sydney where he was to work under Stan Bennett, MDA's finance director, who had been put in charge of finance for Mojo MDA, Coombs (1990, p. 31) describes the situation and what followed.

Thorley was one of the original Mojo employees and, as such, did not really think of himself as an employee, more as a partner. That he was not a partner was brought home forcefully at the time of the merger. Like the rest of the staff he had no warning that Mojo was going to merge with MDA and was shocked and angered by the announcement.

Thorley was referred to as the shop steward of Mojo: he looked after the staff, moulded them into a team, and was at least partly responsible for giving the agency its character. However, after the merger he was banished to North Sydney to work for Stan Bennett. He did not go quietly.

To try to make the Paddington people feel at home in North Sydney at MDA, management installed a bar so the staff could follow their usual custom of a few drinks after work. But it was a modern black laminate structure running around the edge of the room. It looked like some upmarket suburban pub. It was nothing like the solid white bench in the kitchen at Paddington and it seemed to Thorley that it summed up the differences between the two agencies: it was a symbol of how Mojo had let its people down. In an act of defiance he took a chainsaw to work one morning and cut the bar in two.

1. *Why was value destroyed in the Mojo merger?*
2. *How might MDA have managed this situation better?*

The merger in 'Adland' case is adapted from one written by Richard Dunford, *Organisational Behaviour: An Organisational Analysis Perspective* (Sydney: Addison-Wesley, 1992, pp. 12–13).

In addition to organizational culture clash, other layers of complexity arise with the huge increase in cross-border M&A. Differences in national culture can affect the way in which deals unfold. This is not just recognition of differences in language, but that at a fundamental level firms are embedded in their social contexts and this influences behaviours and assumptions over how business is done and for what purpose. A classic example is the merger between pharmaceutical firms, Pharmacia of Sweden and Upjohn of America in 1995. Many rows ensued, with great loss in productivity, due to the Americans banning alcohol at lunchtime and scheduling meetings during the Swedes' national holidays, which caused uproar. There was additional friction between decision styles as the Swedes preferred open and full discussion of issues in meetings to arrive at consensus, whereas the Americans preferred short meetings to rubber stamp decisions made informally in advance. As neither side trusted the other, a new head office was set up in London, but neither the Americans nor Swedes would shut down their own offices and so the result was another layer of management that duplicated existing structures. Particularly in acquisitions, there is an assumption that there must be one right way of doing things, which tends to ignore that the acquired business is heavily customized to its operating environment. This is a prime reason for the fear felt by local employees and communities when foreign firms move in, and underlies the argument that cross-border acquisitions, such as Vodafone's takeover of Mannesmann, are corrosive of local social and economic fabric. In the context of the exploration of the Americas, the indigenous Indians were semi-nomadic for good reason and the imposition of Spanish settlements and systems caused significant hardship to both peoples.

How often have directors said, a couple of years after a deal, why did we take over that firm? – and the rationale having been lost in the mists of time. While an acquisition does allow the gaining of territory and increasing group size, the evidence regarding whether the acquisition actually creates value in the way intended is not so clear. Often the broad strategic picture before the deal was well set out, but adding value during implementation stumbles over a myriad of unforeseen problems. Rather like the Spanish, this is not to say that gold does not exist, but it may exist in smaller quantities than the acquirer and acquiree led investors to believe, and require far more effort to extract than anticipated. The actual realization of the phenomenal potential of the crops of the Americas also shows that surprising unintended discoveries can happen, provided the parties have eyes to see. Intellect and tacit knowledge, embedded in the fabric of the acquired organization, may create new, unanticipated wealth. It is not at all unusual for companies to go into a deal with one agenda and then during the integration phase, discover that other things become possible.

It is well known that around 50 per cent of deals fail to succeed, based upon on a wide variety of criteria, and some would put this figure far higher. Reasons for these problems occurring are over-optimistic assessment of potential, a process that places too much attention upon doing the deal, and not enough on how value will be achieved after the deal. Post-acquisition integration is perceived as trouble-free, acting out the original logic of the takeover. However, as the exploration image has shown, taking possession of a territory is just the beginning. The challenge is to create value now possession has occurred. In recognition of this difficulty and the need to anticipate how value can be realized after the deal, different styles of post-acquisition integration have been identified which suggest quite different approaches for the parent company.

The acquirer needs to decide whether the unique configuration of the target company has a value in itself. In some cases, the acquisition may really just represent a collection of assets, which can be unbundled and slotted into the acquirer's organization, and the latter will achieve more value in this way than in keeping the target intact. In other instances, there may be a compelling reason for keeping the acquisition intact, as its unique configuration is critical to its ability to create value. This is expressed in the contingency matrix in Figure 8.4 as the strategic independence of the acquired company; maintenance of its organizational integrity and the ability to make strategic choices for itself. This resonates with the literature upon organizational fit and emphasizes the limitations of bringing together two organizations.

The second decision is whether value from the acquisition will be captured through the market in terms of getting a good price for the target, or whether value will be created through integrating the two businesses. This integration mechanism is the transferring and sharing of resources and assets. The dimension on the contingency matrix is the intended level of interaction in these terms between acquirer and acquired. This resonates with the literature on strategic fit and emphasizes the strategic potential of the deal.

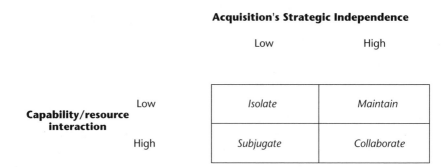

Figure 8.4 Post-acquisition integration styles. *Source*: D.N. Angwin (2000).

These two decisions are portrayed in the framework in Figure 8.4. As the labels indicate, each integration style has different implications for the way in which acquired companies are managed. Styles such as isolation suggest an immediate gain through bargain hunting and a short post-acquisition phase of limited organizational integration. Others, such as collaboration, are reliant upon creating value through a lengthy integration process.

As the exploration image suggests, careful attention to the post-deal integration can lead to considerable if not entirely predictable benefits. This requires companies to move their focus from just doing deals to planning in advance for post-acquisition integration styles. A consistent approach can overcome some of the implementation difficulties experienced by over-focusing upon the deal, and indeed can help to refine pre-acquisition strategies.

The Exploration Cycle

This chapter has argued that exploration and M&A are both cyclical processes, which need to be viewed as such to better understand the phenomena. At the level of the episode itself, I find a curious disjuncture between pre-expedition proclamations and post-expedition results. The former is about convincing investors to back a certain type of future and the latter is often a different sort of future to that envisaged. Columbus' stated aim was to reach Zipangu by sea and during his first voyage in 1492, while cruising through the Bahamas, expressed determination to proceed to the mainland and the city of Hangchow so that he might give the sovereigns' letter to the Great Khan. Later his ability to hear in Amerindian names similarities to those in Marco Polo's account was a severe case of wishful thinking.

Part of this can be explained by an explorer's motivations being only partially exposed and wrapped in a rationale more suited to the tastes of backers than necessarily being an accurate reflection of the expedition. In the same way, an acquirer's motives are often complex, interconnected, and partially submerged from public view. These also are wrapped in an efficient compelling language suitable for investors' tastes. It is of little surprise therefore that the post-deal integration may take quite a different tack from that envisaged pre-deal as it uses different experts to those doing the deal, and they have to cope and live with the reality they find, rather than a higher-level rarefied version. It is where strategy meets practice that interpretation and inter-connectedness distort plans, but may also provide many opportunities. There is a dis-junction then between publicly stated pre-acquisition intentions and post-acquisition outcomes, which make many assessments of performance on this basis highly suspect. It also raises an important issue as to whether deals are assessed more in terms of what is promised rather than what is delivered. It is well known that acquirers are quick to show a few rapid headline results post-deal and proclaim the integration done, to satisfy the markets. Thereafter it is very difficult for external bodies to see what is actually happening in the integration and subsequent acquisitions only serve to further conceal the internal turmoil. One could go further and say that companies are propelled back into the acquisition cycle, to obscure the difficult integration of a previous deal with the dazzling potential of a new deal.

The act of exploration builds legitimacy for further exploration as the explorer returns home to reveal the exotic, the exciting and, most importantly, the new poten-tials. M&A can be seen in the new light as doing a deal, and enacts a range of par-tially stated motives wrapped in a partial rationale as well as legitimating further activity of this sort. If couched in legitimate language, the City is likely to favour action over inaction and look positively upon previous acquisition activity. Doing deals is encour-aged in general and inactivity is penalized.

The M&A deal should be viewed as a process in its own right as well as a cycle of events. There are many positive pressures on organizations to embark on M&A, not least because many professional advisers and investors stand to make substantial profit. The effect of embarking upon a stream of this activity is to focus bystanders' attention upon the new and exciting deals and this distracts effectively from the stage of inte-grating of the previous deals. The deal breeds the deal.

For the explorer, the exploration cycle continues until lack of success, infirmity or death arrives. For the CEO, the boundaries are lack of success in closing deals, and end of term of office. If a CEO remains too long in his position post-deal, there is the risk that poor acquisition integration can raise its head and destabilize the acquisition cycle. Success breeds success, where success is really the ability to continue as a player in the biggest game in town.

Perhaps the most pertinent and contemporary example of exploration, where promises are dissociated from rewards, is NASA's exploration of the Moon and Mars. While the promise is to open up these planets in some way to mankind and extend our boundaries into space, the reality is far more limited. Sending a rocket to Mars legitimates further activities and highlights a boundary to be extended. The tangible benefits, however have been largely in spin-offs from the technology used, such as Teflon in non-stick pans.

Redrawing Boundaries

Explorers are defining the boundaries of geography, redefining our maps and reori-enting our understandings. Before Columbus, most exploration had been in the sight of land and yet he ventured across the 'Ocean Sea' into the unknown. Although people of that time did not believe the world to be flat, the feelings of doubt must have been considerable, rather like the astronauts blasting into space. The impact of perceiving new boundaries and perspectives is startling as we all have our own mental maps of how the world is and how it works. For the fifteenth-century Spanish, these new insights were conveyed by written accounts together with maps, woodcuts and illustrations. The documenters of such momentous discoveries became vital members of exploration teams in their own right, with painters playing an important role up to the beginning of the twentieth century and followed by still and later cine cameras. All these mechanisms performed multiple roles in conveying impressions of the discoveries, emphasizing consciously or unconsciously aspects favourable to the expedition and ultimately were critical in raising further funding. By the time of Shackleton's later voyages to Antarctica, the funds for the expeditions came almost entirely from selling the press, photographic and cinematographic exhibition rights of Hurley's work. These new and striking images have continued to alter our perceptions of the world, perhaps most recently with Apollo's picture of the world and the Hubble Space telescope's view of the heavens.

Explorers generally see publicity as a means to an end, a necessary evil. Indeed, on his historic trek across Antarctica, when Shackleton's ship *Endeavour* was crushed by ice, he decided to leave all the photographic equipment and records behind, even though they were responsible for the funding of the trip!

Acquirers also see the media as an inevitable presence, which can be used to advantage in persuading stakeholders of a new future. With increasingly large deals, this issue of the shape of the future has become particularly germane, as whole industries are restructured, stretching across national boundaries, and are indeed redefined. Exploration is a one-way process in that discovery only adds to the sum of knowledge and previous frontiers fade from sight. In the same way as the Ocean Sea represented the extent of human knowledge for hundreds of years, and indeed our earth, the boundaries of experience for most of human history, we now think nothing of flying over the Bahamas and beyond in a few hours, and we now even have space tourists. In M&A terms, the massive acquisition spree of banks, buying up related financial service providers, led to universal banking and one-stop shopping, where customers previously had to buy products from several distinct providers. Recently the wave of acquisitions among utilities has also removed the boundaries between a multitude of products and their distinct providers.

Explorers break boundaries and redefine our perceptions and expectations in ways that cause seemingly insurmountable barriers to fade quickly. Just as an expedition takes a fraction of time in human experience to redraft our mental maps, acquirers at a stroke can redraw our commercial realities. Acquisitions are a formative force in commercial evolution and are both the method and the strategy for shaping our futures. In the same way that the explorers and colonists of the 'dark continent' drew national boundaries with a singular view, acquirers also redraw industry configurations in the relentless pursuit of increasing performance. However, just as the national boundaries of the 'dark continent' bore little relationship to important political, cultural and geographical differences, and these structural differences have haunted the area for over a century, industry reconfiguration can engage substantial cultural baggage, and can become mired in the sub-texts of social, political and geographical considerations. Ironically, while the singular motive of profit has been portrayed as the death of geography, perhaps all that has happened is for new boundaries and frontiers to emerge at different levels. For one thing is certain, it is a complex interconnected world, where singular views are bound to be clumsy reflections of rich reality. Other dimensions and their boundaries will have their day and appeal to a different breed of explorer.

Conclusion

This chapter has drawn comparisons between exploration and M&A to show how the two phenomena resonate strongly. In so doing, the chapter illuminates the rather limited nature of current M&A literature. The value of the exploration image is in bringing out the complexity of the human condition and emphasizing the role of uncertainty in the process. To date, the human condition in the M&A literature is only really recognized in post-acquisition problems and is largely ignored in all other aspects of the process. This is particularly telling in the motivations ascribed to M&A activity. In terms of uncertainty, ambiguity over outcomes is largely substituted by anticipated benefits and this image from exploration exposes the same unrecognized feature in the M&A literature. This provides evidence for the ideas expressed in Chapter 4, 'Strategy as Intention and Anticipation', which distinguished between intention and anticipation.

Finally, the exploration image raises the issue of interconnectedness between different levels of analysis as well as, with the exploration cycle, across temporal boundaries. In both of these areas, the M&A literature is fragmented in nature both in levels of analysis, treatment of issues and temporally. The implication for the strategist is one of recognizing that the M&A literature, while very extensive and detailed, presents only a very partial view and omits many critical aspects of the M&A process. This is an important reason for many of the paradoxical findings associated with the field. The exploration image tries to redress this balance by reintroducing some complexities and interconnections: complexities and interconnections that have conventionally been ignored or minimized. To our cost.

Case Box 8.4   Vodafone PLC Versus Mannesmann

Vodafone PLC, under Chris Gent, chose November 1999 for the launch of the biggest ever hostile takeover, an offer of DM 135 billion (£83 billion) for Mannesmann of North Rhine Westphalia, Germany.

The announcement of the takeover was met with something approaching hysteria in Germany, which was living through the agonies of BMW wrestling with the 'English Patient', Rover Cars. At the political level, the German Chancellor, Schröder, announced 'hostile takeovers destroy corporate culture'. Similarly Jürgen Ruttgers, leader of the CDU in the North Rhine Westphalia said, 'an unfriendly takeover *does not fit* with the rules of the social market economics which have been very successful for 50 years'. Others remarked that 'we should hold onto our culture and that implies our business culture as well'. Indeed, in the past when foreign companies aimed to buy German firms, such as when the Austrians were close to buying the Salzgitter steel company from Preussag in North Rhine Westphalia, the regional government stepped in with DM 1 billion of public money (their budget for 2000 was DM 90 billion). Comments and actions such as these were bluntly criticized by European Central Bank

President, Wim Duisenberg, who said they did not enhance the image of being an increasingly market-driven economy across the Euro-area.

Klaus Esser, Mannesmann's chairman, took a contrary view, that national culture and historical foundations were unhelpful, 'we could really do without the national pathos; it doesn't suit our time'. Esser was seen as a new breed of German CEO who were used to acquisitions, understood the concept of shareholder value and saw the advantages of Anglo-American financial markets. Controversially, Esser publicly stated that he would fight a clean fight and would concede victory if Vodafone secured more than 50 per cent of the votes – even though in theory he could still frustrate the bid. By eschewing court actions, white knights, poison pills and other US-style defence tactics, Esser laid the foundations for one of the cleanest, fairest and most investor-friendly takeover battles.

For Esser, the case for keeping Mannesmann independent was based largely on the strengths of his own company's prospects. However, he also attacked Vodafone's strategy as well as commented on the volatility of its share price.

Esser's road show through the US argued that Mannesmann was growing more rapidly than Vodafone (forecasting a 39 per cent compound earnings growth for 2000–3 versus 24 per cent), controlled leading mobile operators in three of Europe's four largest markets and was well placed to be European partner of choice. The offer would also involve replacing Orange with Vodafone's UK business, despite the former substantially outperforming the latter. In essence, Esser was arguing predominantly for organic development coupled with strategic alliances.

Gent decided to make the offer under German takeover rules rather UK rules as this allowed Vodafone to raise its all-stock offer at a later stage, although Vodafone stated it had no intention of so doing. His case for the deal was that even if Mannesmann remained independent, it would soon have to merge with a large US player to be able to compete in a fast moving global industry. Indeed, there was concern over Vodafone's continued independence if the deal did not go through. Standing alone and waiting for some future alliance would take time in a world of mobile data and Internet time, where time is of the essence. On this basis, acquisition is the only sustainable approach to growth as organic growth is too slow.

Esser lost some of the early initiative in the deal because some big Mannesmann shareholders were also concerned to protect their investments in Vodafone, which would suffer if the bid failed. In addition, the concerns of shareholder power were not as strong as in the UK and the US, where many investors were based. Throughout the battle there was controversy over the amount of Mannesmann shares held in Germany with Mannesmann suggesting the figure to be around 40 per cent whereas Vodafone believed it to be nearer 25 per cent.

Although Mannesmann revealed excellent preliminary figures on 7 January 2000, showing a 70 per cent rise in earnings (EBITDA) to EURO 2.2 billion, which it argued represented outstanding results for shareholders, they were perceived as being in line with analysts' expectations and appeared to offer little additional support for Mannesmann.

In order to avoid falling foul of the European competition authorities, Vodafone announced its intention to spin off Orange, the UK wireless carrier.

The sentiment in the stock markets at the time was bullish and at the same time, a blockbusting deal between AOL and Time Warner was announced. As the elapsed time of the bid increased, both Mannesmann's and Vodafone's shares increased in value. This proved problematic for Esser, as Mannesmann's defence document stated that Mannesmann was worth EURO 250 a share, and he was on record as saying a fair price would range from EURO 300 to 350, and now they stood at around EURO 350 a share: an increase of 46 per cent on the price at bid launch. He therefore switched focus towards the amount of shares in the combined company that Mannesmann shareholders would receive, arguing for 58 per cent rather than the 47.2 per cent being offered.

On 4 February 2001, Mannesmann capitulated, with the Vodafone offer valuing Mannesmann shares at EURO 353 and the German group's shareholders taking 49.5 per cent of the combined company. Esser became an executive director on Vodafone's board until summer and then became a non-executive deputy chairman. In Chris Gent's words, 'It's been a long run, but it's been a pretty friendly hostile. Mannesmann – a great company – will be better with Vodafone.' The new Vodafone emerges as Europe's largest publicly traded company and the world's largest telecoms group – a global giant to compete with NTT DoCoMo of Japan, WorldCom and AT&T in the US and Deutsche Telekom in Germany. As the undisputed champion of the European telecoms sector, it stands at the centre of the continent's wireless-Internet revolution.

1. *Why did Vodafone make this hostile bid?*
2. *Why did the bid succeed?*
3. *What are the potential implications for cross-border activity in Germany?*

Source Material and Recommended Further Reading

This chapter relates to large-scale M&A where the deal results in a major strategic statement/realignment of the businesses involved. It is not concerned with the myriad of small-scale deals, which can be viewed as bolt-on asset purchases, or the purchasing of undervalued companies as ends in themselves. It also rests upon the assumption that many mergers are in fact zero premium acquisitions.

By now the reader will have gathered that I do not believe there is one adequate all-round text on mergers and acquisitions, but rather that there are unconnected pockets of scholarship. The main academic contributions come from the domains of economics, finance and organizational behaviour, and cluster around the issues of acquisition performance (do acquisitions create value and if so, for whom?), rational explanations for M&A (the relationship between the acquisition and the parent company business, 'strategic fit'), the effects of acquisition upon individuals and organizations ('organizational fit'). This chapter on strategy as exploration has shown that M&A is a much richer tapestry than just these questions and there is a great deal yet to be researched. This will be apparent in viewing the distribution of the following sources which have been structured along the lines of the chapter.

'Explorer motivations' is largely the untold story of M&A, with overwhelming attention being directed toward rational, legitimating explanations covered in the next section. Human motives are critical to the process, but where they are acknowledged, they are portrayed negatively. The classic article on *hubris* is R. Roll, 'The hubris hypothesis of corporate takeovers', *Journal of Business*, 59, 1986, 197–216. Hubris is more closely defined, together with negative corporate performance implications, by M.L.A. Hayward and D.C. Hambrick, 'Explaining the premiums paid for large acquisitions: evidence of CEO hubris', *Administrative Science Quarterly*, 42, 1997, 103–27. The extreme nature of the hubris image is well portrayed by M.J. Kroll, L.A. Toombs and P. Wright, 'Napoleon's tragic march home from Moscow: lessons in hubris', *The Academy of Management Executive*, 14, 2000, 117–28. The limitations of the Hubris interpretation is explained in D.N. Angwin, 'Putting Hubris back in its Box: Shifting the Blame for Success and Failure in M&A (forthcoming).

To fully capture the spirit of human motivation in M&A, the reader will have to venture further afield into journalistic accounts and novels. Two such works which convey the human quality of M&A are B. Burrough and J. Helyar, *Barbarians at the Gate* (London: Arrow Books, 1990); and P. Waine and M. Walker, *Takeover* (Chichester: Wiley, 2000).

My section on motivations suggests that the spirit of exploration can be noble and beneficial and that hubris has become an overused and often wrongly applied descriptor. This argument is articulated in a forthcoming article in the journal of the Institute of Bankers; D.N. Angwin (2003), 'The paradox of performance', *Eclectic*.

The section also emphasizes M&A activity as a result of 'contextual pressures'. An interesting collection of case studies, which suggest the influence of macroeconomic factors upon M&A activity, is contained in S.N. Kaplan (ed.), *Mergers and Productivity* (Chicago: National Bureau of Economic Research/University of Chicago Press, 2000). A useful article which attempts to give weight to different reasons for M&A activity, including contextual influence, is by F. Trautwein, 'Merger motives and merger prescriptions', *Strategic Management Journal*, 11, 1990, 283–95.

On 'launching an expedition': from a macro-perspective on rational motivations for M&A, many texts rehearse the 'M&A waves' of this century. The following diagram of historical merger waves (source: D. DePhamphlis, *Mergers, Acquisitions and Other Restructuring Activities*, New York: Academic Press, 2001) is a useful summary.

| Historical Consolidation 1897–1904 | Increasing Concentration 1916–1929 | Conglomerate Era 1965–1969 | The Dumping Decade 1981–1989 | The Era of Mega-Mergers 1992–2000 |

The period of 'horizontal consolidation' can be described as a Darwinian struggle of survival of the fittest, where drives for efficiency resulted in increased concentration and the creation of industrial giants such as Standard Oil, American Tobacco and General Electric. The wave ended with fraudulent financing and a stock market crash in 1904. The second wave resulted from the US entry into the First World War and the post-war economic boom. The era ended with the stock market crash of 1929 and the passage of the Clayton Act in the US, which defined monopolistic practices. The 'conglomerate era' was driven by the wish to diversify risk. By the early 1970s, conglomerates were trading at a discount, as they were perceived to be difficult to manage. The 'unbundling' decade followed as the parts of conglomerates were deemed to exceed the value of the whole. Hostile takeovers and LBOs predominated and many conglomerates such as British American Tobacco were spurred into substantial divestments. The decade dwindled with slowing economies, the bankruptcy of many LBOs and the demise of Drexel Burnham, the market maker for junk bonds. The current decade of 'mega-deals' has resulted from deregulation, reductions in trade barriers, the global trend towards privatization and a revolution in IT. Each year up to 1999 has seen record levels of activity by value with $3.43 trillion of deals transacted. Noticeable in this current wave are the rise of mega-mergers and the rise of hostile takeovers on the European continent.

At the industry level, a good example of prescriptive approaches for assessing the 'industry attractiveness' for M&A is contained in A.F. Payne, 'Approaching acquisitions strategically', *Journal of General Management*, 13(2), 1987, 5–27.

Reviews of 'economic motives' for M&A are generally well handled in M&A textbooks that are mentioned at the end of this source material section. However, also see W.H. Goldberg, *Mergers, Modes, Methods* (Aldershot: Gower, 1983); and D.J. Ravenscraft and F.M. Scherer, *Mergers, Sell-offs and Economic Efficiency* (Washington, DC: Brookings Institute, 1987).

A good review of 'financial motives' can be found in the text books by P.A. Gaughan, *Mergers, Acquisitions and Corporate Restructurings*, 2nd edn (New York: Wiley, 1999); and in F.A. Weston, J.A. Siu and B.A. Johnson, *Takeovers, Restructuring and Corporate Governance*, 3rd edn (Prentice-Hall, 2001).

At the company level a classical 'strategic taxonomy' of M&A is contained in G.A. Walter and J.B. Barney, 'Research notes and communications: management objectives in mergers and acquisitions', *Strategic Management Journal*, 11(1), 1990, 79–86. Those interested in a more detailed discussion of classical M&A typologies, should consult R. Larsson, *Coordination of Action in Mergers and Acquisitions: Interpretive and Systems Approaches Towards Synergy*, Lund Studies in Economics and Management 10, Institute of Economic Research (Lund: Lund University Press, 1990).

A central concern in the strategy literature is the issue of strategic fit, expressed as the extent of 'relatedness' between the two firms. An important early paper on this issue is by M.S. Salter and W.A. Weinhold, 'Choosing compatible acquisition styles', *Harvard Business Review*, 59(1), 1981, 117–27. This opened a major debate upon the relative merits of related and unrelated acquisitions on which there is a substantial literature. A few key articles are J. Kitching, 'Winning and losing with European acquisitions', *Harvard Business Review*, March–April 1974, 124–36; R.P. Rumelt, 'Diversification strategy and profitability', *Strategic Management Journal*, 3(4), 1982, 359–69; M. Lubatkin, 'Mergers and the performance of the acquiring firm', *Academy of Management Review*, 8, 1983, 218–25; H. Singh and C.A. Montgomery, 'Corporate acquisitions and economic performance', *Strategic Management Journal*, 8, 1987, 377–86; V. Ramanujam and P. Varadarajan, 'Research on corporate diversification', *Strategic Management Journal*, 10, 1989, 523–51; S. Chatterjee, 'Sources of value in take-overs: synergy or restructuring – implications for target and bidder firms', *Strategic Management Journal*, 13, 1992, 267–86.

On 'styles of exploring': the dynamic of doing a deal is not well represented in the academic literature. However, a classic paper that brings out the 'processual nature' of the acquisition process and illustrates some difficulties that stem from this dynamic is by D.B. Jemison and S.B. Sitkin, 'Acquisitions: the process can be a problem', *Harvard Business Review*, 64(2), 1986, 107–16.

'Negotiations' are a crucial aspect of the M&A process, but is very under-researched, largely, one suspects, due to the difficulties of gaining access in real time. Consequently little, if anything, of depth has been written on this issue. However, an interesting article which sets out some bases for M&A negotiation is by J.K. Sebenius, 'Six habits of merely effective negotiators', *Harvard Business Review*, April 2001, 87–95. An article that attempts to assess the implications of negotiations for top management retention is J.P. Walsh, 'Doing a deal: mergers and acquisitions negotiations and target company top management retention', *Strategic Management Journal*, 10(4), 1989, 307–22.

The textbook by D. DePhamphlis, *Mergers, Acquisitions and Other Restructuring Activities* (Academic Press, 2001), does a better job than many in trying to sketch out the actual 'predeal actions' and sequence of events leading up the signing of a deal. There are many books on discrete parts of this process, aimed at practising managers, such as due diligence, financing and structuring deals, valuation techniques, tax planning, legal and regulatory considerations, takeover and defence tactics. These books are often produced or sponsored by professional adviser firms and professional institutes. There are also series such as the one called Executive Briefings by the Financial Times/Prentice-Hall, which aims to address most of these topics.

On 'possession and a hero's welcome': the importance of planting the flag is, for financial economists, the ability to assess success over a short period of time around the deal announcement date (event window), to assess who benefits. Any immediate increase in market value, after correcting for normal market fluctuations, and avoiding arbitrageur effects, is an indicator of success. Important papers in this area are F.R. Franks and R.S. Harris, 'Shareholder wealth effects of corporate takeovers: the UK experience 1955–1985', *Journal of Financial Economics*, 23, 1989; and the review paper by M.C. Jensen and R. Ruback, 'The market for corporate control: the scientific evidence', *Journal of Financial Economics*, 11, 1983, 5–50.

There are likely to be other effects of achieving the acquisition, perhaps in terms of adding to corporate capital, in a social sense, enabling the company and management to achieve further goals. The importance of the deal in a symbolic and reputational sense requires investigation.

On 'searching for gold': the importance of quick wins shows the widely perceived need for seed in extracting benefits from the deal. This stems from the work by G. Stalk, 'Time – the next source of competitive advantage', *Harvard Business Review*, July–August 1988, 41–52. In an M&A context this imperative is clear to see underlying the entertaining read by M.L. Feldman and M.F. Spratt, *Five Frogs on a Log: A CEO's Field Guide to Accelerating the Transition in Mergers and Acquisitions and Gut Wrenching Change* (London: PriceWaterhouseCoopers/Harper Business, 1999). However, I have questioned the dogma that speed is critical for surcess. See D.N. Angwin, 'Fast-tracking M&A Integration: The First 100 Days', *British Academy of Management Conference*, London, September, 2002.

In generic terms, 'acquisition performance' has been strikingly poor. Those who have taken into consideration the post-acquisition period, such as the industrial economists, who have examined long-run profitability, using accounting measures, show declines. A useful book to illustrate this is D.J. Ravenscraft and F.M. Scherer, *Mergers, Sell-offs, and Economic Efficiency* (Washington, DC: Brookings Institute, 1987). Others have examined market share measures: D.C. Mueller, 'Mergers and market share', *The Review of Economics and Statistics*, 67, 1985, 259–67; and divestiture rates: M.E. Porter, 'From competitive advantage to corporate strategy', *Harvard Business Review*, May–June 1987, 2–21; all showing ostensibly poor performance. A good review of these enquiries can be found in A. Hughes, 'Mergers and economic performance in the UK: a survey of the empirical evidence 1950–1990', in M. Bishop and J. Kay (eds), *European Mergers and Merger Policy* (Oxford: Oxford University Press, 1993).

Poor acquisition performance has focused attention upon post-acquisition management. Ownership brings the image of 'taking charge' of the acquired company and attempting to integrate in some way to create value. The strategists working in this field have produced a more refined understanding of the post-acquisition phase than is currently used by the performance studies mentioned above. The key work in this area is by P. Haspeslagh and D. Jemison, *Managing Acquisitions* (New York: Free Press/Macmillan, 1991), which sets up a typology of styles and gives an indication of how these may be managed. This conceptual work has been empirically tested and extended in my own book which seeks to give practising managers guidance on the sorts of changes associated with each style and timing implications: D.N. Angwin, *Implementing Successful Post-acquisition Management* (London: Financial Times/Prentice-Hall, 2000). Few articles have been written on the timing of change in the post-acquisition period, but that by J.F. Bragado, 'Setting the correct speed for post-merger integration', *M&A Europe*, March–April 1992, 24–31, is of interest.

The image of the 'psychological shockwaves' hitting acquired companies from the first moment of the takeover is well brought out in P.H. Mirvis and M.L. Marks, *Managing the Merger: Making it Work* (Englewood Cliffs, NJ: Prentice-Hall, 1992).

The problems of two 'colliding organizational cultures' is vividly described in A.F. Buono and J.L. Bowditch, *The Human Side of Mergers and Acquisitions: Managing Collisions between People and Organizations* (San Francisco: Jossey-Bass, 1989). Attempts to find ways of identifying and working with different corporate cultures have been explored by A. Nahavandi and A.R. Malekzadeh, 'Acculturation in mergers and acquisitions', *Academy of Management Review*, 13(1), 1988, 79–90, and S. Cartwright and C. Cooper, *Acquisitions: The Human Factor* (Oxford: Butterworth-Heinemann, 1996).

The rise in cross-border M&A has raised the image of colliding national cultures. In generic terms this has been well brought out in works such as F. Trompenaars and C. Hampden-Turner, *Riding the Waves of Culture: Understanding Cultural Diversity in Business*, 2nd edn (London: Brealey, 1997). These differences are now being empirically examined in the M&A literature, focusing upon the post-acquisition context, with articles by R. Calori, M. Lubatkin and P. Very, 'Control mechanisms in cross-border acquisitions: an international comparison', *Organisation Studies*, 15(3), 1994, 361–79; R. Schoenburg, 'European cross-border acquisitions: the impact of management style differences on performance', in F. Burton, M. Yamin and S. Young (eds), *International Business and Europe in Transition* (London: Macmillan Business, 1996); D. Angwin and B. Savill, 'Strategic perspectives on European cross-border acquisitions: a view from top European executives', *European Management Journal*, 15(4), 1997, 423–35; and J. Child, R. Pitkethly and D. Faulkner, 'Changes in management practice and post-acquisition performance achieved by direct investors in the UK', *British Journal of Management*, 10(3), 1999, 185–98. To date, my own recent paper is alone in suggesting that we also examine these differences in the pre-acquisition period: D.N. Angwin, 'Mergers and acquisitions across European borders: national perspectives on pre-acquisition due diligence and the use of professional advisers', *Journal of World Business*, Special Issue, Spring 2001.

For an overview of the M&A area, and mindful of my view that these books tend to emphasize a partial coverage of the area, the following are recommended: D. DePhamphlis *Mergers, Acquisitions and Other Restructuring Activities* (New York: Academic Press, 2001); F.A. Weston, J.A. Siu and B.A. Johnson, *Takeovers, Restructuring and Corporate Governance*, 3rd edn (Englewood Cliffs, NJ: Prentice-Hall, 2001) *The Economist, Making Mergers Work* (London: The Economist Newspapers Ltd, 2000); P.A. Gaughan, *Mergers, Acquisitions and Corporate Restructurings*, 2nd edn (New York: Wiley, 1999).

For those interested in explorers, the main sources used throughout the chapter on explorers and exploration are: J. Cummins, *The Voyage of Christopher Columbus* (London: Weidenfeld and Nicolson, 1992); M. Estensen, *Discovery: The Quest for the Great South Land* (London: Conway Maritime Press, 1998); C. Hibbert, *Africa Explored: Europeans in the Dark Continent, 1769–1889* (Harmondsworth: Penguin, 1982); J.F. Kirk, *Prescott's Conquest of Peru and Miscellanies* (London: Routledge, 1893). J.H. Parry, *The Age of Reconnaissance: Discovery, Exploration and Settlement 1450–1650* (Berkeley, CA: University of California Press, 1963); W.D. Phillips, and C.R. Phillips, *The Worlds of Christopher Columbus* (Cambridge: Cambridge University Press, 1992); W.H. Prescott, *The Conquest of Mexico*, Everymans Library (London: Dent Dutton, 1978); A.G. Price (ed.), *The Explorations of Captain James Cook in the Pacific as Told by Selections of his Own Journals 1768–1779* (New York: Dover Publications, 1971); B. Riffenburg, *The Myth and the Explorer: The Press, Sensationalism and Geographical Discovery* (Oxford: Oxford University Press, 1994); O. Riviere, *Christopher Columbus* (Gloucester: Sutton Publishing, 1998); L.B. Simpson, *Many Mexicos* (Berkeley, CA: University of California Press, 1964); P. Van der Merwe, D. Preston, R.E. Feeney and L. McKernan, *South: The Race to the Pole* (London: National Maritime Museum, 2000).

Figure 8.4 is taken from Duncan Angwin, *Implementing Successful Acquisition Management* (London: Pearson Education, 2000).

*Previous chapters have examined how our notions of what customers want and how we configure organizations are fragmenting, and how, given this scenario, thinking outside of the box, managing connections and information and orchestrating interrelations are increasingly crucial to a company's strategic progress. This chapter picks up on this theme, using the image of **systems thinking** to explore the interface between organizing and strategizing. It subsequently demonstrates the importance of seeing these fragments and interrelations as an organic whole and how systems ideas can provide useful frames for seeing strategic decisions and development. From the simple interconnecting of things with arrows to the most complex diagrams, systems frameworks can help people think through the particular strengths and weaknesses of an organization and stimulate discussion as to what should be changed. In addition, recent biological research on the reflexive nature of organic systems provides an exciting new avenue for reflecting upon how complex systems like people and organizations are not objective appliers of frameworks nor completely open to change – a process of reflection that can enable strategic thinkers to be far more effective in their interventions.*

9 Strategy as Systems Thinking

JOHN BROCKLESBY AND STEPHEN CUMMINGS

Think of a leading company. Either the one for which you work or one you know. Take a sheet of paper and answer this: what makes that company's strategy successful?

Chances are that you have written a single statement, or list of factors. So, what's wrong with that?

We often run a case on Cooper Industries (a manufacturing company that has achieved consistent growth through acquiring mature low-technology companies) with our MBA students, asking them to outline Cooper's sources of 'competitive advantage'. They generally come back with a checklist something like this:

✓ It is diversified in such a way as to focus its energies *and* enable growth.
✓ It has a clear view of the companies that it wants to acquire.
✓ It has a good reputation within the industries that it operates.
✓ It takes a long-term view to growing the companies it acquires.
✓ It buys new companies without paying over the odds.
✓ It has a clear plan of action when it acquires and transforms a company.
✓ It has a special team of people devoted to carrying out that plan.
✓ It knows the industries that it operates within.
✓ It acts quickly to acquire its targets.

✓ Knowledge of other subsidiaries spreads quickly throughout Coopers.
✓ It cuts costs by getting actively involved in the companies it acquires rather than just acting as an 'investment company'.

These points are all correct. But something is missing. What gets left off a list is the complex interrelationship between points. If you take the above list for Coopers and begin to draw arrows to depict how these points relate to and reinforce each other, you begin to see the real strength of the company. Soon you see how all of the points above add to one another. Over time these interrelationships have built up to make the company what it is today. While competitors could copy the individual points, the embedded relationships between them within Cooper's context are impossible to manufacture. It is this that makes a competitive advantage sustainable.

We can explore these conventional limitations further. One of strategy's most widely used tools is SWOT analysis. This is also about discrete lists of points arranged into four particular categories:

• a company's internal *S*trengths,
• a company's internal *W*eaknesses,
• the *O*pportunities that exist in a company's external environment, and
• the *T*hreats that exist in its external environment.

SWOT lists are also not particularly good at dealing with a complex and often paradoxical world. For example, once you have listed something as a strength then you can not really use it in another category; right? Looking at the mesh of self-referential arrows again one can recognize the problem with this sort of listing in terms of general classifications. Cooper's greatest *strength* is paradoxically also its greatest *weakness*, and potentially its greatest *threat*. Its *system* of competitive advantage is so connected, such a tangled web, that it is 'closed'. It knows very well what it does and how it does it, but does this come at the expense of not questioning this system as the environment in the 'wider world' changes? Being the best acquirer of low-tech mature manufacturing companies is a sustainable route to growth, so long as the environment remains constant and that market keeps expanding. What do Coopers do if it does not? Its strength is a clear vision of what it does. Its weakness is that this clarity of vision can, over time, diminish its ability to see other *opportunities* or develop other strengths. Cooper's greatest threat is that the environment will change without this being recognized, and without its strengths being questioned. Rather than discrete categories of separate points, strengths, weaknesses, opportunities and threats are very interrelated.

This double-edged sword of strengths potentially being weaknesses is often referred to as the *Icarus Paradox*. This is named after a character in Greek mythology who was so pleased with the wax wings that he had made that he kept flying up and up, increasing in confidence and proficiency – until he got so close to the sun that his wings melted and he fell to earth. It is often used to explain the problems faced by IBM in the 1980s. The moral of the story is that having a tightly interrelated set of abilities gives you the confidence to move very quickly, but the ability to do one set of things particular well often makes you less likely to stop and think about the relevance of what you do. (See Chapter 12, 'Strategy as Numbers', for a further application of the Icarus Paradox.) In systems terms this is often expressed by comparing 'single-loop' and 'double-loop' learning. Most companies are good at single-loop learning, but, like Icarus, are not so good at double-looping.

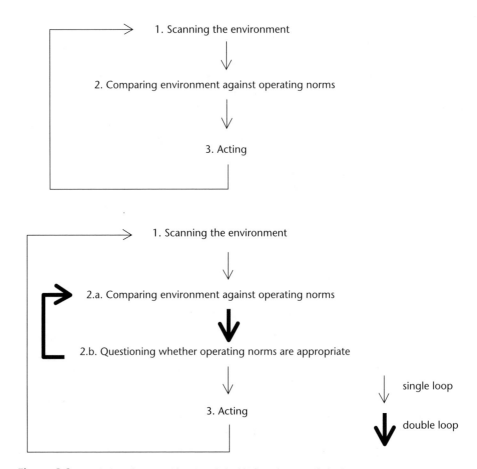

Figure 9.1 Single-loop learning (above) and double-loop learning (below)

From a fairly straightforward list of things that a company does well we have quickly moved into a fairly deep discussion as to the nature of competitive advantage, just by adding a few arrows and questioning complex interrelationships. This is the power of systems thinking. However, before we move into a more substantive discussion of systems ideas and how they may be applied to thinking about strategy, we first provide a basic systems thinking 'starter kit'.

Systems Thinking: The Basic Concepts

The 'will-to-list' and our predilection to categorize rather than think in systems terms, is a legacy of a set of modern Western beliefs as to 'how things work'. This legacy encourages us to see things in the light of two assumptions that are now over 300 years old:

(1)   The notion that there is one universal God, and that He is akin to an all-seeing, all-knowing mechanical designer, a 'watchmaker' as some historians of science

have described Him. Hence, His design must exhibit an underlying pattern – and a linearity of cause and effect. *Knowledge*, in our modern 'age of reason', *comes to be about deciphering God's linear design.*

(2)   The idea, pioneered by René Descartes, that to understand the complexity of this design, and the elements within it, one should detach oneself from the emotions of the situation so as to be objective, not unlike a rational God, and break things down to their component parts. *Understand the parts and you can see the line of cause and effect and understand the whole.*

Thus, historians such as Richard Dawkins name 'the machine' as the analogy upon which modern science is based. That these assumptions continue to influence our thinking can be seen in expressions such as 'the wheels of government', 'we're all cogs', and 'that guy works like a machine'.

Taking a 'systems approach is fundamentally different. It is premised an the following:

(a)   A system is a network of components that interact with one another to constitute a whole. Thus, a system is more than the sum of its parts, which, in and of themselves have little meaning out of their context (e.g., a human hand cannot be understood severed from a body). A system, therefore, 'lives, breathes and develops' and is a product of *interaction*.

(b)   Just as a system subsumes its components, it too will be a component of wider systems. Consequently, where a system's boundaries lie depend on the subjective eye of the observer (one can legitimately take 'the thumb', 'the hand', 'the individual', 'the family', 'society', and so on as 'the system in focus'). Thus, the distinction often made between 'an organization's strategy' and 'the environment' (the basis of much strategic analysis) is, from a systems' perspective, arbitrary.

Despite the fact that people tend to use lists to describe successful strategic approaches (e.g., 'the seven habits of highly effective people'), systems concepts are by no means foreign to us. In fact, they seem to resonate with our experiences of everyday life. The continuation of systems thinking in our language, and the ease with which we use systems expressions, seem to indicate that we retain a natural affinity with systemic notions. Think, for example, of everyday expressions such as 'can't see the wood for the trees'; 'vicious circle'; 'we're on a roll'; 'downward spiral'; 'self-fulfilling prophecy'; 'domino effect' and 'what goes around comes around'. These all embody aspects of systems thinking.

Those who are now applying systems thinking to strategy are thus tapping a rich vein, but one that has gone unexplored for quite some time. In fact, many of the last decade's most successful management gurus owe their success to the systemic nature of their ideas. While these gurus have benefited by drawing upon a much older 'systems tradition', they have translated this tradition in such a way as to enable it to be brought to a mainstream audience.

An understanding of how systems has begun to enter the mainstream provides a good background with which to look further into the tradition of systems in order to learn from more complex, but often overlooked, frameworks. Toward this end, the later parts of this chapter investigate Stafford Beer's 'viable systems model' (VSM) and the systems thinking of Chilean biologist Humberto Maturana. Both of these sets of ideas generate a whole new set of insights into the way in which companies develop strategies.

Systems Enters the Mainstream

In this section of the chapter we outline five approaches that utilize systems thinking concepts: the resource-based view of the firm; the Porter 'diamond of national competitiveness'; the 'seven-S' framework; the 'fifth discipline'; and 'organigraphs'. These are increasingly utilized as tools for analysing strategy in ways that go beyond the conventional microeconomic theory of the firm as a discrete or stand-alone input-process-output function.

The resource-based view

Perhaps the most visible application of systems type thinking in strategy in recent times has been the 'resource-based view' (RBV) of the firm. Throughout the 1990s, this approach, popularized through a series of papers by Jay Barney, has gathered momentum within strategic management circles. The RBV, in contrast to traditional economic models, argues that each organization is made up of a unique constellation of *resources* and the relationships between these resources. 'Resources' being broadly understood to incorporate:

- *physical resources* such as land and machinery;
- *financial resources*;
- *human resources* such as experience and expertise; and
- intangible *organizational resources* such as reputation, ethos and traditional relationships).

Generally, the best way to record these resources and relations is in a systems diagram showing how the various resources build upon and reinforce one another; how the tangible and intangible resources of a business stitch themselves together to make the whole stronger (see Figure 9.2).

Because these resources, relationships and capabilities are reflective of a particular geographical location, a particular history, particular and emergent relations between employees within the firm and then between them and suppliers and customers and so forth, each organization's web of resources will be unique. In strategic terms this is important, because in an age of best practice benchmarking and reverse engineering, firms have become very good at copying what they can copy (see Chapter 2, 'Strategy as Ethos'). Hence, as with the Cooper example at the head of this chapter, it is such historically determined interrelationships that will increasingly provide companies with the routes to sustainable competitive advantage.

It may be a useful exercise at this point to draw an RBV diagram for the firm for which you work or for one with which you are familiar. As with the examples provided in Chapter 7, 'Strategy as Creativity', this approach is especially useful as a discussion aid. Once you have your diagram others can add in, or 'whiteboard up', their contributions as to how the company 'works'. This can enable a rich shared understanding of an organization to emerge organically. (Note: the RBV provides a more sober approach for those not so comfortable with the prospect of presenting their company in terms of ray-guns and knitting needles!).

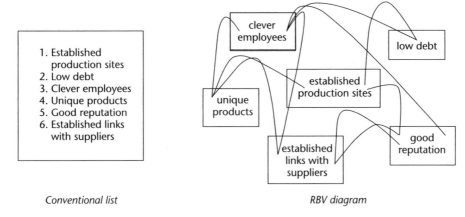

Figure 9.2   A standard list of corporate resources compared to an RBV diagram

The Porter diamond

One can also see systems thinking in less obvious sources. Michael Porter's 'diamond of national competitiveness', for example, provides a useful framework for analysing how some firms can develop a competitive advantage through their being able to tap into the relations that have emerged in a particular geographic location. Why Belgian companies lead the world in the manufacture of chocolates and beer is difficult to explain using the logic of traditional economics, it makes perfect sense however when one analyses the interrelationships active in these industries using Porter's diamond model (see Figure 9.3).

Intense inter-firm *rivalry* in these industries in Belgium and sophisticated consumer *demand* have meant that companies that survive in this environment have a clear *strategic* and *structural* focus. This is aided by being able to draw upon *factor conditions* such as close proximity to key high-quality ingredients and staff who, through specialized education, are extremely proficient in these fields. This education has been aided for decades by a *government* that also helps stimulate local demand by keeping the taxes and excise duties on these products low. Finally, Belgian brewers and chocolatiers gain from the strength of *related and supporting* operators such as distribution and haulage companies (whose development has been aided by *chance* events, such as wars and treaties, that put Belgium at the heart of Europe's markets).

The seven-S framework

Even further back in the history of strategic thinking, Pascale, Athos, Peters and Waterman's 'seven-S framework' illustrated the power of systems thinking. This simple model, which became the starting point for Peters and Waterman's *In Search of Excellence*, provides a nice framework for looking at how organizational success can be understood by exploring the interrelationships between a company's:

- *s*trategy,
- *s*tructure,
- information *s*ystems,

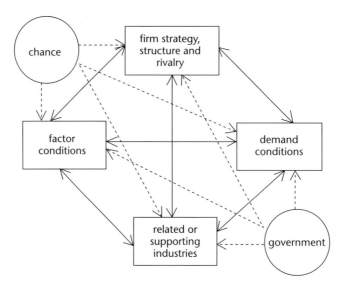

Figure 9.3   The Porter diamond of national competitiveness
Source: Michael E. Porter, *The Competitive Advantage of Nations* (New York: Simon & Schuster), p. 72.
© 1990, 1998 by Michael E. Porter.

- corporate *s*tyle,
- *s*taff,
- *s*kills and
- *s*uperordinate goals or vision for the future.

The fifth discipline

While these approaches and others (see, for example, David Wilson's discussion of Pierre Wack's thinking in Chapter 7, 'Strategy as Creativity') exhibit, but are not explicit in their use of, systems thinking, Peter Senge is. Senge describes systems thinking by analogy:

> A cloud masses, the sky darkens, leaves twist upward, and we know that it will rain. We also know that after the storm, the runoff will feed into groundwater miles away . . . All these events are distant in time and space, and yet they are all connected within the same pattern. Each has an influence on the rest, an influence that is usually hidden from view. You can only understand the system of a rainstorm by contemplating the whole, not any individual part of the pattern.

He then argues that business endeavours are just as systemic as the weather:

> They, too, are bound by invisible fabrics of interrelated actions, which often take years to fully play out their effects on each other. Since we are part of that lacework ourselves, it's doubly hard to see the whole pattern of change. Instead we tend to focus on snap-shots of isolated parts of the system, and wonder why our deepest problems never seem to get solved.

Building upon the pioneering work of Jay Forrester and other Massachusetts Institute of Technology (MIT) colleagues Senge sought to bring systems thinking ideas to managers and strategists to help them better understand systemic patterns and influence them more effectively.

The link between systems thinking and strategy became clear to Senge as he focused on the increasing need for companies to become 'learning organizations'. Here strategy development would need to come from interactive groups of people from diverse backgrounds constantly double-loop learning and developing new ideas unique to their particular circumstances. Senge developed this thinking in his book *The Fifth Discipline*. This provided ideas as to how companies could become learning organizations and how 'future leaders' might use systems thinking to develop strategy.

Senge's systems background helped him identify five 'disciplines' that were necessary to build a learning organization: *learning org!*

(1) *Personal mastery*: because shared visions emerge from personal visions, this first discipline is about both creating personal goals and an organizational environment that encouraged groups of people to develop a sense of purpose.

(2) *Surfacing mental models*: which is about reflecting upon the pictures, maps and models (like the many discussed in this book) that the people in the organization use to make sense of the world and question how these frameworks influence decision making.

(3) *Developing shared vision*: which is about involving the group in developing a shared vision out of personal visions and surfacing, questioning and applying mental models.

(4) *Team learning*: ensuring that the dynamics are in place to make the 'whole' knowledge of the group greater than the sum of individual knowledge within the organization.

(5) *Systems thinking*: the 'fifth discipline', reflecting on, describing, understanding and acting upon the 'big picture' or how the relationships and interactions between the elements of the organization and the environment affect the whole.

According to Senge, this systems thinking should entail:

(i) seeing interrelationships and processes rather than things and snapshots;

(ii) recognizing that individual 'cogs' are not to blame for poor performance – they can only do what the various systems allow them to do;

(iii) distinguishing which parts of the system have high impact on strategy and which are only minor details;

(iv) through paying attention to (iii), one can focus on areas of 'high leverage' – the 20 per cent of things that will make 80 per cent of difference;   *20%. 80%*

(v) look beyond solving 'symptoms' and 'outcomes' through popular 'quick fixes' or applying generic buzzwords. Poorly performing systems require systematic solutions.

Mintzberg's organigraphs

Despite the notion of organization form being taken as given in most strategy textbooks, the idea that the way we see organization will influence the way we view strategy is a theme that runs through this book. Mintzberg's earlier notions of an organic organization were criticized in Chapter 1 for reinforcing the notion of organ-

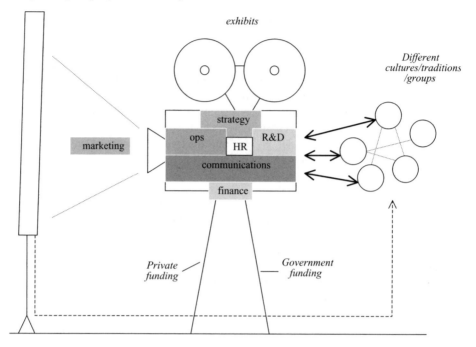

Figure 9.4 An organigraph of a national museum

ization as generically triangular. However, his idea that strategy emerges through particular micro-interactions forming patterns of behaviour, indicates his systemic leanings. Moreover his new 'organigraphic' approach provides a simple method of drawing organization that incorporates systems thinking, and enables us to think strategy as a more idiosyncratic and less generic process.

Mintzberg and his co-author Ludo Van der Heyden argue that organigraphs do not eliminate boxes altogether, but they add other elements into them such as networks, hubs, and other shapes that reflect how a particular place works and interacts with its environment. 'Organigraphs are more than just pictures', they explain, 'they are also maps. They provide an overview of a company's territory – its mountains, rivers, and towns, and the roads that connect them.'

We can illustrate the approach through the example shown in Figure 9.4. This organigraph of a national museum shows how the organization has some elements of a typical value chain running from left to right (see chapter 1) with a feedback loop added on. But it also illustrates how its different sets of components interact with one another along the chain in a more iterative, hub and spoke or web-like way. While the sequential relationships might best be managed through centralized planning, the more web-like relationships may call for a decentralized approach. 'Seeing such relationships illustrated can help a company understand the need for different managerial mind-sets throughout the organization', Mintzberg and Van der Heyden explain.

Mintzberg and Van der Heyden's ideas are not new. While they note precedents of people drawing organizations and 'starbursts' and 'shamrocks' in the early 1990s (a theme developed in Chapter 5, 'Strategy as Orchestrating Knowledge'), there is a much older systems tradition, developed by Peter Checkland in the 1970s and 1980s, which does more or less the same thing. Checkland's 'rich picture analysis', which forms part of his 'soft systems methodology', encourages people to draw their organizations in terms of the people, structures and processes that reflect the 'everyday life' of the organization. Stakeholders are then encouraged to draw how things might be. This actual versus ideal systems drawing approach is one that we shall pick up upon in exploring the viable systems model in the next section. But, first, the case below provides you with an opportunity to practise drawing in a systemic way in order to more accurately reflect an organization's particular strategy.

Case Box 9.1   Drawing the New Aquaparts System

Craig French has a problem and an opportunity. As managing director at *Aquaparts*, one of the world's largest whiteware components companies, he is faced with a fast changing environment that is rapidly making the company's traditional structure (bequeathed to it when it was incorporated within the global giant *Whitespin Corporation*) seem out of step. However, he now has the chance to work on an MBA dissertation focused on this issue. He is required to make recommendations as to what a new structure for *Aquaparts* might look like.

Whitespin, an American corporation, grew into a global powerhouse by focusing on vertical integration, choosing, wherever possible, to source development and manufacture components in house. Hence its value chain was tightly controlled and very long. This provided many cost and scale advantages, but toward the end of the 1990s it was decided that the costs of holding systems and components development in house (e.g., the lack of exposure to competition and different customers and the learning that this would encourage) had begun to outweigh the benefits. *Whitespin* made the decision to spin off its supply divisions, and in June 2001 *Aquaparts* was born. Overnight it became one of the world's three largest white-ware component suppliers.

However, size alone would not guarantee *Aquaparts'* future. In Craig's words the challenge was to 'take the best of the traditional size and strengths through its association with *Whitespin*, while making the most of the new changes and opportunities'. *Whitespin* management's initial objectives for *Aquaparts* were similar, but more precise:

'*Aquaparts* must maintain existing *Whitespin*-group revenues while growing non *Whitespin*-group business towards one third of its total revenues.'

Craig began by reviewing *Aquaparts'* strengths, weaknesses, opportunities and threats:

- *Aquaparts* inherited many **strengths** through being a part of *Whitespin*. Its sheer size, for one thing. Moreover, *Whitespin*'s long history and the tacit knowledge built up over the decades, in combination with this size, made *Aquaparts* able to offer clients integrated solutions which incorporated the whole range of automotive systems. 'Having the skill set to deal with all the different products and technologies is a great advantage as manufacturers look for integrated ways to reduce costs, weight and technology and improve the fit between the parts of the automobile and the whole of its identity or image', Craig mused.

However, he wondered whether this total systems ability was now hindered by the organization's original configuration of four strategic business units (see below). Although these units were linked to a central technology office, whose role it was to work on new technologies to be transferred across the units, they had, over time, become insular and somewhat separate.

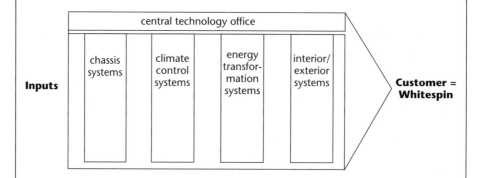

- While this was an entirely efficient, integrated and value-adding chain when *Aquaparts* only sold internally to *Whitespin*, it now presented certain **weaknesses**. It was obvious that the company, so configured, did not have an external focus, and that resources needed to be allocated toward winning non-*Whitespin* business.

In Craig's words, the new company would need to 'move outside of the comfort zone represented by the old structure that existed when it was within *Whitespin* – to connect to and build relationships with other manufacturers'. In order to meet their external targets, *Aquaparts* needed to build relationships and develop a portfolio in Europe in particular.

Craig knew from personal experience that European clients operated with a different mindset to those in the US, thus building new relationships would require particular sensitivities. In addition, *Aquaparts* would need to respond to the different identities that each manufacturer tries to purvey through its white-goods. This would probably necessitate the development of different 'value configurations' rather than seeking to get different entities to conform to the same model.

Given its 'youth' an additional weakness was *Aquaparts*' current lack of brand image. The company needed to work hard to create an identity that different manufacturers wanted to relate to.

- However, changes in the environment also provide some interesting **opportunities**. The move from long value chains to constellations and value-webs, which the creation of *Aquaparts* is, in part, responding to, has also led to reconfigurations among whiteware manufacturers. It is subsequently more meaningful now to talk of manufacturing 'families' rather than independent companies: 'We are down to nine key producer groups, and the theory is that we will soon reach a point where the whiteware industry is served by five global manufacturering families', Craig figures.

The ensuing platform deproliferation and modularization, with companies trying to reduce costs by adopting common platform strategies to be deployed on many models, are leading to the consolidation of a product range across a smaller number of basic design structures, component sets or production architectures. This means that while *Aquaparts* must look outward and begin to customise its products, the number of configuration solutions desired in the marketplace is reducing.

This would suggest that while *Aquaparts* has to offer more than one 'face' to the world, it would not need to develop an infinite number of 'faces' to achieve its targets. The creation of these constellations or families also provides more routes into the companies that *Aquaparts* now needs to connect to. For example, a good relationship with the key player in a network provides an immediate connection with four or five other manufacturers. Or, a connection with a player that *Aquaparts* is traditionally more comfortable with could lead on to others within its 'family'.

- At the same time Craig foresees the following **threats** that *Aquaparts* could fall prey to. In seeking to develop new relationships, it should not just place manufacturers together into traditional stereotypical categories or groupings (e.g., mass market/prestige or Asia/European/US), which seem to mean less and less, but to consider how *Aquaparts* wants to appear to every individual manufacturer or manufacturing family.

Moreover, *Aquaparts* must steer between two potential vices: moving too far too fast and upsetting its traditional *Whitespin* business and established reputation, or not moving far or fast enough to capture new markets before they are secured by the competition.

Consequently, as Craig concluded, 'the question for us for the next ten years is to align ourselves or network ourselves into key customers, to form tight strategies around the needs of key customers, to work at developing links with new families – often with very different cultures from our traditional customers. But we must keep costs down and structure ourselves in such a way as to give potential new customers a sense of *Aquaparts*' traditional strengths because this is our best chance for building our identity in the marketplace. Paradoxically, we must seek to have a strong global identity that can be sensitive to local differences and tailor solutions to particular customer needs, and we should do this by responding to the new opportunities and the new vision by building upon our old *Whitespin* strengths.'

After scouring countless books and articles outlining companies organized along national or product divisions, and generic matrix organization structures, he thought, 'what I really need is to develop some sort of individualized diagram that expresses a structure that relates to our particular challenges – then I could get my head around what we need to do to make a new structure a reality.'

1. *Combine the RBV or organigraphs concepts with the creative individualized drawing approach from the 'Strategy as Creativity' chapter to create a picture or map that illustrates what you think* Aquaparts *should look like.*

2. *How does this form communicate* Aquaparts' *strategy in ways that a typical generic organization chart or list of strengths or sources of competitive advantage could not?*

Note: (The names of the people and companies described in this case have been disguised.)

Delving Deeper Into the Systems Image: 1 – The Viable Systems Model

While the popular ideas of Barney, Senge, and Mintzberg provide some means for liberating our thinking from the modern reductionist assumptions that we outlined earlier in this chapter, they do have some important shortcomings. The first of these is that often they either do not pay much regard to the biological underpinnings of systems thinking, or they unquestioningly accept dated biological thinking. In other words, they carry forward fairly rational, mechanistic or robotic views of how organisms work. This is particularly so in strategic management. Traditionally, the literature has taken strategy to be a process through which actors scan the environment and then on the basis of assessments about what is 'going on', act with intent in relation to a predetermined set of purposes. This conception of strategy mimics the dominant 'open systems' perspective on human cognition. 'Cognitivism' as it is known, considers the nervous system to be an instrument through which humans obtain information from the environment and construct a model of the 'outside world', which they then use to compute appropriate behaviour. On this view, there is a clear separation between the cognitive system and the external world, and cognition involves the former objectively constructing and manipulating representations of the latter. Over the past few decades this view of cognition has increasingly been called into question.

The second shortcoming of the recent take-up of systems ideas by strategy scholars is that they provide little in the way of formal structures, models or templates that provide the basis for convergent dialogue among stakeholders who are interested in the strategic alignment of organizations with their environments. This is an issue since, as earlier chapters of this book have shown, there is often nothing as liberating as a structure that enables people to organize and debate their ideas.

Against this background, the work of systems thinker and cybernetician Stafford Beer is interesting for two reasons. First, because his 'viable systems model' (VSM) provides exactly the sort of organizing device that *Images of Strategy* suggests people need in seeking to make sense of complex ideas and data. Second, because this structure arose out of a very detailed study of how complex adaptive systems behave. Although Beer arrived at his theory of viable systems through studying the way in which the nervous system organizes the human body, he claims that he could have reached the same conclusions had he employed as a model other systems such as single biological cells, whole animal species, or complex social systems. All of these, he submits, are *known-to-be-viable* systems. This makes his VSM an ideal template for looking at organizations as organic systems. However, as we shall see, the VSM is still based upon a number of cognitive assumptions. Hence, the following section investigates a more advanced biological systems approach in which cognitivism is not taken for granted.

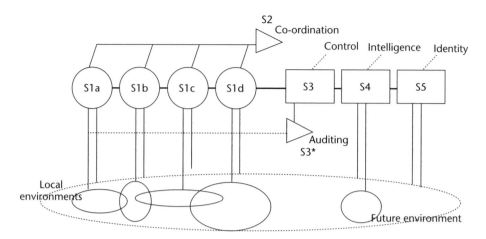

Figure 9.5 The viable systems model
Source: Stafford Beer, *Diagnosing the System for Organizations* (NJ: John Wiley & Sons Inc., 1985).

Although we have found the VSM to be an exceedingly useful tool for helping stakeholders reflect on their organizational structures and processes, it never became a mainstream framework in strategy. Partly this can be put down to the inaccessibility of some of the VSM literature. Hence, what is presented here is just enough to enable you to grasp the following case box where the model is related to practice. From here you should be able to apply the model to your own concerns.

Beer sought a systems framework that could be used to explain and analyse organizational viability (defined as 'the capability to maintain an independent existence across the long-term'). He proposes that all viable systems share five basic properties:

(1) *Operational elements*, that directly interface with the external environment, that enact the identity of the system.
(2) *Co-ordination* functions, that ensure that the operational elements work in sync.
(3) *Control* activities, that maintain and allocate resources to the operational elements.
(4) *Intelligence* functions, that consider the system as a whole – its strategic opportunities, threats and future direction; and an
(5) *Identity* element, that formulates the purpose or *raison d'être* of the system, its soul, 'place' and direction in the world.

As an example, one can think of a human being as a viable system through its exhibition of, and interplay between, *operational elements* such as skin, limbs and vital organs; *co-ordination* functions like the nervous system; *control*, though the *pons medula* at the base of the brain allocating resources, like blood; *intelligence*, characterized by the brain's use of the sense and thought; and *identity* in what might be described as an individual's particular sense of self. A viable human, like any organism, requires all five elements to be in place, interrelated and working in unison.

Beer incorporated these five systemic functions into the framework of the VSM (see Figure 9.5). This illustration depicts the following five systemic functions:

- operations (S1),
- co-ordination (S2),
- control (S3),
- intelligence (S4), and
- identity (S5).

Another element worth noting is S3★. This is an adjunct to the control function concerned with the sporadic auditing of the interaction between operational elements and their local environments.

The S1 operations function will likely be divided into a number of units (the number will vary according to circumstances). From a strategy perspective, S4 is particularly interesting because it is here where the traditional environmental scanning activities take place. Moreover, it is here where the cognitivist underpinning to the VSM is most apparent. The VSM, according to Beer, operates on the premise that systems are embedded in a pre-existing environment, that 'is full of challenges and opportunities (and) the VSM must respond to this environment'. One should thus note the primacy afforded the environment, with which the system interacts, and the *communication channels* (lines) between the various functions and aspects of the environment, in the VSM diagram.

How then do viable systems respond to their environments? According to VSM logic, autonomy is ceded to the system's operational units so that they can take responsibility for understanding the needs of their own local environments, and have the capacity to act on such knowledge without undue constraints or wider interference from the system as a whole. Beyond this, the VSM's logic for adaptation maps almost precisely on to the cognitivist logic just described. S4 collects information from the environment, processes this information and builds models. Thereafter it is a case of S4 communicating the results of its deliberations through the system such that action may be taken to sustain adaptability and survival, and to promote advancement.

Returning to the model as a whole, each VSM, including business organizations, should exhibit each of the five systemic functions described above. In addition, effective channels of communication ensure that these functions operate in sync with the others, and with the environment. To understand Beer's conception of the effective operation of these channels, one needs to understand the cybernetic concept of *requisite variety*.

'Variety', in cybernetic thinking, is the number of distinguishable environmental states or scenarios, present and potential that have a bearing on the purposes of the system in focus. The founding father of the science of co-ordination and control in mechanical and biological systems, or cybernetics, W. Ross Ashby, in his *Law of Requisite Variety*, states that 'only variety can destroy variety'. This can be better understood when placed in the context of the evolution of Ashby's ideas. During the Second World War, Ashby worked on anti-missile defence systems for the US military. His precept was that in order to destroy its targets a defence missile must be able to go as low and as high, as fast and as slow, as the target which it seeks to 'match and destroy'. In order for such a system to be viable, it must be able to match all the states that its incoming targets could bring to bear. In the same way, in order to become, and remain, viable, an organization must achieve *requisite variety* by maintaining the capacity to *match* the present and potential systemic states within its operating environment that may impact upon its purpose.

At this point it is useful to refer back to the drawing of the VSM and conceive of it in three parts. The environment, the operational elements, and the metasystem (S2–S5). In relation to a defined set of purposes the environment will exhibit a number of variety states which the operational elements must be able to *match*. Moreover the metasystem (co-ordination, control, intelligence, and identity functions), must have the variety to *match* those things that the operational elements require to maintain their ability to *match* the demands of their local environments.

Beer argues that the conditions outlined above – the five systemic elements and the effective communication channels running between them, and between them and the environment – must be present in all viable systems. Consequently, the VSM provides a useful tool for thinking about the workings of any complex adaptive system, particularly business organizations. It focuses a strategist's mind on pertinent, but often overlooked questions such as What is this organization's particular identity? (S5); What are the elements that act-out this identity (S1 units), that the system's purpose directly fulfill. What are the elements in this company that carry out co-ordination (S2), control (S3), auditing (S3★) and intelligence (S4) functions? Does the metasystem embodied in these functions have the requisite variety to service the operational elements that directly carry out the organization's primary purpose? Does the organization appear to be lacking in any of the necessary VSM requirements?

The VSM framework also provides a pictorial representation of possible answers to these sorts of questions. They can then be more effectively communicated and discussed by relevant stakeholders. One can consider the VSM shown in Figure 9.5 as a theoretically ideal viable system. One can then use this as a template to draw a real organization and demonstrate the things that are lacking, undersized, oversized, confused, etc. Figure 9.6 (see page 286) shows how some of the most common VSM faults might be illustrated.

The case study in Case Box 9.2 demonstrates how the VSM can be an insightful tool for organizational and strategic analysis. We encourage readers to use it as a means of getting comfortable with the model before using it to better understand organizations with which they are familiar. In our experience, few real systems will exhibit perfect VSM characteristics and no two organizations will have exactly the same VSM profile. Herein lies the strength of the model. It provides a common framework that allows one to examine each organization's unique systemic strengths and weaknesses.

Case Box 9.2   Telecom NZ (A)

During the 1980s the New Zealand Labour Government instituted a massive programme of economic and commercial reforms that included the corporatization (and subsequent privatization) of state trading organizations. In 1987, as part of this process, Telecom (NZ) was formed to operate the telecommunications business of what was the New Zealand Post Office, a government department. Whereas the NZPO had traditionally fulfilled a number of social and political objectives, Telecom was required to operate as a commercial concern. Its vision statement became 'To satisfy the needs of our customers, shareholders and employees with exceptional business efficiency and superior service'. Yet at the time of the change the company was ill equipped to compete in the new competitive environment, into which a number of network providers and equipment suppliers had already entered. Telecom's network technology was out of date, its management structure highly centralized and bureaucratic, its operations were inefficient, and customers perceived that it offered poor quality service.

Over the next few years the company made several key strategic responses to this situation. These changes were embodied in a complete re-organization of the company's structure. Autonomous regional operating companies (ROCs) were created to operate the main business of the Telecom network. Under this structure the four ROCs were made responsible for business in their geographical area, a fifth unit provided common network services. All other business units were established as new venture companies. Thus, many functions previously carried out at head office were decentralized. The company moved with breathtaking speed from a highly centralized bureaucracy to a decentralized collection of very autonomous business units where decision-making responsibility was devolved down the organization in an attempt to get 'closer to the customer'.

Telecom did, however, recognize that this extreme decentralization could well lead to dis-economies of scale and inconsistent policy development and implementation across the company. In response, the company sought to 'cross' the ROC structure with a number of 'Functional Councils' (FCs), to create a matrix-type organization. Each FC had an area of concern such as human resource management, information systems, finance, commercial, and business planning. Their purpose was to bring people with relevant expertise from across the company to co-ordinate and develop consistency in these areas across the corporation. The standard organizational chart depiction of Telecom used to illustrate the new structure is presented below.

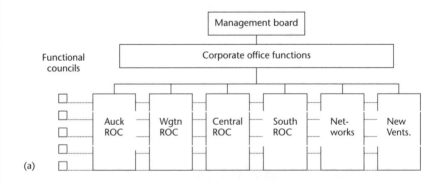

(a)

The chart above might lead one to conclude that the company had come through the difficult changes and was now operating with a structure that would ensure its future viability. Unfortunately this proved not to be the case. The new structure had been up and running for a little over a year when we were commissioned to put together a consultancy team to undertake a review.

Our VSM analysis enabled us to see that things were not so rosy at Telecom. The review resulted in a report that highlighted five major areas of weakness.

The first step in a VSM analysis is to define the purpose of the system in focus. This becomes the basis for determining the system's operational elements.

Telecom's vision statement 'To satisfy the needs of our customers, shareholders and employees with exceptional business efficiency and superior service', was somewhat 'generic' and did not in our view capture the company's unique *raison d'être*. Hence, we framed Telecom's primary purpose as broadly being the provision and servicing of telecommunications technology. Subsequently, the operational elements, those things that actually carried out this purpose, were identified as the four regional operating companies and the Networks and New Ventures business units.

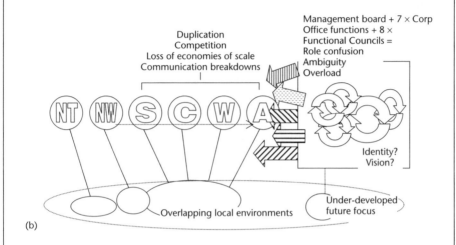

(b)

These differences between our various drawings of Telecom and the ideal VSM represent the system's cybernetic weaknesses:

A – Operational Overlap

On the surface, the thinking behind the autonomy ceded to the ROCs appeared to be consistent with viable systems logic that operational units should be capable of embodying sufficient variety to match that in its immediate environment. Organizationally this made sense, because previously the hierarchical and bureaucratic features of the New Zealand Post Office had severely constrained the ability of operational units to match the increasingly complex technological and market environments. However, our research revealed that most managers believed that the pendulum had swung too far in favour of decentralization, leading to diseconomies of scale and inconsistencies in certain areas. For instance, each ROC had its own marketing arms and consultants that were all spending money developing different ways of promoting what were essentially the same products and services. Thus, the company was consuming far more resources than were necessary, and customers began to wonder why they often could not get 'deals' that people in some other parts of the country could. In addition, some employees interviewed claimed that the ROCs, which were now evaluated and rewarded on individual financial performance, were beginning to compete with each other across geographic boundaries for market share.

In our analysis the division of the four operating companies along geographic grounds appeared to be ill-founded for a communications company in a small country in the 1990s. The local environments with which each ROC sought to interact, did not exhibit variety states that were sufficiently different to warrant separate units. Hence, the costs of diseconomies of scale were not outweighed by the advantages of 'getting closer' to the needs of unique customers. For example, inquiries about telephone billing in Auckland were essentially the same as inquiries made in Wellington. Yet the information technology, that Telecom itself was promoting, made it both possible and cost effective to field such inquiries from a centralized base.

B – Metasystem Confusion

In theory the Functional Councils (FCs) were charged with carrying out what amounted to a 'co-ordination' function – ensuring consistency across the operating units. However, over time, the FCs had grown to become 'jacks-of-all-trades' – developing intelligence (S4), seeking to control resource allocation (S3), monitoring performance (S3*), and developing broad policy or identity guidelines (S5). In practice, most FCs were uncertain about what their role in the organization should be. This ambiguity had allowed them to define their roles in ways that suited the predilections of their members. This was aided and abetted by a management board that was overloaded, through also doing all of the S2–S5 functions simultaneously and which was happy to devolve responsibility to the FCs. Not to be outdone, the remaining corporate office departments (there still remained seven, filling largely advisory roles), also issued advice, policy directives, strategy papers, and sought to monitor performance. The overall picture was of massive metasystemic confusion and a barrage of mixed signals being sent to the operational elements.

C – Uncertain Identity

Telecom's stated vision 'To satisfy the needs of our customers, shareholders and employees with exceptional business efficiency and superior service', did not frame the strategic arena in which the company saw itself, or give any guidance as to its future strategic direction. Beyond this, it contained conflicting signals leading to confusion, especially among front-line staff who felt that it was not always possible to satisfy both the objectives of 'exceptional business efficiency' and 'superior service' concurrently. The *primary* purpose was not known.

D – Operational Inconsistencies

The metasystemic confusion outlined in the previous two points provided opportunities for the S1 units to develop into 'feifdoms'. The confusion 'above', and the mixed messages that emanated from it, enabled them to either choose the alternative messages that suited their own agendas and disregard others, or to switch off altogether and do their own thing. Local managers claimed that they would listen to the FCs and others when these bodies 'got their act together'. This problem is depicted in the figure above by the large number of wayward signals sent to the operational elements and the lack of 'connection' between the various units themselves. Over time this led to some interesting scenarios.

For instance, some ROCs had independently purchased information systems that were incompatible with those running in other parts of the company. In addition, there was some embarrassment when it was discovered that one of the ROCs had adopted a different set of accounting procedures that made preparing the consolidated accounts later in the financial year extremely difficult.

E – Overload

Most of the top ten or so executives within the company found themselves carrying out all sorts of systemic functions at once. They were overburdened and, at times, unable to distinguish between their many roles in the new structure. A ROC manager, for example, would likely be expected to head his or her operational unit, be a part of one or more functional councils, advise corporate office functions, and sit on the management board. Although excessive workload worried senior managers, their inability to conceptualize their various formal roles was a greater concern. Roles frequently became 'contaminated' by extraneous concerns, where for example, metasystemic company-wide matters were allowed to interfere with S1 management, and metasystemic functions were purloined by narrow S1 agendas. These managers found it increasingly difficult to separate the collective wood from their individual trees.

Among the senior management team there was a strong feeling that the management board was not functioning properly because it was preoccupied with detail. In response to the question of what role the board should play, the group unanimously supported the idea that its main responsibility should be direction setting (S5). However, the research revealed these functions were being compromised by the inclusion of agenda items relating to a range of S1–S3 business. As it stood, the metasystem did not possess the variety needed to adequately manage and provide for the system as a whole.

1. *Given the analysis outlined above, what recommendations would you make to the Telecom NZ board?*
2. *Can you use the VSM to provide a more structured view of* Aquaparts *than the one you created in answering the questions to Case Box 9.1?*

Delving Deeper Into the Systems Image:
2 – Autopoesis, Change and Continuity

There are many aspects of the practice of strategic management, as it is currently understood, that fit comfortably with the basic principles of cognitivism and open systems thinking. Moreover, the *modus operandi* of many companies broadly mirrors the viability principles of the VSM that we have just been considering. Thus during the last few decades as the business environment has become increasingly complex and the pace of change has increased, many companies have evolved highly elaborate mechanisms for environmental scanning geared towards understanding and matching present and anticipated customer requirements (or variety). Thereafter, in order to maximize the ability of the firm to match this variety, autonomy has increasingly been ceded to operational units. In order to manage this autonomy, mechanisms – formal and informal – are put

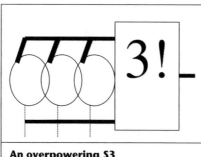

An overpowering S3
Likely strategic implications
S1 units squashed by bureaucracy;
resources allocated without a working
knowledge of customers.

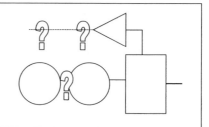

**No S2 functions, no communication
between S1s**
Likely strategic implications
Negative competition between S1 units;
failure to achieve economies of scale
though sharing resources.

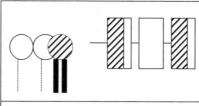

**One S1 unit having disproportionate
influence**
Likely strategic implications
One S1 unit furthers its own ends to the
detriment of others.

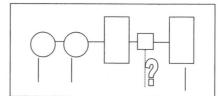

**Under-developed intelligence
functions**
Likely strategic implications
Organization stagnates as competition
moves to meet changing environmental
conditions.

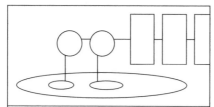

No local environment overlap
likely strategic implications
Lack of synergy between S1 units;
confusion as to where the organization's
loyalties lie.

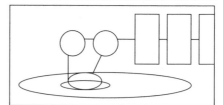

Too much environment overlap
Likely strategic implications
S1s competing for the same markets
indicating that economies of scale could
be achieved by merging units.

Figure 9.6 Pictorial depictions of common threats to viability

in place to ensure adequate co-ordination, control and corporate identity. In true cognitivist fashion, many companies' planning processes now show how it is possible to
design an ideal organizational system with specific purposes in mind and/or to enact
a particular identity. Overall we can say that achieving predetermined goals in the face
of continually changing environmental opportunities and threats, is something that
strategists need to continually work on analytically, culturally, and structurally. And there
are signs that this is exactly what they are doing.

However, while we have used open systems cognitivist models such as the VSM and those other approaches mentioned earlier in this chapter for many years, our latest research (see the reading list for further details) confirms a nagging suspicion that there are aspects of cognitivism that do not sit comfortably with how many companies actually operate and change. For instance, even if there is a good deal of this purposeful thinking, strategic planning, and organizational system-building activity going on, it does not necessarily follow that these activities adequately explain why a company is performing at a particular level in some competitive niche; nor does it necessarily explain how/why it got there.

To some extent, organizations *are* like robots that have been carefully designed to achieve specific purposes or to realize a particular vision. But thinking about them in this way also obscures much of what is interesting about them. Without these 'blinkers' we might better appreciate that organizations are inhabited by relatively autonomous human beings who tend to operate more according to their own dynamics than according to what those who seek to direct them may have in mind. And at the aggregate organization level, even if there is a clear sense of identity, and organizational structures and processes are carefully crafted with this in mind, there may be other reasons why a company achieves or fails to achieve the level of success that it has. For some companies that we have investigated, the cognitivist analyse–decide–act model of corporate development does not sit comfortably with their somewhat haphazard and indeterminate evolutionary path. One of our case companies, for example, developed a global capability in security systems from a base in the manufacturing of mechanical pumps – two seemingly unrelated areas. Another developed a capability in waste management out of a resource capability in resin production and floor coverings. Neither development resulted from the cognitive processes of strategists planning, directing, organizing and controlling the evolution of routines and resources.

In the light of these observations we now ask whether more advanced biological systems thinking might account for aspects of strategic management that the open systems perspective finds difficult to explain. One such source of theoretical inspiration turns on its head the idea of cognition as an open system/information-processing activity. This body of work – known as 'autopoietic theory' – is based largely on work carried out by South American biologists Humberto Maturana and Francisco Varela. In the remainder of this chapter we use this theory to deconstruct three sets of conventional assumptions about strategic development. The first two we categorize as 'biological', the third 'phenomenological'.

Biological aspects of autopoietic theory

Structure determinism and structural coupling

Literally translated 'autopoiesis' means 'self-producing'. Building upon this autopoietic theory calls into question the idea that the human nervous system is wholly open to information from the environment, that it works with picture-perfect representations, and that intentional behaviour is largely guided by a knowledge of how the world 'is' in relation to a particular set of predetermined purposes. Indeed, experimental evidence now shows that to the internal components of the nervous system there is no 'outside', there are only internal correlations of neuronal activity. This is not to say that the 'outside world' has no effect on the nervous system. It is merely saying that there is no direct link between the two. A useful analogy is to think of a balloon that is filled with water. The membrane of the balloon provides a barrier between the water inside and the external world and there are no 'gaps' through which 'information' or matter flows. In this sense it is a closed system. Yet the flow of the water inside the balloon is not completely immune to external events. If you were to poke a finger into the balloon then something would happen – the flow of water would alter. But there would be no direct imprinting of the finger inside the balloon. If we take human experience to correspond with variations in the flow of water, this challenges the cognitivist view that experience mirrors external events. Extending this thinking, Maturana claims that complex systems such as the nervous system are 'structure determined', that in the face of external perturbations what happens to a complex system depends on its structural predisposition. Jump on a rock and nothing happens; jump on an egg of similar size and shape and you crush it; poke a jelly-filled balloon and what happens is different from poking a water-filled balloon. These examples show that it is the structure of a system that determines how external forces *can* perturb it, and what the outcome might be. It counters the idea that external perturbations acting on a system can determine the effect.

This portrayal of the nervous system as operationally closed and structure-determined means that it cannot directly mirror independently existing objects. If this is correct, if the nervous system does not work with representations, then it raises the perplexing question of what accounts for the extraordinary degree of adaptability between human beings and their environments.

The answer to this question revolves around a process of mutual adjustment and co-evolution that is known as *structural coupling*. This term is used to describe the 'interconnection' or 'working together' of two operationally independent complex systems – for example, between an organism and its environment. As long as there are recurrent interactions between the two systems, they both change as a result. However, whereas in the cognitivist model there is a strong sense of there being an independently existing 'outside world' that imprints itself on the 'cognizing system', here more emphasis is placed on how the structure of the system determines what aspects of the environment can perturb it and what the outcome of these perturbations will be. By way of example, think about the process through which a leather shoe becomes more comfortable having been worn for a period of time. Structural changes take place in the shoe as a result of the recurrent interactions between it and the foot, and these changes are determined by the perturbations of the foot interacting with the structure of the shoe. Thus when the shoe comes to the end of its useful life, even a cursory glance at its distorted contours reveals the specific encounters that it has had with the foot of its owner over its lifetime. The location of areas of hard skin on the foot might allow us to say the same about the foot. Through a process of adaptive co-evolution, the two systems have developed congruently each according to its own structure determinism. A different person wearing the same shoe would have had their foot changed in different ways and, at the same time, produced a different shoe as a result of the interaction.

On that basis, structural coupling provides an explanation of how complex systems of common origin (be they human beings or companies) become differentiated as a result of the interplay between the historical conditions in which they live, and their intrinsic structural characteristics.

So much for systems differentiation, but what insights night the concepts of structure determinism and structural coupling generate in relation to the evolution of corporate strategy?

First, the above ideas indicate that different companies might use the same models to analyse the same environment and come to quite different conclusions. Even within companies, different people in different departments can use a framework such as Porter's five forces to come to completely different conclusions. This is something that we have often observed in organizations. Often it is greeted with surprise, consternation and seen as indicative of flaws in the organization's processes. It usually results in frustration, argument, in-fighting and recrimination. However, the idea of structure determinism suggests that it is entirely normal; that what is seen in the environment through a model depends not just on the environment or the model as a representative frame, but on what the people doing the looking are predisposed to see. For example, we have found that if the impact of the Internet has been a popular topic of discussion within the company, this will be seen as part of any environmental scan. If it has not, it will not. If someone has just been to a marketing seminar, what they have heard will impact on what they see in their organization's environment. Autopoiesis encourages us to expect this, so we may *internally reflect* upon, discuss and work with it.

Second, this line of thinking questions the idea that strategists can take what one company has done and apply it, 'best practice' style, to other companies. Even if you see a friend wearing what looks like an exceedingly comfortable pair of shoes, you can be fairly certain that they will not be comfortable on you. You may use this example to question your own shoe-buying policy, but you cannot, literally, step into another man's shoes. In other words, analysis should be *subjective* – in terms of your company's structural predispositions – rather than objective.

Third, the idea that the structure of a system reflects the history of its interactions confirms our observation that firms' emergent capabilities, and the competitive niches that they occupy, are grounded in local historic contexts, each firm having been shaped by these contexts. At any point in time, the resource–routine capabilities of companies mirror its past interactions. In this regard, the competitive positioning of companies is neither arbitrary, nor just a consequence of intent on the part of strategists and/or the firm's internal dynamics. The firm is where it is because of the interplay between all of its past historical interactions and its structural characteristics.

Although this line of argumentation seriously challenges the idea that corporate evolution and competitive position are primarily a consequence of strategic intent that results from scan–analyse–act activities, it is not meant to imply that managers are powerless to affect the evolutionary course of their firms. To illustrate, imagine having a plastic model of a mountain attached to a tray with two handles. Imagine standing outside with a gusty wind blowing. You are holding the tray under a leaky tap. Every now and then a droplet of water lands on the peak of the mountain. Your object is to direct one of these droplets towards a particular target at the mountain's base. You do this by *tilting* the tray to the left and the right, and by tipping it forwards and backwards. In this exercise the water droplet represents the organization, the force of gravity represents the passage of time, the target represents a position of competitive strength in a particular market, and the model of the mountain with its peaks, troughs, valleys, obstructions and varying textures represents the business environment. You may seek to direct the flow of water towards a narrow gully where it picks up momentum towards a pre-defined target. However, since the water droplet cannot fight gravity and the amount of control exerted is less than complete, it may be necessary to confront unexpected events such as an unexpected gust of wind or a 'hidden' obstacle that sets the droplet off on a new and/or unexpected trajectory. This may have undesirable consequences, or it may open up new avenues of opportunity.

Table 9.1 Comparing conventional open-systems thinking with autopoiesis, I

Conventional open-systems logic suggests	Closed-system autopoietic suggests
scanning → objective analysis → decision → act toward ideal	internal reflection → subjective analysis → 'tilting'

If the object of the exercise is to maximize the chances of hitting a particular target as quickly as possible, one needs two types of knowledge. First, in classic environmental scanning style, it is necessary to have a clear understanding of the terrain over which the droplet must travel. Without such knowledge the flow of water is in the lap of the gods. But how the flow of water interfaces with and responds to the terrain requires a second type of knowledge, in this case about the structure of the droplet itself. Indeed the 'behaviour' of the droplet – its direction and speed of flow – depends as much on it as it does on the nature of the terrain. A small droplet might be blown off course by a sudden gust of wind, but a large droplet may be unaffected. In the world of business, a sudden perturbation, for example a short-term fluctuation in exchange and/or interest rates, might cripple one company but have little effect on another.

This analogy suggests that those involved in strategic management need to appreciate that external events, no matter how compelling or powerful, do not determine the substance, direction and/or the timing of organizational change. Moreover, it means that when changes are made to enhance a firm's competitive position, attempting to 'work against' the system's predisposition can be counterproductive. This places the onus on managers to understand the structural characteristics of their firms, and, in terms of both the substance and timing of change, to resist forcing actions on the organization, even when a particular environmental circumstance might appear to 'demand' a particular response. Instead, it is more useful to think in terms of 'tilting' things in the light of the structure of the organization so as to build upon the system's momentum, rather than bringing in wholesale idealized changes.

Table 9.1 summarizes some of the key themes outlined in the paragraphs above. Open-system cognitivist logic suggests that organizations as systems, having established what objectives are being pursued, *scan* and *objectively analyse* the environment, make *rational decisions* and then act toward an *ideal state*. The closed-system perspective, in contrast, suggests that competitive capability rests as much on *internal reflection* on what one is predisposed to see, *subjectively* knowing the organization and analysing the environment accordingly, and then attempting to *tilt* things so as to build upon the capabilities that are embedded in the structure of the system.

The nature of cognition

When we look at processes of adaptation from an autopoietic theory perspective, structural coupling plays the role that, in human beings, conventional wisdom attributes to having a mirror image of the world in one's head. For organisms that possess a nervous system, this conventional cognitivist open-system perspective sounds eminently plausible. But autopoietic theory casts further doubt on this by asking about organisms that are not endowed with a nervous system. How is it that they are often just as well adapted to their medium? And, does the absence of a nervous system mean that these organisms are not 'cognitive' beings?

One can answer the first of these questions using cognitivist logic. An observer might regard physical movement in an amoeba – as it surrounds a source of nourishment in its medium – in terms of this single cell having somehow 'perceived' its environment and having computed an appropriate response. Yet this is unsatisfactory since the absence of a nervous system and the inability to operate in language precludes the amoeba carrying out the necessary 'perceive and compute' functions. Despite this, the amoeba's behaviour seems adequate in its environment. It is adapted to its medium, and one might even say that it 'knows' its environment. How does this work? Instead of perception, *structural* changes in the chemical composition of the medium trigger changes at the sensory surface of the amoeba. This sets up an internal dynamic that, through its highly attuned coupling, results in the amoeba altering its position in relation to the food source and eventually 'swallowing it'. In its most basic form then, cognition is not just a mentalistic phenomenon. It can involve the whole organism and may thus be better defined as 'effective action in a particular domain'.

This inter-linkage between cognition and structural coupling adds weight to the increasingly popular idea that cognition is an integral part of our normal everyday mindful and unmindful activity. According to this line of thought, action that looks like adaptation to an observer, and which the cognitivist perspective would explain in mentalistic terms, may just be the system operating in a relationship of structural coupling with an environment. On this view, cognition is not detached thinking, it is 'situated practical action'. The way in which we deal with the world is a subconscious attitude socialized into us and embodied in our everyday actions and skills, so much more of our lives is spent in skilled unmindful behaviour than in deliberate, intentional analysis. Yet it is this latter category that we notice and which has been the focus of scientific, and subsequently management attention.

Structural coupling then is a form of 'knowing'. It is a form of knowing that is associated not just with the brain or, in organizational terms with rational planning, but with the whole process of individual and organizational living. Certainly knowledge is constituted through conventional cognitivist processes such as sensing and reasoning, but also through physically *doing* things. Thus, in human beings, effective action depends upon having a body with various *orienting* capacities that allow the agent to act, perceive, and sense in distinctive ways. To use examples developed by the philosopher Paul Feyerabend, the singer's particular knowledge and skill exist from the pit of her stomach, through her larynx and into her mouth; the dancer's knowledge lives in his limbs. How did it get there? Through natural skill, plus guidance and encouragement, determination, practice, trial and error, and, importantly, repetition of success. These things combined *orient* the dancer and the singer to 'flow' in a particular performance in combination with others, and to develop further as an artist generally. Relatedly, experiments have shown that batsmen in cricket physiologically do not have time to 'compute' what shot to play when facing a fast bowler. How do they cope? Where does their skill lie? It seems that practice, trial and error, and repetition have oriented and coupled their limbs to their task so successfully that they 'feel' or anticipate and act without thinking. And, in addition, this is what gives the truly great batsmen time and space to create and improvise (see Chapter 4, 'Strategy as Intention and Anticipation'). Indeed, John McEnroe claims that he played his best tennis when he entered a 'zone' where he stopped thinking altogether.

A company's strategy then, should not just be thought of as its policy or its planning, but how all of its 'doing' orients it, or sets it up to deal with the present and face the future. Organizationally, what counts is not just what strategic managers think, or what they analyse, or what they decide; it is about organization-wide action and orientation to act. If the organization has not learned how to orient itself in such a way that the relevant cues are picked up, then it risks failing to perform. Consequently, managers must ensure that they nurture an environment where their people are actively 'looking in the right direction' so to speak.

Correspondingly, direct experience and intuition are crucial to the strategy process. Cognitivism, with its emphasis on rational, objective, logical thinking, pays little regard to the knowledge or understanding that arises out of accumulated organizational experience. Yet as a manager recently put it to us, 'It doesn't matter what the data says, if we do not have direct experience that something works, or if it doesn't feel right, we do not do it.' This is tantamount to saying that while formal inquiry processes have their place, the main source of relevant knowledge is through direct interactions and interconnections with particular local environments. Hence, new ideas about manufacturing processes or working practices often emerge less out of detailed analysis or theoretical consistency and more through a highly pragmatic process of trial and error where combinations of ideas are stitched together primarily on the basis of 'we'll use it if it works'. We have observed similar processes at work in marketing and as companies shift their focus from domestic to global markets. Instead of undertaking expensive and time-consuming market analysis, we have observed companies adopt a 'scatter and see what comes up' approach for entering overseas markets. The seeds for future business are scattered around many possible markets; when one of these 'takes' then the firm focuses its efforts there rather than in another location.

On the view being developed here, knowledge is as much a consequence of past actions as it is an antecedent of strategic action. Knowledge-development capabilities might be embodied in spontaneous actions that are dispersed through the whole organization and not confined to elaborate search activities or in traditional strategic scanning processes. This is an argument for a more passive approach to strategy formulation in which it is assumed that spontaneous micro-level adaptive processes will, if oriented, generate whatever knowledge is necessary.

Whereas the traditional cognitivist approach has strategic actors purposively *planting* initiatives based on their reading of the competitive environment, here the focus is more on identifying and *pruning* elements that seem to be 'non-adapted' once they have emerged. For example, if a new development is failing, the challenge is for managers to proactively remove it rather than allowing it to continue to swallow up resources and killing off more than just its own stem. (This view resonates with 'Tom Peters' claim that successful organizations fail, but when this happens, it happens quickly.)

The second aspect of this more passive approach to strategic management involves a shift away from trying to predetermine what developments are needed to ensure competitiveness, towards providing an environment and frameworks that orient the organization in a particular direction but which allows developments to be less imposed and more spontaneous and organic. In gardening terms it is less like *training* in the sense that one might predetermine the best direction for a plant to grow and then tie it to a stake pointing that way, and more like *trellising*.

Table 9.2 Comparing conventional open-systems thinking with autopoiesis, II

Conventional open-systems thinking suggests	Closed-system autopoietic logic suggests
scanning → objective analysis → decision → act toward ideal	internal reflection → subjective analysis → 'tilting'
planting and 'training'	pruning and 'trellising'

Phenomenological aspects of autopoietic theory

From 'observe, aim and fire' to 'helming'

Although autopoietic theory's distinctive perspective on strategy takes cognition to be a process that extends beyond the rational-analytic externally focused perspective that is promulgated through the conventional literature, it would not deny that such processes take place in most organizations. What then does it have to say about these? In order to answer this question it is necessary to shift emphasis away from the biological aspects of the theory to its consequent phenomenological aspects.

Here, Maturana extends the idea of structural coupling between a single cell or organism and its medium, to a coupling between two or more cells, or between living systems. In the case of living systems, structural coupling then becomes the basis of Maturana's theory of 'languaging' (note emphasis). Languaging is conceptualized as the process of behavioural co-ordinations across two or more structurally coupled systems. In its most basic form, it occurs when there is a further co-ordination of behaviour between organisms whose behaviour is already co-ordinated. In humans, many further recursions of behavioural co-ordinations are possible. The possibility then arises for 'objects' to emerge in language as tokens for these co-ordinated behaviours. Once objects are possible, so too are notions of 'self'. The whole process culminates in the ability of human beings to become self-aware, and to develop 'observing' capabilities such as being able to reflect, to explain phenomena, and to act purposefully on the basis of these.

On this view, the traditional process of environmental scanning and strategy development is but a specialized form of observing/explaining. The key insight however has more to do with the *context* in which observing takes place and the parameters that surround it than it has to do with the nature of observing per se.

The key aspect of the context of observing revolves around Maturana's notion of *conversation*. This includes the vernacular meaning of the term, but is extended to convey the idea of a flow of *emotioning* and *languaging*. Here Maturana's point is that as the flow of a conversation changes through time, as the flow of emotions and distinctions evolves, people's observations, their explanations and hence their decisions and actions alter. On this view, what strategic actors 'see' is not something that is fixed or something that mirrors independently existing phenomena, it is something that reflects the flow of the conversation – the emotions and language – that they share with others and with themselves about 'what is going on out there'. Furthermore, conversations take place in social groupings, that is in networks of structural coupling. This means that as the configuration of these social networks changes, so too do the conversations. And as new people enter conversations and others leave, or as one conversation ends and another begins, different observations are possible.

Thus, language is not an abstract symbolic system of communication about the world in which each symbol corresponds to an aspect of the world or an object in it. Instead, as we have already said, language is grounded in historically, spatially and temporally grounded actions and behaviours. It, like cognition, is about doing things in particular contexts.

This perspective suggests that what people 'see', 'say' and 'feel' is tied up with what they 'do', and this has major implications for strategic management. At a basic level the idea is quite straightforward. In some firms, for example, there is a view that if looking for opportunities and threats is not enshrined in daily practices and infused through the whole organization, then no amount of search and analysis at the 'head' of the firm will recompense for this. As one chief executive put it to us recently, 'some people seize opportunities, other people do not even notice them, when you have 250 people *always* looking for and talking about new ideas, now that is a creative force'.

Translating this idea further raises some interesting insights. One is that strategic decisions are very much a product of the specific conversations through which they are arrived at. Hence, strategic initiatives such as a new product innovation or a decision to globalize are very much a function of the emotional predispositions of their creators and the circumstances of their creation. They are much less to do with rational-analytic processes and/or what may be thought to be external imperatives. What really counts in strategic management is the real embodied people who are involved in the pivotal conversations. On this view it is the personalities, personal qualities, preferences, language, emotions and interactions of the key actors involved in corporate life that explains corporate evolution, it is not the detailed analytical work that appears in planning documents.

Emotions are particularly important. Like the gears in a car, emotions – or 'bodily predispositions' as Maturana calls them – determine the things that people can and will do, and the things that they will not do, or will do only reluctantly. When a car is in first gear it cannot go backwards; nor can it move quickly. When it is in reverse, no amount of 'pumping' or 'hurry up' can move it forwards. These emotions are partly personal and partly shared, but it is the shared emotional predispositions, learned as people have conversations and go about their daily business, that become enshrined in the fabric of corporate life. These predispositions lead people to do things in a certain way. They act as they do not because of some job description or planning report or strategic initiative, but because that is what they have learned and that is what they are predisposed to do.

It follows that it is oversimplistic, for example, to think that strategic opportunities and threats just exist 'out there'. The opportunities and threats that do exist depend on who is doing 'the looking' and on the various processes through which this is done. To the extent that there is a 'world outside', we characterize it on the basis of ourselves, on the basis of the language that we use and – by implication – on the basis of our actions and daily practices. In this sense the firm's strategic environment – which people seek to know, to understand, to predict and control, is not something *in* which they exist. Rather it is something that exists *through* them.

The basic idea that observing reveals as much about the observer and the process of observing as it does about something that might exist independently, has been further refined by other autopoietic theory scholars such as Niklas Luhmann. Put simply,

Luhmann asserts that it is possible to characterize social systems (including organizations) by a circular process in which favoured distinctions and patterns of conversation create new distinctions that reinforce the very patterns that created them in the first place. In the strategic management context this suggests that the 'knowledge' that inputs into key decisions may be a product of habitual and largely subconscious distinctions and preferences that are embodied in entrenched organizational conversations. In extreme cases this circular self-referential process can pose a serious threat to the viability of the firm. When the environment in which a long-established organization operates suddenly becomes much less stable, it conjures up an image of a situation in which, by the time the relevant distinctions are made (if they are made at all), it may be a case of too little too late.

At this point we are back to the Icarus paradox mentioned at the beginning of the chapter. When strategic practices are repeated day after day, people become more adept at them and are more likely to see or find ways of continuing to use them. Even though models and procedures that were once selected for a particular context can become irrelevant or dysfunctional under changed circumstances, people carry on doing what they do best rather than looking for more effective options.

This suggests that there is a need for companies to be very active in questioning their observations and conversations, their institutionalized frames and their traditional ways of thinking. When we combine this insight with the need to recognize that strategic management requires a relatively passive, tilting, pruning and trellising approach, we can see that strategists require quite a deft touch, one that is both active and passive. Within the boundaries of what is structurally possible, companies have to find ways of reinventing themselves as the world changes. Existing identities need to provide a springboard for developing new identities, while not acting as a set of unquestioned blinkers that blind people to radically changed external circumstances that might threaten the viability of the firm.

The analogy that we think best describes this active/passive approach is a very old one. As Chapter 1 of this book demonstrated, the word 'strategy' derives from the Ancient Greek position of 'strategos'. The image that the Greeks liked to use to convey the skill of a great strategos was that of the *kubernetes* – the helmsperson on an inshore fighting ship. The *kubernetes*' skill lay in his recognizing that because he could not make waves he had to passively accept the currents, but at the same time he was active working the rudders so as to change direction within the parameters of what was possible. (This may be related to the analogy that developing an ethos is rather like 'surfing' developed in Chapter 2, 'Strategy as Ethos' and the ideas with regard to continuity and change in Chapter 10. 'Strategy as Process, Power and Change'.)

By a strange twist of fate (or foresight), *kubernetes* is also the root of our word 'cybernetics', the field that became somewhat mechanistic in the hands of the likes of Ashby and Beer. Perhaps by returning to the root of the concept we can make systems thinking a more sensitive and organic field of knowledge.

Case Box 9.3 presents a brief example to help you reflect on the influence of structural coupling and the subjective worlds that we develop. Case Box 9.4 revisits what happened at Telecom NZ after the consultancy project described in Case Box 9.2. It enables you to use this framework outlined in Table 9.3, and the autoiepoetic theory behind it, to see how it might make you think differently about systems interventions and the recommendations for change that stem from them.

Table 9.3 Comparing conventional open-systems thinking with autopoiesis, III

Conventional open-systems thinking suggests	Closed-system autopoietic logic suggests
scanning → objective analysis → decision → act toward ideal	internal reflection → subjective analysis → 'tilting'
planting and 'training'	pruning and 'trellising'
observe, aim and fire	'helming'

Case Box 9.3 The Efficiency (and Limited Viewpoint) of Structural Couplings

Read the following statement at normal speed and count how many times you see the letter 'F' (the correct answer is listed at the end of 'Source Material'):

> FINISHED FILES ARE THE RESULT
> OF YEARS OF SCIENTIFIC
> STUDY COMBINED WITH THE
> EXPERIENCE OF MANY YEARS

Now that you have read and guessed, turn to the back of the chapter to find the correct number.

1. Most people guess three 'Fs'. What structural couplings, built up over time, might explain this? Can you relate your reasons to the Icarus paradox mentioned in the early part of this chapter?
2. People for whom English is a second language and children who are still learning to read tend to be more likely to see more than three 'Fs'. How might you explain this?
3. What strategies might you employ that would make people more likely to see more than three 'Fs' when looking at this statement?

Case Box 9.4 Telecom NZ (B) – Revisiting the Telecom Intervention Through an Autopoietic Lens

At Telecom we saw our brief as employing the VSM to identify objective deficiencies in the company's structure and to come up with a blueprint for a 'better' organization. Thus, having carried out a round of interviews, and digesting the content of a large number of documents, the great bulk of our team's time was spent in discussing among ourselves what Telecom 'looked like' in VSM terms; in identifying weaknesses in its functioning; and, in debating the veracity of various structural solutions. While we did try to incorporate Telecom people into our discussions, they found the language we were using difficult to follow, so we often had to interpret what we thought they meant back into VSM terms.

Much attention was given to ensuring that we came up with 'correct' diagnosis of difficulties, and being able to represent these through carefully crafted VSM diagrams. Very soon the location in which we were working began to resemble an engineering design office. Guided by the thought that our clients would demand an exemplary diagrammatic presentation of our analysis, we consumed copious quantities of flip charts and pieces of A3 paper as we gradually worked our way towards a clearer appreciation of the problems facing Telecom, and what might be done about these.

We did not stop to consider where the company was at in its evolutionary development. Our approach was consistent with the guidelines provided by the VSM literature that almost exclusively amounts to working with a snapshot of organizational systems at a particular point in time. As it turned out, we did attempt to acquaint ourselves with the recent history of the company. However, this was primarily for the purpose of understanding some of the recent structural changes that had taken place. We made no serious attempt to place Telecom's current predicament within a broader evolutionary/historical context either as a means of explaining what changes may and may not be possible, or in understanding how existing trends might manifest themselves in the future.

The team saw itself as having a capacity to identify deficiencies in the functioning of the company and we were sure that our recommendations would lead to an improvement over existing arrangements. Subsequently, our report to Telecom NZ consisted of the following recommendations (it would be interesting to compare them to the recommendations that were made after reading Case Box 9.2):

- Recentralize factors such as treasury, sales and marketing, human resource management, purchasing and information systems. All activities that need to be close to the customer, for example, installation and maintenance, remain decentralized.
- Strengthen communication channels between the ROCs.
- Functional Councils to refocus their activities on a S2 co-ordination function.
- ROC managers required to give primary consideration to their S1 role, and to conceptualize their other roles in VSM terms, to prevent further role contamination.
- The board to refocus its activities on S5 identity-type functions.

Two further broad ideas were also put to Telecom's management team:

First, we did not believe that a clarification of the S5 role of the board coupled with an improvement in the way meetings were to be run, in themselves, would be sufficient to deal with the overload problem. Under the existing structure, there were 17 direct reports to the board. We argued that even a clearly focused and well-organized board could not match this amount of variety. There was a need for another body between the board and the operational elements to carry out control-type resource allocation functions, thereby freeing up the board to deal with S5 business for the company as a whole.

Second, we argued that a fundamentally different structure should be put in place. According to VSM logic, the amount of autonomy and independence ceded to S1 units is partly a function of the diversity existing across S1 environments. In simple terms, the greater the 'market' diversity, the more autonomy S1s need to provide 'specialized' service. If S1 units are serving the same or very similar environments, the decentralization argument is harder to sustain, and, under these circumstances it is tempting to reap the benefits of economies of scale by allowing many functions to remain centralized. In Telecom's case, the ROC's environments had too much in common. Our recommendation for a more systemically logical S1 structure required that we identify activities within the total market that warranted specialized attention. On this criterion the most obvious distinction was between the residential and business segments. Although some core products traverse both markets, the needs of these two groups were distinctly different.

Despite the apparent reasonableness of our recommendations and ideas, the company did not act upon them.

1. *In the light of the discussion in this chapter, what reasons might you suggest for our recommendations for change not being followed?*
2. *In this same light, how might you seek to use a systems model like the VSM in a situation like Telecom NZ differently so as to be more effective?*

Conclusion

The interface between ways of organizing and strategy is a theme that runs throughout this book. This chapter has demonstrated how systems ideas and frameworks can provide useful frames for analysing how the way we organize or connect and disconnect things influences the way we strategize and vice versa.

We arranged images of systems that can help you think at junction of the 'figure 8' shown in Figure 9.7 into three parts in this chapter:

(1) Popular models, underpinned by systems ideas, which are increasingly becoming part of conventional management toolkit;
(2) The VSM as a more advanced 'open-systems' form of thinking and modelling; and

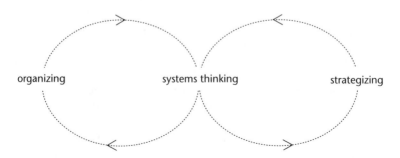

Figure 9.7 Systems thinking as an interface between organizing and strategizing

(3) Autopoietic theory as a more advanced means of 'closed-systems' thinking that is useful for understanding more complex processes of change, and for appreciating some of the processes that are involved in observing and explaining phenomena.

From the simplest interconnecting of corporate capabilities with arrows to the most complex VSM depiction, systems thinking can help people work through the particular strategic strengths and weaknesses of an organization and stimulate discussion as to what should be changed. In addition, we believe that autopoietic theory provides an exciting new avenue for reflecting upon how complex systems such as people and organizations are not objective appliers of frameworks nor completely open to change, no matter how objectively rational those changes may seem. This reflection can enable strategic thinkers to be more effective in their interventions. In our experience, an understanding of these two things combined, closed and open systems thinking, makes for more effective strategists and more effective strategies.

Source Material and Recommended Further Reading

We are indebted to K.E. Maani and R.Y. Cavana's *Systems Thinking and Modelling: Understanding Change and Complexity* (Auckland: Prentice Hall, 1999) for our opening 'gambit' and for parts of our 'Systems Toolkit' section. The Cooper's case that we refer to at the outset is a Harvard Business School case, entitled *Cooper Industries' Corporate Strategy (A)* (no. 9-391-095). Nobody knows for sure who actually invented SWOT analysis. However, it has featured in strategy textbooks since the early 1970s and has been faithfully reproduced ever since.

Richard Dawkins' ideas are described in his *The Blind Watchmaker* (Harmondsworth: Penguin, 1988).

D. Miller first compared Icarus' story to strategic failure in *The Icarus Paradox* (New York: Harper Business, 1990). A good summary of this book is provided in Miller's 'The Icarus paradox: how exceptional companies bring about their own downfall', *Business Horizons*, 35(1), January–February 1992, 24–35.

A good summary of double loop learning is provided in G. Morgan, 'Learning and self-organization: organizations as brains', Chapter 4 in his *Images of Organization* (Thousand Oaks, CA: Sage, 1997).

The origins of Soft Systems Methodology can be found in Peter Checkland 'OR and the systems movement: mapping the conflict', *Journal of the Operational Research Society*, 34(8), 661–76.

The Law of Requisite Variety, which argues that an organization must continue to adapt to its environment and will succeed when the control system it puts in place enables a match between complexity and the speed of organizational changes with those occurring in the environment, can be found in W. Ross Ashby, *Introduction to Cybernetics* (New York: Wiley, 1956).

Key works on resource-based theory include B. Wernerfelt, 'A resource-based view of the firm', *Strategic Management Journal*, 5, 1984, 171–80; J.B. Barney, 'Organizational culture: can it be a source of sustained competitive advantage?', *Academy of Management Review*, 11, 1986, 656–65; 'Firm resources and sustained competitive advantage', *Journal of Management*, 17, 1991, 99–120.

'The Porter diamond' is comprehensively outlined in M. Porter, *The Competitive Advantage of Nations* (London: Macmillan, 1990).

The 'seven-S framework' appeared almost simultaneously in R. Pascale and T. Athos, *The Art of Japanese Management* (London: Allen Lane, 1982) and T. Peters and R. Waterman, *In Search of Excellence* (New York: HarperCollins, 1982).

For more on Peter Senge's ideas, see *The Fifth Discipline: The Art and Practice of the Learning Organization* (New York: Doubleday, 1990). For a more condensed version see 'The leader's new work: building learning organizations', *Sloan Management Review*, Fall 1990, 7–23.

The organigraph concept is taken from H. Mintzberg and L. Van der Heyden, 'Organigraphs: drawing how companies really work', *Harvard Business Review*, September–October, 1999, 87–94.

Much has been written on the VSM and most of it is difficult. Beer's 'masterworks': *The Heart of Enterprise* (Chichester: Wiley, 1979) and *Brain of the Firm* (Chichester: Wiley, 1981) are heavy going, but they do repay the enthusiast. His *Diagnosing the System for Organization* (Chichester: Wiley, 1985) has a more practical 'workbook'-style orientation which incorporates dozens of helpful illustrations. It is probably a better place to start learning more about Beer's thinking. R. Espejo and R. Harnden (eds), *The Viable Systems Model: Interpretations and Applications* (Chichester: Wiley, 1989), is a good collection of other people's approaches to using the VSM. Our own attempt to simplify the VSM may be found in J. Brocklesby, S. Cummings and J. Davies, 'Demystifying the viable systems model as a tool for organizational analysis', *Asia Pacific Journal of Operational Research*, 12, 1995, 65–86. The 'common VSM faults' figures are adapted from this paper. The material in Case Box 9.2 on applying the VSM to Telecom NZ is covered in more detail in J. Brocklesby and S. Cummings, 'Designing a viable organization structure', *Long-Range Planning*, 29(1), 1996, 49–57. For those who are interested in a very useful software adaptation of the VSM see Raul Espejo's 'Viplan' which is produced by Syncho Limited, at the Aston University Science Park.

These sources depict the VSM 'standing up', with S5 above S4, S4 above S3 and so on. We have laid the VSM on its side to encourage people to think beyond the standard hierarchies that the 'standing up' depiction can reinforce.

The literature on autopoiesis presents an even greater challenge to the reader than that of viable systems theory. However, it is worth persevering with since many of the insights are novel and it provides a breadth of perspective across topics such as cognition, language, emotion, epistemology, ethics, and the observer, that is extremely rare.

For a serious introduction to Maturana and Varela's work, we recommend John Mingers, *Self-Producing Systems: Implications and Applications of Autopoiesis'* (New York: Plenum Press, 1995). Randall Whitaker's *Observer Web* ⟨http://www.enolagaia.com⟩ is an excellent on-line resource. This provides a useful set of introductory tutorials as well as a detailed guide to autopoiesis and related literatures.

Having gained a basic understanding of the key concepts we recommend that you then tackle some of the key primary sources. These include Maturana and Varela's *Autopoiesis and Cognition* (New York: Reidel Publishing, 1980) and also Francisco Varela's *Principles of Biological Autonomy* (Amsterdam: Elsevier, 1979). This book provides a comprehensive reference on autopoietic theory, autonomy, and the application of George Spencer Brown's calculus of indications. The reference to Luhmann is taken from N. Lumann, "The Autopoesis of Social Systems" in F. Geyer and J. Van Der Zoewen (eds) *Sociological Paradoxes* (London: Sage, 1986).

Moving from the mainly biological and physical aspects of autopoietic theory to its phenomenological and epistemological dimensions, Maturana's 'Reality: the search for objectivity or the quest for a compelling argument', *The Irish Journal of Psychology*, 9, 1988, 53–97, provides a highly detailed account of key concepts such as the observer, language, cognition, emotion, and ethics. This paper is not for the faint-hearted, but is a landmark contribution to the autopoietic theory literature.

The statement in Case Box 9.3 contains six 'Fs'. People tend to miss the three Fs in the words 'of'.

*Despite the best intentions of economists, strategy is context- and time-dependent. This chapter explores how the content of an organization's strategy does not stand alone, but emerges as a result of a behavioural **process** embedded in a historical context. The content or outcomes of a company's strategy may be seen as concrete or objective facts, but how we see organizational contexts is subjective and processes are multiple. Hence, the content and context of strategy may be interpreted differently and contested within organizational domains, making these domains ripe for **power** and politics. All of these elements have an impact on an organization's ability to **change** vis-à-vis its need for continuity, an aspect of increasingly strategic significance in these uncertain times. The resourceful strategist must, therefore, be part historian, part politician or political analyst, and part social anthropologist. This chapter provides both ways and means of developing your skills in all three arenas.*

10 Strategy as Process, Power and Change

ANDREW PETTIGREW

Being-in-the-world projects itself upon possibilities into which it has been thrown [by the past].

Martin Heidegger, Being and Time

An organization's strategy is the result of a process embedded in a context. At the beginning of the twenty-first century this seems like a fairly unremarkable statement. But when I made my way across what was then a fairly rickety (and in places non-existent) bridge from sociology to strategy by way of organization theory it was, at the very least, an unusual thing to be saying. At that time those with backgrounds in industrial economics ruled the roost and there was an overuse of simple distinctions such as 'strategy formulation' and 'strategy implementation', and 'strategy content' and 'strategy process' research. Figure 10.1 illustrates the ensuing fragmented state of affairs in the field.

For many years now it has been my aim, in collaboration with many bright associates with whom I have been privileged to work, to go beyond these simplistic dichotomies, distinctions and relationships so as to capture the dynamic quality of human conduct in organizational settings. Three decades of empirical research toward this aim has highlighted three things in particular:

(1) The link between formulation and implementation is not unilinear or straightforward: they form interrelated parts of the strategy *process*. This process cannot be properly understood unless one understands the *context* within which the process has emerged and this context cannot be properly understood unless one studies it *over time*.

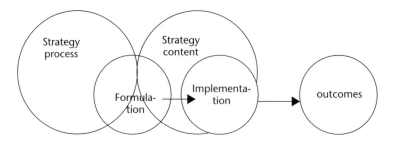

Figure 10.1. The once conventional view

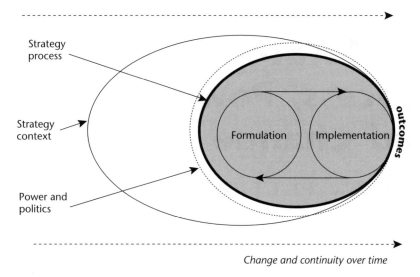

Figure 10.2. Strategy in flight

(2) Anyone concerned with how organizations evolve or *change* must be aware of the factors outlined above, and thus recognize that in human organizations and societies the *past* projects the *present* toward the *future* in a particular way making some outcomes more likely than others. Hence, understanding change is also about understanding continuity over time.

(3) Because the past can be interpreted in many different ways and future outcomes are contested, the system in the present is subject to the 'filtering' of information brought about by relations of *power and politics*. Moreover strategic outcomes are shaped by the balance of power and the use of power in organizational settings.

Recognizing these things leads us to quite a different image of strategy. I have attempted to illustrate this in Figure 10.2. This image of strategy suggests three inter-related lenses that the resourceful and effective strategist should develop:

• First, in order to understand how strategy unfolds as a process over time, he or she must look as a historian.

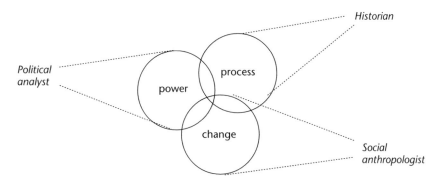

Figure 10.3.   Three lenses of strategy

- Second, in order to understand how humans in organizational settings enact, enable, resist and react to change, he or she must look as a social anthropologist.
- Third, in order to understand the influence of relations of power upon the un-folding process of strategy and organizational change, he or she must look as a political analyst. See Figure 10.3.

In keeping, the structure of this chapter traces my explorations of, and through, these lenses. I begin by describing some formative experiences in seeing strategy and organizational development as a historical process. I focus in particular on my first ever piece of research: on cultural change in Uganda; and on my study of a private board-ing school: Gordonstoun in Scotland. This background has, more by good luck than good planning, not only provided the inclination to look at strategy in an unusual way, it has also provided the ability to analyse the processes and contexts that I came to see.

Second, I move on to discuss the development of change drawing particularly on the experience provided by my work on Imperial Chemical Industries (ICI). This study, more than any other, led me to understand that theoretically sound and practically useful research on change needs to involve the simultaneous analysis of the contexts, process and content of change. Building upon this basis, the remainder of this section reviews further ways and means of examining and understanding successful strategic change and continuity.

My studies of change led me to recognize the importance of leaders as gate-keepers, enablers or thwarters of change, and to consequently see the role played by power and politics in corporate governance, and subsequently in the development of strategy and change. My investigation of these elements forms this chapter's third section.

Finally, I relate what has gone before to my latest work on strategizing/organizing and new organizational forms, finding that given the increasing blurring of organ-izational boundaries, ambiguity of roles and uncertainty of outcomes, mastering the three lenses described in this chapter has never been more important. I conclude the chapter by discussing where the field of strategy could and, in my opinion, should go as we enter the twenty-first century.

While clear presentation requires that I outline the elements described above in a linear fashion, the themes that they bring up should be seen as interconnected. When exploring strategy, it is far more useful to examine the interrelationships between elements than to try and determine 'which comes first'. The linear presentation of these elements roughly follows my intellectual development, but here too one should be wary of oversimplification. As Kierkegaard said, 'we live life forwards but understand it backwards', and in seeking to simplify things we often ascribe a little too much linear rationality to events, thereby missing the contextual circularity and interconnectedness of things. Thus, while I have spent a good portion of the last decade looking at the role of power and politics in the boardroom and beyond, this work reconnected me with the interests expressed in my very first academic publications on *The Politics of Organizational Decision Making* (1973). And, while I have never had the time to do justice to my investigation of Gordonstoun (I still have all the data from this study and remain determined to develop a book on the social and organizational history of the school), the insights and method developed to investigate this institution have shaped much of what I have done since. As it is with an individual's strategic development, so it is with that of an organization.

An Historian of Process: Early Influences, Some Definitions and an Enduring Method

Early influences

Quite by chance, my first exposure to the social sciences in action involved a time series study of cultural change. It was not, however, a typical organizational analysis, and perhaps it was the better for it. Just before I left Corby Grammar School, my mountaineering activities led to an invitation to join a Brathay Exploration Group expedition to Uganda. This expedition, financed by the BBC and the Royal Geographic Society, took a group of 12 boys from various social and educational backgrounds to East Africa to work with local archaeologists and social anthropologists.

On the northern slopes of Mount Elgon, between 9,000 and 11,000 feet, the Musopisiek people of the Sebei kept cattle and sheep in clearings in the forest. The rest of the Sebei lived on the plateau at between 5,000 and 6,000 feet. The Musopisiek lived in long, low rectangular flat-roofed houses, which did not occur elsewhere in Uganda. In the late 1950s, round conical-roofed houses, characteristic of many other parts of East Africa, were beginning to emerge on Elgon in addition to the flat houses. My task was to survey the distribution of the flat houses and their contents. Supported by Royal Air Force aerial photographs and a local guide, I set off to complete my mission. The next step was to conduct a later survey to measure the spread of the round houses as an indicator of the break-up or continuity of the old Musopisiek culture.

A degree in sociology at Liverpool University begun after returning from Africa, a research fellowship and resulting PhD in industrial sociology under the tutelage of Enid Mumford at the newly opened Manchester Business School, and two years developing my ideas in the 'intellectual hothouse' of Yale University's Administrative Science Department, all enabled me to understand what we did, and what more could have been done, in Uganda to a far greater extent than I ever could have as a fresh-faced student. However, looking back that trip to Africa does seem extraordinarily prescient. Its themes can be seen to resonate throughout much of my academic work.

As my PhD publications on the politics of decision making were being completed at Yale, I began to think of my next empirical research projects. I had noticed a small newspaper article describing how a rather famous private boarding school in Scotland, Gordonstoun School, was changing from single-sex to co-education. I knew the head-master, John Kempe, from his time as headmaster at Corby Grammar and I wrote to him asking if I could study this process of change. I returned to England later that year to take up a lectureship in organizational behaviour at London Business School, and continued my correspondence with John. After several visits to Gordonstoun, the School's governing body approved my proposal. Will McQuillan and I began inter-viewing staff in 1972.

Kurt Hahn, a German educationalist who had fled to England in 1933, had founded Gordonstoun in 1934. His behaviour as an 'educational entrepreneur' fascinated me and I began to read widely on the things that influenced him and the birth processes and early development of educational, religious and other organizations. Hahn was an idiosyncratic personality who possessed a definite and well-grounded vision of what kind of organizational structures, mechanisms, people and processes could realize his educational beliefs and aims. Curiously, the more one studied Hahn and the context within which he formulated his views, the more one was able to understand the patterns of behaviour present in 1972 as the school made the transition to co-ed.

Already having recognized the importance of seeing organizational behaviour in context, I had resolved to study Gordonstoun over time, or 'longitudinally', so as to appreciate the richness and influence of this context. The only problem with this was that much of the context that was still influential happened before Will and I arrived. However, Gordonstoun represented an opportunity to develop a method I had used earlier in my Manchester PhD to study capital investment decisions.

As a researcher working with Enid Mumford at Manchester Business School, I was given the task of studying, through participant observation and other means, the implementation of a large new computer system at Littlewoods, a major UK retailer. Unfortunately (or fortunately in hindsight), Littlewoods' decision to purchase the computers was so protracted and full of conflict that I was unable to study its imple-mentation within the time boundaries of my research contract. Left with the choice of doing nothing with the data already gathered or reconfiguring the research on the hoof, we turned the project into a study of decision making rather than implementation.

I had much data relating to a current decision, the investment in the computer system, observed in real time over two years. However, to provide points of compar-ison and contrast, more was needed. I decided to reconstruct other decision-making processes in Littlewoods. Using interviewing and documentary analysis, I investigated three other important computer purchase decisions made over the ten-year period before I started observing Littlewoods directly. This added up to four decisions over a 12-year period. This form of historical analysis of organizational processes was then adapted and taken into the Gordonstoun study.

Because of the tight-knit nature of the Gordonstoun community, it was possible to find former masters, governors and pupils with experience that dated all the way back to the school's inception. Following the Littlewoods approach, I sought to supplement the interviews and questionnaires administered to current staff and students in real time with a historical analysis of the evolution of the school from the 1930s to 1972. This retrospective analysis was based on interviews combined with documentary sources including private papers, speeches, administrative documents, and other archival materials. As an aside, two of the former pupils I interviewed were Prince Philip and Prince Charles. So far as I am aware these were the first (and maybe last) social scientific interviews with senior members of the British royal family.

In order to add some 'width' to this longitudinal 'depth', without getting buried in the morass of available data, I again looked back to the Littlewoods studies. Here I had picked out four important 'capital investment decisions' to give focus to my analysis. This business language did not quite fit the evolution of Gordonstoun but the heightened activity that surrounds big decisions is common to any organization. I had long been interested in Victor Turner's work on 'social dramas' and the relative continuity of routine that intersperses them. Instead of 'capital investment decisions' I would pick out the major 'dramas' that had interspersed the evolution of Gordonstoun. Subsequently, the depth of 61 years, from the birth of the school to the end point of our real-time data collection in 1975, was crossed with the width provided by four dramas: the departure of Kurt Hahn in 1953, the retirement of his successors in 1958 and 1968 respectively and 1972's structural change to co-ed.

Towards an enduring method

Looking back with the benefit of hindsight, my interest since my earliest studies has been in the dynamic quality of human conduct in organizational settings and the overriding intellectual purpose of my work has been to 'catch reality in flight'. However, this emphasis on the dynamic quality of human behaviour has been coupled with the analytical principle that human action should always be studied in context, and a subsequent quest for embeddedness in social analysis. Understanding the embeddedness of social action can only be achieved by locating present behaviour in its historical antecedents. Thus, I have tried to make time for time in my work, not only to reveal the temporal character of human conduct but to expose the relationship between human behaviour and the changing contexts in which it is embedded. Consequently, the process studies associated with my name have all treated time seriously.

A paper published in *Administrative Science Quarterly* in 1979 entitled 'On Studying Organizational Cultures', represented the structure of my Gordonstoun method by way of explaining what I termed the 'longitudinal-processual approach to the study of organizations'. This diagram is reproduced as Figure 10.4. As I explained in the article, this processual method demonstrated many advantages:

- The length of time that one can cover enables the analyst to appreciate strategic decision-making processes in context, thereby providing a richer or more rounded understanding that may help predict and/or influence future outcomes.
- Each 'drama' provides a clear point of data collection, an important practical consideration in such an extended stream of time and data.
- While each drama can act as an in-depth case of a process in its own right, the longitudinal series of dramas allows the development of the organization to be charted. Thus, the kinds of mechanisms that lead to, accentuate, and regulate the impact of each drama can be deduced and the impact of one drama process on successive, and even consequent, dramas as it sinks into an organization's fabric to become part of the decision-making context may all be seen.

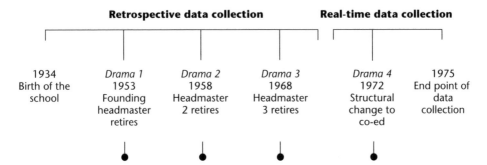

Figure 10.4. A longitudinal-processual research design

- This longitudinal-processual method allows for comparison and contrast while certain things remain constant. Hence, it enables one to see and understand continuity and change over time (more on this in the next section).

I have used this method in various forms throughout my subsequent working life and believe these advantages still mark it out as a superior approach to understanding the strategy process.

What is a processual analysis?

Issues of time, context, emergence and development have been recognized as crucial in human conduct and have subsequently been developed by philosophers since time began. The social sciences are gradually waking up to this, and the past twenty years have seen an increasing number of seminal works on time and social analysis emanating from scholars such as Adam and Sztompka. More recently, important contributions on this theme have come from the likes of Clark, Whipp and Hassard, operating in the narrower field of management. While these writings epitomize a growing awareness of time, history and process in fields that are increasingly influencing our understanding of strategy, they do not in themselves overturn the convention that most social scientists do not appear to give much time to time in their empirical studies and theorizing. Indeed, for many, the social sciences are still an exercise in comparative statics! This does not mark them out as people that we should look to follow if we wish to become astute observers of the process of strategy over time.

Who else might we look to then? Historians were concerning themselves with issues of time and social development long before the last century's group of social scientists had their impact and certainly long before contemporary management theory was thought of. But, unfortunately, their ability to contribute to our understanding of management and strategy is often overlooked, largely because of our simplistic and implicit assumptions of what they do. We dismiss them as mere storytellers, or as worker drones – fit only for burrowing in to dusty archives and hence only concerned with a past probably quite removed from reality. This misguided characterization not only drives out the historical method from strategic analysis, but also tends to exclude antecedent conditions from our explanations of strategy and retrospective data as a pragmatic source of useful information.

Historians are not only interested in poring over artifacts, deep texture and events, but they are also interested in discerning how these things are alive in the present and shaping the emerging future. Certainly historians seek to reconstruct past contexts, processes and decisions, but superior historians do much more. In particular, they exhibit three behaviours that we, as analysers of strategy, could learn much from:

- First, they search for patterns and often attempt to compare and contrast patterns (e.g., the pattern in case A with that in case B) toward drawing some conclusions.
- Second, they seek to find the underlying 'mechanisms' or 'triggers' that shape patterns. Such mechanisms may be discernible in the conscious thoughts and actions of the key players involved in the processes under investigation or they could be a feature of the context that needs to be 'teased out'.
- Third, they combine this *inductive* search for patterns and mechanisms with *deductive* reason and realize the importance of balancing the two. Nobody can develop an understanding by entering a field with a head completely empty and wait for it to be filled with knowledge. This inductive process must be combined with deduction based on prior experience, models or other preconceptions so as to order what one sees. But, at the same time, one must be wary of one's preconceptions forcing what one observes into predetermined categories. A new case may not fit models based on previous cases.

This image of a historian is perhaps our best guide as to what we need to be when we look at the process of strategy in context over time. But having outlined the nature of the observer, perhaps we need to define a little more clearly the nature of the objects we need to observe: what do we mean exactly by 'process' and 'context'?

Some sixteen years after the publication of the *ASQ* article and the consequent widespread application of the method it outlined, I led a workshop on processual analysis at the University of Tampere. I asked the participants to express the key words they associated with the term process. The key phrases and words that followed were:

> flow of events, chronology, mechanism, unfolding, two forces interacting, time, language, context, outcomes, linking things together, individuals and collectives, history, consistent story, change and long period.

This led to the ironic remark that 'If process is all of that, what is not process?'

I have argued elsewhere against rushing to define things too quickly and too narrowly, lest they limit our ability to see interesting things that we may not have been aware enough to understand at the beginning of a journey. (For example, in the late 1970s, as 'culture' was becoming a hot topic in management, I reasoned against determining a strict mechanistic definition of culture, no matter how much easier it would make subsequent observation, and 'scientific' findings.) However, I also recognize that well-thought-out working definitions help provide focus. Hence, in a 1997 paper written as part of a special issue of the *Scandinavian Journal of Management*, based on the Tampere workshop, I sought to outline a 'tighter' working definition of process.

Andrew Van de Ven's formal definition of process provided a useful starting point. Van de Ven highlighted the three ways in which process had been used in the literature: (1) as a logic used to explain a causal relationship in variance theory; (2) as a category of concepts that refer to the activities of individuals; and (3) as a sequence of events that describes how things change over time. Of these three approaches only the third explicitly and directly observes process in action and thereby would lead to one being able to describe and account for how some entity or issue develops and changes over time. Thus, I arrived at the following working definition of process: *a process is a sequence of individual and collective events, actions and activities unfolding over time in context.*

If this is 'process', how then to define the 'context' in which it unfolds? The best means that I have found to explain the nature of context in relation to process is through the following dual analogy. If process is a river, replete with interrelating streams, flows, eddies and swirls, the context is the bank and river bed: that which directs the flow of the process. *Context is, therefore, anything that may be seen to shape a process.* However, in order to capture the duality of bounded development and human agency it is useful to think of this bank and bed as silty and shifting. Thus, while the wider context shapes and directs the flow of process, the movement of this flow can, in turn, shape the context (i.e., terrain) over time.

Further on in the *Scandinavian Journal of Management* article I outlined five internally consistent guiding assumptions for viewing strategy as a process historian, based on my experience over the decades:

- To appreciate the *embeddedness* of the strategy process one must look across many different contextual levels. For example, elements internal to the organization such as structure and culture; but also elements beyond the organization including industry factors, using frameworks such as Porter's five forces; national factors, using frameworks such as the Porter diamond; and broader aspects, using frameworks such as PEST analysis (which basically involves looking at the influence of *political, economic, social* and *technological* changes).
- To appreciate the *temporal interconnectedness* of the strategy process we must study the connections between past, present and future. As Heidegger has argued, too often we see the past as the 'has been', that which is no longer with us. As historians of processes we must see the past as still with us, providing a particular trajectory in the present that projects us into the future.
- However, as B.J. Loasby so eloquently put it, 'If choice is real, the future cannot be certain; if the future is certain there can be no choice.' To appreciate the *interconnectedness between human agency and context* in the strategy process we must move beyond the common urge to present the two as a dichotomy. Process historians recognize Anthony Giddens' theoretical contribution of superseding the polarization of structure and agency by creating a 'third way' whereby we appreciate the duality between the two. We should observe how organizations are shaped by the past but not imprisoned by it. In fact, by reflecting on how we are 'thrown by the past' in certain ways we can increase our ability to act as effective strategic agents.
- To appreciate the *causal interconnectedness* of the strategy process we must seek holistic rather than linear explanations. Hence I am very much in favour of trying to understand processes systemically (see Chapter 9, 'Strategy as Systems Thinking' again).
- To appreciate that *particular strategy processes influence particular outcomes* we must link our studies to the explanation of outcomes. How particular processes and contexts shape strategy outcomes must be our key contribution. Moreover, linking processes to particular outcomes helps simplify and gives focus to our research. In the

Gordonstoun example the outcome was making the transition to co-ed. In the case of your business it might be an increase (or decrease) in sales or some other performance outcome.

To these I would add a sixth element which incorporates my recent work with David Webb on language. In a paper published in *Organization Science* in 1999, we argue that the language of strategy has become locked into the vocabulary of static states. We tend to use nouns rather than verbs, saying that we are interested in strategy, organization, structure, management, decentralization; rather than strategizing, organizing, structuring, managing or decentralizing. Exposing process requires a process vocabulary; we should use a language of becoming rather than being when we look at strategy (or should I say strategizing).

The elements outlined in this section may seem somewhat exhaustive to a practising strategist and it is worth bearing in mind that they were originally designed to aid those engaged as professional researchers. Of course, the practising strategist may not have the time to delve in such depths. However, bearing in mind some of the points made here, and viewing strategy as a historian of process would, may enable you to see things coming that you might not have seen if you only had your eyes fixed on the future.

It also (and you may have already sensed this emerging) provides the necessary sensitivity to better understand the nature of strategic change in organizations.

A Social Anthropologist of Change: The Content, Process and Context of Strategic Change and Continuity

For some time I have been preoccupied with the relationship between continuity and change in organizations. While one might trace the antecedents of this preoccupation all the way back to the context provided by my early experiences in Uganda, I perhaps first became fully conscious of the intricacies of the relationship while working on a longitudinal study of ICI. This work, carried out during 1975–85, became the book for which I am perhaps best known: *The Awakening Giant*.

In 1975 a chance encounter with Mike Browning, then personnel manager in ICI's Agricultural Division, opened up the possibility of a study of ICI. Mike was a delegate on a one-week executive course at London Business School and heard me talking about a model of the evolution of specialized activities in organizations. Afterwards he drew me aside and said, 'You have just described and analysed the development of the Organizational Development (OD) group in my Division, would you consider doing a study of us and then feedback the results in a team workshop?'

After a few days reflection, I phoned Mike to say that I would be more interested if the study could be comparative, if we compared and contrasted the birth and development of the OD groups in different parts of ICI. Within a few months we had negotiated access to the corporate headquarters of ICI, and the Petrochemical and Plastics divisions in addition to Agriculture (a fourth division, Mond, became part of the study in 1978). I also sought to develop the study away from only observing the emergence of OD groups to looking at the wider process of strategic change. *The Awakening Giant* was underway.

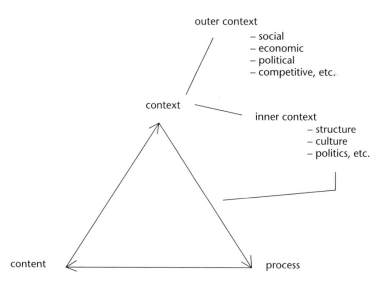

Figure 10.5. A broad framework for understanding change

The research design built upon and further developed that described in Figure 10.4. We would study the five parts of ICI in real time over the period 1975–84 and reconstruct the events in the company during 1960–75, focusing, in particular, on key decisions, 'dramas' and change processes. If I was to draw this method it would look like five 'Gordonstouns' on top of one another, the 'outcome' analysed for each of the five cases being their levels of strategic change. It was a vast undertaking, but the ICI study would not only enable horizontal comparison and analysis, but vertical contrasts too.

At the time we began at ICI, research on organization change was ahistorical, aprocessual and acontextual in character. Even by the time we finished, there were remarkably few studies of change that actually allowed the change process to reveal itself in any kind of substantially temporal or contextual manner. Where the change project was treated as the unit of analysis, the focus was generally on a single event or a set of discrete episodes somehow separate from the immediate and more distant antecedents that give those events form, meaning and substance. Such episodic views of change not only treated innovations as if they had a clear beginning and clear end, they also tend not to provide data on the mechanisms through which changes are created. These sorts of studies of transformation are, therefore, often preoccupied with the intricacies of narrow *changes* rather than the holistic and dynamic analysis of *changing*.

The ICI study reconfirmed all that I have learned from previous studies as to the need to study organizational processes embedded in context over time if one was to gain a full understanding of how and why a strategy and strategic change unfolds in the way it does. But the study also gave birth to a new model of change. This model is represented graphically in Figure 10.5.

This framework represents a major analytical outcome from the ICI study. The message was that one can only understand how and why change occurs (or, for that matter, does not occur) if one simultaneously analyses the contexts, process, and content of change and the interplay between these spheres over time. Figure 10.5 divides the *context* of change into 'outer', referring to the social, political, economic and technological environment the industry and the firm operates in; and 'inner', relating to the structural, cultural and political influences on the process of change. The *process* of change refers to the actions, reactions and interactions from the various interested parties as they seek to move the firm from its present to its future state. The *content* of change refers to the particular areas of transformation that the firm is seeking to change, be it technology, manpower, products, geographical positioning or indeed corporate culture. Broadly, the *what* of change, or the outcomes of change, is encapsulated under the label *content*; the *how* of change can be understood from an analysis of *process*; and much of the *why* of change is derived from an analysis of the inner and outer *contexts*.

This framework illustrates how change occurs as a cycle from context, to process, to content and then these outcomes can, in turn, become part of the context which influences further processes and outcomes. Often change is spurred by outer contextual factors, such as an oil price rise or changing social attitudes, or inner contextual factors, such as a new CEO or a fall in profits (see Chapter 12, 'Strategy as Numbers'). However, how such changes are perceived, received, ignored, debated, accounted for or acted upon depends on the process by which decisions are made. Some processes enable particular changes; others hinder them. The outcomes or content that stem from this process (e.g., diversification), then change the contextual nature of the industry, the company's processes, and so on. The varying pace and degree of change in each of the five ICI cases could be traced to the varying interrelationships between contexts, processes, and contents of change (I describe my ICI experiences further in Case Box 10.1).

One aspect that seemed crucial in the context–process cycle of change was power and politics. Often change 'gets stuck' because processes have become so hardened, hardened in ways that do not create a receptivity to change. In other words, over time, the power of the people involved in the process becomes so linked to the existing nature of the process that it becomes entrenched and people's gaze becomes blinkered to certain things. Any change means that existing power relations may be threatened, however, changing process is usually a key means of enabling change. One can only fight power with power, hence politics and political behaviour and its outcomes become a key factor in the change process.

The effective leaders of change that we observed understood that if they wanted to achieve certain outcomes they would often have to 'double back' and create a processual environment that was more likely to lead to them. Effectively, they recognized that while structure follows strategy (as Chandler famously said), often one had to step back and change the structure of the process before one was able to change the strategy that would then reinforce structural changes. They also had the patience and eye for opportunity that this political, and hence long-term, approach required. As Sir John Harvey-Jones, the radical and highly successful CEO of ICI in the early 1980s put it, 'I never missed the chance to make the point that basically I'm an operator.' The ICI study opened our eyes to the extent to which effective leaders of change have to be astute politicians and political analysts, more of which follows in the next section.

Case Box 10.1 ICI – The Awakening Giant

Imperial Chemical Industries (ICI) was one of Britain's largest manufacturing firms. In 1981 it was ranked the fifth largest of the world's chemical companies. *The Awakening Giant* project examined ICI's attempts to change its strategy, structure and culture over the period 1960–84. ICI's four largest divisions and its corporate headquarters were studied. However, this case box only summarizes some of the key elements of the corporate headquarters case.

ICI had developed its scale and scope early in the development of the global chemicals industry. It had been a great technological innovator and its position was helped through its market dominance in 'The British Empire', which had been ensured by the pre-Second World War cartels that dominated the industry. After the war, with the cartels and other political agreements dissolving and a wide range of new players entering the industry with newer and larger plant, ICI found itself in a more competitive context. Spurred by the increasing success of US chemical companies in Europe, the platform for growth in Europe provided by the birth of the EEC, pressures from within ICI for innovation coming from some of the newer divisions such as organics, plastics and synthetic fibres, and some inauspicious financial results in 1958 and 1961, ICI began the new decade in an atmosphere of challenge and change. Thus, around the early 1960s, ICI began to cohere around four strategic changes that it hoped would improve its competitive position:

(1) Dramatic improvement in the size and efficiency of ICI's manufacturing plants.
(2) Energetic attempts to improve labour productivity.
(3) Repositioning market focus away from Britain and old Empire markets towards Europe and North America.
(4) Moving ICI's culture and organization toward a greater concern with marketing and financial competences and away from its technocratic culture and power system and purely functional bureaucracy.

This context coincided with the appointment of Sir Paul Chambers as chairman: the first 'outsider' to occupy the position within ICI.

By 1972, ICI was still Britain's biggest industrial company, and, according to prevailing rates of exchange, the biggest chemicals company in the world. However, not all of the above strategic changes were realized with the purpose and energy that many within and outside ICI would have liked. It still had scale and it had scope. It was still active in all major industrial and most non-industrial countries and was, product-wise, one of the most diversified chemical companies in the world. However, ICI was in culture and management almost entirely British. About two-thirds of the total workforce was employed in Britain, British factories were by far the most important part of ICI's manufacturing interests, and 63 per cent of total sales were derived from UK assets. ICI remained divided into nine largely autonomous and profit-accountable divisions, answering to the main board. The board and executive directors were resident at ICI's head office in Millbank, London, SW1. They maintained effective strategic control over the divisions through having the final say over the investment decisions that determined ICI's future shape and being the final arbiter of personnel policy.

As ICI entered the 1970s, Anthony Sampson had placed the jibe 'slumbering giant' around ICI's neck. During the 1970s it would increasingly find itself prone to its dependence on an inflation-ridden and declining British economy, and an industry where the premium of chemical growth over general rates of growth was reduced and in some sectors eliminated. By the end of the 1970s there was massive over-capacity in the European fibres, petrochemicals and plastics industries and ICI was having to learn to live with the increasingly confident use of trade union power and government intervention in business. Some within the company had seen these problems coming. One of Chambers' likely successors, Lord Beeching, departed rapidly from ICI in 1967 for sensing problem areas and recommending action which his board colleagues could neither appreciate or act on. Many of Beeching's recommendations were not to be implemented until 12 years later.

The outer-context took a further dramatic turn around 1980. The arrival of the Thatcher government and its pursuit of strict monetarist economics led to high interest rates, a recession in industrial production and mounting unemployment. The further fall in ICI's UK customer base and the sharply rising value of sterling in relation to the US dollar and Deutschmark meant cheaper chemical imports from Europe and the US and a trend for British chemical prices to move out of line with those on the Continent. The net effect was a dramatic worsening of ICI's performance in the early 1980s and an end to the belief that success would come from investment in huge, efficient complexes producing heavy chemicals. The context was once again ripe for major change.

John Harvey-Jones had joined ICI in his early 30s from a career in the Royal Navy. Harvey-Jones, like Chambers before him, was not 'an ICI man'. He was appointed to the main board in 1973 and spent much of the 1970s orchestrating an 'educational process' – trying to 'open ICI up to change'. Crucial to this process was a need to change the mode, style, composition and problem-solving processes of the board. This required persistence and patience as well as the articulation of an imprecise vision of a better future for ICI. However, Harvey-Jones had no simple-minded or clear-cut vision for ICI. Insofar as there was a vision among Harvey-Jones and the 'for change caucus' on the board, it was clarified through additive implementation. Harvey-Jones became chairman of the board in 1982 as the context for change, outlined above, was ripening.

The new chairman and other key executives sought to replace some of the old beliefs about the potency of capital expenditure, cash management, and a risk-averse, consensual and operational style of management with a new ideology. This emphasized a sharpening of market focus, a greater entrepreneurial emphasis on decentralized units, and a lessening of bureaucracy and central control. This cultural shift was linked to major changes in structure, systems and human resource management.

Changes in the content of ICI's strategy followed. Assets in the two biggest loss-making divisions, Petrochemicals and Plastics were closed, and then the two were merged. Three other divisions all lost assets. Service functions such as engineering, R&D, purchasing and personnel were rationalized. ICI's UK employees fell by 31 per cent between 1979 and 1983. In 1986, all of the UK heavy chemicals divisions: Agricultural, Mond, Petrochemicals and Plastics, were merged into one group, allowing further fixed costs to be taken out. In addition, ICI finally began to realize the intentions of the 1970s and significantly increase its business in high added-value products, consolidate its position in Europe and build up its presence in the US. Towards the end of the 1980s, ICI was actively seeking new acquisitions and was cultivating high growth in new markets in the Pacific Basin.

1. What contextual factors had made ICI the company it was at the end of the 1950s?
2. What factors led to the two major pushes for change, at the end of the 1950s and at the end of the 1970s, at ICI?
3. How might you explain the greater degree of change achieved under Harvey-Jones in the 1980s as opposed to what was achieved in the 1960s?
4. What does the ICI case teach us about the nature of strategic change?

In the early 1980s, the dominating policy issue in all aspects of organizational life was change. In Margaret Thatcher, Britain had a right-wing Conservative leader with a revolutionary agenda and who looked like she was going to maintain power long enough to drive through a programme of transformation in both the public and private sectors. This context combined with the interest created by *The Awakening Giant*, provided a momentum that aided me greatly in the successful establishment of the Centre for Corporate Strategy and Change at the University of Warwick. Over a ten-year period, in collaboration with a series of talented and energetic young scholars, I was able to devote myself to further projects exploring the nature of strategic change under the auspices of the centre. The ensuing projects are too numerous to mention in the short space available here. However, three particular outcomes that really have made a difference in the way that people think about change are well worth outlining.

In the late 1980s, Richard Whipp, Robert Rosenfeld and I analysed the behaviour of one higher and one lesser performing firm in four different sectors over thirty years (five years real time and twenty-five years retrospective across eight different firms). The study addressed two linked questions. Why do firms operating in broadly similar industry, country and product markets record different performances? And what contribution did the way that those firms manage strategic change have on their performance? We found that the management of five interrelated factors explained the relative performance of the companies:

- how they dealt with environmental or contextual assessment;
- how key people within the company led change;
- how they managed strategic and operational change and the link between the two;
- the extent to which they treated their human resources as assets or liabilities (see Chapter 3, 'Strategy as Organizing', for more on this); and,
- whether the whole process was coherent, that the elements reinforced rather than ran counter to one another (see Figure 10.6).

A team comprising Chris Hendry, Paul Sparrow and me looked further at the crucial role played by human resource factors in facilitating change. We found that organizational attention to human resource matters was often reactive rather than proactive. In other words, firms would go ahead and make fairly fundamental business changes,

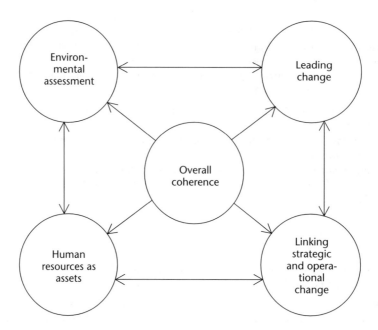

Figure 10.6.   Five interrelated factors influencing the relative performance of companies

focusing on product market, technological and other material capital requirements. Only after the fact would they recognize that they had quite severe human resource deficiencies in these processes of change. They would have then to build in the necessary skill and knowledge base required after the fact, thus dramatically slowing down change. However, there were exceptions to this pattern of reactivity. Some firms were more proactive, and we found that these firms enacted significant human resource changes in advance of, or simultaneous with, broader business strategy change programmes as a result of a strong philosophical and value position adopted by the chief executive and his or her team.

Ewan Ferlie, Lorna McKee and I looked further at the differential pace of change, but this time in the public sector. It was well known that when very large organizations attempted across-the-board changes, there could be quite significant differences in the pace of change in different parts of the organization. However, no research team at that time had gone in-depth to explore why and how these different speeds of change occurred. Ewan, Lorna and I studied different part of Britain's NHS (National Health Service) to explore receptive and non-receptive context for change to see what might account for different degrees of receptivity and therefore speed of change.

We found (among other things) that the interaction between the quality and coherence of policy in the change setting; the availability of key people leading change; the existence of a supportive organizational culture for change; the simplicity and clarity of change goals; and, the ability to persist towards these goals, were key. This is simplified in Figure 10.7. Importantly, we found that these receptive conditions took many years to build up, but could be quickly dissipated by ill-considered, inconsistent, or non-coherent, actions by managers. Receptivity for change is hard won, but easily lost.

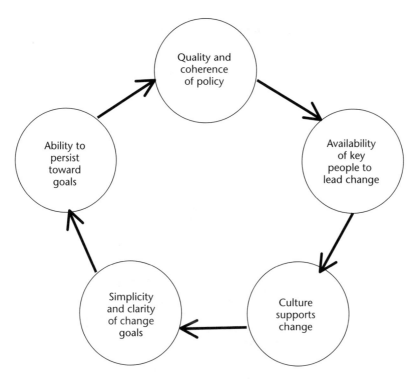

Figure 10.7. Elements influencing the receptivity for change

The 'model' of managing successful change that emerged in the book *Managing Change for Competitive Success*, written by Richard Whipp and me, involved paying attention to nine interrelated aspects:

(1)   building a receptive context for change;
(2)   creating a capacity for change;
(3)   constructing the content and direction of change;
(4)   operationalizing the change agenda;
(5)   creating a critical mass for change within senior management;
(6)   communicating the need for change and detailed requirements;
(7)   achieving and reinforcing success;
(8)   balancing the need for continuity and change;
(9)   sustaining coherence.

It has subsequently been pointed out to me that this framework is remarkably similar to what is seen to be the 'state of the art' model of change to have come out of the United States in the past decade. John P. Kotter's 'Eight steps to transforming your organization', was published in the *Harvard Business Review*, four years after the publication of the book by Richard and me. One may compare the two by examining Kotter's model presented here in Figure 10.8.

While there is some satisfaction to be gained from having prefigured Kotter's work, more interesting to me is the one element present in Richard's and my work that is not replicated in Kotter's: 'balancing continuity and change'. Kotter's model builds on a long tradition of change models dating all the way back to Kurt Lewin's famous unfreeze→

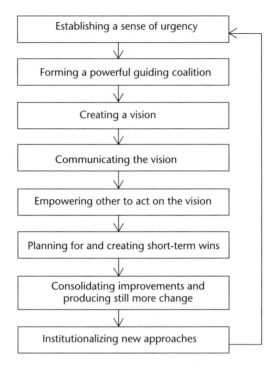

Figure 10.8. Kotter's 'eight steps' to successful change

change→refreeze. Here, because of the infectious American enthusiasm for the future and the belief that it will be better than the past, the emphasis is often on revolutionary change, and change and continuity are implicitly seen as dichotomous opposites.

While America leads the way in many aspects of knowledge creation in strategy, looking in an evolutionary manner, and thus backwards as well as forwards is, I believe, a deeply European trait. I have always felt that European (and Asian) cultures have a deep texture that is not shared in North America and this has had an enormous impact on scholarship in these societies. Reading much (but thankfully not all) US management literature there is an unwitting preference for the present and the future. The past is reserved for historians. The world of business starts from today. The combination of my European background and an historical, sociological and anthropological way of looking at how people behave in groups has led me to recognize the value of seeing continuity and change as necessarily intertwined.

A Political Analyst of Power

> *Man is a political animal.*
> Aristotle

Following this period of intensive research on change, my energies were directed toward two closely related themes, the importance of which had become increasingly apparent through my previous work: leadership and power.

The study that I undertook with Terry McNulty looked at power and influence in UK boards. Before this study there had been an obsession with the structure and composition of boards but a corresponding failure to understand the conduct of boards. There was a suspicion that the structural changes being demanded by reports written by external bodies and subsequently demanded by government were not delivering the required changes in the conduct and behaviour of boards. Indeed, one could see that boards with exactly the same structure and composition behaved quite differently, indicating that something else was at work. Hence we focused our study on power and politics in and around the boardroom.

We found that the stereotype that boards only have influence in crises, and for the rest of the time they are passive to be compliant, was not wholly true. There was evidence of a wide spectrum of involvement of boards in strategy. While we found that most boards took strategic decisions as the final point of approval, others did shape strategic decisions by shaping the assumptions behind strategic options. While very few boards were directly involved in the content and technical process of strategy making, we picked up on an emerging trend that was leading to an increase in board involvement. We characterized this as a move from *minimalist* to *maximalist* boards.

Traditional minimalist boards did not have the information, the time, the processes, or the power to oversee the performance of the company or to assist the executive management to shape the values, identity and strategic development of it. There were often major power asymmetries on this sort of board and an individual or a small faction generally ran it. Non-executive directors were given low legitimacy and often only selected to complement and facilitate the power asymmetries. They were starved of information and often isolated from the strategy process and from the rest of the business below the board. The board agenda was often stylized and predictable, there was no space for issue spotting and even less for dealing with issues. There was little or no challenge or dissent. The atmosphere was 'don't rock the boat', and in the unlikely event of a conflict, 'withdraw and regroup'.

Maximalist boards exhibited a different system of power and process. Interestingly, the trigger to move from a minimalist to a maximalist board was often a performance crisis. The crisis would break the old power culture, with old power figures often being removed. Then there was a more explicit attempt to agree on board purposes and to distinguish people's roles much more clearly. As this happened there was a desire to recruit a different quality of non-executive director and to allow them much greater influence. The board process and agenda were opened up, there was more space for discussing issues and the board as a whole were given the necessary information (or the licence to 'roam' throughout the company to get information) to enter into the strategy process and did so. Their confidence grew and they began to intervene in strategic issues before they became foregone conclusions.

In the maximalist boards there were not the same power asymmetries that were found in minimalist boards. However, there was still tension about power and ensuing political behaviour because non-executives were prepared to use it and executives were feeling its use. Indeed, without such tension there would be no checks and balances in the boardroom and it would be impossible for them to realize the greater level of effective involvement in strategy that people were calling for. For good and for bad, in both types of boards as in all types of organizations, understanding the dynamics of power in play was key to understanding how strategy was shaped.

This finding brought me back to some of my earliest academic works on power and politics and connected me again with change. The threat of change means a potential unscrambling of organizations' resource systems. Hence, people fear that their 'empires' may be dissolved and this prospect is a great source of political energy for those who have something to lose and for those who feel they have a lot to gain. Then it becomes a battle for hearts and minds. Change processes can thus be seen as elaborate influence and communication processes. It is for this reason that boards or other senior executives may not influence change to the extent that they would like – you do not necessarily need to be the chairman to capture hearts and minds. As linking the 'strategic' and the 'operational' in any change process is key, people who may not have rational or bureaucratic authority 'further down' the organization may also be key. It became clear to us in our studies of change that effective change processes were not led just by heroic transformational leaders but teams of leaders. For this reason we stopped using the term 'leadership' in some of our later research studies moving toward the more inclusive 'change leaders'. These people, effectively gatekeepers of change, may be found in all areas and levels of the organization.

All of this highlighted how crucial things not necessarily associated with the formal structure of an organization were in shaping strategy: that power, politics and change are bedfellows. I had been concerned with how communication systems were carriers of power, and how information control or the ability to filter information, or the ability to manage meaning with the clever use of language or corporate myths and stories, were subsequently key determinants of organizational action, since I published my first academic articles in sociology journals in the early 1970s. But the later studies described above had really brought home how the effective strategist or strategic analyst must be an effective political analyst and a politician in addition to being a historian and a social anthropologist.

Strategizing/Organizing

At the beginning of the twenty-first century there is a developing interest by researchers and managers in the boundary of strategy and organization, or, as we would prefer, strategizing/organizing. In the past, organizational structure was always seen as the poor neighbour of strategy. Remember Chandler's famous 1960s' dictum that managerial consideration of structure should follow consideration of strategy. Strategy was the chubby cousin sitting on top of the table swinging the well-polished boots. Structure was the other cousin, slightly in the shadows, and under the table. A fast changing business, economic and political context has altered this asymmetrical relationship between strategy and structure. As this has happened, scholars and managers alike are much less likely to confine matters of organization just to the structural form of the organization. They are more likely to take a more inclusive and holistic view and to see organization as structure, systems, processes and in some cases a whole range of organizational practices. So strategy and organization are now seen much more as equal partners. Some would go further and contend that so central is the form of organizing to performance in today's competitive context that the form of organizing is virtually equivalent to the strategy. This point has been well rehearsed in studies of global professional service firms – the classic example of a knowledge-rich firm. But this is not just the preserve of the newer, knowledge-based industries. Lord Browne, the CEO of BP, that very mature energy business, has recently commented that 'our strategy is our organization'.

The use of the verb forms organizing and strategizing captures well the process theme in this chapter. The pace of change in industry now makes static notions and nouns of strategy and organization increasingly crude and imprecise. In today's world there are few fixed points and end states. The use of verbs gives emphasis to the imperfect and incomplete character of contemporary attempts at strategizing and organizing. Furthermore, the use of the oblique mark in strategizing/organizing emphasizes that these processes are best treated as inextricably linked together, a single duality rather than as two discrete sets of practices and processes.

Treating organizing and strategizing as truly complementary processes and activities is one of the big intellectual and policy themes in my latest research on new forms of organizing and company performance. This research is quite different in character from any others I have carried out in the past thirty years. It involved the surveying of very large samples of firms in the United Kingdom, Continental Western Europe, Japan and the United States. We also carried out eighteen detailed case studies of major European firms. So we have enormous quantitative and qualitative databases to explore our three research questions. The research had a progress aim, a performance aim and a process aim. The progress aim was to map the extent of innovation in forms of organizing in a large sample of firms in Europe, Japan and the United States in 1992–3 and in 1996–7. The performance aim was to test for the performance consequences of these new forms of organizing. The process aim was to examine the managerial and organizational processes of moving from more traditional forms of organizing. Another key feature of the work was its network character. I always used to say we were a network studying networks. The Warwick–Oxford team on this project was Richard Whittington, Evelyn Fenton, Silvia Massini, Simon Peck and me. In addition, the research was carried out with the active co-operation of a university in Japan and the United States and six universities in Europe. It would have been quite impossible to do this research from a single university in the UK. Figure 10.9 captures the multiple indicators of new forms of organizing/strategizing we explored in this very big international study.

The overwhelming finding from our research is a common direction of change but from different starting points and involving some variation in pace across the three regions. There is evident structural change with movement towards flatter, more fluid and decentralized structures with especially strong development of project structures and operational decentralization in Europe. Underlying these structural changes were considerable process changes most notably in the development of both vertical and horizontal linkages and investment in IT to improve intra-firm and between-firm networking. Across the three regions there was greater evidence of boundary and process changes than structural changes in the period 1992–7. Although there is evidence of parallel organizational changes across the three regions, our findings did not support the thesis that firms are converging towards a single type or set of organizational practices. We assessed incremental and radical organizational changes in the three regions. European and US firms show much higher percentages of radical change compared with their Japanese comparators over the period 1992–7. These results do not confirm previous conjecture about revolutionary change in forms of organizing. New forms of organizing are emerging across the three regions but they are supplementing rather than supplanting existing forms.

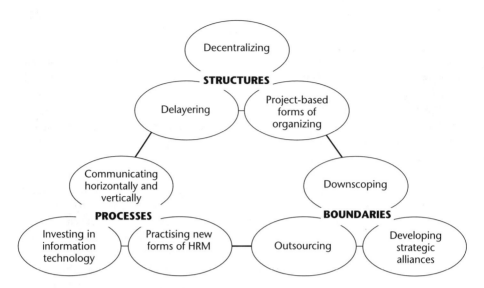

Figure 10.9.   New forms of organizing: the multiple indicators

In our European sample we found a clear link between whole system change and company performance. In other words, companies that made the whole raft of complementary changes, seeking to alter their structures, their processes and their boundaries were higher performers. Organizations that made partial changes were often lesser performers. In particular, firms that changed their structures and boundaries but did not change their processes often created negative performance effects for themselves. The European results of this research are published in *The Innovating Organization* (2000) and the cross-regional analysis will be published in 2003 in *Innovative Forms of Organizing*.

Case Box 10.2   Strategizing/Organizing and Performance in BP, 1990–2000

By the beginning of the twenty-first century, the UK-headquartered energy giant BP was the largest UK company and the second biggest energy company in the world. But size was not everything. It was also now one of the most profitable and best managed in its industry, and its group chief executive (Lord Browne) had been voted for three years running the most successful CEO of a UK-headquartered company. All these plaudits were a relatively new experience for BP. For most of the 1980s and 1990s, BP's financial performance had lagged behind its most obvious comparators – Exxon, Shell and Mobil. This case vignette explores these changes in fortunes for BP.

But what determines the performance of energy giants such as BP, Shell and Exxon? The price of oil obviously matters. Over the time period from 1985 to 2000 there are three points 1986–7, 1992–3, and 1998–9, when the performance of all the oil majors took a hammering. These are all points when the world price of oil took substantial drops, in 1985 to 1986 from $27 to $14 per barrel, in 1992 to 1994 from $19 to $15 per barrel and from 1998 to 1999 from $19 to $10 per barrel. However, by 1995 BP (as measured by return on capital employment) had begun to overtake Shell and then in 1996–8 it began to overhaul its two big US competitors, Exxon and Mobil.

So what did BP do differently in the 1990s that impacted on its relative performance? The four most crucial determinants of BP's performance are oil prices, gas prices, and refining and chemical margins. However, beyond these four determinants there are a number of controllables over which BP executives have some discretion: their strategizing/organizing, their control over costs, their tax policies, and the level and direction of their capital expenditure.

The story of BP's strategizing/organizing is told more fully in the second book from our big international project on new forms of organizing and company performance (see source material at the end of this chapter). Of the 18 European case studies we did in that research project, BP represents the best contemporary example of the sustained and consistent attempt to deliver radical performance change over the period 1990–2000 (and continuing now). BP has changed its structures, processes and boundaries.

The boundary changes had started in the late 1980s with early attempts to downscope. When Robert Horton became chairman/CEO in 1990, these changes accelerated and by 1994 BP had dropped its 1980s' portfolio of eleven businesses down to three. Horton also encouraged massive outsourcing of its service activities. Throughout the David Simon era as CEO (1992–5), boundary changes continued with a number of joint ventures and alliances. However, it was in the John Browne era that this process extended from alliances with Mobil to the era of massive acquisitions, when in 1999–2000 BP acquired first Amoco, then Arco and then Burmah Castrol. These processes of strategizing/organizing began to change the competitive landscape in the whole industry and triggered similar behaviour by Exxon and Total. But the BP changes were not just boundary changes to affect market share and power, they also represented crucial opportunities for cost-driven efficiencies. By the late 1990s a more-or-less continuous succession of organizing changes (mainly in structures, processes and performance systems) had produced an organizing machine that set new standards for the industry and absorbed three other energy companies with enormous speed and efficiency.

But all this did not happen in one jump, over a short period of time and under the leadership and guidance of one CEO or board of directors. This process was inspired and aspirational, but it was never smooth or easy. There were many organizational casualties along the way, the most notable being Robert Horton, who was asked by the BP board to resign in June 1992, only two years and three months after he had assumed the top job. Big changes release large amounts of political energy and if this energy is not controlled and re-directed it can even lead to the dethronement of the principal architect of change.

Complementary Change in Action: The Horton, Simon and Browne Eras in BP

The starting point for this account of BP's organizational transformation is Robert Horton's return from the United States in March 1989 to become first deputy chairman and then chairman and chief executive of BP. By this time Robert Horton had a reputation as a hard-driving, no-nonsense executive who had in turn rationalized BP's chemicals operation, sought unsuccessfully to downscope BP's 1970s diversification in minerals, coal and nutrition and then had been sent out to the USA to sort out BP's acquisitions of Standard Oil in the mid-1980s. With the acquiescence of Peter Walters, and before he was formally appointed chairman, Robert Horton set in train the strategic thinking and action which led to the launch in March 1990 of Project 1990 on BP's 'sleepy' institutional form. Project 1990 was commissioned by Robert Horton in July 1989 to:

(1) Reduce complexity;
(2) Redesign the central organization; and
(3) Reposition the corporation in approach and style for the 1990s.

Project 1990 was an attempt at comprehensive and holistic change. It was driven from the top by Horton (aided by a specially chosen group of high-flying middle managers) and designed to reduce the complexity of BP. Of the corporation's three-dimensional matrix organization – the business streams were to be strengthened and the functional regional and national systems reduced in size and influence. The purpose and size of the group and centre HQ in London were to be reduced by cutting back large functional departments, transferring the remnants into the business streams (at that time four – exploration, oil, chemicals and nutrition) and the residue of centre staff was formed into specially constructed teams. There was to be a devolution of responsibility and decision making to the four business areas and the number of central committees was to be drastically reduced. Horizontal networking through a team-based structure was to replace the slow cascading of information up and down the previously extended hierarchy and the new more open flows of information were to be enabled by a large investment in the IT infrastructure.

Crucial to the success and aim of Project 1990 was the cultural change it prescribed. Doing things with the new BP style involved first signalling and encouraging new behaviours encapsulated in the slogan OPEN: Open thinking, Personal impact, Empowering and Networking. After the top 300 executives in BP had all been through a 'Leadership in Change' programme, a series of cultural change workshops were then rolled out through BP's international presence in 70 countries. This central plank of human resource change was to be reinforced by a new performance review and reward system tied to soft (values-driven) criteria, as well as hard. Personal development plans were introduced for all staff and all this was tied to the first explicit statement of corporate vision and values.

Boundary changes were also part of the strategic intent. BP's vast central information systems section of 1,000-plus employees was outsourced and renewed attention was given to downscoping the business to take out non-core businesses such as minerals, coal and nutrition. Horton aimed to 'reduce the cost of complexity, yet maintain an integrated corporation' that he hoped would as a result become 'the most successful oil company of the 1990s'.

Here was the grandest, most aspirational programme of complementary change involving significant alterations in structure, process and boundaries yet attempted in UK business. Yet in the short term it was all to end in tears. In June 1992, Robert Horton was asked to resign by the BP board. His successors, David Simon and John Browne, were able to build upon and reformulate Horton's vision and eventually bring about the complementary changes Horton could intellectually envisage but not strategically and operationally deliver.

But why in the short term did Horton fail, if indeed the case is now clear he prepared the ground for future success? Big outcomes are rarely explained by single causes. When Robert Horton was asked to resign in June 1992, it was not just because of any doubts about the appropriateness of Project 1990, or because of his hubris, or because of accumulating weaknesses in BP's perform-ance and reputation, it was because of a volatile mixture of all these factors. Additionally there was the process and tenor with which Project 1990 was introduced and justified to a BP that was at that time ill-equipped to handle large-scale holistic change.

But when Robert Horton fell on his sword in June 1992, his successor shrewdly judged that this was a moment not just for change but also for continuity. A fellow director described the change-over in these terms:

> There was a big reaction around Bob's call to resign . . . his demise was a signal for us to go into penury mood. The six of us sat down and we went through it all down to the pictures on the wall saying we can't afford this – we can't afford that. And that lasted ferociously – it is still around – but it lasted to the exclusion of almost any strategic sensible long-term debate for about 2–3 years. We got profitability up and we benefited from a lot of the pluses that Bob brought in because of Project 1990. It still lives. Nobody talks about it anymore, of course, but he was way ahead of his time in a lot of his thinking. And he was right about many of the organizational things.

The message now was encapsulated in the simple slogan from David Simon – PRT – performance, reputation and teamwork. There was to be no growth without performance, and no survival without performance. A senior manager described David Simon's first large meeting as CEO with an anxious London office immediately after Robert Horton resigned. 'The stylistic differences were apparent immediately. Here was "the great communicator", "Mr Everyman". There was no nuclear science – just a series of simple messages, conceptually easy but hard to deliver.' David Simon, jacket off, microphone in hand, left the platform and walked through the tense and troubled audience trying to deal with questions about why and where next. He relaxed his audience but only as a prelude to an orgy of blood on the carpet.

In 1995 David Simon stepped down as CEO and John Browne succeeded him. Simon in turn succeeded Lord Ashburton as non-executive chairman. But the changing of the guard was more than just continuity of top personnel; there was more telling evidence of continuity in underlying philosophy alongside again a change in direction, this time to strategically re-position BP in the world oil industry and begin to change the rules of the game in that industry. But before the big strategic changes came another round of structure, systems and to a lesser extent process changes. John Browne turned BP's three big businesses – oil, exploration and chemicals – into 91 business units all focusing relentlessly on performance. The idea was to break BP – into smaller more, accountable and responsible performance centres, while simultaneously obtaining the benefits of scale and knowledge transfer by building corporate group leadership meetings and problem solving through peer groups. So there is some fragmentation and glue.

While John Browne was simultaneously fragmenting and complicating BP, he was also integrating and simplifying it. After several years of decentralizing, this emphasis was maintained in the context of a drive to create a stronger strategic centre. All this was focused on the organizational obsession with performance. Hierarchy had disappeared in the layered status sense, but had massively increased in the immediacy of the performance targets and the incentive systems which buttressed them. Further evidence of the centralizing tendencies in BP was Browne's imposition of a common operating environment for IT – a signal weakness until then in the company's IT infrastructure. In 1997 there was now nowhere to hide among BP's slimmed-down staff of 55,000. But the message was underlying continuity and building up the complements.

By 1997 the strategic thinking and acting of Browne were now harnessed to re-positioning BP in the industry and then applying the fiercesome organizational capabilities to drive performance to even greater scale. All this was to be focused on the impending acquisitions of Amoco, Arco and Burmah Castrol. By the end of 1998, BP was a very long way in scale, performance and respectability from what it had been in the low point of summer 1992.

1.   *What features of the outer and inner context of BP mobilized and perpetuated the climate for change in the 1990s?*
2.   *How important were leader effects in the process of strategic change?*
3.   *What are the limits of senior executive action in strategizing/organizing?*
4.   *What were the key complementary changes in BP in the 1990s, how were they built and linked to firm performance?*

Conclusion

Twenty years ago the themes of process, power and change would have appeared out of place in a strategic management text. However, with each passing decade it has been pleasing to see these themes progress further into the mainstream of our field. Today:

- as organizational structures, processes and boundaries have become less bureaucratic, bounded and rationally determined and more ambiguous, uncertain and dynamic, the use of power has become more influential, and strategic thinkers increasingly need to be *political analysts*;
- as the pace of change has quickened and increasingly grates against people's desire and ability to cope with change, strategic thinkers increasingly need to be *social anthropologists* of the relationship between change and continuity;
- as firms have engaged more in 'best practice' copying, emphasis has shifted toward things such as the networks of tacit knowledge contained in human resources (see

Chapter 3, 'Strategy as Organizing') and an organization's heritage (see Chapter 2, 'Strategy as Ethos'), things that are difficult to 'reverse engineer', strategic thinkers increasingly need to be *historians* that can recognize, evaluate and take advantage of how an organization's strategy emerges as a unique process in particular context;

- as firms are challenged by greater complexity and dynamism in their contexts, so *managerial skill in thinking and acting holistically* are core leader attributes in delivering complementary change.

Strategy making is not just about acquiring and using the conventional industrial economics-based techniques. In this chapter I have emphasized how and why the making and practising of strategy are bounded by many considerations of which history, politics, power, process sensitivity and change capability are central.

Think of history. Can you imagine the prime ministers of Israel, or senior politicians in the north of Ireland waking up on a Monday morning and thinking and acting strategically without consideration of the heavy hand of the past? National history, identity and culture are crucial shapers of what political and business leaders are capable of seeing, saying and strategizing about. Direction, therefore, is not just about thinking and acting about the future, it is also about the subtle processes of linking the past, the present and the future. If this is the case in practice, it is surely time we as analysts of strategy making conducted research which seeks to catch reality in flight.

Features of the outer and inner context of organizations also fundamentally shape the timing and process of making strategy. External threats and crises are great enablers and disablers of strategic thinking and action. Often it takes the appearance of the barbarians at the gate for the past to be overturned, the old guard to lose power, and the new regime with the new strategic recipe to have their voices heard. External threats from new competition and new competitive standards can thereby trigger internal change. So new strategies often emerge from a cocktail of pressure arising from changes in the outer and inner context of the firm.

I have also argued that the prospect and reality of changing have the potential to unscramble the existing distribution of resources in the organization. As empires are threatened, so the existing distribution of power may be endangered and this will release political energy in the strategic decision-making and change processes of the firm. External strategy consultants may be brought in as unstated referees or arbitrators in such power battles, or are used to impose a veneer of rationality on the self-interested pleadings of one of the factions. Strategy making can be a battle of ideas and interests where coalition formation and bargaining are crucial human processes in shaping the outcome.

Making strategy is also about justifying and delivering timely change. Here above all process sensitivity and skill and will in shaping change are crucial. The management of strategic change is one of the most contextually sensitive of organizational tasks. Customization of change strategies to fit the context and time of the change is crucial. Building receptivity for change is often hard won but easily lost by ill considered and precipitous action. Managing change is also fundamentally about balancing continuity and change – keeping one foot in the present while tempting a coalition of real and potential supporters of change into the future. In all these processes sensitivity to time and place are of the essence. The wise strategist does indeed need to gaze down the lenses of the historian, the politician and the anthropologist and to act judiciously and wilfully with a keen sense of time and space.

But what of the future? I have been fortunate over the past three years to be involved in the creation of the *Handbook of Strategy and Management*, a collaborative work involving leading strategy academics from all over the globe. On reflecting on the contributions, the other editors (Howard Thomas and Richard Whittington) and I concluded that the future of strategy and management would lie in its capacity to meet a number of conditions. We considered the rapid growth of the field had occurred at the expense of a developed absence of reflexivity and critical reflection. So we would like to see more challenge and more creativity in the field. The field is also being challenged empirically to move from the preoccupation with firms and sectors as the prime units of analysis and to engage with the new empirical reality of networks and webs of firms (see Chapter 5, 'Strategy as Orchestrating Knowledge'). We also developed in the *Handbook* conclusions about the important themes about strategizing/organizing and challenged scholars outside of the United States to bring forward the varieties of strategic thought and action which exist throughout the world. The tremendous power and influence of the social sciences in North America are mirrored in the great influence of US scholars (in particular) in developing the field of strategy. But we need to confront any easy or implicit assumption that the social sciences have made America the universal pattern. As I have emphasized throughout this chapter, truth is the daughter of time and space. There are many different expressions of strategy being shaped by country and company cultures and more of this variety needs to be exposed. And without doubt we need an approach to strategic analysis that is more dynamic, processual, holistic and contextual than hitherto.

While the *Handbook* works towards such aims from a research and theoretical perspective, *Images of Strategy* much to my delight, carries this torch of creativity and diversity with a different emphasis. In contributing to it, this chapter has offered a personal and therefore partial, collection of frames of reference or images of strategy. You have eleven other alternatives against which to juxtapose it towards drawing your own conclusions as to where you want to take strategy.

Source Material and Recommended Further Reading

The quotation from Martin Heidegger is from the difficult but brilliant *Being and Time* (Oxford: Blackwell, 1962) in which he critiques, among other things, our linear view of past, present and future as separate and discrete objects.

The story of my academic development is told in greater detail in 'Catching Reality in Flight' in A. Bedeian (ed.) *Management Laureates*, vol. 5 (Greenwood, CT: JAI Press, 1998, pp. 171–206). The findings of the Uganda study were written up by the expedition leader Ioan Thomas in *Uganda Journal*, 27, 1963, 111–22. My early work on politics and power in Littlewoods was published in *The Politics of Organizational Decision Making* (London: Tavistock, 1973). While the Gordonstoun study has never been written up in 'all its glory', the method related to it and outlined in Figure 10.4 is developed in 'On Studying Organizational Cultures', *Administrative Science Quarterly*, 24, 1979, 570–80. I also outline a rationale here for not defining terms such as 'organizational culture' too rigidly.

The discussion on historians as role models and definitions of process and context borrows from 'What is a Processual Analysis?', *Scandinavian Journal of Management*, 13, 1997, 337–48. Good sources looking at time with regard to sociological and management research include: B. Adam,

Time and Social Theory (Cambridge: Polity, 1990); P. Clark, 'A Review of the Theories of Time and Structure for Organizational Sociology', in S.B. Bacharach and S.M. Mitchell (eds), *Research in the Sociology of Organizations* (London: Greenwich, 1985); J. Hassard, 'Images of Time and Work in Organization', in S. Clegg, C. Hardy and W.R. Nord (eds), *Handbook of Organization Studies* (London: Sage, 1996); P. Sztompka, *Society in Action: The Theory of Social Becoming* (Chicago: University of Chicago Press, 1991) and *The Sociology of Social Change* (Oxford: Blackwell, 1993); and R. Whipp, 'A Time to be Concerned', *Time and Society*, 3, 1994, 99–116. Loasby's work on time can be found in Brian J. Loasby, *Choice, Complexity and Ignorance* (Cambridge: Cambridge University Press, 1976).

Andrew Van de Ven's definition of processes comes from his paper 'Suggestions for Studying Strategy Process: A Research Note', *Strategic Management Journal*, 13, 1992, 169–88. With regard to ideas on the staticness of strategic language, see David Webb and Andrew Pettigrew, 'The Temporal Development of Strategy', *Organization Science*, 10(5), 1999, 601–21. These ideas may be connected to Robert Chia's analysis in 'From Modern to Postmodern Organizational Analysis', *Organization Studies*, 16, 1995, 579–604; and 'The Problem of Reflexivity in Organizational Research: Towards a Postmodern Science of Organization', *Organization*, 3, 1996, 31–59.

The Awakening Giant: Continuity and Change in ICI is published by Blackwell (Oxford, 1985). For those of you in a hurry, 'Context and Action in the Transformation of the Firm', *Journal of Management Studies*, 24, 1987, 649–70, summarizes some of the key themes of the ICI study.

For extra background to the section 'A social anthropologist of change', see R. Whipp, R. Rosenfeld and A. Pettigrew, 'Culture and Competitiveness: Evidence from Mature UK Industries', *Journal of Management Studies*, 26, 1989, 561–85; and A. Pettigrew, C. Hendry and P.R. Sparrow, 'Linking Strategic Change, Competitive Performance and Human Resource Management: Results from a UK Empirical Study', in R. Mansfield (ed.), *New Frontiers of Management* (London: Routledge, 1989); A. Pettigrew and C. Hendry, 'Human Resource Management: An Agenda for the 1990s', *International Journal of Human Resource Management*, 1, 1990, 17–43; A. Pettigrew, 'Studying Strategic Choice and Strategic Change', *Organization Studies*, 11, 1990, 6–11, and 'Longitudinal Field Research on Change: Theory and Practice', *Organization Science*, 1, 1990, 267–92; A. Pettigrew, E. Ferlie and L. McKee, *Shaping Strategic Change* (London: Sage, 1992); and A. Pettigrew and R. Whipp, *Managing Change for Competitive Success* (Oxford: Blackwell, 1991).

The 'process–content–context' framework has now been widely applied as a means of looking at strategy. A good example is Bob de Wit and Ron Meyer's best-selling textbook *Strategy: Process, Content, Context* (London: Thompson, 1998).

John Kotter's 'eight steps' can be found in 'Leading Change: Why Transformation Efforts Fail', *Harvard Business Review*, March–April 1995, 59–67. His model is contrasted with Richard and mine's in S. Cummings, 'ReGenerating Change', the final chapter of *ReCreating Strategy* (London: Sage, 2002). This work also traces the development and critiques conventional linear models of change.

Terry McNulty's and my work on boards is presented in 'Power and Influence in and around the Boardroom', *Human Relations*, 48, 1995, 1–29 and 'Strategists on the Board', *Organization Studies*, 20(1), 1999, 47–74.

Gareth Morgan's *Images of Organization* (London: Sage, 1997) contains an excellent review of political models for analysing organizational behaviour. See also Jeffrey Pfeffer, *Power in Organizations* (Marshfield, MA: Pitman, 1981). See also A. Pettigrew, 'Information Control as a Power Resource', *Sociology*, 6, 1972, 187–204, and 'Strategy Formulation as a Political Process', *International Studies of Management and Organization*, 7, 1977, 78–87.

Anthony Giddens's work on the inter-relationships between structure and agency became crystallized in 'structuration' theory. Further reading can be found in Anthony Giddens, *The Consti-*

tution of Society: Outline of the Theory of Structuration (Berkeley: University of California Press, 1984).

The findings from the INNFORM international research project on new forms of organizing and firm performance have been published in *The Innovating Organization*, A. Pettigrew and E. Fenton (eds) (London: Sage, 2000), and in the forthcoming book, *Innovative Forms of Organizing*, A. Pettigrew et al. (eds) (London: Sage, 2003). The BP case is discussed in much more detail in Chapter 8 of that book.

Our concluding thoughts on the future of the strategy field are given greater vent in the first and last chapters of A. Pettigrew, H. Thomas and R. Whittington (eds), *Handbook of Strategy and Management* (London: Sage, 2002).

A good overview of a lot of the ideas covered in this chapter is provided in 'Andrew Pettigrew on Executives and Strategy', *European Journal of Management*, February 2002.

Finally, I would like to express my appreciation to Stephen Cummings for his assistance in compiling and editing this chapter.

Progress, from a modernist point of view, leads to specialization (see Chapter 1). This then leads to the fragmentation of things that were once one. Hence, as management has become more 'scientific' the field has disintegrated into different sub-units, much like the fragmentation of corporate bodies described in Chapter 4. However, as other chapters in this book have made clear, we must orchestrate, explore, connect and re-centre these fragmenting pieces, and find ways of continuing to see them as systems. Following the modern march of progress, strategy and marketing have become separate

fiefdoms. This next paper deconstructs the largely fruitless path that marketing has sought to carve out for itself by defining its role as 'meeting customer needs'. Doyle suggests a mutually beneficial reconnection of strategy and marketing by redefining marketing as 'the process of creating a competitive advantage by developing relationships with valued customers'. Here marketing, and by implication strategy, should be about managing the process of increasing the long-term future value of the company for its owners.

11 Strategy as Marketing

PETER DOYLE

There is a paradox in how top management (we could say strategic management) views marketing. On the one hand, marketing has become accepted as the central driver of shareholder value. Every world-class company now puts building long-term relationships with customers, based on satisfying their needs, at the forefront of strategy. Three factors have increased the primacy of marketing in strategy:

(1) The emergence of excess production capacity in more and more industries from manufacturing sectors like textiles and steel, to services like banking and air transport. This has meant that marketing rather than production capabilities have emerged as the primary determinants of value added.

(2) The deregulation of industry, the decline of trade barriers and the emergence of increasingly global competition, mean that today there is no place to hide if your company cannot satisfy customers.

(3) The information revolution has driven a renewed drive to get closer to customers. The Internet, in particular, is shaping a new business model that allows suppliers to strip out distribution costs and develop one-to-one relationships with customers.

However, while the central role of marketing in achieving competitiveness and creating shareholder value is now undisputed, the role of marketing professionals is increasingly questioned. A widely reported research study from the top consultants, McKinsey and Company was entitled 'Marketing's mid-life crisis' and concluded that marketing departments are 'often a millstone around an organisation's neck'. A study by Coopers & Lybrand concluded that the marketing department is 'critically ill'. Research by the Boston Consulting Group found that 90 per cent of major companies claimed to have restructured their marketing departments. Even Unilever and Procter & Gamble were abolishing marketing directors' jobs.

A recent survey of major companies by the Marketing Society echoed this marginalization of marketing professionals. Only 12 out of 100 chief executives had previous experience in a marketing position. Only 57 per cent of the companies surveyed had a marketing director on the board.

The marketing profession's response to these studies has not been convincing. One response has been exhorting the government and senior executives to 'understand the importance of satisfying customers'. But to quote Dr Johnson, 'what is true about this argument is not new, and what is new is not true'. The case for the necessity of satisfying customers in competitive markets was made very familiar to us by Adam Smith, over 200 years ago. Some marketing professionals want to go further, suggesting the firm should focus everything upon maximizing customer satisfaction. But such a view is absurd (as the Dilbert cartoon below illustrates). Lowering prices and increasing service levels can always increase customer satisfaction further, but such a policy would be a quick route to bankruptcy.

Another tack, tried by some marketing managers to make their contributions more appreciated, has been to seek to justify marketing investments by showing how they increase corporate earnings or return on capital employed. But such an approach is invariably counterproductive for marketing. Cutting, rather than increasing, marketing expenditures will almost always boost short-term profitability. Because of the lagged effects of most marketing investments, encouraging these expenditures to be treated as accounting costs is a dead-end for marketers.

Subsequently, marketing has not had the impact on strategy that its importance justifies. To a significant extent this is due to marketing's lack of a clear objective. As a

Reprinted from *Dogbert's Big Book of Business*. © Knight features.

consequence, top management is often sceptical about the contribution of marketing in creating shareholder value. Marketing professionals too, generally do not know how to support their plans in strategic terms. Often they make the mistake of believing that market share or customer satisfaction are ends in themselves, or worse, try to justify marketing investments in terms of improving current earnings.

It was not always this way though. In the 1970s, when we might say that marketing as an academic field of inquiry was in its infancy, concepts such as the 'product life cycle' were developed with a mind to connect marketing to other elements of the firm and its stakeholders toward developing value for the long term.

In 1976 I published a paper titled 'The Realities of the Product Life Cycle'. In the early 1980s the ideas developed in this work were combined with others from both the strategy and marketing domains: Harold Fox, Charles Hofer, Philip Kotler and Charles Wasson in Table 11.1. The product life cycle and the growth-share matrix (BCG), which is often associated with it (see Chapter 4, 'Strategy as Intention and Anticipation') has its weaknesses (for starters, it indicates a somewhat defeatist attitude in suggesting that all products must decline and implies, rather simplistically, only four different marketing strategies that can be followed 'by numbers'). However, Table 11.1 demonstrates how marketing can been seen as about proving a unifying focus by balancing what customers want with internal realities (design capabilities, production capacity, financial leverage, etc.) and external realities (like providing returns for the owners of the business).

In an attempt to get marketing back on track and in an attempt to join marketing and strategic management (concerns which by becoming sub-fields, specializations, and subsequently silos, have had increasingly little to say to one another), this chapter introduces the concept of value-based marketing. It proposes that the real objective of marketing in the business enterprise is to develop and implement customer-led strategies that create shareholder value. We illustrate the way shareholder value analysis can provide a powerful technique for demonstrating how marketing strategies can increase the value of the firm. It provides a framework and a language for integrating marketing more effectively with other functions within the business. Value-based marketing also gives the subject a stronger theoretical base, which puts marketing as a pivotal role in the strategy formulation process.

The application of shareholder value analysis encourages profitable marketing investments. Brand-building investments that would be discouraged under conventional accounting procedures because they reduce current profits, can be shown as having a clear positive impact on the share price, using value-based marketing analysis. Finally, value-based analysis penalizes arbitrary cuts in marketing budgets. Management found that cutting marketing investment is an easy target when it needed to boost current profits. Now shareholder value analysis gives marketing a powerful tool to demonstrate that these short-term cuts destroy rather than build value. Such cutbacks are more likely to erode rather than raise the share price.

Back to First Principles

The basic problem with marketing management, as indicated above, is that its objectives are unclear. Marketing managers have come up with a variety of metrics to evaluate campaigns and justify their performance. The most common criteria for measuring

Table 11.1 Sources of distinctive strategic and functional competence at different stages of product or industry evolution

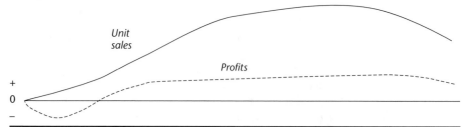

Functional area	Introduction	Growth	Maturity	Decline
Marketing	Resources/skills to create widespread awareness and find acceptance from customers; advantageous access access to distribution	Ability to establish brand recognition, find niche, reduce price, solidify, strong distribution relations, and develop new channels	Skills in aggressively promoting products to new markets and holding existing markets; pricing flexibility; skills in differentiating products and holding customer loyalty	Cost-effective means of efficient access to selected channels and markets; strong customer loyalty or dependence; strong company image
Production operations	Ability to expand capacity effectively, limit number of designs, develop standards	Ability to add product variants, centralize production, or otherwise lower costs; ability to improve product quality; seasonal subcontracting capacity	Ability to improve product and reduce costs; ability to share or reduce capacity; advantageous supplier relationships; subcontracting	Ability to prune product line; cost advantage in production location or simplified inventory control; subcontracting or long production runs
Finance	Resources to support high net cash overflow and initial losses; ability to use leverage effectively	Ability to finance rapid expansion, to have net cash outflows but increasing profits; resources to support product improvements	Ability to generate and redistribute increasing net cash inflows; effective cost control systems	Ability to reuse or liquidate unneeded equipment; advantage in cost of facilities; control system accuracy; streamlined management control
Personnel	Flexibility in staffing and training new management; existence of employees with key skills in new products or markets	Existence of and ability to add skilled personnel; motivated and loyal work force	Ability to cost effectively, reduce work force, increase efficiency	Capacity to reduce and reallocate personnel; cost advantage
Engineering and research and development	Ability to make engineering changes, have technical bugs in product and process resolved	Skill in quality and new feature development; ability to start developing successor product	Ability to reduce costs, develop variants differentiate products	Ability to support other grown areas or to apply product to unique customer needs.
Key functional area and strategy focus	Engineering; market penetration	Sales; consumer loyalty; market share	Production efficiency successor products	Finance; maximum investment recovery

the effectiveness of marketing are increases in sales and market share. Unfortunately, any first year economics student can demonstrate that such growth may as easily decrease, as increase, profits. Sales growth increases profits only if the operating margin on the additional sales covers the higher costs and investment incurred to achieve the growth. Chasing profitless growth has been one of the most common sources of corporate failure.

A number of other criteria for justifying marketing strategies have become increasingly popular. These include brand awareness, consumer attitudes, repeat buying, and ratings of customer satisfaction.

Marketing academics and professionals have become increasingly sophisticated in their measuring of these things (as a quick scan of leading academic journals such as *Marketing Science* or *The Journal of Marketing Research* will demonstrate). But, unfortunately, these aspects generally have relatively weak relationships to sales, and almost none to profitability. Increasing advertising, for example, will generally raise brand awareness and in many situations will increase sales, but whether these incremental sales will be profitable is very hard to say. The same criticisms apply to all the conventional marketing metrics.

Marketing management's lack of credibility in the boardroom is much to do with its failure to quantify the contribution of marketing strategy to corporate performance. Claims that investment in a new campaign will increase sales or brand awareness do not rate highly for boards struggling to increase their share price in a hostile capital market. Other business functions such as operations, sales, finance, and even human resources management, thus appear or are believed to make more significant contributions to the bottom-line.

The starting point for reasserting the role of marketing management begins with properly defining its objective. Major business firms now almost universally accept that the primary task of management is to maximize returns to shareholders. The rationales for this goal lie in the property rights of shareholders and in capital market pressures to oust management that does not deliver competitive returns. The driving force for the adoption of the shareholder value concept was the dissatisfaction of investors with the results of the growth strategies pursued by so many companies in the 1960s and 1970s. Many managers, driven by a quest for size, diversified into markets where they had no competitive advantage, took on unprofitable customers, and launched arrays of products that did not create value. The result was that while many companies grew greatly in size, shareholders saw the value of the holdings stagnate or decline. The reaction in the 1980s and 1990s was a stricter code of corporate governance that defined the central responsibility of managers as creating value for shareholders.

This new 'value-based management' has three elements: beliefs, principles and processes.

- The *beliefs* are the wholehearted acceptance by management that maximizing shareholder returns is the governing objective of the firm and that this can be planned for in a systematic way.
- The *principles* are the strategic foundations upon which value is determined. These are, first, targeting those markets where positive economic returns can be made, and second, developing a competitive advantage that enables both customer and the firm to create value.

- The *processes* are the activities necessary to implement the beliefs and principles. These concern how strategies should be developed, resources allocated and performance evaluated.

Marketing can be at the centre of value-based management if managers embrace this statement of beliefs, principles and processes. This acceptance in no way weakens the traditional contribution of marketing, rather, it enormously strengthens it by providing a sound intellectual base. This approach states that the role of marketing is to contribute to increasing shareholder value. It suggests a new definition of marketing, which I have outlined below:

> Marketing is the management process that seeks to maximize returns to shareholders by developing relationships with valued customers and creating competitive advantage in the long term.

I term this new concept *value-based marketing*. This definition clearly defines the objective of marketing and how its performance should be evaluated. The specific contribution of marketing to strategy lies in the formulation of policies to choose the right customers, build relationships of trust with them and to create what strategy people like to call a *sustainable competitive advantage*.

The paragraphs below outline the development of a value-based marketing (VBM) approach in four sections. I begin by discussing the determinants of shareholder value, then describe the four main types of marketing assets. Following on from this, I examine how these marketing assets are linked to, and in many respects determine, shareholder value. Finally, the ways in which marketing's contribution to strategic decision making toward increasing shareholder value, through things such as advertising and valuing brands, can be justified and communicated are explored. Throughout the discussion I have provided examples relating to a fictional company called *Warwick Inc.* To aid the building of your understanding of VBM, I urge you to work through these examples in your own mind before moving on to the next section.

VBM 1: Determinants of Shareholder Value

Value-based management is based on the belief that management should evaluate strategies in the same way that outsiders do. Investors assess strategies on their ability to create shareholder value. The company's share price reflects investors' evaluations of whether the current strategy of management will create value in the future. To explore the implications for marketing we need to review how finance professionals estimate value and value creation.

Modern finance is based on four principles: the importance of cash flow, the time value of money, the opportunity cost of capital and the concept of net present value. *Cash* is the basis of value − it is what is left over for shareholders after all the bills have been paid. Cash has a *time value* because a pound today is worth more than a pound tomorrow. The *opportunity cost of capital* is the return investors could obtain if they invested elsewhere in companies of similar risk. The *net present value* concept calculates the value of an asset as the sum of the net cash flows discounted by the opportunity cost of capital. By maximizing the net present value of a business managers are pursuing those strategies most likely to maximize the returns to shareholders.

Table 11.2   Warwick Inc.: Shareholder value analysis (£ million)

Year	Base	1	2	3	4	5
Sales	100.0	110.0	121.0	133.1	146.4	161.1
Operating margin	10.0	11.0	12.1	13.3	14.6	16.1
Tax (30%)	3.0	3.3	3.6	4.0	4.4	4.8
NOPAT	7.0	7.7	8.5	9.3	10.2	11.3
Net investment		4.0	4.4	4.8	5.3	5.9
Cash flow		3.7	4.1	4.5	4.9	5.4
Discount factor (r = 10%)		0.909	0.826	0.751	0.683	0.621
Present value of cash flow		3.4	3.4	3.4	3.4	3.4
Cumulative present value						16.8
PV of continuing value						70.0
Other investments						7.0
Value of debt						−25.0
Shareholder value						68.8
Initial shareholder value						52.0
Shareholder value added						16.8
Implied share price £						3.44
Initial share price £						2.60

To illustrate the calculations, consider *Warwick Inc.* (see Table 11.2). Its current sales and net operating profit after tax (NOPAT) are shown in the first or base column. Management has developed a new marketing strategy and it believes sales will grow by 10 per cent annually. To arrive at net cash flow we have to deduct the investment in working capital and fixed assets that will be needed to support this growth. This is forecast to be 40 per cent of incremental sales. Shareholder value is obtained by discounting this cash flow by the opportunity cost of capital, r, which is taken here to be 10 per cent. The annual discount factor is $1/(1 + r)i$ where $i = 1, 2, \ldots$ is the year.

The shareholder value calculation divides the estimation of the value created by a strategy into two components. The first is the present value of cash flows during the planning period. Generally, managers feel it reasonable to plan ahead in some detail for a period of around five years. Here they forecast a cumulative cash flow in the planning period with a present value of £16.8 million. The second component is the residual or terminal value, which is the present value of cash flow after the end of the planning period. The residual value is calculated by the standard perpetuity method, which is NOPAT/r. This method effectively assumes that beyond the five-year planning period, competition will drive down profits to a level such that new investment just earns the company's cost of capital, so that there will be no additional shareholder value created.

When the residual value is multiplied by the discount factor, we arrive at its present value, £70 million. Adding any non-operating investments the firm owns and deducting the market value of any debt leads to the shareholder value of £68.8 million. If there were 20 million shares outstanding this would produce any expected share price of £3.44. If the current share price is below this figure, then analysts would recommend the shares for purchase. If the company had not introduced the new growth strategy and remained at its present level, the implied share price would have stayed at £2.60 (i.e., its residual value in the base year).

The significance of shareholder value analysis is that it provides a highly effective vehicle for demonstrating the contribution of marketing to the company's strategy and financial performance. To explore this further we need to show how marketing adds value.

VBM 2: Marketing Assets

The task of marketing is to create shareholder value. Marketing expenditure adds value when it creates assets that generate future cash flows with a positive net present value. Marketing assets are what link marketing activities to value creation. Accountants define assets as economic resources, owned by an entity, whose cost at the time of acquisition can be objectively measured. Unfortunately, this definition generally leads accountants to only include tangible assets such as cash, stock, debtors, plant and equipment in their balance sheets. Yet, in modern companies, such tangible assets account for only a small proportion of the market value of companies. The 'market-to-book' ratio in Britain's largest companies averages three, which suggests that two-thirds of the market value of these companies lies in intangible assets.

Of course, not all such intangible assets derive from marketing activities, they may arise in the skills of the employees, the value of patents and licences, or the possession of scarce resources. But in most companies, it is in the value of their customer relationships that long-term cash flow is primarily based. Marketing assets can be divided into four types:

- *Marketing knowledge.* Superior marketing knowledge provides a core competency consisting of skills, systems and information that convey a competitive advantage to the firm in terms of identifying market opportunities and developing marketing strategies.
- *Brands.* Successful brand names convey powerful images to customers that make them more desirable than competitive products. Owners of strong brands possess assets that attract customers, often earn premium prices and can be enduring generators of cash.
- *Customer loyalty.* If a company has built a satisfied loyal customer base, it will be more profitable and should grow faster than other companies. Many studies have shown that loyal customers buy more of the company's products, are cheaper to serve, are less sensitive to price, and bring in new customers.
- *Strategic relationships.* A company's network of relationships with channel partners can provide incremental sales, access to new markets and allow the firm to leverage its competencies in additional areas.

Marketing assets are no different from the firm's tangible assets in that their value lies in their contribution to generating future cash flow. However, marketing assets are often more valuable to the firm for two reasons. First, they are harder to acquire than tangible assets. Normally they take years of investment and are closely integrated into the firm's culture, which makes them difficult to buy or reproduce. Second, the worth of marketing assets derives solely from the value customers attach to them. Since customers are the ultimate source of cash flow, marketing assets can be considered the primary source of customer preference and competitive advantage.

Marketing assets do not normally appear on the balance sheet because accountants believe that their value cannot be measured with sufficient accuracy. Commentators have speculated whether this matters. While accountants do not measure intangible assets, the discrepancy between market and book values shows that investors do. Most accountants recognize that balance sheets no longer give meaningful information about values, instead they record historical details of transactions. It has been suggested, on the other hand, that because marketing assets are not recorded, their values are under-estimated. Because they are treated as costs rather than investments that are depreciated, this then leads to insufficient spending on developing brands, retaining customers and creating channel partnerships.

Fortunately, shareholder value analysis (SVA) avoids such possibilities of bias. This values strategies and companies in the same way outside investors do. SVA is not based on accounting conventions, instead it is based on cash. While profits are subjective, cash is a fact. Investments and costs are treated identically as deductions from cash flow, at the time they are paid. Like investors, managers have to judge their strategies in terms of their impact on *future* cash flow. Expenditures to develop marketing assets make sense if the sum of the discounted cash flow they generate is positive.

VBM 3: Marketing Assets Determine Shareholder Value

Turning around failing companies has conventionally been seen as a financial problem. But the significance of SVA is that it shows value creation is much more to do with the firm's effectiveness in developing marketing assets.

The model illustrated in Table 11.2 (presented in the 'VBM1: Determinants of Shareholder Value' section above) shows that the amount of shareholder value created depends upon four factors:

(1) level of future cash flow;
(2) timing of cash flow;
(3) risk attached to the business; and
(4) residual value.

And marketing assets are the principal drivers of all four of these determinants of value as we shall explore in the paragraphs that follow.

Effects on the level of future cash flow

Table 11.2 shows that the level of cash flow is a function of sales growth, the after-tax operating profit margin and the net investment required to fund the growth of sales, i.e.:

Cash flow = sales × net operating margin − net investment

Faster *sales growth* drives up returns to shareholders as long as the additional sales deliver economic profit. While cost-cutting and downsizing can temporarily boost cash flow, only sales growth can deliver long-run growth in cash flow. Growing sales is the main task of marketing. Growth is accelerated where the firm has strong marketing assets:

Table 11.3 Simulation of the impact of marketing on shareholder value (£ million)

	Discounted cash flow	Present value of residual	Shareholder value	Shareholder value added	Share price	Change in value(%)
No sales growth 0% pa	26.5	43.5	52.0	0.0	£2.60	0
Sales growth +10% pa	16.8	70.0	68.8	16.8	3.44	32
Sales growth +20% pa	2.2	108.2	92.3	40.3	4.62	78
Price increase +10%	51.3	86.9	120.2	68.9	6.01	131
Operating costs cut −10%	33.4	54.8	70.2	33.6	3.51	35
Investment rate cut −10%	30.2	43.5	55.6	3.6	2.78	7
Accelerated cash flow	18.2	70.0	70.2	18.2	3.51	2*
Cost of capital cut −10%	27.2	45.5	54.7	2.7	2.74	5
Extending growth period	20.5	70.0	72.5	20.5	3.63	5*

Note: * compared to 10% sales growth base case.

marketing knowledge, powerful brands, loyal customers and strategic partnerships with channel members. To understand the role of growth in creating shareholder value, Table 11.3 simulates the effects of different growth rates on the company illustrated in Table 11.2. (These calculations can easily be checked by entering Table 11.2 in a spreadsheet such as Microsoft Excel, and simulating the changes discussed.)

If the company remains static over the five-year planning period, the value of the company does not change and the equity value of the business remains at £52 million. If sales grow at 10 per cent annually and the operating margin remains constant, then the value of the company and its share price rise by 32 per cent. At 20 per cent annual growth, the value of the company rises by 78 per cent.

Note that while faster growth greatly increases the value of the company, during the first five years the cash flow is reduced as profits are reinvested to drive growth. Creating value is about sacrificing immediate cash flow to build a greater cash generating potential for the future. The second determinant of the level of cash flow is the after-tax *operating margin*. This is a function of the size of the company's sales, its costs, and the average prices it is able to charge for its products and services. Profitable sales growth should improve the operating margin by spreading fixed costs. Strong marketing assets should also lead to higher prices and lower costs. This means the effect of growth could be greater than shown in Table 11.3. There is much evidence that strong brands are associated with price premiums. Studies have found that brand leaders in the United Kingdom sell on average at prices 40 per cent above regular brands. Strong brands also tend to possess higher advertising and promotional elasticities, implying that the costs of acquiring additional sales will be lower. There is also evidence that well-established brand names permit line and brand extensions that lower entry costs.

Table 11.3 shows the enormous effect price premiums can have on shareholder value. A 10 per cent price premium more than doubles the projected share price and equity value of the company. It greatly boosts cash flow during the planning period as well as leaving a significantly higher terminal figure for profits. Putting it another way, if managers neglect to invest in marketing assets and suffer a loss of brand premium as a result, the share price can be expected to drop dramatically, as investors figure out the implications for future cash flow. There is no more dramatic proof of the power of brands than simulating on a spreadsheet the effects of brand premiums on shareholder value. Table 11.3 also looks at the impact of marketing assets in lowering operating or fixed costs. If these costs amount to 50 per cent of total costs, and they are reduced by 10 per cent as a result of significant marketing assets, then shareholder value is increased by 35 per cent.

The third determinant of the level of cash flow is *investment*. Recent years have seen a growing recognition of the importance of customer partnerships in augmenting cash flow by reducing working capital and fixed investment. Stimulated by new information technology, particularly the Internet, marketing-orientated suppliers are forging closer links with key customers to eliminate the amount of stock and capital tied up in the supply chain. Customer partnerships are marketing assets built through carefully listening to customers and meeting their needs. They generate a return in enhanced cash flow through lowering investment requirements. For example, stock reductions of 15–20 per cent are commonly reported by companies with effective channel partnerships. Table 11.3 simulates the effect of a 10 per cent cut in investment requirements. This adds £3.6 million to shareholder value.

The effects of marketing assets on the level of cash flow have been looked at individually. The effects are of course cumulative. If price premiums and growth are combined the effects on the value of the company are additive. Such cumulative effects account for the very high market-to-book value ratios earned by companies such as Microsoft, Nokia, Coca-Cola and Vodafone. Similarly, the failure to achieve growth or price premiums accounts for the poor returns to shareholders in such companies as ICI, Safeway and United Biscuits.

Effects in accelerating cash flow

Because cash has a time value, cash flows are discounted. Shareholder value is increased if cash flows can be generated quicker. Table 11.3 shows the effect of accelerating the cash flow by one year. If the year 2 sales of Table 11.2 were achieved in year 1, year 3 sales in year 2, etc., shareholder value would increase from £68.8 million to £70.2 million, even though final year sales and profits are unchanged. Again marketing assets are often designed to achieve such acceleration.

In many cases Table 11.3 underestimates the effect of accelerated market penetration. Fast penetration can lead to first mover advantages. These include higher prices, greater customer loyalty, access to the best distribution channels and network effects that enable the innovator to become the specification standard. These feed back into both higher sales and higher operating margins. Many studies have shown that brands with strong images can expect customers to adopt their next generation products significantly earlier than those with weaker images. Companies now place much greater emphasis on 'pre-marketing' activities that focus on increasing awareness among opinion leaders even before the product launch to speed up the product life cycle and therefor accelerate cash flow.

Brands are not the only marketing assets that can accelerate cash flows. Strategic relationships and co-marketing partnerships can also speed up market penetration. Alliances can enable the firm to open up overseas markets faster. A firm with good marketing networks can use these assets to more quickly capitalize on emerging market opportunities. Boots, for example, has an arrangement to place its pharmacies in Tesco supermarkets, enabling it to penetrate faster this new growth area. By demonstrating how such investments accelerate cash flow, marketers can quantify their efficacy in enhancing shareholder value.

Effect on business risk

The third factor determining the value of the business is the opportunity cost of capital used to discount future cash flows. This discount rate depends upon market interest rates plus the special risks attached to the specific business unit. The risk attached to a business is determined by the volatility and vulnerability of its cash flows compared to the market average. Investors expect a higher return to justify investment in risky businesses. Because investors discount risky cash flows with a higher cost of capital, their value is reduced.

Again there is evidence that an important function of marketing assets is to reduce the risk attached to future cash flows. Strong brands operate by building layers of value that make them less vulnerable to competition. This is a key reason why leading investors rate companies with strong brand portfolios at a premium in their industries. Many studies have also demonstrated the dramatic effects on the company's net present value of increasing customer loyalty. A major focus of marketing today is on increasing customer loyalty, shareholder value analysis provides a powerful mechanism for demonstrating the financial contribution of these activities. Table 11.3 illustrates this by showing, if the opportunity cost of capital is reduced from 10 to 9 per cent, as a result of marketing activities which reduce the vulnerability of cash flows, then shareholder value is boosted by £2.7 million.

Effect on residual value

Shareholder value is made up of two components: the present value of cash flows during the planning period and the present value of the company at the end of the planning period. Not surprisingly, since a company potentially has an infinite life, the residual value normally greatly exceeds the value of the cash flows over the planning period. In the example of Table 11.2, the residual value accounts for over 70 per cent of the corporate value. Figure 11.1 shows that this is a typical figure across industry, indeed in high growth industries the residual value is an even higher proportion of total value.

The problem is valuing the business at the end of the planning period. The most common approach is to use the perpetuity method, as in Table 11.2. This assumes that at the end of the planning period, the company earns a return on net investment equivalent only to the cost of capital, so that shareholder value remains constant. An alternative assumption is that the business can continue to earn returns that exceed the cost of capital. Another more pessimistic assumption is that after the planning period the cash flows turns negative as competition intensifies. The choice depends upon two factors: the sustainability of the firm's *competitive advantage* and the *real options* for growth it has created. Microsoft and Coca-Cola, for example, have very high residual values because investors perceive them having very long-term brand strengths that can be leveraged to future growth opportunities in new markets or product areas.

Strong marketing assets, such as new product development expertise, brands, customer loyalty and strategic partnerships should create competitive advantage and growth options that will often endure beyond the normal period for which a company plans. Because such assets are difficult to copy and create, and offer lasting advantages, they should enhance residual values and so have a marked effect on shareholder value. Table 11.3 illustrates this by showing the effect of extending the period over which

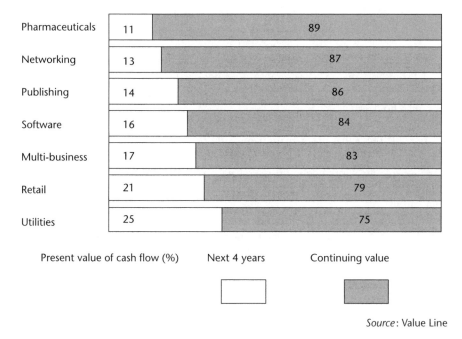

Figure 11.1 Structure of cash flow by industry

the company earns positive net cash flow by one year, from five to six years. This adds £3.7 million to shareholder value (from £68.8 million to £72.5 million).

VBM 4: Demonstrating Marketing's Contribution

Shareholder value analysis allows marketing professionals to communicate the expected results of their marketing strategies in terms that make sense for top management. In particular, it allows them to quantify how investments in marketing assets may affect the share price. Measures such as sales, market share or consumer attitudes have little value as criteria for judging marketing strategies since they have no necessary correlation with how investors value the business.

Valuing marketing strategies

Marketers need a simple decision rule to understand when additional sales will increase shareholder value. Sales are valuable if the operating margin on these sales exceed a threshold margin. The *threshold margin* is the minimum operating profit margin needed to maintain shareholder value. As can be seen from Table 11.2, it is a function of the added investment required to fund sales growth, the rate of tax the company pays, and its cost of capital. Specifically, it is defined as:

$$\text{Threshold margin} = \frac{\text{Investment rate} \times \text{Cost of capital}}{(1 + \text{cost of capital})(1 - \text{tax rate})}$$

In the example of Table 11.2, the threshold margin is $(40\% \times 10\%)/(1.1 \times 0.7) =$ 5.2%. Since the actual operating margin is constant at 10 per cent, additional sales are earning returns well above the investors' cost of capital and shareholder value is being consistently created. The key point for marketers is that when a business is operating at *below* the threshold margin sales growth does not create value. But top management should appreciate that sales growth achieved at *above* the threshold margin does create value for shareholders.

This concept leads to another useful tool for marketers, the threshold spread. The *threshold spread* is the actual profit margin on additional sales less the threshold margin. In the example of *Warwick Inc.* this is 4.8 per cent $(10 - 5.2)$. Its significance is that once the investment requirements and risk characteristics of a strategy have been established, shareholder value is determined by two factors: (1) sales growth, and (2) the threshold spread.

Most marketers in developing strategy focus on the marketing value drivers. For example, the strategy might involve new creative ideas and new above- and below-the-line initiatives aimed at increasing customer loyalty, winning bigger shares of the customers' spend and gaining new customers. These marketing drivers then need to be translated into financial value drivers.

For example, suppose *Warwick Inc.* management must choose between the strategy proposed in Table 11.2 and an alternative strategy proposed by the new marketing director. This new strategy centres on a comprehensive relationship marketing programme. The marketing department believed this would add an additional 2 per cent to annual sales, and to discount reductions amounting to 1 per cent of sales (effectively this is the equivalent to 1 per cent on the ex-factory price). They also believed higher customer retention would reduce the cost of sales by 1.5 per cent. The additional cost of the marketing programme would be an up-front investment of £5 million in the first year and an on-cost of £2 million annually.

Table 11.4 evaluates the new strategy. While the new strategy reduces operating profits in the first year, and reduces cash flow for the first three years of the planning period, shareholder value is substantially increased.

At £83.7 million, equity value is 22 per cent higher than in the original plan due to the higher long-term profits created and which are reflected in the higher residual value *of the business*. The example also illustrates the value of shareholder value for advocating aggressive marketing strategies. If management were orientated to maximizing profits or earnings per share, they would reject the new marketing strategy. But a proper analysis decisively demonstrates that such a short-term orientation is in the interest of neither shareholders nor the long-term competitiveness of the business.

Justifying advertising budgets

Many companies treat the advertising budget as a cushion; something that may be expanded in good times, but which is ruthlessly cut back when profit budgets are under threat. Top management appears to believe that advertising has no demonstrable impact on shareholder value. But proper analysis can show that this is a prime example of short-term thinking: while cutting advertising will normally increase immediate earnings, it has a deleterious impact on shareholder value. This is why cuts in advertising often lead to a fall in the share price even though short-term profits increase.

Table 11.4 Valuing a new marketing strategy for Warwick inc. (£ million)

Year	Base	1	2	3	4	5
Units	100.00	112.20	125.89	141.25	158.48	177.81
price	1.00	1.01	1.01	1.01	1.01	1.01
Sales	100.0	113.3	127.1	142.7	160.1	179.6
Costs	90.0	99.5	111.6	125.2	140.5	157.6
Initial margin	10.0	13.9	15.5	17.4	19.6	22.0
Additional marketing		5.0	2.0	2.0	2.0	2.0
Operating margin	10.0	8.9	13.5	15.4	17.6	20.0
Tax (30%)	3.0	2.7	4.1	4.6	5.3	6.0
NOPAT	7.0	6.2	9.5	10.8	12.3	14.0
Net investment		5.3	5.5	6.2	7.0	7.8
Cash flow		0.9	4.0	4.6	5.3	6.2
Discount factor (r = 10%)		0.909	0.826	0.751	0.683	0.621
Present value of cash flow		0.8	3.3	3.5	3.6	3.8
Cumulative present value						15.0
PV of continuing value						86.8
Other investments						7.0
Value of debt						−25.0
Shareholder value						83.7
Shareholder value added						31.7
Implied share price under new strategy £						4.19
Share price under original strategy £						3.44

The problems in justifying advertising budgets occur because sales are affected by many other factors in addition to advertising. All the studies of advertising agree that the effects of advertising on sales are small, certainly much smaller than the effects of price or promotion. The maximum advertising elasticities reported are around 0.2, meaning that a 10 per cent increase in advertising would increase sales by 2 per cent. Another problem making the effects of advertising even more difficult to calculate is its lagged effects. Sales today are not just affected by current advertising but by the customer's memories of past advertising. This means the short-run impact of advertising may underestimate its total impact on sales.

Demonstrating the effect of advertising on shareholder value depends on understanding the function of the advertising. There are two main approaches to explaining how advertising works: the persuasive hierarchy model and the low-involvement model. The former is sometimes called the aggressive theory of advertising, which sees it as first informing consumers about the product and then persuading them to try it. The ultimate test of whether such advertising has been effective is the resultant increase in sales. The shareholder value created by such an advertising campaign can be gauged by first estimating the advertising effect, generally through some form of econometric model, and then feeding the incremental sales attributed to advertising into the type of financial model illustrated in Table 11.2.

A more difficult case is justifying advertising for established brands in mature markets. While the persuasive hierarchy model of advertising might fit new products seeking to attract new customers, it hardly describes the role of advertising for brands such as Coca-Cola, Persil or Flora margarine. Virtually everyone buying these brands has bought

Table 11.5 Effect of eliminating advertising on shareholder value (£ million)

Year	Base	1	2	3	4	5
Sales (units)	100.0	90.00	85.5	83.4	82.3	82.3
Price	1.00	0.99	0.98	0.97	0.96	0.95
Revenue	100.0	89.1	83.8	80.9	79.0	78.1
Variable costs	66.7	60.0	57.0	55.6	54.9	54.8
Fixed costs	23.3	18.3	18.3	18.3	18.3	18.3
Operating profit	10.0	10.8	8.5	7.0	5.8	5.0
NOPAT	7.0	7.5	5.9	4.9	4.1	3.5
Net Investment		−4.0	−1.8	−0.9	−0.4	−0.0
Cash flow	7.0	11.5	7.7	5.7	4.5	3.5
Discount factor	1.0	0.909	0.826	0.751	0.683	0.621
Present value of cash flow	7.0	10.5	6.4	4.3	3.1	2.2
Cumulative present value						26.4
PV of continuing value						21.6
Shareholder value						48.0
Original shareholder value						70.0

them before; they are familiar with them; and have already been persuaded to buy. The low-involvement model best describes the role of advertising here. This sees advertising as being essentially defensive: the object is to *maintain* the brand's market share and price premium, through reinforcing current buying behaviour. Advertising in these mature markets does not increase sales but it prevents them declining and preserves the brands as long-term generators of cash for the shareholders.

Table 11.5 illustrates how shareholder analysis can be used to justify advertising, even though advertising does not create incremental sales. Initially the brand has stable sales at £100 million and a 10 per cent operating margin. In an effort to increase profits and cash-flow management decide to eliminate the £5 million advertising spend. A previous econometric analysis has estimated the advertising elasticity at 0.1, implying that eliminating advertising would only cut sales by 10 per cent. Since two-thirds of costs were variable, management believed profits were bound to rise.

However, management ignored sales effects after the first year. In the second and subsequent years the brand increasingly loses saliency to consumers without the benefit of advertising to reinforce and update the brand's associations. The model of Table 11.5 assumes diminishing advertising effects: the first year the loss is 10 per cent; the second year 5 per cent; and so on. In addition, management failed to take into account the loss of volume on the brand premium. Faced with declining sales and margin the major retailers will demand bigger allowances. The effect was estimated to take 1 per cent off the ex-factory price each year. In the first year profits were indeed up as a result of the £5 million saving on marketing. There was also a marked increase in cash flow in the first two years as lower sales resulted in declining working capital requirements. But from the second year, profits fall precipitously as declining margins and the drag of fixed costs take their toll.

If advertising had been maintained, the shareholder value of the brand would have been worth £70 million. Eliminating advertising produces a short-term jump in profits and cash flow, but a sharp decline in the long-run value of the business. The value of the business to shareholders drops by one third to £48 million.

Table 11.6 Valuing the brand (£ million)

Year	Base	1	2	3	4	5
Sales	250.0	262.5	275.6	289.4	303.9	319.1
Operating margin	37.5	39.4	41.3	43.4	45.6	47.9
NOPAT	26.3	27.6	28.9	30.4	31.9	33.5
Net investment		6.3	6.6	6.9	7.2	7.6
Cash flow		21.3	22.4	23.5	24.7	25.9
Brand cash flow		14.7	15.4	16.2	17.0	17.9
Discount factor (r = 12%)	0.893	0.797	0.712	0.636	0.567	
Discounted cash flow		13.1	12.3	11.5	10.8	10.1
Cumulative present value						57.9
PV of continuing value						84.5
Brand value						142.4

Valuing brands

The increasingly obvious gap between the balance sheet valuations of companies and their market values has led to a growing interest in valuing brands, which are seen as a major component in the difference. Brand valuations can be particularly useful in acquisitions both for the acquirer wanting to know what parts of the company may be worth, and for the defender wanting to justify its stewardship. Brand valuations are also used to calculate royalty rates in licensing deals. Tax authorities are now asking companies to charge their subsidiaries for the use of their bands and proper valuations assist negotiations. Finally, convinced of the importance of brands, many companies want regular valuations to track that their strategies reinforce the value of these assets.

Table 11.6 illustrates the process of valuing a brand. The first step is to forecast brand sales, operating margins and cash flow over a reasonable period, such as five years. It is important that the forecasts are based solely on brand sales and not any unbranded products that may be produced in parallel. Here brand sales are predicted to grow at 5 per cent a year, the operating margin is 15 per cent, the tax rate 30 per cent, and net investment is estimated at 50 per cent of incremental revenue. The second step is to calculate the percentage of the earnings that accrue from the use of the brand name. A brand name creates value by adding emotive associations, over and above the product, that lead to additional sales or higher prices. There are a variety of methods for estimating this increment, depending on the type of brand and its market. Where the brand operates by enhancing the margin, the most direct approach is to compare the operating margin on the brand with the estimated margin on similar unbranded products. This difference (i.e. $OM_{branded} - OM_{unbranded}$) should be attributable to the company's unique assets: its brands, patents, channel partnerships, and so on. In heavily branded markets, any residual earnings will be predominantly due to brands; in hi-tech markets other intangible assets may be more critical. In Table 11.6, the margin on unbranded products is estimated at 7 per cent, implying earnings from intangibles account for 8 per cent of sales (i.e. 15–7 per cent). In this market, since there are no quality differences, it is assumed that the brand premium accounts for this residual. The brand cash flow associated with this premium is in any one year is then:

$$CF_{brand} = Sales(OM_{branded} - OM_{unbranded})(I - tax\ rate).$$

The final step is to estimate the brand discount rate. This will not be identical to the company's overall cost of capital since the brand's earnings may be more or less volatile than the average of the portfolio. The Interbrand Group, a pioneer of brand valuation methods, calculated the discount rate on the basis of a 'brand strength score', which measures the security that the brand name adds to the earnings stream. This rates such factors as the stability of the market, the brand's market share, its geographic spread, legal protection, etc. In the example, the discount rate is calculated at 12 per cent.

The brand value is calculated by applying the discount rate to the expected future brand cash flows. As with all shareholder analyses, sensitivity analysis is important to explore alternative scenarios using different price and growth assumptions and different brand investment policies. This allows an assessment of the robustness of the brand and the problems and opportunities it may face in the future.

Implications for Strategy

Shareholder value has become a new standard because of an increasing realization of the defects of conventional accounting. A myopic focus on accounting profits encourages an excessively short-term view of business. It leads to an under-investment in intangible or information-based assets such as:

- staff;
- brands;
- customer relationships; and
- supplier relationships.

In today's information age, the accounting focus on tangible assets makes little sense now that intangible assets are the overwhelming source of value. Shareholder value analysis can avoid both these biases. But to achieve its potential in guiding the formulation of strategy in firms, SVA needs marketing. Similarly, marketing needs SVA if it is to make a greater contribution to strategy. And, I conclude, strategy needs both marketing and SVA.

Shareholder value needs marketing

Shareholder value is tautological without a creative marketing strategy. It provides a tool for calculating the value added from any given growth, profit and investment projections. But what drives these projections is outside the financial model. SVA does not address how managers can identify and develop the strategic value drivers that accelerate growth, increase profit margins and lever investments. These tasks are the province of marketing. At the heart of SVA is the concept of competitive advantage. In competitive markets, only by creating customer preference through lower costs or a superior offer, can a company earn profits above the cost of capital, that is create shareholder value. Marketing provides the tools for creating such a competitive advantage. These are frameworks for analysing customer needs and identifying opportunities for growth, techniques of competitive analysis, and systems for measuring and enhancing customer loyalty.

Because many companies have lacked a market orientation, SVA has been taken over by the finance function. Lacking the concepts and experience to build value through strategies to develop competitive advantage and growth, financial directors have relied upon what they can control. In a majority of companies, shareholder value has become synonymous with rationalization and downsizing. Such strategies rarely create value because investors can usually see that while they produce a temporary fillip to profits and cash flow, they do not offer sustained growth in profits. Today, stock markets are offering the most dramatic rewards to innovative companies that promise growth and competitive advantage, almost irrespective of whether or not they are currently profitable or generating cash. Only when married to effective marketing can SVA be dynamic and growth-orientated. Without marketing, SVA is just another accounting tool that sacrifices long-term competitiveness for short-term profits.

Marketing needs shareholder value

Shareholder value is a great opportunity for marketing professionals. Traditional accounting, by focusing on short-term profits and ignoring intangible assets, marginalizes marketing. In contrast, SVA can bring to the fore the real strategic value drivers in today's markets in four ways.

First, SVA roots marketing into a central role in the boardroom process of strategy formulation. The language of the modern board is finance. Actions have to be justified in terms of their ability to increase the financial value of the business. In the past marketing has not been able to measure and communicate to other disciplines the financial value created by marketing activities. This has resulted in marketing professionals being undervalued and sidelined. Now SVA offers marketing a direct way to show how marketing strategies increase the value of the firm. It provides the framework and language for integrating marketing more effectively with the other functions in the business.

Second, SVA provides marketing with a stronger theoretical base. Traditionally, marketing has tended to see increasing customer loyalty and market share as ends in themselves. But today, top management requires that marketing view its ultimate purpose as contributing to increasing shareholder value. No longer can marketers afford to rely on the untested assumptions that increases in customer satisfaction and share will translate automatically into higher financial performance. This dilemma now suggests a reformulation of the marketing discipline as about developing and managing intangible assets – marketing expertise, customer and channel relationships and brands – to maximize economic value. This view of marketing is both theoretically appealing and places marketing activities in a pivotal role in the strategy formulation process.

Third, SVA encourages profitable marketing investments. Conventional accounting has treated marketing expenditures as costs rather than investments in intangible assets. Because the long-term profit streams generated by such investments are ignored, marketing in many businesses is underfunded. SVA, however, is future-orientated: it encourages the long-term effects of marketing expenditures to be explicitly estimated. As we have illustrated, brand-building investments that would be discouraged under conventional accounting procedures because they reduce current profits, are shown as value creating under SVA.

Finally, SVA penalizes arbitrary cuts in marketing budgets. Management have found marketing budgets an easy target when they needed to improve short-term profits. For example, cutting brand support will normally boost profitability without significantly affecting sales in the short run. The fact that such policies invariable lead to longer-term erosion in market share and price premiums has been ignored. Now SVA gives marketing management the tool to demonstrate that these short-term cuts destroy rather than build value. Informed shareholders are likely to react to ad hoc cuts in brand support by reducing the market value of the company.

Strategy needs shareholder value and marketing

Like any technique, SVA is no panacea, and in particular it is only as good as the assumptions that are fed in as input. The key inputs are:

- forecasts of sales growth;
- operating margins; and
- investment requirements for at least five years ahead.

These all depend upon good judgements about the evolution of the market and the firm's ability to sustain a competitive advantage. The cost of capital is also a critical variable and again depends upon assessments, particularly upon the degree of risk the unit or brand faces. Different judgements can lead to significant differences in estimates of the shareholder value created from a particular strategy.

Another key issue is the estimate of terminal or residual value. SVA splits the estimation of shareholder value into two components:

(1)   The present value of cash flow during the planning period; and
(2)   The residual value, which is the present value of the cash flow that occurs after the planning period.

For growth businesses the overwhelming proportion of value arises in the terminal value. Unfortunately, it is difficult to be confident about this value. The reason for splitting the estimation into two components is that managers cannot forecast much beyond five years or so. So how can one decide the reasonableness of the terminal value, which is making an assumption about cash flows up to 20 or more years ahead? Different assumptions can give quite different estimates of shareholder value.

Finally, a concern has been that SVA underestimates the value of new ventures by overestimating the risks involved. In practice, the risks are not as high as they appear because managers can often proceed step-by-step, piloting on a small scale new projects before major investment have to be made. More recently, SVA has been extended with the development of real options analysis (see Chapter 4, 'Strategy as Intention and Anticipation') to fill this important gap.

While, as with any model, good practitioners will recognize its limitations (Chapter 12 explores these a little further), SVA is genuinely important for the development of marketing and strategy. Both as an intellectual discipline and a business function, marketing has not had the impact on strategy that its importance justifies. To a significant measure this has been due to the lack of definition of the objectives of marketing and to its failure to become integrated with the overall value-creating goal of the firm. Value-based marketing overcomes much of this deficiency by redefining the objective of marketing as creating value for shareholders and adopting the tools of SVA to evaluate proposed marketing strategies.

Similarly, if levels of disagreement as to what strategy is about is as it was described in Chapter 1 (or, indeed, if the many perspectives and musing grasped at by my co-authors here), are anything to go by, strategy currently seems like a rabble in search of

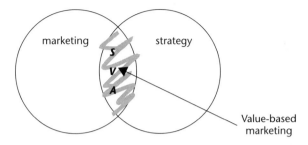

Figure 11.2   Strategy and marketing connected by SVA and value-based marketing

a unifying purpose. If we take value-based marketing seriously it can be seen as reconnecting the multiple directions that strategy and marketing have added to their ambits
through SVA. Thus, it can provide strategic thinkers in organizations with a clear objective goal. A goal that provides a basis external to the particular whims or specific subjective backgrounds or views of individual managers, or simply moving the flow of
decisions past. A goal beyond leaving things to chance and clever hindsight after the
fact (as implied in the Dilbert cartoon near to the head of this chapter). A goal that
can provide a centralizing, or unifying, focus on adding value for the owners of organizations for the long term.

Case Box 11.1   Sigma Biscuits

Sigma, from Associated Biscuits, is a brand leader in the impulse biscuit market.
It had succeeded in maintaining sales despite the growth of retailer own label
brands and competitive new product launches from Cadbury and Nestlé. Awareness is very high and consumer attitude and usage studies confirm the brand's
strong profile and franchise. However, a newly appointed finance director is less
impressed about the brand, pointing to its low operating margin, lack of growth
in recent years, and heavy spending on advertising and marketing. He observed
that spending on communications amounted to 10 per cent of sales and ex-
ceeded profits by 150 per cent.

You are the marketing manager, and you have proposed a communications
budget of £3 million; the same as in the previous year. But your finance director has calculated that the break-even on this expenditure amounted to
£7.5 million (£3 million divided by the contribution margin of 50 per cent) and
was unwilling to endorse the budget unless marketing could promise such a
sales increase. He has duly stated that profits would be higher without the campaign, with a cost saving of up to £3 million. He has demonstrated this on a
spreadsheet to you:

Column A shows the budget as it stands;
Column B shows the profits with no communications support;
Column C shows the budget with the communications budget halved; and
Column D shows profits if advertising is eliminated and sales decline as a result
by 5 per cent.

	A	**B**	**C**	**D**
Sales (£ million)	30	30	30	28.5
Variable costs	18	18	18	17.1
Contribution	12	12	12	11.4
Communications and marketing	3	0	1.5	0
Overheads	7	7	7	7
Operating profits	2	5	3.5	4.4

You are alarmed since this all clearly showed – to your surprise – that profits were significantly higher without the advertising and communications support. You also know that there is no way that sales next year will increase by the 25 per cent necessary to achieve the break-even on the communications budget.

You decide to discuss the problem with a friend who is a City analyst.

The analyst criticizes the financial director's approach. She says the director was using an old-fashioned accountancy approach that investors jettisoned years ago. Investors, she says, were interested in long-run performance, not just next year's results. Also, she claims that shareholders are interested in cash, which is a much more objective and relevant figure than accounting profit. Finally, she thinks that the financial director is taking a very naive and short-term view of marketing and consumer behaviour. Surely, she points out, cutting marketing support will lead to a long-term erosion of the brand. It will also hit margins because retailers will need to be offered more discounts to give shelf space to a declining brand.

Drawing a small calculator from her handbag, she suggests exploring three valuations: the value of the brand to shareholder's with the past strategy being continued; the value using the financial director's plan; and an alternative strategy to boost operating profits.

1.   Value with the Continuing Strategy

Under the continuing strategy, you believe that Sigma can hold market share and profits will remain around the present level for the foreseeable future. This means that shareholder value could be estimated by the perpetuity method. Assuming a tax rate of 30 per cent and a cost of capital of 10 per cent, then the value of the business was now worth £14 million (after tax profit or NOPAT is £1.4 million. Dividing by the cost of capital at 10 per cent gives £14 million).

2.   Value under the Financial Director's Plan

You reconsider the implications of the financial director's plan. He thought that the idea of losing 5 per cent of sales if advertising and brand support was abandoned was reasonable. But if there was no brand support in the future years he thought it obvious that sales would continue to decline. He estimated this decline as around 2.5 per cent a year. Having negotiated with the major retail chains he knew that a declining brand would become unattractive to them and he would have to pay higher discounts to retain shelf space. He figured this would have the effect of eroding prices by 2 per cent a year. The table below shows the new scenario.

In the first year, the financial director is correct: profits and cash flow were higher if the advertising and marketing budget are cut. But from the second year, profits and cash flow fall precipitously as market share and prices erode. At £9.56 million, shareholder value is one-third less under this policy than under the current strategy.

Implications of eliminating discretionary communications spending (£m)

Year	0	1	2	3	4	5
Cases (m. units)	20.00	19.00	18.53	18.06	17.61	17.17
Unit price (£)	1.50	1.47	1.44	1.41	1.38	1.36
Sales	30.00	27.93	26.69	25.50	24.36	23.28
Variable costs	15.00	14.25	13.89	13.55	13.21	12.88
Contribution	15.00	13.68	12.79	11.95	11.16	10.40
Comms & mkg	3.00	0.00	0.00	0.00	0.00	0.00
Overheads	10.00	10.00	10.00	10.00	10.00	10.00
Operating profit	2.00	3.68	2.79	1.95	1.16	0.40
NOPAT	1.40	2.58	1.96	1.37	0.81	0.28
Net investment		−0.83	−0.50	−0.48	−0.45	−0.43
Cash flow	1.40	3.40	2.45	1.84	1.26	0.72
Df		0.91	0.83	0.75	0.68	0.62
DCF	1.40	3.09	2.03	1.38	0.86	0.44

Cumulative present value	7.81
PV of continuing value	1.75
Shareholder value	**9.56**

3.   *Value under an Alternative Strategy*

The analyst suggests that if the financial director is determined to improve short-term profits, then a strategy that might do less permanent damage to the brand would be to raise the price by 5 per cent. She suggests that a leading brand such as Sigma would be expected to have a lower than average price elasticity, say around −1, suggesting this might erode the number of cases sold by around 5 per cent. You and the analyst are pleased with the numbers that are generated from these assumptions: operating profits jump by nearly 40 per cent to £2.77 million and shareholder value increases to £19.38 million. The market share loss over the planning period is only 5 per cent as against nearly 15 per cent under the financial director's plan.

In summary, the three options gave the following figures:

	Shareholder value	Market share (year 5)
Current policy	£14,000,000	34 per cent
Finance director	£9,560,000	29 per cent
Alternative policy	£19,380,000	32 per cent

1.   Assess the assumptions behind your financial director's calculations.
2.   What do you think the future strategy for Sigma Biscuits should be?
3.   How would you present your thinking back to your financial director?

Names used in this case have been disguised.

Source Material and Recommended Further Reading

Marketing emerged as a separate subject of study at the beginning of the twentieth century. These early years are often called the *production era*, when the economic focus was on increasing production and product quality. Marketing in these years was concerned mostly with distribution and logistics – how to efficiently make the goods available to a waiting market. The production era gave way to a *sales era* as increasing competition made it more difficult to find markets for the volumes modern factories could produce. Marketing in this era became concerned with advertising and sales promotion techniques – how to create customer awareness and convert sales.

Modern marketing proper started with the articulation of the *marketing concept* by writers such as Peter Drucker and Theodore Levitt. The marketing concept argued the key to corporate growth and profits was researching the customers' needs and developing products to meet these needs. Levitt's 1960 article, 'Marketing Myopia', in *Harvard Business Review*, was particularly influential in raising awareness of the importance of marketing. So too were the works of Peter Drucker, which articulated a theory and practice of management that put marketing at the centre of business strategy. The marketing concept led to the development of sophisticated market research tools and a focus on market segmentation and branding. The most influential textbook of the past 20 years which has mirrored and described these trends is Philip Kotler, *Marketing Management*, 10th edn (Englewood Cliffs, NJ: Prentice-Hall, 2000).

The table shown here as Table 11.1 is adapted from J.A. Pearce and R.B. Robinson Jr, *Strategic Management. Formulation and Implementation*, 3rd edn (Homewood, IL: Irwin, 1988). They incorporated ideas from P. Doyle, 'The Realities of the Product Life Cycle', *Quarterly Review of Marketing*, Summer 1976, 1–6; H. Fox, 'A Framework for Functional Coordination', *Atlantic Economic Review*, November–December 1973, 21–30; C.W. Hofer, *Conceptual Constructs for Formulating Corporate and Business Strategy* (Boston: Intercollegiate Case Clearing House, 1977); P. Kotler, *Marketing Management* (Englewood Cliffs, NJ: Prentice-Hall, 1988); and C. Wason, *Dynamic Competitive Strategy and Product Life Cycles* (Austin, TX: Austin Press, 1978).

The Internet era has led to a further refocusing of marketing towards an *individualized marketing concept*. This argues that the information revolution and direct marketing techniques now allows firms to talk and customize products to individual customers. Don Peppers and Martha Rogers' *Enterprise One to One* (New York: Doubleday, 1997) describes these ideas.

Over the past decade at least, the marketing literature has reflected a lack of confidence about the contribution of marketing and where it is heading. Concerns are expressed about its lack of original contributions, whether it has a distinct body of knowledge or whether it simply applied economics or psychology, whether it should be a separate function in the firm, and what types of activities and organizations should be marketing orientated. The most important academic journal is the American Marketing Association's *Journal of Marketing*, which has regularly debated these issues. For a recent discussion of the controversies see the special issue, 'Fundamental Issues and Directions for Marketing,' *Journal of Marketing*, 63, 1999. Criticisms about the relevance and contribution of marketing have also come from managers and consultants. See, for example, John Brady and Ian Davis, 'Marketing's Mid-Life Crisis', *McKinsey Quarterly*, 2, 1993, 110–21.

Modern shareholder value analysis is usually dated from Alfred Rappaport's *Creating Shareholder Value* (New York: Free Press, 1986). However, the basic ideas of discounted cash flow analysis go back much earlier. The distinctive idea of shareholder value analysis was that the financial techniques that had been applied to individual investment projects could be developed and applied to business strategies as a whole. Another influential work was that G. Bennett Stewart, *The Quest for Value* (London: Harper Business, 1990), which described the parallel concept of economic value added popularized by consultants Stern Stewart. Tom Copeland, Tim Koller and Jack Murrin, *Valuation. Measuring and Managing the Value of Companies* 3rd edn (Chichester: Wiley, 2000), is a comprehensive review of the theory. Consultants have developed much of the practical work on shareholder value. One of the most successful groups has been Marakon Associates. Their approach is described in James M. McTaggart, Peter W. Kontes and Michael C. Mankins, *The Value Imperative* (New York: Free Press, 1994).

The ideas in this chapter are explained in greater detail in Peter Doyle, *Value-Based Marketing: Marketing Strategies for Corporate Growth and Shareholder Value* (Chichester: Wiley, 2000).

This chapter argues that despite all the emergent 'new-age' approaches to strategy and MBA students who spurn 'harder' subjects like financial management, companies, while they may talk this soft strategy talk, still walk the **numbers** walk. This chapter, following on from Chapter 11, examines how strategy, rather than just being measured by the interpretation of market data, economic value added (EVA), shareholder value (SHV) and other 'financials', is actually driven by these numbers. Hence, if we wish to understand where strategy comes from we ignore them at our peril. This chapter argues that we have been led to ignore them because of an unfortunate schism between the world of strategy theory and the real world of managers. This chapter seeks to reconnect these two realms. If you tend to avoid or downplay 'the numbers' then you are doing yourself and your company a disservice. You will be a more resourceful strategist for understanding and confronting this split and critiquing how numbers are used and followed in your organization.

12 Strategy as Numbers

CHRIS SMITH

Engineer:	My analysis shows that your pet project isn't feasible.
Boss:	Try working the numbers.
Engineer:	That wouldn't change the underlying reality.
Boss:	What if we massaged the numbers?
Engineer:	Massaging the numbers means the same thing as working the numbers. You can't make the impossible possible by hallucinating new numbers. . . . do you have any other ideas?
Boss:	That depends on what the phrase 'fiddle with the numbers' means.

(Dilbert)

A case I teach on MBA courses concerns a travel company in Europe. The students enjoy it as they are all holidaymakers and have intrinsic interest in the products and the industry. The competitive advantage enjoyed by the company is that it is the lowest cost operator and the participants narrate and debate the qualitative issues with typical confidence and panache. Then I ask them to *quantify* the degree of cost superiority and guide them through some elementary arithmetic deduction to show it to be of the order of 15–19 per cent. Generally all hell breaks loose as I am accused of the unspeakable crime of bringing 'accounting' into a 'strategy' course. Guarantees are demanded that such a dirty trick will not be played in the examinations. A course on strategy is not about numbers!

In this chapter I am going to suggest that this response is more than a reflection of educational reductionism or departmental silos. Somehow, over the years, a crack became a gap and then a chasm between what is put forward as strategy and strategizing by the *academic* world, and the most ubiquitous model-in-use in the *real* one – hitting the numbers. This book is an example.

By now you will have absorbed, skimmed or skipped other chapters to reach this one. You will have been told that strategy is ethos, decision, anticipation and so on (and practised mainly by Greek divinities!). You will have gained a sense that 'strategy' is clever, important, perhaps even noble and certainly ethereal. In such a vein a manufacturing director once requested authorization to hire additional subordinates so that he could get away from 'being an operator' and become 'more strategic'. I asked him what he thought was more 'strategic' than running the factories to ever-increasing standards of quality, efficiency and safety as he was currently doing. He did not know but, whatever it was, he wanted time to find out and the increase in fixed overhead (subordinates) would be worth it – he failed to convince me.

Implicit in the views of my students and the manufacturing director is a sense that 'strategy' is the really important thing that they need to grapple with and that financial and operating parameters, that is, numbers, are secondary and less worthy of their time. Many of you in the real world of business may feel vaguely uneasy that this does not reflect the firm you are in, a firm that seems to have an opposite orientation: that is, get the numbers right and let the strategy take care of itself. Fear not, you are not alone, and you are not bereft of all (strategic) wit.

I begin this chapter by describing the polarization of strategy and numbers and then outline some past and current models of numbers-as-strategy. I suggest that the modern equivalents of the profit and loss statements, that is, shareholder value (SHV) and economic value added (EVA), have once again made 'numbers' a respectable focus but 'strategists' still underestimate their short- and long-term driving power on organizational behaviour. I offer British Airways as an example of a company that has talked much strategy talk over the past quarter of a decade and challenge the reader to identify the underlying numbers model that has actually driven the organization's actions. I conclude by examining some generally accepted company characteristics that have often puzzled strategists but make perfect sense from a numbers-as-strategy perspective.

The Gap Between Those Who Teach Strategy and Those Who do Strategy

Social science began as attempts to develop generalizable understanding of real-world phenomena. Theories were tested in practice and the results fed back to debunk, develop and test again. In disciplines such as medicine, this model is as generally robust today as it was when Pasteur fought battles against bacteria in his mind, in his lab and in the field. In some arenas, however, a subtle re-orientation emerged. Theory and theorizing became an end in themselves, and a lack of congruence with the real world was seen as a problem with the real world. Psychology, for example, developed a world-view based on controlled experiments with rodents and/or undergraduates (the 'compare and contrast' jokes are legion) while ignoring the notorious lack of transfer to the blooming, buzzing confusion outside the lab. Economics erected pristine models of exchange and utility-maximization on the illusionary foundation of the rational (wo)man. In both disciplines, methods and assumptions that began as learning supports became the infrastructure of knowledge.

Some of the manifest gaps between theory and practice were unilaterally closed by shifting theorizing from an empirical/normative orientation, that is, this is how it *is*, to a prescriptive/ideological orientation, that is, this is how it *should be*. While preserving the internal validity of the models, this move reinforced the ivory tower reputation of academics who met the 'but it ain't like that!' arguments of practitioners with the cool disdain of 'but that's your fault'.

This picture has changed. In this 'postmodern' era it is non-controversial to question the ecological validity of ideology dressed as theory, and psychologists and economists have been doing just this. In the field of strategy, however, a subject richly informed by these two disciplines, we have yet to come to grips with some of the large gaps between what we proselytize for idealized firms and what happens in real firms.

One of the most important contributions of strategy theory, and some would claim its only contribution, is the explanation and ultimately, the prediction, of corporate success and failure. Naturally enough, managers also see this as important and they have evolved their own generic theory of success and failure that can be seen in operation in most annual reports. These attribute corporate over-performance to managerial inputs ('aren't we the clever ones?') and under-performance to malevolent, external forces ('you can't help bad luck!'). Given that bonuses and job tenure are often contingent on firm success it is hardly surprising that executives are self-serving in their assessment of causality as they are not stupid people. Strategy academics, however, who are very clever people, also have difficulty in convincingly explaining the links between strategy and success as anything but idiosyncrasy; and idiosyncrasy, while vastly interesting and entertaining, is not theory.

Research continues to confirm that no single, generalizable variable has any more than a 10 per cent explanatory value in terms of long-term profitability. Notwithstanding this, we academics continue to develop and defend different causal perspectives with the only integrating hope being that we are examining different parts of the same whole (such as Mintzberg's elephant) and that, one day, all will be revealed. So, for example, different strategy authors have attributed Honda's initial success in the United States to different strategic rationales. While one suggests that Honda was just lucky, another praises the company's logically incremental approach. To one the company is a prime example of classical positioning/market segmentation while to another the way that the managers leveraged the firm's core competencies is its obvious strategy success factor. With so many explanations it begins to looks suspiciously as if 'strategy' is no more than *post-hoc* rationalization couched in our particular beliefs and language for our own ends. In other words, we are just like managers when it comes to explaining company success and failure.

I suggest that one of the reasons for the lack of connectedness between strategic theory and practice outcomes is that the dominant theory-in-use of managers has been demoted to a theory of measurement. Archilochus (*c*.650 BC) a Greek poet and soldier wrote, 'the fox knows many things – the hedgehog one *big* thing'. Academics are cunning foxes but managers are canny hedgehogs and they know one very big thing: *all life in the corporate world is a function of the money that is being made or not made.*

We have become increasingly divided, convoluted and arcane in our theorizing as we struggle to escape from the 'banal' view that strategy is, for the typical real-world executive, about the numbers, for the numbers and by the numbers. Academics have tended to explain this orientation, and its attendant behaviours, in dismissively patronizing and pathologizing terms, that is:

- managers are driven by the short-term and the urgent (read 'short-sighted');
- focused on content and the concrete ('not that bright'); and
- shaped by measurement and reward ('greedy').

Such polarizing descriptions are matched by the 'academic-as-airhead' beliefs of a large proportion of the management population. The time has come to reunite practice with our ideas about it.

How Managers Learned to Talk 'Strategy' and Walk 'Profits'

When the giants of the early US industry landscape were building their retailing, railway or automobile empires they had no doubts about the purpose of their existence. Alfred Sloan Jr, one of the earliest 'captains of industry' put it this way:

> The strategic aim of a business [is] to earn a return on capital, and if in any particular case the return in the long term is not satisfactory, the deficiency should be corrected or the activity abandoned for a more favorable one.

These early executives, as with their counterparts today, believed that being in business was first and foremost about making money (profits/cash/return on investment) – everything else followed. However, with the emergence of business 'strategy' as a stand-alone, academic discipline in the 1960s, a shift of emphasis occurred that rapidly gained momentum and prominence. Aiming to loosen the perceived constrictions of an accounting perspective on business, strategy teachers and consultants argued that profits were 'only' a *measure* of the success of *strategy*. Get the strategy right and the money, and everything else, would follow. A focus on the numbers was demeaned as 'operational' and the route to eventual failure unless executed within the framework of a long-term, over-the-horizon, all-encompassing, visionary 'strategy'. Longevity was guaranteed by 'effectiveness' whereas efficiency led to an early or lingering demise. This separation and privileging of 'strategy' over the 'operational numbers' are made manifest in many of strategies earliest distinctions and frameworks (see, for example, Figure 12.1).

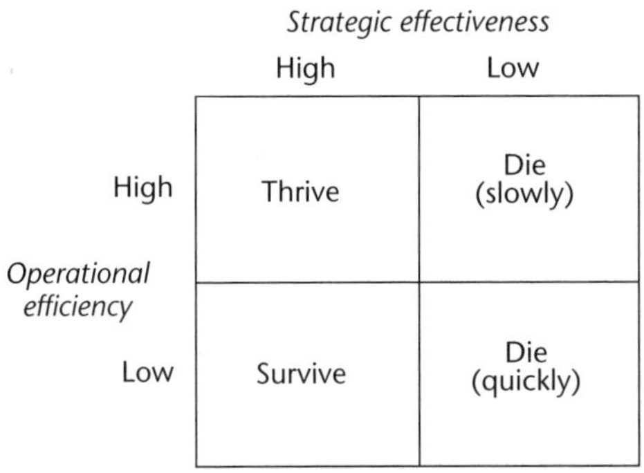

	Strategic effectiveness	
	High	Low
High	Thrive	Die (slowly)
Low	Survive	Die (quickly)

Operational efficiency

Figure 12.1 The effectiveness–efficiency relationship

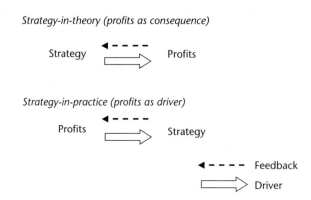

Figure 12.2 Strategy–profit causal links

Business executives seem Odysseus-like in their resourcefulness and they soon learned to chant the mantra of 'strategy first, profits second' in tuneful unison, even adopting slogans such as 'Profits are Nothing, Customer Service is Everything!' to affirm their credentials as strategists (see Chapter 11, Strategy as Marketing for a related argument). However, this is not how they behaved. In the 'good' (i.e. profitable) times 'strategy' was espoused as the *sine qua non* of business success but in downturns (and a 'downturn' for the typical profit-centre executive is any profit achievement below budget) it was ditched. Spending on 'strategic' activities such as advertising, R&D, training, etc. was reduced to bring the profit figure back to where it was supposed to be.

This is still an ongoing aspect of business today. In June 1998, Sir Christopher Bland, the new chairman of a UK-based transport group, explained the cost cutting programme the company was undertaking to deal with a slump in profitability from a £50.7 million annual profit to a £200,000 loss, by remarking that 'We can't afford any more strategy'. Teams of consultants and the previous management team had subjected the National Freight Corporation (NFC) strategy to detailed analysis without noticeable effect. Now it was time to get down to 'real' business.

Note the paradox here. If 'strategy' drives profits, then a downturn in profits should signal an increase in (spending on) 'strategy' but experience and the daily financial headlines tell us otherwise. There are few long-serving executives who have not smiled wryly over this contradiction as it has manifested itself in their arena. The paradox only exists, however, if we continue to insist on a unidirectional link between 'strategy' and 'profit numbers'. The dilemma disappears if we consider the perspective that 'strategy' is a consequence of profits, that is, profits are the chicken and strategy the egg or, for those of a less ornithological persuasion, 'strategy', not profits, is the dependent variable (see Figure 12.2).

Some Numbers-as-Strategy Models

Most causality in social science is recursive in the same way that chickens lay eggs that become chickens that lay eggs ad infinitum, that is, each phenomenon influences and is influenced by the other simultaneously. But in the minds of most people it is

Sales
  – Costs
  ────────
Margin
  – Expenses
  ────────
  Profit
  ════════

Figure 12.3   The standard profit and loss (income) statement

chickens that lay eggs and not eggs that lay chickens. In the same sense the models that follow are logically predicated on some form of profit making activities involving markets, customers, competitors, etc. However, the argument being presented in this chapter is that, in the minds of most managers, it is 'performance' as defined by the underlying model that drives the activities and work of managers and these in turn drive the numbers in the models.

Profits rule!

The most venerable and enduring strategy paradigm in practice is the sales − cost = profits relationship (see Figure 12.3). This has been with us since the ancient trading nations were sending their galleys around the known world in search of profitable exchange.

'Costs' are the traditional 'variable' costs, that is, those that tend to vary with the level of sales volume or operating activity (e.g. labour, material, fuel) and 'expenses' the traditional fixed outgoings that tend to be stable over a wider range of outputs (e.g. rent, depreciation, management). These categories are based on day-to-day reality because, as we are all aware, over the long term all costs are variable. The 'bottom line', a colloquial expression signifying the final, most important condition is accounting slang for 'profit'. 'Profit' has a variety of formulations but in the no-frills world it is what is left after all costs have been subtracted from total sales revenue. There are no 'strategic' competitive or marketing activities that are not derived from sustaining or growing the profit line by either increasing sales revenue (by price or volume) or by reducing either costs or expenses. These fundamental strategic relationships are represented as the classic break-even chart (see Figure 12.4). What this chart illustrates is that, when trying to grow or protect profits, there are 'only' three interrelated factors and their associated mechanisms to be considered:

(1)   Price: how the company increases its prices and/or;
(2)   Volume: how the company sells more goods/services and/or;
(3)   Costs: how the company reduces its costs.

'Only', written thus, signifies that such considerations are neither trivial nor simple. These factors are, after all, the heart of 'strategy' and are linked in a complex and dynamic relationship both inside the firm and within the external environment. Increasing prices may result in such a level of volume decline that total revenues diminish and profits fall. Reducing costs will improve profitability provided those 'costs' are not an important part of maintaining sales. It is easy to get these things spectacularly wrong as the following examples indicate:

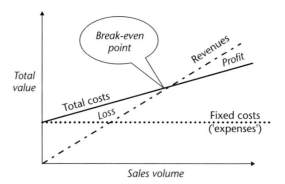

Figure 12.4 The classic break-even chart

(1) Most of the Internet-based business models in evidence over the past decade focused on driving sales through lower prices. Ensuing profits were predicated on lower structural and transaction costs (search, evaluation, order, etc.) then those of earth bound competitors. The problem for most e-businesses was that their marketing and branding 'strategies' proved so costly that the structural and transaction benefits were trivial by comparison and so they went broke in droves. In terms of Figure 12.4, the total costs line remained above the revenue line throughout the (short) life of the businesses.

(2) A UK company acquired a rival in the US. The company now had significant market share and two well-known brands: one UK-based, one US-based. Corporate managers reduced the level of fixed costs of the new company considerably by blending the two accounting/finance, manufacturing, sales, etc. functions into one and retrenching the surplus staff. Operating profits improved immediately. It was too late when they finally realized that the two brands were so different, that is, they sold into different distribution channels, had different 'values', different delivery systems, different pricing, etc., that they could not be co-managed by the same sales people. Sales of both brands declined sharply and the ensuing significant losses more than wiped out the 'savings' in fixed overhead reduction. With reference to Figure 12.4, the total costs line had moved down as the fixed costs level was reduced sharply. Unfortunately the resulting loss of sales volume drove the company below its break-even.

(3) Many 'brand leaders' have attempted to keep their prices high against the prevailing tide of price reduction. Their 'strategies' of higher quality, image, technological advance, etc., were 'differentiators' that were supposed to enable them to maintain a price premium against their less sophisticated competitors. Companies such as Marlboro (cigarettes) and Compaq (personal computers) maintained these premiums until plunging volumes, as customers eschewed differentiation in favour of lower priced options and more spending money, brought new strategic insight, that is, 'you can't fool all of the consumers all of the time'. Using Figure 12.4 again, these companies maintained the slope of the total revenue line until loss of volume drove them below break-even. They then reduced price (decreased the slope of the revenue line) with the result that the break-even point occurred at

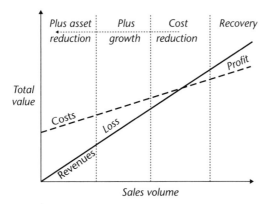

Figure 12.5 Influence of firm's break-even on profit recovery strategy
Source: S. Slatter, *Corporate Recovery: A Guide to Turnaround Management* (Penguin, 1984).

a higher sales volume! (They also undertook cost-reduction programmes to reduce their break-even point.)

When companies are achieving their profit goals they tend to espouse the ensuing, or coincidental 'strategies' as primary causal factors and de-emphasize the underlying profit and loss model. However, when profits falter then the fundamental model re-emerges and drives the necessary actions. As the mapping of various turnaround strategies onto the break-even chart indicates (Figure 12.5), the actions needed are contingent on the degree of negative profit variance. Cost reduction (reduce employee levels, pay less for materials, do less advertising, make executives travel economy instead of business class, etc.) will suffice when the company is just below its break-even. The bigger the gap, however, the more the cost surgery becomes structural (e.g. asset sales) rather than cosmetic, and revenue growth becomes essential (e.g. through price reduction) to keep the stricken organization breathing.

Even when dressed in the language of markets, customer segments, capabilities, etc., the basic (i.e., real) strategy model of the practising manager is never far below the surface as the driver of his/her actions. The quest for 'higher value-added' products by manufacturing companies is an example of the profit and loss model disguised as 'strategy'. Some companies seek to change their product mix to increase their overall margin. Since its demerger from its pharmaceutical arm Zenecca in 1993, the UK chemical company ICI has been seeking such higher margin sanctuaries. It has moved into new industries in which higher margins are generally available and into segments of its existing industries with similar characteristics. At the same time it has exited low margin, commodity sectors. A significant fall back in revenues and profits accompanied by a bold advance in debt have resulted from this margin-retreat 'strategy' and these factors leave the company facing a real challenge to survive in the early 2000s.

Furthermore, and by way of concluding this sub-section, aggregating the sales, costs and profits of all the companies in an industry gives the margins and the overall profitability of that industry and its component strategic groups. Unsurprisingly

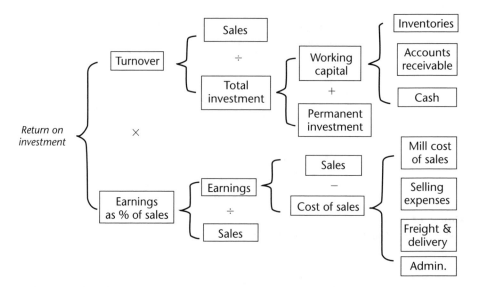

Figure 12.6   The DuPont return on investment format
Source: H.T. Johnson and R.S. Kaplan, *Relevance Lost: The Rise and Fall of Management Accounting* (Boston, MA: Harvard Business School Press, 1987).

'unattractive' industries like 'unattractive' groups and 'unattractive' companies have 'unattractive' margins/profits. Equally unsurprisingly, companies try to extricate themselves from such unattractive places or make them more attractive, that is even at the industry level the income model drives choice and implementation.

Cash (and opportunity cost) is king! – towards economic value added (EVA) and shareholder value (SHV).

Chapter 11, 'Strategy as Marketing', developed a theme by connecting the realms of strategy and marketing by way of the concept of added shareholder value (SHV). The next few paragraphs take a step back to examine the emergence of SHV, and the related concept of economic value added (EVA), and look at why such concepts have become increasingly popular.

The DuPont Company, in the form of its famous 'return on investment' charts, beefed up the basic profit and loss model and made the connections shown in Figure 12.6.

The company had over 350 different charts along these lines in a special chart room and these served as diagnostics and guides for company-wide policy and action by top management. The formulae acted as a constant reminder to managers that profits per se are meaningless without being made relative to the value of the investments used to bring about those profits.

Return on investment (ROI), return on capital employed (ROCE), return on equity (ROE), return on assets managed (ROAM), and so on, are all variants of relative profitability the relative merits/weaknesses of each the interested reader can explore in any standard finance text (see the reading list at the end of this chapter for a selection).

Hurdle rates of relative profitability incorporated the opportunity cost of the capital invested. This reflected the fact that a company is a wealth-creation vehicle *for its investors*. Investors are interested in gaining a return on their capital that is higher than keeping it in the bank or putting it to other uses. This is the 'opportunity' they forgo in order to take a stake in a company and any return needs to take this forgone opportunity into account.

Basic or extended 'profits' models such as those listed above drive managers to perform short-, medium- and long-term activities to protect and grow absolute and relative measures of profitability. Human beings are at their most creative when seeking to maximize their own well-being. Hence it is a cause of little surprise that operating managers, whose bonuses and promotions are contingent on profitable performance each year, soon learned how to optimize the appearance of the numbers per se. Two such tricks of the trade became sufficiently institutionalized to cause major problems for investors.

(1) The practice of under-investing in operating businesses to ensure that the denominator of the ROI equation decreased, hence the income required to achieve the hurdle rate of return became easier to attain.
(2) Focusing on corporate growth in earnings per share (EPS) as a major indicator of firm, and hence shareholder, wealth. Thus, while EPS grows as profits within a company grow, it is also 'enhanced' by buying other profitable companies with an EPS higher than that of the purchasing firm. The demand for perpetual EPS growth led to demand for further acquisitions. Eventually mighty conglomerate edifices collapsed under the weight of debt servicing costs, leaving investors out-of-pocket and in need of more valid valuation models.

The investors' perspective subsequently became the major driver of company valuation and measurement. At one time the 'owners' of most businesses really did own them legally and psychologically in the sense of 'this is me and mine'. These owners, often part of a family dynasty, also managed their businesses at the most senior levels with the whippersnapper offspring having to endure a rite of passage to the executive suite through various of the company's departments, functions and territories. Hence the demands for performance from the firm depended on the particular motivations of its particular owners. While some aspired to higher financial returns, others followed more eclectic drivers. Because of this a problem often arose for the managers of publicly listed companies who have to compete with owner-managed companies. One CEO complained that while he is forced to manage to a profit hurdle of 20 per cent ROI, his owner-managed (male) competitors have lower, self-evolved aspirations of 'the 3Ms – the mistress, the (luxury) motor and the mortgage (on the luxury home)'. As long as profits cover the financing of these lifestyle investments they are deemed satisfactory.

Professional (i.e. non-owner) managers now run the medium and large firms in the Western world, and increasingly, in other parts of the globe. 'Owners' are *shareholders* – investors who have legal title to part of the paper manifestation of the company solely on the presumption (hope) of financial gain from increases in the stock price or dividend. Most of these investors are not individuals but investment firms for whom the only drivers are *profitability* and *growth*. Wealth appreciation, through adroit investment, is the only inducement they offer to their own subscriber/investor/shareholder 'owners'. Hence the 'ownership' of a company has become dispersed to the extent that most of its 'owners-in-remove' do not even know of their 'ownership' and do not care as long as their investment increases in value over time. This means, referring back to the diagram in Figure 12.2, that numbers now drive strategy more than ever rather than the other way around which 'strategy-in-theory' assumes. This is a worrying disparity if our aim is to understand how strategy happens and to subsequently influence its happening.

The importance of the wealth-growth driver on modern businesses cannot be overstated. Many millions of individuals, either through their own actions or through the pension contributions they make at work, are investing money today in the hope that it will grow to enable them to lead a comfortably self-sufficient life when they retire. This is being encouraged, and sometimes mandated, by governments as actuarial calculations indicate that welfare contributions from existing and future taxpayers cannot sustain government payments to a retired sector that is growing substantially as a proportion of the population. For example, all employers in Australia must, by law, be paying at least 8 per cent of each employee's wage into a fund to be invested for that employee's retirement. Billions of dollars collected in this way are invested in stocks and shares on the assumption of growth in the value of that security. What this means for listed companies is that *no matter how profitable the company is today it must be more profitable tomorrow* or its investors will sell their shares to buy more growth-promising firms. This is because today's share price reflects today's profitability and the 'normal' growth inherent in that profit stream. To drive growth in the share price, profit streams over and above this 'normal' level must be promised. Like perpetual motion, perpetual growth in profitability is a challenging dynamic that forces managers to pay unremitting attention to numbers.

Using SHV and EVA

The shareholder value (SHV) and economic value added (EVA), which have become especially popular models of measuring performance over the past few years, specifically take the investor's welfare as the main driver for managerial action. Their popularity initially derived from dissatisfaction with traditional methods of assessing return to investment (ROI and ROE) and to shareholders (EPS). These parameters had proven unreliable and, more importantly, too susceptible to managerial 'spin' as the two 'tricks' described above make clear. Also 'profits' or 'earnings', as well as being defined differently under different methods take no account of risk, investment requirements, dividend policy or the time value of money, that is, valuation models moved from an accounting to an economic perspective.

Economic value added and shareholder value are models that address the accounting derived problems by making two major refinements to profit-based paradigms:

(1) First, they emphasize that a rate of return is needed that takes into account the risk-related, opportunity cost of the money being invested to generate that return. The fundamental premise is that, unless the return generated is at least as great as the total cost of capital invested, then the value of the shareholders funds is being eroded. While this philosophy was well established at the level of capital investment *within* companies it had not been applied to the company as a capital investment itself until EVA and SHV became prominent in the 1990s.

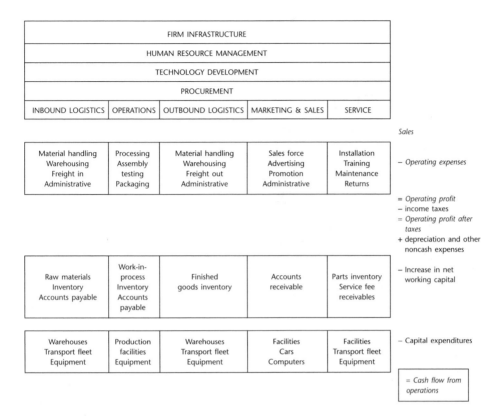

Figure 12.7 Links between value chain and cash flows
Source: A. Rappaport, *Creating Shareholder Value: the New Standard for Business performance* (New York: Free Press, 1986).

(2)   Second, they assume current and future *cash flows* as being the major strategic goal of the company rather than profits. Cash is the ultimate, hard measure of wealth and has the advantage of not being as subject to variable definition or to as many manipulations (without direct lying – see the Dilbert quote at the head of the chapter).

The SHV of a company is defined as its corporate value (the present value of current and future cash flows from operations discounted at the weighted average cost of debt and equity) minus its current debt. The technicalities of calculation demand the addition of discounted cash flows from operations in the forecast period plus a figure for the residual value after this period. The use of discounted cash flow as the main driver of value is not as straightforward as it might seem as changes in assumptions about hurdle rates, forecast cash flows and the forecasting horizon cause significant variations in the final figure.

Shareholder value caught the eye of the investing community and large companies began to use the measure, as well as the associated clichés about shareholders being the centre of the universe, to drive the espoused content and conduct of 'strategy'. Figure 12.7 shows how a specific link was made by Alfred Rappaport between the SHV model and Porter's value chain, one of the mainstream models of value-adding strategy that is discussed in Chapter 1. It is notable that the equation which runs down the right-hand side and breaks up the typical distinctions of the value chain into vertical segments, still follows the basic 'sales − costs = profits' core, although the emphasis has shifted to cash generation.

The EVA model, based even more stringently on increasing the wealth of shareholders through share price appreciation, differs in nuance and emphasis from the SHV variant but has the same fundamental underpinnings. EVA is what remains after the total cost of capital, calculated by multiplying the weighted percentage cost of capital by the total capital invested, is subtracted from net operating profits. While the SHV of the company is the actual calculation of the net present value (NPV) of all future cash flows, the EVA model accepts the market capitalization of the company as (the market's assessment of) its net present value.

While both models promote share ownership for employees, and particularly managers, EVA supporters emphasize to a greater extent the importance of having EVA-linked, but uncapped, incentive schemes. Hence employees become shareholders but are also directly rewarded for having unlimited horizons for growth in investor wealth. Proponents of EVA claim a high rate of conversion of major corporations from ROI/EPS orientations and, more significantly, rapidly increased market capitalization of those companies. So powerful is the aura of EVA, that even the announcement of its planned adoption by a firm has resulted in share price increases of as much as 30 per cent in the next week.

The sophisticated terminology and quasi-scientific calculations of these models have made managers' focus on strategy-as-numbers more respectable. Before this, they risked being denigrated as 'short-term', 'accountancy-driven', or worst of all 'non-strategic' if they articulated their underlying strategic model as being the income statement. Now they are eulogized for dedicating their companies to the pursuit of SHV/EVA. Companies such as Coca-Cola and Varity have finally found that the 'profit-based' music to which they danced and the 'strategy' song they sang has the same tune. But where does this leave the various schools of strategy process and content described elsewhere in this book? More sophisticated valuation-based models as the basis of 'strategy' are no better, from a theoretical perspective, than profits being the fundamental driver. Whatever happened to 'strategy first profits second'? What happened is that *it was never true in the first place*, as close inspection of the strategic forays of British Airways (Case Box 12.1) illustrates.

Case Box 12.1 British Airways – Profits in Flight

British Airways (BA) is the flagship airline of the UK. On April fool's day, 1984, the government passed a bill that made BA a public limited company and, in early 1987, shares were sold to an enthusiastic public. Before that and since, the behaviour of BA's management is a good example of a company that, while in reality driven by its profit and loss, balance sheet and cash flow statements, has alternatively beguiled and calmed analysts and shareholders with the seductive language of strategy.

The Airline Industry and Governments

Airlines are part of a global, capital-intensive industry subject to significant national and international regulation. The industry suffers from low margins and is subject to cyclical swings as economic slowdowns bring over-capacity and price pressures. In 'booming' economic conditions more people holiday abroad and executives fly at the (expensive) front of the aircraft. In recessions or during periods of international tension people stay at home and corporate controllers restrict travel costs by reducing travelling and moving those executives who do travel, closer to the (cheaper) tail.

While most free-market oriented countries have privatized their national carriers, others are more reluctant to do so. Even some privatized carriers, however, benefit from various forms of official and unofficial government assistance. Assistance ranges from loans to technically bankrupt carriers to 'nod-and-wink' protection of monopoly positions at beneficially located airports (hubs) or on important routes. In the case of BA, the British government has practised studied non-interference with the airline's domination of the landing slots at Heathrow, one of the world's most important airports. This 'competitive advantage' enables BA to charge significantly higher business fares for trans-Atlantic flights than European or American competitors operating from less strategically located hubs in their own countries.

Market Segmentation of Airline Passengers

Many people use air travel either as part of a holiday or on business. Like any companies in any industry the airlines have many ways of segmenting their markets or customers. 'Market segmentation' often assumes a mystical property when expounded by marketing acolytes.

However, in the case of big airlines it is fundamentally a way of attempting to benefit from legal price discrimination (i.e., some people will pay more than others for the same thing). The trick is to get them to do so without them finding out and hence getting upset. The way this is done is to disguise the sameness of the 'product' by dressing it in fancy frills.

The basic segmentation of airline customers splits them into two groups: those who are using their own money to pay for the ticket (mainly leisure travellers) and those who are using someone else's money (mainly business travellers). Needless to say this is not how the airlines would put it. It will come as no great surprise that the latter group is prepared to spend more to go from A to B than the former, or to use the parlance of the marketer/strategist, the business traveller is less price sensitive. Clearly the airlines cannot simply ask, 'Are you a business traveller?' and then charge *far more* than the leisure fare if the answer is in the affirmative.

As examples of 'far more', consider that in early 2002 the Heathrow–New York business class return fare on BA was quoted at US$5,562, for the same flight the economy ('coach') fare 'without restrictions' was US$1,244.50 and 'with restrictions' it was $490.50. The truly flexible 'take it when you can get it' traveller could do the Heathrow–New York trip with BA for US$206! 'Flexibility' (i.e. being allowed to not turn up and not lose your fare) and frills such as access to airport lounges, more leg-room, edible food and frequent flyer points (a form of legal bribery) are part of business class travel. In this way the higher price of going from A to B can be represented as 'added-value' over the torture of being herded into 'cattle class'.

Whatever the 'added-value' the added costs of these extras are minor compared to the added margins obtained from the higher fares (apply Figure 12.3). The *real* 'added value' can be ascertained by the extent to which business people pay for business class when paying for themselves for their vacation flights. I leave the reader to do his/her own informal survey to test this point.

Profitability Model in Airlines

The profitability model for airlines may be described as:

Profitability = Yield × load factor − cost

This is an industry-specific version of profit = average price × volume − costs, where:

Profitability is measured as the operating income per available seat mile (ASM) where an ASM is one seat flown one mile with or without a passenger.

Yield is the total operating revenues divided by the number of revenue passenger miles (RPM). This measure captures the average sales revenue being made from each mile that a passenger travels, as one RPM is one seat flown one mile with a passenger in it.

Load factor is the ratio between RPMs and APMs and is a capacity utilization measure for the (expensive) aircraft.

Cost is the total operating expenses per ASM.

i.e. $\dfrac{\text{Income}}{\text{ASMs}} = \dfrac{\text{Revenue}}{\text{RPMs}} \times \dfrac{\text{RPMs}}{\text{ASMs}} - \dfrac{\text{Expenses}}{\text{ASMs}}$

Hence to increase profitability, 'strategy' means increasing the average price being obtained and/or increasing the volume of passengers and/or reducing costs. The reader might be forgiven for thinking that this is hardly Nobel Prize material. It is not, but it *is* the underlying model that drives every executive in the airline industry and all the strategies devised and implemented in that industry, as we shall see in the case of BA.

The Strategies of BA

The turnaround of BA from moribund, inefficient, over-staffed, disinterested state-owned behemoth to energetic, productive, lean, customer-driven privatized giant of the industry is the stuff of corporate legend and MBA business case. Prior to 1981, BA was a profitable airline despite its inefficiency, over-staffing and customer-unfriendliness. But the airline world was changing as deregulation began to remove the government-based barriers that protected state-owned ineptitude from competition. In 1981 the company was losing money at the rate of nearly £200 a minute. Unfortunately for the British Government, this was two years after it had announced plans to privatize its airline.

The company's newly appointed chairman Sir John (now Lord) King settled on the most common of actions to stem the losses – he made swingeing cost cuts (i.e., he reduced the 'expenses' component of the airline profitability equation above). He imposed salary freezes, closed loss-making routes, offices, staff clubs, etc., and, most significantly, reduced the staff numbers to an eventual 36,000 in 1984 compared with 56,000 in 1980. He achieved much of this by the use of generous inducements for people to leave. The newly appointed chief finance officer, Gordon Dunlop, took these and future redundancy costs against the 1981–2 profits as, at the same time, he wrote down the value of the fleet (this was to ease the impost of depreciation charges in future years). Thus by the generous use of taxpayers' money King was able to announce a record loss for the year to 31 March 1981 of £545 million. In this way he stemmed current losses but also set up a less onerous operating and asset cost base for the future privatized company.

Having carried out this financial 'housekeeping', it was time for 'strategy' – time to become 'The World's Favourite Airline'. Colin Marshall (now Sir Colin) was appointed chief executive in February 1983 and became a crusader for good customer service – a novel idea it seems for the company at the time. A series of workshops were run for all staff throughout the mid-1980s and these 'Putting People First' (PPF) and then 'Managing People First' (MPF) sessions became the catalyst for attitude and behaviour change throughout the company. Other symbols of the new approach were a new advertising agency/campaign, new uniforms, 'awards for excellence' as well as others.

At the same time King fought and won a major political battle to prevent British Caledonian, another UK airline, from winning the rights to some of BA's routes. Clearly, customer service was good but monopoly rights, and the ensuing yield and profitability increases, were better. Having passengers with no choice but to use BA helped with the load factor and income (prices) component of the equation with more certainty than trying to woo them by being customer focused. Following privatization, BA eventually bought Caledonian as it grew through acquisition and partnerships. While this growth was in response to BA's own drivers, increased consolidation and hence concentration of players is typical in capital-intensive industries with the margin-destroying threat of over-capacity perennially in the air; in this case literally.

From 1983 onwards the airline returned to profitability to become one of the world's most profitable airlines in the early–mid 1990s. This was reflected in the soaring share price and happy shareholders. Much was made of customer orientation and employee involvement as the 'strategy' behind this financial good health, culminating in articles on customer service and customer championing in the *Harvard Business Review* in November 1995. Maybe it was those articles that provoked the gods of hubris to respond.

Robert Ayling became chief executive in 1996 and a market capitalization of BA of over £7 billion at that time became one of little more than £3 billion by the time his resignation was announced in early 2000. The share price plunged as profits declined and problem upon problem seemed to beset the company.

Nemesis took various forms. It included a public relations blunder in removing the British flag from the tail fins of the planes. Added to this a three-day strike by disgruntled cabin crew cost the company £125 million and its 'happy employee' reputation. Finally a protracted attempt to form an alliance with American Airlines was scuppered by regulators in Brussels and Washington but not before BA's competitors had taken advantage of their distraction to form alliances of their own. By 1999, BA was the fifth largest airline in the world in terms of passenger miles flown but its profitability was sagging. Whether Ayling was a contributor to the demise or a scapegoat is not an issue here. CEOs are paid what they are paid to be accountable and hence, if things go wrong on their watch they cannot complain at being offered as ritual sacrifice to angry shareholders and analysts. The £1 million plus payout Mr Ayling is reported to have taken with him would have gone some way to ease his disappointment and regret.

In 2000 British Airways changed 'strategic' direction. Profits had declined and the much-lauded 'strategy' of customer service seemed to be having little impact. In particular it seemed to be having little effect on the leisure traveller who was paying with his/her own money and who seemed to persist with the non-strategic belief that a flight is a flight is a flight and hence the cheaper the better. Robert Ayling's last strategic hurrah in 1999 was to unveil that BA was going to become smaller in order to get richer. It was buying smaller planes and planned to pack them with business people who would be pampered into paying business class fares. No longer will the airline struggle to fill two-thirds of its aircraft with ungrateful, low-fare holidaymakers because the planes will not be big enough to need them.

Unfortunately the increasing penetration of the low-fare, no-frills airlines, combined with declining availability in other passenger segments (exacerbated by the events of 11 September 2001) led to increasing losses at BA. And so the new Australian boss Rod Eddington announced yet another strategic analysis in early 2002; the so-called 'Future Size and Shape Project'. At the time of writing this 'new' direction appears to involve more cost cutting (staff and marginal routes to be axed) and wooing back (perhaps with differently branded tickets) those cheapskates who want to fly from A to B as cheaply and quickly as possible. Numbers rule!

1. Can you argue that BA's various 'strategies' are in actual fact the outcomes of the basic profitability equation for airlines outlined above?
2. Can service strategies also be argued to be the result of pricing models (rather than vice versa)?
3. How can you reconcile the paradox of, for example, a 'people first' strategy with recurrent headcount reduction?

A Numbers-Driving-Strategy Perspective on BA

The case box above is not meant to suggest that British Airways (BA) is in any way an abnormal or bad company – quite the contrary. Rather, what it shows is what I believe to be a typical company whose dissonance is caused by the belief that the numbers should follow its strategy. Overall, it is interesting the way that BA management, while manifestly driven by the numbers (i.e., load factors, expenses, RPM, etc.), extolled the *strategies* of 'people first', customer orientation, etc., as the reasons for their profitability. Perhaps they would do better to think through how the later actually follows the former? Below are my thoughts with regard to the questions posed at the end of the case.

Expense reduction was always an ongoing focus within BA and will always have to be in a low-margin, capital-intensive and cyclical industry. Even after all the cost reductions throughout the 1980s and early 1990s another three-year programme to take £1 billion out of costs began in 1996. Included was the planned outsourcing of various services such as catering, which caused high friction with staff and employee antagonism towards Ayling. In 1999, even more cost-cutting targets were announced and these included the plan to reduce headcount by a further 1,000 and so it continues to the present day. It defies rational belief that employees who are viewed as perpetual *costs* to be reduced in pursuit of more viable expense ratios will remain dewy-eyed on being lauded as 'our most valued *assets*'. 'Valued' they *may* be, but (too) expensive they certainly are. Training and employee programmes as 'strategy' help to maintain morale against the deleterious influence of profit-and-loss-driven action (headcount reduction). Of course if such 'strategy' were truly value adding, then its incremental effect would be to require more staff to cope with all those extra passengers.

Revenue per passenger mile (RPM) also remains a key driver and 'customer service' the espoused 'strategy' behind maintaining and developing prices and sales. However, it remains easier and more lucrative to protect prices and sales through monopoly effects. The main source of profits for BA continues to be those price-insensitive executives paying high prices to travel business class from Heathrow and particularly those that travel across the Atlantic. So the all-important Heathrow slots remain firmly in BA's control and the company fights tooth and nail to protect them. The aborted merger with American Airlines, as well reducing costs, would have broadened the monopolistic power of the merged companies. Whatever the intent of BA/American this would have been the natural consequences of the deal.

So where does 'strategy' as customer service fit here? It is a *consequence* of pricing, that is, pricing drives 'strategy'. Where BA is forced to compete away its margin it forgoes all but the most basic of services – 'What do you expect at these prices?' This applies to the people at the back of its normal scheduled flights but BA also created and then sold off 'Go', its own 'no frills' (i.e. seat only) line, to compete directly with the new breed of lower cost/low price carriers. However, when BA is able to exercise its monopoly power with busy executives whose companies are paying the bill the added services are a secondary *distracter* and then merely a *justification* – 'At these prices we better give them something more than a seat!'.

Many of the actions of BA management seem inconsistent and even strange if we look at them through the strategy-drives-profits lens. The 'strategy' is clearly to gain wholehearted commitment from employees to the ideals and practices that will ensure the highest levels of customer service and hence customer satisfaction. High customer satisfaction will then, assumedly, drive repeat business and premium pricing over competitors whose level of customer service lags behind that of BA. This is a well-known strategy mantra that is repeated in many businesses.

The problem is that it is a mantra, and the point of a mantra is that the mantra is not the point. A mantra is a banal verbal aid to help concentrate the mind on the real business of meditation. The real business of business is business, and business is about making money; about increasing volumes and/or increasing prices and/or decreasing costs. If we take this as the start point, then everything that BA management has done as 'strategy' and is doing (except perhaps painting the tail fins with strange designs – see Chapter 2, 'Strategy as Ethos', for more on this) is understandable and, perhaps even predictable. Even the newest tweak to its 'strategy' makes sense from the start point of the components of BA's profitability equation. I leave you to play with this idea further in terms of BA's most recent strategic direction.

It may seem a survival truism that in bad times companies cut costs, reduce assets, freeze spending and so on. It can be argued that this is not a case of profits driving strategy but more a case of necessity suspending strategic initiatives for a while. An analogy might be the case of a yacht dropping its sales (*sic*) during a storm. This does not mean that the crew have ceased trying to reach their destination (achieve their strategy); they are merely ensuring that they survive a tough short-term weather pattern in order to be able to continue on course after it has passed. I think that there are other patterns in firm behaviour, however, that can be argued to support the idea that the numbers (profits/cash) drive strategy.

Further Evidence of Profit Numbers Driving Strategy Patterns

An organization is its long-term patterns of actions (and inactions). It is at this level that some well-established organizational behaviour patterns constitute clumps of evidence that reflect the extent to which numbers drive strategy. As well as those already mentioned we might consider:

- the tendency of successful companies to hang on for too long to former mechanisms of success (the 'buggy whip syndrome' or the Icarus paradox);
- the general consensus that frame-breaking innovation is not driven by big businesses and is in fact resisted by them; and,
- the tendency for executives in difficult times to resort to and accept 'hockey stick' forecasts.

The Icarus paradox and the buggy whip syndrome

The term 'Icarus paradox' is taken from the legend of Icarus, a youth in Greek mythology who defied the gods by flying with wings attached to his back by wax. He flew too near the sun and this melted the wax, causing him to fall to his death. In modern times it describes the tendency of high performing companies to meet their downfall by continuing with the same success formula despite changes in markets or industries that make it obsolete.

Marks & Spencer in the United Kingdom, Chrysler in the United States, and Scandinavian Airline Systems (SAS) in Sweden, are current and past examples as were many of the original 'excellent' companies in Tom Peters' best-seller. A traditional version of this tale concerns the company that was the world's most esteemed maker of fine leather whips for use by the drivers of horse-drawn buggies when these conveyances were the principal means of non-pedestrian transport. The company managers failed to notice the impact of the car on the demand for horse-drawn buggies and hence the demand for buggy whips. The firm continued to make the best buggy whips in the world right up to bankruptcy.

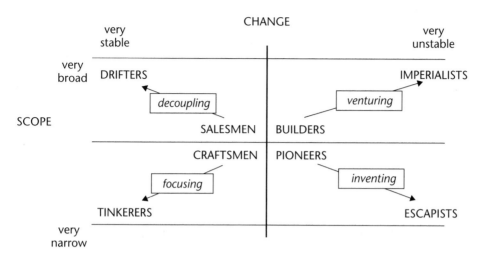

Figure 12.8 The configurations and trajectories arrayed
Source: D. Miller, *The Icarus paradox: How Exceptional Companies Bring About Their Own Downfall* (New York: HarperCollins, 1990).

This 'myth' was popularized in the strategy arena by Danny Miller whose book *The Icarus Paradox: How Exceptional Companies Bring About Their Own Downfall*, became a best-seller. The book develops a very useful table (shown here as Figure 12.8). This examines how managers who set off as useful salesmen, builders, craftsmen and pioneers tend to become not so useful drifters, imperialists, tinkerers and escapists respectively by continuing to do what they did in the past without question even in the light of changed circumstances.

This, like all simple frameworks, can help stimulate debate about how managers, strategists and companies behave. However, the problem with the way it and the Icarus and buggy whip analogies are used is that they tend to lay the blame on managers. The manifestly circular explanation for corporate failures is often that their managers followed the 'wrong' strategy. They failed to look over the horizon and see the changes that were about to engulf them. Even when in decline many of them still continued with their old ways even more vigorously. *Post-hoc* rationales from academic observers tend to be some (thinly disguised) derivative of the 'managers are greedy, short-sighted idiots' school of analysis. It should be noted that these losers were the self-same geniuses of prior success.

Like managers everywhere, these managers were simply adhering to the strategy-as-numbers paradigm. For an extended period the profits/cash figures had been high and growing and hence reinforced the particular actions of the company and the managers. Even during the occasional downturn renewed vigour in pursuing the same actions had always produced the desired effect in the past (i.e., the profits had gone back up). Psychologists call it 'superstitious' behaviour when animals or people engage in behaviours that are correlated with a desired outcome but not causal of it. Thus 'strategy' in these cases is superstitious behaviour based on divining from the numbers. When the final decline commences (and remember no one knows it to be 'final' until afterwards) the managers and hence the company do what they have always done, but this time their redoubled efforts in branding, new products, engineering or whatever do not work.

Profit and 'strategy' have been fellow travellers and while they have appeared to be arm in arm, it has always been profit that has been the guide and leader. Instead of blaming managers, which is too easy, we should understand and question the wider institutional pressures acting upon them; pressures that we all contribute to as members of capitalist societies. Managers who succumb to the Icarus paradox are those who are effective enough to satisfy the criteria held up by these institutional pressures for long enough. The more long-sighted or academically minded questioners of this process generally do not last long enough to have any noticeable impact on their companies.

Big companies do not innovate

Some strategy authors see innovation as the *sine qua non* of long-term strategic success. As Schumpeter highlighted nearly 70 years ago, 'gales of creative destruction' blow away the old ways in society and business, to make way for the new. The problem, from a strategic perspective, is that while God might be on the side of the big battalions on the battlefield of business, it is the small fry that come up with the new weapons of strategic warfare – the frame-breaking products and processes that transform the nature of battle. In fact it is often the case that the big companies do not even recognize innovation and the opportunities offered by it when it is thrust upon them:

- IBM failed to notice the significance of the PC;
- Microsoft missed the significance of the Internet (and then used tried and true 'steamroller' strategy to make up lost ground); and
- even the ultra-innovative 3M tried repeatedly, but to little avail, to avoid putting yellow markers all over the universe.

Not surprisingly most inventions that transform industries are invented outside of that industry's major players.

Take shaving for example. In the beginning these was one blade. Then, 'the twin blade'. Then nothing much happened for a long time, until . . . three blades. Where to next? The big companies who have the capital to invest in new technologies have too much invested in shaving with blades to do much differently. In the same vein, they have too much invested in foams and gels to be too interested in the idea of 'shaving oils'. So smaller companies with less to lose take the risk and the bigger companies eventually cherry-pick their ensuing 'tried and tested' new formulas to their existing product portfolios.

Of course big companies are slow to take up frame-breaking innovations outside of their usual way of doing business. It is obvious if you have a look at the two technology 'S' curves in Figure 12.9 and imagine you are running your large, successful company at position A on the technology curve 'old' where this curve represents the standard enabling technology of the industry.

Say some smart-Alec has invented the technology process labelled 'new' and the big company is fully aware of the long-term ('strategic') implications of this process. Now, what sort of an idiot of a senior manager would proactively take his/her company from A to B at the current time? Profit performance would plunge, SHV/EVA would diminish and he/she would be collecting unemployment benefits shortly afterwards

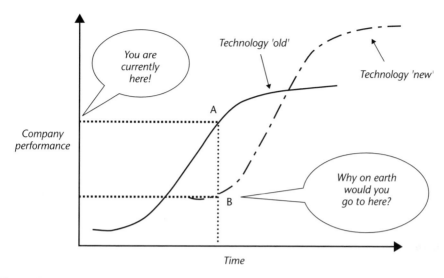

Figure 12.9 The dilemma of moving from technology 'old' to technology 'new'

with the dubious comfort of being a 'visionary' ahead of his/her time. In the long term, of course, the company's profits and shareholder value would be higher than ever but, as the great economist Keynes reminded us, the long term is made up of a lot of short terms and in the long term we are all dead.

So which big companies are more likely to jump to the new technology immediately?: those with nothing to lose. In other words, those with a level of performance that so lags behind their aspirations and/or their competitors that the additional, short-term performance decrement is hardly noticeable, particularly given the possible gains that might accrue. The profit statement dictates that the sensible technology strategy for successful big firms is to hang in there with the old way until the new way is manifestly more profitable and then buy it in.

Hockey stick forecasting

Known in Britain as 'jam tomorrow', this phrase describes the tendency of forecasts of share price, profits, market share, margins, etc., in under-performing businesses to show dramatic improvement in the longer term, while staying constant or continuing to decline in the short term (Figure 12.10). Reality (the ongoing momentum in the numbers) clouds the short term but then the 'strategy' kicks in a year or so later and the sun breaks through. Over several budgeting periods, the same managers make the same shaped forecasts to the same directors with jam remaining on the horizon, but never quite making it onto the plate. The numbers are real and cannot be ignored in the short term. 'Strategy' is unreal but this can only be reflected in the dreamtime of the distant future when all competitors are dead and all customers rounded up and held captive. Notice that management at all levels colludes in this use of strategy-as-hope. The senior people do not toss the budget out because of yet another delusional hockey stick, because the alternative is for managers to 'plan for decline' or to 'plan to do nothing' (can there be any more foolhardy pitch for highly paid strategists to make?)

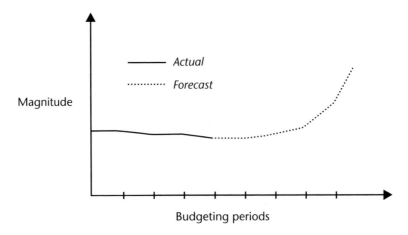

Figure 12.10   'Hockey stick' forecasting

and pray that the board accept, or fail to notice, this. Neither managers nor board would accept such a 'defeatist' or 'idle' stance and if they did then their replacements would certainly not.

I have deliberately used the expression 'strategy-as-hope' because while outside observer might conclude that managers are lying, I have not found this to be common. What I have been surprised at is the extent to which managers believe in these strategic visions of a desired future sometimes to their personal cost. A managerial colleague once showed me his proposed budget presentation based on an outlandish 'hockey stick' of a sales forecast (i.e., one that lacked the necessary and self-preserving time-lag built into the Dilbert cartoon). Despite my reasoning, my entreaties and my bleak assessment of his future career should he persist with his (unnecessarily) overoptimistic presentation, he would not alter the plan. He firmly believed in the numbers he was proposing and paid for that misplaced belief with his job.

Dilbert cartoon reprinted with permission. © Knight features.

The optimism and hope that the jam tomorrow vision inspires are often reflected at the post-budget dinner when everyone shares a sense of accomplishment – as if finalizing the budget and vision is tantamount to achieving both. For a brief, warm evening the reality of the numbers can be put aside, we can all start again with a 'strategy' for the next financial year. The next day those same managers go back to working to improve the numbers bit by bit, hour by hour because in the cold light of day it is the numbers that rule. (Chapter 13, 'Strategy as Decision Making', examines how this combination of the uncertainty and desire for hope in a business combined with the seeming solidity of numbers leads to the control and presentation of 'the numbers' often being a highly politicized realm.)

Conclusion

By now you will have grasped the point I have been making in this chapter. I am sure that some of you will have chortled in recognition, while others will be affronted at the banality of the ideas. But the numbers-to-strategy (versus the strategy-to-numbers) dynamic is one that academic and practising strategists ignore at their peril. The major problem is that the power of profits to drive strategy and strategizing only really becomes *apparent* when companies are doing badly, when 'strategy' is jettisoned as all hands are put to the profit pumps. I write 'all hands' when I should really write 'all *remaining* hands' because one of the first responses to profit decline is often to lighten the load by jettisoning people who, by some miracle, have suddenly become surplus ballast rather than important crew members. Activities that are strategically *critical* when the oceans are calm, for example, advertising, R&D, training programmes, become flotsam and jetsam in stormy seas.

Consequently, and by way of a summary, this 'images of strategy' suggests that those involved with strategy should note the following:

(1)   Recognize that 'the numbers' are drivers and not just measures of strategy.
(2)   Being conscious of the above point means that strategists can begin to see how the numbers can be knowingly 'co-evolved' with a company's strategic develop-ment. Or, using plainer language, they can argue against developments that follow the numbers blindly or unknowingly if such knee-jerk reactions and the sub-sequent to-ing and fro-ing between different strategies (we might term this 'number-chasing') are not in their organization's best interests. Or, alternatively, they can argue against strategies, or statements about strategies, that fail to reflect the reality of the numbers. More to the point, if strategic activities depend on the money available then this needs to be made crystal clear within the company. If absolutism is preached, for example 'Customer service is everything!' and rela-tivism is practised, for example 'Customer service is everything (when we can afford it)!', then cynicism is the rational response. Cynical people, for self-protective reasons, then become adept at lip service rather than customer service because their perspective is that this is what the company *really* wants.
(3)   Finally, from an academic perspective, we need to keep our theorizing firmly con-nected with the profits-as-drivers model of day-to-day management. This model is not pathology to be cured by taking the strategy potion but a long-established, deep-rooted, path-dependent, tacit culture that enables personal wealth and advancement every day and which, when all else fails, *works!*

A well-established observation among strategists is that the failure of a strategy is almost always due to faulty implementation rather than faulty formulation. Another way of viewing this is that when 'strategy' meets real life then real life almost always prevails. For managers, numbers are the stuff of real life so, notwithstanding the complaints of my MBA students and the apparent ambivalence of most of my fellow chapter authors, let us reconnect them with strategy.

Case Box 12.2   Who's Driving Who?

On 12 November 2001, *The Birmingham Post* ran a story entitled 'Restructuring will target cutting costs and airfares.' It reported on how Britain's second largest airline BMI (British Midland International) was set to undergo a major strategic shift and restructure itself into a low-cost airline. A BMI spokeswoman said: 'We are restructuring the airline into a low-cost business. We know our costs are too high and we are looking to see how they can be reduced.' She said the move was part of a restructuring programme that had actually begun earlier, and stressed that, while the group was cutting costs, it had no plans to relaunch itself as a no-frills airline such as rivals Go, EasyJet or Ryanair.

Other national papers followed up the story. *The Guardian* reported Austin Reed, chief executive of BMI, saying that airlines needed to reinvent themselves and cut costs if they were to survive in the current market. Hence, BMI would follow a new strategy of adopting low cost principles and building alliances with other airlines. Mr Reed's statements followed the remarks of British Airways' chief executive, Rod Eddington, who said that BA might have to examine some of the methods of the low-cost airlines. Mr Reed warned that if BMI was to survive, it would have to consider the cost of its entire operation, however, he stressed that BMI had no plans to become a low-cost carrier.

The Independent also described BMI's 'radical plans to transform itself into a "low-cost, full-frills" carrier'. Here Mr Reed was reported as claiming that BMI was likely to make a loss next year and a rethink of the way it operated was necessary if it was to return to profitability. 'BMI remains and will continue to remain a full-service airline and we have no intention of becoming a budget carrier,' he said. 'However, it is vital that if we are to survive in the current climate we have to continually examine the cost of the operation as a whole . . . If we are still going to be profitable we have to adjust our cost base and if we are going to compete, our prices will have to be lower and more transparent.' Mr Reed concluded that BMI would remain a full-service airline but one which operated on 'low-cost principles' offering cheaper fares.

However, an editorial piece in the same paper sounded a note of caution. It claimed that the post-11 September environment had spelled bad news for the bigger full-service scheduled carriers but not necessarily for the low-cost operators such as EasyJet and Ryanair. BMI, it claimed, 'fits, uncomfortably, in between the two ends of the spectrum – neither a flag-carrier for all its transatlantic ambitions, nor a budget airline for all the low fares it offers in comparison with the likes of British Airways'. In response to this, 'BMI has now decided to move closer to the low-cost model, while still retaining its full service status. Pilots will work more hours and planes will stay in the air for longer. The airline will fly to fewer destinations but more often and the fleet will eventually consist of a single aircraft type. The money saved will be used to offer cheaper fares. At the same time there will still be a curtain half-way down the cabin separating business class from the plebs, an executive lounge to call into and a frequent flyer programme . . . It will be fascinating to see whether BMI can pull off this hybrid concept of a low-cost, full-frills airline. The last time it was tried, with [a British airline called] Debonair, it ended in disaster.'

1. By what logic, or equation, do you think do you think BMI may have arrived at the conclusion that their cost structure was too high?
2. What do you think is driving BMI's strategy process?
3. If you were advising BMI would you raise any concerns about how their strategy appears to be being developed in this instance?
4. Select another company that you are familiar with and plot its profits over a timeline. Underneath this graph note any key strategic shifts. Would you say that this company's strategy is driving the numbers, the numbers are driving the strategy, or both?

The case is based on 'Restructuring will target cutting costs and airfares', *The Birmingham Post* (12 November 2001); 'EU denies slots to low-fare airlines: Markets rate pounds 3bn Ryanair number 1 in Europe', *The Guardian* (13 November 2001); 'BMI launches "low-cost, full-frills" restructuring', *The Independent* (13 November 2001); and, 'Outlook: Sir Michael plots new path through turbulence', *The Independent* (13 November 2001)

Source Material and Recommended Further Reading

Nobody makes the point about no single, generalizable variable having any more than a 10 per cent explanatory value in terms of long-term profitability better than my fellow chapter writer Robin Wensley in his 1997 article 'Explaining Success: The Rule of Ten Percent and the Example of Market Share', *Business Strategy Review*, 8(1), 63–70.

See the 1996 summer edition of *Californian Management Review* for alternative explanations of Honda's success. This special issue debates Honda's development at great length and concludes that each of the many reasons that people have linked to Honda's success are valid.

The Alfred Sloan quotation at the beginning of 'How Managers Learned to Talk "Strategy" and Walk "Profits",' comes from Sloan's *My Years with General Motors* (London: Sedgewick & Jackson, 1963). This is one of the first of a long line of 'hero CEO' books.

Figure 12.1 is one of the many contributions to our thinking made by management and strategy pioneer Peter Drucker. His list of publications is prodigious but his 1994 text *Managing for Results: Economic Tasks and Risk-taking Decisions* (London: Butterworth-Heinemann), updates most of his important ideas.

Figure 12.5 is taken from S. Slatter, *Corporate Recovery: Successful Turnaround Strategies and their Implementation* (Harmondsworth: Penguin, 1984). This is a classic text in the corporate decline literature. Its US orientation may be complemented by a series of UK studies in P. Grinyer, D. Mayes and P. McKiernan, *Sharpbenders: the Secrets of Unleashing Corporate Potential* (Oxford: Blackwell, 1988).

The DuPont chart in Figure 12.6 is taken from the challenging view of the accounting discipline offered by H.T. Johnson and R.S. Kaplan's *Relevance Lost: The Rise and Fall of Management Accounting* (Boston, MA: Harvard Business School Press, 1987).

A.H. Vause, *Guide to Analysing Companies* (London: Economist Books, 1997), is a good source book for guiding readers through the application of basic profit ratios.

Alfred Rappaport has been most influential in spreading the SHV gospel. For more on his work, see his *Creating Shareholder Value: The New Standard for Business Performance* (New York: Free Press, 1986); 'Linking Competitive Strategy and Shareholder Value Analysis', *The Journal of Business Strategy*, 7, 1987, 58–68; and 'CFOs and Strategists: Forging a Common Framework', *Harvard Business Review*, January–February 1992, 84–91.

The main developer and proponent of EVA has been the Stern Stewart Consultancy and its approach is captured in A. Ehrbar, *EVA: the Real Key to Creating Wealth* (New York: Wiley, 1998). A typical 'real-business' lauding of the approach is the article 'EVA: The Real Key to Creating Wealth', in *Fortune*, 20 September 1993, 38–50.

While the airline profit model described in the first case box is general, I have taken the specifics from R. Grant, *Contemporary Strategy Analysis*, 3rd edn (Oxford: Blackwell, 1998). This book is close to the standard strategy analysis in the 'classical' (i.e. money comes first) tradition.

There has been a great deal of very good quality business journalism focused on the airline industry since the terrible events of 11 September. Searching ⟨www.ft.com⟩ or scanning recent issues of *The Economist* and *Business Week* will provide much more background on the business model responses by companies such as BMI and British Airways to the ensuing downturn.

The Dilbert cartoon is from Scott Adams, *The Dilbert Principle* (London: Boxtree Press, 1997).

Previous chapters have demonstrated how the environment within which strategy takes place has become faster and more dynamic, more complex and uncertain, and how our understanding of strategy has become more pluralistic or multiple. However, this chapter cautions against taking this to mean that strategy is now at the behest of these contextual changes or that this new complexity simply requires more philosophical or semantic debate or throwing in more information technology. Within the parameters described above, strategy, at its core, still means people in organizations **making decisions**. This chapter argues that in times of increasing uncertainty the importance of strategic decisions increases. Hence, the successful strategists of the future will be those that exhibit the 'analytical intelligence' to sift through competing images and increasing levels of information to make the key decisions that provide organizational clarity and certainty in turbulent times. In order to help build your analytical intelligence in this regard, this chapter is arranged in two parts. First, it reviews some of the classical theories of decision making: while environmental parameters have changed greatly, the basic social process of decision making has remained relatively constant, hence we would be wise to be aware of existing understanding in this regard. Second, because environmental change **is** significant, this chapter reviews and updates these models in the light of the increasing speed and complexity of change that all organizations now must face.

13 **Strategy as Decision Making**

DAVID WILSON

Economics and Psychology are all about how people make choices; Sociology, Anthropology and Political Science are all about how they don't have any choices to make. Students of Organizational Decisions locate themselves happily in the midst of this distinction trying to understand decisions as instruments of conflict and consciousness and trying to understand conflict and consciousness as embedded in social relations.

J.G. March, 1999

Strategy is the handful of decisions which drive or shape most of a company's subsequent actions, are not easily changed once made, and have the greatest impact on whether a company's strategic objectives are met.

K. Coyne and S. Subramaniam, 1996

Strategy, as a subject, has the advantage (or disadvantage, depending on your view) of being grand, macro in perspective and, by definition, 'important'. Strategy is the jugular of the organization. It is a mixture of many processes by which social and economic organizations assimilate and process information; how they interpret their environments; how they imitate or differentiate themselves from others and how they learn by doing. Strategy is thus at the heart of organizational activity and this heart must be kept healthy. It must be kept pumping. Strategies can be focused, generic or specific, competitive or co-operative, planned or can emerge, to mention just a few perspectives which have developed from that virtual industry of describing strategy (Mintzberg's

Strategy Safari, which is referred to often in this book, provides a very good overview of these descriptions). On many occasions, I have been with managers who speak the language of strategy and share this abstract and codified vocabulary among themselves. The cognoscenti nod their heads as each descriptor trips off the tongue and the knowing elite of the strategists make their pronouncements.

Make strategy but hesitate to put it in practice

Yet, ask these same strategists to make a specific decision (e.g., should we invest, make or buy, change suppliers or outsource?), and they hesitate. The rules and descriptors by which one can characterize corporate strategy are of little help when it comes to making choices over specific decisions. Managers (indeed, all individuals) know that decisions can just as easily go wrong as they can succeed and when they fail they are costly and sometimes irrevocably damage the organization. More importantly, it is sometimes extremely unclear why the decision went wrong or worked out well. The final paradox is that it is only at the very end of the decision process that its ultimate success or failure can be judged. Yet significant investment has to be made up front with the expectation that this will yield future returns.

It is in these ways that strategic decision making differs in key ways from more generic descriptions of strategy itself. They are more specific, are likely to be more immediate in their impact upon the organization and they are processes that occur in specific time-frames, and are evaluated by the extent to which they have achieved goals and objectives which may be unclear and ill-specified at the beginning of the process. In addition, strategic decision making is a process characterized by three complicating factors:

- *Partial knowledge* (not everything can be known in advance).
- *Power and conflict* (mutually conflicting interests are attached to the decision and its potential outcomes). and
- *Ambiguity* (preferences and evaluation are unclear; are subject to change and are not exogenous).

The latter characteristic leads to decisions being potentially evaluated very differently before and after the process. Later claims for insight may rest more on serendipity than analysis (and vice versa)! Strategic decision making is primarily about *thinking* strategically (deciding what to decide about) and *acting* strategically (putting it into practice). A characterization that brings us back to the distinction we made in the introductory chapter between orientation and animation. I shall return to these two 'sides' in the latter sections of this chapter.

With two colleagues (David Hickson and Sue Miller), I have been studying how strategic decisions might be characterized and understood. My own work spans 25 years and that was preceded by decades of earlier studies, most of these from the USA, including some world-famous scholars such as James March, Richard Cyert and Herbert Simon (who won a Nobel Prize for his studies of decision making). We know a great deal about decisions, how they are made and how successful they might be. The images of strategy that this decision-making perspective offers are explored in this chapter.

What Are Strategic Decisions and Why Do We Need to Study Them?

The pursuit of modernism in management theory, outlined in some detail in Chapter 1, very nearly rendered the study of strategic decision making seemingly redundant. There were analysts who argued that the practice of strategic decision making was almost totally out of the hands of decision makers, since the operating environment of the organization ultimately structured and decided which organizations would survive and which would not.

Organization theorists will be familiar with this approach as the 'population ecology' perspective, in essence, the survival of the fittest of a set of organizations (Michael Hannan and John Freeman are leading exponents of this perspective). In this and parallel modernist perspectives, decision makers are perceived as being passive agents with minimal influence over organizational development and change.

Such macro-level analyses found favour with the emerging trend toward modernism happening at the time in studies of management. Common, underlying causes, which bridged local differences, were becoming increasingly popular and decision makers, as agents of activity at the local level, were relegated to a back seat. In particular, strategic management, as a sub-discipline, began to eschew strategic decision making as a perspective worth pursuing preferring, instead, to focus on the meta-narratives of sector, industry and portfolios that drew heavily on economic theories of the firm (where the outputs of decisions rather than the processes and practices of decision making are used to explain firm behaviour in competitive environments). These meta-narratives, in turn, relegated strategic decision making to a rather mechanical set of activities that were dependent upon a set of global environmental conditions. Subsequently, people operating in the sub-discipline of organization theory explored what I would call the really interesting aspects of decision making. And, as managers and strategists become more aware of the complexity of decision making, these people began to bridge across from organization theory (OT) into strategic management.

Local differences

It was once generically assumed that strategic decision making will be more objective, rational and sequential (e.g., a strict sequence of activities such as define the problem, seek alternatives, choose alternatives, implement, monitor) in stable and predictable environments and that strategic decision making was less rational, less sequential and considered fewer alternatives when decision makers faced unpredictable and high velocity environments. However, those from the more 'behavioural' sides of management theory and my own studies led to very different conclusions. We consistently observed how strategic decision making differed within and between organizations, as well as between different countries. There seemed to be little evidence of universalism or generic global consistency.

For example, Peter Drucker had identified that there were key differences in the meaning of the words 'making a decision' in particular between Western cultures and the Japanese:

- In Western cultures, the emphasis is mostly on finding an *answer to the problem*.
- To the Japanese, the primary meaning is about *defining the question*.

Consequently, Japanese managers will spend a great deal of time considering whether or not there is a need to make a decision and what that decision should be about. Western cultures are more fixated on achieving outcomes to specific problems.

Between Western nations there are also key differences which emerge at the local levels. With my colleagues Runo Axelsson (a Swede) and Geoff Mallory, we examined similarities and differences in the ways in which Swedish and British managers engaged in strategic decision-making activities. Key differences were that the Swedes took significantly longer to get to the point of authorization than the British. Consistently, they took at least six months longer than their British counterparts. They spent longer negotiating and analysing the problem (and usually identified a few additional problems in the process). 'We like to achieve both high participation levels and consensus,' a Swedish manager told me, 'so we invest time in working the problem before we commit ourselves, then we can implement the decision quickly and without much further conflict or negotiation.' Case Box 13.1 explores this research further (and your answers to the questions it poses might make it worth revisiting the case boxes in Chapter 9, 'Strategy as Discovery and Interconnection').

Similarly, Teddy Weinshall observed that the way in which French managers typically approached strategic decisions was an almost perfect mirror image of North American managers. To the French, the question or problem itself is as important as the potential solution. Simple and fast solutions to complex problems cause mistrust in French managers. The reverse is true of North American managers who seek action that is decisive and, at best, swift.

Finally, Francisco Barbosa, one of my Latin American colleagues, points out that many 'Latin' managers view time spent on decision making in very different ways to many Western European managers. Latin managers will devote as much time as it takes to problem solving, even if this means cancelling previously arranged outings to the theatre or restaurants with family. Such a life by values (rather than a life by time) is accepted by all parties. The decision takes precedence. Western European managers are far more likely to adjourn the meeting, go to the cinema and reconvene the next day.

The majority of these managers were subject to the same information, similar problems, similar problem solving technologies, information systems and had equal access to what Levitt and others were terming 'global' best practices. Yet, all approached strategic decision making in very different ways. This coincides with a review of the research on strategic decision making by Vassilis Papadakis and his colleagues at London Business School. This emphasized the crucial importance of specific local processes in decision making and demonstrated that there was little evidence of more macro (e.g., organizational, markets) or global factors common across the field.

The emphasis is on local differences where the local context predominates and where the global solutions and analyses of 'modern' strategic management appear misguided at best and wrong at worst. As Lyotard argued (and as we suggested at the outset of this book), homogenization of decision-making tools, such as information technologies, was leading to an increazed localization (rather than globalization) in the different ways such information was processed and utilized in postmodern environments.

Case Box 13.1 A Clash of Cultures in Steel-Making Decisions

A few years ago, I was discussing strategic decision making with the senior managers of a Swedish–British company (a steel-making organization). In many respects the merger was highly successful. They had joint HRM policies, had agreed on a common organizational structure and had put in place a large number of cross-postings with Swedish managers working in Britain and vice versa. However, it was when strategic decisions over what was core business and to what extent the firm should outsource key activities (for example) were presented that difficulties began to emerge.

The Swedes approached strategic decision making just as Axelsson and his colleagues described in the paragraphs above this case box. On the one hand, British managers approached the same problems by seeking closure at every meeting. They wanted to narrow down the alternatives quickly so that the decision could be about a choice between a very small number of alternatives. The Swedes, on the other hand, specialized in opening up the number of alternatives at the same meetings and, in turn, raising fresh problems. This was one of the commonest causes of frustration and conflict between the British and Swedish managers. The tensions thus caused were a key factor in the eventual de-merger of the organization only a few years after the merger had taken place.

1. *Consider how decisions are generally made in your organization. What are the relationships between problems and solutions – and how are alternatives handled?*
2. *Why do you think your organization makes strategic decisions as you describe?*
3. *Are all decisions made in the same way, or does it depend on the topic for decision?*
4. *What changes, if any, would you recommend to the ways in which decisions are handled?*

The nature of strategic decisions and decision-making processes

The level of analysis of the strategic decision itself is important and the local influences on its processes bear investigation. However, the nature of both strategic decisions and their processes is hotly contested and has evolved over at least the past fifty years or so. In the following paragraphs, I try to delineate some of the important features and variables in these different images of strategic decision making.

The word *strategic* refers to the characteristics of the problem to be solved. Problems have been characterized as '*wicked*' or '*tame*' (Bob de Wit and Ron Meyer provide a good overview of this literature). Strategic decisions tend toward the characteristics of wicked problems, while operational decisions tend toward those which are tame. Wicked problems are complex. They are permeated with uncertainty. More prosaically, David Hickson and his colleagues characterized decisions as complex, political (or both):

- Complex decisions are those which are unprecedented, carry high levels of uncertainty and may have fundamental precedent-setting consequences for subsequent decisions. They may also require information of a different type and from a different source to be gathered and interpreted.
- Political decisions are those which draw in a specific set of stakeholders (inside and outside of the organization). The more interests are represented in the decision (multiple and conflicting voices), the more political is the strategic decision.

In my experience, however, strategic decisions tend to exhibit both political and complexity dimensions (see Table 13.1).

Table 13.1   Characteristics of strategic decisions

Strategic decisions

- Are difficult to define.
- Are difficult to assess in terms of performance, since they tend to continue through the organization without a clear final end point.
- Are highly interconnected with other decisions in the organization.
- Have high levels of uncertainty associated with them.
- Once made, are difficult to reverse.
- Are likely to be discontinuous and political, with different competing interests trying to influence the outcome in line with their preferences.
- Involves understanding the problem as also part of understanding the solution.
- Rarely have one best solution, but a series of possible solutions.
- Are associated with different trade-offs and priorities.
- Are accompanied by fairly high degrees of risk.
- Set precedents for subsequent decisions (such as procedures and establishing evaluation criteria).

Having a definition of 'strategic-ness' is necessary but not sufficient. Equally import-ant is how decision makers perceive or make sense of the decision process. This view will influence both the ways in which managers approach decision making and will inform them of which criteria of evaluation are likely to be used. Henry Mintzberg and colleagues identified five different 'angles' on strategy making that can usefully be applied to different decision-making processes. These are listed below:

- *A plan:* The decision is the outcome of a consciously intended course of action. Decision making is a process, therefore, which is carried out in advance of the action and is developed with a clear purpose.
- *A ploy:* The decision is the outcome of a set of actions designed to outwit the com-petition and may not necessarily be the 'obvious' content of the decision. There are obvious connections here with game theory (see Chapter 4, 'Strategy as Intention and Anticipation'), which examines the choices players make in every possible situ-ation. Forcing one's opponents to move (to achieve a short-term win) so that this puts them at a longer-term disadvantage is an example of such a ploy. Equally, there are connections with strategy as conceived in its military roots, where the plans of campaigns may have similar intentions to the game analogy.
- *A pattern:* Decisions are not necessarily taken with such purpose and decision makers do not always have access to the range of knowledge required to plan wholly in advance. What happens is that multiple decisions taken (or indeed deferred – consciously or unconsciously) over time form a pattern. It is this pattern of resulting behaviour that we call the strategy of the firm. Strategy is therefore characterized as a pattern in a stream of decisions to act or not act in particular ways.
- *A position:* Decisions emerge from a process of trying to achieve a match between the organization and its environment. This position can be one of alignment, so that the organization matches its environment (e.g. highly decentralized structures to match a turbulent and unpredictable environment) or one of competitive advan-tage (where the organization achieves a unique position in the market for some

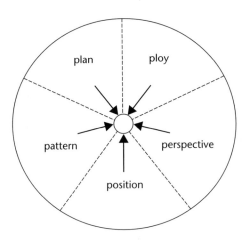

Figure 13.1   Mintzberg's five perspectives of strategy related to a decision point

time). Positions can, of course, be planned, emerge or be a combination of both processes.

- *A perspective*: Decisions here are characterized by how the senior strategists inside the organization see and perceive the world and their organization. Often aligned with the organizational vision, this perspective, if pervasive enough, can influence the kinds of decisions taken in respect of their content and their processes. Porac and colleagues, for example, showed how the mental models of strategists in the Scottish garment industry are formed and how these shared perspectives shape the ways in which they perceive and make sense of strategic problems. Feldman also demonstrated how such perspectives can permeate whole organizations and become strong influences on the mental maps of all individuals in an organization and not just its strategic decision makers.

Each of these perspectives does not necessarily preclude any of the others and strategic decision making can be, therefore, a combination of two or more. The key question for understanding strategic decision making is to try and identify any predominance of one or more of these perspectives in an organization, since these will inevitably shape strategic decisions and thus thinking and acting or orientation and animation in the organization. They will create the image of decision making. Above all, however, these perspectives describe how individual managers both relate to and interpret strategic decision making. I explore this further in the next section.

'Making Sense' and Strategic Decisions

One characteristic of 'traditional' strategic management is that the interpretive processes of individuals and the relationships between individuals and the wider structures, of which they are a part, are mostly omitted since they are not a part of the global, generic overview that characterizes much of strategy. But we have already seen how managers from different nations act differently in decision-making activities. We can explore this further drawing upon the work of Karl Weick – in particular his work on different types of sense-making (see Chapter 6, 'Strategy as Data Plus Sense-Making' for further background).

Intra-subjective sense-making

Of course, individuals engage with and participate in decision processes from an *intra-subjective* perspective. They make sense of the world from a predominantly subjective and personal point of view. From this perspective, the key analytical construct is inter-pretive. To understand decision making we need to uncover how individuals interpret and define their world. Logically, something called a strategic decision does not exist independently of those multiple (and possibly conflicting) perceptions. A theory of decision making therefore becomes a theory of interpretation.

However, Weick also alerts us to *inter*-subjective interpretation. Here, thinking and acting (as well as feelings and intentions) are merged between individuals. Terminology such as 'we' think this way substitutes for statements such as 'I' believe. Such inter-subjectivities are not just created by social structures (such as teams or other forms of structured interaction), they are created and maintained by a shared level of social reality. Such reality develops over time (as in Porac's study of Scottish garment man-ufacturers described as an example of 'choosing a perspective' above) and it shapes and places boundaries around decision making. Case Box 13.2 provides an example that can help you see how this interpretative process emerges in an organizational setting.

Case Box 13.2 Interpretive Processes and Inter-subjectivity in Decision Making

As some readers may know, I am a guitarist as well as a decision analyst and play music in a band (an organization). The latter is often more enjoyable than the former! The band's decision making processes on what material we play are heavily influenced by such inter-subjectivity. 'We' play particular material and, by definition, not other sorts of material. 'We' articulate this to audiences who might ask for a tune which does not fit our repertoire. 'We' say 'we' don't play that song.

But this is completely different from saying we can't play that song. As individual players, we are quite capable of playing a wide variety of music and styles. Yet as an organization which is constantly evolving by adding new material, 'we' play only selected material and in a style which conforms to (and is created by) the shared meaning and interpretation of the band's members. Change the band, of course, and you are likely to change the shared collective conscious-ness, but it too will evolve into a new shared inter-subjectivity.

1. *In your organization, reflect on the use of the term 'we'. Does it correspond to the above examples?*
2. *If so, then part of your understanding of the parameters around strategic deci-sion making will lie in the collective consciousness of your organization. Can you describe this collective consciousness and the influence it has on decision making?*

Generic–subjective sense-making

The process of decision making (like the process of organizing) also codifies inter-subjectivities over time. These codifications in turn become abstracted from either individuals or collective consciousness. They become embodied in structures such as networks, or in roles. These, to use a literary analogy, become 'standard plots' which events will follow regardless of the individuals in the story. This form of *generic-*subjectivity is also a powerful influence on decision making. Michael Cohen, Johan Olsen and J. March showed how standard plots could shape decision making by reversing the problem–solution sequence. They showed how the standard plot could often present a ready-made solution to a problem before it had occurred. As soon as new problem occurs, then a ready-made solution is attached to it. Consider the following scenarios:

- Standard plots and patterns of behaviour are encapsulated in your organization's collective memory. Arguably, the longer your organization has been in existence, the more ready-made solutions it will have potentially to address any new problem. Can you be sure that when you engage in strategic decision making you are looking forward, rather than looking backward and delving into the memory of the organization for a ready-made solution? How would you distinguish between these two activities in your organization?
- Think also what would happen if you decided to leave your organization. How would they process the decision to replace you? One way (that characterizes the strength of inter-subjectivities) is simply to produce a role description. The decision is to replace a role rather than an individual. In the most extreme case of this, all you will leave behind, therefore, is your role description. (See Chapter 9, 'Strategy as Systems Thinking', particularly the section on resource-based networks, on the importance of interconnectivity in this sense as a sustainable – that is, difficult to replicate – competitive advantage.)

Extra-subjective sense-making

At the most abstract, but perhaps most obvious levels, are *extra*-subjective sense-making processes. These are what Karl Popper has referred to as 'pure' meanings that are generally devoid of a single knowing subject. Weick argues that mathematics or capitalism corresponds to these extra-subjective characterizations.

It is clear that these processes and levels of analysis are both complex and not always easy to see in any organization. I hope the above examples help to clarify some instances where you might see such subjectivities of all kinds in action.

It is nevertheless central to the topic of this book. The first image of strategy from the decision-making perspective is one that is characterized by *multiple levels of analysis*, from individual cognition to patterns of meaning which are largely devoid of subjective approaches. The second image is that irrespective of whether we examine decision making from an interpretive or a generic standpoint, some form of action will take place over time. In other words, strategy as decision making enables us to focus upon and observe the *process* of a strategic decision.

Decision-making Processes

Although the majority of authors on decision making agree that understanding process is central (a good part of Chapter 10, 'Strategy as Process, Power and Change' deals directly with this issue), there has been a wide range of approaches to delineating these processes, even across the short history of five decades. The following paragraphs and corresponding figure outline this range:

- The 1950s and 1960s saw the emergence and the emphasis on the planning approach to decision making. Processes were about planning. The predominant focus was on tools and techniques to help managers make informed decisions about future business directions. Such tools included industry structure analyses, portfolio matrices (popularized by Igor Ansoff and the Boston Consulting Group) and saw the origins of what we call today the core competences of the organization.
- The 1970s onwards saw work on decisions that were supposed to yield pay-offs to organizations if they pursued different strategic directions. The most usual were diversification decisions, but this was also an era of innovation (R&D), acquisition, joint venture and internationalization decisions. Processes from this perspective were about designing mechanisms and a calculus for deciding on the content of strategic decisions.
- The 1980s saw a move away from examining the content of strategic decisions (i.e. what they were about) to examining them exclusively as processes. David Hickson and colleagues characterized such processes as sporadic (discontinuous), fluid (continuous and smooth) or constricted (restricted to a small group of stakeholders).
- The 1990s onwards have seen a continuing interest in unfolding the characteristics of strategic decision processes, but now there is a strong interest in the ultimate dependent variable of strategy – performance. The aim today is to try and establish what links there may be (if any) between how decisions are processed and whether they are more or less successful.

Following the 'postmodern' philosophy outlined in the introductory chapter, we might speculate that the decade beyond 2000 will be one of seeing all these approaches as viable images and mixing and matching them to suit particular individual decision-making needs. This chapter will expand on the emerging work in this field, but first we need to examine in a little more detail the links between strategic problems and decision making, since these are not always simple nor obvious.

Strategic Decision Making and Problem Solving

The practice of managers making decisions can appear deceptively like actions formulated toward the solution of a particular problem. There may be actions and there may be outcomes, However, as Chapter 4, 'Strategy as Intention and Anticipation' indicated, such things are not necessarily wholly related to one another in a linear causal fashion. Problems, for example, may be solved by other factors than strategic decisions and, sometimes, taking a strategic decision can create a whole new set of problems (without solving the initial problem the decision was supposed to address).

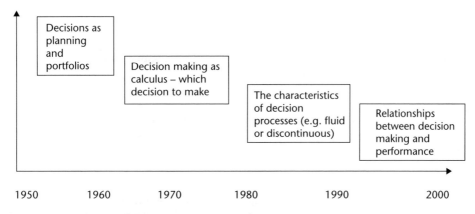

Figure 13.2   A timeline of favoured decision-making approaches

These polar views represent the *planning* versus the *chaos* perspectives on strategic decision making:

- Planning perspectives assume dyadic and direct relations between x (the problem to be solved) and y (the decision taken).
- Chaos perspectives make no such assumption, arguing for a more complex and multivariate view.

These two are extreme views, of course, and most decisions lie somewhere between the planned and the chaotic. Indeed, we believe it is better not to see them as an either/or choice but, rather, as a 'both/and'. The perspectives that flow from each image are useful for the practice of strategic management and for refining the image of strategy thus created as their different emphases highlight different aspect of decision making. The strengths of each are outlined below.

The *planning model* helps managers to:

- analyse and codify complex problems;
- question and challenge current practice;
- involve others and create higher levels of ownership;
- communicate as fully as possible;
- set up key performance indicators by which progress can be monitored and judged.

The chaos model (see the references to Michael Cohen and Ralph Stacey's work at the end of this chapter for more on this) turns the planning model on its head. The argument is that instead of viewing the firm as an 'organization', it is more useful to see it as an 'anarchy' or as a system with chaotic tendencies. This means that managers can neither understand fully nor control internal processes. Nor are means and ends necessarily coupled. Actions do not lead to expected outcomes and are swayed one way and another by other decisions, other actions and unforeseen circumstances. The main components of a strategic decision-making process (problems, solutions, participants and choice situations) interact in an apparently haphazard way, a stream of demands for the fluid attention and energies of managers. Participants move in and out of the decision-making process (every entrance is an exit elsewhere) and this can

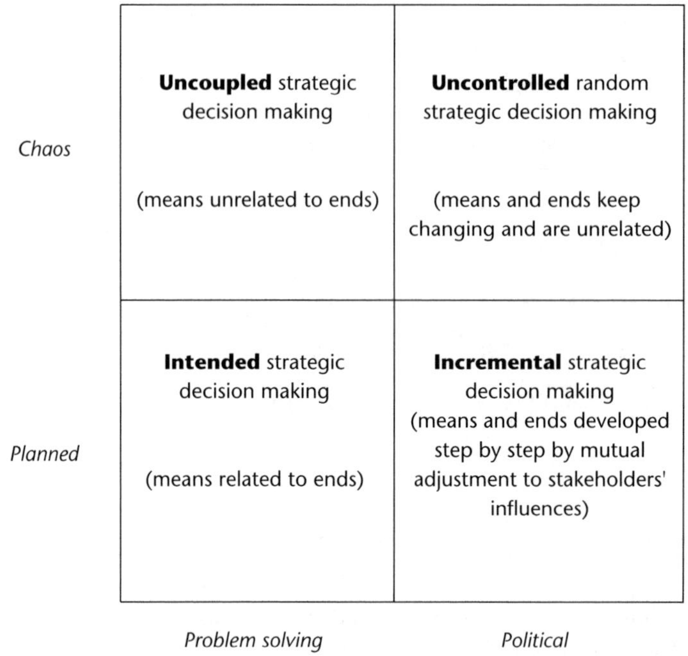

Chaos	**Uncoupled** strategic decision making (means unrelated to ends)	**Uncontrolled** random strategic decision making (means and ends keep changing and are unrelated)
Planned	**Intended** strategic decision making (means related to ends)	**Incremental** strategic decision making (means and ends developed step by step by mutual adjustment to stakeholders' influences)
	Problem solving	*Political*

Figure 13.3 A typology of decision process characteristics

create discontinuity. At other times, participants fight for the right to become involved and then never exercise their influence.

The *chaos model* helps managers to:

- avoid oversimplifying the process;
- avoid means–ends errors;
- appreciate more fully the role of *politics and influence* where different stakeholders try to influence the decision process and its outcomes in ways conducive to their interests;
- think creatively around complex problems;
- avoid thinking solely in linear sequences and appreciate that it is sometimes useful to take actions off at a tangent;
- appreciate the influence of the context in which strategic decision making takes place.

The above characterizations highlight four key characterizations of strategic decision making. These are problem solving versus political process and planning versus chaos. Decision making can then be classified into four generic types: uncoupled, uncontrolled, intended and incremental, as shown in Figure 13.3. It may be useful at this point to reflect on how your organization, or an organization with which you are familiar, might be categorized according to this typology – and what the advantages and disadvantages of their generic approach to decision making may be.

Strategic Decision Making: Managerial Choice, Influence and Control

The above characterization would perhaps indicate that the prevalence of managerial agency – who decides? – would be restricted to incremental or problem-solving activities since in more chaotic environments it is elements beyond managerial control that steer and shape the decision. However, this is only partially the case, since those managers who can examine and analyse accurately the nature and the impact of such externalities will be able to appreciate the likely influence of such elements and the direction in which they may also steer the decision. Consequently, this section looks at the context in which strategic decision making takes place with a particular emphasis on the role played by leaders in organizations.

Making choices can reflect the personal characteristics of decision makers, making them seem relatively context-free. John Child, in his well-known theory of strategic choice, argued that managers had a degree of choice (the environment was not all deterministic) and that the behaviours of managers would be one element in the extent of this choice. Strategic choices are also, of course, a reflection of top teams, such as boards, trustees or policy-making committees. How boards are structured and who they comprise can have a strong influence on what choices are made and which strategic decisions are given priority (for more on this see Chapter 10, 'Strategy as Process, Power and Change', which deals directly with issues of governance).

In terms of behaviours, the role of leadership is central to strategic choice. Many authors, such as Warren Bennis and Don Hambrick, have pointed to the influence that strong individual leaders exert over strategic decision making. We can all think of high profile or charismatic leaders who exert such influence (e.g., Richard Branson, CEO of Virgin). These leaders shape, influence or orchestrate (to borrow a phrase from Chapter 5, 'Strategy as Orchestrating Knowledge') strategic decisions sometimes so strongly that they become personally associated with the decision and, often, the organization. In other organizations, it is a combination of influential managers (a *dominant coalition* to use James March and Richard Cyert's apt words) who together shape and influence strategic decision making. The example shown in Case Box 13.3 is one of the best I have ever seen (literally, since it was filmed as it happened) in depicting the influences exerted by dominant coalitions. In answering the questions it poses it may be particularly useful to connect the ideas developed here to those outlined in Chapter 12, 'Strategy as Numbers'.

Case Box 13.2   Decision Steel – The Korf Contract*

This was a strategic investment decision in new technology made in the British Steel Corporation (now part of the Corus Group) and filmed as it happened by Roger Graef (a television and radio programme maker). The decision was whether or not to invest in the new gas-fired reduction of steel (known as direct reduction) or to stick with the existing process of using a coal-fired blast furnace. The gas plants were manufactured by a German company – Korf.

If this new technology were to be invested in, then there would be a question about the level of investment (one plant or two). There were significant savings to be made if two plants were purchased together.

The key players in this decision were the chairman (Monty Finniston), the board and the policy committee which was charged with making a decision and recommending it to the board. Discussions in the policy committee and informally in corridors revealed sharp divisions between influential coalitions.

Some senior managers favoured no investment, with other favouring one or two plants. Ron Atkin, the chief negotiator with Korf and also the director of project engineering (something of a role conflict one would have thought), favoured two plants and presented this internally as getting a great deal. He also emphasized that the current prices for the plant were only available for a very short time – there was a deadline.

Others, such as John Grieve-Smith, director of planning, took an initially 'rational' approach arguing that no good reasons had been put forward for investment even in one plant. However, when it became clear that the board was favouring the purchase of two plants, Grieve-Smith also backed two, contrary to his own department's advice.

Herbert Morley (Atkin's immediate boss) was initially unsure what to think since he had been given very piecemeal and selective information from Atkin. For example, Atkin argued the deadline was non-negotiable (despite this turning out not to be the case) and kept very quiet the fact that Korf would be quite happy to switch from two plants to one if this was what British Steel decided was best.

It became clear during the decision that Finniston favoured two plants although this was mostly based upon the need for a quick decision since in the early stages he seemed uncommitted to any outcome.

Subsequently, Morley was pressured from both above (Finniston) and below (Atkin) to re-calculate data that initially indicated that the one plant option was the best. He did this by 'cooking' the data until it emerged that two plants were the only option. Even though the finance director (Lionel Pugh) fought hard against this decision, he was one man alone against a board committed to two plants and seemingly happy to accept the 'revised' data presented by Morley.

Finniston used his formal authority to get the figures re-jigged by Morley. He then supported the new figures at the crucial final board meeting at which the decision was made. Atkin controlled the process of the decision by restricting information and by influencing Morley who was able, in turn, to convince the board. Pugh was isolated both by being the lone voice against a dominant coalition (the board) and by his (erroneous) assumption that the decision-making process was intended to be rational. The two plants were purchased and never used (due to the massive fall in demand for steel that followed immediately afterwards). They were eventually disassembled and sold to a North American concern at an estimated loss of over £70 million.

1. *Consider the role of data in decisions made in your organization. Its presentation and interpretation are likely to be coloured and heavily influenced by individuals and coalitions that have conflicting interests. What would you*

> *recommend to ensure that these different interests did not distort the decision-making process and influence the eventual outcome?*
> 2. *Once you have read the section on 'The Influence of Politics' toward the end of this chapter, return to this case and see if you can use the frameworks presented there to analyze why this decision went the way it did.*
>
> **Even though this film is now over 25 years old it may still be purchased from Granada Television in the UK. We highly recommend it as a classroom teaching aid and its use can greatly flesh out the issues discussed in this chapter.*

Not all individual leaders (rather than dominant coalitions) have such an influence, however, and strategic decision making goes on independently of their individual influence. In the Korf case above, the chairman was relatively ineffectual as an individual leader, only becoming powerful once he 'joined' forces with a coalition that favoured the purchase of two plants. As Brian Leavy and myself discovered, individual leaders are 'tenants of time and context'. That is, they operate in organizations at particular points in history and at particular points in the organizational life cycle. As a result, the influence a particular leader can bring to bear on strategic decision making varies, depending, for example, on whether they are the initiators of new ideas or are inheritors of the ideas of others who preceded them in that role. This is called the locus of influence, and this can be internal or external to the leadership role (or a combination of both). Internal locus of influence means that the leadership role has the capacity to influence strategic decision making directly. An external locus of influence means that the leadership role has very little or no capacity to influence strategic decision making directly.

Figure 13.4 summarizes the six major roles that we found in our study of leaders and strategy. This is a simplified table, since the study was conducted to examine over a 40-year period in each organization. Therefore, any one organization may have several leaders in that time, each of whom display different role characteristics. (In fact we would suggest that having such a range of leadership skills within an organization is a very good thing as the dynamic this creates can help alleviate the unquestioning single-loop learning described in a number of earlier chapters in this book.) In some years, the influence of leadership upon strategic decision making is minimal and in other years almost total (in the same organization in different time periods). The six roles span a continuum ranging from organizational change to continuity.

Having explored the nature of strategic decisions and different decision making processes, the role played by broader cultural contexts and approaches to sense-making, the evolution of views regarding the process of decision making, the relationship between decision-making processes and problem solving, and the influence of different styles of leadership or management, the last three sections of this chapter investigate how particular organizational characteristics can:

(1) influence decision making (or strategic orientation);
(2) influence the implementation of decisions (or strategic animation); and
(3) reveal how political behaviour can influence both decisions and their implementation.

CHANGE

**LEADERSHIP
ROLE:**

Builder: The creators and developers of their respective organizations at the formative stage of the organization's development. (Influence predominantly internal.)

Transformer: Leaders who radically change the strategic direction of their organization, for example, they take it into a new area of core business. (Influence predominantly internal.)

Revitalizer: Leaders who operate within the already established basic characteristics of their organization, but who try to raise it to a new plane of development, for example, more of the same, but more effective. (A combination of internal/external influence.)

Turnarounder: Leaders who chop and change the basic already established characteristics of the organization, for example, emphasize one or more areas of the core business and de-emphasize others. (Influence a combination of internal and external.)

Defender: Leaders where the organization is well into maturity and whose role is to protect market position, for example, ensure sustained competitiveness. (Influence external.)

Inheritor: Leaders who consolidate and build on the progress made by their predecessors. (Influence external.)

CONTINUITY

Figure 13.4   The locus of influence of leadership on strategic decision making
Source: Adapted from B. Leavy and D. Wilson (1994).

Strategic Decision Making: Organizational Influences on Orientation

We saw earlier in this chapter how the particular organizational settings in which strategic decision making is practised can have a strong influence on strategic decision making. This can occur independently of direct managerial control. David Hickson, Richard Butler and I noticed some of these key influences when we collected our research work together a couple of years ago. I have listed the key influences below under the sub-headings: internal systems; organizational structure; ownership and control; and, organizational culture.

Internal systems

Internal systems, such as information or formal planning processes, both influence the flow of information across the organization and to some extent determine the nature and context of human interaction. It is not surprising, then, that they have a strong influence over strategic decision making and its practice. Control systems and measurement and reward systems also prescribe what is given priority and therefore what decision makers focus most of their attention upon. In decision making, such systems will set parameters around trade-offs and what levels of risk are tolerable, for example.

- The more regulated the formal systems, the more strategic decision making tends to be routine and predictable and the more it will have to accommodate a large number of specialist functions.
- The more complex the systems, the more decision making becomes reliant on knowledge experts and information gathering and synthesis.
- The more automated systems become, the more flexibility and space there is for strategic decision making that relies upon expertise (or the intellectual capital of the organization). The obsession with control tends to be reduced since controlled systems do not require watching over (when they go wrong, however, they can cause havoc!).
- The greater is the scope of the system, the greater is the reliance on expertise and intellectual capital. This is true of e-commerce and e-business, for example, where the scope of information goes beyond the single organizational unit.

Organizational structure

The structure of an organization also has an impact on strategic decision making. The most obvious example of the interrelationship between strategy and structure is the debate (which still rages) about whether structure follows strategy or vice versa (this is addressed at the head of Chapter 5, 'Strategy as Orchestrating Knowledge'). Whichever comes first (strategy or structure) or whether they are inextricably interrelated, strategy and structure are like two legs. You need both to walk. Whether you lead with the left or the right leg is fairly arbitrary, you are still walking:

- Formalized structures are associated mainly with older organizations. Decision making becomes formalized and has a tendency to become more predictable. This is especially so in the 'seen it all before' attitudes that may pervade and in the dragging up of what was done in the past as solutions to today's problems.
- Larger organizations formalize processes more, even if they are structured into smaller business units. Strategic decision making becomes more about rule following than rule bending (or breaking) practice.
- Decentralized structures may appear to avoid the above, but decision making can become dominated by trying to ensure co-ordination and communication across the decentralized organization (rather than putting effort into producing new products and service, for example). Decentralized structures often require more, rather than less, hands-on management before they can become effective and efficient.
- Organizational structures reflect the age of the industry from its founding date. Industries that predate the Industrial Revolution (e.g., railways, the church or the military) are characterized by centralized and formal structures (whatever the age of the organization in the industry). It seems that industry age is a better predictor of the organizational structure of even a new entrant into the industry.
- In terms of organizational size, the main effect on strategic decision making appears to be formalization rather than size itself. David Hickson found no differences in

strategic decision-making processes that could be attributed to organizational size. So large organizations that manage to retain less formal structures may not necessarily exhibit the rule following strategic decision-making processes of their more formalized counterparts.

Ownership and control

Ownership and control exert separate influences over strategic decision making. In family-owned firms, for example, the overlap between the two social systems of the family and the firm creates decision processes in which personal stakes are high and delegation may be rare since decision-making authority and the strategic direction of the firm are controlled by the owners.

Interestingly, there is strong evidence to show that public versus private ownership seems to make little difference to the ways in which strategic decision making occurs (at least in the UK). Public sector organizations take no longer to make strategic decisions, do not have more committees and do not have significantly more stakeholders than private sector organizations.

Two of my colleagues at Warwick, Sue Bridgewater and Andrew Hardwick, are engaged in a project analysing strategic decision making in a very different set of organizations: English football clubs. We await with interest their findings in terms of whether football clubs exhibit any noticeable differences in decision-making processes relative to other organizations. It may be that in comparing (say) BPAmoco with the National Health Service in Britain, one would expect few differences. They are both large organizations with many similar structural and processual features. However, football clubs are very different in these respects and may thus yield greater differences that those observed so far.

Organizational culture

The culture of an organization is where many of the underlying assumptions that inform strategic decision making are to be found. Culture embodies what is taken for granted in organizational processes and is continually reinforced by symbols, stories, routines as well as by structures and power plays between individuals and groups. Gerry Johnson and Kevan Scholes' notion of the 'cultural web' in organizations usefully captures the main ingredients of organizational culture as stories, routines, symbols, structures, power and control.

The important aspect from the cultural web for strategic decision making is that of coherence. Johnson and Scholes argue that in order to operate effectively, decision makers must be working where there is some degree of coherence among all the factors which make up the cultural web. The greater is the level of coherence, the greater is the likely advantage to the organization in competitive markets, since such coherence is very difficult to imitate. Strong cultures can therefore be a potent source of competitive advantage since they allow decisions to be made that would be more difficult in other organizations with less cultural coherence.

On the other hand, organizations can become trapped by their coherent cultures into routines that impair the development of new and different strategies. The practice of strategic decision making, therefore, becomes trapped rather than enhanced by the organizational culture. Decision makers can only think along the rigid lines demarcated by the strong culture. Innovation and creative thinking are precluded and invoking learning into the organization becomes very difficult, since the culture resists new ideas (see Chapter 7, 'Strategy as Creativity').

Implementing Strategic Decisions so as to Animate

It would be only painting half the picture if we did not couple the practice of strategic decision making to performance. Put another way, what are the relationships between process and outcomes? Does what managers do in the strategic decision-making process matter? And to what?

For nearly thirty years, practitioners and scholars alike have argued about what brings success. So complex have some of these arguments become, that there is virtually a whole industry of analysts devoted to arguing whether planned or emergent strategies (for example) capture the essence of strategy and whether the effective positioning of the organization in its industry and value chain led to greater or lesser performance. Sub-industries also sprung up including, for example, focusing on whether organizations could learn from failures and successes and whether key technological advancements (e.g., killer applications) rendered any form of strategic planning redundant. Other analysts focused on the levels of uncertainty facing decision makers arguing that, faced with extreme uncertainties, success was more probable if managers took action (leaps of faith in the dark) than no action at all. Of course this rich analysis has not only provided a large number of industry overviews and industry shake-outs (e.g., in the telecommunications industry) but has also provided many case studies and war stories for others to pick over and make sense of.

As pointed out at the outset of this book, strategic *orientation* and *animation* should be seen in tandem. And, as I stressed at the outset of this chapter, strategic decision making focuses on *thinking* and *acting* strategically. The many slips that can occur 'between cup and lip' (i.e., between thinking and acting) have been well documented. Failure to achieve can be a result of decisions that:

- fail to address the original problem;
- make the problem worse rather than better;
- are irreversible when they begin to go wrong;
- are beyond the knowledge base of the organization;
- are too big a leap in the dark;
- are counter-cultural for the organization.

It seems that it is more in the implementation stages of decision making that things can go wrong, despite what may have seemed like good ideas during formulation. Of course, there is a critical temporal element here. Before implementation, it is extremely difficult to differentiate what will be an effective strategy from one that ultimately fails. Despite all the attempts to assess the degree of future risk (through techniques such as risk analysis), strategic decisions seemingly succeed or fail independently of such criteria.

We are beginning to identify patterns of implementation that indicate key factors associated with higher achieving decisions. These factors are a combination of features of the decision process itself: such as its duration. And of organizational features: such as structures and the receptiveness of organizational culture to the decision. And of features of what actions managers take during the process: such as how far they can specify what must be done in advance or whether the required expertise can be accessed inside the organization.

The duration and processes of decisions

David Hickson and colleagues produced an empirical classification of strategic-decision processes up to the point of authorization. One aspect of process was duration. They found that from first mention to the point of authorization, the bulk of decisions take between four and twenty-four months to process. The mean for 150 cases was 12.4 months. The question is, to what extent this mean duration also applied to the implementation phase of a strategic decision.

Implementation is defined here as the time taken from the point of authorization to when the decision was put into practice (e.g., the new building was built or the reorganization put in place). It is also where the greatest time variations occur. Perhaps unsurprisingly, implementations take longer on average than it takes to get to the point of decision. *Acting* strategically takes significantly longer than *thinking* strategically. However, surprisingly, duration of implementation is *not associated* directly with achievement. It seems the time taken to implement strategic decisions matters little in terms of performance. Long, drawn-out implementation processes can be associated with very successful decisions, while faster implementation times are no guarantee of success.

Equally, the processes and events that led up to the point of authorization for any strategic decision have little or no influence over the characteristics of implementation and no influence at all over whether the decision subsequently achieved stated objectives or not (achievement). Knowing how a decision was made (thinking-orientation) is of little help to managers who have to implement it (acting-animation).

So what makes a difference? Two factors – the first captures the receptivity of the organizational culture to the strategic decision and the second the knowledge base of managers.

The receptivity of organizational culture

The key factor here is how ready is the organization to adopt the changes incurred by the strategic decision? The greater is the readiness in the 'cultural web' to undertake the change, the easier it is for managers to take action and to begin to prioritize their various strategic decisions.

However, even a high state of cultural readiness can be blocked by organizational structures that are overly formal or bureaucratic. Hence, both organizational culture and structure have to be co-aligned if higher levels of performance are to be expected from the strategic decision-making process.

The knowledge base of managers

The key factors that emerge as related to performance cluster around how familiar managers are with the problem to be addressed. Where managers are clear about the parameters of the problems and what information is needed to address it, then they can begin to take action toward implementation. Two other processes are associated

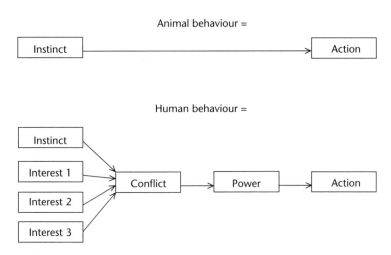

Figure 13.5 Different interests, conflict, and power in the individual

with this knowledge base. They are the ability to plan and resource strategic decisions. Knowledge facilitates planning and argues a good case for resourcing. Strategic decisions do not succeed on knowledge alone, they need resources to back them up.

Equally (and perhaps not surprisingly) it is important for managers to convince stakeholders in the decision and get them on their side. It seems that there is a positive relationship between how well managers can specify and plan strategically and the extent to which the variety of stakeholders involved in the process concur with the strategic decision.

The Influence of Politics on Decision Making (Orientation) and Decision Implementation (Animation)

As Aristotle remarked, 'Man is a political animal'. In so doing, Aristotle defined human beings by arguing that they belonged to a different category from other animals because they engaged in political behaviour. Ever since (and probably long before) people have been interested in the relations between power, politics and human action.

Aristotle subsequently explained that predicting an animal's behaviour was easy. Understand its *instincts* under certain conditions and one would know how the animal would act. Humans are more complicated. We not only act on *instinct*, but also attempt to balance other different *interests* (being a good partner, or a good student, or a good tennis player and so on). Because different interests would lead to different actions and we cannot be all things to all people; we are in *conflict*. If we are to act, this conflict must be resolved, certain interests must win out over others. Hence, certain interests, or a coalition of interests, must over-*power* others (see Figure 13.5).

Because humans have different interests, general human behaviour is almost impossible to predict. Conflict occurs not only within individuals, but also between individuals (as the 'Decision steel' case exemplifies). The interplay of interests, conflict and power means that processes such as strategic decision making and implementing strategic decisions can be characterized as essentially political in nature.

Of course, political behaviour between and within groups has been a central theme of the social sciences. In organizational theory, one of the earliest pieces of research to exemplify the dynamic of politics in power and decision making was William Foote Whyte's ground-breaking ethnographic study *Street Corner Society*. He built diagrams mapping the interactions between individuals to understand relationships between group structure and individual performance (we could say that these diagrams were the forebears of those outlined in Chapter 7, 'Strategy as Creativity' and in Chapter 9, 'Strategy as Systems Thinking'). Whyte found that people who influenced outcomes were generally those with the most key 'connections' to others. Being 'networked' and having many linkages to others was an important source of power. In the Decision steel case, we can see how Ron Atkin uses this power of connections and being networked to his advantage in securing the decision to buy two plants.

To describe and analyse power in organizations fully would take at least another book. For readers interested in exploring the topic of power, some further reading is suggested in the endnotes to this chapter. Here, we will limit ourselves to providing some simple images for understanding and delineating interests, conflict and power in organizations which may help your reflections on strategy.

Interests

First, coalition building is key as we have indicated above, and the most effective way to build coalitions is to connect with people who have similar *interests* or whose interests may be shown to be compatible with your own. Gareth Morgan provides a very simple way of drawing individuals' interests as a first step in seeing potential allies. Morgan suggests that individuals at work have three main spheres of interest:

- Task interests (e.g., an interest in being a good auditor by doing the auditing task to the utmost).
- Career interests (e.g., wanting to 'get ahead', which, while overlapping with one's task interests, will at times conflict with doing one's job description or task 'to the letter').
- Extramural interests (e.g., social and other external interests, which may at times conflict with furthering one's career or doing one's task thoroughly).

By drawing an individual's spheres of interests relative to each other you can delineate to what extent they have a much bigger extramural circle, or task circle, etc. This picture helps inform those areas which a coalition builder could potentially connect with, or target, as a series of first steps to increasing their influence (see Figure 13.6).

Conflict: different interest orientations

Not everybody's interests will be compatible or connectable and this leads to *conflict*. According to Jeffery Pfeffer, conflict is resolved in different ways in different organizations, depending on the 'decision-making model' present in that organization. This 'model' is likely be relatively implicit, so it requires some interpretation to ascertain its characteristics. As a guide, Pfeffer describes four main models: rational, bureaucratic,

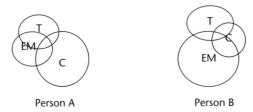

Figure 13.6 Examples of different spheres of interest

decision process, and political. Each exhibits different modes of goal setting, control and ideology that feed into, and stem from, a particular type of decision-making process. Interpreting what type of model, or combination of models (e.g., rational/bureaucratic, process/power, bureaucratic/power) is important if one wants to understand how an organization's strategy develops, and, consequently, how one might influence strategy outcomes to a greater extent.

If the game is chess then there is not much value in having a great backhand. By the same token, Pfeffer's schema suggests that no matter how compelling your, or your coalition's interests may be, they will not hold much sway if you are not playing by the rules of the model in operation. For example, there may be less value in preparing a perfect rationally argued presentation to the board if you are operating in a process/power situation.

The Decision steel case described earlier in this chapter is a good example of this. Lionel Pugh presented a perfectly rational argument against the concocted figures presented. By rational criteria, the decision should have been to invest in only one direct-reduction plant. However, the decision rules in operation were much more process and power orientated and the rational voice was ignored (despite Pugh being a powerful figure in terms of hierarchy). Pugh might have been better advised to spend more time bargaining behind the scenes and trying to shape preferences before the formal meetings took place. Figure 13.7 illustrates a simplified adaptation of Pfeffer's typology.

Power

If more that one individual or faction is 'playing the right game', how then does conflict get resolved? It usually comes down to who can muster the most *power*. Each of the eight sources of power listed below can provide organizational members with a variety of means of enhancing their interests and resolving or perpetuating organizational conflict.

(1) *Formal authority* (FA): Formal authority plays an important part in resolving conflict in organization. Those 'higher up' have greater ability to promote or demote potential initiatives if they see fit. They also often have a greater ability to control decision processes by keeping them ring-fenced and restricted to a small but elite group.

(2) *Control of formal decision processes and structures* (FDP): Being responsible for setting deadlines, agendas, chairing meetings, controlling how minutes of meetings are scripted; having the authority to 'sign off' on certain decisions; all can influence decision processes and outcomes.

	DECISION-MAKING MODEL			
Dimension	**Rational**	**Bureaucratic**	**Decision process**	**Political power**
Goals, preferences	Consistent within and across social actors	Reasonably consistent	Unclear, ambiguous may be constructed *ex post* to rationalize action	Consistent within social actors; inconsistent, pluralistic within the organization
Power and control	Centralized	Less centralized with greater reliance on rules	Very decentralized	Shifting coalitions and interest groups
Decision processes	Orderly, substantively rational	Rational programmes and standard operating procedures	Ad hoc	Disorderly, characterized by push and pull of interests
Decisions	Follow from value-maximizing choice	Follow from programmes and routines	Not linked to intention; result of intersection of persons, solutions, problems	Result of bargaining and interplay among interests
Ideology	Efficiency and effectiveness	Stability, fairness, predictability	Playfulness, loose coupling, randomness	Struggle, conflict, winners and losers

Figure 13.7   An adaptation of Pfeffer's decision-making models
Source: Pfeffer (1981).

(3) *Control of scarce resources* (SR): Having control or influence over tangibles like capital budgets, or intangibles like specialist knowledge and key information that can be revealed or concealed when 'the time is right'. A sense of timing, as in when to reveal one's hand, can be both a tactical and extremely political act in decision making.

(4) *Control of boundaries* (B): Controlling the links or flows of information between departments or between different companies that may have input into final decisions can influence the presentation of alternatives. Such 'framing' of alternatives can favour some and disfavour others in the organization.

(5) *Control of technology* (T): The most notable example of the control of technology as a source of power influencing strategy in recent times relates to the way in which companies decided that 'the web was the future'. Those who had expert knowledge about how web-based technologies could be utilized found their power to influence strategy greatly increased.

(6) *Interpersonal alliances and networks* (IA): The philosopher Michel Foucault challenged preconceptions about power by arguing that power does not exist in 'bodies of authority' (e.g., the government, the police, the media, the CEO, the CFO), but lies in the often unseen relationships or 'networks' running between these bodies. Protesting through directly confronting such bodies may cause the network to manufacture opinion against the protest and make traditional bonds stronger. The best form of resistance, therefore, is to organize alternative networks linking the interests of like-minded individuals who can help 'the cause' behind

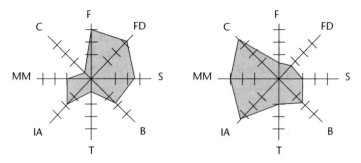

Figure 13.8 Examples of different power profiles

the scenes. (Perhaps this was Lionel Pugh's problem in the Decision steel case depicted above?)

(7) *Symbolism, language and the management of meaning* (MM): Instead of linking one's interests directly to the interests of others, this source of power derives from the ability of individuals and groups to align with symbols or myths of an organization's glorious past or prevailing language. At the same time, the ability to link one's opponents interests to 'the bad old days' or things 'which don't seem in keeping with the spirit of the company', for example, can be equally powerful in the negative sense.

(8) *Charisma and the ability to cope with uncertainty* (C): In an uncertain world people look for certainty. Hence, as Max Weber described so well, they gravitate toward charismatic people who seem to have a clear sense of purpose. Having such a character can be a great source of power, since by creating a sense of certainty for others, groups or individuals accrue substantial influence and perceived power. Gurus, wizards and soothsayers all operate in this way.

One useful way of depicting the power of an individual or group is to use a radar graph or 'spidergram' (a tool that we will utilize further in the next concluding chapter) to demonstrate their level of power in each of these eight categories relative to other factions or individuals (see Figure 13.8).

These sources of power profiles can then be linked back to decision-making modes. In organizations which tend toward the more *rational* or *bureaucratic*, the profile represented in the graph on the left is likely to have greater influence potential. However, in organizations which tend toward the *decision process* or *political* end of the spectrum the profile in the graph on the right will be potentially more influential.

Conclusion

The analysis of strategic decision making reveals how interrelated features of decisions, managers, power, and organizations interact. It is this interaction which forms what we commonly term organizational strategy. Whether strategy is planned, or emerges as a pattern of strategic decisions (which are rationalized after the event), individual strategic decisions are at the heart of the process. Most organizations have a handful of strategic decisions running through them at any point in time, usually ranging between three and seven strategic issues (which may or may not be interrelated). There is strong evidence that the characteristics of implementation (i.e., *acting* strategically or animation as we have referred to it in this book) have a greater influence over the success of strategic decisions than formulation (i.e., *thinking* strategically or orientation). Hence the need to focus on decision making beyond (i.e., both before and after) the actual point of decision itself.

The strategic decision level of analysis brings into sharp focus the need for a combination of high levels of intellectual capital (the knowledge base of the organization) and open and malleable organizational features such as culture, structure and political control. It is this combination which seems to offer the greatest chance of success and hence the stronger overall strategic positioning of the organization. Decisions are at the heart of organizational strategy. Without an understanding of how decisions are made and what influences both their processes and their outcomes, we cannot fully analyse the concept we term strategy. The image of the decision is fundamental to understanding strategy.

Moreover, in general terms, we can continue this logic as a means of reflecting back on the chapters that have preceded this. Increasingly, we believe, successful strategies will be developed through the combination of high levels of intellectual capital like those embedded in the different myriad images of strategy that have been put forward here. Our next and final chapter provides you with further food for thought as to how you might develop your skills for doing this.

Source Material and Recommended Further Reading

The opening quotation is taken from James G. March, *The Pursuit of Organizational Intelligence* (Oxford: Blackwell, 1999). The multiple references to strategy perspectives can be found in H. Mintzberg, P. Ahlstrand and J. Lampel, *A Strategy Safari* (London: Prentice-Hall, 1996). The Population Ecology School is derived from Michael Hannan and John Freeman 'The Population Ecology of Organisations', *Sociology* 82 (1977) 4, 929–64. Peter Drucker's work is extensive but his *Managing in Turbulent Times* (London: Pan, 1981) is a good source for decision enthusiasts. As an antidote to modernist approaches to strategic management see J-F. Lyotard, *The Condition of Postmodernity* (Manchester: Manchester University Press: 1983).

The topics covered in this chapter are extensive and are often treated as separate subjects in their own right. Accordingly, I have grouped topics together here under three main headings which, while they interrelate, can be read in-depth separately.

Understanding decision making
This chapter relies quite heavily on the work of the 'Bradford' studies (led by David Hickson), the work of Henry Mintzberg and the various reviews of decision theory that have appeared more recently. Devotees might consult the numerous publications by David Hickson and his colleagues in *The Bradford Studies of Strategic Decision Making* (Aldershot: Ashgate, 2001), which contains many of the original papers from the research. Although out of print, a second-hand copy of *Top Decisions* (Oxford: Blackwell, 1986), by D.J. Hickson et al. is a useful source for the characterization of processes. K. Coyne and S. Subramaniam (1996) 'Bringing Discipline to Strategy', *The McKinsey Quarterly*, 4, 1996, 14–25, argues the case strongly for approaching strategy from the level of analysis of the strategic decision rather than aggregate to the levels of corporate strategy. H. Mintzberg, B. Quinn and S. Ghoshal, *The Strategy Process* (New York: Prentice-Hall, 1998), provides a good overview and competing perspectives on strategic decision making and Mintzberg's earlier work (with Raisinghani and André Theoret) was seminal in capturing the characteristics of the decision processes. You can read this in 'The Structure of

Unstructured Decisions', *Administrative Science Quarterly*, 21(2), 1976, 246–75. Paul Nutt is a prolific author on decision making and, in particular, is very effective at making the links between processes, outcomes and success. I would recommend looking at the following papers by Paul Nutt: 'Tactics of Implementation', *Academy of Management Journal*, 29(2), 1986, 230–61; 'Identifying and Appraising How Managers Install Strategy', *Strategic Management Journal*, 8(1), 1987, 1–14; 'Selecting Tactics to Implement Strategic Plans', *Strategic Management Journal*, 10(3), 1989, 145–61; 'The Formulation Processes and Tactics Used in Organizational Decision Making', *Organization Science*, 4(2), 1993, 226–51; 'Leverage, Resistance and the Success of Implementation Approaches', *Journal of Management Studies*, 35(2), 1998, 213–40; 'Surprising But True: Half the Decisions in Organizations Fail', *Academy of Management Executive*, 13(4), 1999, 75–90. Overview material can be accessed in V. Papadakis and P. Barwise (eds), *Strategic Decisions* (London: Kluwer, 1997); and N. Rajagopalan et al., 'Strategic Decision Processes: Critical Review and Future Directions', *Journal of Management*, 19(2), 1993, 349–84. Also very accessible and useful papers have been written by J. Dean and M. Sharfman. These include 'Procedural Rationality in the Strategic Decision Making Process', *Journal of Management Studies*, 30, 1993, 607–30, and 'Does Decision Process Matter? A Study of Strategic Decision Making Effectiveness', *Academy of Management Journal*, 39(2), 1996, 368–96.

On the question of how much autonomy managers do have in decision making (as opposed to environmental determinism) the well-known paper on strategic choice by John Child cannot be beaten: J. Child, 'Organisational Structure, Environment and Performance: the Role of Strategic Choice', *Sociology*, 6, 1972, 1–22. Rational planning, game theory and militaristic models can be found in C.W. Hofer and D. Schendel, *Strategy Formulation: Analytical Concepts* (Chicago: West Publishing, 1978); C. von Clausewitz *On War*, translated by M. Howard and P. Paret (Princeton, NJ: Princeton University Press, 1976); and J. van Neumann and O. Morgenstern, *Theory of Games and Economic Behaviour* (Princeton, NJ: Princeton University Press, 1944).

Chaos and complexity versus rational planning
Here, the literature is extensive, especially where discussions of systems occurs. When strategic planning (or strategic prescriptions) takes place, then we are making assumptions about both the linearity and the sequence of processes as well as about the nature of the organizational system. For example, in strategic planning the dominant systemic assumption is that organizations exist in negative feedback loops which maintain the organization in states of relatively stable equilibrium. Hence patterns of decision making and change are regular and predictable. In addition, thinking precedes action. Authors who have queried such assumptions include R. Stacey, *Strategic Management and Organizational Dynamics* (London: Pitman, 1993); and M. Cohen, J. March and J. Olsen, 'A Garbage Can Model of Organizational Choice', *Administrative Science Quarterly*, 17, 1972, 1–25. Stacey points out that organizations are capable of existing far from states of equilibrium, a state of paradox that combines both conditions of stability and instability. There are acute tensions between the needs to plan, integrate and maintain the system and the needs constantly to change it. Cohen and his colleagues point out that solutions often precede the occurrence of problems in organizations and that decision making may be more accurately described as attaching ready-made solutions to new problems rather than seeking a solution through a rational choice sequence. The older the organization generally, the more ready-made solutions it will have in its repertoire.

Power and decision making
This is a wide area of study. In this chapter, the basic ideas surrounding the articulation and accommodation of interests have been outlined in some detail, building on the work of Jeffrey Pfeffer, *Power in Organizations* (Marshfield, MA: Pitman, 1981); Gareth Morgan, *Images of Organization* (London: Sage, 1986). The chapter also noted the importance of language as a political tool in decision making and this was drawn from the work of Andrew Pettigrew, *The Awakening Giant: Continuity and Change in ICI* (Oxford: Blackwell, 1985). Another useful text in the

vein of language is P. Daudi, *Power in the Organization: The Discourse of Power in Managerial Practice* (Oxford: Blackwell, 1986). On the political advantages of being networked see William Foole Whyte. *Street Corner Society* (New York: Harper, 1957). The notion of charismatic attraction is from Max Weber, *Theory of Economic and Social Organisation* (London: Routledge and Kegan Paul, 1947).

However, the chapter, of necessity limited by space, only dealt with overt aspects of power and influence. Many sociologists, philosophers and political scientists have pointed out that the most potent forces of influence lie hidden from view. They are covert. Those people, systems and structures which influence what is not open to decision have a very strong influence. These are the issues which are not debated in the overt managerial arena, but which are issues nevertheless and are kept off the agenda by powerful players or systems.

The two best references for this aspect of power can be found in P. Bachrach and M. Baratz, *Power and Poverty: Theory and Practice* (Oxford: Oxford University Press, 1970); and S. Lukes, *Power: A Radical View* (London: Macmillan, 1974); and S. Clegg and D. Dunkerley, *Organization, Class and Control* (London: Routledge, 1980). The work of the French philosopher, Michel Foucault is also drawn upon in this chapter. In a wide range of works, Foucault draws our attention to the fact that what it is 'we all know' and how we make sense of some categorizations and not others are contextually sensitive and may have been very different in earlier periods of history. In particular, Foucault traces the shift into the modern world (post-eighteenth century) where God lost his place as the firm centre of all power and the spotlight shifted to mankind, as the source of knowing. Social sciences now examined mankind as both the object and subject of study. As decision maker, mankind had to come to some view about what was normal and what was considered abnormal. Foucault called these normalizing judgements. He pointed out that, for example, the law traditionally puts limits on behaviour and therefore concludes what is unacceptable behaviour by default, since it rarely talks about what behaviour is desired. Such negative 'normality' exists in organizations but so also does the ability to punish and to reward individuals. Foucault viewed this ability as a key element of 'disciplinary power' (drawing his own empirical evidence from the madhouse) but these ideas readily translate into modern organizations, in particular through the notions of surveillance. Here, people and decisions can be monitored (often quite literally by digital means or on computer screens) by remote managerial cadres who can see (but not be seen). Parameters are placed not only on behaviours but also upon what is considered the norm. Punishment and reward (e.g. promotion) keep the system going. Foucault is not easy reading, but for the purposes of this chapter, *Discipline and Punish: The Birth of the Prison* (London: Routledge, 1975), and *The Archaeology of Knowledge* (London: Routledge, 1972), are perhaps the most relevant.

This chapter has also drawn upon the following authors: Gerry Johnson and Kevan Scholes, *Exploring Corporate Strategy*, 6th edn (London: Financial Times, Prentice-Hall, 2001); Richard Cyert and James March, *A Behavioral Theory of the Firm* (New Jersey: Prentice-Hall, 1963); Brian Leavy and David Wilson, *Strategy and Leadership* (London: Routledge, 1994); H. Igor Ansoff, *Corporate Strategy* (London: McGraw-Hill, 1965); Warren Bennis et al., *Beyond Leadership* (Oxford: Blackwell, 1994); Karl Weick, *Sensemaking in Organization* (London: Sage, 1995); Theodore Weinshall, *Societal Culture and Management* (Berlin: de Gruyter, 1993); David Hickson and Derek Pugh, *Management Worldwide* (Harmondsworth: Penguin, 2001); Bob de Wit and Ron Meyer, *Strategy Synthesis* (London: International Thomson, 1999); M.S. Feldman and J.G. March, 'Information in Organizations as Signal and Symbol', *Administrative Science Quarterly*, 26, 1981, 171–86; B. Levitt and C. Nass, 'The Lid on the Garbage Can: Institutional Constraints on Decision Making in the Technical Core of College-Text Publishers', *Administrative Science Quarterly*, 34, 1989, 190–207; J. Porac, H. Thomas and C. Bade-Fuller, 'Competitive groups as cognitive communities: the case of Scottish knitwear manufacturers', *Journal of Management Studies*, 26(4), 1989, 397–416.

Our final chapter provides an opportunity to reflect back on all that has gone before and practise seeing strategy in terms of the images put forward here toward developing and implementing strategies that can **orient** *and* **animate** *organizational development (to hark back to the philosophy outlined in Chapter 1). Toward this end, we develop an organizing schema that categorizes each of the previous twelve chapter's key images; we provide a case that you can analyse in terms of this schema; and then invite you to analyse this case using the images and ideas developed in the preceding chapters.*

14 Strategy as Orientation and Animation

EDITED BY STEPHEN CUMMINGS AND DAVID WILSON

Knowledge so conceived is not a series of self-consistent theories that converge towards an ideal view; it is not a gradual approach to the truth. It is rather an ever increasing ocean of mutually incompatible alternatives, each single theory, each fairy-tale, each myth that is part of the collection forcing others into greater articulation and all of them contributing, via this process of competition, to the development of our consciousness. Nothing is ever settled, no view can ever be omitted from a comprehensive account.

Paul Feyerabend, Against Method.

Orient – Animate

A criticism often levelled at the multi-perspective books that have inspired this one (*Strategy Safari* and *Images of Organization* to name two) is that they provide an interesting range of alternatives, but give little indication as to how these might develop our consciousness toward making decisions that could help orient and animate real organizations. In other words, readers are often left thinking, 'That's interesting, but so what? How does this change the way that I develop, influence or implement strategy in my company?' In an attempt to get beyond this quite valid response this concluding chapter introduces a framework that relates the images of strategy focused upon in each of the twelve chapters of this book to one another, and provides a schema by which they can be applied to animate and orient strategy. We provide a case based on a 'live' organization (Marks & Spencer) that can be examined by working through this schema and the opportunity to analyse this case using the images and frameworks presented and developed in this book. And, the opportunity to compare your analysis with contributions from each of the chapter authors on this book's website, whereby they apply images from their chapters to analyse the case. These contributions do not result in us settling upon the 'right answer', 'ideal view' or 'self-consistent general truth'. What has already been said in this book should act as a warning against believing that such things exist in strategy. And, given that any settled collection of views will not be the whole story and that alternatives will always exist and should not be omitted – hopefully what we have done here will inspire you to add your own images for analysing strategic situations to those that we put forward (again the website also provides the opportunity to do this). What this exercise does provide is a tangible example of how different images of strategy, forcing one another into greater articulation, can contribute, by way of this process of competition, to the development of your consciousness of strategic situations. Through such a process we believe that you can make more informed strategic decisions.

An Integrating Schema: A Wheel of Strategy Images

As this book emerged we, as editors, recognized that we would eventually have to face up to a problem of our own making, if we wanted *Images of Strategy* to do what we had intended it to do. On the one hand, we wanted the individual authors to write from their own subjective perspectives – to incorporate the best and most useful images picked up on their own particular travels through strategy. Much to our delight, this is what the chapter authors have done, and, as a result, many of the chapters have spread far and wide, incorporating a broad range of perspectives under the auspices of their chapter title 'image'. However, on the other hand, for the reasons described in the introductory paragraphs of this chapter and in Chapter 1, we did want to provide out of these images a tangible schema that would aid people in taking the ideas outlined in this book 'to work', as it were.

As a result, we have come up with a schema. But we preface it by saying that it of necessity simplifies and classifies each *Images of Strategy* chapter in ways that do not do justice to their richness and complexity. Thus, we present it as a 'memento'. Or 'a division or generalization to help you speak and think about strategy', to paraphrase Plato's words from our introductory chapter. We discourage you from simply referring to this schema as a stand-alone entity and jettisoning the chapters themselves. It is best used as a key to take you back into the chapters when faced with particular situations.

A wheel crossed with a 2 × 2 matrix

Influenced by the 12 linked microcosms from Chapter 1 (Plates 1.3 and 1.11) and the many arms of Ganesh (see cover illustration), we started with the idea of a wheel with many spokes. In keeping with much that has gone on in the earlier chapters in this book, we then sought to create a 2 × 2 matrix by developing two axes.

Vertical axis

Drawing on work we had done earlier, we set the vertical axis as the 'locus of influence on strategy' with an *internal* locus positioned at the top of the axis and *external* at the bottom. This was developed by combining work done by Brian Leavy and David Wilson on *voluntarist* and *determinist* views of leadership and strategy, and Stephen Cummings and John Davies' work on the strengths of mission versus vision, with the later based on an *existentialist* ontology and the former on a *structuralist* view. At the internal influence end of our spectrum lies a belief that our *independent choices and actions* determine our futures. At the external influence end, lies a belief that our destinies are *determined or structured* by things external to us.

Horizontal axis

We then set the horizontal axis to be the 'effect of strategy', with a *centring* effect on the left and a *decentring effect on the right*. This was developed by combining Stephen Cummings' analysis of how firms must focus on both *centralization* and *decentralization*, rather than seeing the two as an either/or choice; Brian Leavy and David Wilson's spectrum from *continuity* and *change* (see Chapter 13 for a fuller description of this), and Susan Miller, David Hickson and David Wilson's action dimension spectrum, which has an axis that runs from *coherence* to *chaos*.

Classifications

As we began to review the twelve chapters in the light of this framework we could begin to make the following general classifications:

(1) The chapters on *ethos*, *organizing* and *intention and anticipation*, by and large, bring out images that look within the company to see how certain choices and actions can have a centring effect which builds coherence and aids continuity – for better or for worse.

(2) The chapters on *orchestrating knowledge*, *data + meaning*, and *creativity*, by and large, examine how we as strategists can control our own destinies but that we should seek to do things that challenge and decentre our organizations and our conventions so long as we continue to co-ordinate and communicate between the decentring elements.

(3) The chapters on *exploration and interconnection*, *systems thinking* and *power, process and change*, by and large, investigate how we should think beyond the conventional boundaries of an organization to see the things that can motivate or effect strategic change and development.

(4) The chapters on *marketing*, *numbers* and *decision making*, by and large, bring things back to a head, looking at how external stimuli such as market value and financial figures can give an organization a central focus that promotes strategic decision making – again, for better or for worse.

The resulting schema is represented diagrammatically in Figure 14.1. If this order seems a little too neat and convenient (with our schema neatly following the order in which the chapters of the book have been presented), we can assure the reader that this was a more organic and emergent process than our final presentation suggests. The chapters were to appear in quite a different order until we developed this schema and reset the running order.

This 'images of strategy wheel' indicates that all of the images addressed here are equally valid, and that the resourceful strategist, following the philosophy outlined in the introductory chapter, would work around the wheel: from ethos, all the way around and out to creativity, and then back to using what has been gathered to feed into decision making.

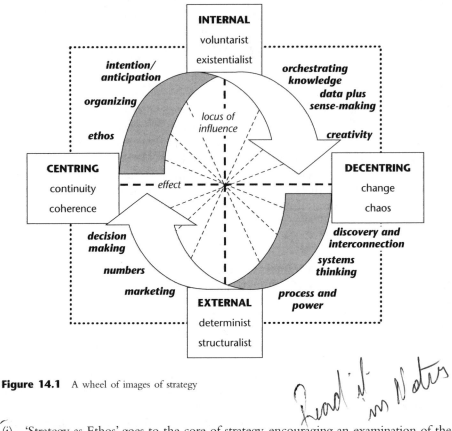

Figure 14.1   A wheel of images of strategy

(i) 'Strategy as Ethos' goes to the core of strategy, encouraging an examination of the identity or character of an organization. Here 'knowing thyself', developing by surfing positive aspects of one's background, and consistency, are strategically more important than attempting to copy or adhere to a 'best practice' type of 'goodness'.

(ii) 'Strategy as Organizing' focuses the reader upon the ways in which 'human resources' are organized within a firm and how this can, often unwittingly, indicate a corporate strategy. Organizations would then be wise to reflect on whether their organizing rhetoric is consistent with the internal culture or cultures that they would like to promote.

(iii) 'Strategy as Intention and Anticipation' emphasizes how we are often unified in our strategic actions in a complex world through a shared sense of intention in the present in combination with developing an ability to anticipate and adapt to the future. Different circumstances require different combinations of anticipation and intention.

(iv) 'Strategy as Orchestrating Knowledge' highlights how the changing shape of economics leads to a fragmentation of traditional forms of organizing. This means that old forms of command and control are less appropriate and that we must embrace new approaches to orchestrating strategy.

(v) 'Strategy as Data Plus Sense-Making' looks at the importance of information systems in a world of decentring fragmentation and interconnectivity. However, this is approached from a unique angle – one that encourages us to consider the interaction between humans and data in the development of knowledge and then integrate these considerations into the formulation of a coherent business strategy.

(vi) 'Strategy as Creativity' is probably the chapter that pushes boat out furthest toward decentring the way we think about strategy. Its author writes about the importance of connecting with people from different perspectives to think outside of the box and think beyond conventional views of strategy.

(vii) 'Strategy as Exploration and Interconnection' is another that looks a conventional subject but from an 'added-value' angle. While most writing on how firms look for external mergers and acquisitions focuses on financial data, it forces us to also consider the human influences on M&A: ambition, power, lust, greed, hubris, restlessness, jealousy and so on, using examples of great explorers.

(viii) 'Strategy as Systems Thinking' also encourages thinking outside of the conventional boundaries of an organization. It promotes reflecting on how relationships within our heads, within our organizations and between these things and our environments are interrelated as we develop, or fail to develop, strategy.

(ix) 'Strategy as Process, Power and Change' was especially broad-ranging and hence difficult to categorize. For example, the material on power and governance would perhaps sit better on the 'centring' side of our wheel. However, we focused upon the author's ideas with regard to the importance of external context and process in shaping strategy, and the importance of change – but with one eye on continuity – to place this chapter where we did.

(x) 'Strategy as Marketing' seeks to reunite strategy and marketing by redefining marketing as 'the process of creating a competitive advantage by developing relationships with valued customers'. As an external measure of a company's progress in this regard, it put forward the notion of increased market value for the long term. This can provide a much-needed central focus for strategic decision makers.

(xi) 'Strategy as Numbers' reasserts the part played by numbers in strategic analysis. However, in so doing, it also seeks to alert us to the ways in which financial and other market figures are not simply the outcomes of organizational behaviour, they also drive our strategic decision making, often without our recognizing this.

(xii) 'Strategy as Decision Making' brought us around full circle. It cautioned us against letting the complexity of views outlined in the previous chapters tie us up in philosophical or semantic debate. Strategy, when it comes to the crunch, still means people in organizations making decisions. Thus we need to focus on making decisions that centre or orient, and implementation plans that animate strategic action. This means being aware of the influence of things such as organizational structure, culture, and politics, on how decisions are made and how implementation may be enabled or disabled.

This statement of the importance of all of these images should not, however, detract from your own analytical abilities to see what is most important in a particular industry or company and place your energies accordingly. For one thing, more may be required than simply working around the wheel once and acting according to a single

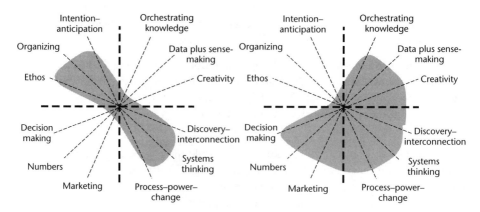

Figure 14.2   Examples of different image emphases

iteration of analyses. Your recommended actions may force reactions, and the environment has a habit of changing, so you will likely want to follow up going around these images at a later stage by revisiting some or all of them in the light of changes over time.

We may borrow the spidergram concept to illustrate how in some industries emphasis needs to be placed on building a strong corporate identity and then using this to build out externally from this base (the left-hand diagram in Figure 14.2), whereas for some companies at some time they may have a strong internal sense of purpose but need to change and develop by focusing on external influences and then make some strong decisions (the right-hand diagram in Figure 14.2). You should use your own informed judgement to determine which images are most useful given your individual circumstances. The section that follows provides you with an opportunity to practise using this simple key and the many images of strategy put forward in this book on a live business case.

Integration Case 1: The Rise and Fall and Future of Marks & Spencer

There are three reasons why the Marks & Spencer (M&S) story provides a particularly good integration case for *Images of Strategy*. First, despite being primarily a British retailer, M&S it is well known internationally (particularly since so much has been written about the company's rise and fall in the world's business press over the past decade). Second, the amount that has been written, and continues to be written, on M&S gives you an opportunity, through web-sites such as <www.ft.com>, to gain further information on, and background to, the case to aid your analyses and add to case as we move through time. As we have already said, this should be viewed as a 'live' developing case not one that is fixed in time. Finally, it has, or at least had, problems along all 12 spokes of our wheel of images of strategy spidergram (Figure 14.3).

We urge you to read the case and think through why M&S was successful, why it declined, and how it might succeed again, using the images, perspectives and frameworks you have read about in this book.

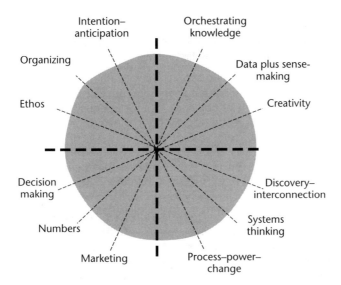

Figure 14.3   Wheels of images of strategy spidergram applied to Marks & Spencer (*c*.2000)

Case Box 14.1   The Rise and Fall and Future of M&S

What was to become Britain's largest retailer began in Leeds in 1884 as a market stall. The story goes that Michael Marks, a Jewish refugee from Eastern Europe, penniless and looking for factory work, bumped in to factory owner Isaac Dewhurst in the street. He asked Dewhurst for a job. Dewhurst invited Marks in to his offices for tea. He took a liking to the young immigrant, but for reasons unknown Dewhurst helped Marks set up as a peddler with a small stall in Leeds Market instead of offering him a factory job. Marks' marketing concept was 'everything for a penny' and to grow his business he started taking his wares on tour around Yorkshire's market towns.

A few reasonably successful years later, Marks decided to set up permanent stores, but for this he would need more capital. He came back to Dewhurst and asked if he wanted to go into business with him. Dewhurst refused, so Marks approached Dewhurst's accountant Tom Spencer. Together, Marks and Spencer raised £600 and set up a network of shops in the surrounding area that came to be called 'Marks & Spencer's Penny Bazaars'. Their strategy was simple but innovative for its time: penny pricing and 'courteous and charming shop girls' who were made to feel part of a family and whose loyalty thus encouraged loyalty among customers.

Until very recently, M&S thrived by following a model that built upon Michael Marks and Tom Spencer's original concept. Its staff viewed the company with pride and they and M&S's suppliers all saw themselves as part of something very special – part of a collective. It had built a reputation among customers for quality, dependability and classic, if functional, styling. It grew to over

70,000 employees, to be the most visible retailer in Britain's high streets, to be the provider of 40 per cent of all women's underwear and 25 per cent of men's suits sold in the UK, and to be the first retailer in Britain to gross over £1 billion in annual profits.

M&S managed to achieve something very rare: the City, the Press, its suppliers, its employers and the general public all loved it in equal measure. The level of affection felt by people is evidenced by the nicknames given to the company: M&S, Marks', Marks and Sparks; that have become part of the vernacular. Even hard-nosed business analysts described them as 'one of Britain's most cherished institutions'. Their reports uncharacteristically note that 'people really love them'; that 'shopping at M&S is a matter of tradition'; and that 'it is a total institution'.

However, the past few years have seen M&S fall on hard times in a quite spectacular fashion. In what seemed like a matter of just a few weeks it went from darling to duffer. In a television programme produced by the BBC, shown toward the end of 2000, an impassioned great-grandson of Michael Marks claimed that his ancestors would spin in their graves if they could see what had happened. The same programme captured the feelings of the British public thus:

> Since its foundation . . . this company came to be loved and respected like an indispensable part of the family. Everyone had an opinion about its food, its clothes ranges. You couldn't avoid it. Even if you didn't shop there as a teenager, half your deliveries from Santa every December would bear a M&S label. So when a company like this falls on hard times, it is rather like the feeling you get at the end of rousing tragic theatre. When Hamlet or Othello bites the dust, you feel that part of you has gone with them. You sense, still, a very deep desire on behalf of the British public, to turn things around and revive the brand.

This case examines the rise, the fall and what the future might hold for M&S.

1900–1940 – The Establishment of an Institution

Michael Marks died aged 44. His son Simon was only 19 at the time, but he managed to buy up enough shares in M&S to take control of the company and with his good friend Israel Sieff, Simon set about making M&S into what it would become. Along the way, the ties between Marks and Sieff grew stronger, with Simon marrying Israel's sister and Israel marrying Simon's. By 1924 Simon Marks, aged 36, was the owner-manager of chain of penny bazaars that spread throughout England.

In that same year, Simon took a visit to America to investigate leading retailers there and the fledgling field of 'scientific retailing'. His findings either confirmed or added to his very keen 'gut-feel'. Retailing, he concluded, was about making tough choices. One must invest in branding and building a particular image. One must measure sales and margins per square foot and discontinue lines that under-performed.

Marks returned from the US, managed to borrow a large sum from *The Prudential*, and set about turning his penny bazaars into the department stores that we would recognize today. Previously, such stores were the preserve of the wealthy, but, borrowing from his father, Marks adopted a 'nothing over five-shillings' policy. He introduced the logo 'St Michael' as a quality mark and backed this up with a 'no quibble' return and exchange or refund policy. He went against his financial advisers in opening a store next to Selfridges in the grandeur of London's Oxford Street, claiming that the publicity alone would offset the investment.

Israel Sieff built up the external architecture of the company. He employed his considerable charm to bypass the traditional textile industry middle-men and do deals direct with suppliers who were all British, mostly small, and little known in their own right. M&S managers became a part of their suppliers, visiting them regularly to discuss delivery systems, styles and fabrics, stitch lengths, production routines and quality control. (Sieff and Marks became renowned sticklers for quality; one former associate said that Marks told him 'our garments should sell arse-up', i.e., that they should sell even if displayed inside out with their seams showing.) So long as a supplier met M&S's strict standards they would continue to be linked – in perpetuity. Because the suppliers were generally small and M&S was increasingly big the relationship was one of benevolent paternalism. Many suppliers knew that they would be out of business if not for their M&S contracts and subsequently put their M&S runs first.

Internally, at the other end of the value chain, Simon Marks created a unique camaraderie. His regular store visits would combine silent moments – where he would simply stand and listen to the sound and frequency of the tills (Marks claimed to be able to tell much about a store from this) – with boisterous interaction with staff and products. It was said that Marks 'loved the goods in the store – they were his!' Indeed, he took personal umbrage when he felt 'his' goods where not up to scratch or poorly presented.

Marks took the same paternal attitude to store employees. Hence, not only were there more M&S assistants per square foot than in most other establishments, M&S people were better trained, better paid, and otherwise better looked after, than those who worked for their high street rivals. Right up until the 1990s, assistants wore tape measures for assisting and advising customers as a symbol of their skill being greater than the average 'till-jockey'. Marks even employed chiropodists to advise assistants on how to look after their feet and treat any complaints. It was a stark contrast to the attitude of other British employers of the time. One retired 'M&S girl' told the BBC that 'we were a different class altogether – there were sales assistants and then there were M&S girls – they were totally different'. Marks boasted that whereas 'shop girls' were 'once pale and wan, you could now not tell M&S staff from the daughters of Dukes and Earls'. As a result M&S built up a high-quality, highly motivated staff who made their careers with the company.

Behind the scenes, Marks ran his managers hard. They were the centralizing glue that held things together and he expected much of them. On the board, Marks, the great patriarch, oversaw a group that until the late 1970s would only consist of family members.

M&S provide a direct link between supplier and customers that guaranteed quality from a fragmented textile industry. It offered customers a selective range of the basic essentials that every customer needed, that were stylish and well-designed as well as functional, and backed up with the St Michael guarantee of consistency and quality. Prices were reasonable because of M&S's highly centralized and simplified operating procedures. Supply lines and information systems were established so that every branch of M&S provided the same range of the same quality to enable customers to buy with confidence and exchange goods with ease.

These policies tapped into the aspirations of a growing 'middle class', and by the 1930s Marks & Spencer was a household name. By the beginning of the Second World War, one-third of all undergarments in Britain were sold by M&S. Indeed, by working closely with suppliers and investing in R&D on new fibres, fabrics and materials to increase comfort and durability, fashion historians now claim that M&S was starting to reshape the way the British wore underwear.

1940–1964 – Growth and National Adoration

Simon Marks' patriotism came to the fore during the war years. Sixteen M&S stores were bombed during the conflict. Marks 'hit back' by doing whatever he could to switch production and sales facilities over to the provision of utility clothing to meet war needs, and the company donated a Spitfire aircraft to the Royal Air Force.

In the postwar years, Marks blended patriotism with his canniness for emerging social trends and a dash of opportunism to move further ahead. In a world of scarcity and products that were functional at best, the St Michael's brand offered customers 'something better'. And, to further 'treat' the British public in these austere times Marks and Sieff used their connections in the newly formed state of Israel, and advances in refrigeration, to deliver 'exotic' foods such as avocado pears, oranges and figs to the British people. The success of these items would lead M&S into a gap in the market for fancy convenience foods.

As with 'his' clothes, Simon Marks insisted that M&S's food business be quality led, not cost led, and he took food that was not of a high quality as a personal affront. He and his managers regularly tasted for M&S. One important M&S ritual in this regard was the 'chicken test'. If most people did not think that M&S chicken had better flavour than its rivals, Marks would immediately send everybody back to the drawing board to put things right. And by this time this was a fairly substantial drawing board. Marks had realized that war technology could be channelled into producing goods of a higher calibre for Britain as it regained prosperity, and had hired many technologists who fled continental Europe into Britain after the war. Before long M&S had built up a 200-strong army of food and clothing scientists.

To this day, food is seen as a bright spot in the M&S portfolio. Its success capitalized on a growing demand for food of a higher quality and technologically advanced 'easy-to-cook' ready meals in increasingly busy and convenience-oriented households, and the fact that food generates high revenues per square foot of floor space (while food takes up 15 per cent of M&S floor space it accounts for 40 per cent of sales). By 1998, food sales were £3.1 billion compared to £4.8 billion for clothing and footwear with analysts claiming that M&S could further boost their fortunes by opening more food shops.

Just before Christmas 1964, Simon Marks collapsed during a store tour and died. He, and those he worked with, had created an institution that fulfilled its mission every day. This mission, first articulated in the 1950s long before such statements became the fashion, was:

To continually raise the standards of the working man and woman.

1965–1988 – From Strength to Strength

Israel, and then Israel's two sons Teddy and Marcus Sieff, took over the M&S legacy and the late 1960s and 1970s continued in the vein established by the Marks's. The British people continued to shop at M&S in ever-increasing numbers. Postwar baby boomers were beginning to have money of their own and spend it. They remained loyal to the brand they had grown up with and brought their children up on it too. Moreover, many sought to become a part of M&S by buying shares in the company. Ninety per cent, some 300,000 shareholders in M&S, are individuals, and even despite the recent tough times many continue to regard the company with an unreasonable affection. Moira, who cleaned our offices and generally looked after us while we were preparing this book (and for many years before), is a good example: she had had M&S shares for decades and, as her retirement approached, she was sticking with them despite their plunge in value.

It is written that for people from Leeds, M&S meant even more. As one Leeds journalist recently noted, along with Alan Bennet and Billy Bremner, M&S is one of the few notable names that the city has ever produced, and that M&S: 'grew into Britain's mightiest retailer in the days when Leeds proudest boast was "Motorway City of the 70s". It sometimes [even] seemed a bit too posh, what with its overpriced knits and tea and crumpet cafes, for its own home town.'

The late 1970s and early 1980s saw the appointment of Sir Derek Rayner as M&S's first non-family chairman and international expansion into the Far East and North America which included the purchase of the high-profile Brooks Brothers clothing chain. Maggie Thatcher was widely reported as having a soft spot for M&S's 'sensible and stylish classics that were a cut above'. And M&S seemed well placed to benefit from the increased individualism and consumerism that were said to characterize the culture that the 'Thatcher years' ushered in.

1988–1997 – The Greenbury Years

Sir Richard Greenbury, a Simon Marks protégé, joined M&S in 1952 and rose through the ranks to become joint managing director in 1978, chief operating officer in 1986 and chief executive in 1988. In 1991 he took over as chairman while remaining CEO, later claiming that his holding of the two positions at once happened 'almost by accident'.

From the late 1980s to the mid-1990s, M&S appeared to go from strength to strength under Greenbury's leadership. Despite a nationwide recession, Greenbury's autocratic, tough, 'in your face' approach and legendary hands-on control of the company (his office was a clutter of jumpers and fabric samples waiting for his approval), took M&S's profits before tax from £615 million to £1.168 billion. Greenbury had used his firm hand to work through changes that would see M&S take far greater control of costs during the downturn. For example, he decided that there should be fewer full-time sales assistants in stores and encouraged M&S's overseas acquisitions to trim their cost structures.

Greenbury's success in steering M&S through difficult times in the early 1990s and taking M&S through the psychologically impressive £1 billion profits barrier, led to him being encouraged to stay on as both chairman and CEO beyond his earlier agreed retirement date. He and M&S seemed, according to one associate, 'boomproof'.

M&S came out of the recession full of gusto. In the mid-1990s, it embarked on an ambitious £2 billion expansion scheme. Plans for its other interests in the US sought an increase in retail space there by 17 per cent. More M&S stores were opened in the Far East. Furthermore, M&S ambitiously moved to establish a beachhead in Europe, opening 40 stores in France, Germany, Spain and Belgium. At home, M&S spent £192 million acquiring 19 stores from *Littlewoods*, another UK chain, and set aside more money for refurbishing these into M&S stores. This and other initiatives would increase the size of M&S's average store by more than a third. Moreover, Simon Marks's self-imposed limit of '240 UK stores' was easily surpassed as M&S pushed toward 300. Further growth was planned through diversification into financial services (even though M&S still held on to an unusual policy of not accepting credit cards in their own stores). Here M&S sought to position itself as a low-cost alternative to traditional providers of unit trusts, pensions and life assurance. Furniture, luggage, sandwiches, mobile phones and jewellery also became new M&S lines.

Toward the end of the 1990s, M&S were still pointing to results that were the envy of other retailers as the comparison of sales, profits and margins among Britain's leading retailers in 1998 makes clear.

	Core business	Sales (£M)	Pre-tax Profit (£M)	Margin (%)
Marks & Spencer	Dept. stores	8,243	1,168	14.2
Boots	Chemists	5,022	432	8.6
Dixons	Electronics	2,774	219	7.9
W.H. Smith	Books	2,850	143	5.0
Asda	Grocery	7,620	405	5.3
J. Sainsbury's	Grocery	14,500	719	4.9
Tesco	Grocery	16,452	728	4.4

The wheels, however, were about to fall off.

1998–1999 – The Past Catches Up?

On 3 November 1998, M&S announced a 23 per cent fall in half-year operating profit from £428 million to £327 million. This figure was further reduced by a £64 million write-off for 'reduced value of overseas assets'. An admission, in other words, that M&S had overpaid for overseas acquisitions. This was the first drop in profits in 30 years and it was the first time in M&S history that sales had declined significantly. In Britain, market share slipped to 12 per cent from 15 per cent during 1998. Despite increasing floor space, sales in the 15 weeks to 9 February 1999 were 6.4 per cent below the same period in the previous year. By the end of that financial year annual pre-tax profits had halved from

£1.2 billion to £546 million. Almost £400 million of the decline was in the core UK retail business.

The Autumn '98 range of clothing needed to be a 'fight back', a return to form but was, instead a damp squib. As a spokesman for the company reflected:

> Grey was the fashion colour so we bought it, but the mistake we made was that we bought it for everybody. Older customers wanted colour and we were missing it. By the time we realised, it was too late to buy more colour. We'd had a successful year previously, so we were confident and bullish about buying.

The autumn season went flat and M&S was forced to heavily discount stock (something it had never engaged in before, relying instead on tightly managed and responsive supply chains) in order to clear space for its Christmas stock and try and recoup some cash. Unfortunately, this was in vain. M&S's trading results in 1998's crucial Christmas period were dire.

The previously bombproof Greenbury was placed under increasing pressure from City investors to split his roles as both chairman and CEO and to make M&S's succession plans plain. Greenbury, who was notoriously grumpy in his dealings with the City (he perceived it as being unable to understand the complexities of his business and overly short-term in outlook), dug in. Much infighting and jockeying for position ensued. Two main candidates emerged. Greenbury's deputy Keith Oates, and another senior director Peter Salsbury, who had worked his way up through M&S's clothing divisions – but Greenbury would not budge. A provocative letter written by Oates saying that Greenbury's roles should be split and directly challenging his authority was leaked to the press.

In November 1998, after months of speculation, uncertainty and very public infighting, Greenbury, under pressure from the board, announced he would be stepping down from his role as CEO. There then ensued further fracas between Oates and Salsbury, who was seen as Greenbury's preferred choice. Seventeen acrimonious days later Salsbury was eventually appointed and a bitter Oates took early retirement.

The appointment was poorly received, both by the City and by many within M&S. One senior executive was happy to tell *The Sunday Times* that 'Salsbury is seen as the knight in shining armour but he has only worked at Marks & Spencer's and if he continues to be surrounded by M&S clones, his task may be too great. Do remember that Salsbury was the man in charge of clothing when that department went off the cliff.' M&S shares fell by 25 pence the day the news broke. Reflecting on a rather ungentlemanly and amateurish transition, Simon Marks's grandson was reported as saying that his grandfather would have turned in his grave: 'This is not the way things are done at M&S.'

Analysts, wise in hindsight, were quick to provide a multitude of reasons for M&S's and Greenbury's spectacular demise. Social, economic, external issues relating to the industry, and internal reasons relating to the nature of the firm, were thrown up as the British media raked over the coals.

From a social environmental perspective, changing demographics and spending patterns were pointed to: overall demand for clothing had stabilized or declined, as an ever-higher share of consumer spending was being done by the affluent over-45s who were less inclined to spend a high proportion of their disposable income on clothes. Moreover, the under-45s were increasingly discerning, individual in taste, and aware of fashion and fashion labels.

Economic factors such as the growing strength of Sterling on global currency markets, making M&S products increasingly expensive, a substantial slowdown in retail spending at home, and economic turmoil in the Far East did not help matters.

Two revolutions in the 'high street' were identified. The first saw M&S losing ground on two sides. On the one hand, heavy discounters and supermarkets such as Asda and Tesco moved into M&S's segments, utilizing aggressive marketing, cheaper overseas production facilities, and/or mail-order or Internet distribution channels. On the other hand, newer retailers such as Next and Debenhams were also utilizing cheaper production, but combining this with more fashion-conscious branding and design, then feeding back data as to what people were actually buying, to provide clothes that were significantly more targeted and desirable to most people than M&S, but not significantly more expensive.

As UK retailing became more international, M&S's failings were further highlighted in contrast to more style-conscious rivals such as Sweden's H&M, Spain's Zara and America's Gap. Curiously, in a world where people seemed to want to embrace local differences in style, M&S's overseas store seemed to lack 'Britishness'. In hindsight, *BusinessWeek* argued that M&S on the Continent seemed destined to fail because M&S was just another bland store. They claimed that M&S might have fared better had it concentrated on playing up its 'Britishness' while concentrating on its two traditional British strengths: lingerie and convenience food.

A second revolution saw a move away from the proportion spent on items like clothes toward consumer electronics where companies such as Dixons and Currys dominated the UK market. M&S had picked the wrong horse in the diversification game.

The internal environment at M&S made its managers unable to see or act upon these changes. Some analysts claimed that Greenbury's focus on the day-to-day operations saw M&S take its eye off strategy for the long term; some that Greenbury's autocratic style and longevity had made the company increasingly more risk-averse, leaving it without the ability to innovate. Others pointed to a general cultural malaise, whereby 'in-bred' top management was so immersed in M&S's ways and loved them so much that they could not see what was wrong, and when they did they went into denial or lacked the stomach to change. Some claimed that M&S's rigid top-down 'head office knows best' culture built on M&S's proud record was out of date. It resulted in managers who rested on their laurels and harked back to old glories. Although most of its customers were women, some analysts pointed out that men dominated top management at M&S.

This culture had led M&S to become increasingly inward-looking with regard to relying on traditional UK suppliers without looking at what customers wanted. According to one analyst, 'M&S had behaved like a wholesale buyer of products such as shirts and trousers, rather than thinking about the sort of person that was buying that item.' To make matters worse, this culture also made M&S

complacent with regard to working with suppliers to improve. George Davies, founder of Next explained that 'The customer looks in the [fashion] magazine and will not wait . . . you have got to have a structure with your supply partners that can cope with ridiculously quick turnarounds.' At one time, Israel Sieff and Simon Marks had developed a relationship designed to do just this, but M&S had gone off the boil in this respect.

At the other end of the value-chain, the increase in average shop space turned out to be a curse rather than a blessing. M&S found it had to offer more products just to fill the empty space. It subsequently moved into areas such as mobile phones and jewellery where it had little expertise and subsequently could only be lower-quality 'me-too players'. One widely reported story told of an M&S branch manager who called his opposite in another department store to ask what to do with a table that had been scratched during home delivery. 'Send round your French polisher' was the answer. Unfortunately M&S did not have one, and the manager was not sure where to begin to find one, or even sure if his leg was just being pulled.

Other attempts to grow were seen as poorly thought out. By 1996, M&S was trading in Canada under three different names with only 47 stores. The Canadian operation lost money in 24 of the 25 years between 1973 and 1998 due to the lack of strong brands and supply lines as in the UK, and a lack of the M&S culture among staff who had joined the firm by being 'acquired'.

Finally, through a combination of not investing in their brand and sticking to a generalized one-model-fits-all view of the market instead of trying to tailor their offering to various segments, M&S fell between two stools. Older traditional customers were depressed by the decreasing quality and quick-fire approaches to make the product appear more fashionable, while younger potential customers saw M&S as dull and dowdy.

1999–2000 – All Change

In January 1999 M&S issued a further profits warning and Peter Salsbury set to work changing M&S. Three board directors and 31 of the company's top 125 managers were sacked. The company was reorganized into three units: UK retail, overseas business and financial services (which had grown to provide 18 per cent of group profits), these were crossed by a new organization-wide marketing department. Brooks Brothers was instructed to cut its spending. Salsbury even started to do the once unthinkable; bringing 'outside branding' into M&S stores. But there was no quick turnaround. By May, Salsbury had to announce a severe drop in trading and a further halving of profits.

Relations between Salsbury and his chairman soured. Greenbury seemed to feel 'out of the loop' and he particularly disliked the army of consultants that Salsbury had brought into the company (so many that a new position – 'consultant co-ordinator' – had to be created). On 22 June 1999, Greenbury announced that he would retire immediately from the chairmanship.

July saw the closure of six of M&S's European stores and the closure of all of its Canadian stores. In the UK, design consultants were commissioned to create a glossy new store image. In-store cappuccino bars were developed and the distinctive green M&S carrier bag was questioned. A department dedicated to identifying new business opportunities was established and M&S diversified further into home catalogue and Internet shopping. The marketing department came up with a new approach to discounting that involved giving away £5 with every £25 spent. The company finally decided to allow people to purchase goods with credit cards.

Barry Morris, who was in charge of food, the one part of the business consistently performing well, was transferred to womenswear, leaving food without a main board director. The food offering was then revamped, but rather than leading the way as it once did, M&S copied rivals' features by introducing in-house bakeries, delis and meat counters. Unfortunately, food sales stayed flat and operating margins fell (from £247 million in 1997 to £137 million in 1999) as a result of the extra space and staff needed for the new services.

Unfortunately, 1999's Christmas results were even worse than 1998's. Leaks from insiders said sales at the flagship Oxford Street store had collapsed by 27 per cent. The overseas retail business reported an overall loss of £15 million after posting profits of £67 million in 1998. In November 1999, M&S shares fell to £2.50 – their lowest price since 1991 and some felt that this was artificially high on account of rumours of a takeover. At the end of 1999, M&S announced that it was slashing the proportion of goods it bought from British suppliers in a bid to cut costs.

In January 2000, M&S announced a replacement for Greenbury. Belgian-born Luc Vandevelde from French retailer Promodes, part of huge Carrefour conglomerate, became chairman. Unfortunately for Vandevelde, he arrived just as the British press was finally beginning to lose patience with M&S. After posting its worst half-year results in living memory toward for the first half of 2000, one report described M&S as besieged by a 'sort of chaos'. *The Economist* asked whether 'M&S had a future?'; claiming that 'things have become so bad that M&S, until recently a national icon, is in danger of becoming a national joke'. Given this sort of press 'you almost expect Mr Vandevelde to don a hard hat to greet visitors', wrote the *Independent*.

Public ill will grew as 2,000 jobs were lost at long-term M&S supplier Coats Viyella. This followed closures and large-scale redundancies at other M&S favourites William Baird and Courtaulds. Even though M&S still claimed to be the biggest buyers of UK-made clothes, many accused the company of 'deserting Britain' and of 'shamefully jettisoning' its suppliers. In response, M&S accused its suppliers of failing to keep up with fashion. Making matters worse, M&S suppliers overseas were accused of unethical practices. All M&S could do was claim that having only just started to do business with these suppliers it was unaware of such practices.

The BBC's *Money Programme* released the results of a customer satisfaction survey that showed both that the rot had set in some time ago, and that things were getting worse rather than better (see below).

Still more change would be implemented. A headline in the *Independent on Sunday* claimed 'Nothing Sacred at St Michael'. The tally of departing directors rose to eleven. In February 2000, M&S promised to bring an extra 4,000 shop floor staff on stream – although where they would come from and when they would arrive was not clear. In March, a dramatic brand overhaul was declared, the famous green carrier bags would be discontinued, the St Michael brand would be downgraded and there was even talk of dropping the Marks & Spencer name in favour of a new brand. The selling of newspapers and magazines was mooted and M&S launched a downmarket concept offering clothes at discounted prices in factory outlet malls.

BBC Money Programme *M&S customer satisfaction survey results*

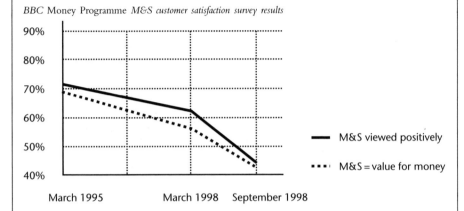

For the year ended March 2000, profits again fell dramatically: to £417 million. The share price had melted from a peak of around £6.65 at the end of 1997 to less than £2. By the middle of 2000, M&S's share price was languishing around £1.70. Even taking a generally retailing slump into account, M&S was under-performing the FTSE 100 index by 52 per cent. The company's market capitalization shrank to around £5 billion, no more than the book value of its assets, making it ripe for takeover.

Vandevelde was under pressure to sell Brooks Brothers and Kings supermarkets business in the US. However, while he admitted that they were hardly a good fit, nothing was done with regard to their sale.

Before the profits crash, M&S did not stoop to advertise. But in 2000 is unveiled a bold multi-media campaign. 'I'm normal', as it was officially named, featured a woman in increasingly exuberant mood running up a hill tearing off her clothes as she discovers that her size (16) is the UK average. Several miles of newspaper columns over many years had bemoaned the fashion industry's stubborn insistence on promoting its clothes on stick-thin lanky models. So, one would have thought this would have been seen as proof that someone was finally listening to the data. However, instead of a chorus of 'Good old Marks and Sparks', a flurry of articles appeared critiquing the company: on the one hand for not waking up sooner, and on the other questioning whether 'real' women really wanted to be reminded of their true curvy selves.

One executive later claimed that 'We might as well have run a campaign saying: "are you a lumpy lard arse? Do you want to look, er, normal? We're the store for you".' A journalist noted that 'More sensitive shoppers may prefer not to be seen with a carrier bag that might as well be a placard reading "I'm Outsize, Me".'

'I'm normal' made M&S look patronizing and frumpy in one swoop. It also made them look inconsistent. At the same time as 'I'm normal', well-known society 'skinny girl' about town Tara Palmer-Topkinson was being used as the face of a new website devoted to selling M&S lingerie online. Meanwhile, the BBC's *Watchdog* programme was savaging M&S for overcharging and poor quality in its range of garments for the fuller figure.

Vandevelde somewhat sheepishly claimed to have supported 'I'm normal', although he distanced himself somewhat by saying that it would not have been his ideal choice.

By Christmas 2000 things were bleak. Catherine Bennet writing for *The Guardian* (16 November 2000) had this to say about a visit to the Oxford Street branch:

> Expanses of this vast shop were deserted, great vistas of tops and troos opened up, empty of both shoppers and shop assistants. No one was looking at the slippers. No one showed an interest in the 'looks like sheep-skin' coats that looked more like fuzzy felt. No one was checking out the reading glasses, nor the teddies, nor the financial services . . . nor the Bart Simpson advent calendars, nor the thick-pile lavatory seat covers . . . nor the beige 'secret support' ski pants, the sludgy mid-length anoraks, the yoked nightie marked 'cosy'.

How M&S so quickly reversed from profitability to its current pitiful state was still a matter for conjecture, but the reasons seemed obvious to Bennet as she walked the store:

> [M&S] isn't selling enough clothes because many of its clothes are now tacky, rather than dull or dowdy, without being cheap. The children's clothes have been colonized by *Disney*, the lingerie by *Agent Provocateur*. Even when a decent conventional M&S idea such as a plain jumper has emerged, it has been executed in vile knitting-shop colours.
>
> Last week, with the news that sales were still in decline, the company sounded contrite. 'We are still working to improve our clothing offer, par-ticularly in womenswear and menswear.' It seems unlikely to improve its 'offer' though, unless it decides which particular kinds of women or men it is aiming at. Young or old? Extravagant or frugal? Staid or showy? The current female target appears to be a fantastic hybrid, part-Gran, part-slapper: an impecunious, size 22 slack-and-slipper wearing Simpsons fan in her 60s who exists on a diet of prepared Caesar salad and jam roly poly and is currently saving up for a baby blue pashmina and a pair of Salon Rose Embroidered Mesh High Leg Briefs.
>
> If such beasts exist, they were not, I'm afraid, shopping in the Oxford Street branch last Tuesday . . . Then again nor was anyone else. That's because the over-50s think it's for the 14-year olds, and the 14-year olds think it's for the over-50s. Last month sales of clothes and footwear fell by a further 17 per cent.

Bennet's analysis is backed up by earlier more sober, but just as critical, *Financial Times* reports:

> There are so many items here to find and they don't tend to segregate it out, so there's something I might like next to something my granny might like (28 September 1999).

An hour walking around Marks and Spencer's London show-case spring/ summer collection leaves you unclear who was meant to be there . . . The range is not unwearable, but navigating an M&S store would test a Magellan . . . The collection seems desperate, disorganised and derivative (20 January 2000).

2001 – Vandevelde Settles In

Salsbury retired from M&S at the end of 2000. Vandevelde admitted that 'nine months into the job its "British side" is more overwhelming than I originally thought', but during 2001 he appeared to grow in confidence as he became more familiar with his new surroundings and the peculiarities of M&S. His vision for the future became clearer and he started to outline key decisions.

After results were posted at the end of 2000, Vandevelde announced that it was closing six of its 287 stores. Most analysts seemed either disappointed or perplexed, having expected M&S to shut at least 20 and saw this as further evidence of M&S not facing up to the tough decisions that needed to be made. Vandevelde admitted that if you had applied a strict economic test you might have closed up to 40 stores. But M&S could not do that, he said. 'You cannot underestimate the impact of public opinion on our commercial decisions,' he claimed. From across the English Channel, he had viewed the outrage that greeted M&S's decision to follow other retailers in buying from low-cost countries and seemed to have taken this to heart. Vandevelde said he wanted changes to be 'evolutionary rather than revolutionary'. He claimed to love M&S history, referring to 'the glory days of M&S everybody felt proud to be associated with'. And he believed that M&S has huge reserves of expertise.

At the end of March 2001, M&S announced it plans to withdraw completely from Europe and America. Brooks Brothers and its European stores were put up for sale. Its stores in Hong Kong were sold to franchises. M&S also closed its home and Internet catalogue operations at a loss of £300 million. Vandevelde claimed that M&S needed to focus on its core business. And, for the first time in its history, M&S cut the dividend paid to shareholders. In a letter to shareholders, 90 per cent of whom are individuals who have seen their savings tumble, Vandevelde asked them to be patient and claimed that he needs the money saved to boost investment. Vandevelde said that he wanted to revitalize the domestic brand before taking that brand back overseas.

Vandevelde reorganized M&S into five operating divisions: UK retail, international retail, financial services, property, and ventures. And in an attempt to make M&S more customer-focused, UK retail was organized into seven units: womenswear, menswear, children's wear, lingerie, food, home and beauty.

After extensive store visits, Vandevelde set aside £77 million of 2001's budget for modernizing stores in Britain, arguing that reverberation should have been started 8–10 years ago. Traditionally, M&S has taken a 'one-size-fits-all' approach to its stores, so that what is offered in the Norwich branch is a scaled-down version of what is available in the flagship store at Marble Arch, but Vandevelde wants M&S to become a 'multi-format' retailer. He identified 10 different types of M&S including big city outlets, smaller city stores, new concept shops (of which there will be 25 by the end of the year), bigger outlet stores, food-only stores and small-clothing and food stores. These stores will also be grouped on the basis of demographic characteristics and lifestyle patterns.

In accordance with this reconfiguration, Vandevelde's team sought to reorganize supply chains and make them more reactive again. Decision making, once dictated by head office, is now set at individual stores and based on local tastes, with store managers not only being responsible for the goods they sell but also for feeding information back up the supply chain. To measure performance, Vandevelde returned to Simon Marks' measure of revenue and profit per square foot.

The City wondered if Vandevelde, who has talked about size being important in food retailing while at Carrefour, would make acquisitions in this area. But he dismissed this with a quip that updated Simon Marks' 'chicken test': 'I don't think we need more stores to be competitive. We don't want to get into a price war with *Tesco*. But my crispy duck can stand up to anyone's.'

After finding that customers were confused between Marks & Spencer and St Michael, it was also decided that branding should be reconfigured. A revitalized M&S logo was developed and then displayed in a range of seven colours each indicating different departments. The St Michael logo was placed inside garments as a quality mark – which is what it was originally intended to be.

However, by the end of 2001 Vandevelde had also made some harsher decisions. He had slashed 4,000 jobs and removed every single member of the board, many of whom had been with M&S for the best part of their working lives, and he continued to look to source M&S products from abroad. And, despite the bad press that met him on arrival, and the bad press that would accompany decisions such as these, Vandevelde continued to conduct dozens of interviews with the press in an attempt to raise awareness of what was happening at M&S.

Upon arrival in January 2000, Vandevelde had told the press that he would quit if he did not meet profit goals and turn the company around within two years. Insiders whispered that this sort of learning curve was too steep and that Vandevelde was setting himself up for failure. But, in addition to his own skill and that of the management team he was rebuilding around him, Vandevelde also put his faith in the British people: 'Most of the people in this country want us to succeed,' he says. 'Most of the people will continue to shop with us. They may not buy as much as they used to, but that is because we have lost touch with them. But if we listen to the customers, we will get it right.' Ex-chairman Greenbury was not so confident. In an interview with Radio 4 he remarked: 'Do I think in the foreseeable future [M&S] will go back to making those kind of returns? The answer is, I think, it is extremely unlikely.'

The first results in 2002 were awaited with interest.

Marks & Spencer financial highlights 1997–2000 (£ million)

	1997	**1998**	**1999**	**2000**
Turnover	7,841	8,243	8,224	8,195
Profit on ordinary activities before tax	1,102	1,155	546	417
Dividends	−368	−409	−413	−258
Retained profit/loss	386	406	−41	0
Fixed assets	3,646	4,034	4,448	4,298
Net current assets	3,204	3,401	3,355	3,717
Short-term creditors	1,775	2,345	2,029	2,162
Long-term creditors	495	187	772	804
Earnings per share (pence)	27	29	13	9
Dividend per share (pence)	13	14	14	9

2002 – New Hope or False Dawn?

On 21 January 2002, *BusinessWeek* published a lead article under the heading 'A sigh of relief at Marks and Sparks: Vandevelde's restructuring has cash registers ringing again'. It reported the share price having moved from £2 to £3.60 in the year to January 2002. Analysts estimated that the M&S's same-store sales increased as much as 6 per cent in the third quarter of the 2001 financial year. For the year ending March 2002 pre-tax profits should rise more than 35 per cent to £550 million on sales of £0.8 billion, according to Goldman, Sachs & Co. analyst Keith Wills. 'They're now on a genuine recovery track', said analyst John Ballie of SG Securities in London.

Perhaps more importantly for the long term, Vandevelde's team also seems to be ushering in a new culture. The firm's Baker Street headquarters have been transformed. Instead of special blue carpets in the executive corridors, oil paintings of past dignitaries and security guards to repel ordinary staff, the powerful are approached on stripped wooden floors past photographs of models wearing the product.

Taking advantage of the residual affection felt for M&S in the UK, Vandevelde has been able to blend old faces and new people keen to be associated with revitalizing the company. In combination with a younger and more mixed management team, Vandevelde has hired George Davies, a stalwart of Next and the designer of a range for Asda that did much to take the wind out of M&S sails, to design a new 'Per Una' range. Davies insisted on differentiation within M&S: 'I wanted different hangers, different changing room and different carrier bags [within M&S stores].' And he got them. Per Una was launched in September 2001. Sales were so strong that M&S had to delay rolling out the brand into all of its stores, arousing great publicity.

Having learned too from the failed 'I'm normal' campaign, things on the advertising front also started to look more focused. At the beginning of 2002, hand-picked British celebrities were enlisted and depicted bringing their historical affection for the corporation up to date: DJ Zoe Ball for the aspiration, trendy twenties and thirties; Honor Blackman for the Home Counties' ladies, Sir Stephen Redgrave and George Best for 'blokes'; comedian Julian Clary for others.

'The new [M&S] team are excellent,' said one industry commentator. 'They listen well, are incredibly focused, work well together and are making the right moves. The atmosphere is totally different.' Other insiders say that M&S has learnt a little humility and taken lessons from being overtaken by rivals that gave customers what they really wanted: classic, stylish basics in quality fabrics at reasonable prices. And a humbled M&S seems to be returning to its roots with gusto.

'Perfect', a massively publicized collection of quality basics: white shirts cut well and soft, black jumpers that will go through the wash, shot off the shelves to the extent that Vandevelde was able to go before City journalists with the headline grabbing fact that the firm was selling 10,000 Perfect white shirts and 10,000 black polo-necks a week. Along with rebuilding its image for basics differentiated on quality, M&S is also placing more emphasis on integrating its ranges so that all of its clothes work together, enabling its customers to pick-and-mix with confidence.

The decline in clothing sales has now been halted. They rose 0.8 per cent in the quarter ending 30 September 2001. A year previously they were down 9.1 per cent. Merrill Lynch & Co. figures that every percentage point increase adds £29 million to pre-tax profits. In keeping, profits for the six months to the end of 2001 rose by 19 per cent.

Indeed, the tone of reporting on M&S has changed from those dark days when everybody seemed to want to put the boot in. The name 'Vandevelde' now regularly appears alongside 'the man reviving M&S' captions, and the company is receiving its best reviews for years: 'M&S reclaims its high street throne', gushed the *Daily Telegraph*, whose readership would appear to be a key M&S middle-England constituency. Sandra Halliday of Worth Global Style Network claimed that 'It's early days but M&S is back on the up. The collections are more stylish, the quality is better, and the stores no longer look like something out of *Are You Being Served?*'

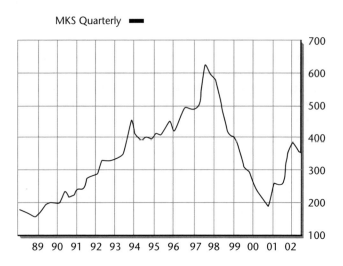

MKS Quarterly ━

At the beginning of 2002, M&S is still the biggest player on the UK High Street and it looks like Vandevelde and M&S might just be able to stick around for a little while yet. However, while the charts outlining M&S share price 1988–2002 and M&S's share price change relative to other FSTE retailers over the past decade (see below) indicates a recovery, it is not all rosy. M&S is by no means out of the woods yet and much remains to be done. And, in a highly publicized review, published in *The Sunday Times* on 24 March 2002, of 'The 100 best places to work in Britain', which linked employee satisfaction to long-term share price increases, M&S did not even rate a mention. Asda was number one and Debenhams and Tesco were also well placed. Simon Marks would not be best pleased.

Integration Case 2: Twelve Images of M&S

In this section we take the M&S case described above and invite you to analyse it by using the images and frameworks provided by and in the preceding chapters. We suggest working your way around our images of strategy wheel (Figure 14.1), from ethos to decision making. Below is a discussion applying some of the classic framework introduced in Chapter 1 in a postmodern way (as in Case Box 1.1). Combining the cost + margin = selling price equation, Porter's value chain, generic strategy matrix and five forces of industry frameworks, we can offer the following three snapshot-maps of M&S's past, which focus, in particular, on the clothing side of their business. It might help you get started.

Circa 1930–1980s

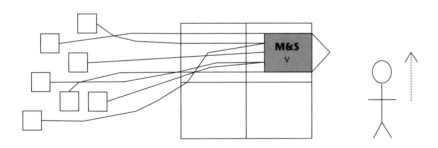

1. Simon Marks and Israel Sieff built the company by networking and working closely with numerous small suppliers to add value by improving quality standards and fashionability, thereby providing wares for the general public that raised the norm and sold at a healthy price. While cost was important, the company was clearly led by differentiating on quality.

Circa 1990s

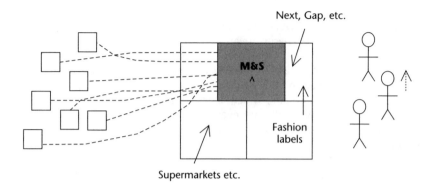

2. The competitive environment changed and the M&S recipe was no longer a sustainable competitive advantage. New players such as Next and Gap entered the high street, matching M&S in quality and beating them on fashion and price. Supermarkets diversified and began to provide a substitute to traditional clothing retailers at the low end of the market. High fashion labels began to develop more of a retailing presence. In response to these movements, and a general retailing downturn, M&S focused on growing bigger through diversification and on growing margins through cost reduction. However, it lacked expertise in many of the new areas in which it was seeking to compete, and, unlike many of the new entrants in their existing businesses, was laden with extensive fixed costs. Over time, it had also lost the ability to work as one with suppliers on efficiency and on other aspects, and it had lost touch with customers whose standards were generally rising faster than M&S's, and who, in any case, could no longer be treated as one.

Circa 2000

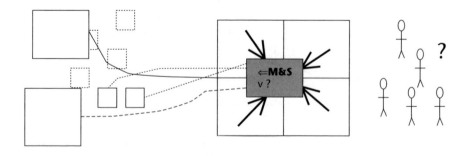

3. M&S is now being attacked by the competition on all fronts. It sought to take action but this has left it seeming somewhat confused and stuck between being a cost or a differentiating company. Customers' wants were fragmenting further, but M&S still seemed to want to lump them all together, satisfying nobody – hence its unit sales and margins declined. Other retailers seem better at targeting particular segments. Some traditional suppliers go to the wall as M&S switches to

larger overseas manufacturers. Because this is not handled well, relationships with those suppliers that remain continue to diminish and because its overseas supply lines are new and distant, these new relationships take time to gel. This means that even those customers who remain loyal to M&S are often disappointed and disillusioned by what they find in the stores.

The big question

The big question is: 'What, having done your own analysis and having read the analysis outlined above, would you do if you were running or advising M&S?' By consulting the *Images of Strategy* website at <www.blackwell.co.uk/resources/images> you can read what each of the chapter authors would suggest through applying the ideas developed in their own chapters. You will see that their views are not necessarily consistent with one another. But strategy is often about making choices in environments where there is rarely a general consensus. However, by oscillating between their views and your own we hope that your analysis and recommendations are forced into greater articulation.

Given that the future strategic environment cannot be fully predicted, there is no one right answer. Even if M&S does well over the next five years by following a particular strategy, there is nothing to say that it could not have done better by following an alternative. However, if you believe that how you would answer the question posed above now is better and more informed than what it would have been before you read this book, then *Images of Strategy* has fulfilled its purpose.

Conclusion

Hopefully, after years of debating which map or perspective or recipe best represents the way strategy really is, we might now see the value in having many images at our disposal. Most of the maps that strategy has drawn upon have been based on the fields of economics, psychology and statistics. However, this is more due to particular historical contingencies than fundamental necessities. Recognizing this should encourage us to begin to incorporate frameworks from other fields that we may be familiar with *in combination with* those already widely used, to help us articulate and discuss potential courses of action. This survey has considered strategy as ethos, as organizing human resources, as anticipation and intention, as orchestrating knowledge, as combining data and sense-making, as creative thinking, as exploration and connection, as systems thinking, as process, power and change, as marketing and adding market value, as numbers, and as decision making. *Images of Strategy* encourages development through an oscillation between maps or frameworks such as those provided by these images and practical chaotic realities in order to inspire us toward taking particular courses.

While there are many maps that can help refresh one's strategic visions, none of these should prescribe what you must do, each individual must bring his or her particular purpose and understanding into the mix in order to analyse his or her situations. To return to the cooking analogy with which we began this book in Chapter 1, Nigella Lawson provides a useful parallel in bemoaning the 'tyranny of the recipe' in her recently published *How to Eat*. Having several good recipes is a starting point, she explains, but a good chef must be more than this – he or she must have their 'own individual sense of what food is about'. Too often in the past managers have fallen under the spell of the tyranny of this year's recipe for corporate success, just seeking to replicate it before realizing that everybody is doing the same inferior copy of the original. A recipe can inspire added value, but only if it is infused with a different approach and given a new twist. Thus, it is better to focus on one's individuality before and during the preparation and 'cooking' process. In any event, postmodern paradoxes and the realization that organizations must increasingly accentuate their 'difference', mean that it may no longer be useful for consultants, academics or chefs to prescribe what others must do. That is a matter for those who determine particular goals in specific contexts, those who, in Foucault's words 'do the fighting' – that is, you. The M&S case presented above, and the many case boxes throughout the book, gave you an opportunity to practise with some different tools, but it is up to you to now take these into your own 'battles'.

Plutarch contended that we should view the ideas and models of others not in order to copy them but as a means of stimulating and refreshing our own vision, our own unique style. Hence, while we might find the views of the contributors to this book refreshing, it is important to recognize that they are not fundamentally more useful than anyone else's. You harbour just as many interesting metaphors for strategy as we have been able to relate here. We finish this book by urging you to write your own sequels; to add to the spokes of your strategy wheel by thinking up other images; not to just be consumers of knowledge but producers of knowledge too. In fact, if you would like to share these images with other readers we, in association with the good people at Blackwell, have even provided space on the above-mentioned website for doing so. Please continue this book at <www.blackwell.co.uk/resources/images>.

Source Material and Recommended Further Reading

The epigraph is taken from Paul Feyerabend, *Against Method*, 3rd edition (London: Verso, 1993).

The dimensions on our 'images of strategy wheel' are inspired by B. Leavy and D. Wilson's *Strategy and Leadership* (London: Routledge, 1994); S. Cummings and J. Davies, 'Mission, vision, fusion', *Long Range Planning*, 27(6), 1994, 146–51; S. Cummings, 'Centralization and decentralization: the never-ending story of separation and betrayal', *Scandinavian Journal of Management*, 11(2), 1995, 103–17; S.J. Miller, D.J. Hickson and D.C. Wilson, 'Decision-making in organizations', in S.R. Clegg, C. Hardy and W.R. Nord (eds), *Handbook of Organization Studies* (London: Sage, 1996); and S. Cummings, *ReCreating Strategy* (London: Sage, 2002).

'The rise and fall and future of M&S' draws on many sources including the television programmes described in the case, Marks & Spencer annual reports, and: 'Bras, knickers and well hidden talents', *The Guardian*, 22 December 1999; 'M&S in "make or break" reshuffle', *The Guardian*, 22 December 1999; 'Competitive advantage, corporate governance and reputation management: the case of Marks and Spencer', *Journal of Communication Management*, 4(2), 1999, 185–96; 'Does M&S have a future?', *The Economist*, 28 October 2000; 'Nothing sacred at St Michael', *Independent on Sunday*, 12 November 2000; 'M&S plans to drop name at 50 stores', *Independent on Sunday*, 12 November 2000; Catherine Bennett, 'It's all over the shop', *The Guardian*, 16 November 2000; H. Macmillan and M. Tampoe, 'Hard times for Marks & Spencer', *Strategic Management*, 2000, 313–22; 'Focus: the empire's new clothes – it's full marks for effort',

Observer, 18 November 2001; N. Collies, 'Marks and Spencer', in G. Johnson and K. Scholes (eds), *Exploring Corporate Strategy* (London: Prentice-Hall); 'A sigh of relief at Marks and Sparks: Vandevelde's restructuring has cash registers ringing again', *BusinessWeek*, 21 January 2002. The following web sites were also consulted: BBC Knowledge and <ft.com>.

For references cited in 'An integration case II', please refer to each author's original chapters. For references cited in 'Conclusion' please refer to Chapter 1.

Index

Commitment to efficiency, calculability, predictability
and Control embodied
in FF

4th
5th Sep